DATE DUE

BRODART, CO.   Cat. No. 23-221

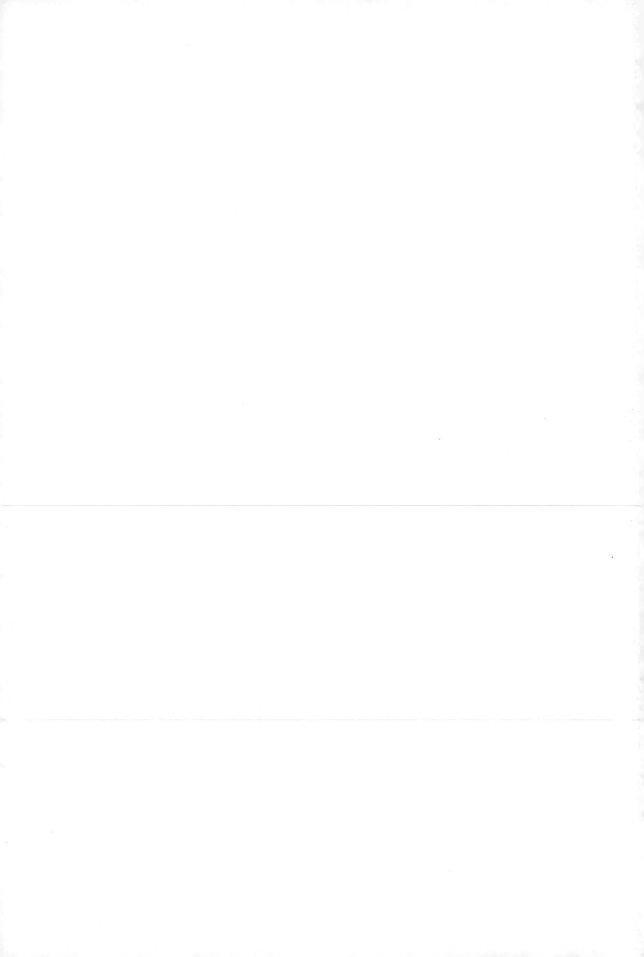

American Reference Books Annual

Volume 45

2014 Edition

American Reference Books Annual
Advisory Board

2014
EDITION

AMERICAN
REFERENCE
BOOKS
ANNUAL

Volume 45

Shannon Graff Hysell, Associate Editor

 LIBRARIES UNLIMITED

AN IMPRINT OF ABC-CLIO, LLC
Santa Barbara, California • Denver, Colorado • Oxford, England

LIBRARIES UNLIMITED
An Imprint of ABC-CLIO, LLC
130 Cremona Drive
P.O. Box 1911
Santa Barbara, California 93116-1911
www.abc-clio.com

Library of Congress Cataloging-in-Publication Data

American reference books annual, 1970-
    Santa Barbara, CA, Libraries Unlimited.

        v. 19x26 cm.

Indexes:
    1970-74. 1v.
    1975-79. 1v.
    1980-84. 1v.
    1985-89. 1v.
    1990-94. 1v.
    1995-99. 1v.
    2000-04. lv.
    2005-09. lv.
    2010-14. lv.

        I. Reference books--Bibliography--Periodicals.
I. Hysell, Shannon Graff
Z1035.1.A55   011'.02
ISBN 978-1-61069-548-0 (2014 edition)
ISSN 0065-9959

Contents

14—Psychology, Parapsychology, and Occultism

15—Recreation and Sports

16—Sociology

17—Statistics, Demography, and Urban Studies

18—Women's Studies

Part III
HUMANITIES

19—Humanities in General

20—Communication and Mass Media

21—Decorative Arts

Introduction

Purpose and Scope

We are pleased to provide you with volume 45 of *American Reference Books Annual*, a far-reaching review service for reference books and electronic resources. The 45th volume of ARBA provides users with reviews of 1,308 books, databases, and free Internet sites covering the years 2012 and 2013, as well as some from 2014 that were received in time for review in the publication. In the 45 volumes of ARBA published since 1970, a total of 70,235 resources have been reviewed. Nine cumulative indexes for ARBA cover the years 1970-1974, 1975-1979, 1980-1984, 1985-1989, 1990-1994, 1995-1999, 2000-2004, 2005-2009, and 2010-2014. These indexes expedite the use of the annual print volumes.

In 2002 Libraries Unlimited debuted ARBAonline, an authoritative database with more than 26,000 reviews of print and electronic resources of interest to academic, public, and school libraries. ARBAonline provides all reviews published in the print version of ARBA since 1997. Its availability significantly increases ARBA's value to librarians by helping them select quality reference products for their library with confidence, while at the same time ensuring they will have access to the most up-to-date materials and depth of coverage. ARBA is extending its coverage to electronic resources by expanding the number of reviews of Websites and databases, both subscription based and free, in ARBA and ARBAonline. Our goal is to provide coverage for electronic reference resources that is as comprehensive as it is for print resources. Future editions will continue to expand the number of reviews for these electronic resources in a variety of subject areas.

ARBA differs significantly from other reviewing media in its basic purpose, which is to provide comprehensive coverage of English-language reference books published in the United States and Canada during a single year. The categories of reference books reviewed in ARBA and the policy regarding them can be summarized as follows: (1) Dictionaries, encyclopedias, indexes, directories, bibliographies, guides, concordances, atlases, gazetteers, and other types of ready-reference tools are routinely reviewed in each volume of ARBA; coverage of these categories of reference materials is nearly complete. (2) Generally encyclopedias that are updated annually, yearbooks, almanacs, indexing and abstracting services, and other annuals or serials are usually reviewed at intervals of two to three years. The first review of such works generally provides an appropriate historical background. Subsequent reviews of these publications attempt to point out changes in scope or editorial policy. (3) New editions of reference books are ordinarily reviewed with appropriate comparisons to older editions. (4) Products that are published in both print and online versions are typically reviewed together to provide the user with a comparative analysis that will allow them to select the right product for their library's needs. (5) Traditionally, foreign reference titles have been reviewed only if they had an exclusive distributor in the United States. Substantial coverage of Canadian reference publications has been achieved and will continue until it is as complete for Canada as it is for the United States. Other foreign-title coverage is restricted to English-language publications from Great Britain, as well as a few select sources from Australia and other countries. (6) Reprints are reviewed in ARBA on a selective basis as they often are produced in limited quantities. (7) Titles produced for the mass market in the areas of collectibles, travel guides, and genealogy receive selective coverage.

Certain categories of reference sources are usually not reviewed in ARBA: those of fewer than 48 pages that are not part of a larger set, those produced by vanity presses or by the author as publisher, and those generated by library staffs for internal use. Highly specialized reference works printed in a limited number of copies and that do not appeal to the general library audience ARBA serves may also be omitted.

In the 2000 edition of ARBA reviews of sources intended specifically for the library professional were added to our publication. These include monographs and handbooks that address the concerns of library and information specialists. Much like the acclaimed *Library and Information Science Annual*, these reviews provide critical analyses of library literature. These reviews can be found in chapter 11, titled "Library and Information Science and Publishing and Bookselling."

Since 2013 ARBA has teamed up with another highly esteemed reviewing source, *Library Media Connection* (LMC), to recognize the Best of Reference in the areas of children's and young adult library resources. Both publications are known for featuring high-quality, critical reviews that enable librarians to select the best reference sources for their young researchers' needs. In the coming year we will be announcing the "best of the best" in the areas of children's reference, young adult reference, electronic reference for K-12, and best professional guide for school and youth librarians. The editors and reviewers of ARBA look forward to celebrating the best in children's and youth reference in the coming year.

Reviewing Policy

To ensure well-written, balanced reviews of high quality, the ARBA staff maintains a roster of more than 400 scholars, practitioners, and library educators in all subject specialties at libraries and universities throughout the United States and Canada. Because ARBA is a comprehensive reviewing source, unlike *Choice* or *Library Journal*, the reviews are generally longer and more critical, to detail the strengths and weaknesses of important reference works. Reviewers are asked to examine books and provide well-documented critical comments, both positive and negative. Coverage usually includes the usefulness of a given work; organization, execution, and pertinence of contents; prose style; format; availability of supplementary materials (e.g., indexes, appendixes); and similarity to other works and previous editions. Reviewers are encouraged to address the intended audience but not necessarily to give specific recommendations for purchase. An adequate description and evaluation of the reference source are sufficient.

Arrangement

ARBA 2014 consists of 37 chapters, an author/title index, and a subject index. It is divided into four alphabetically arranged parts: "General Reference Works," "Social Sciences," "Humanities," and "Science and Technology." "General Reference Works" is subdivided by form: bibliography, biography, dictionaries and encyclopedias, government publications, handbooks and yearbooks, and so on. Within the remaining three parts, chapters are organized by topic. Thus, under "Social Sciences" the reader will find chapters titled "Economics and Business," "Education," "History," "Law," "Sociology," and so on.

Each chapter is subdivided to reflect the arrangement strategy of the entire volume. There is a section on general works followed by a topical breakdown. For example, in the chapter titled "Literature," "General Works" is followed by "Children's and Young Adult Literature," "Fiction," and "National Literature." These sections are divided into subsections by format, such as "Bibliography" and "Dictionaries and Encyclopedias." Subsections are based on the amount of material available on a given topic and vary from year to year. Users should keep in mind that many materials may fall under several different chapter topics. The comprehensive author/title and subject indexes found at the end of the volume will assist users in finding specific works that could fall under several different chapters.

Acknowledgments

In closing, we wish to express our gratitude to the many talented contributors without whose support this volume of ARBA could not have been compiled. Many thanks also go out to our distinguished Advisory Board members whose contributions greatly enhance ARBA and ARBAonline. We would also like to thank the members of our staff who were instrumental in its preparation.

Contributors

Gordon J. Aamot, Head, Foster Business Library, Univ. of Washington, Seattle.

Stephen H. Aby, Education Bibliographer, Bierce Library, Univ. of Akron, Ohio.

Anthony J. Adam, Director, Institutional Assessment, Blinn College, Brenham, Tex.

Melinda A. Adams, Library Teacher, Upper Cape Cod Regional Technical School, Bourne, Mass.

Michael Adams, Reference Librarian, City Univ. of New York Graduate Center.

Bev Cummings Agnew, Asst. Distance Learning Librarian, Regis Univ., Colorado Springs Library, Colo.

Karen Alexander, Lake Fenton High School, Linden, Mich.

Adrienne Antink, Medical Group Management Association, Lakewood, Colo.

Noriko Asato, Assoc. Professor of Library and Information Science, Univ. of Hawaii at Manoa.

Susan C. Awe, Asst. Director, Univ. of New Mexico, Albuquerque.

Thomas E. Baker, Assoc. Professor, Department of Criminal Justice, Univ. of Scranton, Pa.

Laurie Balderson, English Teacher, Hamilton-Holmes Middle School, King William, Va.

Catherine Barr, Editor, Children's and Young Adult Literature Reference Series, Libraries Unlimited

Daniel R. Beach, Teaching Librarian, Concord Elementary School, Anderson, S.C.

Suzanne Bell, Economics/Data Librarian, Rush Rhees Library Reference Dept. Univ. of Rochester, N.Y.

Michael Francis Bemis, Asst. Librarian, Washington County Library, Woodbury, Minn.

Laura J. Bender, Librarian, Univ. of Arizona, Tucson.

Helen Margaret Bernard, Reference and Interlibrary Loan Librarian, Writing Center Director, Southwestern Baptist Theological Seminary, Fort Worth, Tex.

Allison L. Bernstein, Educational Materials Reviewer, Cortlandt Manor, N.Y.

John B. Beston, (former) Professor of English, Santa Fe, N.Mex.

Barbara M. Bibel, Reference Librarian, Science/Business/Sociology Dept., Main Library, Oakland Public Library, Calif.

Sally Bickley, Coordinator of Reference Services, Texas A&M Univ.-Corpus Christi, Corpus Christi, Tex.

Daniel K. Blewett, Reference Librarian, College of DuPage Library, College of DuPage, Glen Ellyn, Ill.

James E. Bobick, (former) Head of the Science and Technology Dept., Carnegie Library of Pittsburgh, Pa.

Polly D. Boruff-Jones, Director of Library and Information Services, Drury Univ., Springfield, Mo.

Anne Bozievich, Library Media Specialist, Friendship Elementary School, Glen Rock, Pa.

Alicia Brillon, Reference Librarian, S. J. Quinney Law Library, Univ. of Utah.

Georgia Briscoe, Assoc. Director and Head of Technical Services, Law Library, Univ. of Colorado, Boulder.

Simon J. Bronner, Distinguished Professor of Folklore and American Studies, Capitol College, Pennsylvania State Univ., Middletown.

Janet Dagenais Brown, Assoc. Professor and Education and Social Sciences Librarian, Wichita State Univ., Kans.

Kate Brundage, Library Media Specialist, Singapore American School, Singapore.

Patrick J. Brunet, (retired) Library Manager, Western Wisconsin Technical College, La Crosse.

John R. Burch Jr., Dean of Distance Learning and Library Services, Cambellsville Univ., Ky.

Frederic F. Burchsted, Reference Librarian, Widener Library, Harvard Univ., Cambridge, Mass.

Mike Burgmeier, Reference Librarian, Northern Michigan Univ., Marquette.

Joanna M. Burkhardt, Head Librarian, College of Continuing Education Library, Univ. of Rhode Island, Providence.

Diane M. Calabrese, Freelance Writer and Contributor, Silver Springs, Md.

Delilah R. Caldwell, Online Services Librarian and Adjunct Instructor, Southwestern College, Winfield, Kans.

Robert M. Campbell, Social Studies Teacher, Olympic Middle School, Shelton, Wash.

Joseph L. Carlson, Library Director, Vandenberg Air Force Base, Calif.

Lourdes Cervantes, Hemphill Elementary School, Kyle, Tex.

Bert Chapman, Government Publications Coordinator, Purdue Univ., West Lafayette, Ind.

Boyd Childress, Reference Librarian, Ralph B. Draughon Library, Auburn Univ., Ala.

Hui Hua Chua, U.S. Documents Librarian, Michigan State Univ. Libraries, East Lansing.

Dene L. Clark, (retired) Reference Librarian, Auraria Library, Denver, Colo.

Donald E. Collins, Assoc. Professor, History Dept., East Carolina Univ., Greenville, N.C.

Martha Cooney, Director, Center for Business Research, C. W. Post Campus, Long Island Univ., Brookville, N.Y.

Rosanne M. Cordell, (formerly) Head of Reference Services, Franklin D. Schurz Library, Indiana Univ., South Bend.

Paul B. Cors, Catalog Librarian, Univ. of Wyoming, Laramie.

Gregory A. Crawford, Head of Public Services, Penn State Harrisburg, Middletown, Pa.

Alice Crosetto, Coordinator, Collection Development and Acquisitions Librarian, Univ. of Toledo, Ohio.

Gregory Curtis, Regional Federal Depository Librarian for Maine, New Hampshire, and Vermont, Fogler Library, Univ. of Maine, Presque Isle.

Barbara Delzell, Librarian, St. Gregorys Univ., Shawnee, Okla.

Norman Desmarais, Acquisitions Librarian, Providence College, R.I.

Wendy Diamond, Business and Economics Librarian and Head of Reference at California State Univ.—Chico.

R. K. Dickson, Asst. Professor of Fine Arts, Wilson College, Chambersburg, Pa.

Scott R. DiMarco, Director of Library Services and Information Resources, Mansfield Univ., Mansfield, Pa.

Margaret F. Dominy, Information Services Librarian, Drexel Univ., Philadelphia, Pa.

Lucy Duhon, Serials Librarian, Univ. of Toledo, Ohio.

Joe P. Dunn, Charles A. Dana Professor of History and Politics, Converse College, Spartanburg, S.C.

Bradford Lee Eden, Assoc. University Librarian for Technical Services and Scholarly Communication, Univ. of California, Santa Barbara.

Benet Steven Exton, St. Gregorys Univ. Library, Shawnee, Okla.

Elaine Ezell, Library Media Specialist, Bowling Green Jr. High School, Ohio.

Judith J. Field, Senior Lecturer, Program for Library and Information Science, Wayne State Univ., Detroit.

Josh Eugene Finnell, Reference Librarian, William Howard Doane Library, Denison Univ., Granville, Ohio.

Michael A. Foley, Honors Director, Marywood College, Scranton, Pa.

Charlotte Ford, Asst. Professor, School of Library and Information Science, San Jose State Univ., Calif.

Eric Forte, Member Services Consultant with OCLC.

Kenneth M. Frankel, Assoc. University Librarian, Florida Atlantic Univ., Boca Raton.

Julia Frankosky, Government Information Librarian, Michigan State Univ., East Lansing.

David K. Frasier, Asst. Librarian, Reference Dept., Indiana Univ., Bloomington.

David O. Friedrichs, Professor, Univ. of Scranton, Pa.

Linda Friend, Head Libraries Information Technology, Pennsylvania State Univ., University Park.

Zev Garber, Professor and Chair, Jewish Studies, Los Angeles Valley College, Calif.

Denise A. Garofalo, Systems and Catalog Services Librarian, Curtin Memorial Library, Mount Saint Mary College, Newburgh, N.Y.

Karen Gedeon, Roberts Middle School, Cuyahoga Falls, Ohio.

John T. Gillespie, College Professor and Writer, New York.

Lois Gilmer, (formerly) Library Director, Univ. of West Florida, Fort Walton Beach.

Caroline L. Gilson, Coordinator, Prevo Science Library, DePauw Univ., Greencastle, Ind.

Michelle Glatt, Librarian, Chiddix Junior High School, Normal, Ill.

Ann M. G. Gray, Library Media Specialist, Pittsburg School, N.H.

Beth Green, School Library Media Specialist, Wappingers Junior High School, Wappingers Falls, N.Y.

Richard W. Grefrath, Reference Librarian, Univ. of Nevada, Reno.

Sue Ellen Griffiths, Public Services Librarian 1, Pasco County Library System, Hudson, Fla.

Linda W. Hacker, Reference Librarian, SUNY Brockport, Brockport, N.Y.

Patrick Hall, Director of the Library, Univ. of Pittsburgh, Pa.

Diane S. Hance, NBCT Librarian, Grisham Middle School, Austin, Tex.

Ralph Hartsock, Senior Music Catalog Librarian, Univ. of North Texas, Denton.

Karen D. Harvey, Assoc. Dean for Academic Affairs, Univ. College, Univ. of Denver, Colo.

Muhammed Hassanali, Independent Consultant, Shaker Heights, Ohio.

Maris L. Hayashi, Asst. University Librarian, Florida Atlantic Univ., Boca Raton, Fla.

Lucy Heckman, Reference Librarian (Business-Economics), St. John's Univ. Library, Jamaica, N.Y.

Robin Henry, Librarian, Wakeland High School, Frisco, Tex.

Mark Y. Herring, Dean of Library Services, Winthrop Univ., Dacus Library, Rock Hill, S.C.

Joseph P. Hester, SRO-Learning, Claremont, N.C.

Ladyjane Hickey, Reference Librarian, Austin College, Tex.

Susan Tower Hollis, Assoc. Dean and Center Director, Central New York Center of the State Univ. of New York.

Sara Anne Hook, Professor of Informatics and Assoc. Dean for Academic Affairs and Undergraduate Studies, UP School of Informatics, Indiana Univ., Purdue Univ., Indianapolis.

Mihoko Hosoi, Public Services Librarian, Cornell Univ., Ithaca, N.Y.

Ma Lei Hsieh, Librarian, Rider Univ., N.J.

Lisa Hunt, NBCT Elementary Library Media Specialist, Apple Creek Elementary, Moore, Okla.

Jonathan F. Husband, Program Chair of the Library/Reader Services Librarian, Henry Whittemore Library, Framingham State College, Mass.

Shannon Graff Hysell, Staff, Libraries Unlimited.

Amanda Izenstark, Asst. Professor, Reference and Instructional Design Librarian, Univ. of Rhode Island, Kingston.

Barbara Johnson, Technology Resource Teacher, Colchester Public Schools, Conn.

Mary J. Johnson, Retired School Librarian and Education Consultant, Colorado Springs, Colo.

Melissa M. Johnson, Reference Services, NOVA Southeastern Univ., Alvin Sherman Library, Ft. Lauderdale, Fla.

Elizabeth Kahn, Librarian, Patrick F. Taylor Sci Tech Academy, Jefferson, La.

Thomas A. Karel, Assoc. Director for Public Services, Shadek-Fackenthal Library, Franklin and Marshall College, Lancaster, Pa.

Craig Mury Keeney, Cataloging Librarian, South Caroliniana Library, Univ. of South Carolina.

Edmund D. Keiser Jr., Professor of Biology, Univ. of Mississippi, University.

John Laurence Kelland, Reference Bibliographer for Life Sciences, Univ. of Rhode Island Library, Kingston.

Sue C. Kimmel, Old Dominion Univ., Norfolk, Va.

Michael Knee, Science Library, Univ. of Albany, SUNY.

Lori D. Kranz, Freelance Editor, Chambersburg, Pa.

Betsy J. Kraus, Librarian, Lovelace Respiratory Research Institute, National Environmental Respiratory Center, Albuquerque, N.Mex.

Marlene M. Kuhl, Library Manager, Baltimore County Public Library, Reisterstown Branch, Md.

George Thomas Kurian, President, Encyclopedia Society, Baldwin Place, N.Y.

Robert V. Labaree, Reference/Public Services Librarian, Von KleinSmid Library, Univ. of Southern California, Los Angeles.

Lizbeth Langston, Reference Librarian, Univ. of California, Riverside.

Rob Laurich, Head of Reference and Collection Development, The City College of New York.

Martha Lawler, Assoc. Librarian, Louisiana State Univ., Shreveport.

Chris LeBeau, Asst. Teaching Professor, Univ. of Missouri, School of Information Science and Learning Technologies.

Charles Leck, Professor of Biological Sciences, Rutgers Univ., New Brunswick, N.J.

Polin P. Lei, Silver Springs, Md.

Karen Leon, Librarian, Roslyn High School, Roslyn Heights, N.Y.

Judyth Lessee, Librarian, Schutz American School, Alexandria, Egypt

Tze-chung Li, Professor and Dean Emeritus, Dominican Univ.

Charlotte Lindgren, Professor Emerita of English, Emerson College, Boston, Mass.

Megan W. Lowe, Reference/Instruction Librarian, University Library, Univ. of Louisiana at Monroe.

W. Bernard Lukenbill, Professor Emeritus in the School of Information, Univ. of Texas at Austin

Barbara MacAlpine, Science Librarian, Coates Library, Trinity Univ., San Antonio, Tex.

Marty Magee, Medical Librarian, National Network of Libraries of Medicine, MidContinental Region based at the McGoogan Library of Medicine at the Univ. of Nebraska Medical Center.

Theresa Maggio, Head of Public Services, Southwest Georgia Regional Library, Bainbridge.

Tyler Manolovitz, Digital Resources Coordinator, Sam Houston State Univ.—Newton Gresham Library, Huntsville, Tex.

Sara Marcus, Asst. Professor of Education, Touro Univ. International, N.Y.

Ron Marinucci, Adjunct Professor of History, Mott and Oakland Community Colleges, Mich.

LJ Martin, Elementary Librarian, Dubai, United Arab Emirates.

Michelle Martinez, Librarian, Newton Gresham Library, Sam Houston State Univ., Huntsville, Tex.

Melinda F. Matthews, Interlibrary Loan/Reference Librarian, Univ. of Louisiana at Monroe.

John Maxymuk, Reference Librarian, Paul Robeson Library, Rutgers Univ., Camden, N.J.

Kevin McDonough, Reference and Electronic Resources Librarian, Northern Michigan Univ.—Olson Library, Marquette.

Peter Zachary McKay, Business Librarian, Assoc. Chair for the Social Sciences, Univ. of Florida Libraries, Gainesville.

Susan C. McNair, NBCT librarian, Lugoff-Elgin High School, Lugoff, S.C.

Lillian R. Mesner, Arbor City Indexing, Nebraska City, Nebr.

G. Douglas Meyers, Chair, Dept. of English, Univ. of Texas, El Paso.

Elizabeth M. Mezick, CPA/Asst. Professor, Long Island Univ., Brookville, N.Y.

Seiko Mieczkowski, Cocoa Beach, Fla.

Melinda W. Miller, K-12 Library Media Specialist, Colton-Pierrepont Central School, Colton, N.Y.

Janet Mongan, Research Officer, Cleveland State Univ. Library, Ohio.

Susan E. Montgomery, Instruction Librarian, Lynn Univ., Boca Raton, Fla.

Terry Ann Mood, Professor Emeritus, Univ. of Colorado, Denver.

Rita W. Moss, Business and Economics Librarian, Univ. of North Carolina, Chapel Hill.

Craig A. Munsart, Teacher, Jefferson County Public Schools, Golden, Colo.

Paul M. Murphy III, Director of Marketing, PMX Medical, Denver, Colo.

Ann Bryan Nelson, Volunteer Media Specialist and Guest Teacher, Thompson Ranch Elementary School, Surprise, Ariz.

Charles Neuringer, Professor of Psychology and Theatre and Film, Univ. of Kansas, Lawrence.

Carol L. Noll, Volunteer Librarian, Schimelpfenig Middle School, Plano, Tex.

Margot Note, Information Manager and Archivist, World Monuments Fund, New York.

Herbert W. Ockerman, Professor, Ohio State Univ., Columbus.

Lawrence Olszewski, Director, OCLC Library and Information Center, Dublin, Ohio.

Ray Olszewski, Independent Consultant, Palo Alto, Calif.

John Howard Oxley, Faculty, American Intercontinental Univ., Atlanta, Ga.

Mike Parchinski, Brookfield, Conn.

Amy B. Parsons, Reference and Catalog Librarian, Courtright Memorial Library, Otterbein College, Westerville, Ohio.

Gary L. Parsons, Reference Librarian, Florida Atlantic Univ., Boca Raton.

Stefanie S. Pearlman, Asst. Professor of Law Library and Reference Librarian, Schmid Law Library, Univ. of Nebraska, Lincoln.

Anna H. Perrault, Assoc. Professor, Univ. of South Florida, Tampa.

Christina K. Pikas, Technical Librarian, Johns Hopkins Univ., Applied Physics Laboratory, Laurel, Md.

Jack Ray, Asst. Director, Loyola/Notre Dame Library, Baltimore, Md.

Patrick J. Reakes, Journalism/Mass Communications Librarian, Univ. of Florida, Gainesville.

Donna Reed, NBCT Library Media Specialist, Newark High School, Del.

Allen Reichert, Electronic Access Librarian, Courtright Memorial Library, Otterbein College, Westerville, Ohio.

John B. Romeiser, Professor of French and Dept. Head, Univ. of Tennessee, Knoxville.

Barbara Ripp Safford, Assoc. Professor at the School Library Media Studies, Univ. of Northern Iowa, Cedar Falls.

Nadine Salmons, (retired) Technical Services Librarian, Fort Carson's Grant Library, Colo.

William O. Scheeren, Lecturer in Education at St. Vincent College, Latrobe, Pa.

Diane Schmidt, Biology Librarian, Univ. of Illinois, Urbana.

Ralph Lee Scott, Assoc. Professor, East Carolina Univ. Library, Greenville, N.C.

Robert A. Seal, Univ. Librarian, Texas Christian Univ., Fort Worth.

Colleen Seale, Humanities and Social Sciences Services, George A. Smathers Libraries, Univ. of Florida, Gainesville.

Shanna Shadoan, McGill Univ., Montreal, Quebec, Canada.

Ravindra Nath Sharma, Dean of Library, Monmouth University Library, West Long Branch, N.J.

Scott Alan Sheidlower, Asst. Professor, York College/City Univ. of New York, Jamaica.

Brian J. Sherman, Head of Access Services and Systems, Noel Memorial Library, Louisiana State Univ.—Shreveport.

Susan Shultz, Reference and Instruction Librarian, DePaul Univ., Chicago, Ill.

Leena Siegelbaum, (formerly) Bibliographer of Eastern European Law, Harvard Univ., Cambridge, Mass.

Kay Stebbins Slattery, Coordinator Librarian, Louisiana State Univ., Shreveport.

Mary Ellen Snodgrass, Freelance Writer, Charlotte, N.C.

Steven W. Sowards, Asst. Director for Collections, Michigan State Univ. Libraries, East Lansing.

Lisa Kay Speer, Special Collections Librarian, Southeast Missouri State Univ., Cape Girardeau.

Ellen Spring, Library Media Specialist, Rockland District Middle School, Maine.

Sandhya D. Srivastava, Asst. Professor, Serials Librarian, Hofstra Univ., Hempstead, N.Y.

John P. Stierman, Reference Librarian, Western Illinois Univ., Macomb.

John W. Storey, Professor of History, Lamar Univ., Beaumont, Tex.

William C. Struning, Professor, Seton Hall Univ., South Orange, N.J.

Mila C. Su, Assoc./Women's Studies Librarian, Pennsylvania State Univ., Altoona.

Philip G. Swan, Head Librarian, Hunter College, School of Social Work Library, New York.

Martha Tarlton, Head, Reference and Information Services, Univ. of North Texas Libraries, Denton.

Marit S. Taylor, Reference Librarian, Auraria Libraries, Univ. of Colorado, Denver.

Rosalind Tedford, Asst. Head for Research and Instruction, Z.Smith Reynolds Library, Wake Forest Univ., Winston-Salem, N.C.

Annette B. Thibodeaux, Librarian, Archbishop Chapelle High School Library, Metairie, La.

Paul H. Thomas, Head, Catalog Dept., Hoover Institution Library, Stanford Univ., Calif.

Susan E. Thomas, Head of Collection Development/Assoc. Librarian, Indiana Univ. South Bend.

Mary Ann Thompson, Asst. Professor of Nursing, Saint Joseph College, West Hartford, Conn.

Linda D. Tietjen, Senior Instructor, Arts and Architecture Bibliographer, Auraria Library, Denver, Colo.

Elizabeth Kay Tompkins, Asst. Professor, Kingsborough Community College—CUNY, Brooklyn, N.Y.

Megan Toups, Instruction/Liaison Librarian , Trinity Univ., San Antonio, Tex.

Martha A. Tucker, Head Librarian, Mathematics Research Library, Univ. of Washington, Seattle.

Elias H. Tuma, Professor of Economics, Univ. of California, Davis.

Diane J. Turner, Science/Engineering Liaison, Auraria Library, Univ. of Colorado, Denver.

Robert L. Turner Jr., Librarian and Assoc. Professor, Radford Univ., Va.

Linda M. Turney, E-Resources Cataloging Librarian, Walker Library, Middle Tennessee State Univ., Murfreesboro.

Nancy L. Van Atta, Dayton, Ohio.

Stephanie Vie, Univ. of Central Florida, Winter Park, Fla.

J. E. Weaver, Dept. of Economics, Drake Univ., Des Moines, Iowa.

Karen T. Wei, Head, Asian Library, Univ. of Illinois, Urbana.

Jennifer Welch, Librarian, Thomas Crossroads Elementary School, Sharpsburg, Ga.

Gary W. White, Head, Schreyer Business Library, Pennsylvania State Univ.

Maren Williams, Reference Librarian, Univ. of Louisiana at Monroe.

Mark A. Wilson, Professor of Geology, College of Wooster, Ohio.

Julienne L. Wood, Head, Research Services, Noel Memorial Library, Louisiana State Univ. in Shreveport.

Eileen Wright, Reference Librarian, Montana State Univ., Billings.

Henry E. York, Head, Collection Management, Cleveland State Univ., Ohio.

Anita Zutis, Adjunct Librarian, Queensborough Community College, Bayside, N.Y.

Journals Cited

FORM OF CITATION	JOURNAL TITLE
AG	*Against the Grain*
BL	*Booklist*
BR	*Book Report*
Choice	*Choice*
JAL	*Journal of Academic Librarianship*
LJ	*Library Journal*
LMC	*Library Media Connection*
RUSQ	*Reference & User Services Quarterly*
SLJ	*School Library Journal*
TL	*Teacher Librarian*
VOYA	*Voice of Youth Advocates*

Part I

GENERAL
REFERENCE
WORKS

1 General Reference Works

Almanacs

1. **Factmonster.com. http://www.factmonster.com/.** [Website]. Upper Saddle River, N.J., Pearson Education. Free. Date reviewed: 2013.

Factmonster.com is a freely available almanac for children online. It draws on the contents of the print *Time for Kids Almanac* and offers information in various categories: World, United States, People, Science, Math and Money, Word Wise, and Sports. The Cool Stuff link includes information on art, architecture, business, entertainment, fashion, holidays, music, and worldwide dating and marriage customs. *Factmonster.com* also offers a Game and Quizzes area and a Homework Center. The Word Wise section includes information on children's literature, language facts, and a handy grammar and spelling resource. This reference also has a Reference Desk area. One can search all the information on the site through a simple keyword search box on the homepage. For general information for children this is a good online source to consult.—**Adrienne Antink**

2. **Information Please Almanac Online. http://www.infoplease.com.** [Website]. Free. Date reviewed: 2013.

The *Information Please Almanac* online (http://www.infoplease.com) includes information from the *Time Almanac* and the *ESPN Sports Almanac*. The almanac information is integrated with the *Random House Unabridged Dictionary* and the *Columbia Encyclopedia* (6th edition) into a single reference source with a wealth of facts. The search page offers several ways to find information, including a keyword box, an index of topics, and a directory of information divided into the following categories: World and News, United States, History and Government, Biography, Sports, Arts and Entertainment, Business, Calendars and Holidays, Health and Science, Homework Center, and Fact Monster. One can click the Daily Almanac link near the top of the search page to access such features as "This Day in History," "Today's Word Quiz," "Today's Weather Fact," and "Today's Birthdays." The site is continuously updated, offering more recent information than can be found in the paper edition.—**Adrienne Antink**

3. **The World Almanac and Book of Facts 2014.** New York, Infobase Publishing, 2014. 1007p. illus. maps. index. $34.95. ISBN 13: 978-1-60057-181-7.

This almanac is a powerhouse of statistics, facts, lists, and stories covering the economy, crime, the military, health, notable personalities, the arts and media, science, consumer information, the U.S. Government, U.S. history, American cities and states, world history, geography, religion, education, sports, and more. For example, there are tables for determining the rising and setting of the planets for 2014, identifying past Academy Award winners, directories of associations, universities and colleges, businesses and corporations as well as listings for U.S. government departments and agencies. Interesting features include 2013 in Pictures, the World at a Glance section that picks out key statistics and little-known facts from the body of the book, Top 10 News Stories of 2013, obituaries from the past year, historical anniversaries coming up in 2014 (100th, 50th, 25th), and the editors' whimsical selections for a 2013 time capsule. This edition has special features on voting in the United States that features key election dates and information on the new voter-ID laws adopted by many states. It also has a special section on memorable Winter Olympic moments of the past in honor of the 2014 games. It is hard to imagine a question you might have that is not covered by this reference, which makes it an obvious choice for the ready-reference collection of most academic, school, and public libraries.—**Adrienne Antink**

4.   **The World Almanac for Kids 2014.** New York, Infobase Publishing, 2014. 352p. illus. index. $24.95. ISBN 13: 978-1-60057-176-3.

The World Almanac for Kids 2014 is an information-packed volume with the perfect content and presentation for the late-elementary to middle-school-aged child. This ready reference provides a good balance of history, current events, general knowledge, and statistics. The book begins with a "Faces & Places" section covering important topics from the past year in news and entertainment. From there, sections are presented alphabetically from animals to world history and cover a variety of topics, such as the arts, books, geography, language, movies and television, religion, science, sports, the United States, and weather. To cater to today's technologically savvy child, the book has stunning color pictures, maps, illustrations, Q&A's, quizzes, and puzzles to keep the user engaged. A child might actually enjoy just thumbing through the book for curiosity's sake. This volume achieves its objective and then some; it is a great example of what an almanac should be. Every child should have access to *The World Almanac for Kids 2011.*—**Sue Ellen Griffiths**

5.   **The World Almanac Online. http://www.worldalmanac.com/.** [Website]. New York, Infobase Publishing. Price negotiated by site. Date reviewed: 2013.

6.   **The World Almanac for Kids Online. http://www.worldalmanacforkids.com/.** [Website]. New York, Infobase Publishing. Price negotiated by site. Date reviewed: 2013.

Almanacs are handy collections of fascinating facts about a wide variety of people, places, and things. *The World Almanac and Book of Facts* is an excellent example of this type of reference source and for the first time Facts on File has made it available in an easy-to-navigate online resource. The publisher offers it in two formats: *The World Almanac Online* (for users from high school age and up) and *The World Almanac for Kids Online* (for kindergarten through middle school ages).

The World Almanac Online can be searched by keyword or browsed by category (e.g., Year in Review, Crime, Military Affairs, Health and Vital Statistics, Consumer Information, Science and Technology). It includes many additional features apart from the print edition such as daily articles on "This Day in History," "This Day in Sports," and "Quote of the Day." In addition users can export data into Excel; see full-color maps, flags, and graphs; and get citation help in the forms of MLA and *Chicago Manual of Style*.

The World Almanac for Kids Online provides extensive resources for students that goes well beyond what the print edition provides. These include: resources for homework, reports, and projects; image and video galleries; interactive games and quizzes; Homework Help tools; and Search Assistant technology that will help kids figure out the best way to research a topic. The site can be searched by keyword or browsed by topic (e.g., Animals, Career Ideas, Space and the Solar System, U.S. Presidents). There is also a Reader's Corner where children can discover books in particular genres, by specific authors, or best-sellers. The homepage is filled with news of the day, such as famous person's birthdays, "Today in History," and "Today in Sports."—**Shannon Graff Hysell**

Bibliography

Bibliographic Guides

7. **Book Index with Reviews (BIR). http://www.ebscohost.com/public/book-index-with-reviews.** [Website]. Ipswich, Mass., EBSCO. Price negotiated by site. Date reviewed: 2013.

8. **Book Review Digest Retrospective. 1905-1982. http://ebscohost.com/wilson.** [Website]. Bronx, N.Y., H. W. Wilson. Price negotiated by site. Date reviewed: 2013.

Book Index with Reviews is primarily a tool for information professionals. The site can be used for collection development and readers' advisory. Booklists and subject guides can be searched to find new titles for acquisition, replacement copies, and reviews. BIR includes over five million book titles, with thousands of fiction series, and with more constantly being added. NoveList, a readers' advisory section, includes readers' advisory training, feature articles by notable librarians and subject matter experts, access to NoveList newsletters, genre outlines, an online product tour, and more. BIR also includes the BIR Entertainment component, which provides information on 450,000 music titles and over 200,000 DVD/video titles with more being added regularly. Searching is simple with a basic search by title, author, or keyword. At the search results users can further narrow their searches in a variety of ways, such as by subject headings, publication date, in-print status, fiction/nonfiction, and more. Reviews are linked to the works in the library catalog. Library users can have their own My BIR site with options for saving searches, lists, and alerts. The My BIR alert service lets users know about new editions, forthcoming titles from popular authors, or new releases on hot topics.—**Anna H. Perrault**

9. **Early English Books Online (EEBO). http://eebo.chadwyck.com/home.** [Website]. Alexandria, Va., Chadwyck-Healey. Price negotiated by site. Date reviewed: 2013.

From the first book published in English through the age of Spenser and Shakespeare, this collection now contains more than 125,000 titles listed in Pollard & Redgrave's *Short-Title Catalogue (1475-1640)* and Wing's *Short-Title Catalogue (1641-1700)* and their revised editions, as well as the *Thomason Tracts (1640-1661)* collection and the *Early English Books Tract Supplement.* The works preserved here cover a broad range of topics, including literature, religion, politics, science, and social sciences, making them an in-depth resource for those scholars concerned with any aspect of English history and culture from this era. Previously these collections were only available to the public for those willing to seek out a library large enough to own these works on microfilm. The images are available in PDF files for easy printing; some books have also been keyed in, allowing display of the plaintext, which is a relief to anyone with aging eyes.

The keyed texts are fully searchable, allowing retrieval on any word in the text. The site's search functions are easy to use. Common typographical variants can be accounted for simply by clicking a box, a useful feature considering the era's reputation for having unconventional approaches to spelling even the most common of words. EEBO remains a work in progress, as titles are continuously being converted from microfilm; there are bound to be some records for which no online image or text is available. For libraries that can afford it, EEBO is a superb resource for scholarly study of this crucial historical period and is highly recommended for undergraduate through graduate level libraries.—**ARBA Staff Reviewer**

10. **Early European Books. http://www.proquest.com/en-US/catalogs/databases/detail/eeb.shtml.** [Website]. Alexandria, Va., Chadwyck-Healey. Price negotiated by site. Date reviewed: 2012.

Following in the footsteps of *Early English Books Online* (see ARBA 2013, entry 5), *Early European Books* provides scholars with extended access to more than 250 years of print culture from across Europe for the same time period 1450-1700. The project began by digitizing holdings from the Danish Royal Library's national collection of fifteenth- and sixteenth-century rare and valuable imprints. *Early European Books* is issued in collection units. Collection 1 has 2,600 books. The online database features high-resolution color images of all pages, bindings and clasps, image viewing, panning and zooming, a multilingual interface, and references to bibliographic sources. Indexing extends beyond text to include features such as illuminated lettering and marginalia.—**Anna H. Perrault**

11.   **FRANCIS. http://www.proquest.co.uk/en-UK/catalogs/databases/detail/francis-set-c.shtml.** [Website]. Bethesda, Md., ProQuest. Price negotiated by site. Date reviewed: 2013.

Art, art history, and archaeology are covered in the FRANCIS database for the humanities and social sciences, which contains 2,600,000 records from 4,300 journals dating from 1972 to the present. FRANCIS continues the content indexed by the earlier RAA (Repertoire d'Art et d'Archeologie), published from 1973 to 1989,and RILA (International Repertory of the Literature of Art), published from 1975 to 1989, both of which were merged to form *The Bibliography of the History of Art*,which was subsequently subsumed by the *International Bibliography of Art*.

FRANCIS contains over 2.6 million bibliographic records with coverage from 1972 to present. FRANCIS is strong in religion, the history of art, psychology, and sociology. Language and linguistics are well covered with psycholinguistics, sociolinguistics, ethno-linguistics, historical linguistics, semiotics, and communications. Other subject areas include archaeology, ethnology, geography, information science, and philosophy. Journal articles make up approximately 80 percent of source documents with books at 9 percent. It also indexes books and book chapters, and offers noteworthy coverage of grey literature, including conference papers, French dissertations, exhibition catalogs, and teaching materials. With its strong emphasis of French and European literature, there is the possibility to obtain bibliography records not contained in databases produced in the United States. Anyone endeavoring to conduct thorough research for retrospective materials in the humanities and arts needs to include FRANCIS in their research.—**Anna H. Perrault**

12.   **Oxford Bibliographies Online (OBO). http:/oxfordbibliographiesonline.com/.** [Website]. New York, Oxford University Press. Price negotiated by site. Date reviewed: 2013.

This resource indexes bibliographic resources of all types and makes them accessible to the researcher. OBO is primarily designed to provide bibliographic information, but the organization and introductory descriptions serve an encyclopedia function as well. The publisher's description of the resource indicates that it is a scholar-curated library of discipline-based subject modules. Each article has subject headings related to the topic, a commentary essay, citations to relevant resources with annotations, and links where available. The user is guided through the resource to the chapter, book, Website, archive, or dataset needed. It is the intent of the editors to combine the best aspects of online bibliographic databases and print bibliographies and their goal has been realized in this helpful and unique resource.—**Anna H. Perrault**

National and Trade Bibliography

13.   **Readers' Guide Full Text. http://ebscohost.com/academic/readers-guide-full-text-mega.** [Website]. Bronx, N.Y., H. W. Wilson. Price negotiated by site. Date reviewed: 2013.

14.   **Readers' Guide Retrospective, 1890-1994. http://ebscohost.com/academic/readers-guide-retrospective.** [Website]. Bronx, N.Y., H. W. Wilson. Price negotiated by site. Date reviewed: 2013.

The *Readers' Guide* is the most well-known general indexing tool found in nearly all public, academic, and school libraries. The online version is a full-text database with articles from hundreds of magazines back as far as 1994, plus article abstracts and indexing. The *Readers' Guide Retrospective* is a separate file that contains the texts of more than 3 million articles as far back as 1890, the beginnings of the index, "tracking modern U.S. cultural and history over more than 100 years." The *Readers' Guide* should be included in any thorough literature search for retrospective topics in the humanities and the arts.—**ARBA Staff Reviewer**

15.   **Wilson Book Review Digest Plus. http://ebscohost.com/wilson.** [Website]. Bronx, N.Y., H. W. Wilson. Price negotiated by site. Date reviewed: 2013.

   Wilson Book Review Digest Plus is the online version of the long-running *Book Review Digest*. The database contains over 100,000 full-text reviews, plus review excerpts, book summaries, and bibliographic data updated daily. Entries encompass some 1,300,000 reviews from sources back to 1983, covering over 660,000 books. *Book Review Digest Retrospective* contains the volumes of the title from 1905-1982 with 1.5 million reviews, covering more than 300,000 books (see entry 8).—**ARBA Staff Reviewer**

Biography

United States

16.   **American Academy of Achievement. http://www.achievement.org.** [Website]. Free. Date reviewed: 2013.

   This Website provides biographies of high achievers in the arts, business, public service, science and exploration, sports, and more. The goal of the Academy of Achievement is to put students face-to-face with the leaders and visionaries that have shaped our modern world. They do this by providing high-quality videos, Webinars, podcasts, photographs, and profiles of some of the world's most influential achievers. Students will be able to access this site for research and for inspiration.—**ARBA Staff Reviewer**

International

17.   **Biography Reference Bank. http://ebscohost.com/academic/biography-reference-bank.** [Website]. Bronx, N.Y., H. W. Wilson. Price negotiated by site. Date reviewed: 2013.

   Biography Reference Bank is a single online resource that combines the content of five H.W. Wilson biographical databases: Biography Index, Current Biography, Wilson Biographies Plus Illustrated, and Junior Authors & Illustrators; as well as biographical full-text articles, page images, and abstracts from all Wilson databases. Additional content is published through agreements with other major publishers. About 1,500 new names are added each year. The graphical interface is user-friendly; searching is by name, profession, place of origin, gender, ethnicity, birth/death dates, titles of works, or keywords. Both full-text articles and article citations can be retrieved. The database can be used by any level of reader in any discipline and is well suited for research in multidisciplinary fields, such as women's studies, cultural studies, media studies, and more.—**Anna H. Perrault**

18.   **Crabtree Groundbreaker Biographies Series.** New York, Crabtree, 2012. multivolume. illus. index. $33.27/vol.

   These books cover a diverse group of people—both male and female, fashion designers and sports stars, people from the United States and from Canada. Each inspirational story tells of a leader in their field. Whether one is interested in political activism, law, astronomy, sports, or fashion, there is a story for all. Those newly profiled in the series include The Beatles and Muhammad Ali. Each book has a chronology, glossary, sources for further information, and index. The narratives have black-and-white photographs and pictures, although not all images are clearly captioned, leading a reader to lack contextual connections at times. Grey boxes indicate shorter pieces on related material to the main topic of the book, providing visual guidance to help keep the reader on track. Despite different authors, all books follow the same layout, making it easy to go from one book to another. Suitable for grades five to eight, these books will entertain as they educate, providing biographical, historical, and social studies tie-ins.—**Sara Marcus**

19.   **Current Biography Illustrated. http://www.ebscohost.com/academic/current-biography-illustrated.** [Website]. Bronx, N.Y., H. W. Wilson. Price negotiated by site. Date reviewed: 2013.

This is a database of more than 25,000 biographies and obituaries that have appeared in *Current Biography* since 1940, as well as updated biographies and articles not in the print edition. The profiles are written in an entertaining and informative style. The biography's remain unchanged, but more than 19,500 illustrations are included on those profiled. Each year nearly 450 new biographies are added. Users can search by name, profession, place of origin, birth or death date, ethnicity, gender, or popular works. A bibliography provides users with new resources for further study. Building on its solid reputation, *Current Biography Illustrated* is an essential purchase for reference collections at all levels.—**Catherine Barr**

20.   **Thinkers 50. http://www.thinkers50.com.** [Website]. Free. Date reviewed: 2013.

This Website ranks the top 50 business thinkers of all time and includes biographical information on each key innovator. The Thinkers50 consists of leaders that are considered to be engaged, accomplished, creative, and inspiring. The staff at Thinkers50 follows books being published, apps being developed, ideas being explored and refined, and topics appearing in the media from this remarkable group as well as up-and-coming leaders in the business world. Under Access Ideas users will find videos and interviews with the key leaders and will learn more about their approach to business, their creative process, and their vision for the future.—**ARBA Staff Reviewer**

Dictionaries and Encyclopedias

21.   **National Geographic: People, Animals and the World. http://www.gale.cengage.com/.** [Website]. Stamford, Conn., Gale/Cengage Learning, 2013. Price negotiated by site. Date reviewed: 2013.

National Geographic is working with Gale to create digital access to their collection of information, images, and maps. Hundreds of magazine issues, special inserts and maps, images from award-winning photographers, and videos are now available from one resource. The feature *People, Animals and the World* allows users to search the site by topic: animals, science and technology, environment, history, people and cultures, and travel. Materials are listed in category types; full-text books include bookmarking, printing, and citation tools. Brief videos provide transcribed text; maps can be adjusted for size. The content is rich and varied with easy access, and the subscription allows for multiple users. Additional tools are available to create saved lists, search history, and graph the topical searches over time. This easily accessible site is recommended for dependable use and authority of information.—**Lisa Hunt**

22.   **Oxford English Dictionary Online. http://www.oed.com.** [Website]. New York, Oxford University Press. Price negotiated by site. Date reviewed: 2013.

The *Oxford English Dictionary* is widely regarded as the accepted authority on the English language, and this online version is keeping with this claim. This easily accessible database provides over 600,000 word meanings, histories, and pronunciations. Quarterly updates revise existing entries and add new words. Researchers will find fascinating commentaries, articles, and scholarly essays, all of which pertain to the English language in the context of use, time and place, the people who shaped the language, and word stories. The Historical Thesaurus contains 800,000 words and meanings in 235,000 entry categories. It is the first comprehensive historical thesaurus ever produced. Librarians will find a fully searchable resource section complete with ways of marketing the OED to patrons. The Resource section for teachers is sparse and lacks lesson plans, which would have truly enhanced the database. In spite of this, it is a great addition to both high school and public libraries.—**Melinda A. Adams**

23.   **Social Studies Power. http://www.worldbookonline.com/wb.2001.** [Website]. Chicago, World Book. Price negotiated by site. Date reviewed: 2013.

Part of World Book Classroom, *Social Studies Power* is best suited for middle school students. It is easy to navigate with interactive maps, quizzes, and multimedia. Users can search by keyword or pre-selected strand. Literacy tools include extension activities, inquiry projects, official thinking, and graphic organizers. Information can be e-mailed or saved, and a downloading option is quite helpful. In the Teacher section, one can correlate curriculum standards with World Book entries. The reading level of most entries is middle school and the database is text heavy. Many features are already available in the World Book Student database, so this product is not necessary for those subscribers.—**Judyth Lessee**

24.   **World Book Discovery Encyclopedia.** Chicago, World Book, 2013. 13v. illus. maps. index. $389.00/set. ISBN 13: 978-0-7166-7417-7.

This is a general encyclopedia written expressly for primary or middle school children. With eye-catching visuals in the form of illustrations, diagrams, and maps, this set will appeal to this age group. The vocabulary range is carefully limited, but there is no hint of talking down to readers. Certainly a tool to encourage a child's curiosity and independence, it will also enhance alphabetic searching skills and the ability of students to make alphabetic lists of their own. The content of the articles is directed toward the interests of children and the writers/editors have done a good job of outlining events such as World War I, or identifying primary attributes of a subject. It is particularly interesting to note the fairness in treatment of controversial subjects.

Every entry is accompanied by one or more color illustrations. The encyclopedia is an excellent source of illustrations for people of any age. The set will be easy for young people to navigate due to the many features the publisher has added: guide words at the top of each page, cross-references to related articles, section headings within the longer articles, pronunciation guides, and sidebars with special information geared toward kids. The average length of an article is two to three paragraphs, each consisting of two to three sentences, but there are longer articles of two to four pages. New to this 2013 edition are updated state and province information as well as city population data; revised state and provincial flags and seals; 2012 U.S. presidential election results; and updated global population data and maps. This encyclopedia, written for children to enjoy and beautifully illustrated, would be an excellent addition to any educational library for children, at home, at school, or at a public library.—**Shannon Graff Hysell**

25.   **World Book Discovery Science Encyclopedia.** Chicago, World Book, 2014. 13v. illus. maps. index. $9,999.00/set. ISBN 13: 978-0-7166-7507-5.

World Book Discovery Science Encyclopedia is a multivolume set compiled by the World Book staff and that draws its information from World Book. The subject matter includes a mixture of human, animal, and marine biology; geology; astronomy; chemistry; and prominent people in the field of science.

There are also entries on computer science, botany, ecology, entomology, dinosaurs, mechanics, and concepts, such as emotions and dreams. The volumes also contain special feature articles and suggested experiments; these sections are clearly distinguished from the entries. The entries are generally brief and informative.

Volumes 1-12 contain the entries with volume 13 providing the index and additional science resources, such as facts and theories and useful Websites. Entries are generally a half a page with the longest being about four pages. The language is simple and clear. All entries generally have an accompanying photograph or graphic and include related article lists and cross-references where applicable. The volumes themselves are slim with sturdy binding. Each one runs from slightly over 100 pages with the thicker volumes at a little over 200 pages. The pages are glossy and thick. Since the set is geared toward children in elementary school the individual books are built to take a bit of abuse. This is a good resource for elementary school media centers.—**Melissa M. Johnson**

26.   **The World Book Encyclopedia 2014.** Chicago, World Book, 2014. 22v. illus. maps. index. $999.00/set. ISBN 13: 978-0-7166-0114-2.

In publication since 1917, this well-known and well-respected encyclopedia now comprises 22 volumes, including a special research guide and index volume. With each new edition a significant amount of material is revised and many new entries are added. This volume has dozens of new and expanded articles with new entries on Cyberbullying, electricity, Kim Jong-un, kit-in, Xi Jinping, and many more. It also includes updates for each state's representatives of Congress and electoral votes, and population data on all of the United States major ethnic groups. Contributing to this update, more than 25,000 illustrations, photographs, and maps are presented here, including reproductions of fine art and well-drawn illustrations of the human anatomy. Dozens of QR codes have been added that link users to videos that provide related content.

Another key element of *The World Book Encyclopedia* is the plethora of research aids provided. Some examples include: "Facts in Brief" tables, which highlight important facts on counties; "Tables of Terms," which define highly technical entries; "Table of Important Dates," which provide a chronology of historical dates; lists of "Additional Resources" (arranged by difficulty); and a listing of "Related Articles."

World Book has a roster of 4,000 experts who work as contributors, authenticators, reviewers, and consultants. Content of the encyclopedia is determined by what the publisher refers to as the Classroom Research Project. This project allows for the publisher to poll students in kindergarten through high school classrooms and find out what they are researching, how they are researching, and if *The World Book Encyclopedia* is useful in their research. This encyclopedia is based on the schools' curriculum needs and national and state standards. For this reason, this *Encyclopedia* is most useful in K-12 school media centers and children's reference departments of public libraries. The work uses questions, outlines, and timelines to enhance student retention of information.

The World Book Encyclopedia is available on an Internet version (by subscription) so libraries will have a choice of the most useful format for their library. The online edition offers hundreds of thousands of encyclopedia articles and primary source documents. It also includes thousands of complete e-books to help students with research. The e-books can be accessed in English as well as Spanish, French, German, Italian, Dutch, Latin, Flemish, and Portuguese. Research tools include an atlas, dictionary, and local and country research guides. Users can create and save their personal research along with their notes and citations. The Timeline Builder allows students to create their own illustrated timeline with content pulled from the *Encyclopedia*. Although the print version is bulky, it does provide stunning illustrations and will teach young users valuable research skills.—**Shannon Graff Hysell**

Directories

27. **Associations Yellow Book: Who's Who at the Leading U.S. Trade and Professional Associations. Winter 2013 ed.** New York, Leadership Directories, 2013. 1425p. illus. index. $445.00pa. (annual subscription); $423.00pa. (automatic renewal). ISSN 1054-4070.

This detail-filled, informative directory includes a user's guide, A-Z listing of associations, an industry index, a geographical index, a budget index, a political action committee index, a foundation index, a name index, an acronym index, and an organization index. Each entry on an association provides acronyms, addresses, telephone numbers, e-mail addresses, thorough paragraphs explaining the associations, members, goals, how many workers, finances, date originated, and annual conferences. The entries feature a picture of the president of the group and the president's credentials. The listing provides the other employees, secretaries, and contact data. The catalog shows the affiliated government department and contact information. Foundation research is mentioned. Divisions of the corporations throughout the United States and other countries are given. The listing reveals any items published. Committee and board members are highlighted.

The eight indexes with page numbers go the extra mile. The industry index uncovers associations by type of subject. The geographical index categorizes associations by state. The budget index records organizations by millions in finances. The political action committee index reports groups by politics and causes. The foundation index features foundations supporting the organizations. The name index supplies all people included in the association directory. The acronym index notes association acronyms. The organization index points out all organizations in the book. Clearly, *Associations Yellow Book* is one of the best complete catalogs of associations for any type of library.—**Melinda F. Matthews**

28. **Awards, Honors & Prizes.** 33d ed. Stamford, Conn., Gale/Cengage Learning, 2013. 2v. index. $543.00/set. ISBN 13: 978-1-4144-7720-6.

Descriptions of nearly 25,000 awards are attractively presented in two volumes. The work contains over 4,500 organizations from the United States and Canada and their some 16,000 awards bestowed as well as describes over 3,000 international organizations and their corresponding awards.

The awards are arranged alphabetically by awarding organization, with organization and award names set in bold. Each entry is numbered and provides name, address, telephone and toll-free numbers, fax number, e-mail address, and Web address. Former names of organizations are provided when applicable. A typical entry includes award name, purpose, type, frequency, year established, and sponsor. Indexed by subject, organization, and award name. Each volume contains primarily the same 15 pages of introductory material, which explains the type of achievement the awards cover, reasons why one might consult the work, examples of awards to demonstrate the depth and breadth of coverage, how the information was collected, and how to find information in each volume. The publisher disclaims any and all inaccuracies in the publication, and inaccuracies are to be expected with a work of this size.

This is still the most comprehensive work of its kind and is now available in electronic format through the Gale Directory Library. Large academic and public libraries might consider the value of the information versus the price.—**ARBA Staff Reviewer**

29. **The Grey House Homeland Security Directory, 2013.** 9th ed. Millerton, N.Y., Grey House Publishing, 2013. 1078p. index. $195.00pa.; $400.00 (electronic edition; single user); $500.00 (print and electronic editions). ISBN 13: 978-1-59237-757-2.

The 9th edition of *The Grey House Homeland Security Directory* represents the ultimate resource for accessing Homeland Security federal and state agencies. Grey House accomplished the coordination of multiple resources: consultants, products, and services; associations; magazines and newsletters; trade shows; and directories and databases. The *Directory* offers contemporary, comprehensive data on every facet of Homeland Security administration, on both federal and state levels. It is thorough in its detailed profiles of private sector companies that provide products and services to the Homeland Security industry. The joint endeavor has earned the respect of professionals as the most comprehensive resource on Homeland Security for the past seven years. The handsomely bound paperback volume represents 5,242 listings and the names of 11,21372 Homeland Security professionals.

The *Directory* is divided into five main sections: Federal Agencies, State Agencies, Manufactures and Supplies, Industry Resources, and Indexes. Grey House editors enhanced information retrieval by dividing the five main sections into chapters and subchapters. Readers immediately gain access to relevant subject matter that initiates further inquiry or answers queries. The *Directory* saves time and serves as a desktop reference for any agency or individual who requires up-to-date information on Homeland Security resources, services, and products.

Section 1, "Federal Agencies," includes 18 primary chapters and 12 subchapters that include 510 listings. These chapters address the Department of Homeland Security, its directorates, and relevant branches of the federal government. Individual chapters commence with listing the department or branch headquarters, highlighted in gray shading for speedy recognition and retrieval. Each listing is supported by a clear and concise account of the agency's involvement in Homeland Security. In addition, all listings include the names of key officials. Official contact information is offered as well, including telephone number and e-mail address.

Section 2, "State Agencies," includes 788 entries that are arranged in alphabetic state chapters. The initial entry in each state chapter provides the main Homeland Security Office, including the Governor, Lieutenant Governor, Attorney General, and the individual who shoulders the foremost responsibility for Homeland Security. Again, contact information is provided for further information. The main entry is followed by an alphabetic inventory of state agencies with Homeland Security responsibilities: emergency management, state police, emergency services agencies, the National Guards, and other state contingency planning agencies.

Section 3, "Manufactures and Supplies," includes an alphabetic listing of the 753 products and services provided by the over 3,000 companies listed in this section. The safety- and security-related products and services documented range from access control locking systems to work station security software. Individual company profiles include: company description, address, telephone number, fax and Website, and a list of available products and services.

Section 4, "Industry Resources," documents 728 industry resources, including associations, periodicals, shows and seminars, directories, databases, and supplementary resources. The entries offer full contact information, a description of the resource, and the names of at least one prominent executive. Section 5 includes three indexes to further enhance reader accessibility and retrieval of pertinent information: entry name index (alphabetic list of all directory entries); key personnel index (alphabetic list of all government officials and key executives who have responsibilities related to Homeland Security); and a products and services index (an alphabetic list of products and services presented in section 3).

The Grey House Homeland Security Directory offers readers a clear and concise format that applies legible fonts, appropriate bolding, and highlighting that enhance readability. Adequate text spacing offers an easy-to-read format and entices continued investigation. The publishers should be applauded for their efforts to offer readers a well-organized and significant contribution to the field of Homeland Security. The *Directory* will primarily serve the needs of federal, state, and local law enforcement agencies. Moreover, this resource will have INTERPOL and international law enforcement agency applications. Universities, colleges, and community colleges world benefit by placing this book at the reference desk. Private libraries might find the text an excellent resource document.—**Thomas E. Baker**

30.　　**National 5-Digit Zip Code and Post Office Directory, 2013.** Lanham, Md., Bernan Press, 2013. 2v. $79.00pa./set. ISBN 13: 978-1-60175-882-8.

This directory to the national five-digit ZIP Codes of the United States is updated annually to reflect the changes in the U.S. Postal Service's geographic distribution system ZIP Codes help in the distribution of letters and other types of mail to more than 37,000 post offices, which in turn serve some 141 million homes and businesses across the United States. The work is organized alphabetically by state and then by city or town name. It then alphabetically lists each street's name in the city and provides the ZIP Code associated with the street and the street numbers. The work also offers other interesting supplementary material such as delivery statistics for each city, a list of new ZIP Codes approved, a list of discontinued post offices and ZIP Codes, and tips on how to mail military personnel overseas, just to name a few.— **Shannon Graff Hysell**

31.   **Nonprofit Sector Yellow Book: Who's Who in the Management of the Leading Foundations Universities, Museums, and Other Nonprofit Organizations., Winter 2013 ed.** New York, Leadership Directories, 2013. 1440p. index. $445.00pa. (annual subscription); $423.00pa. (automatic renewal). ISSN 1520-9148.

Published semiannually, the *Nonprofit Sector Yellow Book* provides information on over 1,400 U.S. nonprofit organizations. Listed here are foundations, colleges and universities, museums, performing arts groups, medical institutions, library systems, preparatory schools, and charitable service organizations. The opening introduction, "The Nonprofit Sector News," outlines the criteria for selection of nonprofits featured here. Also listed in the introduction are new listings and any name changes since the last volume.

The entries are arranged into sections by nonprofit type (e.g., foundation, museum). The nonprofits are listed alphabetically by name within each section. Each entry includes the nonprofits contact information (e.g., address, telephone and fax numbers, Web address); a brief mission statement; total net assets; year founded; type of organization; biographical information on the president of chief executive (sometimes with a photograph); and names, educational information, and telephone numbers of officers and managers and persons on the board of trustees. Geographical, name, and organization indexes at the back of the volume will aid users in finding the information they need quickly. This work will be useful for those looking for the specific names and contact information for board members, executives, and trustees for nonprofit groups.

This is a worthwhile directory for those needing this specific type of information. It is also available online where updates are made available daily.—**Shannon Graff Hysell**

32.   **SIRS Discoverer. http://www.proquest.com.** [Website]. North Salt Lake, Utah, ProQuest, 2012. Price negotiated by site. Date reviewed: 2013.

SIRS Discoverer has been around for years and there is a very good explanation for its longevity; it delivers effective research strategies and tools for young learners, and is an extensive interactive reference database that supports student research. This online resource provides over 1,600 full-text articles and graphics from newspapers, magazines, and U.S. government documents. WebFind enables kids to safely search over 9,000 educationally reviewed, age-appropriate Websites. The home screen menu options make it easy to navigate and fun to use. With the exception of some of the maps, the online materials are remarkably up-to-date. Educators can limit student search criteria by reading level. Full-text articles can be e-mailed and young researchers can export article citations. Colorful icons help the student identify article features such as pictures. The Educators Guide can be used to design student research activities. The main advantage of this resource is that it has a large collection of age-appropriate materials.—**Kate Brundage**

Government Information

33.   **USA.gov. http://www.usa.gov/.** [Website]. Free. Date reviewed: 2013.

The U.S. General Services Administration is responsible for a third federal resource that functions as the primary portal to federal government information online, as a government services directory, and as a reference tool and also points to basic directory information. USA.gov was begun as Firstgov.gov by entrepreneur Eric Brewer in 2000 and, after some uncertainty, became the official single portal to federal government information (the E-Government Act of 2002 further pushed development of government Internet sites and services and effectively served to provide funding for, and legitimize, USA.gov). It became know as USA.gov in 2007. USA.gov offers subject-based access to government information, as well as a series of in-depth, user-friendly portals aimed at seniors, student, exporters, workers, small businesspeople, and people with disabilities, to name a few. It also provides access to state, local, and tribal government Websites. It is organized centrally by broad topics, such as Consumer Guides, Jobs and Education, Science and Technology, and Travel and Recreation, to name a few. Convenient interactions with government are facilitated. "Shop Government Auctions," "Passport Application," "Flu Clinic Locator—Get Your Flu Shot," and "Loans—GovLoans.gov" are examples illustrative of its service-delivery focus. USA.gov features specialty portals for citizens, business and nonprofits, government employees, seniors, military and veterans, and visitors to the United States. USA.gov also includes a Spanish-language version.—**Julienne L. Wood**

Handbooks and Yearbooks

34.   **The Europa World Year Book 2013.** 54th ed. Florence, Ky., Europa Publications/Taylor & Francis Group, 2013. 2v. index. $1,675.00/set. ISBN 13: 978-1-85743-679-2.

35.   **Europa World Online. http://www.europaworld.com/.** [Website]. Florence, Ky., Europa Publications/Taylor & Francis Group. Price negotiated by site. Date reviewed: 2014.

The 54th edition of *The Europa World Year Book* carries on the tradition of earlier editions by presenting timely, accurate information on political, economic, and commercial institutions around the world. Volume 1 begins by listing over 1,900 international organizations, including the United Nations and the European Union. It then provides an alphabetic survey of more than 250 countries and territories. For each country the following information is provided: an introductory survey on the country's history, government, defense, economic affairs, education, and holidays; statistical survey on area and population, health and welfare, agriculture, industry, external trade, transportation, tourism, and education; and directory information for government, legislature, diplomatic representation, religious centers, the press, finance, and trade and industry. The set concludes with a three-page index of territories. New to this edition is information on the transfer of power to the next generation of leadership in the People's Republic of China, coverage of the 2012 U.S. presidential and legislative elections, an update on the conflict going on in Syria, and details the election Pope Francis in March 2013.

The online version of this work is *Europa World Online*, which provides the same information but in an easy-to-search database format. The online edition also provides additional statistical surveys and is updated on a regular basis to ensure accuracy of information. Links to related sites are also made available with this database, saving the user much time in their research. Subscribers can now download archival content from *The Europa World Year Book*. The print and online editions of this valuable resource continue to be worthwhile investments for public and academic libraries, business and international organizations, and media and research organizations. It will be a boon especially to students, scholars, and journalists needing quick, up-to-date information.—**Shannon Graff Hysell**

36.   **Information Explorer Junior Series.** North Mankato, Minn., Cherry Lake, 2013. multivolume. illus. index. $28.50/vol.

This series provides young students with valuable information for researching. The title *Join Forces* features projects involving collaborative work by teaching children how to use wikis. With primary sources being an emphasis of Common Core, *Find Out Firsthand* offers practical examples of primary sources. *Post It!* gives children instructions for taking good photographs and using them to create photo journals, greeting cards, and thank you notes. *Record It!* guides students in creating movies. This series provides a strong foundation for encouraging students, even in early grades, to become creators and users of media. The series provides teachers and students opportunities to integrate technology and meet Common Core goals.—**Daniel R. Beach**

37.   **The Research Virtuoso: How To Find Anything You Need to Know.** rev. ed. By the Toronto Public Library. Toronto, Ont., Annick Press. 2012. 128p. $14.95pa. 978-1-55451-394-9.

This handy guide, written by two experienced professional librarians, is divided into four major sections: research preparations, information location, information evaluation, and research presentation. At the end of each section are highly useful "Grab and Go" templates that allow users to organize their findings. These templates include checklists, diagrams, charts, and other similar tools that will prove helpful to researchers. Suggestions are provided for the most efficient ways to approach a variety of sources including libraries, archives, the Internet, people, and more. The guide also suggests possible ways to present findings. This guide would be useful to individual researchers and to instructors who provide research guidance.—**Annette b. Thibodeaux**

38.   **Terra Maxima: The Records of Humankind.** Wolfgang Kunth, ed. Richmond Hills, Ont., Firefly Books, 2012. 576p. illus. index. $49.95. ISBN 13: 978-1-77085-242-6.

Edited by Wolfgang Kunth, this reference is intended to celebrate humankind's technological achievements through the presentation of records, which are organized as lists. They include such eclectic topics as "The Most Important Pilgrimage Destinations in Hinduism," "The Highest Mountain Roads and Passes in Oceania and Africa," "The Largest Powered Tall Ships and Sailing Ships in the World," and "The Most Important Natural History Museums in the World." Some of the criteria used to identify certain accomplishments, such as the tallest tower, are based on hard analytic data. Other records are determined subjectively without any real explanation of how the individual compiling the list came to his or her conclusion. The records are grouped into 10 categories: "Countries and Nations"; "Languages and Scripts"; "Faith and Religion"; "Cities and Metropolises"; "Urban Megastructures"; "Transportation and Traffic"; "Aviation and Space Travel"; "Arts and Culture"; "Science and Research"; and "Sports and Leisure."

The strength of the work is the more than 3,000 full-color photographs used to illustrate the respective records. Each record entry has at least one two-page photograph that shows a record holder, along with smaller photographs showing unique details. For example, the Hermitage is presented as one of the selections in "The Most Important Museums of the World." The two-page spread is a jaw-dropping picture of the Hermitage's Winter Palace at night. The smaller pictures surrounding it are "The Jordan Staircase in the Winter Palace," "Ceremonial Hall in the Winter Palace," the "White Hall" in the Winter Palace," and "War Gallery of 1812 in the Hermitage's Winter Palace." Although it is technically a reference title, it is best used for browsing since it can also function as a coffee-table book due to the beauty of its copious photographs. This work is highly recommended for the reference collections of public and school libraries. Since the book is very reasonably priced, all libraries should consider adding a copy to their circulating collection.—**John R. Burch Jr.**

39.   **A True Book—Information Literacy Series.** Danbury, Conn., Scholastic Library Publishing, 2013. multivolume. illus. index. $29.00/vol.

Each book in this series provides background information on the featured topic with photographs and a clear explanation of each. For example, *Reading Maps* includes online maps and how they are developed, making this a very up-to-date resource. The series emphasizes that all the information provided is true and can be verified. Adding these to an elementary school library or classroom collection as supplemental information would be recommended. The works are supplemented with a bibliography, glossary, lists of Websites, and an index.—**Lourdes Cervantes**

40. **Yearbook of the United Nations 2008.** 62d ed. New York, United Nations, 2012. 1776p. $175.00. ISBN 13: 978-92-11012-27-9.

The 62d edition of this yearbook continues the tradition of providing the most comprehensive coverage of the activities of the United Nations. The *Yearbook* is divided into six parts: political and security questions; human rights; economic and social questions; legal questions; institutional, administrative, and budgetary questions; and intergovernmental organizations related to the United Nations. The appendixes include, among others, a roster of the United Nations, the Charter of the United Nations and the Statute of the International Court of Justice, and the structure of the United Nation's. Access to the contents is provided through a subject index, an index to resolutions and decisions, and an index to Security Council presidential statements.

The year 2008 provided a variety of challenges that the United Nations faced, many of which resulted in UN actions that are included in the *Yearbook*. The volume contains information on the conflicts in the Democratic Republic of the Congo, the Georgian province of Abkhazia, and the Sudan. It also discusses the challenges presented by the global food security crisis, the global economic recession, natural disasters, climate change, and piracy and terrorism.

As the leading source of information related to the United Nations, the *Yearbook* remains an essential part of most reference collections, especially in larger public and all academic libraries.— **Gregory A. Crawford**

Museums

41. **CoOL. Conservation Online: Resources for Conservation Professionals. http://preservation-us.org/.** [Website]. Free. Date reviewed: 2013.

The play on words here is for real; CoOL is a really "cool" site, a full-text library of conservation information, covering a wide spectrum of topics of interest to those involved with the conservation of library, archives, and museum materials. Sponsored by the Foundation of the American Institute for the Conservation and Preservation of Historic Works (FAIC), the site has links to conservation organizations, news, job listings, directory of professionals, conferences, bibliographies, library resources, and more. Subject areas covered include cultural property such as art books, paintings, paper, photographic materials, sculpture, wood, and textiles. Materials and formats offered are electronic media, architectural materials, archives, artifacts, manuscripts, and natural history collections. Subjects include but are not limited to biodeterioriation, conservation, education and training, digital imaging, disaster planning, ethics, mold, pest management, and restoration. The Website will be of interest to anyone involve with or interested in conservation and preservation.—**Anna H. Perrault**

42. Danilov, Victor J. **Famous Americans: A Directory of Museums, Historic Sites, and Memorials.** Lanham, Md., Scarecrow, 2013. 419p. illus. index. $95.00; $94.99 (e-book). ISBN 13: 978-0-8108-9185-2; 978-0-8108-9186-9 (e-book).

This well-written directory showcases the places where visitors can be entertained and educated about the lives, accomplishments, failures, impact, and historical contributions of over 407 Americans and 9 European poets and writers with ties to the United States. The book features museums, historical sites and homesteads, and memorials in 48 states, Washington, D.C., and Puerto Rico.

The biographical essays are divided into 26 categories from Actors to Socialites, with Presidents being the largest category, and President Lincoln being honored with the most sites (21). Each biography contains pertinent contact information, hours of operation, admission fees, e-mail and street addresses, and average attendance numbers. A geographical guide follows these categories to facilitate finding sites by location. In addition to literature and government, the famous people featured in this book have affected many fields such as the arts, religion, civil rights, medicine, sports, and industry, just to name a few. Their tributes help researchers and general readers have a better understanding of our nation's history and its role in the world. A selected bibliography of 32 reference sources is included on page 405, and an index begins on page 407. Danilov's directory would be a valuable addition to public, community college, and academic library reference collections.—**Laura J. Bender**

43.   Oldfield, Molly. **The Secret Museum.** Richmond Hills, Ont., Firefly Books, 2013. 352p. illus. index. $35. ISBN 13: 978-1-77085-257-0.

Molly Oldfield is a storyteller. She takes the reader on a journey through the hidden collections of museums around the world via a descriptive, breezy vernacular. Many of the world's greatest museums harbor vast numbers of rare and unique items that are only seen by curators or researchers. Oldfield exposes these hidden treasures, and shows us how curious citizens could avail themselves of them simply by asking the librarians and curators who work in the museums. This book describes collections that consist of items too precious, too large, too small, or too fragile to display. Those that can be displayed are rotated among other exhibited items over time. The reader will visit Massachusetts, New York, various cities in England, Italy, Monaco, Brazil, Scotland, Germany, Sweden, Canada, Norway, the Netherlands and France, to be introduced to a total of what the author calls, 60 "objects."

The illustrations by Hennie Haworth are vivid and fun, and help readers find the magic in objects such as "Tools that belonged to Queen Victoria's Dentist," glass models of jellyfish and plants, Livingstone and Stanley's hats, an original draft of "Auld Lang Syne," and many more. A complete index begins on page 344, and picture credits on 352.

It is evident that this work is a product of the author's emotional, personal discovery, and yet reflects great attention to detail and fastidious research. *The Secret Museum* is recommended for public, community college, and academic libraries.—**Laura J. Bender**

44.   **PreservationDirectory.com. http://www.preservationdirectory.com/.** [Website]. Free. Date reviewed: 2014.

PreservationDirectory.com is an online resource for historic preservation, building restoration, and cultural resource management in the United States and Canada. Its goal is to encourage the preservation of historic buildings, historic downtowns and neighborhoods, and promote tourism by providing an avenue of communication between preservationists, historical societies, and state and federal historic preservation offices. In doing so this site provides directories and links to historical societies' revitalization groups, historic properties for sale, restoration businesses, historical events, conferences, historic tours, and more. Users will have access to 4,500 historical societies and more the 7,000 historical museums and houses through this site. There is also an extensive "News" section listed here as well as job listings with historical associations and museums.—**ARBA Staff Reviewer**

Periodicals and Serials

45.   **The Modernist Journals Project (MJP). http://dl.lib.brown.edu/mjp/.** Free. Date reviewed: 2013.

The Modernist Journals Project is a joint project of Brown University and the University of Tulsa. The MJP is intended to become a major resource for the study of the rise of modernism in the English-speaking world. The project has begun with periodical literature in a chronological range of 1890 to 1922 and a geographical range that extends to English-language periodicals, where ever they were published. On the Website, a list is being compiled of all of the periodicals within the period. There is a database of biographies of the authors and editors of the periodicals. Another section of the site contains the text of essays about the Modernist period. The project has made a good start on a long-term endeavor.—**ARBA Staff Reviewer**

46. **Periodicals Index Online.** http://www.proquest.com/en-US/catalogs/databases/detail/periodicals_index.shtml. [Website]. Bethesda, Md., ProQuest. Price negotiated by site. Date reviewed: 2014.

Periodicals Index Online in an electronic database with more than 300 years of fully indexed articles from journals in the arts, humanities, and social sciences providing access to more than 10 million citations. It provides abstracting and indexing for more than 3,000 journals from their inception to 1991. The overall dates of coverage are 1770-1991 with separate records for over 10 million journal articles. More than one million records are added each year. Users can search for articles by words or phrases in the title, by author, and by journal title. The search can be restricted to the language of the article, the journal's subject, the year of publication, or a range of dates. In addition, researchers can access a list of issues for each journal and a table of contents for each issue. The broad coverage of this index provides researchers access to originally published materials and to articles on historical topics.

For many of the citations in the *PIO*, UMI's *American Periodicals Series Online, 1741-1900* provides full text. The American Periodicals series were microfilm projects begun in the 1970s: *American Periodicals I*, 1741-1800, and *American Periodicals II*, 1800-1850. The first microfilm series contained 89 titles, such as Benjamin Franklin's *General Magazine* and Tom Paine's *Pennsylvania Magazine*. The 911 titles in the second series covered the issue of slavery and events leading up to the Civil War. The titles are now available in full text in the APS Online, which contains 89 journals published between 1740 and 1800, and 118 periodicals published during the Civil War and Reconstruction. Many women's and children's magazines are contained in the collection. Because the database contains digitized images of the magazines pages, researchers can see the original typography, drawings, and layouts. Together, the *Periodicals Index Online* and the *American Periodicals Series Online* provide easy access to a broad range of periodicals important in American history. These products cover the eighteenth and nineteenth centuries up to the period in which the *Readers' Guide* began. There is overlap with the indexing provided by the *19th Century Masterfile* Web database. Researchers will be wise to utilize both databases.—**Anna H. Perrault**

Quotations

47. **John F. Kennedy in Quotations: A Topical Dictionary, with Sources.** David B. Frost, comp. Jefferson, N.C., McFarland, 2013. 207p. index. $75.00pa. ISBN 13: 978-0-7864-7492-9.

The work reveals 2,019 quotes by John F. Kennedy along with information on the occasion of each quote. After an introduction the work is organized into categories, including: Agriculture, American Leadership, American Spirit, Arts and Humanities, Berlin, Budgetary and Fiscal Policies, Business, Civic Duty, Communism and the Cold War, Cuba, Democracy, Domestic Social Issues, Economic Policies, Education, Energy Policy, Environment, Equal Opportunity and Civil Rights, Foreign Assistance, Foreign Policy, Founding Fathers, Free Enterprise System, Freedom and Liberty, God and Country, Government, Healthcare, Human Rights, International Relations, International Trade, Kennedy on Kennedy, Labor Unions, National Security, NATO, New Frontier, News Media, Nuclear Weapons, Peace, Peace Corps, Physical Fitness, Political Leadership, Politics, Presidency, Public Service, Science and Technology, Senior Citizens, Soviet Union, Space Exploration, United Nations, Voluntarism, and Washington D.C. The index is accurate providing item numbers for quotes. As an example of what can be found within this work, the category of Freedom and Liberty has the following Kennedy quote: "My fellow citizens of the world: ask not what America will do for you, but what together we can do for the freedom of man." Inaugural Address (January 20, 1961). Another legendary statement is from the section Civic Duty: "And so, my fellow Americans: ask not what your country can do for you-ask what you can do for your country" (Inaugural Address (January 20, 1961). The jewel of quotes and occasions of quotes from John F. Kennedy is invaluable for Kennedy researchers and will be useful in public and academic libraries.—**Melinda F. Matthews**

48.	**The Quotable Henry Ford.** Michele Wehrwein Albion, ed. Gainesville, Fla., University Press of Florida, 2014. 262p. illus. $24.95pa. ISBN 13: 978-0-8130-4405-7.

One of the great American Captains of Industry, Henry Ford was a man of contradictions. He changed the way Americans worked with his assembly line and his progressive management practices that included the eight-hour day, the five-day week, and profit sharing. He supported women's rights; hired African Americans, ex-cons, and the handicapped; yet was a vehement anti-Semitic who Hitler said was a personal inspiration. Lacking a formal education, Ford was not a skilled communicator but that did not mean he did not have plenty to say. After the Model-T made him famous, Ford began to see himself as a folksy philosopher and kept a notebook of his thoughts and sayings. The press and public listened to him, hoping to discover the secret to fame and fortune. This book brings together a selection of his quotations on topics ranging from automobiles; machines and technology; his company, money, and economics; employees; politics, war and peace; the law; education; the arts; the press; religion; nationalities and ethnic groups; health; science; his family; himself; and more. Each section of quotations starts with a brief historical note to set the context. To give a sampling: "A business absolutely devoted to service will have only one worry about profits. They will be embarrassingly large." And, "Society does not owe any man a living, but society does owe him a chance to work." Features include a chronology of his life, and quotes of others on Ford and Ford on others. John Dillinger, the bank robber, is quoted as saying: "I want to thank you for making an excellent car. If I am ever captured it will have to be someone in another Ford." This collection helps us to understand the complexity of Ford—a man who helped to shape the twentieth century.—**Adrienne Antink**

49.	**The Quotable Kierkegaard.** Gordon Marino, ed. Princeton, N.J., Princeton University Press, 2014. 234p. index. $24.95. ISBN 13: 978-0-691-15530-2.

That a philosopher would get his own quotation book should be news enough to make you rush out to buy it. That the philosopher in question is referred to as "quotable" is a stop-the-presses kind of news, although today we would say "update Twitter" or "Post to Huffington" since newspapers are fading like so many snows in a spring thaw. That Twitter post would, however, be ironic since Kierkegaard maintained 100 years ago that most of what was said was so much chattering anyway.

Marino's 40-plus page introduction is quite excellent and should be read by anyone using the book. It puts into context the work of this great philosopher. The chronology included also gives users a sense of the sage's life, and the index makes locating known quotes quick and easy. The idea to include a map of Copenhagen, Kierkegaard's birthplace and really a place he rarely left, is also helpful.

The quotes are, of course, the meat of the book, and they are tasty morsels, too. Arranged topically (anxiety, freedom, despair, guilt, envy, truth, God, Christianity and so on), these are not sound bites or "zingers" so much as they are meatier topics that must be ruminated, chewed on, and for some time. While most readers will recognize the titles of the books from which they come (Either-Or, Fear and Trembling, The Sickness unto Death) most probably have never read them or any of the dozens of works for which Kierkegaard is rightly remembered. Kierkegaard's works are not instantly accessible, and even his famous "leap of faith" is better known than it is understood. Further, Kierkegaard was a deeply religious thinker, yet another *bete noire* to the modern mind.

While dipping into these pages will not reward readers with the perfect "toastmaster" opening or a great cocktail conversation line, it will enlarge the mind, demand reflection, and haunt readers for years on end.—**Mark Y. Herring**

Part II
SOCIAL SCIENCES

2 Social Sciences in General

General Works

Catalogs and Collections

50   **PebbleGo Social Studies. http://www.PebbleGo.com** [Website] North Mankato, Minn., Capstone. $395.00 (annual subscription). Date reviewed: 2013.

Pebble Books has a reputation for producing high-quality print materials for the primary student (PreK-3), and this easy-to-access Website is no exception. Child appeal is achieved through colorful photographs, bold colors, easy-to-read font, and easy navigation. Users may choose a feature that reads the simple paragraphs aloud as it highlights each word. Multiple games for each subject provide a review of materials with kid appeal. This new social studies database covers holidays, U.S. government, U.S. symbols, good citizenship, and more. Each of these curricular subjects explore six to eight topics, and each topic is linked to five or six other exploratory questions plus several video links. Information goes beyond the expected to include careers, safety, and defining vocabulary. The depth of coverage enables this site to be appropriate for primary and intermediate students with varying degrees of student support available as needed. The printable graphic organizer allows students to share what they know, helping the primary student build useful research skills. Other databases in the PebbleGo series include Biographies, Earth and Space, and Animals. Users can purchase one database for $395 per year, two for $695 per year, three for $895 per year, or all four for $995 per year.—**ARBA Staff Reviewer**

Dictionaries and Encyclopedias

51.   **Culture Wars in America: An Encyclopedia of Issues, Viewpoints, and Voices.** 2d ed. Roger Chapman and James Ciment, eds. Armonk, N.Y., M. E. Sharpe, 2014. 3v. illus. index. $349.00/set. ISBN 13: 978-0-7656-8302-1.

This three-volume set on "culture wars" provide the reader with an array of articles pointing to the historical significance of the political and cultural divisions in American society and perhaps around the world, particularly the moral issues that have divided the religious from the secular and the conservative from the more progressive; perhaps even from those who are committed to absolute truth and value from those who sense some relativity in value choices. The editor provides a short, but inadequate, introduction to these volumes. Considering the spread of topics for the reader to think over, the introduction could have been more inclusive and definitive. The editors rightly point out that the labels used in the political, religious, and secular arenas oversimplify many issues by failing to acknowledge the rational, moral, and religious complexities involved. Along with the 640 main entries, this new edition includes 120 supporting primary documents that will be useful to students, teachers, and researchers. Many popular and newsworthy topics are included; however, more editorial analysis linking them to the culture war thesis would have been useful for the intended audience of high school and undergraduate students. It will serve nicely as a jumping off point for research for these students and will have appeal for the general public as well. This work is recommended for high school and undergraduate libraries.—**Joseph P. Hester**

52.   **Human Geography: People and the Environment.** K. Lee Lerner, Brenda Wilmoth Lerner, and Sonia Benson, eds. Stamford, Conn., Gale/Cengage Learning, 2013. 2v. illus. maps. index. $270.00/set. ISBN 13: 978-1-4144-9135-6; 978-1-4144-9138-7 (e-book).

    This two-volume reference set effectively combines sociology, anthropology, and geography to provide a comprehensive study of human culture and its environmental and physical relationships. Written for the high school Advanced Placement course in human geography, these volumes will also make an excellent resource for college freshmen and sophomores in such courses as sociology and introduction to anthropology. The substance of these volumes demonstrates the connections and interdependency of the physical and human environments. Resources in these volumes include pictures, maps, models, theories, spatial and population data, the cultural tissue of language, religion, agricultural, industrial, urban, and economic and political forces. The authors and editors have achieved their purpose of demonstrating how human activity leaves an unmistakable stamp on the physical and nonphysical world. The articles in these two volumes are clearly and concisely written including sidebars, pull quotes, maps, timelines, and important biographical sources that include books, periodicals, and Websites. They do not burden the student with nonessential material as these volumes include an extensive glossary. [R: LJ, 15 June 13, p. 114]—**Joseph P. Hester**

Handbooks and Yearbooks

53.   **At Issue Series.** Farmington Hills, Mich., Greenhaven Press/Gale/Cengage Learning, 2013. multivolume. index. $35.45/vol.; $25.45pa./vol.

    Published since 2001, Greenhaven's At Issue Series is one of the publisher's largest series with nearly 500 titles in print (both in hardcover and in paperback). The series is grouped into smaller subtopics, including health, civil liberties, and crime. The goal of the series is to provide a wide range of opinions on specific social issues. The titles vary greatly in the breadth or narrowness of each topic discussed; for example, users will find a title on the very broad topic of teenage suicide as well as a title on the much more narrowly focused subject of age of consent. To provide opinions for each side to the argument the book uses eyewitness accounts, governmental views, scientific analysis, and newspaper and magazine accounts. A bibliography and a list of organizations at the back of each book points readers to other sources for further information. More than 50 new titles have been published recently or in the months to come and include the topics of: animal experimentation, self defense laws, Mexico's war on drugs, adaptation and climate change, and fair wage and women.

    These books are an excellent source for middle and high school readers to enhance their critical thinking skills. They could easily be used as jumping off points for research projects and debate topics. At $35.45 for the hardcover copies and $25.45 for the paperback versions this set as a whole is expensive. School librarians will most likely need to be selective if they choose to purchase books within this series.—**Shannon Graff Hysell**

54.   **Current Controversies Series.** Farmington Hills, Mich., Greenhaven Press/Gale/Cengage Learning, 2013. multivolume. $42.45/vol.; $29.95pa./vol.

    Greenhaven Press's Current Controversies series is designed for middle to high school age students. It takes current social and political issues and, with the use of primary sources, presents the pros and cons of each side of these hotly debated topics. Some of the most recently published volumes discuss oil spills, mobile apps, violence in the media, e-books, factory farming, and family violence. In all, more than 25 new titles have been recently added or are planned for to be released in the new year. The titles are arranged into chapters that pose controversial questions. Following the questions are several pro and con responses that come directly from politicians, activists, and other interested parties. The books are ideal for teens researching topics for debates or research papers. The topics are current enough that many teens will want to browse through the books on their favorite topics. At $42.45 per volume for the hardback editions and $29.95 per volume for the paperbacks, however, the series is expense; most school and public libraries will need to be selective in their choices when adding these titles to their collections.—**Shannon Graff Hysell**

55.   **The Gallup Poll: Public Opinion 2011.** Frank Newport, ed. Lanham, Md., Rowman & Littlefield, 2013. 496p. index. $130.00; $129.99 (e-book). ISBN 13: 978-1-44222-033-1; 978-1-4422-2034-8 (e-book).

This 2011 edition marks the 38th volume of Gallup's Public Opinion annual series, which publishes the results of questions asked of the public throughout the calendar year. These questions usually cover issues surrounding major news events, presidential and political campaigns, and American lifestyles. The more than 600 poll reports for this volume were released in 2011 by major news broadcasting outlets including CNN, *USA Today,* and the Chicago Tribune Newspaper Syndicate. The volume lists poll results in chronological order by the interview date, and each entry features a detailed analysis of the topic. It also includes a subject index and a brief timeline of major events that took place in 2011 and late 2010. With the introduction of *The Gallup Brain*, a searchable electronic database of *The Gallup Poll* findings since 1935, the print volumes may become unnecessary.—**Maris L. Hayashi**

56.   **Global Viewpoints Series.** Farmington Hills, Mich., Greenhaven Press/Gale/Cengage Learning, 2013. multivolume. illus. maps. index. $44.95/vol.; $30.95pa./vol.

The Global Viewpoints Series from Greenhaven Press can serve as a go-to resource for hot topics in global issues for young adults. This series focuses on the social issues facing the world as a whole—politically, environmentally, and in the area of public health. Less emphasis is placed on the U.S. perspective and more on the impact of issues in other countries. New titles within the series include the topics of genetic engineering, organ donation, capitalism, and genocide. All of the topics in this series are on timely topics that spark debate from all sides of the issue. The books use primary sources (e.g., speeches, government documents) as well as essays from international magazines and news sources to present the information in a unique way. Supplementary materials in each book include black-and-white maps and charts, a bibliography, topics for further discussion, and an index. These books provide a unique perspective to today's social issues and are recommended for school library collections. The titles are available in both hard cover and paperback editions as well as in e-book editions. But at $44.95 and $30.95 respectively, this will be an expensive set to collect in full; libraries may need to pick and choose the most relevant titles for their patrons' use.—**Shannon Graff Hysell**

57.   **Human Development Report 2012: The Rise of the South—Human Progress in a Diverse World.** New York, United Nations, 2012. 200p. $30.00pa. ISBN 13: 978-92-11263-40-4.

Beginning in 1990, the United Nations Development Programme has published the *Human Development Report* annually, treating a different issue related to development each year. It is one of the world's major statements of global opinion and policy, and has helped to focus attention on the multiple dimensions of human potential, discussing not simply economic, but also social and political aspects. Since the UN's Millennium Development Goals were promulgated, it has also tracked MDG indicators. It follows the same pattern as other flagship international publications like the World Bank's *World Development Report* or the International Monetary Fund's *World Economic Outlook* by combining an authoritative but opinionated policy document with extensive statistical compilations. This year's report takes an in-depth look at the rapid emergence of the South and how it is projected to transform twenty-first century economics and politics. This report seeks to identify how the dynamics of power, voice, and wealth in the world are changing. It aims to identify the policies and institutions necessary to address these twenty-first century realities and promote greater social equity, sustainability, and cohesion. Text boxes enliven the report with additional perspectives from world leaders. The document's signature statistic is the Human Development Index, which weighs GDP per capita alongside literacy, life expectancy, and education. The texts tables are packed with essential country-level data on inequality, health, gender issues, and more. The extensive notes and references provide a comprehensive entry point into the literature of development. Since this title is one that any informed student or citizen of the world may wish to consult, it is an important title to acquire for all but the smallest libraries.—**ARBA Staff Reviewer**

58.	**Introducing Issues with Opposing Viewpoints Series.** Farmington Hills, Mich., Greenhaven Press/Gale/Cengage Learning, 2013. multivolume. illus. maps. index. $38.45/vol.

Greenhaven Press has been publishing the Opposing Viewpoints series for over 35 years. It was introduced to help students develop critical thinking skills about social issues of the day. The Introducing Issues with Opposing Viewpoints, a relatively new subset of this series, was designed to continue the tradition by presenting viewpoints on current social issues. The text tends to be a bit more conversational than the original series, which may make it more user friendly for its intended audience—middle and high school students. New titles in this series include the topics of drug legalization, fast food, homelessness, human rights, teen driving, and athletes and drug use, just to name a few. In all, more than 25 titles have been added in the past year and are planned for the months ahead. A variety of viewpoints and "solutions" are offered in each title as well as lists of organizations to contact for more information, further reading lists, and a "Fast Facts" section. The titles in this series will be useful for students studying debate topics or researching for papers. It also teaches the valuable lesson that there are two (or more) sides to every issue. At $38.45 per volume this is an expensive series to collect. Most libraries needing this type of material will want to select the volumes that will be most useful for their specific collection.—**Shannon Graff Hysell**

59.	**Issues That Concern You Series.** Farmington Hills, Mich., Greenhaven Press/Gale/Cengage Learning, 2013. multivolume. illus. index. $36.95/vol.

These volumes have both pro and con essays on the topic covered by the book. New topics covered in the series include medical marijuana, career and technical education, date rape, dropping out of school, electronic devises in school, and gun violence. Each has between 8 and 12 brief readings that are reprints from other sources. An issue with this is that the copyright dates of the enclosed readings are often older than the copyright of the volume, causing problems for the more time-sensitive topics. There are many full-color photographs, images, charts, graphs, and other imagery to assist the visual learner in gaining the knowledge. The volumes conclude with annotated lists of organizations to contact, annotated bibliographies of both books and periodicals, and lengthy subject indexes. These are valuable to the middle school and high school libraries where students need brief yet scholarly information on issues of concern to them.—**Sara Marcus**

60.	**Opposing Viewpoints Series.** Farmington Hills, Mich., Greenhaven Press/Gale/Cengage Learning, 2013. multivolume. illus. maps. index. $42.95/vol.; $24.95pa./vol.

These volumes provide valuable, well-researched, and documented articles on their intended issues from both sides. Each article is an edited reprint from other scholarly sources, pulling together relevant and related information into a single volume. An issue with this collection of materials is that the copyright of the volume itself is misleading as the enclosed entries are older, an issue of importance when dealing with timely matters. Regardless, this series is valuable in its presenting both sides of numerous arguments on often highly controversial topics. New topics covered in the series include: birth defects, hackers and hacking, mass media, multiracial America, North and South Korea, and professional athletes. Topical volumes of interest to patrons are invaluable additions to any young adult, public, or undergraduate library collection where teenagers, college students, or others are seeking a single book that has information on a controversial topic. In all, nearly 50 new titles are recently released or soon to be released in the coming year.—**Sara Marcus**

3 Area Studies

General Works

61. **Country at a Glance. http://www.un.org/Pubs/CyberSchoolBus/res.html.** [Website]. New York, United Nations. Free. Date reviewed: 2013.

This site provides United National data including flag, latitude and longitude, area, population, population density, capital city, languages, largest city, currency, UN membership date, GDP, and GDP per capita. The companion site, Infonation, allows one to view and compare statistical data for the Member States of the United Nations. This is a useful and reliable international site for students and young researchers.—**ARBA Staff Reviewer**

62. **Nations of the World, 2013: A Political, Economic, and Business Handbook.** 12th ed. Millerton, N.Y., Grey House Publishing, 2013. 2112p. maps. index. $180.00pa. ISBN 13: 978-1-59237-875-3.

The contributors of this work are primarily journalist writing in a concise, engaging, and informal style. Entries are in alphabetic order and range from two to several pages with each country's information broken down into short captions. The entries begin with brief introductions that are occasionally frank and opinionated. Most country profiles include a map and a section of key facts, including rudimentary information such as ruling party, population, and Gross Domestic Product. Typical entries then go on to provide a condensed historical profile and risk assessment covering politics, economy, and regional stability. Economic information is provided covering major industries and financial markets. Most entries then provide a treasure trove of political, business, and cultural tidbits that are very useful to students and professionals. This includes sections on dress codes, health advisories, entry requirements, personal security, and social customs. Sections conclude with information on getting to a desired destination, getting around the country, and a business directory with useful Websites. Entries are not signed.

The monograph concludes with brief essays on different world regions and a list of U.S. embassies. There is no index and all illustrations are black and white. The binding is paper and glue and reasonably sturdy for a book of over 2,000 pages. This is a wonderful addition to public and academic library reference collections.—**Melissa M. Johnson**

63. **Social Studies Explorer: It's Cool to Learn About Countries.** North Mankato, Minn., Cherry Lake Publishing, 2013. multivolume. illus. maps. index $31.36/vol.

Vivid photographs engage the reader throughout each book, depicting the people, places, animals, and the history of each country. Each title contains a succinct table of contents that includes a welcome chapter, one on business and government, one of celebrations, and one of food. The series will be more engaging than the average "country study" book with its learning activities, craft activities, and recipes. Quality color maps give the young reader an idea of the country's relative size and location. History and current issues are delivered using "postcards" with a summary of a historic event or pressing social concern. Lacking is a "quick facts" listing of the country's capital, currency, population, and more, which is common in most "country books." Each title contains a bibliography, glossary, and index, and all volumes are available in e-book version.—**Robert M. Campbell**

64.   **Spotlight on My Country Series.** New York, Crabtree, 2013. multivolume. illus. maps. index. $26.60/vol.; $8.95pa./vol.

This multivolume series from Crabtree Publishing, a company known for their multivolume, nonfiction series designed specifically for children, provides cultural and geographic information on 19 of the world's countries. The newest volumes in the series discuss: France, Kenya, South Korea, and Argentina. The volumes focus on the people and culture of the country as well as the geography, the plants and wildlife, landmarks, religions and beliefs, a brief history, and food. Within each volume are plenty of color photographs and illustrations as well as sidebars full of additional information. Each volume ends with a glossary and a very short index, both of which can be used to teach young students basic researching skills. This series could be of use in elementary school libraries and juvenile collections in public libraries. They provide a good, but very basic introduction to the geography and history behind these countries and how they have evolved.—**Shannon Graff Hysell**

United States

General Works

65.   **America's Top Rated Cities, 2013: A Statistical Handbook.** 20th ed. Millerton, N.Y., Grey House Publishing, 2013. 4v. maps. index. $275.00pa./set; $75.00pa./vol. ISBN 13: 978-1-61925-120-5.

Now in its 20th edition, this reference tool clearly has proven its worth to a wide audience ranging from businesspeople and corporations planning to launch, relocate, or expand their operations to market researchers, real estate professionals, urban planners, job-seekers, students, and anyone else interested in access to more than 3,600 pages of reliable, attractively presented statistical information about larger U.S. cities. All of the 100 cities included have populations of 100,000 or more. Cities are ranked by the publisher's weighting system reflecting data from 231 sources defining top-rated cities in numerous categories. Both the four regional volumes and the individual city chapters follow a standard format enabling users to quickly and easily review "Background," "Rankings," and 120 "Business" and "Living" statistical tables for cities of interest. Ninety percent of the statistical data have been updated from the previous edition. New ranking topics presented here are Education, Pets, Technology, and Transportation. The five appendixes common to all four volumes yield information on government type and county, metropolitan statistical areas, chambers of commerce, state departments of labor, and comparative statistics. Public, academic, and business libraries that purchase this useful set may also wish to acquire the publisher's similar two-volume set titled *America's Top-Rated Smaller Cities* (2010 ed.; see ARBA 2011, entry 796).—**Julienne L. Wood**

66.   **Country Reports: United States Edition. http://www.countryreports.org/unitedstates.** [Website]. Price negotiated by site. Date reviewed: 2013.

This database is an add-on product, available to subscribers of Country Reports. Its focus is to provide information about individual states; each state entry includes basic facts, figures, and photographs. Entries need additional proofreading, as this reviewer found typographical errors as well as major omissions. Because of these flaws, I do not, as a Country Reports subscriber, plan to purchase this add-on.—**Michelle Glatt**

67.   **Junior Worldmark Encyclopedia of the States.** 6th ed. Drew Johnson and Cynthia Johnson, eds. Farmington Hills, Mich., U*X*L/Gale, 2013. 4v. illus. maps. index. $321.00/set. ISBN 13: 978-1-4144-9859-1; 978-1-4144-9864-5 (e-book).

Based on the latest edition of the *Worldmark Encyclopedia of the States* (7th ed.; see ARBA 2008, entry 72), this encyclopedia offers accurate information on each of the 50 states plus the District of Columbia, Puerto Rico, and the U.S. Pacific and Caribbean dependencies in a format designed for children but appropriate for all library users seeking quick access to basic facts. The new edition features full-color photographs, updated information on political leaders, and population data from 2011. Volume 1 provides a handy reader's guide and a guide to state articles. Volume 4 contains a U.S. overview article plus a subject index to all four volumes. Each volume includes a glossary and a list of abbreviations and acronyms.

The distinctive structure of the *Worldmark* encyclopedia with its 40 standard numbered headings within each article, permits easy comparison of data across topics and states. Data categories for each state range from the traditional size, climate, and history to environmental protection, religions, public finance, and press. Item 40 at the end of each article yields a useful bibliography of books and Websites current as of early 2012. Endpapers feature color reproductions of state flags and seals. Maps and tables within each article enhance the visual appeal of this set. Attractively designed and well researched, this encyclopedia belongs in the children's section of every public library and in K-12 school libraries as well.—**Julienne L. Wood**

68.   **State Profiles, 2013: The Population and Economy of Each U.S. State.** Shana Hertz Hattis, ed. Lanham, Md., Bernan Press, 2013. 555p. index. $165.00; $164.99 (e-book). ISBN 13: 978-1-59888-640-5; 978-1-59888-641-2 (e-book).

State Profiles: The Population and Economy of Each U.S. State provides a convenient source to obtain essential population and economic data for each of the 50 states and the District of Columbia. In addition to population, aggregate as well as major groups, each state profile contains information on health, households, labor, economic activity, exports, agriculture, energy, state finance, education, and voter participation. Individual state data have been aggregated to national level in an overview of the United States, providing an opportunity to compare state information with national data. Comparison among states is offered by means of tables that rank states by some 24 characteristics. Presentation is largely in the form of tables, supported by graphs. Relevance and priority are given to the large amount of data provided in the tables and graphs by brief, but pertinent, textual explanations. Major developments and trends are highlighted, placing introductory bullets at the beginning of each state chapter. Data have been drawn from government sources, and are quite current, largely through 2012. A useful section on notes and definitions is included, which also contains source information that would be helpful for those seeking further details. A table of contents, a list of tables, an index, a preface, and suggestions for using the volume are included to enhance understanding and to ease the task of searching for specific information.—**William C. Struning**

69.   **The World Today Series, 2013: The USA & the World.** By David M. Keithly. Lanham, Md., Rowman & Littlefield, 2013. 276p. illus. maps. $18.50pa.; $16.99 (e-book). ISBN 13: 978-1-4758-0497-3; 978-1-4758-0504-8 [e-book].

Unlike other titles in this series, this title on the United States is arranged into topical chapters rather than sections on individual states. After a short introduction the section is arranged into the following chapters: National Interest Priorities, National Expansion, Ascent to Globalism, The Anguish of Power, Political Ideas and the Political System, The U.S. Economy, A Nation of Nations, and The Future. This arrangement allows for a very broad, basic overview of each topic. The chapters are well written and explain in general terms difficult concepts surrounding U.S. history. There is a selected bibliography of key English-language sources for the last section of the book as well as Websites that the user can use for additional research. It provides important current and historical information that affect the current status of our world dynamics.—**Kay Stebbins Slattery**

California

70.   **Profiles of California.** 3d ed. Millerton, N.Y., Grey House Publishing, 2013. 1002p. maps. index. $149.00pa. ISBN 13: 978-1-61925-140-3; 978-1-61925-159-5 (e-book).

This 3d edition of *Profiles of California* provides a comprehensive, data-rich guide to 1,782 populated places, and 266 unincorporated communities throughout the state of California. The volume is divided into five sections. Section 1 provides information on the state's history, government, natural resources, and maps. Section 2 contains 1,782 profiles of places organized alphabetically by county. County profiles include statistical data on geography, climate, and demographics as well as information about the economy, taxes, and housing. Also included are Websites and telephone numbers to cities and various Chambers of Commerce. Each place profile includes data on the following: geographical characteristics, history, population, economic data, income, taxes per capita, education, housing, hospitals, crime rate, newspapers, transportation and airports, and general contact information. All data are obtained from the 2010 Census, with some projection data. Section 3 contains a profile of public school education in California and all districts with a student population over 1,500. Important data includes migrant student numbers, student-teacher ratios, current spending per student, and high school drop-out rate. Section 4 provides a detailed look at the ancestral, Hispanic, and racial makeup of California's 200-plus ethnic categories. Section 6 provides a detailed overview of climate based on analysis of statistics from the National Climatic Data Center. Sixteen data elements are presented based on weather station data. The user guide outlines in detail each section of the book. Although it could be argued that the information contained in this book could be found elsewhere, nowhere is it compiled so conveniently and comprehensively, making this item well worth the price. *Profiles of California* is highly recommended. The title is updated every four years to ensure that data is up to date and relevant for the user.—**Robert V. Labaree**

New York

71.   **The New York State Directory, 2013/2014.** Millerton, N.Y., Grey House Publishing, 2013. 898p. maps. $145.00pa.; $300.00 (online edition; single user); $400.00 (print and online editions). ISBN 13: 978-1-61925-125-0.

From 1983 until 2004 *The New York State Directory* was published annually by Walker's Research. In 2004 Grey House Publishing became the publisher of this title and this is their 9th edition. The content is similar to what you would expect to find if you consulted other state government manuals. In the first section users are provided with the organization of the executive, legislative, and judicial branches. The second section provides information related to 25 major policy areas. It is in this section that the user can find which key individuals in the New York state government, federal government, and the private sector have the expertise in specific policy areas with the standard contact information provided. The third section provides listings for state government public information officers and contact information for the New York delegation in Washington (including their committee assignments). Senior government officials for the counties and municipalities whose population is greater than 20,000 greater are also included. Additionally, users can find contact information regarding the political parties, chambers of commerce, media contacts, information on administrators in higher education, and public school administrators. A nice feature is the biography section that profiles nearly 250 key officials.

The work is thoroughly indexed by name, organization, Websites, and geography. At the back of the volume are 45 full-color demographic maps that visually display such items as the congressional districts, percent of different ethnic groups, median age, and education levels. This book is for a specialized audience such as other state's legislative bureaus or political parties and lobbyists wanting to influence public policy in New York. This resource is available online from the publisher's GOLD database (http://

gold.greyhouse.com). Here users can search the information by government branch, personnel name, keyword, geographic area, and more.—**Judith J. Field**

72.   Panchyk, Richard. **New York City History for Kids: From New Amsterdam to the Big Apple with 21 Activities.** Chicago, Chicago Review Press, 2013. 144p. illus. $16.95pa. ISBN 13: 978-1-88305-293-5.

This book opens with a timeline from Giovanni da Verrazano landing in New York Harbor in 1524 and marks important events through the building of Freedom Tower in 2013. There are pen-and-ink drawings, photographs, original maps, and an overview of historical events throughout the eighteenth and nineteenth centuries. Interspersed with age-appropriate historical accounts are related activities such as tracing family history, producing a Broadway play, graphing a neighborhood walking tour, and building a replica of Fort Amsterdam. This is a comprehensive look at history as well as a dynamic source of engaging topics. The text and graphics are attractive and invite the reader to delve deeper. This guide will be a valuable addition to public libraries and school libraries as well as home libraries.—**Jennifer Welch**

73.   **Profiles of New York State, 2013/2014.** 9th ed. Millerton, N.Y., Grey House Publishing, 2013. 980p. $149.00pa. ISBN 13: 978-1-61925-127-4.

This 2013/2014 edition of this title provides data on all populated communities and counties in New York State as well as individual statistics from the U.S. Census. It is divided into seven major sections that cover everything from ethnic backgrounds to climate. All sections include comprehensive statistics or rankings and full-color maps. Section 2, Profiles, is organized by county and gives "detailed profiles of more than 2,500 places plus 62 counties." Major fields include: Geography, Housing, Education, Religion, Ancestry, Transportation, Population, Climate, Economy, Industry, and Health. Also included are an alphabetic place index and comparative statistics that compare the 100 largest New York communities. Section 2, Education, summarizes the number of schools, students, diplomas granted, and educational dollars spent. Section 3, Education, summarizes the number of schools, students, diplomas granted, and money spent. Section 4, Ancestry, looks at 217 ethnic categories that are ranked in three different ways. Section 5, Climate, provides a summary of the state's weather patterns, information on weather stations in the area, and lots of interesting details on New York weather. The work concludes with full-color maps covering a variety of topics and subjects. Overall, this work is especially useful for those needing information on the state of New York. It should be included in all New York libraries.—**ARBA Staff Reviewer**

Wisconsin

74.   **Profiles of Wisconsin.** 3d ed. Millerton, N.Y., Grey House Publishing, 2013. 845p. maps. index. $149.00pa. ISBN 13: 978-1-61925-141-0; 978-1-61925-160-1pa.

Profiles of Wisconsin is a useful reference that briefly profiles the history, statistics, and demographics for the 2,082 populated places in Wisconsin. Profiles are organized alphabetically by county and include such details as the latitude and longitude, population from the 2010 census with demographic detail, history, employment, income, education, housing, hospitals, newspapers, additional information contacts, taxes, safety, and transportation information. There is an excellent user guide and introduction at the beginning of the book, which is helpful in adding more depth and detail to the short profiles found for each populated place. By far the best feature of this reference tool is the comparative statistics section. This includes comparisons of areas such as population, education, school district rankings, demographic breakdown, ancestry, and weather service as well as others. The layout and topics are much the same as the last edition; however, all data have been updated to reflect the most current data available at the time of publication. This book can be recommended to a public library or school library to purchase as it is well organized, well researched, informative, and would be a good addition to a quick reference collection.—**ARBA Staff Reviewer**

Africa

General Works

75.   Dickovick, J. Tyler. **The World Today Series, 2013: Africa.** Lanham, Md., Rowman & Littlefield, 2013. 344p. illus. maps. $18.50pa.; $16.95 (e-book). ISBN 13: 978-1-4758-0471-3; 978-1-4758-0472-0 (e-book).

This volume starts with an overview of the situation in Africa in 2013. It is followed by a brief essay of the pre-colonial period. The colonial period, broken down by the Portuguese, British, French, Americans, King Leopold II, Spanish, Germans, South Africans and Italians, comes next. The bulk of the book is reports on the 54 individual countries in Africa, grouped by region. For each country the pattern is to start with basic facts. Then a short description of the land and people is given, followed by the past political and economic history, regimes, contemporary issues (where appropriate), and the future. There has been considerable change in many African countries in recent years. This volume is a convenient source to learn what has happened in specific countries.—**J. E. Weaver**

Burkino Faso

76.   Rupley, Lawrence, Lamissa Bangali, and Boureima Diamitani. **Historical Dictionary of Burkina Faso.** Lanham, Md., Scarecrow, 2013. 317p. (Historical Dictionary of Africa). $109.99. ISBN 13: 978-0-8108-6770-3; 978-0-8108-8010-8 (e-book).

This, the 3d edition, updates the *Historical Dictionary of Burkina Faso* last published in 1997 (see ARBA 99, entry 96). The more than 1,000 entries, on people (such as political and military leaders, clerics, and teachers), places, events, organizations, and more comprise the bulk of the book. They provide information on politics, religion, economics, history, literature, cinema, and finance in Burkina Faso. The dictionary entries are preceded by a list of acronyms and abbreviations, a chronology from 700 B.C.E.-2012 C.E. and a short introduction to Burkina Faso. The book ends with a bibliography that includes works on history, politics, the economy, culture, society, and science. It also includes reference works and online sources. This book is a good resource for those wanting to know about Burkina Faso, including students and researchers.—**J. E. Weaver**

Ethiopia

77.   Shinn, David H., and Thomas P. Ofcansky. **Historical Dictionary of Ethiopia.** 2d ed. Lanham, Md., Scarecrow, 2013. 649p. (Historical Dictionaries of Africa). $145.00; $139.99 (e-book). ISBN 13: 978-0-8108-7194-6; 978-0-8108-7457-2 (e-book).

The authors David H. Shinn and Thomas P. Ofcansky provide the reader with a concise yet scholarly treatment of the history and related subjects germane to the country of Ethiopia. The *Historical Dictionary of Ethiopia* outlines essential information on a wide array of subjects, including, but not limited to the history, culture, religion, and politics of this African country. In a series of short to medium length essays, the user is presented with a myriad of facts, dates, philosophical, and political observations, which go beyond the normal pedantic coverage that characterizes other historical dictionaries. An outstanding feature of this text is its over 200-page bibliography of sources, which is extremely helpful to academic researchers and students wishing to further their knowledge of the historical nomenclature of Ethiopia and its people. The dictionary also provides maps, chronology tables, and appendixes as well as numerous cross-references following each essay. This work is highly recommended for both college and high school collections looking to enhance their African studies area.—**Patrick Hall**

Guinea

78.   Camara, Mohamed Saliou, Thomas O'Toole, and Janice E. Baker. **Historical Dictionary of Guinea.** 5th ed. Lanham, Md., Scarecrow, 2014. 392p. (Historical Dictionaries of Africa). $120.00; $119.99 (e-book). ISBN 13: 978-0-8108-7823-5; 978-0-8108-7969-0 (e-book).

It has been a 9 years now since the 4th edition of this title was published, and Dr. O'Toole (Professor of Anthropology and African Studies, St. Cloud State University, Minnesota) continues his long authorship of this work. For this edition he is joined by Camara, a Guinea native and professor of history at Embry-Riddle Aeronautical University in Florida, and Baker, a retired public servant who has written on Africa. As with many Third World nations, there is more information available for the turbulent post-1945 period, while the earlier eras suffer in comparison. The dictionary's information has been revised and updated to reflect the changes in the last 10 years, and there are now over 800 alphabetically arranged entries—twice as many as published in the last edition. A chronology (3500 B.C.E. - 2013 C.E.) supplements the introduction that briefly describes the land and people, the pre-colonial history, and the more recent period since 1984. There is no index (which would have aided subject access to the information), but there are *see* references, and plentiful cross-references embedded within the text are identified by their heavy black print. The value-added features include a list of acronyms and abbreviations, and lists of government officials (e.g., presidents, prime ministers, governors). The lengthy bibliography is important as it provides a selection of citations to European and African materials not easily found elsewhere. The two maps found at the beginning of the book are not enough to do this country justice; physical features and ethnic groups could have been illustrated along with cities and rivers. However, there really are very few reference books on this poor West African country. This item is necessary for all African collections, and suitable for all other academic and large public library reference collections.—**Daniel K. Blewett**

Lesotho

79.   Rosenberg, Scott, and Richard F. Weisfelder. **Historical Dictionary of Lesotho.** 2d ed. Lanham, Md., Scarecrow, 2013. 620p. maps. (Historical Dictionaries of Africa). $150.00; $149.99 (e-book). ISBN 13: 978-0-8108-6795-6; 978-0-8108-7982-9 (e-book).

This thorough successor to the authors' 2004 work of the same title brings reference coverage of the Kingdom of Lesotho's complex history up to contemporary times and fills a long-standing gap in Africana (see ARBA 2005, entry 88). At nearly twice the size of its predecessor, it reflects the social conditions of the region during the past decade, emphasizing detailed coverage of the Basotho responsible for many of the political and historical events, their internal cultural institutions and organizations, and less the prominent colonial era figures and institutions. Entries are clearly written, with detailed cross-references indicated in bold type. A lengthy bibliography of recent publications greatly expands awareness of what has actually been written about Lesotho, while the chronology reaches from the early nineteenth-century formation of the Basotho kingdom through 2012, and is accompanied by maps, a royal genealogy, and heads of government. This work is most useful for college and university libraries supporting degree programs in political science, history, and African studies.—**ARBA Staff Reviewer**

Republic of Guinea-Bissau

80.   Mendy, Peter Karibe, and Richard A. Lobban Jr. **Historical Dictionary of the Republic of Guinea-Bissau.** 4th ed. Lanham, Md., Scarecrow, 2014. 560p. (Historical Dictionaries of Africa). $150.00; $149.99 (e-book). ISBN 13: 978-0-8108-5310-2; 978-0-8108-8027-6 (e-book).

This volume is another updated edition in the African Historical Dictionaries series. Like other entries in the series, the dictionary proper is preceded by a historical chronology, a list of acronyms and abbreviations, and a general introduction, and in this case is followed by several appendixes, including a list of Portuguese governors, lists of heads of state and prime ministers, several reprints of primary documents, and a modicum of cultural information. A few maps of varying quality are scattered throughout. The bibliography is substantial but, paradoxically, overmatches the likely usership of the work—many citations are to works in French and Portuguese, much of which are in turn virtually unobtainable. Overall, this volume does a good job of relating the long and oftentimes difficult history of this African country that includes a collapsing infrastructure, a dilapidated economy, and military coups d'etat.—**ARBA Staff Reviewer**

South Africa

81.   Beck, Roger B. **A History of South Africa.** 2d ed. Santa Barbara, Calif., Greenwood Press/ABC-CLIO, 2014. 301p. illus. index. (The Greenwood Histories of the Modern Nations). $58.00. ISBN 13: 978-1-61069-526-8; 978-1-61069-527-5 (e-book).

The author of this work, who teaches African and world history at Eastern Illinois University, has updated his 2000 monograph on South African history. Given the complexity of the topic, this is no mean feat. Although it begins with the prehistoric period, it is current enough that it can discuss not only the development of the post-apartheid constitution and the post-Mandela era, as well as more current political news. As one might expect, however, the twentieth century garners half the book.

This book is, of necessity, startlingly terse at times. Yet, that is not meant to be a criticism since it was written as an introductory text, especially for students, probably of high school or college age. It is also quite suitable as a reference work. It has a good index, a list of notable people in the history of South Africa (65 in all), a glossary of terms (primarily Afrikaans and African words), and a brief bibliographic essay that could have been expanded. Also included are a timeline of historical events and a list of abbreviations.

There are very few illustrations and the maps are few and at best adequate. More maps, especially in the beginning of the text, would have been helpful. On the other hand, the initial chapter discusses South Africa today, its geography, population, economic conditions, mass media, and much more to set the stage for what follows. Overall, the text is well written, easy to follow, and a good place to start for readers who have no prior knowledge of South African history. This work is recommended for most libraries, but especially high school, college, and public libraries.—**Paul H. Thomas**

Sudan

82.   Kramer, Robert S., Richard A. Lobban Jr., and Carolyn Fluehr-Lobban. **Historical Dictionary of the Sudan.** 4th ed. Lanham, Md., Scarecrow, 2013. 546p. (Historical Dictionaries of Africa). $145.00; $139.99 (e-book). ISBN 13: 978-0-8108-6180-0; 978-0-8108-7940-9.

The *Historical Dictionary of Sudan*, like its predecessor, starts with the rise of Islam. It concludes with Sudan partitioned into two countries. As with other Historical Dictionaries in the series, it begins with a chronology that has brief entries for the period from 5000 B.C.E. to the 1400s (the time period covered in the *Historical Dictionary of Ancient Nubia*) and fuller ones from 1504 to 2012 (the time period of this volume). An introductory essay precedes the alphabetic entries about people, places, events, and more. The seven appendixes are: a current factfile; ethno-linguistic groups in or adjoining the Sudan; sultans; eighteenth- and nineteenth-century administrators; 1890 agreement for the administration of the Sudan; political structure and administration; and educational institutions. There is an extensive bibliography broken down into areas such as historical, political, economic, cultural, and more. It includes electronic sources as well as books, journal entries, and audio-visual materials. This work is intended to be a comprehensive reference and research tool for undergraduates and generalist researchers and helpful to specialists in Sudan and African/Middle Eastern studies.—**J. E. Weaver**

Tanzania

83.   Otiso, Kefa M. **Culture and Customs of Tanzania.** Santa Barbara, Calif., Greenwood Press/ABC-CLIO, 2013. 250p. illus. index. (Culture and Customs of Africa). $50.00. ISBN 13: 978-0-313-33978-3; 978-0-313-08708-0.

This book provides a concise and yet thorough overview of Tanzanian culture. Divided into eight chapters, the reader is presented with a host of facts concerning Tanzania's social life and customs, religious beliefs, and geopolitical worldview. Especially illuminating is chapter 6, dealing with gender roles in Tanzanian society. From the traditional extended family model, to a more open view of men's and women's roles precipitated by global influences, researchers interested in the dynamics of cultural change will find this an invaluable chapter. A chronology highlighting key historical events and people is also included. Another notable feature of this work is the inclusion of a bibliographic essay. This essay, covering such areas as Tanzanian religion, art and architecture, gender roles, social customs, music, and worldview, can direct the serious researcher to pertinent books and journal articles explicating the country of Tanzania. In short, this work is highly recommended for any library supporting a multicultural or African studies program.—**Patrick Hall**

Asia

General Works

Bibliography

84.   **Asia-Studies Full-Text Online. http://www.asia-studies.com/.** [Website]. International Information Services. Price negotiated by site. Date reviewed: 2013.

Asia-Studies Full-Text Online offers full-text reports and analyses from research institutions on 55 countries regarding public and private sector issues. Examples of specific subject coverage include finance, trade, environment, human resources development, best practices in government, fisheries, tourism, education and women's studies, to name a few. The average study is 50 pages long, and contains statistics, research, analysis, and forecasts. Most contain statistical tables, charts, and/or graphs. The database search engine offers advanced search features for experienced researchers while delivering excellent results for novices.—**Noriko Asato**

85.   **Handbook for Asian Studies Specialists: A Guide to Research Materials and Collection Building Tools.** Noriko Asato, ed. Santa Barbara, Calif., Libraries Unlimited/ABC-CLIO, 2013. 466p. index. $105.00pa. ISBN 13: 978-1-59884-842-7; 978-1-59884-843-4 (e-book).

This reference provides a bibliography of key print and electronic East Asian resources in English, Chinese, Japanese, and Korean. In addition it provides guidance on the development, cataloging, and management of an Asian Studies collection. The target audience for this introductory handbook is librarians just entering this field of specialization. For the countries of China, Japan, and Korea, entries are categorized by types of sources such as encyclopedias, dictionaries, atlases, catalogs, directories, and yearbooks, under subject headings like the arts, religion, literature, history, sociology, language and linguistics, philosophy, geography, business and economics, political science, anthropology, and more. As an example of the comprehensiveness of this work, if a librarian should be asked for facsimiles of real-size signatures or seals of major Japanese historical figures, a dictionary of North Korean artists, or an online database of Korean movies, they can be found in this reference. This bibliography is unusual in that within each subject heading, items are not listed alphabetically but instead they are given in order of importance or ease of use. The goal is to make it easier for the new East Asian Studies librarian to respond to reference questions. Among the unique dimensions of Asian Studies librarianship discussed, we learn about the additional classification systems specifically developed for the complexities of this specialty, such as the Harvard-Yenching scheme, and the need for consistent transliteration schemes to Romanize Chinese, Japanese, and Korean material for effective online searches.—**Adrienne Antink**

Catalogs and Collections

86.   **AccessAsia. http://accessasia.org/.** [Website]. National Bureau of Asian Research. Free. Date reviewed: 2013.

This site provides thousands of links to contemporary Asian affairs experts' Websites ranging from Afghanistan to Uzbekistan with an emphasis on policy, health security, economics, trade, and energy. To find links to experts in AccessAsia, simply type a search term in the search box located on the AccessAsia homepage. Recommended search terms are last names, regions, and specializations (for instance, China or Security).—**Noriko Asato**

87.   **Image Database to Enhance Asian Studies (IDEAS). http://ideasproject.org/.** [Website]. Free. Date reviewed: 2013.

This database offers instructors a range of historical and contemporary images of Asia. The goal of the Image Database to Enhance Asian Studies (IDEAS) is to unify digitizing efforts already in progress at various campuses into a shared searchable database. IDEAS focuses on the generally underrepresented area of Asia in an attempt to make multi-media materials more widely available for specialists and non-specialists alike. The scope of the IDEAS project will allow for the continued addition of new materials over time, encouraging participation in both use as well as development of the database through faculty and staff workshops. IDEAS is the first multi-institutional, interdisciplinary, pan-Asian searchable database in the country.—**Noriko Asato**

Handbooks and Yearbooks

88.   **The World Today Series, 2013: East & Southeast Asia.** 46th ed. By Steven A. Leibo. Lanham, Md., Rowman & Littlefield, 2013. 314p. illus. maps. $18.50pa.; $16.95 (e-book). ISBN 13: 978-1-4758-

0475-1; 978-1-4758-0476-8 (e-book).

East & Southeast Asia are presented as a mosaic of countries in the title *The World Today Series: East & Southeast Asia*. The first chapter is an overview of Southeast Asia in the world today, the politics, its relationship with the United States, the various cultures, the economies, and the histories. Each of the countries has an entry, and is described by political name, geographic information, capital city, population, neighboring countries, official language and other languages spoken, ethnic background, principle religion, chief commercial products, former colonial status, its independence day, its chief of state, and flag description. Each country begins with a short history and ends with the current state of affairs through April 2013. Black-and-white photographs and outline maps accompany the text information. Since the entries are in alphabetic order, there is no index. Also, there is a selected bibliography of key English-language sources for the last section of the book. I would recommend this East and Southeast Asian compendium for large public and academic libraries' country studies collections. It provides current and very important information on the current status of our world dynamics.—**Kay Stebbins Slattery**

China

89.   Song, Yuwu. **Biographical Dictionary of the People's Republic of China.** Jefferson, N.C., McFarland, 2013. 443p. index. $95.00pa. ISBN 13: 978-0-7864-3582-1; 978-1-4766-0298-1 (e-book).

This biographical dictionary provides key information on nearly 600 Chinese individuals who have made significant contributions to the development of life in China over the past seven decades. While the focus leans heavily toward political figures, users will also find biographies on people in business, the military, academia, medicine, social movements, entertainment, the arts, and sports. Not everyone on this list has contributed to Chinas progress in a worthwhile way—the focus of the work is to highlight all key people, not just those that have done good. For each person the user will find an objective description of their life and an analysis of their individual contributions and importance in the modern history of China.—**Ma Lei Hsieh**

Japan

90.   **East Asia Image Collection. http://digital.lafayette.edu/collections/eastasia.** [Website]. Lafayette College Libraries. Free. Date reviewed: 2013.

This is an open-access digital repository of photographs, postcards, and slides of Japan and its Asian colonies, as well as the occupation of Japan. Rare materials include prewar picture postcards, high-quality commercial prints, and colonial era picture books. Each record in the East Asia Image Collection has been assigned subject headings, hyper-linked metadata, and, to the fullest extent possible, historiographical, bibliographical and technical data.—**Noriko Asato**

Thailand

91.   Fry, Gerald W., Gayla S. Nieminen, and Harold E. Smith. **Historical Dictionary of Thailand.** 3d ed. Lanham, Md., Scarecrow, 2013. 662p. (Historical Dictionaries of Asia, Oceania, and the Middle East). $140.00; $139.99 (e-book). ISBN 13: 978-0-8108-7802-0; 978-0-8108-7525-8 (e-book).

Since the publication of the 2d edition in 2005, much has changed in Thailand in all sectors of the country. This 3d edition has a revised introduction and many updates from 2005-2013. In addition, there are new entries that discuss many significant recent events, including politics, economics, and foreign relations.

Besides the introduction and the main body of dictionary, the chronology is concise and useful. The 16 appendixes—including such information as kings, population statistics, principal agricultural crops, economic indicators, gross domestic products, elections, Coups d'Etats in modern Thailand, and prime ministers—are simple compilations suitable to nonspecialist readers for quick reference and general information. The bibliography is a selective and classified one that also provides a list of relevant Websites on Thailand. This historical dictionary is useful as a beginning-level reference book on Thailand.—**Tze-chung Li**

Tibet

92.   **Sources of Tibetan Tradition.** Kurtis R. Schaeffer, Matthew T. Kapstein, and Gray Tuttle, eds. Irvington, N.Y., Columbia University Press, 2013. 810p. index. $120.00; $40.00pa.; $39.99 (e-book). ISBN 13: 978-0-231-13598-6; 978-0-231-13599-3; 978-0-231-50978-7 (e-book).

This is a collection of more than 180 translated writings from over the centuries on various topics such as art, literature, politics, religion, philosophy, history, travel, geography, music, and government. Some of these are just excerpts from longer documents, while others are the complete text of the item. Naturally, the role of Buddhism is central to the history of this mountainous region in Central Asia. There is a chronology (247 B.C.E. to Oct. 24, 1951, when Tibet was forcibly incorporated into China), four maps, a bibliography of the source materials, and another one for those desiring additional materials on this topic. A glossary of important Tibetan terms would have been useful. This valuable work is part of a series, Introduction to Asian Civilizations, and is a companion to the earlier *Sources of Chinese Tradition* (2d ed., 1999 and 2000), and *Sources of Indian Tradition* (2d ed., 1988). These collections are very useful for those seeking important foundational documents that illustrate or highlight some aspect of those societies, and can supplement reference works such as the *Historical Dictionary of Tibet* (see ARBA 2013, entry 94). When searching by the official subject headings, such as Tibet Region—Civilization—Sources or Tibet Region—Intellectual Life—Sources, one finds few items in English, so this is a welcome addition for the literature of this subject area. Schaeffer and Tuttle also jointly edited *The Tibetan History Reader* (Columbia University Press, 2013). The item under review is suitable for academic and public libraries that support religion or Asian Studies programs, or a Tibetan population. Unless there is high demand for this information, it should be located in the circulating rather than the reference collection.—**Daniel K. Blewett**

Canada

93.   **The World Today Series, 2013: Canada.** By Wayne C. Thompson. Lanham, Md., Rowman & Littlefield, 2013. 215p. illus. maps. $18.50pa.; $16.99 (e-book). ISBN 13: 978-1-4758-0473-7; 978-1-4758-0474-4 [e-book].

The first chapter of this work is an overview of Canada in the world today, the politics, its relationship with the United States, the various cultures, the economy, and the history. Politics is an important feature of this book as well as geographic information, capital city, population, neighboring countries, official language and other languages spoken, ethnic background, principle religion, chief commercial products, its independence day, its chief of state, and flag description. Black-and-white photographs and outline maps accompany the text information. There is no index. Also, there is a selected bibliography of key English-language sources for the last section of the book. I would recommend this Canadian compendium for large public and academic libraries' country studies collections. It provides current and very important information on the current status of our world dynamics.—**Kay Stebbins Slattery**

Developing Countries

94. **Atlas of Global Development: A Visual Guide to the World's Greatest Challenges.** 4th ed. Lanham, Md., Bernan Press, 2013. 144p. illus. maps. index. $29.95pa. ISBN 13: 978-0-8213-9757-2.

The 4th edition of the *Atlas of Global Development* provides a graphic overview of the social and economic status of the world and its people as of the first 13 years of the twenty-first century. Key issues addressed are population, income, education, health, economic development, and challenges to the environment. Those issues are considered on a geographical basis, thus emphasizing the importance of geography in human and economic development. Topics are presented largely by means of maps, charts, tables, and summarizing sidebars, supported by brief explanatory insertions of text. Although primarily a portrayal of world development as of from the early 2000s to 2013, time series graphics and tables have been added to help in identifying trends. Since the intention of the publisher was to provide a broad perspective, sources of further information on individual topics are indicated by Internet links. However, the guide contains much statistical data, gathered from the resources of the World Bank, and thus can serve as a reference as well as an introduction to, or refresher on, global development. Also included is a listing of Millennium Development Goals established by the United Nations with indications for monitoring progress. A glossary of relevant terms and an index offer useful assistance to readers. The use of color in the graphics add to the readability of possibly drab statistics.—**William C. Struning**

95. **The Least Developed Countries Report 2011: Exploring the Role of South-South Cooperation and Integration for Inclusive Growth and Sustainable Development.** New York, United Nations, 2012. 280p. $50.00pa. ISBN 13: 978-92-1-112835-2.

This is a report by UNCTAD on least developed countries (LDC), those countries that meet the criteria of: low income based on Gross National Income per capita; human assets based on nutrition, health, school enrolment, and literacy indicators that comprise the Human Assets Index; and economic vulnerability based natural shocks, trade shocks, exposure to shocks, economic smallness, and economic remoteness that make up the Economic Vulnerability Index. The report finds that developing productive capacity is the key to achieving sustained economic growth in the LDC. While recently LDC have had greater economic growth than in the past, unfortunately, it is not translating effectively into poverty reduction and improved human well being. Productive capacities are defined as the productive resources, entrepreneurial capacities and production linkages which together determine the capacity of a country to produce goods and services and enable it to grow and develop. These develop within a country through capital accumulation, technological progress, and structural change. This edition explores the reasons behind the difficulties the LDC countries have experienced in breaking into the international market place. It explores the role of cooperation among nearby countries for regional support in development and that new government policies need to be put into place to tap into economic potential. The book is intended as a resource for policy makers in LDC and their development partners. It is a useful volume for anyone interested in LDC and development economics.—**J. E. Weaver**

Europe

General Works

96. **American Bibliography of Slavic and East European Studies: EBSEES 1990-Present.** http://www.ebscohost.com/academic/american-bibliography-of-slavic-eastern-european-studies. [Website]. Ipswich, Mass., EBSCO. Price negotiated by site. Date reviewed: 2013.

This bibliography, covering East-Central Europe and the former Soviet Union, is produced at the University of Illinois at Urbana-Champaign and made available through EBSCO. It includes articles, books, dissertations, and journals in all disciplines as well as online resources and government publications from the United States and Canada that focus on Eastern Europe. This site works well in conjunction with the *Bibliography of Slavic Literature* (see ARBA 2002, entry 1125), in which the bibliographic entries represent literature from the middle ages to the present.—**Anna H. Perrault**

97.   **Austria, Croatia, and Slovenia.** Lorraine Murray, ed. New York, Rosen Publishing, 2014. 224p. illus. maps. index. (The Britannica Guide to Countries of the European Union). $53.00/vol.; $689.00/set. ISBN 13: 978-1-61530-970-2; 978-1-61530-974-0/set.

98.   **Belgium, Luxembourg, and the Netherlands.** Jeff Wallenfeldt, ed. New York, Rosen Publishing, 2014. 224p. illus. maps. index. (The Britannica Guide to Countries of the European Union). $53.00/vol.; $689.00/set. ISBN 13: 978-1-61530-973-3; 978-1-61530-974-0/set.

99.   **Bulgaria, Hungary, Romania, the Czech Republic, and Slovakia.** Lorraine Murray, ed. New York, Rosen Publishing, 2014. 360p. illus. maps. index. (The Britannica Guide to Countries of the European Union). $53.00/vol.; $689.00/set. ISBN 13: 978-1-61530-968-9; 978-1-61530-974-0/set.

100.   **Cyprus, Greece, and Malta.** Noah Tesch, ed. New York, Rosen Publishing, 2014. 178p. illus. maps. index. (The Britannica Guide to Countries of the European Union). $53.00/vol.; $689.00/set. ISBN 13: 978-1-61530-972-6; 978-1-61530-974-0/set.

101.   **Denmark, Finland, and Sweden.** Amy McKenna, ed. New York, Rosen Publishing, 2014. 232p. illus. maps. index. (The Britannica Guide to Countries of the European Union). $53.00/vol.; $689.00/set. ISBN 13: 978-1-61530-969-6; 978-1-61530-974-0/set.

102.   **Estonia, Latvia, Lithuania, and Poland.** Amy McKenna, ed. New York, Rosen Publishing, 2014. 216p. illus. maps. index. (The Britannica Guide to Countries of the European Union). $53.00/vol.; $689.00/set. ISBN 13: 978-1-61530-971-9; 978-1-61530-974-0/set.

103.   **France.** Michael Ray, ed. New York, Rosen Publishing, 2014. 353p. illus. maps. index. (The Britannica Guide to Countries of the European Union). $53.00/vol.; $689.00/set. ISBN 13: 978-1-61530-964-1; 978-1-61530-974-0/set.

104.   **Germany.** Michael Ray, ed. New York, Rosen Publishing, 2014. 334p. illus. maps. index. (The Britannica Guide to Countries of the European Union). $53.00/vol.; $689.00/set. ISBN 13: 978-1-61530-965-8; 978-1-61530-974-0/set.

105.   **Ireland.** Jeff Wallenfeldt, ed. New York, Rosen Publishing, 2014. 120p. illus. maps. index. (The Britannica Guide to Countries of the European Union). $53.00/vol.;$689.00/set. ISBN 13: 978-1-62275-058-0; 978-1-61530-974-0/set.

106.   **Italy.** Lorraine Murray, ed. New York, Rosen Publishing, 2014. 301p. illus. maps. index. (The Britannica Guide to Countries of the European Union). $53.00/vol.; $689.00/set. ISBN 13: 978-1-61530-966-5; 978-1-61530-974-0/set.

107.   **Portugal and Spain.** Michael Ray, ed. New York, Rosen Publishing, 2014. 322p. illus. maps. index. (The Britannica Guide to Countries of the European Union). $53.00/vol.; $689.00/set. ISBN 13: 978-1-61530-967-2; 978-1-61530-974-0/set.

108.   **The United Kingdom: England.** Jeff Wallenfeldt, ed. New York, Rosen Publishing, 2014. 378p. illus. maps. index. (The Britannica Guide to Countries of the European Union). $53.00/vol.; $689.00/set. ISBN 13: 978-1-61530-963-4; 978-1-61530-974-0/set.

109.   **The United Kingdom: Northern Ireland, Scotland, and Wales.** Jeff Wallenfeldt, ed. New York, Rosen Publishing, 2014. 184p. illus. maps. index. (The Britannica Guide to Countries of the European Union). $53.00/vol.; $689.00/set. ISBN 13: 978-1-62275-055-9; 978-1-61530-974-0/set.

Britannica Educational Publishing and Rosen Publishing have teamed up to offer this impressive 13-volume set that provides information on the countries of the European Union. In spite of their differing histories, varying languages, and different cultural norms, these countries have come together to form a unique union that allows them to share their common goals and work toward a better future for their citizens. Each volume provides information on the featured countries' geography, culture, economy, government, ancient and modern history, religion, and conflicts throughout history. The language is appropriate for advanced middle school students or high school age students. Full-color maps, illustrations, and photographs are used to enhance learning. Sidebars are used throughout to highlight important events, people, and newsworthy items. The use of the photographs and sidebars make this series fun to browse, while also very appropriate for research. The volumes conclude with a glossary of key terms, a bibliography, and an index. This series will be an expensive addition for most libraries so cost will be a consideration. For those libraries interested in specific countries, the volumes can be purchased separately for $53 each.—**Shannon Graff Hysell**

110.   **The World Today Series, 2013: Nordic, Central, & Southeastern Europe.** 13th ed. By Wayne C. Thompson. Lanham, Md., Rowman & Littlefield, 2013. 578p. illus. maps. $19.00pa.; $17.99 (e-book). ISBN 13: 978-1-4758-0488-1; 978-1-4758-0489-8 [e-book].

111.   **The World Today Series, 2013: Western Europe.** 32d ed. By Wayne C. Thompson. Lanham, Md., Rowman & Littlefield, 2013. 451p. illus. maps. $19.00pa.; $17.99 (e-book). ISBN 13: 978-1-4758-0606-5; 978-1-4758-0507-9 [e-book].

Western, Central, Southeaster, and Nordic Europe are presented as a mosaic of countries in these two compilation titles. The *Western Europe* title begins with an overview of the titles that comprise Western Europe, including the region's role in the world today, the politics, its relationship with the United States, the various cultures, the economies, and the histories. Unfortunately, the volume on the other regions of Europe does not provide an overview, which would have been useful. Divided into region, each of the countries has an entry, and is described by political name, geographic information, capital city, population, neighboring countries, official language and other languages spoken, ethnic background, principle religion, chief commercial products, its independence day, its chief of state, and flag description. Each country begins with a short history and ends with the current state of affairs. Black-and-white photographs and outline maps accompany the text information. Since the entries are in alphabetic order, there is no index. Also, there is a selected bibliography of key English-language print and Web sources for the last section of each book. I would recommend these compendium for large public and academic libraries' country studies collections. They provide current and very important information on the current status of our world dynamics.—**Kay Stebbins Slattery**

Ireland

112.   Biletz, Frank A. **Historical Dictionary of Ireland.** new ed. Lanham, Md., Scarecrow, 2014. 571p. (Historical Dictionaries of Europe). $140.00; $139.99 (e-book). ISBN 13: 978-0-8108-5077-4; 978-0-8108-7091-8 (e-book).

This volume in the European Historical Dictionaries series continues this series' tradition of excellence. The dictionary is a scholarly, clearly written work, packed full of useful information. The main section consists of an A to Z annotated dictionary with entries covering the main events, people, and places in Irish history. The 20-page introduction provides a concise overview of Irish history from the Neolithic period until 1922. Four appendixes list the presidents of Ireland; the prime ministers of the Irish Free State and Irish Republic; the prime ministers of Northern Ireland; and the first ministers and deputy first ministers of Northern Ireland. The work concludes with an extensive bibliography. This dictionary is a useful book that any institution or individual with an interest in Irish studies should acquire.—**Adrienne Antink**

Russia

113.   **The World Today Series, 2013: Russia & the Commonwealth of Independent States'.** 44th ed. By M. Wesley Shoemaker. Lanham, Md., Rowman & Littlefield, 2013. 318p. illus. maps. $18.00pa.; $16.99 (e-book). ISBN 13: 978-1-4758-0490-4; 978-1-4758-0491-1 (e-book).

Russia and the Commonwealth of Independent States are presented as a mosaic of countries in the title *The World Today Series: Russia and the Commonwealth of Independent States*. The first chapter is an overview of this region in the world today, including the politics, the relationship with the United States, the various cultures, the economies, and the histories. Arranged by region, each of the countries has an entry and is described by political name, geographic information, capital city, population, neighboring countries, official language and other languages spoken, ethnic background, principle religion, chief commercial products, its independence day, its chief of state, and flag description. Each country begins with a short history and ends with the current state of affairs. Black-and-white photographs and outline maps accompany the text information. Since the entries are in alphabetic order, there is no index. There is a selected bibliography of key English-language sources for the last section of the book. I would recommend this inexpensive compendium for large public and academic libraries' country studies collections. It provides current and very important information on the current status of our world dynamics.—**Kay Stebbins Slattery**

Slovakia

114.   Kirschbaum, Stanislav J. **Historical Dictionary of Slovakia.** 3d ed. Lanham, Md., Scarecrow, 2014. 415p. (Historical Dictionaries of Europe). $125.00; $119.99 (e-book). ISBN 13: 978-0-8108-8029-0; 978-0-8108-8030-6 (e-book).

This is an update to the 2007 *Historical Dictionary of Slovakia* by the same author. The book includes a very detailed chronology of Slovak history from 179 C.E.-January 2013 followed by a substantial historical overview that includes information on the development of Slovakia politically and economically since 1993. Entries include people, places, concepts, key events, organizations and political parties, and even important periodical publications. January 2013 marked two decades of democratic government within the country, the longest period of democracy in the country's history. An appendix contains a list of all of the rulers of the Slovak lands, from 623 C.E.-2013. The book also contains an extensive bibliographic essay of works on Slovak history in English, Slovak and several other languages, as well as helpful Websites for archives, libraries, and Slovak ministries. Overall, this is an important update that most large university libraries will want to acquire.—**ARBA Staff Reviewer**

Ukraine

115.   Katchanovski, Ivan, Zenon E. Kohut, Bohdan Y. Nebesio, and Myroslav Yurkevich. **Historical Dictionary of Ukraine.** 2d ed. Lanham, Md., Scarecrow, 2013. 914p. (Historical Dictionaries of Europe). $165.00; $159.99 (e-book). ISBN 13: 978-0-8108-7845-7; 978-0-8108-7847-1 (e-book).

This is the 2d edition of this work on Ukrainian history in English. It has more than 725 entries that cover biographies, places, historical events, institutions, economics, and social and cultural aspects of Ukraine. The book has a list of acronyms and abbreviations, nine maps, a chronology, and an introduction that summarizes the history of Ukraine. Then it goes into the entries, which are in the traditional A-to-Z format. The entries vary in length. Cross-references are indicated by having the topic or term in bold print. The authors use the modified Library of Congress system to transliterate Ukrainian and other East Slavic words and names. The authors are associated with the Canadian Institute of Ukrainian Studies (CIUS) at the University of Alberta. The book ends with an extensive bibliography that has its own introduction. The bibliography is subdivided into various subjects. Books, articles, and Internet sites are included. It does not have illustrations. This is a great one-volume reference on Ukrainian history that belongs in academic and larger public libraries with a Ukrainian or Eastern European reference section.—**Benet Steven Exton**

Latin America and the Caribbean

General Works

116.   Buckman, Robert T. **The World Today Series, 2013: Latin America.** 4th ed. Lanham, Md., Rowman & Littlefield, 2013. 434p. illus. maps. $19.00pa.; $17.95 (e-book). ISBN 13: 978-1-4758-0477-5; 978-1-4758-0481-2 (e-book).

Latin America is presented as a mosaic of countries in our Southern Hemisphere in the title *The World Today Series: Latin America*. The first chapter is an overview of Latin America in the world today, the politics, its relationship with the United States, the various cultures, the economies, and the histories. Each of the Latin and South American countries has an entry, and are described by political name, geographic information, capital city, population, neighboring countries, official language and other languages spoken, ethnic background, principle religion, chief commercial products, former colonial status, its independence day, its chief of state, and flag description. Each country begins with a short history and ends with the current state of affairs through April 2013. Black-and-white photographs and outline maps accompany the text information. Since the entries are in alphabetic order, there is no index. There is a chapter entitled "Smaller Nations and Dependent Territories of Latin America," which provides information about he island territories of the CARICOM. This is a common market of the 15 members of the Caribbean community. Also, there is a selected bibliography of key English-language sources for the last section of the book. I would recommend this Latin American compendium for large public and academic libraries' country studies collections. It provides current and very important information on the current status of our world dynamics.—**Kay Stebbins Slattery**

Cuba

117.   **Cuba.** Ted A. Henken, Miriam Celaya, and Dimas Castellanos, eds. Santa Barbara, Calif., ABC-CLIO, 2013. 596p. illus. index. (Latin America in Focus). $89.00. ISBN 13: 978-1-61069-011-9; 978-1-61069-012-6 (e-book).

The editors of this work have tried to present Cuba's new reality as the Cuban people deal with modern changes in politics, economics, society, and culture. The authors provide a discussion and evaluation of these issues to help readers understand the Cuba of today.

The work is organized into seven topical chapters covering geography, history, politics and government, the economy, society, culture, and contemporary issues. The chapters are broken down into sections that dissect the topic on a closer level; for example, in the chapter on Society, users will find additional information class structure and inequality, family and gender, migration and diaspora, and the impact of the Internet and social media. There are several helpful sidebars of information throughout the text. A glossary of terms associated with Cuba, basic facts and figures of country information, demographics, geography, the economy, communications and transportation, and census information. There is a list of country-related organizations and an index.

This book is written very honestly with thought-provoking facts about one of our more interesting Latin American neighbors. This title is recommended for large public libraries and academic libraries.—**Kay Stebbins Slattery**

Middle East

General Works

118.   **The World Today Series, 2013: The Middle East & South Asia.** By Malcolm B. Russell. Lanham, Md., Rowman & Littlefield, 2012. 283p. illus. maps. $18.50pa.; $16.99 (e-book). ISBN 13: 978-1-4758-0486-7; 978-1-4758-0487-4 [e-book].

The Middle East and South Asia are presented as a mosaic of countries in the title *The World Today Series: The Middle East & South Asia.* The first chapter is an overview of the history of the region, the Arab Spring and its effects on regional and world politics, and the impact of oil in this region of the world. Separated into region, first the Middle East and then South Asia, each of the countries has an entry, and is described by political name, geographic information, capital city, population, neighboring countries, official language and other languages spoken, ethnic background, principle religion, chief commercial products, its independence day, its chief of state, and flag description. Each country begins with a short history and ends with the current state of affairs. Black-and-white photographs and outline maps accompany the text information. Since the entries are in alphabetic order, there is no index. Also, there is a selected bibliography of key English-language sources for the last section of the book. I would recommend this Middle East and South Asia compendium for large public and academic libraries' country studies collections. It provides current and very important information on the current status of our world dynamics.—**Kay Stebbins Slattery**

Egypt

119.   Goldschmidt, Arthur, Jr. **Historical Dictionary of Egypt.** 4th ed. Lanham, Md., Scarecrow, 2013. 535p. (Historical Dictionaries of Africa). $145.00; $139.99 (e-book). ISBN 13: 978-0-8108-6189-3; 978-0-8108-8025-2 (e-book).

This updated dictionary, written by a well-known scholar of Middle Eastern history, focuses on the people, places, and institutions of the last two centuries of Egyptian history. This work covers Egypt's history from its emergences during the reign of Ali Bey (1760-1772) up to the first two years of the Arab Spring. It includes information on the leadership of Jamal Abd al-Nasir and Anwar al-Sadat as well as the recent demonstrations in Cairo's Tahrir Square that have become an iconic movement in the Middle East. It is enhanced by a complete list of political leaders since 1878, followed by an extensive bibliographic essay and a bibliography ordered by time period. The bibliography refers the reader to Websites as well as to print materials and is organized by themes (e.g., theater, women). Because of its comprehensiveness and its currency, this volume belongs in every central public library and the libraries of every college and university, as well as in libraries easily accessible to media researchers, legislators, and other government officials so that they may not only have ready access to the historical background of the area but also may check quickly on virtually any aspect of this important crossroads country.—**Susan Tower Hollis**

120.   Russell, Mona. **Egypt.** Santa Barbara, Calif., ABC-CLIO, 2013. 508p. illus. maps. index. (Middle East in Focus). $100.00. ISBN 13: 978-1-59884-233-3; 978-1-59884-234-0 (e-book).

Egypt, an evolving ancient civilization, is discussed in depth in this new analysis for the Middle East in Focus series. Every aspect of this Middle Eastern country is covered, beginning with geography and history, continuing with the government and politics, the economy, society, religions, social classes and ethnicities, women, and education. The chapters on the Egyptian culture covers the language, literature, art and architecture, food, sports and leisure, popular youth and consumer culture, and finally, its performing arts, theater, dance, and film.

Each area begins with its history and brings the reader up-to-date to the beginning of 2012, before the Arab Spring unfolded. The last chapter, entitled "Contemporary Issues," provides the reader with an up-to-date scenario on the present political situation in Egypt. The issues discussed in this last section are about the January 25 Movement, when Hosni Mubarak, the Egyptian Prime Minister, for over 30 years was arrested and new elections were held to elect a new government under President Mohammed Morsi.

The appendixes include a glossary and abbreviations as well as basic facts and figures, which defines Egypt's geography, population, official names, government officials, political parties and organizations, demographics, economy, communications and transportation, military, education, weather, labor, and agriculture. There is a calendar of religions and secular holidays. The final sections are an annotated bibliography, thematic index, and a regular index.

This reviewer highly recommends this overview of Egypt for all libraries. It covers the panoramic history and provides an update on all aspects of Egypt, as a crossroad of the world as well as a key player in the world and regional geopolitics, particularly in the Palestinian-Arab-Israeli conflict.—**Kay Stebbins Slattery**

Iraq

121.   Dougherty, Beth K., and Edmund A. Ghareeb. **Historical Dictionary of Iraq.** 2d ed. Lanham, Md., Scarecrow, 2014. 811p. (Historical Dictionaries of Asia, Oceania, and the Middle East). $150.00; $149.99 (e-book). ISBN 13: 978-0-8108-6845-8; 978-0-8108-7942-3 (e-book)

I have reviewed several of the historical dictionaries in this series and they are outstanding works. This timely volume is no exception. The scope covers the long span of history from ancient Mesopotamia through 2013, with attention to ethnic, religious, political, and ideological groups; individuals; cultural elements; and much more. Besides the hundreds of well-crafted entries, the volume includes a lengthy chronology, maps (including a tribal area breakdown), a fine historical essay, and several useful appendixes. The appendixes include the structures and individuals of political leadership since 1920 and the important Iraqi individuals, organizations, and election results from 2005-2013. The general bibliography and an extensive topical bibliography are both quite good. This edition has considerably more entries than the last edition published in 2004 and the bibliography has also been significantly expanded. The compiler, Edmund Ghareeb, is a leading scholar of Kurdish Studies and a prolific author on many aspects of the region. Beth Dougherty specializes in ethnic conflict and human rights. Iraq will continue to be in the forefront for many years to come and this source will be a valuable one for libraries to have available.—**Joe P. Dunn**

Syria

122. Commins, David, and David W. Lesch. **Historical Dictionary of Syria.** 3d ed. Lanham, Md., Scarecrow, 2014. 485p. (Historical Dictionaries of Asia, Oceania, and the Middle East). $125.00; $119.99 (e-book). ISBN 13: 978-0-8108-7820-4; 978-0-8108-7966-9 (e-book).

Syria, one of the most important countries in the Middle East, has undergone tremendous change since the 2d edition (2004) of this valuable reference work, the only volume in English specifically devoted to the country. Particularly significant changes have transpired since 2011 with the Arab uprising when Syrians took to the streets demanding a new regime. Tens of thousands of Syrians have been killed, some 25 percent of the population has fled the country, and much of the government has deteriorated. The new edition contains more than 500 entries on the most important political figures and events, religious groups and movements, economic sectors, social institutions, and cultural facets. Nearly 150 new entries have been added and more than 50 entries have been updated. Greater attention is given to social institutions, cultural aspects, and economic issues.

Besides the alphabetically arranged entries, the volume contains a chronology; extensive bibliography; Websites and Internet resources; and a specific section dedicated to the Syrian uprising. The author is a specialist who first studied in Syria as an undergraduate and has resided there for extensive periods of time. This very fine reference work should be acquired in all large libraries with full coverage of Middle East reference tools.—**Joe P. Dunn**

Yemen

123. **Yemen.** Steven C. Caton, ed. Santa Barbara, Calif., ABC-CLIO, 2013. 317p. illus. maps. index. (Middle East in Focus). $89.00. ISBN 13: 978-1-59884-927-1; 978-1-59884-928-8 (e-book).

The third volume in the ABC-CLIO Middle East in Focus series (the first two on Saudi Arabia and Egypt) maintains the excellence of quality expected from this prestigious publisher and series. Editor, Steven C. Caton, professor of contemporary Arab Studies at Harvard and expert on Yemen, laments in the introduction that the complex reality of the country is often reduced to stereotypes, simple-minded generalizations, and frankly false impressions. Today the country is generally considered by many in the West as peripheral, backward, chaotic, dangerous, and unworkable, indeed a failed state. Caton counters that the country is unique, beautiful, and fascinating, with an impressive past and a future worthy of hope. This comprehensive encyclopedia makes an impressive case for this perspective.

Few observers would challenge that Yemen is unique in the Arab world, the region, and the globe. As just one example, its magnificent multi-story mud houses are a marvel unmatched on the planet. The volume, the product of seven Yemen experts, treats the important geography, long history, turbulent politics and government, challenging economy, complex society, and rich culture. The final chapter addresses the myriad of contemporary issues facing the nation. Although it is a reference work, it is not hard to become captivated by the book and read it from cover to cover. Supplementary attributes include a glossary, facts and figures about the country, major Yemeni holidays, a listing of organizations that deal with the country, an annotated bibliography, and both a thematic and a subject index. Pictures, maps, and boxed highlighted information add to the value of the volume. The volume joins Robert D.

Burrowes' *Historical Dictionary of Yemen* (2d ed.; see ARBA 2011, entry 123) as the sources on this little understood country.

The Middle East in Focus Series is part of a larger ABC-CLIO effort to publish volumes on all the countries of the world by region—Latin America, Africa, Asia, and more. It is a grand task and the products thus far are outstanding.—**Joe P. Dunn**

Polar Regions

124.   Day, David. **Antarctica: A Biography.** New York, Oxford University Press, 2013. 624p. illus. maps. index. $34.95. ISBN 13: 978-0-19-986145-3.

Cleverly titled a "biography," this area study on the history of Antarctica provides readers with a thorough study of this continent. The author, a research associate at La Trobe University, organized the volume chronologically beginning with the early exploration of James Cook in the 1770s, who circled the continent but never actually made it to land (or ice). The work also discusses how various countries have profited off Antarctica's resources, including the history of hunting seals and whales of the region. All of the explorers who made contributions to our knowledge of this region are mentioned here, with their expedition documents serving as the basis of the work. The work closes with a look at the international treaties, scientific research, and tourism at work in Antarctica today. This book provides a comprehensive overview of the history of Antarctica that will appeal mainly to students and scholars, making it appropriate for academic libraries. [R: LJ, 15 June 13, p. 101]—**Marlene M. Kuhl**

4   Economics and Business

General Works

Bibliography

125.   **Factiva. http://factiva.com/.** [Website]. Free. Date reviewed: 2013.

Dow Jones Factiva is a leading provider of global business news and information with full-text content from more than 28,000 sources, from 157 countries in 23 languages. Date ranges vary for individual publications. The "News Page" feature allows users to browse the current day's front page headlines from major U.S. newspapers and magazines, including the *Wall Street Journal,* and is customizable. The "Company/Markets" section allows user to search for company information and current and historical stock quotes.—**Gary W. White**

Biography

126.   **Economic Thinkers: A Biographical Encyclopedia.** David A. Dieterle, ed. Santa Barbara, Calif., Greenwood Press/ABC-CLIO, 2013. 552p. illus. index. $100.00. ISBN 13: 978-0-313-39746-2; 978-0-313-39747-9 (e-book).

This is a compendium of current and historical economists. It begins with Qin Shi Huang (259-210 B.C.E.) and continues through the twenty-first century (2000-present) with Emily Oster. There are three guides. A chronology guide listing the century the economic thinkers lived, a geography guide listing what country and region they lived, and a guide to their economic concepts and their philosophies. The 210 main entries for economists are in an alphabetic arrangement. The entries are biographical and begin with discussion of Qin Shi Huang in the centuries before Christ, and how the Chinese established a money system. It continues on to our current Nobel Prize winners for economics, Alvin Roth and Lloyd Shapley. The authors call this a "family tree" of historical economic thinkers that influenced other economic thinkers throughout time and to carry their concepts and philosophies to the current science of economics.

This book was written to bring a better understanding of the economic world. There is a list of the Nobel Prize laureates beginning with 1969 and going through 2012. There is a glossary of terms, a selected bibliography, and an index.

This reviewer recommends this economic history for school and academic libraries for their business and economic collections. This book fulfills the "missing" history of economics in our library collections.—**Kay Stebbins Slattery**

Catalogs and Collections

127. **Business Source Premier. http://www.ebscohost.com/academic/business-source-premier.** [Website]. Ipswich, Mass., EBSCO. Price negotiated by site. Date reviewed: 2013.

Business Source Premier fills the need for access to general business journals, magazines, and trade journals. Its 3,300 titles cover the fields of marketing, management, MIS, production, operations, accounting, finance, and economics. A little more than 50 percent of the titles are academic, one-quarter are trade titles, and the remainder are business magazines. The database has expanded its content to encompass nearly 100 books, including the Blue Ibex "Doing Business in …" series, case studies mostly from Datamonitor, country reports from sources including Business Monitor International, ICON Group International, Country Watch, Economist Intelligence Unit, and the Superintendent of Documents, domestic and international industry reports from Datamonitor, and company profiles containing SWOT analyses. Market research reports are dated and very limited. *Business Source Premier* carries some unique titles, particularly *Harvard Business Review*.—**Chris LeBeau**

128. **BusinessTown.com. http://www.businesstown.com.** [Website]. Free. Date reviewed: 2013.

This extensive business information site has sections on Managing a Business, Home Businesses, Internet businesses, Accounting, Selling a Business, and more. The articles are not lengthy but quite thoroughly cover their subject. Under Home Business, you will find ideas for home businesses, how to set one up, and articles on getting started right. Under Accounting, you will learn basic concepts, how to budget, how to plan and project, and more. Also has links to a variety of Financial Calculators at www. dinkytown.net. This is a useful site, noncommercial, that can be used to help you in any area where you need more information on starting or running a business.—**Susan C. Awe**

129. **EconPapers. http://econpapers.repec.org/.** [Website]. By Sune Karlsson. Free. Date reviewed: 2013.

This site is self-described as the world's largest collection of online economics working papers, journal articles, and software, with most full-text files available for free. Typically journal articles require that users or their organization subscribe to the service providing the full-text. RePEc, where the bibliographic and author data originate, is a distributed data set residing in over 1,100 archives operated by research organizations, academic departments, and publishers. EconPapers would not be possible without the effort of the maintainers of these archives. Citation data and reference lists are provided by the CitEc, Citations in Economics, project.—**Noriko Asato**

130. **Edward Lowe's Entrepreneurs Resource Center. http://www.edwardlowe.org/ERC/.** [Website]. Free. Date reviewed: 2013.

This well-known small business site contains a large section on Defining and Serving a Market. One of the articles here is "Gathering Market Research" and it walks users through identifying data sources, gathering customer and competitor information, and gathering information on suppliers. Real-life examples of successful marketing are also provided. Additional resources are often provided at the end of the articles. Find also information on branding, direct mail marketing, social media, and in general, providing a promotional mix for your new business. An outstanding article under the topic of Defining and Serving a Market, is on How to Conduct and Prepare a Competitive Analysis. It is an excellent place for new entrepreneurs to begin learning about how to monitor the competition. This site can be used frequently for those looking for help running or marketing a business.—**Susan C. Awe**

131. **Entrepreneurs' Resource Center. http://www.edwardlowe.org/ERC.** [Website]. Free. Date reviewed: 2013.

This nonprofit organization promotes entrepreneurship by providing information, research, and education. The Acquiring and Managing Finances section will help new entrepreneurs learn more about all aspects related to their business's financial situation. The section of this useful site entitled Building and Inspiring an Organization, will lead users to articles on crisis management, communication skills, management development, organizational structure, and more. Use this site also to find practical articles on marketing, finances, human resources management, and legal issues and taxes. Networking possibilities include conferences and educational seminars listed here.—**Susan C. Awe**

132.   **Gale Business Insights: Global. http://www.gale.cengage.com/businessinsights/academic. htm.** [Website]. Stamford, Conn., Gale/Cengage Learning. Price negotiated by site. Date reviewed: 2013.

   Gale Business Insights: Global is a new online international business reference database that discusses such topics as global companies, rankings and statistics, company histories, market share data, and industry research reports. It is full of full-text articles from academic journals, business periodicals, newswires, and media outlets and provides hundreds of economic indicators that allow users to analyze various economies, companies, and industries across the globe. Case studies have been included from the publisher's *CaseBase* (see ARBA 2012, entry 232) as well as from other publishing partners. In all, text and resources from nearly 2,500 resources have been pulled into this searchable database. There is video provided on management and leadership tips, as well as live charts for economic and business indicators that will allow researchers to generate their own analyses and custom charts for reports and presentations. It will be most useful for students and researchers needing information on international business and trade. It will aid in business research and help them interpret their findings. It would be a useful research tool in academic libraries but libraries are encouraged to register for the publisher's free trial to see if the material and the functions of the database are right for your clientele and reference needs.—**Shannon Graff Hysell**

133.   **Market Research, Industry Research, Business Research. http://www.virtualpet.com/ industry.** [Website]. Free. Date reviewed: 2013.

   This major portal for researching companies and industries presents a step-by-step process to begin researching an industry. Here you can find sources to help you learn about legal issues, regulatory issues, competition, markets, and even history of the industry for your new business. Additional links to industry portals are also available. Three other linked sites offer help on "How to Learn about a Company by Examining its Products," "How to Review, Evaluate, Critique a Web Site," and "How to Conduct a Patent Search."—**Susan C. Awe**

134.   **ProQuest Entrepreneurship. http://www.proquest.com.** [Website]. Bethesda, Md., ProQuest. Price negotiated by site. Date reviewed: 2013.

   The audience for *ProQuest Entrepreneurship* spans the needs of the practitioner to the educator and student. This well-designed database features menus with major business concepts the average entrepreneur or small-business owner would seek. The topical approach lists sources for start-ups, management, legal issues, marketing and sales, operations, product development, and profit and financial management. Topic links connect searchers to 115 journals, 50 trade publications, working papers, conference papers—in all, a little over 400 sources are included.

   The practitioner or business planner has access to forms, tips from successful business owners, and start-up toolkits and guides. The basic search screen walks searchers through topics such as product development and design, innovations, business planning issues, marketing, advertising, pricing, sales, cash flow, purchasing, and technology use. Expectedly, there is a topic heading for start-ups. Start-up information covers idea creation, feasibility, and industry and competitor analysis. It also includes forms of ownership and franchising. Users can find business models, as well as location and planning resources. A special section is devoted to family-owned business, women-owned and minority-owned business, Web-based business, and native and aboriginal business.

   But there is even more content. The database also includes approximately 60 books and journals. Also included are very short video clips on topics such as business valuation, exit strategies, and promotion. These come complete with a text copy of the video.—**Chris LeBeau**

Dictionaries and Encyclopedias

135.   **The AMA Dictionary of Business and Management.** By George Thomas Kurian. New York, AMACOM/American Management Association, 2013. 292p. $24.95. ISBN 13: 978-0-8144-2028-7.

The AMA Dictionary of Business and Management provides concise and authoritative definitions for more than 6,000 currently used business and management terms and phrases. Definitions are clearly presented without resorting to excessive use of technical jargon. Where appropriate, terms are given fuller, more detailed treatment. Also included are brief biographies of those who have made notable contributions to, or have had significant influence on, the fields of business, management, or related fields such as economics. Cross-references are provided that are particularly useful in relating contributors to contributions. The dictionary not only serves as a comprehensive reference for deriving meanings, but also as a top-line overview of the modern business world. The book should be useful to students, instructors, and business practitioners as well as those in other fields who require understanding of business terminology.—**William C. Struning**

136.   **Encyclopedia of Global Brands.** 2d ed. Farmington Hills, Mich., St. James Press/Gale Group, 2013. 2v. index. $768.00/set. ISBN 13: 978-1-55862-227-2; 978-1-55862-854-0 (e-book).

The *Encyclopedia of Global Brands* now in its 2d edition is, according to its editors: "intended as a reference for students, businesspeople, librarians, historians, economists, investors, job seekers, researchers and others who want to learn more about the world's most influential brands. " The brands covered are 269 of the most popular brands worldwide and include such notables as Amazon.com, Apple, Facebook, the Gap, AT&T, Barclays, Colgate, Nescafe, Taco Bell, Twitter, IBM, and Toyota. Brands were selected for inclusion by editors and advisory board members based on the following criteria: public awareness, dominance in sales and market share within the product's category, high financial valuation, and its potential for future success and global awareness. Research of each brand was based on study of marketing textbooks, discussions with business school professors, brand management services, and articles in business and trade journals. Each entry includes: an At a Glance section which features brand synopsis, parent company, sector, industry group, performance (market share), and principal competitors; Brand origins, which provides a history and background; Brand Elements (including description of logo) ; Brand Identity; Brand Strategy; Brand Equity; Brand Outlook (future projections), and a list of resources for further reading. Included are a Brand Sector Index (listing brands under their specific category), Person/Company Index, and Geographic Index.

The *Encyclopedia of Global Brands* is a source that should be purchased by academic libraries supporting business schools and larger public libraries. It provides an excellent starting point for researchers of companies and their products/brands and some background history and key information is included. It can be used in conjunction with the company's annual reports and business directories online including Hoover's, Mergent, Dun & Bradstreet, and Standard & Poor's.—**Lucy Heckman**

Directories

137.   **AllBusiness. http://www.allbusiness.com/.** [Website]. Short Hills, N.J., Dun and Bradstreet. Free (some content for sale). Date reviewed: 2013.

AllBusiness covers the finer aspects of starting and operating a new business, and it does so in a very consolidated way. The Dun & Bradstreet site offers tools for the new business owner, short multimedia clips covering tips, and more than 5 million journal articles written by in-house staff and by the Gale Cengage Learning staff. While the main body of content is free, there is much for sale on the site offered through memberships. One must wind a path through the advertising of related products such as forms.

An entire section is devoted to franchises. The franchise directory lists several hundred franchise opportunities. Franchise entries give brief information, including required investment amounts, business descriptions, an all-star ranking, and the number of employees needed to operate a franchise. Entries also include a three-year growth rate based on the numbers of units, the franchise and royalty fee, the net worth and capital requirements, and franchise-sponsored financing. *AllBusiness* runs an all-star ranking of 300 listed franchises. All of this is accompanied by feature articles with tips for buying, growing, and franchising a business. The franchise directory is a particularly good addition to this well-organized site, packed with valuable content for the new business owner.—**Chris LeBeau**

138.   **Corporate Yellow Book: Who's Who at the Leading U.S. Companies. Winter 2013 ed.** New York, Leadership Directories, 2013. 1290p. index. $595.00pa. (annual subscription); $566.00pa. (automatic renewal). ISSN 1058-2908.

The *Corporate Yellow Book* provides contact and brief biographical information for executives and board members of high-growth corporations with revenues over $500 million in manufacturing, services, and utilities industries. This translates to information for nearly 1,000 companies and over 5,000 subsidiaries and divisions. Published quarterly, the directory is arranged alphabetically by official company name. For most companies the following information is provided: the physical and mailing addresses with telephone, fax, and company Website; the line of business; stock exchange and ticker symbol; number of employees; annual revenue; shareholder meeting date; state and date of incorporation; independent auditor; and general counsel. For the chief officer, a photograph, title, and brief biographical information is provided (e.g., education, date of birth, career). The Officers and Management section lists company officers in a hierarchical arrangement with full name, title, functional area, direct telephone and e-mail, education, and executive assistant. The Administrative Services section provides the names and contact information for managers of key departments and services within the company, including benefits, corporate communications, corporate contributions, purchasing, recruitment, shareholder relations, training and development, and more. The Major Subsidiaries and Divisions and the Board of Directors sections provides the names, brief education information, and career highlights for each individual listed. There are separate indexes by organization, industry, geography, and personal name.

Information included in the directory has been verified at printing. Changes that have occurred since the previous update are listed in a quarterly report at the front of the directory. The online version of the *Corporate Yellow Book* along with the other Yellow Books published by Leadership Directories, Inc. are available by subscription and updated daily. Highlights of daily changes may be viewed at the publisher's Website (http://www.leadershipdirectories.com/). The *Corporate Yellow Book* is an authoritative who's who of corporate leaders. Although some of the book's information is freely available on the Web, the detailed corporate hierarchy, contact, and biographical information it provides is not easily found on the Internet, making it a desirable purchase for large business collections or corporate libraries.—**Colleen Seale**

139.   **The Directory of Business Information Resources, 2013.** 20th ed. Millerton, N.Y., Grey House Publishing, 2013. 1883p. index. $195.00pa.; $475.00 (online database; single user); $575.00 (print and online editions). ISBN 13: 978-1-61925-009-3.

The 20th edition of *The Directory of Business Information Resources*, provides a convenient and efficient vehicle for locating sources of information on U.S. businesses. The directory contains more than 23,000 entries, each with access data, key personnel, brief description of activities, as well as other pertinent information. Entries are presented in 99 chapters, each covering an industrial category. Resources for each industry are grouped into associations, newsletters, magazines and journals, trade shows, directories and database, and industry Websites. To enable readers to locate specific entries, the directory contains a table of contents (basically a list of industries or chapters), a summary or list of topics included in each industry, a table that cross-references standard industrial codes to chapters, an alphabetic index of all entries, an index of publishers mentioned in the directory, an introduction, and a brief user guide. A special feature of this edition is the an article on the "Economic Environment of 2012." The directory is also available as an online database for those requiring quick access or who wish to search with respect to specific criteria. The directory offers a vast quantity of accessible information in a single volume.—**William C. Struning**

140.   **ORBIS.   http://www.bvdinfo.com/Products/Company-Information/International/ORBIS. aspx.** [Website]. Amsterdam, Netherlands, Bureau Van Dijk. Price negotiated by site. Date reviewed: 2013.

ORBIS has information on more than 80 million companies, both publicly quoted and privately held, in about 203 countries around the world. For the more than 65,000 publically quoted companies, the nearly 30,000 banks, and more than 11,000 insurance companies, information includes: typical directory facts, detailed or summary financial and ownership information, listings of subsidiaries, names and titles for executives and directors, and more. For the privately held companies, summary information includes much of the information that is included for the public companies except for the financial information.—**Rita W. Moss**

141.   **Osiris.   http://www.bvdinfo.com/Products/Compnay-Information/International/OSIRIS. aspx.** [Website]. Amsterdam, Netherlands, Bureau Van Dijk. Price negotiated by site. Date reviewed: 2013.

Osiris contains information on more than 65,000 listed (publically traded) companies, banks, and insurance companies from about 200 countries around the world. In addition to up to 20 yeas of income statements, balance sheets, cash flow statements, and ratios, Osiris provides ownership, subsidiaries, stock, and bond ratings from Fitch Moody's and Standard & Poor's, country risk ratings from the EIU earnings estimates, and stock data. In addition to the existing ratios you can create your own that you can display in the reports and also use in your searches and analysis. Osiris contains specific report formats for industrial companies, banks, and insurance companies and also has reports that reflect accounting procedures in the major world regions. Both standardized and "as reported" financials are provided.—**Rita W. Moss**

Handbooks and Yearbooks

142.   **Business Statistics of the United States, 2013: Patterns of Economic Change.** 18th ed. Cornelia J. Strawser, ed. Lanham, Md., Bernan Press, 2014. 568p. index. $165.00; $164.99 (e-book). ISBN 13: 089-1-59888-635-1; 978-1-59888-636-8 (e-book).

Bernan Press's *Business Statistics of the United States: Patterns of Economic Change* is a comprehensive source for important economic and financial data produced by United States government agencies. The 18th edition contains income and product accounts from the Bureau of Economic Analysis (BEA), price and labor data from the Bureau of Labor Statistics (BLS), and financial market data from the Federal Reserve. The statistics generally cover annual time periods from the end of World War II through 2012. Although nearly all data in *Business Statistics of the United States* can be downloaded from individual government agency Websites, the single-volume format serves as a useful compilation.

Bernan Press began publishing this title in 1995 after budgetary constraints led the Bureau of Economic Analysis to cease publication of a biennial reference source with the same name and similar content. Current editor Cornelia J. Strawser has skillfully incorporated explanatory articles that enhance the data sets. This edition incorporates fully revised data for more than 700 series from the National Income and Product Accounts (NIPAs) that were revised in 2013. Also included is the comprehensive August 2013 revision of the productivity and cost series that are based on the revised NIPAs. Clearly labeled tables display statistics in an easy-to-use format. Librarians and researchers will find *Business Statistics of the United States* a valuable resource.—**ARBA Staff Reviewer**

143. **Entrepreneurship.** New York, Facts on File, 2013. 5v. illus. index. (Student Handbook to Economics). $250.00/set. ISBN 13: 978-1-60413-997-6.

144. **History of Economic Thought.** New York, Facts on File, 2013. 5v. illus. index. (Student Handbook to Economics). $250.00/set. ISBN 13: 978-1-60413-996-9; 978-1-4381-4160-2 (e-book).

145. **International Economics.** New York, Facts on File, 2013. 5v. illus. index. (Student Handbook to Economics). $250.00/set. ISBN 13: 978-1-60413-995-2.

146. **Macroeconomics.** New York, Facts on File, 2013. 166p. illus. index. (Student Handbook to Economics). $250.00/set. ISBN 13: 978-1-60413-993-8; 978-1-4381-4163-3 (e-book).

147. **Microeconomics.** New York, Facts on File, 2013. 5v. illus. index. (Student Handbook to Economics). $250.00/set. ISBN 13: 978-1-60413-994-5; 978-1-4381-4162-6 (e-book).

The Student Handbook to Economics Series from Facts on File is a five-volume set that discusses the basic principles surrounding the study of economics, including the prominent influences over the economy as well as the philosophy behind it. The titles cover such topics as microeconomics, macroeconomics, international economics, entrepreneurship, and the history of economic thought. The set can serve as a supplement to the information that middle and high school students are taught in their civics, economics, and history courses. Users will explore such topics as production and distribution, supply and demand, corporations, globalism, and more. The volumes are supplemented by about 40 full-color photographs and illustrations, sidebars, as well as a glossary, bibliography, and an index. The books are written in an easy-to-understand manner that will be most useful to a high school and possibly undergraduate audience.—**Shannon Graff Hysell**

148. **Gale Business Insights Handbook of Global Business Law. Volume 1.** Stamford, Conn., Gale/Cengage Learning, 2013. 431p. index. (Gale Business Insights). $175.00. ISBN 13: 978-1-4144-9933-8 (e-book).

149. **Gale Business Insights Handbook of Investment Research. Volume 2.** Miranda Herbert Ferrara, ed. Stamford, Conn., Gale/Cengage Learning, 2013. 345p. index. (Gale Business Insights). $175.00pa. ISBN 13: 978-1-4144-9927-7; 978-1-4144-9934-5 (e-book).

150. **Gale Business Insights Handbook of Global Marketing. Volume 3.** Miranda Herbert Ferrara, ed. Stamford, Conn., Gale/Cengage Learning, 2013. 352p. index. (Gale Business Insights). $175.00pa. ISBN 13: 978-1-4144-9928-4; 978-1-4144-9935-2 (e-book).

151. **Gale Business Insights Handbook of Cultural Transformation. Volume 4.** Miranda Herbert Ferrara, ed. Stamford, Conn., Gale/Cengage Learning, 2013. 339p. index. (Gale Business Insights). $175.00pa. ISBN 13: 978-1-4144-9929-1; 978-1-4144-9936-9 (e-book).

152. **Gale Business Insights Handbook of Innovation Management. Volume 5.** Miranda Herbert Ferrara, ed. Stamford, Conn., Gale/Cengage Learning, 2013. 335p. index. $175.00pa. ISBN 13: 978-1-4144-9930-7; 978-1-4144-9937-6 (e-book).

153.   **Gale Business Insights Handbook of Social Media Marketing. Volume 6.** Miranda Herbert Ferrara, ed. Stamford, Conn., Gale/Cengage Learning, 2013. 431p. index. (Gale Business Insights). $175.00pa. ISBN 13: 978-1-4144-9931-4; 978-1-4144-9938-3 (e-book).

The Gale Business Insights Handbooks series are designed with undergraduate and graduate business students in mind. They are meant to serve as an overview of specialized current topics within the business world and provide both a theoretical overview of that topic as well as ideas for practical application. While designed with students in mind they would also be useful for the professional working in the field who needs a refresher on a specific topic or is looking to broaden their scope of knowledge. Currently there are six volumes in the series covering hot topics in the business world. The main topic for each of which was selected based off of topics that are trending in business textbooks, journals, and trade publications, as well as discussions with business school professors and professionals in the field. From this selection process the publisher launched the series with the following topics: cultural transformation, innovation management, social media marketing, investment research, global marketing, and global business law. The entries were compiled from government sources, professional associations, and publically accessible print and online materials as well as some original research. Entries include additional resources accentuated with an icon throughout the text, which include lists of resources for further information, helpful hints, tools, and key terms. An example of the type of information found in this series can be noted in the *Gale Business Insights Handbook of Social Media Marketing* title, which provides chapters on the benefits of social media, creating a social media marketing strategy, choosing the right media of your campaign, and taking advantage of interactivity, among others. Large academic libraries will find these titles useful as will large public libraries that provide service to local business professionals.—**Shannon Graff Hysell**

154.   **Handbook of Innovation Indicators and Measurement.** Fred Gault, ed. Northhampton, Mass., Edward Elgar, 2013. 486p. index. $240.00. ISBN 13: 978-0-85793-364-5.

This handbook focuses on measuring the activity of innovation and "its links to the innovation system" and "is written at a time when the domain of innovation studies in expanding ." As noted in the handbook, the definition of innovation "for the purposes of statistical measurement was codified 20 years ago in the Oslo Manual." The *Handbook* is comprised of a series of scholarly articles and chapters by experts in the field who make measurements and produce indicators or those who are users of the indicators or between production and use. The authors of these essays are internationally based and are from organizations and universities including: National Research University "Higher School of Economics" (Russia); University of Tasmania; National Institute of Statistics (Italy); Massachusetts Institute of Technology; Centre for European Economic Research; the Rockefeller Foundation; and Centre for European Economic Research. The chapters are arranged within seven parts: Why Indicators Matter; Defining Innovation and Implementing the Definitions; Measurement; Developing and Using Indicators; Innovation Strategy; Beyond the Horizon; and Challenges. Specific chapters focus on the Oslo Manual; innovation surveys experience from Japan; OECD measurement agenda for innovation; the United States innovation strategy and policy; indicators for social innovation; and the OECD innovation strategy. Notes and bibliographic references are included with each chapter and some chapters contain statistical tables and charts. A list of abbreviations and an index are also included.

This handbook fills a need in the study of innovation indicators and measurement and is recommended to larger university libraries supporting a program in graduate and doctoral studies in business and economics. For advanced courses in business and economics, faculty and students can learn about results of research studies from scholars in the field.—**Lucy Heckman**

155.   **Handbook of Longitudinal Research Methods in Organisation and Business Studies.** Melanie E. Hassett and Eriikka Paavilainen-Mantymaki, eds. Northhampton, Mass., Edward Elgar, 2013. 362p. index. $225.00. ISBN 13: 978-0-85793-678-3.

This book is encyclopedic in nature. In its 15 chapters the contributors covered many topics, from simple presentation to deep research and analysis. The book would a good Economics 101 text for graduate students who may become professional researchers and methodologists in economics, business, or any social science. A few contributors tried to walk the readers into research methods from the beginning through to its conclusion. The book is divided into four parts. Part 1 covers longitudinal. Part 2 covers quantitative longitudinal research. Part 3 covers research as a process on the assumption that the process approach would help to find the black box, and find solutions to the problems being studied, and answers to the questions being raised. Part 4 covers conducting research by the experts walking the readers their own projects, with emphasis on understanding the objectives and the plan, step by step. Each chapter has its own references. The total references come to about 37 pages, with 25 entries on each page. The editors devote most of the introductory chapter to a summary of each chapter. Chapter 1 summarizes the longitudinal research approach into seven points from the general definition to the conclusion. Thus the reader is offered a choice to decide which chapters are most relevant and useful. Chapter 15 represents an exercise, led by an expert who has devoted much attention and energy to helping those who wish to learn about longitudinal research methods in social science.—**Elias H. Tuma**

156.   **Handbook of Research Methods and Applications in Empirical Macroeconomics.** Nigar Hashimzade and Michael A. Thornton, eds. Northhampton, Mass., Edward Elgar, 2013. 614. index. 261.00. ISBN 13: 9780857931016.

The *Handbook of Research Methods and Applications in Empirical Macroeconomics* is in Edward Elgar's series Handbooks of Research Methods and Applications. The series emphasizes practical application of research methods. The series focuses on identifying and using suitable sources for data, best practices, and interpretation of data.

The *Handbook* provides an overview of research methods in this field for graduate students and researchers. Since it covers recent advances in research methods in addition to established methods, it could be a text for researchers interested in new methods. It is a reference manual of formulas, graphs, charts, and use of real data.

The introduction and a substantive review chapter provide the theoretical concepts, models, and estimation methods. The remainder of the text is arranged in six parts: properties of macroeconomic data; models for macroeconomic data analysis; estimation and evaluation frameworks in macroeconomics; Applications I: dynamic stochastic general equilibrium models; Applications II: vector autoregressive models; and Applications III: calibration and simulations. Each part has several chapters, ranging from two to eight.

Undergraduate libraries supporting majors in economics, with a concentration on econometrics, may choose to consider it as a reference work covering the various methods. It does not provide the definitions and words of explanation for the various formulas that undergraduates need; but it could be used for the formulas and other techniques upper classmen need to address in their own first research project.

This work is highly recommended for graduate school and special libraries.—**Ladyjane Hickey**

157.   **Handbook of Research Methods and Applications in Urban Economies.** Peter Karl Kresl and Jaime Sobrino, eds. Northhampton, Mass., Edward Elgar, 2013. 525p. index. $240.00. ISBN 13: 978-0-85793-461-1.

This is more like an encyclopedia article on urban economies than a research contribution. This is so in terms of the number of contributors, location, and longevity. Each topic has a chapter of its own. For some reason Mexico and China are discussed each in separate chapters. Mexico illustrates the Main obstacles one meets in the process. Governability occupies a fairly large space. This seemed obvious in Mexico with regard to hospitals and school buildings, especially when the federal authority intervened to lobby for its preferred design. Analysis of well-being in China was rapidly distributed among Chinese towns, but inequality was ignored, in contrast to the communist ideology, which calls for equality. Numerical data were not easily accessible and therefore cardinal results and conclusions were not possible. When the data were improved rational methods could be used. Luckily multiple regression was used and answers the question of efficiency and productivity of ethnic migrants. A study in the Netherlands found that ethnicity has little to do with efficiency and productivity of the worker. Migrants with skill and initiative would be better for economic development. Planning was found to be important, but there was little discovered about the wants and needs of the local residents. The question of competitiveness by cities was discussed in detail. There was little support for planning; in fact, there was little attempt to discover what the people wanted. Comparative analysis was practiced in a number of situations, comparing cities in different countries with regard to achieving an objective. Globalization was applied in Europe and its impact on the city of Chicago was assessed. The effect was favorable to diversity and immigration; education and technical knowledge were more important than the ethnicity of the migrant. A large number of pages are devoted to the bibliography. Attempts could have been made to remove duplicates and combine in one set of references at the end of the book. The contributors are from different countries, but they reflect interest in diversity. Some contributors are graduate students, while others are established scholars who fill university endowed chairs. Cities grow in population and in territory. They become metro poles or megacities, in which case their municipalities take over the governance of the establishment. Unfortunately, municipalities are not just urban, or belong in cities over a certain size. For example, I come from a village that has never exceeded 8,000 people in its population. Yet my village has always had a municipal council and they always competed with other villages for benefits for benefits from the national government.—**Elias H. Tuma**

158. **Handbook of Research on Family Business.** 2d ed. Kosmas X. Smyrnios, Panikkos Zata Poutziouris, and Sanjay Goel, eds. Northhampton, Mass., Edward Elgar, 2013. 779p. index. $310.00. ISBN 13: 978-1-84844-322-8.

This 2d edition has 29 new essays and 2 reprints from leading journals on research conducted and/or published in the field since the 1st edition. Any academic discipline provides a conceptual framework for research and study. This 2d edition advances the conceptual theoretical framework, develops critical thinking, and provides empirical studies that exemplify systematic measurement. It identifies advances in the multidisciplinary field of family business.

The *Handbook* is written from an academic perspective with contributors from every continent. The 72 contributors are mostly European with 25 contributors from the United States, Canada, Australia, Japan, Korea, China, Israel, and Brazil combined. Most have an academic background in business administration or one of its specialized subdisciplines, with economics and social sciences also represented. It is written in scholarly language suitable for graduate students, educators, researchers, and consultants.

Surveys or reviews of the literature, hypothesis, methodology, research design, measures, results, discussions, and conclusions are interspersed with well-designed tables, charts, and graphs. They are easy to read and interpret, and they present the research findings in comprehensible forms.

This work is highly recommended for business libraries and academic libraries supporting graduate studies in business administration, economics, or social sciences.—**Ladyjane Hickey**

159. **Handbook of Research on Gender and Economic Life.** Deborah M. Figart and Tonia L. Warnecke, eds. Northhampton, Mass., Edward Elgar, 2013. 571p. index. $270.00. ISBN 13: 978-0-85793-094-1.

The *Handbook of Research on Gender and Economic Life* is comprised of a series of scholarly articles by leading feminist economists and scholars "from related disciplines covering both theory and policy." According to the foreword by Diane Elson of the University of Essex the *Handbook* "goes far beyond mere disaggregation of economic agents by sex to challenge the mainstream definition of economics as the optimum allocation of scarce resources, and to focus instead on economics as a process of provisioning for well-being, shaped by social norms, including gender norms." Contributors are from universities and centers throughout the world including: Bucknell University, the University of Michigan-Dearborn, the University of British Columbia, the World Bank, Rutgers University, the

University of Utrecht, and the University of Muenster (Germany). This resource is divided into seven parts that include analytical tools to "give readers an understanding of possible entry points for gender based analysis" and features essays that include "a social provisioning approach to gender and economic life." Part 2, "Institutional Contexts for Provisioning," examines gendered impacts of formal and informal institutions and essays include "Infrastructure and Gender Equality" and "Gender Provisioning under Different Capitalisms." Part 3, "Formal and Informal Work," contains essays that discuss employment inequalities and firings and discrimination in hiring and promotion based on sex, race and ethnicity, and sexual orientation. Essays include "Gender Inequality in the Workplace," "Occupational Segregation and the Gender Wage Gap in the United States," and "Discrimination in Gay and Lesbian Lives." Part 4, "Employment Policies," focuses on "methods (successful or not) to address these gendered employment outcomes" and includes the essays on low-wage mothers on the edge in the United States and work-family reconciliation policies in Europe. Part 5, " Macroeconomic Policies, Finance, and Credit," links gender to the macroeconomy, bank policies, and credit. Essays include "Central Bank Policy and Gender," "Credit and Self Employment," and "Gender, Debt and the Housing/Financial Crisis." Part 6, "Human-Development Education and Health," examines key issues of human development including education (girls' schooling) and includes essays on "Measuring Gender Disparities in Human Development," "The Health of the Worlds' Women," "Gender and Food Security," and "Intersecting Sources of Education Inequality." Part 7, "Contemporary Global Issues," examines issues of migration, peace, war, violence, and trafficking and includes essays on "Family Migration in the United States" and "Environmental Activism and Gender." Each essay contains notes and a bibliography of references with some containing tables and figures. This resource also includes an index and a list of contributors.

The *Handbook of Research on Gender and Economic Life* is an informative source offering various perspectives on the topic. It is recommended to students and faculty in undergraduate, graduate, and post-graduate business and social studies programs. This work is recommended to libraries supporting advanced programs.—**Lucy Heckman**

160. **Handbook on the Economics of Cultural Heritage.** Ilde Rizzo and Anna Mignosa, eds. Northhampton, Mass., Edward Elgar, 2013. 640. index. 256.50. ISBN 13: 9780857930996.

The aim of this handbook is to stimulate a dialogue about the concept of cultural heritage and the challenges it faces using cultural economics as the framework. That many different disciplines and all parts of the world are part of cultural heritage is seen in the list of contributors. While interest in cultural heritage is not new, academic interest, as reflected in published articles, is approximately 35 years old with a considerable amount of work being done this century. The handbook is divided into nine parts: public intervention and policy analysis; private actors; the international dimension; management: strategies and tools; technology: issues and opportunities; conservation of build heritage; cultural heritage and the economy; values and evaluation; and case studies. Economic theory and its application are evident in many of the papers. Changes and challenges brought by digitization and the Internet are explored. The multiplicity of interests and the complexity of the issues are clearly demonstrated with little repetition in the volume. Each entry has end notes and references. The book has an index. It is a comprehensive source on a large and expanding area of study.—**J. E. Weaver**

161. **Handbook on the Economics of Women in Sports.** Eva Marikova Leeds and Michael A. Leeds, eds. Northhampton, Mass., Edward Elgar, 2013. 443p. index. $225.00. ISBN 13: 978-1-84980-938-2.

This reference brings together academic research studies on the economics of women participating in intercollegiate sports, professional sports, the Olympics, and other international competitions. Although the bulk of the studies look at women as participants, there is also some attention to women as consumers of sports (for example, attendance at sporting events). As a small taste of the breadth of the topics studied, the reader can explore how men and women react differently to tournament settings, why Korean women are a sizeable component of the LGPA, and several studies on the impact of Title IX. For example, since the implementation of Title IX, the number of women's intercollegiate teams has gone from an average of 2.5 per educational institution to an average of 8.64 (over 9,000 teams in total). But, while the number of women college athletes has increased, the number of women coaches has decreased. In 2010, just over 40 percent of women's teams were coached by females as compared to 90 percent before Title IX. The question is: Why? There is a study in this handbook that explores this puzzle. Insights are provided not only into the economics of women's athletics, but this work also helps us explore the questions: Do women behave differently than men in the arena of sports, and does how society view women affect athletic performance? This volume provides a focused resource for students in the fields of sports management and women's studies.—**Adrienne Antink**

162. **World Economic Situation and Prospects 2013.** New York, United Nations, 2013. 200p. $30.00pa. ISBN 13: 978-92-11091-66-3.

This volume provides the cumulative report of the United Nations on the state of the world's economy. This 2013 edition focuses on the continuing Euro debt crisis, the prolonged job crisis that many countries are still experiencing, and the need to find ways to resolve the possibility of the world experiencing a continued recession. The volume provides in-depth reports and up-to-date statistical information. It is jointly produced by the Department of Economic and Social Affairs, the United Nations Conference on Trade and Development, and the five United Nations Regional Commissions. It is highly recommended to academic and research library collections.—**Lucy Heckman**

Indexes

163. **ABI/INFORM Global.** http://www.proquest.com/en-US/catalogs/databases/detail/abi_inform.shtml. [Website]. Ann Arbor, Mich., ProQuest. Price negotiated by site. Date reviewed: 2013.

ABI/Inform is perhaps the largest and best-known business indexing service. It has been published in various electronic formats for approximately 25 years. Currently *ABI/Inform* is available through Bell & Howell's *ProQuest Direct* and various other database aggregators in several varieties, including *ABI/Inform Global*, *ABI/Inform Research*, and *ABI/Inform Select*. The *Global* version currently indexes over 1,500 scholarly and trade titles, the *Research* version has over 1,250 scholarly and trade titles, and the *Select* version has 375 scholarly titles. *ABI/Inform* contains full-text versions of many of the articles included in the database, and *ProQuest Direct* offers some in .pdf format. Dates of full-text availability vary by title. This is the definitive electronic resource for business periodical literature.—**Gary W. White**

164. **Annual Reports at Academic Business Libraries.** http://www.lib.purdue.edu/abldars/. [Website]. Free. Date reviewed: 2013.

This index is the result of a collaboration of 12 academic business libraries who merged the lists of their respective collections of annual reports to shareholders into one database of approximately 38,000 companies—Columbia University, Cornell University, Harvard University, Massachusetts Institute of Technology, Purdue University, Stanford University, University of Alabama, University of California-Berkeley, University of Pennsylvania, University of Western Ontario, Yale University, and the Science/Industry/Business Library of New York Public Library. The index identifies library owns which reports and what years are covered. There is also information on the lending policies of each institution.—**ARBA Staff Reviewer**

Business Services and Investment Guides

Catalogs and Collections

165.   **Investing in Bonds.com. http://investinginbonds.com/.** [Website]. Free. Date reviewed: 2013.

Geared toward many types of investors—from beginners to experienced equity investors who are new to bonds to sophisticated bond investors—Investinginbonds.com is a unique source of bond price information and includes a wide variety of market data, news, commentary, and information about bonds. The site, which as been ranked as a top investor site for bonds by *Money*, CNBC, *Forbes*, and others, was most recently named one of *Kiplinger's Personal Finance* magazine's two 2009 Best Investing Sites for its information for newcomers and data for experts. The site is continually enhanced and updated with new data, information, and features.—**Rita W. Moss**

166.   **Investor's Clearinghouse. http://www.investoreducation.org.** [Website]. Free. Date reviewed: 2013.

Advised by such reputable groups as the Federal Trade Commission, The Board of Governors of the Federal Reserve System, the Securities and Exchange Commission's Office of Investor Education and Assistance, and other reputable investment-related organizations, the Investor's Clearinghouse offers information and reports on consumer finance issues such as senior investment fraud, retirement savings, home equities, and compulsive buying. It is produced by the alliance for Investor Education with the goal of providing an educational platform where people can learn about investing and get solid advice. It is a good place to find out about current topics of interest as well as get basic information on what to be aware of when entering into an investment.—**ARBA Staff Reviewer**

167.   **Morningstar Investment Research Center. http://library.morningstar.com/.** [Website]. Price negotiated by site. Date reviewed: 2013.

The Morningstar Investment Research Center is a subscription database aimed to appeal to institutions, individual investors, business students, faculty, and anyone trying to stay on track toward a financial goal. Many people associate Morningstar with its reports on mutual funds, but the Investment Research Center also covers stocks, bonds, exchange-traded funds, and market indexes. It sorts financial information by stock sectors, indexes investment style, fund category, and industry. The service analyzes portfolios, examines management effectiveness, established fair market value for stocks, describes "economic moats" enjoyed by companies, reports corporate credit rankings, and importantly assigns stars to stocks and mutual funds. The user can search for a stock or mutual fund by entering a name or ticker symbol. The database also has screens to help narrow a search within a certain area of interest, or a user can create his own screens based on data or selected characteristics. Funds also have the Morningstar rankings and analyst reports.—**Rita W. Moss**

Directories

168.   **The Directory of Venture Capital & Private Equity Firms, 2013.** 17th ed. Millerton, N.Y., Grey House Publishing, 2013. 1426p. index. $395.00pa.; $900.00 (online database); $1,100.00 (print and online editions). ISBN 13: 978-1-61925-112-0.

Published since 1996, the 2013 edition of *The Directory of Venture Capital & Private Equity Firms* includes over 3,000 American, Canadian, and international firms, which are presented in A-Z lists. Each listing is assigned an entry number and includes company name, complete contact information (including mailing, e-mail, and Website addresses, and telephone and fax numbers), a company mission statement, geographic preference, fund size, date founded, average and minimum investments, investment criteria (e.g., stages at which the firm is willing to invest, such as seed, startup, first-stage, second-stage, mezzanine, leveraged buyout, management buyout), industry group preferences, portfolio companies (those the firm has invested in to date), and key executives/partners with their e-mail addresses, education, previous work experience, and directorships. A brief directory of national and state trade associations is also included. The *Directory* provides the following indexes (referenced by firm entry number): a geographic index, an executive surname index, a college and university index to group partners by educational affiliation, an industry preference index (including more than 200 industries and the firms that have invested in them), and a portfolio companies index that provides an alphabetic list of over 15,000 companies funded by one of the listed firms.

More than 300 new firms and 1,300 new partners were added in this edition. There is also an online database available to subscribers of the directory through Grey House OnLine databases. With venture capital investment on the rise and continually improving venture capital performance, this comprehensive directory will be a valuable resource for business collections in large academic, public, and corporate libraries.—**Colleen Seale**

169.   **Gale Directory of Early Stage Investment.** Holly M. Selden, ed. Stamford, Conn., Gale/Cengage Learning, 2013. 803p. index. $580.00. ISBN 13: 978-1-4144-9616-0.

The *Gale Directory of Early Stage Investment*, in its 1st edition, is "designed for anyone who has started, or is looking to start a business" and "provide contacts to begin the search for investors." This new directory provides coverage of 586 companies; approximately 2,500 funding sources and over 2,000 firms that enable start-up businesses. Data for the *Directory* were obtained by direct contact with the companies, groups, associations, and agencies,; data from other related Gale publications; and Internet searches. The main sources of early-stage investment are angel investors and venture capital firms and these are covered along with other sources of investment including government resources, business accelerators, associations and resources, business incubators, and investment advisors and consultants. The *Gale Directory of Early Stage Investment* has an alphabetic listing section of companies; the alphabetic listings are arranged within categories of investment sources. The index section allows users of the source to search by the following categories: portfolio (lists portfolio companies that have been incubated by angel investors and venture capital firms), geographic, personal name, market focus, and general index. Included also are a user's guide and a list of standard abbreviations. Each company entry includes name, address, telephone number, e-mail address, fax number, URL, fund size, date founded, description, key personnel, and geographic restrictions (where applicable).

The *Gale Directory of Early Stage Investment* fills a niche for entrepreneurs looking for funding by bringing together, in one source, listings of companies that help start ups. The *Directory* contains clear and succinct definitions of terms used (e.g., business accelerator) in its introduction and includes a background history of how equity investment developed. This resource is highly recommended to business collections in larger public libraries and academic library collections. It provides a wealth of information to those who wish to start up a business as well as students of business who wish to learn more about funding options for entrepreneurs or find information about funding sources will also benefit from this new resource.—**Lucy Heckman**

170.   **Plunkett's Investment & Securities Industry Almanac.** 2014 ed. Jack W. Plunkett, ed. Houston, Tex., Plunkett Research, 2014. 500p. $349.99pa. ISBN 13: 978-1-60879-724-0.

Plunkett's Investment & Securities Industry Almanac covers over 300 companies (referred to as the "Investment 300") in the investment industry and related industry segments. Industry segments include brokers, investments, asset management, exchanges, services, and technology. Most of the companies profiled are based in the United States, but some 80 firms are headquartered elsewhere. All were selected for inclusion because of their prominence in the investment industry.

Company information is presented in the same format found in the earlier Plunkett's title. Listed alphabetically, a full page is devoted to each entry. The amount of white space on each page varies with the company. A standard company profile includes: types of businesses the company is involved in; brands, divisions, or affiliates; contact information and Website; short lists of company officers; summary financial information; salary and benefit information; locations in which the company has a presence, including international; and a "Growth Plans/Special Features" section that provides several paragraphs of narrative information about the companies' business activities, position in the industry, and recent events. Each company entry also shows its ranking within its industry group by sales and profits. The information is also available online. Additional sections include an "Investment & Securities Industry Glossary," a short directory of "Important Investment & Securities Industry Contacts," and several special indexes. These include geographical indexes of firms with operations outside the United States and non-U.S. headquarters by country, an index of "Subsidiaries, Brand Names, and Affiliations," and an index of "Firms Noted as Hot Spots for Advancement for Women & Minorities."

The introduction states that *Plunkett's Investment & Securities Industry Almanac* is intended to be a general guide to a vast industry and suggests that researchers start with this volume for an overview and, if more information is needed, consult the companies themselves or other resources for more in-depth research. It meets its stated goal. Serious researchers often need to dig further to find the company or industry information they need, but the Plunkett's almanacs fill an important niche by combining basic industry overview information and basic company information in one package. This work is recommended for all reference collections serving users with academic or personal interests in the investment industry.—**Gordon J. Aamot**

171.   **TheStreet Ratings' Guide to Bond and Money Market Mutual Funds, Spring 2013.** Millerton, N.Y., Grey House Publishing, 2013. 503p. $249.00pa.; $499.00pa. (4 quarterly editions). ISBN 13: 978-1-61925-032-1.

This is a quarterly publication covering the bond and money market mutual funds. It uses a system that evaluates the mutual funds market offerings with ratings of "A—Excellent" through "E—Very Weak." There is a plus sign and a minus sign to indicate whether a company is in the top third of its letter grade or in the bottom third of its grade. The mutual fund data are collected and consolidated into one opinion of each fund's risk-adjusted performance.

This edition contains 4,600 funds and they are evaluated and updated on a quarterly basis. There are eight sections in this title. Section 1 covers Bond and Money Market Mutual Funds, spread over two pages. The left-hand page covers fund type and name, ticker symbol, overall investment rating, telephone number of the company managing the fund, performance ratings, three and six months ratings returns, one-year total return and percentiles, dividend yields, and expense ratios. The right-hand page covers the risk-rating points, the standard deviation, average duration, net asset value, net assets, cash percentage, government bonds, municipal bonds percentages corporate bonds percentage, portfolio turnover ratio, and average coupon rate the manager-quality percentile, manager tenure, the initial purchase minimum, front-end and back-end load. Section 2 is a summary analysis of the largest retail fixed income mutual funds. Section 3 lists the "Top 200 Bond Mutual Funds." These funds are listed in order by their overall investment rating. These entries include the fund family, symbol, the addresses, telephone number, fund type, and major reporting factors for each company. Tables and graphs are provided to illustrate the last five years performance for each of the funds. Section 4 lists the "Bottom 200 Mutual Funds," and section 5 reports the "Performance: 100 Best and Worst Bond Mutual Funds." Section 7 considers the top-rated bond mutual funds by risk category. Section 8 lists the "Top-Rated Bond Mutual Funds by Fund Type." There is an appendix that defines a mutual fund, provides an investor profile quiz, performance benchmarks, fund type descriptions, and share-class descriptions.

There is a plethora of mutual fund information for the investor and for the business researcher. The evaluation of the funds is thorough and current; therefore, this title is recommended as an essential acquisition. For those libraries needing up-to-date financial information on all of the topics that TheStreet Ratings' offers, Grey House offers a subscription Website (http://www.financialratingsseries.com). It rates more than 21,000 banks, credit unions, and insurance companies, as well as 6,000 stocks and 16,000 mutual funds in an easy-to-search format.—**Kay Stebbins Slattery**

172.   **TheStreet Ratings' Guide to Common Stocks: A Quarterly Compilation of Ratings and Analyses Covering Common Stocks Traded on the NYSE, AMEX, and NASDAQ.** Millerton, N.Y., Grey House Publishing, 2013. 339p. $249.00pa. (single edition); $499.00pa. (4 quarterly editions). ISBN 13: 978-1-61925-016-1.

This quarterly published serial rates stocks commonly traded on the NYSE, AMEX, and NASDAQ exchanges. In all, more than 4,700 stocks are rated in this guide. The benefits of a guide such as this are that it will help users track and evaluate the performance of their common stock holdings; it provides a means of identifying and monitoring other potential stocks for new investments; and it provides users with the ability to analyze their options in a way that is readable and reliable.

This source is divided into eight sections plus an introduction. The eight sections include: Index of Common Stocks; Top 200 Common Stocks; Bottom 200 Common Stocks; Performance: The 100 Best and Worst Common Stocks: Risk: 100 Best and Worst Common Stocks; Top-Rated Stocks by Risk Category; Top Rated Common Stocks by Industry; and 200 Highest Dividend-Yielding Common Stock. Data for each common stock listed is comprised of: industry sector, company name, overall investment rating (plus a recommendation to buy, sell, or hold), stock price as of 3/31/13, 52 week high and low, performance rating, total return percent through 3/31/13, risk rating, earnings, projection, valuation ratios, and size and growth. Appendixes list definitions of key terms, investor profile quiz, and performance benchmarks. The investor quiz allows readers to do a self-assessment on stock buying/selling potential, including questions on income, years until retirement, and other existing investments.

Any library looking at this title would also want to consider *TheStreet Ratings' Guide to Stock Mutual Funds* (2013) and *TheStreet Ratings' Guide to Bond and Money Market Mutual Funds* (2013) in their decision. An overall better investment for libraries needing this type of financial information would be to invest in the online database of the Financial Rating Series (http://www.financialratingsseries.com). The site provides an array of search options and access to 21,000 banks, credit unions, and insurers, as well as 6,000 stocks and 16,000 mutual funds.—**Lucy Heckman**

173.   **TheStreet Ratings' Guide to Exchange-Traded Funds: A Quarterly Compilation of Investment Ratings and Analyses Covering ETFs and Other Closed-End Mutual Funds, Spring, 2013.** Millerton, N.Y., Grey House Publishing, 2013. 766p. $249.00pa.; $499.00 (4 quarterly editions). ISBN 13: 978-1-61925-020-8.

The mission of TheStreet.com, a leading financial media company, is to empower users with high-quality advisory information for selecting or monitoring a financial investment. The company's free flagship Website is a leading provider of financial news, commentary, analysis, ratings, and business and investment content.

Published quarterly, *TheStreet Ratings' Guide to Exchange-Traded Funds* provides investors with a source of investment ratings and analyses of exchange-traded funds and closed-end mutual funds. Investment ratings represent a fund's historical risk-adjusted performance and are based on two primary components: performance rating and risk rating. Since there is always a trade-off between risk and reward, funds that receive the highest overall investment ratings are those that combine the ideal combination of both components. For those investors specifically interested in basing their exchange fund selection on tolerance for risk, the provision in this publication of both the performance and risk ratings, in addition to the overall investment rating, will help them to identify the funds that best meet their individual investment requirements and objectives. The Investor Profile Quiz, included in the appendix, can help users to assess their personal risk tolerance based upon their own personal life situation.

The *Guide* is divided into eight sections, including an informative introductory section with an explanation of the A-F investment ratings system used in the book. The primary section, or Index of ETFs and Other Closed-End Funds, is an analysis of all rated and selected unrated funds listed alphabetically by fund name. Other sections identify top-performing funds based upon risk category, type of fund, and overall risk-adjusted performance. Between quarterly editions of the *Guide*, users can take advantage of a link to the Mutual Fund Screener that may be found under the Portfolio and Tools tab on the company's free Website (http://www.thestreet.com) to check if there has been a change in the ratings of a particular fund.—**Elizabeth M. Mezick**

174.   **TheStreet Ratings' Guide to Stock Mutual Funds, Spring 2013.** Jupiter, Fla., Weiss Rating's, 2013. 771p. $249.00pa.; $499.00 (4 quarterly editions). ISBN 13: 978-1-61925-040-6.

Published quarterly, *TheStreet Ratings' Guide to Stock Mutual Funds* provides investors with a source of investment ratings and analyses of equity and balanced mutual funds. Investment ratings represent a mutual fund's historical risk-adjusted performance and are based on two primary components: performance rating and risk rating. Since there is always a trade-off between risk and reward, funds that receive the highest overall investment ratings are those that combine the ideal combination of both components. For those investors specifically interested in basing their mutual fund selection on tolerance for risk, the provision in this publication of both the performance and risk ratings, in addition to the overall investment rating, will help them to identify the funds that best meet their individual investment requirements and objectives. The Investor Profile Quiz, included in the appendix, can help users to assess their personal risk tolerance based upon their own personal life situation.

The *Guide* is divided into eight sections, including an informative introductory section with an explanation of the A-F investment ratings system used in the book. The primary section, or Index of Stock Mutual Funds, is an analysis of all rated and selected unrated equity mutual funds listed alphabetically by fund name. Other sections identify top-performing mutual funds based upon risk category, type of fund, and overall risk-adjusted performance. For those libraries that need financial information on all of topics in Grey House Publishing's Financial Ratings Series it may be worth investing in the subscription Website (http://www.financialratingsseries.com). Here users will have access to information on over 6,000 stocks and 16,000 mutual funds as well as banks, credit unions, and insurance companies.—**Elizabeth M. Mezick**

Consumer Guides

175.   **Consumer Expenditure Survey. http://www.bls.gov/cex.** [Website]. Free. Date reviewed: 2013.

As important and wide-ranging as the decennial census and the ACS are, neither program answers perhaps the most basic of market research questions: how do people spend their money? The government does measure consumer spending, although not in enough detail to inform most specific products nor in enough volume to provide data for specific, smaller geographies such as cities and ZIP codes. The survey that does exist is the Bureau of Labor Statistic's Consumer Expenditure Survey (CES). As the name implies, the CES addresses how people spend their money. It covers some 20 categories of spending: housing and housing specifics such as mortgages, home repairs, and utilities; transportation expenses such as automobile purchase, gasoline, and mass-transit spending; personal expenditures such as those for apparel, health care, and personal products; and entertainment and recreation expenditures. Like the decennial census, the CES can form the basis of more in-depth, private market research products, but its lack of coverage for smaller geographies limits its application somewhat. Although it does not have data for specific states, it is able to break down data by some market segments for the nation as a whole, such as by age, race, region, broad occupation, and family type (e.g., single, dual earner, married with children).—**Eric Forte**

176.   **Consumer Survival: An Encyclopedia of Consumer Rights, Safety, and Protection.** Wendy Reiboldt and Melanie Horn Mallers, eds. Santa Barbara, Calif., ABC-CLIO, 2014. 2v. illus. index. $189.00/set. ISBN 13: 978-1-59884-936-3; 978-1-59884-937-0 (e-book).

Consumer rights is an important topic in the lives of U.S. citizens; however, very few people know much about the topic or could tell you what their specific rights are. This one-of-a-kind resource focuses solely on consumer rights and their role in protecting people within the marketplace. The volume covers a broad range of topic, with special interest in underrepresented populations such as older adults, veterans, and the homeless. The set reviews the historical development of the consumer rights movement and identifies the agencies and laws in place to safeguard consumers. Entries address such topics as food and product safety, housing, health care, the financial industry, and telecommunications. The contributors use vignettes and case studies throughout to illustrate key points and provide insight into contrasting points of view. This will provide students with the opportunity to use their critical thinking skills. *See also* references are used throughout to guide readers to related entries. This work will be a useful addition to public and academic libraries.—**ARBA Staff Reviewer**

177.   **Weiss Ratings' Consumer Box Set.** Millerton, N.Y., Grey House Publishing, 2013. 9v. $359.00pa./set (single issue); $499.00pa./set (two biennial editions). ISBN 13: 978-1-61925-047-5.

This set of nine guides from Grey House Publishing and Weiss Ratings provides information and recommendations on insurance and health care choices that will help consumers make sound decisions. Each slim volume covers a different area: Medicare supplement insurance, Medicare prescription drug coverage, long-term care insurance, homeowners insurance, automobile insurance, variable annuities, elder care choices, term life insurance, and health savings accounts. The guides use Weiss' rating scale that provides a straight forward A-F grade that can be easily interpreted. The guides are written in a straightforward manner that will be easily understood by an educated public. Step-by-step worksheets and planners are provided in each guide that will provide users with further assistance. In a library setting these guides can be copied for individual use. Each guide provides 50 to 70 pages offering detailed information on the subject, including what consumers should look for when choosing a plan or policy and recommended companies to buy insurance from. This set is recommended for large public libraries. Larger libraries that need more than the insurance listing here may be interested in Grey House Publishing's new Financial Ratings Series (http://www.financialratingsseries.com), which provides this nine-volume set as well as all of the consumer guides from TheStreet Series.—**Shannon Graff Hysell**

Finance and Banking

Catalogs and Collections

178.   **DataStream. http://online.thomsonreuters.com/datastream/.** [Website]. Thomson Reuters. Price negotiated by site. Date reviewed: 2013.

Thomson Reuters DataStream is arguably the largest and most comprehensive financial database. Content includes a broad range of financial statistics that is global in coverage. According to the DataStream Website, content includes daily prices, trading volumes, and return indexes, updated at the end of every trading day, for over 100,000 equities in nearly 200 countries around the world. DataStream includes over 140 million time series containing over 100,000 data types. DataStream also includes information on options, futures, commodities, derivatives, bonds, mutual funds, market indexes, interest and exchange rates, macroeconomic variables, and corporate financial data. There are a number of different options and features available, and results can be download easily into Microsoft Excel, Word, or PowerPoint. Date ranges vary by type of data, but many are available back to the 1970s.—**Gary W. White**

179.   **Dow Jones VentureSource. http://www.venturesource.com.** [Website]. New York, Dow Jones. Price negotiated by site. Date reviewed: 2013.

Many entrepreneurs rely on venture capital for various stages of funding. *VentureSource* is a resource that pulls together 30,000 venture-backed companies and 8,000 private capital firms from the United States, Europe, Israel, and China. Entrepreneurs can use this database to find and research investors. *VentureSource* gives aggregate funding and funding stage details. It is possible to evaluate which industries receive the most funding. The resource can also be used for investment benchmarking. Company records give details about the executives and board members, the target markets of the fund or private equity firm, the region in which they operate, their products and financial status, the funding stages offered, a record of financing, past investments, types, and dates. The source can be used not only to identify funding but also for competitive intelligence purposes.—**Wendy Diamond**

180.   **Federal Reserve Statistics & Historical Data. http://www.federalreserve.gov/econresdata/ releases/statisticsdata.htm.** [Website]. Free. Date reviewed: 2013.

This preeminent producer of popular economic indicators is the Federal Reserve, whose mission is largely to manage the nation's money supply. It and its highly visible chairman have become more prominent in recent decades as their role in managing the economy has become perceived as more influential than may have been the case earlier. Key indicators from the Federal Reserve measure consumer credit and money stocks. Arguably its best-known activity is its control of the interest rate (popularly known as the prime rate or the federal funds rate), which may change after a meeting of the Fed's Open Market Committee. Announcements of changes to the prime rate are very closely watched by business, economic, financial, and even general interests. FRASER—the Federal Reserve Archival System for Economic Research (http://fraser.stlouisfed.org/) also contains data from the Federal reserve, as well as other U.S. economic data.—**Eric Forte**

181.   **Financial Literacy. http://financialliteracy.rosendigital.com/.** [Website]. New York, Rosen Publishing. Price negotiated by site. Date reviewed: 2014.

One thing is certain: it is never too early to begin teaching children the value of money or how to manage their money. This Web resource makes money and finance interesting and easier to understand for middle and high school students. Users can search the database for articles on key financial concepts, such a macroeconomics, microeconomics, and global economics. They can also explore information closer to home, such as terms used in household finance and credit. Students can explore by such categories as Personal Finance, Careers and Entrepreneurship, Financial Institutions, Role of Government, Market Economy, Measure Economic Performance, and Trade and Global Economy. Some of the most popular features of this site will enable students to create their own budgets or develop a saving plan for college. All of the material and tools are curriculum based and support state and national standards. Videos are integrated throughout the site to support student learning and the calculators and quizzes bring the content alive and will continue to challenge students. There is a text-to-speech feature that supports ESL students. This will be a worthwhile addition to middle and high school libraries.—**Shannon Graff Hysell**

182.   **Mergent WebReports. http://www.mergent.com/productsServices-desktopApplications-web.html.** [Website]. Fort Mill, S.C., Mergent. Price negotiated by site. Date reviewed: 2013.

Mergent WebReports provides a comprehensive history of corporate America for almost 100 years. It includes corporate histories, brief financial statements, lists of subsidiaries, descriptions of long-term debt and stock offerings, officers and directors, and so on. Much of the historical data are available in PDF format from the print resources that were once known as the Moody's and Mergent Manuals. Users can search within and across manuals, by company name, manual year, or type. Additional resources in the archive include: corporate annual reports, industry reports, and equity reports.—**Rita W. Moss**

183.   **Valuation & Deal Term Database. http://vcexperts.com/vce/.** [Website]. Shreveport, La., VC Expert. $125 (single user/month); $995.00 (single user/year); $5,000.00 (for academic institutions/year). Date reviewed: 2013.

VC Experts is a major provider of commentary, data, and analytics for those entrepreneurs and investors in private equity and venture capital circles. This resource gives valuation and deal term data on thousands of privately held U.S. companies. Entrepreneurs can identify funding sources that suits their needs, and investors and entrepreneurs alike can use this information to negotiate better valuations, deal terms, and exit strategies.

The resource has three parts. The Valuation & Deal Term Database details more than 2,800 privately held U.S. companies. Unlike other similar resources, this database includes analysis of 13 individual deal terms on more than 3,700 private financing transactions, with comparisons to national and regional averages. Also featured are postmoney valuation estimates on more than 2,000 private financing transactions. "Postmoney" is a term referring to the situation or number of shares after a deal is made. Search criteria include company name, industry, region, financing round, investor, and individual deal term. Valuations and deal terms come from the offices of secretaries of state. There is also a Portfolio Company Analysis tool to model financing and payouts. The third part is *The Encyclopedia of Private Equity & Venture Capital*, covering all aspects of raising and investing money in these ventures with expert commentary. The database may be purchased with or without the Encyclopedia.—**Wendy Diamond**

Dictionaries and Encyclopedias

184.   Tenney, Sarah, and Anne C. Salda. **Historical Dictionary of the World Bank.** 2d ed. Lanham, Md., Scarecrow, 2014. 421p. (Historical Dictionaries of International Organizations). $115.00; $109.99 (e-book). ISBN 13: 978-0-8108-7864-8; 978-0-8108-7865-5 (e-book).

The International Bank for Reconstruction and Development (World Bank) plays an influential and often high-profile role in the economic development of many contemporary developing countries. Not only does it lend money, provide technical assistance, and influence economic and financial policies to these countries, but the adoption of its programs is seen as a stamp of approval that opens access to private international capital for a country. Despite this high-profile and often controversial role played by the bank, there are few sources that provide adequate information about the history, structure, and operation of the bank and its affiliate institutions. *Historical Dictionary of the World Bank* fills this gap. The 421-page book provides copious information about the World Bank that has hitherto not been available in any single volume. Both the entries and the bibliography sections have been significantly expanded since the publication of the 1st edition (1997).

The majority of the book is devoted to the dictionary itself. Each entry gives sufficient detail and is put in a historical context that makes it understandable and enjoyable to read. The work includes four appendixes: a list of World Bank presidents, IBRD operational summary 2008-1012, IDA operational summary 2008-2012, World Bank lending by theme and sector 2007-2012, and subscriptions and voting power of member countries. The work concludes with a detailed bibliography arranged by subject. Perhaps the most interesting and informative part of the book is the introductory chapter covering the first 30 pages. In this short section, the author brilliantly describes the historical context within which the bank was created; the major personalities behind its creation; objectives of the bank, its growth, and changes in objectives; the structure of the bank; and how some of its affiliates came to be created. The historical chronology of events that precede the introduction makes the book user friendly. The book is also well written.

By putting the activities of the World Bank in a historical context, this book will do more to educate the public about the bank than any effort the bank itself may produce. The dictionary is recommended for all who are interested in the activities of the World Bank.—**ARBA Staff Reviewer**

Directories

185. **Financial Yellow Book: Who's Who at the Leading U.S. Financial Institutions. Winter 2013 ed.** New York, Leadership Directories, 2013. 825p. index. $445.00pa. (annual subscription); $423.00pa. (automatic renewal). ISSN 1058-2878.

This semiannual publication is a directory of about 560 public and private financial companies in the United States, with over 1,000 subsidiaries. In addition to its availability in print format, the *Yellow Book* is accessible over the Internet through an annual subscription to *The Leadership Library on the Internet*.

The first section provides a list of companies appearing for the first time, completed mergers since the last edition, pending mergers, company name changes, chief executive officer changes, and the main companies in which major companies are located. The work is divided into four sections for financial institutions, government financial institutions, accounting firms, and exchanges and markets. Companies are arranged alphabetically within each section. Along with providing contact information for personnel at the executive level users can also use the directory to find contact names for those in charge of communications, contributions, foundations, government affairs, libraries and information centers, events and conferences, recruitment, shareholder relations, and facilities.

Each company listing contains its name; ticker symbol (when applicable); address; telephone number; e-mail and Internet addresses; fax number; a brief description of company services; brief biographical information about the chief officer; a list of key executives and administrative staff; major subsidiaries, divisions, and affiliates; and a list of the members of the board of directors. In many entries, a photograph of the chief officer is provided. This directory serves as a good way to stay up-to-date on the financial industry by keeping you up to date on the hiring of new executives; informing you on new mergers, pending mergers; company name changes; and giving you access to contact information for such important information as company benefits, foundations, libraries and information centers, and conferences.

The directory has an industry, a geographical, a name (of all individuals), and an organization index. It is recommended for larger academic library business collections and to research libraries. The value of the work is that it brings together and lists, in one directory, both public and private institutions representing accounting firms, banks, insurance companies, and government agencies.—**Lucy Heckman**

186. **Plunkett's Banking, Mortgages, & Credit Industry Almanac.** 2014 ed. Jack W. Plunkett, ed. Houston, Tex., Plunkett Research, 2013. 450p. index. $349.99pa. ISBN 13: 978-1-60879-720-2.

This is the latest edition of *Plunkett's Banking, Mortgages, & Credit Industry Almanac*. The introduction states that this work was designed to be broad in scope so that it can have value for a diversity of researchers. The organization and content of the *Almanac* support this objective.

The work is divided into two main sections: the "Banking Industry" and the "Banking & Lending 350." This structure allows a researcher to easily locate the specific type of information they are seeking. Also facilitating access are several indexes in the following categories: alphabetical; industry sectors; headquarters by state; non-U.S. headquarters by country; regions of the United States; firms with operations outside the United States; firms that are hot spots for women and minorities; and brand names, affiliates, and subsidiaries.

The first section is a compilation of somewhat disparate industry information. This includes a glossary of financial services industry terms; industry statistics; trends impacting the three sectors; and a short directory of trade associations, Websites, publishers, government agencies, and other organizations that intersect these sectors. The second and lengthiest section of the *Almanac* contains one-page profiles of the "Banking & Lending 350." These are primarily U.S. companies that operate in the banking, mortgage, and credit industry sectors. Companies were selected based on their dominance in their industry sectors. In addition to basic directory information, such as ticker, address, and telephone and fax numbers, company profiles can also include industry designations, brands, divisions, and affiliates, lines of business, key executives, number of employees, up to five years of sales and profit statistics, growth plans, and compensation for the top executives.

While the content in the first section is valuable, the strength of the work is the "Banking & Lending 350" section. A specific aim of the *Almanac*'s design is to support market research, employment searches, and mailing list creation. The "Banking & Lending 350" section will be an excellent tool for these pursuits. This moderately priced almanac is recommended for public libraries as well as academic libraries on limited budgets.—**Susan Shultz**

187. **Weiss Ratings' Guide to Banks: A Quarterly Compilation of Financial Institutions Ratings and Analyses. Summer 2013.** Millerton, N.Y., Grey House Publishing, 2013. 364p. index. $249.00pa. (single edition); $499.00pa. (4 quarterly editions). ISBN 13: 978-1-61925-013-0.

This volume reports Weiss's 2013 safety ratings for almost 9,000 banking institutions. All U.S. federally insured commercial banks, savings banks, and savings and loans are reported in alphabetic order. (Ratings for credit unions are covered in another Weiss Ratings' publication, *Weiss Ratings Guide to Credit Unions* [see entry 188].) This guide is a quarterly compilation. The ratings range from "A+" (excellent financial security) to "E" (very weak) and "F" (failed).

Ratings are based on many factors (emphasizing capitalization, asset quality, profitability, liquidity, and stability) that are measured by an index. Supporting data include size (total assets), growth (one year), asset mix, a capitalization index (downside risk), financial leverage, capital ration (capital divided by assets), an asset quality index, nonperforming loans (percent), ratio of nonperforming loans to capital plus loan reserve, a foreclosure ratio, a profitability index, net income, return on assets, return on equity, net interest spread, overhead divided by total reserve less interest expense, a liquidity index, liquidity ratio, a hot money ratio, and a stability index. The elements making up each index are indicated, but no weighting (e.g., algebraic weighted average) scheme is revealed.

In a separate part, institutions rated "B+" or higher are listed state by state. A third part alphabetically lists upgrades and downgrades during the spring 2012 and 2013 quarters. An appendix lists recent bank and thrift failures (2007-2013). These guides provide excellent, but not infallible, ratings for banks and thrifts.—**ARBA Staff Reviewer**

188. **Weiss Ratings' Guide to Credit Unions: A Quarterly Compilation of Credit Union Ratings and Analyses. Summer 2013.** Millerton, N.Y., Grey House Publishing, 2013. 350p. $249.00pa. (single edition) ; $499.00 (4 quarterly editions). ISBN 13: 978-1-61925-051-2.

In today's financially turbulent world, consumers, professions, and institutions would be well advised to consult *Weiss Ratings' Guide to Credit Unions* before establishing a relationship with a credit union. This new title in the Weiss Ratings collection is now published by Grey House Publishing. Based on the most current information from government and commercial sources, Weiss creates letter grades (A, B, C, D, E, and F) through formulaic interaction of the indexes for each financial institution and then publishes its analyses quarterly. The Spring 2013 issue, which was based on data from the September 30, 2012 reports supplied to federal agencies, was reviewed. Each issue is divided into three principal sections. Section 1, the bulk of the work, is an alphabetic list of all the financial institutions, followed by the city and state in which the firm is headquartered, the most recent Weiss Safety Rating, the Weiss Safety Rating for the preceding 2 years, and financial figures and ratios extended over 2 columnar pages. If the Weiss Rating has changed over the preceding year, a symbol shows an upward or downward revision. Section 2 is a list of "Weiss Recommended Companies" arranged in alphabetic order by state and then city. Section 3 is a list of financial institutions that have undergone a rating upgrade or downgrade. This volume concludes with three appendixes: a list of recent credit union failures from 2010-2012; a chart indicating the differences between commercial banks and credit unions; and a glossary of key terms.

Weiss makes no textual comments, relying instead on universally obvious letter grades for its evaluations. The subscription price puts this title out of reach for many libraries, public as well as academic. But large public and academic libraries most definitely need to acquire the work. Likewise, special libraries in large corporations will find this title indispensable. For larger libraries and corporate libraries that require this type of information for not only credit unions but banks, insurers, mutual funds, and stocks, the publisher offers an online database that combines data from Weiss Ratings' Guides and TheStreet Ratings guides in an easy-to-search database.—**Dene L. Clark**

Handbooks and Yearbooks

189.   **International Debt Statistics 2013.** By The World Bank. Lanham, Md., Bernan Press, 2013. 336p. $75.00pa. ISBN 13: 978-0-82139-787-9.

This work is a continuation of the previously published *Global Development Finance,* a World Bank title distributed by Bernan Press. It provides an in-depth look at how the global financial crisis has affected developing countries and their access to international capital. The book provides data for 128 developing countries, including their trends in capital and their trends in external debt. It includes key debt ratios for individual reporting countries and their external debt stocks. More detailed data are available from the World Bank open database, which provides more than 200 indicators covering the years 1970 to 2011 for most reporting countries. Summary tables of regional and income group aggregates as well and country tables are provided. This report is useful for government collections economists, and investors and financial consultants.—**Shannon Graff Hysell**

190.   **World Economic Outlook, April 2013: Hopes, Realities, Risks.** By the International Monetary Fund. Lanham, Md., Bernan Press, 2013. 250p. $68.00pa. ISBN 13: 978-1-6163-5555-5.

World Economic Outlook, April 2013: Hopes, Realities, Risks is one of an ongoing series of *World Economic Outlook* reviews published by the International Monetary Fund (IMF). Although more recent editions contain updated data, each publication also addresses topics and issues selected by the IMF as being of particular relevance at the time of preparation. Since many of the issues are relevant over a much longer time horizon, the volumes exude both timeliness and timelessness. Roughly 40 percent of the book is comprised of statistical tables that provide current data and historical perspective, as well as projections to the year 2014. The bulk of the book provides well-organized and well-supported discussions of world economies and policies, with attention paid to individual countries and regions.

In this issue the focus is on the economic future of emerging market economies. The work takes a close look at the dynamic developing economies—those that have experienced remarkable economic turnarounds in the past decade. Catalysts for growth in the current global market are explored. The text avoids unnecessary technicalities, thus it can be appreciated by a broad audience. Numerous charts, text tables, and boxes help to illustrate major points. A table of contents and a list of references to other publications are included. The *Outlook* provides much insight and information at a relatively modest cost.—**William C. Struning**

Industry and Manufacturing

Catalogs and Collections

191.   **First Research Industry Profiles. http://www.dnblearn.com/index.php?page=hoover-s-first-research.** [Website]. Parsippany, N.J., Dun & Bradstreet. Price negotiated by site. Date reviewed: 2013.

First Research is a resource with 900 industry profiles. It was acquired by Dun & Bradstreet in 2007. First Research profiles serve the varied needs of the researcher, the business planner, and the business marketer. The reports facilitate market analysis with industry overviews. The report sections include: the competitive landscape, the products, operations and technology, sales and marketing, finance and regulation, human resources, industry indicators, and industry updates. Industry challenges, trends, and opportunities are also covered. The section on executive talking points raises a number of valuable questions that new business owners should consider. Reports end with an opportunity ranking, a list of industry acronyms, and a list of valuable free industry Websites. If small businesses constitute a large part of an industry, data for small business will be displayed apart from the overall aggregate industry data.

Reports draw data from third-party providers: valuation multiples, which are used in business valuations for acquisitions, are provided from business Valuation Resources. Fintel supplies the benchmarking financial ratios for private companies. Inforum provides industry forecasts.

First Research reports appear in ProQuest's ABI/INFORM and in MarketResearch.com. First Research can also be linked to D&B's Hoover's database for libraries that subscribe to the latter.—**Chris LeBeau**

192.   **Pratt's Stats. http://www.bvresources.com/.** [Website]. Portland, Oreg., Business Valuation Resources. $219 .00 (individual pay-per-view); others negotiated by site. Date reviewed: 2011.

This database is a place where entrepreneurs can find private transaction data for sales of privately and closely held companies. This kind of data is commonly referred to as "comps" or comparables and market data. The database collects information on up to 88 data points (valuation multiples and financial ratios) for the financial and transactional details of the sale of a business, which help an investor calculate the financial value and fair price. Searches are relatively easy to conduct by the novice. Data are sourced from a number of "intermediaries" as well as from SEC filings.

Business Valuation Resources (http://www.bvresources.com/) offers two similar products, Bizcomps and Public Stats. The first gives transaction data for very small "main street" companies, and the latter gives sales transaction data for public company sales transactions.—**Chris LeBeau**

Dictionaries and Encyclopedias

193.   Hinshaw, John, and Peter N. Stearns. **Industrialization in the Modern World: From the Industrial Revolution to the Internet.** Santa Barbara, Calif., ABC-CLIO, 2014. 2v. illus. index. $173.00/set. ISBN 13: 978-1-61069-087-4; 978-1-61069-088-1 (e-book).

The Industrial Revolution stands alongside mankind's greatest achievements, utilizing fossil fuels for energy to create new tools and trades for a global community. The other revolutions of discovering fire, developing languages for communication among the human race, and the agricultural revolution that enabled man to process his food more efficiently are the other great human achievements. This is a two-volume encyclopedia of alphabetic entries discussing the various aspects of the industrial revolution.

It historical value begins in 1563 with the "Apprentice Laws" that required guilds to regulate skilled workers and continues to 2011 when Toyota Motors surpasses General Motors in automobile sales. Some of the topics are Artificial Intelligence, Capitalism, Socialism, Foreign Trade, and biographies of personalities who played a part in the Industrial Revolution.

Each entry provides a definition or a profile, accompanied by a *see* or *see also* reference and a short bibliography. The articles are accompanied by primary documents that are made up of essays and speeches of the participants in the Industrial Revolution. There is an index in volume 2 for both volumes. I would recommend this historical encyclopedia to public and academic collections for social history and business collections.—**Kay Stebbins Slattery**

Directories

194.   **Food & Beverage Market Place, 2014.** 13th ed. Millerton, N.Y., Grey House Publishing, 2013. 3v. index. $595.00pa./set; $895.00 (online database; single user); $1,095.00 (print and online editions). ISBN 13: 978-1-61925-128-1.

The 2014 edition of the *Food & Beverage Market Place* provides a wealth of information on the food and beverage industry. Published in three softcover volumes, it contains directory information with company profiles some 45,000 firms in the United States and Canada.

Volume 1 is devoted exclusively to food and ingredient manufacturers, with a hierarchical listing for product categories (including a cross-reference key), as well as indexes for brand names, ethnic foods, state or province, and parent companies with subsidiaries. The second volume is comprised of equipment, supplies and services companies preceded by a product category and company listing; transportation firms; warehouse companies; and wholesalers/distributors. The third volume of the set covers brokers; importers/exporters; consumer catalogs; and industry resources such as associations, trade shows, and publications. At the conclusion of volume 3 are indexes with entry numbers for all brands and all companies covered within the set. While the format may initially appear to be somewhat confusing, the introductory and explanatory material provided by the publisher proves useful.

As is often the case with directories covering a wide gamut of publicly and privately owned companies of various sizes, profiles vary in detail according to the amount of information readily available. The lengthier profiles include e-mail and Web addresses, names of key executives, estimated sales figures, number of employees, facilities square footage, brand names, and parent company information. At a minimum, profiles include mailing address, telephone and fax numbers, and a brief description.

This directory information is also available online via the Grey House Online Database (GOLD). With access to this database users can search the information by subject-specific criteria. All entries provide direct links to listee's Websites and e-mail addresses.

Given its comprehensive coverage, this set is highly valuable to professionals in the food and beverage industry. It should be considered for purchase by academic libraries supporting food service or hospitality management programs and by large public libraries.—**Martha Tarlton**

195.   **Plunkett's Airline, Hotel & Travel Industry Almanac.** 2014 ed. Jack W. Plunkett, ed. Houston, Tex., Plunkett Research, 2013. 480p. $349.99pa. ISBN 13: 978-1-60879-715-8.

This 2014 edition of *Plunkett's Airline, Hotel & Travel Industry Almanac* provides an overview of the travel and hotel industry and the key players. It is intended to be a general guide and offers many easy-to-use charts and tables. Industries covered within this volume include hotels and resorts, cruise ships, the airline industry, theme parks, tour operators, casinos, car rental companies, passenger trains, and personal modes of transportation (e.g., jet, air taxi, business jets).

Chapter 1 describes the major trends affecting the industry. Chapter 2 provides travel statistics from trustful sources such as the World Tourism Organization, trade associations, and government sources. Chapter 3 offers industry contacts, such as associations, publications, and various information sources related to the industry. Chapter 4, "The Travel 300," is the core of this publication, and includes ranking charts and leading company's profiles. There are four different indexes for this chapter. Each profile includes the following: company name; Website address; ranks; types of business; brands/divisions/ affiliations; names and positions of top officers; address; telephone and fax numbers; brief financials; executive salaries; benefits; competitive advantage; number of apparent women officers; growth plans; and office locations. There are two additional indexes at the end of the publications: Index of Hot Spots for Advancement for Women/Minorities; and Index by Subsidiaries, Brand Names and Selected Affiliations. The glossary at the beginning the publication is brief.

This almanac seems especially useful for market research, strategic planning, and job hunting. The inclusion criteria of chapter 4, "The Travel 300," are not clear and the information provided is not in depth, but the volume provides a good overview of the travel industry. This resource is recommended for business reference collections.—**Mihoko Hosoi**

196.   **Plunkett's Apparel & Textile's Industry Almanac.** 2014 ed. Jack W. Plunkett, ed. Houston, Tex., Plunkett Research, 2013. 493p. $349.99pa. ISBN 13: 978-1-60879-702-8.

Plunkett's Apparel & Textile's Industry Almanac promises to be your complete guide to all facets of the apparel and textiles industry. The introduction points out that the *Almanac* is especially useful for market research, strategic planning, employment searching, and sales prospecting.

The book primarily consists of some 350 company profiles, selected for their importance in the industry. The one-page summaries include the following: contact information; type of business; a list of brands, divisions, or affiliates; the names of key executives; sales and profit figures; salaries and benefits; and a narrative discussion of growth plans or special features. Companies are indexed alphabetically, geographically, and by brand name. In addition, rankings by sales compare companies within specific industry groups. The *Almanac* rounds out the work with a discussion of important industry trends, key statistics, and contact information for trade and membership associations. Here users will find out more information on things like the globalization of the apparel and textiles industries, the growing use of private label fashions at major retailers, and clothing distribution logistics. A glossary provides definitions for apparel, textile, fashion, and marketing terms. Access to the online edition is available with purchase of the print edition.

The Plunkett guide deserves high marks for aggregating pertinent information for the apparel and textile industry. The work is clearly organized and accessible, as each chapter begins with a succinct summary of its contents. Additional indexes would be useful, especially by type of business, annual sales, and key officers. Since the $349.99 price tag is hefty, an upgrade in layout and design would improve the work. Nonetheless, the *Almanac* achieves its goal, providing comprehensive industry and company research under one cover. Business and academic libraries needing textile and apparel information will benefit from adding this source to their collection.—**Elizabeth Kay Tompkins**

197.   **Plunkett's Consulting Industry Almanac.** 2014 ed. Jack W. Plunkett, ed. Houston, Tex., Plunkett Research, 2014. 400p. index. $349.99pa. ISBN 13: 978-1-60879-737-0.

Plunkett's Consulting Industry Almanac selectively covers not only the traditional areas of management and human resources consulting but also the less traditional areas of manufacturing, logistics, and transportation along with the emerging areas of IT and e-commerce (marketing) consulting. The competitive job market has presented many changes and challenges to the consulting industry, including consolidation of firms, more competitive bidding, and the ability to serve customers in a global market. The volume begins with a brief glossary of industry terminology followed by chapters covering major trends, statistics and rankings, and a directory of consulting industry contacts with addresses and Websites. The remaining and largest section of the *Almanac* provides information profiles on the biggest, most successful corporations in all segments of the consulting industry. A brief introduction explains selection criteria. Most are U.S.-based, but some international firms are also included. The one-page entries are arranged in alphabetic order. Indexes by subsidiary name, brand name, and selected affiliations are also provided. Profile information includes: company name; addresses; types of consulting; types of business; brands/divisions/affiliates; NAIC industry group code; a narrative on growth plans and special features; a list of company officers (contacts); financials; ticker symbol; number of employees; and brief salaries/benefits information indicating available plans and top executive compensation. An interesting "other thoughts" category briefly examines the firm's success with advancement for women in the organization based on the number of apparent women officers or directors. Indexes of rankings within industry groups as well as an alphabetic listing of the profiled companies and additional geographic indexes also precede the company profiles. Free access to the online version is available with purchase of the print edition. There is no comparable publication with this coverage and price. Gale's *Consultants and Consulting Organizations Directory* (36th ed.; see ARBA 2012, entry 138) and the *Consultants Directory* (Dun & Bradstreet) are both broader in scope, providing directory information for over 25,000 firms each.—**Colleen Seale**

198.   **Plunkett's E-Commerce & Internet Business Almanac.** 2014 ed. Jack W. Plunkett, ed. Houston, Tex., Plunkett Research, 2014. 600p. $349.99pa. ISBN 13: 978-1-60879-728-8.

Plunkett's E-Commerce & Internet Business Almanac is a comprehensive directory and guide to the industry. It is arranged within sections: "The E-Commerce and Internet Industry," an overview of trends (including statistics), a glossary, and a directory of industry contacts including government agencies and industry associations; and the "E-Commerce 400," the directory section of companies. The "E-Commerce and Internet Industry" overview section, other than its narrative of current trends as projections, includes statistics and results of surveys by agencies. The directory section, the "E-Commerce 400" provides information concerning "the largest, most successful, fastest growing firms in e-commerce and related industries in the world." Companies selected must meet the following criteria: U.S. based for profit corporations (also added were about 20 foreign-based companies); publicly held companies (although a number of privately held firms were added to "round-out certain niche sets of companies"); prominence or a significant presence in the industry; and financial data regarding companies must have been available (either from company itself or other sources). Companies did not have to be exclusively in e-commerce and Internet fields. Each company listing provides: Website address; mailing address; telephone number; industry group code (based on NAIC code); type of business; officers; financials; growth plans/special features; locations; and brands/divisions/affiliates. In addition to the directory section, companies are indexed alphabetically by location, by industry group, and by firms with international affiliates. Additionally, there are two additional special indexes: one of firms noted as hot spots for advancement for women and minorities and the other of subsidiaries, brand names, and affiliations.

Plunkett's E-Commerce & Internet Business Almanac is an excellent and thorough source on the industry. It is especially recommended to academic library collections and larger public libraries.—**Lucy Heckman**

199.   **Plunkett's Outsourcing & Offshoring Industry Almanac.** 2014 ed. Jack W. Plunkett, ed. Houston, Tex., Plunkett Research, 2013. 469p. $349.99pa. ISBN 13: 978-1-60879-708-0.

As manufacturing and business services increasingly leave the United States for distant shores, words such as *outsourcing* and *offshoring* will undoubtedly become even more prominent in the media and in our vocabulary. One only needs to examine a product label or call a toll-free number to realize what a global economy we live in. The 2014 edition of *Plunkett's Outsourcing & Offshoring Industry Almanac* is described as a comprehensive guide to this growing industry for researchers of all types. The volume is arranged with a table of contents, followed by a handy glossary of industry terminology, an introduction to the *Almanac*, and a section explaining how to best use it. The largest section of the *Almanac*, highlights the largest, most successful and fastest growing companies in offshoring, outsourcing, and related industries worldwide. About one-third of the companies are housed outside of the United States. The profiles are arranged in alphabetic order by company name, with indexes at the beginning of the chapter providing the following additional listings: industries covered with NAICS codes, rankings within industry group, an alphabetic index, listings of headquarters location by U.S. state, non-U.S. headquarters location by country, regions of the United States where these companies have locations, and firms with operations outside the United States. Data provided for each company profile include: company name, Website, contacts and address, industry group code (NAICS), sales and profits rankings within the company's industry group, types of business, brands/divisions/affiliations, growth plans/special features, financials, (apparent) salaries/benefits (U.S. employers only), locations, and a category ranking the company as favorable to women/minorities. The publisher has taken a liberal view in their coverage of the industry by including companies and sectors that are not exclusively involved in the outsourcing or offshoring business. Types of businesses covered include among others: call centers, contract manufacturing, life sciences, research and development, software development, and third party logistics. Two additional indexes provide information on hotspots for advancement for women and minorities, and subsidiaries, brand names, and selected affiliations.

Data were either provided directly from the company featured or from outside sources deemed reliable and accurate by the editors. The information can be found in the publisher's online version as well, which is free with the purchase of the print volume. As an almanac this reference work fulfills the definition of providing statistical information on a (to date) annual basis. As a directory, it provides much value-added information about an important industry.—**Colleen Seale**

Handbooks and Yearbooks

200.   **Compendium of Tourism Statistics.** 2013 ed. By the World Tourism Ogranization. New York, United Nations, 2013. 664p. $220.00pa. ISBN 13: 978-92-8441-489-5.

201.   **Yearbook of Tourism Statistics 2013.** New York, United Nations, 2013. 898p. $305.00. ISBN 13: 978-92-8441-488-8.

The information, which the World Tourism Organization has been gathering annually for 65 years, comes from data obtained by questionnaires sent to governments and from official national publications. The *Yearbook of Tourism Statistics 2013* presents an overview of worldwide trends in tourism, with country rankings for top destinations, earners, and spenders, among other things. These are followed by regional summaries for Africa, the Americas, East Asia and the Pacific, Europe, and the Middle East. It also presents details for selected countries and territories on total arrivals and overnight stays by country of origin. The years detailed in this current volume are 2007-2011.

The *Compendium of Tourism Statistics* provides statistical data on tourism in 209 countries and territories for the years 2007-2011. It is designed to help tourism professionals analyze and measure the international tourism sector.

These publications are standard reference tools for tourism officials. Large urban public libraries and colleges and universities that provide public administration courses may want to consider their purchase, but the information may be too dated for most.—**ARBA Staff Reviewer**

202.   **Industrial Commodity Statistics Yearbook 2009.** New York, United Nations; distr., Lanham, Md., Bernan Press, 2011. 2v. $160.00/set. ISBN 13: 978-92-1061-316-3.

This UN publication collects and aggregates national data on production of raw materials, manufactured goods, and power (electricity and gas) for the past decade. Nearly 600 industrial commodities are covered. Although subject to data collection limitations derived from the national data it draws on, it is nonetheless a standard reference for worldwide manufacturing and mineral extraction, providing measures that are standardized and reasonably comparable from country to country. Data are provided for the period of 2000-2009 and includes information from 200 countries and territories.

The *Yearbook* is arranged into two volumes: Physical Quantity Data and Monetary Value Data.

The commodities have been selected based on their importance in world production and trade, with this volume providing data on the value of industrial production. Users can link the data provided to other internationally used product classifications by using the correspondence tables provided.

As is typical for UN publications, the data are presented in a clear and consistent way. Data sources are indicated clearly, and when the entries are estimates, the basis for making the estimates is described clearly. This is a basic data reference source, and as such, it belongs in every serious reference collection.—**Ray Olszewski**

203.   **OECD Science, Technology and Industry Outlook 2012.** By the Organisation for Economic Co-operation and Development. Lanham, Md., Bernan Press, 2012. 280p. $84.00pa. ISBN 13: 978-92-41703-2-2.

Based on the latest statistics reported from countries in the Organisation for Economic Co-operation and Development, this yearbook provides information and indicators in science and innovation. It reviews key trends in the policies and performances of these countries in the areas of science and technology. All of the numbers are analyzed across a number of thematic areas. The focus of this edition is the changes that countries are making in their science and technology industries to ensure that they have a key role in creating a sustainable role in economic recovery.—**William C. Struning**

204.   **OECD Tourism Trends and Policies 2012.** New York, United Nations, 2012. 426p. $126.00pa. ISBN 13: 978-92-64177-55-0.

This work, a cooperative publication between the Organisation for Economic Co-operation and Development and the European Commission, provides information on key tourism policy developments. It provides a broad overview and interpretation of tourism trends in these countries and beyond to help users get a better understanding of what innovations are working to draw tourism into the featured countries. It sheds light on policies and practices associated with growth in tourism. Published on a two-year basis, this title may be of interest to those in the tourism industry and large academic libraries.—**ARBA Staff Reviewer**

Insurance

205.   **Plunkett's Insurance Industry Almanac.** 2014 ed. Jack W. Plunkett, ed. Houston, Tex., Plunkett Research, 2014. 480p. $349.99pa. ISBN 13: 978-1-60879-719-6.

Plunkett Research is a well-known publisher of industry directories and almanacs. This particular title covers the insurance industry, and is designed for the general reader to compare the top 300 American insurance companies. An overview of the insurance industry trends is provided and graphs and tables are provided for easy interpretation of the information.

The top 300 insurance companies included here are the largest and most successful companies from all areas of the insurance industry. The alphabetic listing of these top companies provides the industry group, types of business, brands, divisions, subsidiaries, plans for growth, current news, contact information for the officers, annual financials, salaries and benefits, and provides an assessment of the company's hiring and advancement of minorities and women. Indexes to the industry, sales, brand names, and the subsidiaries are provided. The information in this book is also available online through the publisher. This work is recommended as a supplement to other insurance ratings guides, due to its very general overview of the insurance industry.—**Kay Stebbins Slattery**

206.   **Weiss Ratings' Guide to Health Insurers: A Quarterly Compilation of Health Insurance Company Ratings and Analysis. Summer 2013.** Millerton, N.Y., Grey House Publishing, 2013. 513p. $249.00pa. (single edition): $499.00pa. (4 quarterly editions). ISBN 13: 978-1-61925-025-3.

The purpose of the Weiss insurance guides is to provide the consumer with information about various insurance companies that will enable them to make wise choices for their insurance needs. Formerly published the *Weiss Ratings' Guide to Life, Health, and Annuity Insurers*, this guide now focuses solely on the health insurance industry and includes analyses of more than 1,200 health insurers and some 500 health maintenance organizations (HMOs). The Weiss Guides cover only U.S. companies and are updated on a quarterly basis. Weiss Ratings do not accept money for recommendations. Therefore, the ratings are unbiased and are recognized as the insurance industry's leading consumer advocate. The Weiss Ratings range from A-F, with "A+" being the best rating and "F" signifying failure of the company. The volume is divided into eight sections: "Index of Companies"; "Analysis of Largest Companies"; "Weiss Recommended Companies"; "Weiss Recommended Companies By State"; "Long-Term Care Insurers"; "Medicare Supplement Insurance"; "Analysis of Medicare Managed Care Complaints"; and "Rating Upgrades and Downgrades. An appendix with risk-adjusted capital, long-term care insurance planner, Medicare prescription drug planner, recent industry failures, state insurance commissioners, and a glossary of terms concludes this volume. This rating guide is recommended as a priority purchase for large public libraries and academic libraries.—**Kay Stebbins Slattery**

207.   **Weiss Ratings' Guide to Life and Annuity Insurers: A Quarterly Compilation of Insurance Company Ratings and Analyses. Spring 2013.** Millerton, N.Y., Grey House Publishing, 2013. 329p. $249.00pa. (single edition); $499.00pa. (4 quarterly editions). ISBN 13: 978-1-61925-028-4.

Weiss Ratings' Guide to Life and Annuity Insurers is, simply stated, a resource that purchasers of life and annuity insurance from a United States company may consult to assure themselves that a potential insurance carrier is financially sound. The company's rigorous rating standards are designed to show whether an insurer can deal with severe economic adversity and its quarterly publication assures timely reporting. Weiss' rating scale (A to F) is designed for simplicity and its meaning is readily apparent to the general public. Each quarterly publication consists of several sections. Section 1, the "Index of Companies," is sorted alphabetically by company name. It includes a Weiss Safety Rating (A to F) for each company, followed by ratios, indexes, and dollar figures in over 20 different categories. The safety ratings are assigned by analysts who synthesize hundreds of factors into five indexes. The introduction describes the makeup of these indexes. The reader will find a bullet next to the names of the largest companies. These carriers appear in section 2, again in alphabetic order. Here readers will find detailed information on a company's strengths and weaknesses: a five-year summary of factors impacting Weiss Safety Rating plus graphs or indexes further illuminating Weiss' ratings. Following sections address Weiss's recommended companies, the recommended companies by state, all companies listed by rating, and companies that have either had an upgrade or downgraded rating since the last edition. An appendix provides a listing of state guarantee associations; risk-adjusted capital; and recent industry failures. *Weiss Ratings'* is highly recommended for insurance collections in special libraries, medium and large public libraries, and medium and large academic libraries.—**Dene L. Clark**

208.   **Weiss Ratings' Guide to Property and Casualty Insurers: A Quarterly Compilation of Insurance Company Ratings and Analyses. Spring 2013.** Millerton, N.Y., Grey House Publishing, 2013. 438p. $249.00pa. (single edition): $499.00pa. (4 quarterly editions). ISBN 13: 978-1-61925-036-9.

Weiss Ratings' Guide to Property and Casualty Insurers is, simply stated, a resource that purchasers of property and casualty insurance from a United States company may consult to assure themselves that a potential insurance carrier is financially sound. The company's rigorous rating standards are designed to show whether an insurer can deal with severe economic adversity and its quarterly publication assures timely reporting. Weiss' rating scale (A to F) is designed for simplicity and its meaning is readily apparent to the general public. Each quarterly publication consists of several sections. Section 1, the "Index of Companies," is sorted alphabetically by company name. It includes a Weiss Safety Rating (A to F) for each company, followed by ratios, indexes, and dollar figures in over 20 different categories. The safety ratings are assigned by analysts who synthesize hundreds of factors into five indexes. The introduction describes the makeup of these indexes. The reader will find a bullet next to the names of the largest companies. These carriers appear in section 2, again in alphabetic order. Here readers will find detailed information on a company's strengths and weaknesses: a five-year summary of factors impacting Weiss Safety Rating plus graphs or indexes further illuminating Weiss' ratings. Following sections address Weiss's recommended companies, the recommended companies by state, all companies listed by rating, and companies that have either had an upgrade or downgraded rating since the last edition. An appendix provides a listing of state guarantee associations; risk-adjusted capital; and recent industry failures. *Weiss Ratings'* is highly recommended for insurance collections in special libraries, medium and large public libraries, and medium and large academic libraries. [R: LJ, 1 June 02, p. 134]—**Dene L. Clark**

International Business

General Works

Catalogs and Collections

209. **IBISWorld. http://www.ibisworld.com.** [Website]. $8,000 (annual subscription). Date reviewed: 2013.

IBISWorld is a good source for market research and industry analysis. The reports are lengthy, use a clear narrative style with many statistical tables and charts, and are updated on a predictable schedule. All reports share a standardized format so that readers can easily compare industries. IBISWorld covers performance and outlook, industry life cycles, products and markets, competitive landscape, and operating conditions. However, the reports include mostly aggregated discussion of consumer demographics and do not include psychographics or segmentation.

IBISWorld systematically analyzes more than 750 industry sectors across the whole spectrum of the economy. This breadth of coverage is invaluable in settings where students' business plans and marketing papers are driven by innovation, green business, or the latest extreme sports craze. With coverage of such topics as "party rentals," "wind power," or "swimming pool construction," IBISWorld fills a gap in available literature.

The database uses the NAICS codes as its primary navigational structure (searching by keywords and SIC Code numbers is also possible). The "drilldown" format makes the code system easy to understand, and thus supports business research skills. IBISWorld also offers an international option that includes China. Although other countries do not have individualized reports, the Global Industry Research series covers worldwide conditions, highlighting relevant countries and major companies.—**Wendy Diamond**

210. **Political Risk Services (PRS). http://www.prsgroup.com/.** [Website]. Price negotiated by site. Date reviewed: 2013.

PRS produces a number of well-known sources related to international business/political risk and risk forecasting. PRS offers a number of modules, including Country Reports, guides to 100 countries, each assessing potential political, financial, and economic risks to business investments and trade. Country Forecasts, published semiannually in April and October, provides a four-page summary of forecasts and data for each of the 100 countries monitored by PRS. Most institutions subscribe to PRS Online, which includes both Country Reports and Country Forecasts as well as the *Political Risk Letter*, a monthly newsletter covering key events and a summary of the 100 countries covered.—**Gary W. White**

Dictionaries and Encyclopedias

211. **Encyclopedia of Emerging Markets.** Stamford, Conn., Gale/Cengage Learning, 2013. 466p. maps. index. $549.00. ISBN 13: 978-1-4144-9923-9; 978-1-4144-9924-6 (e-book).

Offering rare insight into emerging industries in emerging markets across the globe, this title provides articles highlighting key elements of the rapid growth within these countries. In this first edition 33 countries have been featured, including China, India, Indonesia, Mexico, South Africa, and Vietnam. The essays for each country provide information on the current trends and long-term outlook for that country's growth, the structure of their market industry, and the history and development of their market. For each industry profile within the country highlighted the following is provided: population data, macroeconomic data, gross domestic product (GDP), Nominal GDP, inflation, and consumer price index. Also included are insight into socioeconomic or industrial factors that may have played a role in their emergence within the market, how they rank in the world and within their region, and major industries that comprise the majority of the market's overall GDP. Each essay concludes with a bibliography and a list for further reading. Maps, statistical charts, and tables are scattered throughout the text and add to the reader's understanding. The volume concludes with general, geographic, industrial classification, and ISIC coverage indexes.—**William C. Struning**

Directories

212. **Retail Trade International.** Chicago, Euromonitor International, 2012. 1010p. $785.00pa. ISBN 13: 978-1-84264-581-9.

This is a very comprehensive survey of world retail trade in 52 countries that will be useful to academic libraries supporting international business programs and specialized business libraries. Each country retail profile is lengthy and follows a format that includes: the identification of trends; a description of the operating environment; forecasted retail sales; and data for sectors such as private label, grocery, non-grocery, vending, home shopping, Internet retailing, store and loyalty cards, and direct selling. A particular strength of this survey is that in addition to merely reporting data, it also presents an analysis and evaluation of the data. Each country section has been written by a Euromonitor analyst with specific country and/or retail expertise. Retail statistics are provided for the period 2005 to 2017, and forecasted data is provided to 2018. Source information is included for each table so that additional research or follow-up is possible. Although recommended for many academic or specialized business libraries, the high purchase price will preclude all but the libraries with the greatest need or the best budgets from adding to their collections.—**Martha Cooney**

Handbooks and Yearbooks

213. **Doing Business 2013: Smaller Regulations for Small and Medium-Size Enterprises.** By the World Bank. Lanham, Md., Bernan Press, 2012. 264p. $35.00pa. ISBN 13: 978-0-82139-615-5.

This work is part of a series of titles that compare business regulations in 185 economies (Barbados and Malta are new to this volume). The 10th book in the series, *Doing Business 2013* focuses on new regulations affecting 11 areas of business activity: starting a business, dealing with construction permits, getting electricity, registering property, getting credit, protecting investors, paying taxes, trading across borders, enforcing contracts, closing a business, and employing workers. The book provides rankings of 185 countries to give the reader a clear indication of which countries are improving their regulations to encourage strong new business as well as which countries make it easy to do business across borders. Academic libraries with business and international business collections will find this volume useful.— **Lucy Heckman**

214.   **International Marketing Data and Statistics 2013.** Chicago, Euromonitor International, 2012. 700p. index. $475.00pa. ISBN 13: 978-1-8426-4588-8.

This oversized, well-organized tome provides over 200 tables on 25 data categories for 160 non-European countries. Tables detail demographics, economic trends, banking and finance, external trade, labor, industrial and energy resources and output, consumer expenditure, defense, retailing, advertising, consumer market size and prices, housing and household expenditures, health and living standards, communication, automobiles, transports, travel and tourism, and cultural indicators. Data are presented in easy-to-understand spreadsheet format covering 1980 to 2012, which requires three pages per table, although not all years are included for each table. The directory, selective as it may be, is quite useful for developing countries. In a glance you can compare population size by age, length of the average work week, consumer expenditure on hotels per month, and much more. An index gives better than average access to the often hard to find data. Sources are listed for each table, but, because of the multiyear nature of the tables, only the general title of the source is given. European data are not found in this volume, but it is in the complementary title, *European Marketing Data and Statistics* (49th ed., see entry 236).

The Europa World Year Book (54th ed.; see entry 34) and *The Statesman's Yearbook* (see ARBA 2013, entry 66) contain some of this data as well as national political and economic reviews, but provide it for each individual country, not in tables comparing the 160 potential reporting countries. This comparison of countries for a specific data element is a particular strength. This work is a very useful and strongly recommended tool for graduate and undergraduate libraries as well as those public libraries serving international business and marketing clientele.—**Patrick J. Brunet**

215.   **International Trade Statistics Yearbook 2011. Volume 1: Trade by Country.** New York, United Nations, 2013. 1v. (various paging). $115.00. ISBN 13: 978-92-11515-61-6.

216.   **International Trade Statistics Yearbook 2011. Volume 2: Trade by Commodity.** New York, United Nations, 2013. 1v. (various paging). $115.00. ISBN 13: 978-92-11615-61-6.

This two-volume statistical yearbook from the United Nations is the best source of international trade information available. The volumes are presented at different times of the year. Volume 1 contains 1,150-plus pages of tables with trade information from nearly 175 countries or areas. A major portion covers information on each country such as imports by principle countries, exports by principle countries, imports and exports by principle commodities of each country, imports by broad economic categories, and exports by industrial origin. In most cases, each of these categories covers the last five years. The work also has a number of tables that explain how to use this volume as well as a 71-page index that gives further information. Volume 2 contains 650-plus pages. Tables are proceeded by information on how to use this series as well. This area is subdivided into commodity groups and under this, various principle countries or areas are subdivided. In both volumes, compression data for larger categories in countries are also available. Most of the data in volume 2 represents the last five consecutive years. The paper quality and binding are above average and the font size has been improved from previous editions in order to make the manuscript more readable. This is an essential addition to any library that is interested in international trade.—**Herbert W. Ockerman**

217.   **Trade Policy Review: United States 2012.** Lanham, Md., Bernan Press, 2013. 185p. $90.00pa. ISBN 13: 978-1-59888-652-8. ISSN 1556-2050.

Mandated in the World Trade Organization agreements, Trade Policy Reviews are an effort to examine member countries trade and related policies at regular intervals. Any significant developments in local or global economics that may have impacted the trading system are also monitored in these guides.

Each review has detailed chapters that examine trade policies, describe policy-making institutions, and explain macroeconomic situations. Each volume begins with an introduction from the Secretariat with their observations of that country's trade policies. All WTO members are subject to review; however, the frequency of the review varies depending on the country's size and its impact on global economics. For those studying global economics and international trade, especially the impact of North American countries on global economics, these guides will be a useful. They are recommended for the economics collections in academic libraries.—**Shannon Graff Hysell**

218.   **Trade Profiles 2012.** By the World Trade Organization. New York, United Nations, 2012. 190p. $65.00pa. ISBN 13: 978-92-87038-46-3.

219.   **World Tariff Profiles 2012.** New York, United Nations, 2012. 220p. $65.00pa. ISBN 13: 978-92-87038-43-2.

Trade Profiles 2012, from the World Trade Organization, provides a breakdown of trade policy measures for WTO members as well as those seeking WTO membership. The information is organized by country and includes basic economic indicators (such as gross domestic product), trade policy indicators (e.g., tariffs), merchandise trade (arranged by broad categories), commercial trade, and industry property indicators. The format has been standardized across each country, which allows users to make easy comparisons between countries. This is a concise and easy-to-use guide to global trade among WTO members.

World Tariff Profiles 2012 lists the tariffs imposed by each WTO member on its imports. Alongside this information users will find an analysis of the market access conditions that it faces when compared to other major export markets. The information is organized by country and includes both summary tables as well. The standardized format allows for easy comparison between countries and sectors.

Students of international business and trade will find these two volumes easy to use and the information within is useful in understanding international markets and terms of business. Both volumes will be useful in academic libraries and business collections.—**William C. Struning**

220.   **World Economic Factbook 2013.** Chicago, Euromonitor International, 2012. 474p. $315.00pa. ISBN 13: 978-1-8425-4582-6.

The *Factbook* presents a selection of key economic, political, and demographic data in a standardized format for 207 countries, making it easy to compare countries on these variables. The data in the 2013 edition cover the year 2011 as well as some preceding years. Data sources include national statistical bureaus and multilateral agencies, such as the International Monetary Fund and the United Nations. For each country there is a two-page report. The first page is a textual summary providing the currency unit, the location and area of the country, the Head of State and the Head of Government, the Ruling Party, the Political Structure, the results of the last elections, a quick assessment of political risk, highlights of international disputes, a paragraph summarizing economic developments, a paragraph highlighting the main industries, and an overview of the energy situation.

The numerical data provided are primarily economic measures and population statistics. Economic data include the rate of inflation, the U.S. dollar exchange rate, real GDP growth, GDP in U.S. dollars and the home currency, total and per capita consumption, exports and imports, and tourism receipts and spending. There is also a table listing major trading partners with percentage share of exports and imports and value in U.S. dollars. Population data includes total population, population density, population by age groups, total male and female population, urban population, birth and death rates, male and female life expectancy, infant mortality, and number of households. After a brief introduction that explains the content and layout of the reference work, the first section contains maps of the continents with outlines for individual countries and their capitals. Section 2 contains comparative world rankings with separate tables for rankings by area, population, and economic measures.

Although the price of the volume has gone down considerably (down to $315 from the $475 price tag of the 2011 edition), users may wish to check some of the excellent authoritative sources of data available for free on the Internet such as the CIA's *The World Factbook* (http://www.cia.gov/cia/publications/factbook/) and the *World Development Report* (http://econ.worldbank.org/wdr/).—**Peter Zachary McKay**

221. **World Retail Data and Statistics 2014.** 8th ed. Chicago, Euromonitor International, 2013. 296p. $475.00. ISBN 13: 978-1-84264-622-9; 978-1-84264-631-1 (e-book).

This is a handbook of statistical information on retail trade worldwide for 2007 to 2012. There is a companion volume, *Retail Trade International* (Euromonitor, 2012). In the first two sections summary data on socioeconomic parameters and on world retailing trends are given. Data are not included for all 52 countries in all of the tables. The third section has specifics on world retail rankings on such topics as: grocery retail sales growth at constant prices 2007-2012, number of retail outlets per million inhabitants 2012, and total retail sales per capita 2012. Section 4 focuses specifically on grocery retailers, while section 5 provides statistics for specific countries (organized alphabetically). A variety of types of stores have been included, such as chain store, discount superstore, home shopping, and cooperatives. The data come from government and nongovernment sources. Currency values are given in U.S. dollars. While the publisher has tried to check accuracy and standardize the date, care is urged when using the information. Cross-country comparisons can be difficult. For those interested in retailing, this could be a convenient source of data. It could be a main source or supplement what is known from other sources.—**J. E. Weaver**

222. **World Trade Organization Dispute Settlement Decisions: Bernan's Annotated Reporter.** Jackson C. Pai, Mark Nguyen, and Bryan Cave, eds. Lanham, Md., Bernan Press, 2014. 158p. index. $175.00. ISBN 13: 978-1-59888-651-1.

223. **World Trade Organization Dispute Settlement Decisions. Volume 95: 17 July 2008-27-August 2008.** Lanham, Md., Bernan Press, 2013. 1170p. $175.00. ISBN 13: 978-1-59888-590-3. ISSN 1534-7559.

224. **World Trade Organization Dispute Settlement Decisions. Volume 96: 29 August 2008 - 4 September 2008.** Jackson C. Pai and Mark Nguyen, eds. Lanham, Md., Bernan Press, 2013. 332p. $175.00. ISBN 13: 978-1-59888-649-8. ISSN 1534-7559.

225. **World Trade Organization Dispute Settlement Decisions: Volume 97: Decisions Reported 1 October 2008 - 16 October 2008.** Jackson C. Pai, Mark Nguyen, and Bryan Cave, eds. Lanham, Md., Bernan Press, 2013. 1063p. $175.00. ISBN 13: 978-1-59888-650-4. ISSN 1534-7559.

226. **World Trade Organization Dispute Settlement Decisions. Volume 98.** Jackson C. Pai and Mark Nguyen, eds. Lanham, Md., Bernan Press, 2013. 1007p. $175.00. ISBN 13: 978-1-59888-651-1. ISSN 1534-7559.

These books are an important reference source for a fairly small set of the population. They are produced by the exclusive publisher of the World Trade Organization (WTO). Other volumes will cover later cases. Most of the book gives detailed information on nine cases. After a two-page summary of the complainant, respondent, third parties, decision date, procedural history, conclusion, and annotations, the report of the panel is given. The specific reports vary but generally include factual aspects of the case, the main arguments, submissions by interested parties, interim review findings, conclusions, issues raised in appeal, treaty interpretation, and article interpretation, among other items. The language is very technical and detailed. There are four tables that contain an overview of dispute settlement activity, countries involved in disputes, treaty provisions interpreted, and Basic Instruments and Selected Documents (BISD) and dispute references (by case). An index is provided. The resolution of disputes by the WTO has far-reaching implications, both political and economic. Numerous businesses and industries will be affected by the outcomes. It is also important information for scholars. Although these works of the WTO will affect everyone, this level of detail on the work of the organization will not be desired by many.—**J. E. Weaver**

227. **World Trade Organization International Trade Statistics 2012.** By the World Trade Organization. New York, United Nations, 2012. 250p. $65.00pa. ISBN 13: 978-92-87038-40-1.

Designed with researchers, policy makers, and those interested in international trade in mind, this yearbook from the World Trade Organization (WTO) provides an annual overview of the latest developments in world trade. It includes detailed statistics on trade in commercial services as well as in merchandise trade. The work includes more than 100 tables that breakdown all aspects of trade among WTO members. The charts and maps that accompany the statistical tables highlight the latest developments in world trade over the past year. This work continues to be a valuable addition to large academic libraries with international trade collections.—**ARBA Staff Reviewer**

Africa

228. **African Statistical Yearbook 2012.** New York, United Nations, 2013. 352p. $65.00pa. ISBN 13: 978-92-10251-68-6.

This respected annual offers a wide range of demographic, commercial, and socioeconomic statistics for the countries of Africa. The data in this issue of this book are for the years 2003-2011. Data have been accumulated through a collaborative effort of major African regional organizations in order to promote wider use of country data, reduce costs, and improve the availability and quality of the data in order to monitor and create more economic and social initiatives on the continent. It is one of the few sources to seriously attempt to compile data from many of the nations. Supplementary matter includes a very useful explanation of each data category, a list of principal sources for each country, a list of conversion factors, and a collected data summary for the entire region. There is really no title that compares as an overview of the region and the price is quite reasonable. To get more detailed statistics, one would have to go into national publications. As with most UN publications, no index is provided. This work is strongly recommended for graduate international relations and area studies program.—**Patrick J. Brunet**

229. **Economic Report on Africa 2012: Unleashing Africa's Potential as a Pole of Global Growth.** New York, United Nations, 2012. 250p. $25.00pa. ISBN 13: 978-92-11251-18-0.

First printed in September 2012, the *Economic Report on Africa 2012* is the first of its kind, jointly produced by the African Union Commission and the United Nations Economic Commission for Africa. This work assesses long-term trends in Africa's growth, looks at factors behind recent growth momentum, and addresses key challenges to growth in the future. With close to 50 countries in Africa, it is often useful to work with subsets of countries, such as North Africa and Sub-Saharan Africa; North Africa, East Africa, West Africa, Central Africa, and Southern Africa; and oil exporting countries and oil importing countries. They have different conditions and problems.

The first part of the book discusses recent economic and social developments as well as some current and emerging development issues in Africa. The goal of this publication is to facilitate discussion on policy directions and actions at national and regional levels that can help African realize its growth potential. The second section emphasizes the subtitle of the report, *Unleashing Africa's Potential as a Pole of Global Growth*, with a discussion of how to best address constraints and unlock the potential of the continent to create new growth nationally and internationally. The report, with its data and graphs, provides a good idea how concerned, educated people in Africa see their past performance and prospects for the near future.—**J. E. Weaver**

230.   **Trade Policy Review: Cote d'Ivoire, Guinea-Bissau, and Togo 2012.** Lanham, Md., Bernan Press, 2013. 374p. $90.00pa. ISBN 13: 978-1-59888-604-7. ISSN 1556-2050.

231.   **Trade Policy Review: East African Community 2012.** Lanham, Md., Bernan Press, 2013. 655p. $90.00pa. ISBN 13: 978-1-59888-661-0. ISSN 1556-2050.

Mandated in the World Trade Organization agreements, Trade Policy Reviews are an effort to examine member countries trade and related policies at regular intervals. Any significant developments in local or global economics that may have impacted the trading system are also monitored in these guides. Each review has detailed chapters that examine trade policies, describe policy-making institutions, and explain macroeconomic situations. Each volume begins with an introduction from the Secretariat with their observations of that country's trade policies. All WTO members are subject to review; however, the frequency of the review varies depending on the country's size and its impact on global economics. For those studying global economics and international trade, especially the impact of African countries on global economics, these guides will be a useful. They are recommended for the economics collections in academic libraries.—**Shannon Graff Hysell**

Asia

232.   **Statistical Yearbook for Asia and the Pacific 2012.** New York, United Nations, 2013. 308p. $95.00pa. ISBN 13: 978-92-11206-52-4.

This respected annual offers a wide range of demographic, commercial, and socioeconomic statistics for 58 countries in Asia, Australasia, and Oceania ranging from Armenia in the west to the Cook Islands in the Pacific and from the Russian Federation in the north (including many former Soviet Republics) to Australia in the south. Approximately 675 data elements are grouped under the topics of agriculture, fisheries, forestry, industry, energy, transport, communications, external trade, finance, education, and health, and displayed in a grid for the years 2000-2011. With countries as small as Nauru and closed as Myanmar or North Korea, the amount of coverage ranges widely. Still, it is one of the few sources to seriously attempt to compile data from many of the nations. Supplementary matter includes a very useful explanation of each data category, a list of principal sources for each country, a list of conversion factors, and a collected data summary for the entire ESCAP (Economic and Social Commission for Asia and the Pacific) region. There is really no title that compares as an overview of the region and the price is quite reasonable. To get more detailed statistics, one would have to go into national publications. As with most UN publications, no index is provided. This work is strongly recommended for graduate international relations and area studies program.—**Patrick J. Brunet**

233.   **Trade Policy Review: Bangladesh 2012.** Lanham, Md., Bernan Press, 2013. 142p. $90.00pa. ISBN 13: 978-1-59888-619-1.

234.   **Trade Policy Review: Japan 2013.** Lanham, Md., Bernan Press, 2013. 192p. $90.00pa. ISBN 13: 978-1-59888-664-1. ISSN 1556-2050.

235.   **Trade Policy Review: Republic of Korea 2012.** Lanham, Md., Bernan Press, 2013. 223p. $90.00pa. ISBN 13: 978-1-59888-612-2. ISSN 1556-2050.

Mandated in the World Trade Organization agreements, Trade Policy Reviews are an effort to examine member countries trade and related policies at regular intervals. Any significant developments in local or global economics that may have impacted the trading system are also monitored in these guides. Each review has detailed chapters that examine trade policies, describe policy-making institutions, and explain macroeconomic situations. Each volume begins with an introduction from the Secretariat with their observations of that country's trade policies. All WTO members are subject to review; however, the frequency of the review varies depending on the country's size and its impact on global economics. For those studying global economics and international trade, especially the impact of Asian countries on global economics, these guides will be a useful. They are recommended for the economics collections in academic libraries.—**Shannon Graff Hysell**

Europe

236.   **European Marketing Data and Statistics 2014.** 49th ed. Chicago, Euromonitor International, 2014. 405p. $475.00. ISBN 13: 978-1-84264-619-9; 978-1-84264-629-8 (e-book).

The 49th edition of *European Marketing Data and Statistics*, a comprehensive annual statistical yearbook of business and marketing information, continues to be a valuable and unique resource for those studying and working in international business, and for those seeking more general international economic, social, and demographic data. The book provides data on 24 major subject areas and is especially useful for those looking for consumer expenditure and consumption data on a broad array of specific services and products, much of which is not available for free on the Internet. It contains comparable demographic, economic, and marketing data for 45 European countries, and covers such subjects as health, media, leisure, home ownership, external trade, and population. It has many uses, one of which would be the ability to compare advertising expenditure by medium, annual disposable income, government expenditure on health, and more. An excellent table of contents and index provide easy access to all data sets (as current as 2012, and some as far back as 1977), and a listing of the major international and country-specific organizations that collect and disseminate statistical data provides a wealth of additional resources for the researcher. This is a highly recommended source for academic libraries with programs in international business and for large public libraries serving patrons engaged in or seeking to become involved in international trade.—**Martha Cooney**

237.   **Trade Policy Review: Iceland 2013.** Lanham, Md., Bernan Press, 2013. 106p. $90.00pa. ISBN 13: 978-1-59888-642-9. ISSN 1556-2050.

238.   **Trade Policy Review: Norway 2013.** Lanham, Md., Bernan Press, 2013. 142p. $90.00pa. ISBN 13: 978-1-59888-616-0. ISSN 1556-2050.

Mandated in the World Trade Organization agreements, Trade Policy Reviews are an effort to examine member countries trade and related policies at regular intervals. Any significant developments in local or global economics that may have impacted the trading system are also monitored in these guides. Each review has detailed chapters that examine trade policies, describe policy-making institutions, and explain macroeconomic situations. Each volume begins with an introduction from the Secretariat with their observations of that country's trade policies. All WTO members are subject to review; however, the frequency of the review varies depending on the country's size and its impact on global economics. For those studying global economics and international trade, especially the impact of European countries on global economics, these guides will be a useful. They are recommended for the economics collections in academic libraries.—**Shannon Graff Hysell**

Latin America

239.   **Economic Survey of Latin America and the Caribbean, 2010-2011.** Compiled by the Economic Development Division of the Economic Commission for Latin America and the Caribbean. New York, United Nations, 2013. 156p. $50.00. ISBN 13: 978-92-1-22106-50. ISSN 0257-2184.

This annual survey that reviews regional economic conditions and reports the economic performance of Latin American countries for 2011 and early 2012 remains an essential reference work for those analyzing regional economies. The work assesses the economic policies within this region and discusses the adverse economic factors at play, including increased fuel prices and spiraling food market prices. It tracks investment in this region and asses the challenges this region faces in the international trade market. The work concludes with a bibliography and a statistical annex that provides statistics for all countries in such areas as unemployment and underemployment, external debt, average wages, government fiscal expenditure, and government tax burden, just to name a few. While there is no index, the table of contents and list of illustrations is detailed enough for anyone. As an essential tool for achieving a broad understanding of the regional and global economies, this annual is recommended for academic libraries, particularly those serving scholars in regional studies and international business programs.—**Shannon Graff Hysell**

240.   **Trade Policy Review: Argentina 2013.** Lanham, Md., Bernan Press, 2014. 264p. $90.00pa. ISBN 13: 978-1-69888-671-9.

241.   **Trade Policy Review: Nicaragua 2012.** Lanham, Md., Bernan Press, 2013. 167p. $90.00pa. ISBN 13: 978-1-59888-655-9. ISSN 1556-2050.

Mandated in the World Trade Organization agreements, Trade Policy Reviews are an effort to examine member countries trade and related policies at regular intervals. Any significant developments in local or global economics that may have impacted the trading system are also monitored in these guides. Each review has detailed chapters that examine trade policies, describe policy-making institutions, and explain macroeconomic situations. Each volume begins with an introduction from the Secretariat with their observations of that country's trade policies. All WTO members are subject to review; however, the frequency of the review varies depending on the country's size and its impact on global economics. For those studying global economics and international trade, especially the impact of Central and Latin American countries on global economics, these guides will be a useful. They are recommended for the economics collections in academic libraries.—**Shannon Graff Hysell**

Middle East

242.   **Consumer Middle East and North Africa 2014.** 7th ed. Chicago, Euromonitor International, 2013. 360p. $600.00pa. ISBN 13: 978-1-84264-617-5; 978-1-84264-626-7 (e-book).

This thick paperback is primarily composed of tables concerning information on the Middle East and Northern Africa. The work includes over sections on this region of the world, regional marketing perimeters, and consumer markets. It also covers demographics, economic indicators, standards of living, household characteristics, consumer expenditures, and service industries—including consumer markets broken down into 20 to 30 categories. The following sections cover each individual country and their consumer markets, again broken down into numerous categories.

Tables include economic growth and prospects and regional marketing perimeters, including demographics, economic indicators, standard of living, household characteristics, advertising and media access, retail distribution, consumer expenditures, and service industries. Information on consumer markets is broken down by several categories, such as food, pet food and pet care products, drinks, tobacco, household cleaning products, health care, disposable paper products, cosmetics and toiletries, leisure goods, and automobiles. The binding, paper, and print quality are average and the font size is small but adequate for its purpose. This manuscript contains a massive quantity of information on an area where sources are limited. It should be in all libraries that are considered experts in international perspective, and particularly the Middle East and North Africa.—**Herbert W. Ockerman**

243.　**Trade Policy Review: Israel 2012.** Lanham, Md., Bernan Press, 2013. 126p. $90.00pa. ISBN 13: 978-1-59888-658-0. ISSN 1556-2050.

Mandated in the World Trade Organization agreements, Trade Policy Reviews are an effort to examine member countries trade and related policies at regular intervals. Any significant developments in local or global economics that may have impacted the trading system are also monitored in these guides. Each review has detailed chapters that examine trade policies, describe policy-making institutions, and explain macroeconomic situations. Each volume begins with an introduction from the Secretariat with their observations of that country's trade policies. All WTO members are subject to review; however, the frequency of the review varies depending on the country's size and its impact on global economics. For those studying global economics and international trade, especially the impact of Middle Eastern countries on global economics, these guides will be a useful. They are recommended for the economics collections in academic libraries.—**Shannon Graff Hysell**

Labor

General Works

Catalogs and Collections

244.　**Career Cruising. http://www.careercrusing.com/.** [Website]. Price negotiated by site. Date reviewed: 2014.

Many of the materials located on this site can be found in other free online sources. However, this site pulls the information together in an integrated, seamless system. *Career Cruising* provides students with interest and skills assessments, occupational profiles, college and university information, and financial aid materials in one easy-to-use site. Students can use the site to build an individual portfolio of skills assessments, create a personalized high school plan, document activities and awards, do school searches, and store SAT/ACT scores, essays, and reference letters. Students can create documents, such as résumés and cover letters. The site also provides interview skills information. Career profiles include video clips with individuals who work in the specific occupations, and technical school and university profiles provide links to the school Websites. The site is easy to navigate and available in Spanish. It includes a career advisor management system which schools and guidance staff can use to track student career preparation, suggest high school scheduling options, and alert students to opportunities such as campus visits. This site would be an extremely useful tool for high school students and their advisors as they prepare for their future education and work careers.—**ARBA Staff Reviewer**

Dictionaries and Encyclopedias

245.　Weir, Robert E. **Workers in America: A Historical Encyclopedia.** Santa Barbara, Calif., ABC-CLIO, 2013. 2v. index. $189.00/set. ISBN 13: 978-1-59884-718-5; 978-1-59884-719-2 (e-book).

The author of *Workers in America* acknowledges the difficulty of creating discrete encyclopedia entries for a topic that is interdisciplinary and interconnected between people, movements, and concepts. To capture these connections, the author uses bold type within the text of an entry to designate the inclusion of a separate entry for that term, concept, person, movement, or event rather than using a *see also* note at the end of each entry to indicate those connections. The author's intention is to encourage the reader to cross-reference to the related bold type topic after reading through the text of the essay. This encyclopedia is arranged in two volumes (A to L and M to Y) with *see* (instead) entries for common synonymous terms included in the alphabetic list of entries. Each entry essay is, on average, two to four pages in length; a few are shorter. Although the essays are relatively short, they are well written and concise, and are packed with information. Each entry is followed by a short list of "Suggested Reading" selected for availability and readability by the target audience of nonspecialists. Volume 2 concludes with a combined person, title, subject index. A chronology of workers in America, beginning with the first indentured servants sent to North America in 1607 and ending with the signing into law of health care reform in 2009, is found after the volume 2 entries. This work is intended to be a source for first reference rather than for more advanced research. It is suggested for high school, public, and undergraduate academic libraries.—**Polly D. Boruff-Jones**

Handbooks and Yearbooks

246.   Birkel, Damian. **The Job Search Checklist.** New York, AMACOM/American Management Association, 2013. 264p. index. $16.00pa. ISBN 13: 978-0-8144-3291-4.

Being laid off is a difficult event, both economically and emotionally. The purpose of this book is to guide people who have been laid off through the upheaval and into a new job. Seven steps are laid out, with accompanying checklists to follow from the lay-off to re-employment. One section of the book is devoted to each step.

The author encourages employees to be aware of the possibility of layoffs in their workplaces and offers examples of what warning signs to look for. Section 1 covers warning signs and the emotional stages laid off people go through (not unlike the Kubler-Ross 5 stages of grief). Section 2 covers getting ready to search for a new job—emotional recovery, assessing job skills, gathering information, and time management. Section 3 offers exercises to help focus job skills and job options, and suggestions about building a career plan. Section 4 discusses how to create the best résumé and how to use the Internet to one's advantage. Section 5 discusses the importance of networking and how to build a network. Section 6 gives effective interviewing tips. Section 7 recommends the best strategies for success during the first six months in a new job. Each chapter in a section has two checklists: recommended steps-to-take (at the beginning of the chapter); and a measure-your-progress chart (at the end of each chapter). Endnotes offer citations to additional information on the topics covered. An index is included.

The author of this work is a nationally certified career counselor. He is the founder of Professionals in Transition Support Group Inc. This book offers a framework for the unemployed. It is practical and addresses many of the issues the unexpectedly unemployed may face. While it is pitched to "professional" level job seekers, anyone seeking employment will find solid advice in this book. This title is recommended.—**Joanna M. Burkhardt**

247.   Derks, Scott. **Working Americans 1880-2012. Volume XIII: Educators & Education.** Millerton, N.Y., Grey House Publishing, 2013. 549p. illus. index. $150.00. ISBN 13: 978-1-59237-877-7; 978-1-59237-984-2 (e-book).

This volume, covering 1880 to 2010, focuses on a diverse group of Americans that have educated America's children for over a century in very diverse ways, from one-room school houses to the most innovative schools. Arranged chronologically by decade, this volume includes three profiles per chapter for a total of some 36 biographical profiles as well as 12 news features. By arranging the people chronologically rather than alphabetically users can see how education changed over time and how society changed and innovations built upon each other. Each decade chapter begins with an introduction that discusses the social concerns, economics, and politics of the time. Included are historical snapshots of major milestones of the decade. The news features highlight important events or innovations in education that exemplify that era; for example, the 1920s focuses on the ability of more Americans to go to college, the 1930s chapter discusses the challenges to education in the south, and the 1990s chapter has a feature article on the need to help Hispanics find college opportunities. An example of those profiled within this volume are Dwight Heald Perkins, an architect of school buildings (1909); Emily Strandhope, kindergarten teacher of immigrants (1916); Laura Hargrove, school librarian (1933); Septima Clark, teacher fired for her affiliation with the NAACP (1961); and Viola Chadusky, a vocal skeptic of standardized testing (1999).

Like other volumes in the series, this volume was compiled from both primary and secondary sources, including personal diaries, family histories, government statistics, news features, and commercial advertisements. The text is easy to read and includes many bulleted lists, sidebars, and photographs that add interest.

This volume serves as an outstanding overview of how the U.S. educational system has evolved over time and the innovative techniques it has used and hurdles it has overcome. The author has based his profiles on real people and events, utilizing diaries, letters, biographies, interviews, and magazine articles. This work is highly recommended for school libraries from middle school through high school as well as college libraries from community college through graduate school. It should also be found in public libraries of every size.—**Dene L. Clark**

248.   **Employment, Hours, and Earnings, 2013: States and Areas.** 8th ed. Grewnavere W. Dunn, ed. Lanham, Md., Bernan Press, 2014. 610p. $105.00pa.; $104.99 (e-book). ISBN 13: 978-1-59888-637-5; 978-1-59888-638-2 (e-book).

Based on data from the Bureau of Labor Statistics, this handbook is a special edition to the *Handbook of United States Labor Statistics: Employment, Earnings, Prices, Productivity and Other Labor Data* (16th ed.; see entry 251). It provides estimates on employment, hours, and earnings for each of the 50 states and the District of Columbia. The work is filled with some 300 charts and tables that succinctly provides employment data for a variety of industries, organized by month and year for 1990 and from 2002 to 2012. Each state has an introductory statement that provides information on noteworthy trends in population, civilian labor force estimates, industry growth, and unemployment rates. Seventy-five of the largest metropolitan areas are ranked as well. A very useful addition to this volume are the technical notes that are included with charts and tables that explain important facts about the data, including sources, definitions, and significant changes. This new edition has detailed statistical data on mass layoff events, by state, from 2001-2012. This work can be used in a variety of circumstances, both at the academic level and at the public level. Local and state governments will find much information of use here for public policy updates and businesses could use this resource to select the best states to expand their efforts. It would be a worthwhile addition to both academic and public libraries.—**Joanna M. Burkhardt**

249.   **Global Employment Trends 2013: Recovering from a Second Jobs Dip.** By International Labour Organization. Lanham, Md., Bernan Press, 2013. 140p. $35.00pa. ISBN 13: 978-92-21266-55-6.

250.   **Global Wage Report 2012/2013.** By International Labour Organization. Lanham, Md., Bernan Press, 2012. 122p. $50.00pa. ISBN 13: 978-92-21262-36-7.

These two volumes serve to highlight the employment trends and wage trends in the international market place. The economic recession the world has been experiencing has caused concern in most nations and these titles reflect the reasons for concern in the labor market and what future prospects look like today.

Global Employment Trends 2013 focuses on the high unemployment rate in industrial nations, which is at the root of the economic recession. Investments and employment rates have not shown significant signs of recovery in spite of historically low interest rates. This is also affecting the developing world where there is a decrease in productivity, which is affecting wages and disposable incomes. This book highlights the economic reasons behind these trends.

Global Wage Report 2012/2013 provides economists and scholars with the latest trends in wage statistics and wage policies from around the world. Statistical charts are provided to illustrate how countries vary in the wages they pay prospective workers. The work also provides in-depth essays on hot topics in wage policies, including minimum wage fixing and collective bargaining and in-work benefits. The report links to a statistical appendix that can be accessed through the International Labour Organization Website so that researchers can create their own analyses.—**ARBA Staff Reviewer**

251.   **Handbook of U.S. Labor Statistics, 2013: Employment, Earnings, Prices, Productivity, and Other Labor Data.** 16th ed. Mary Meghan Ryan, ed. Lanham, Md., Bernan Press, 2013. 515p. index. $165.00; $164.99 (e-book). ISBN 13: 978-1-59888-610-8; 978-1-59888-611-5 (e-book).

Bernan Associates, a noted publisher of federal government agencies reports, has been publishing this title since 1997; prior to this it was published by the U.S. Bureau of Labor Statistics. This 16th edition updates the content of approximately 200 statistical tables contained in previous editions, provides some new features, and has included some tables on income that were derived from the Census Bureau. This work is more that just statistical tables, included are some short articles that reflect events that have impacted the economy impacted statistical data. Additionally, before each set of tables is an article that summarizes what the following tables contain and provide some information regarding the methodology used, relevant definitions, and where more current information can be found. The index provides a quick way to get to specific tables without looking at all the tables in a chapter. Depending on the topic, many tables provide information for 25 years, others for 10 years and some for fewer years because they are new categories of statistics.

This is a one-stop indispensable guide to statistics on a wide variety of labor data, such as employment, productivity, prices, and earnings. While it is true much of this information is available on the Bureau of Labor Statistics Website, it is often easier to find the needed tables by using this book. This very useful compilation of statistics and should be acquired by most libraries with strong business and economic collections and those agencies who deal with labor data at least every other year, but preferably every year.—**Judith J. Field**

252.   Mishel, Lawrence, Josh Bivens, Elise Gould, and Heidi Shierholz. **The State of Working America.** Ithaca, N.Y., Cornell University Press, 2013. 505p. index. $24.95pa. ISBN 13: 978-0-8014-7855-0.

The 12th edition of this work was authored and compiled by member of the Economic Policy Institute (EPI). EPI is a nonprofit, nonpartisan think tank, founded in 1986. They focus "on the economic condition of low- and middle-income Americans and their families" (p. 504). The authors are credentialed and experienced economists. In this work the authors document changes in income, taxes, wages, employment, wealth, and poverty over a long period of time. The data are presented in numerous tables and charts with accompanying explanations. The source for the information for each table is cited.

The first chapter provides an overview of the economic well being of the middle class in the United States. The authors conclude from the data presented that there have been an alarming down-turn for the middle class during the past decade. They predict that the coming decade holds more of the same, and blame economic policies that favor the wealthy almost exclusively.

The six chapters that follow provide detailed information on income, mobility, wages, jobs, wealth, and poverty. Many indicators show substantial and growing inequalities between the middle class and the wealthy that have been underway for decades. The final chapter details the almost hopeless situation of those families who live in poverty. Appendix A explains the income measurements used and appendix B explains the wage measurements used. An index and bibliography complete the volume.

As in the previous edition (2008-2009) this unbiased presentation of the data puts the responsibility for the dire condition of the middle-class squarely on the federal economic policies that favor the wealthy. This work is highly recommended for all reference collections.—**Joanna M. Burkhardt**

253.   **Race and Employment in America 2013.** Deirdre A. Gaquin and Gwenavere W. Dunn, eds. Lanham, Md., Bernan Press, 2014. 581p. index. $100.00pa.; $99.99 (e-book). ISBN 13: 978-1-59888-680-1; 978-1-59888-681-8 (e-book).

Race and Employment in America adds to Bernan Press's collection of statistical handbooks on employment and labor in the United States. The first edition of this volume pulls statistical data from the Census Bureau's Equal Employment Opportunity tabulation and is designed to highlight diversity in the labor force and can be used to compare race, ethnicity, and gender composition in the U.S. workforce. Researchers can narrow their findings by geography and by job category. The work includes listings of job categories for all states and metropolitan areas and provides up-to-date statistics on employment from 2006-2010. There are occupational profiles for each race (and Hispanic origin group), broken down into 15 occupations and highlighting the 10 most selected occupations of each sex and race. Educational attainment is also shown for age group and for occupation. This will be a useful resource for researchers and government officials needing current information on the state of the current job market and its trends over the past 10 years. This will be a useful resource for most academic and larger public libraries.— **William C. Struning**

254.   **Research Handbook on the Economics of Labor and Employment Law.** Cynthia L. Estlund and Michael L. Wachter, eds. Northhampton, Mass., Edward Elgar, 2013. 509p. index. $245.00. ISBN 13: 978-1-84980-101-0.

The *Research Handbook on the Economics of Labor and Employment Law* consists of a series of essays about traditional labor laws, the organization of unions, laws governing contracts and termination of employment, discrimination in employment, and how to remedy employment claims. All of the essay topics are varied and each contributor takes a different approach to his or her topic. The essays have been written from a broad range of perspectives: sociologists, organizational psychologists, policy advisors, economics, lawyers, and scholars. The goal of the volume is to explore what lessons we have learned from the past to predict what we can expect in the future of work and employment law. Many of the themes that we deal with today we have dealt with from the past; however, some, such as the need for a collective voice among employees, are new and need further exploration. This is an enlightening text on the subject of employment and work relations that will be useful for students in economics, specifically those studying employment law and labor economics.—**Lucy Heckman**

255.   **World Development Report 2013: Jobs.** Washington, D.C., World Bank, 2013. 300p. index. $60.00; $35.00pa. ISBN 13: 978-0-8213-9620-9; 978-0-8213-9575-2pa.

The annual *World Development Report* has won renown as a source for current information on developing economies. Each year's report has a theme with essays. Recent reports focused on equity and development. This year's theme reports on the hot topic of jobs, including the topics of entrepreneurship, job creation, and job training. Specifically this resource focuses on presenting essays that explore how public policy can change to better help society and government deal with today's changing economy and the need for countries to develop and grow their economies. This book has several key areas of focus. It looks at the area of entrepreneurship, asking whether or not it can be fostered or must people be born with it. It also questions whether the focus on formal higher education is more important than on-the-job training and skill building. And, finally, in a global economy, it questions the policies that support job creation in one country when it comes at the expense of jobs in other countries. The World Bank (http:// www.worldbank.org/) defines its mission as reducing global poverty and improving the standard of living in developing countries. It promotes these goals through lending and grants for economic development and by providing technical assistance.—**ARBA Staff Reviewer**

Career Guides

256.   **CareerOneStop. http://www.careeronestop.org/.** [Website]. Free. Date reviewed: 2013.

Sponsored by the U.S. Department of Labor, this excellent resource provides comprehensive, up-to-date, and reliable information on careers and job opportunities. The site is organized into six major areas: Explore Careers, Salary & Benefits, Education & Training, Job Search, Resumes & Interviews, and People & Places to Help. The home page also contains a link to a section titled Re-Employment Tools, which will be beneficial for those who have recently lost a job; this section also offers specific information on military transition and unemployment assistance following a major disaster. *CareerOneStop* is useful not only for students and job-seekers but for employers as well. Employers can post positions using a very sophisticated Job Description Writer. Two particular features of this site stand out: the comprehensive explore careers section, which encourages viewers to take a step back and really think about their career options; and the links to the One-stop Career Centers, located in all 50 states, which provide job training referrals, career counseling, job listings, and similar employment-related services. One can download or print just about anything on the site, and navigation is quick and easy.

Other major job sites offer some sort of credible career guidance, but they tend to focus more on immediately pairing an inquirer with a job listing or college/university and do not provide crucial information and advice about the front end of the process and found on this site (e.g., spending time thinking about your career, your interests, and perhaps most important, whether your career interests are a real match with your skills). This Website would be very useful for undergraduate students as well as those who work with and advise them.—**ARBA Staff Reviewer**

257.   Friedman, Leonard H. **101 Careers in Healthcare Management.** New York, Springer Publishing, 2013. 332p. index. $25.00pa. ISBN 13: 978-0-82619-334-6.

This work provides job profiles in 101 healthcare management careers. The work will be useful to anyone considering work in one of these fast-growing fields field. Some of the jobs appearing here include academic, government, and clinical positions as well as careers in the private and corporate sectors.

The work begins with general chapters providing an overview of the field and then goes on to describe the details of the job, requirements (including high school, postsecondary training, certification, or other requirements), exploring career options, employers, how to start out, advancement, salary, work environment, and where to go for more information. Several real-life examples of individuals working in the field are provided. The work concludes with information on future trends in the health care management field and a sample job search strategy.

This work will be useful for those seeking to find in-depth information about what career options are available for those seeking meaningful employment in the healthcare management industry. It will be helpful to any career-related collection in guidance offices, academic libraries, and public libraries and is recommended. [R: Choice, June 13, p. 1804]—**Joanna M. Burkhardt**

Management

258.   Evenson, Renee. **Powerful Phrases for Dealing with Difficult People.** New York, AMACOM/ American Management Association, 2013. 226p. $10.95. ISBN 13: 978-0-8144-3298-3.

Renee Evenson, a small-business consultant, has provided a self-help book on dealing with difficult personalities, whether at work or in one's family circle. The book is divided into two parts. The first part deals with "Powerful Phrases + Actions = Successful Work Relationships" and the second part deals with "Effective Conflict Resolution = Strengthened Work Relationships." Each section begins with resolving conflict the wrong way, reasons why it does not work, then turns the situation around by providing phrases of understanding, apology, compromise, resolution, and reconciliation to coming to an understanding and stating the reasons these phrases work. Personal actions that come into play, such as body language, facial expressions, tone of voice, and assertiveness are discussed to provide a complete lesson on resolving problems. This is an all-in-one troubleshooting guide for solving conflict and defusing situations with co-workers, bosses, friends, and relatives. This one-volume book is highly recommended for public, academic, or personal library collections.—**Kay Stebbins Slattery**

259. **Free Management Library. http://www.managementhelp.org/.** [Website]. Free. Date reviewed: 2013.
     The Free Management Library provides easy-to-access, clutter-free, comprehensive resources regarding the leadership and management of yourself, other individuals, groups, and organizations. Content is relevant to most small- and medium-sized organizations. Over the past 10 years, the Library has grown to be one of the world's largest well-organized collections of these types of resources. Approximately 650 topics are included here, spanning 5,000 links. Topics include the most important practices to start, develop, operate, evaluate, and resolve problems in for-profit and nonprofit organizations. Each topic has additionally recommended books and related articles. Grouped alphabetically by subject, the E-Commerce collection is particularly noteworthy.—**Susan C. Awe**

260. **Handbook of Research on Negotiation.** Mara Olekalns and Wendi L. Adair, eds. Northhampton, Mass., Edward Elgar, 2013. 540p. index. $255.00. ISBN 13: 978-1-7810-0589-7.
     The *Handbook of Research on Negotiation* provides an in-depth and comprehensive review of research on negotiation. The contributions of some 37 researchers, largely from academia, are presented in 17 chapters, supplemented by introductory and concluding chapters by the editors The complexity inherent in the negotiating process makes presentation of research efforts challenging, but the editors have succeeded quite well by developing four perspectives within which contributions have been classified: individual process, social-psychological processes, communication processes, and complex negotiations. The book offers useful insights that could be helpful to researchers, instructors, and practitioners, although those involved in negotiating will not find a series of simple steps leading to winning negotiating procedures. The concluding chapter contains an interesting summary of opportunities and directions for further research. Each chapter is concluded by an extensive bibliography that enhances the utility of the book as a basic source of information relating to research on negotiation in a single volume.—**William C. Struning**

Marketing and Trade

Catalogs and Collections

261. **All About Internet Market Research and Marketing. http://www.allaboutmarketresearch. com/.** [Website]. Free. Date reviewed: 2013.
     This directory is a guide to outstanding tools, tips, resources, and services for eCommerce Internet Marketing Research. This well-organized site has areas listed across the top including Blog, Academic Market Research, Associations, Directories, Internet Growth, Library, e-Commerce, and Links. The Library has coaching-type articles on Search Engine Optimization, Internet Writing, Internet Online Advertising, and more. The Associations section has a length list of links to International Market

Research organizations. Internet Growth has a wealth of informative statistics. This site can be used to help business owners improve their online marketing efforts.—**Susan C. Awe**

262.   **Local Market Audience Analyst. http://www.srds.com/frontMatter/ips/lifestyle/index.html.** [Website]. SRDS Media Solutions, 2012. Price negotiated by site. Date reviewed: 2013.

Formerly the print edition of *Lifestyle Market Analyst* (which ceased publication in 2008), this database cross-tabulates demographic attributes such as age, gender, and income against those groups' likelihood to participate in a variety of activities (or, lifestyles). Lifestyles include anything from traveling for business to exercising, owning a dog, gardening, scuba diving, and more. All of the data are survey-based and then broken down by lifestyles and by geographic region and by demographic attributes. The goal in general is to help those in marketing and business entrepreneurship better understand target audiences, the behavior, and their lifestyles.—**ARBA Staff Reviewer**

263.   **MarketResearch.com. http://www.MarketResearch.com/.** [Website]. Price negotiated by site. Date reviewed: 2013.

MarketResearch.com is one of the leading providers of global market intelligence products and services. Presently it is offering more than 300,000 research publications from more than 700 top consulting and advisory firms. One of the attractions of this commercial Website is the ability to search the database at no charge, after free registration, and then buy information "by the slice." One is no longer obligated to purchase full reports but can select only the chapters or sections that are of interest and so cut costs. A full list of market research publishers, complete with a description of their activities and links to their Websites, is available from the MarketResearch.com site. The company also provides academic subscriptions at MarketResearch.com Academic (see entry 264).—**Rita W. Moss**

264.   **MarketResearch.com Academic. http://www.academic.marketresearch.com.** [Website]. Price negotiated by site. Date reviewed: 2013.

MarketResearch.com Academic (MRDC) is a premier source and the oldest market research service for academic libraries. Covering both major industries and niche markets, it aggregates reports from world-class researchers, including Packaged Facts (consumer goods), Kalorama Information (health sciences), Simba (media), and SBI (energy). Significantly, MRDC supports "green" curricula with extensive reports on sustainable technologies and renewable energy.

Full reports from MRDC are the most extensive and specialized available to the academic market. Written for corporate analysis, a typical report can be well over 100 pages and include forecasts, channel trends, demographics, psychographics, performance and challenges, manufacturing components technology, regulations, and competitor comparison. The reports are made available to libraries at the same time as they are released to the private market. Interestingly, the corporate price is transparent so students can understand the true cost of valuable business information. The attractive interface is arranged in topical categories like consumer goods, demographics, heavy industry, life science, technology and media, and more.

In an ideal world, academic libraries might want IBISWorld (http://www.ibisworld.com), Mintel (http://www.mintel.com), and MarketResearch.com Academic to provide coverage of the complete economy, detailed lifestyle analysis, environmental technology, and multipublisher scope. All are models of rigorous research, cogent writing, effective graphics, useable interfaces, and complete documentation. Considering budget limitations, most libraries will have to choose based on their curriculum and clientele. If their marketing projects are in the realm of entrepreneurship and small business, then perhaps IBISWorld with its coverage of all NAICS codes will be preferred. If the curriculum is focused on the disciplines of branding, advertising, new products, strategic innovation, and customer segmentation, Mintel Oxygen may be suitable. If the library needs interdisciplinary, comprehensive coverage of green energy, technology, health care, pharmaceuticals, and international strategies, then MarketResearch.com Academic might be ideal.—**ARBA Staff Reviewer**

265. **WebSite MarketingPlan. http://www.websitemarketingplan.com.** [Website]. Free. Date reviewed: 2013.

This large site contains a wealth of information for small businesses. A large assortment of articles and sample marketing plans are available as well as sample business plans, a newsletter, Internet marketing articles, marketing strategy articles, and more. Featured Directory Categories include articles grouped under Search Engine Marketing, Marketing Strategy, Marketing Plan, and Public Relations. Learn about the four seasons of public relations. Lengthy articles on advertising, using public relations for communicating to customers and finding new ones, and customer retention are outstanding. There are many commercial links here, but plenty of free help for the new entrepreneur can be found as well. Many sample business plans are also available. This site is especially helpful for those interested in e-commerce. Easy to navigate, this site will definitely help entrepreneurs and business owners develop a marketing plan that they can use.—**Susan C. Awe**

Dictionaries and Encyclopedias

266. **Encyclopedia of Major Marketing Strategies. Volume 3.** Matthew Miskelly, ed. Stamford, Conn., Gale/Cengage Learning, 2013. 431p. illus. index. $523.00. ISBN 13: 978-1-4144-9921-5; 978-1-4144-9922-1 (e-book).

Volume 3 of the *Encyclopedia of Major Marketing Strategies* profiles 100 outstanding marketing campaigns that appeared from 2010-2013. It continues the 974 summaries of twentieth-century campaigns that comprised the first and second volumes published in 1999 and 2007. Some of the marketing adds featured in this 3d volume include: Canon USA's "Long Live Imagination," Priceline.com's "The Priceline Negotiator Lives!", and Dos Equis's "Most Interesting Man in the World." Campaigns were selected on the basis of conceptual value or innovation, the significance of the brands involved or the firms that market them, and the resulting effectiveness of the campaigns in selling the promoted products or services. Profiles are presented alphabetically by sponsoring company, and each includes contact information (mail, telephone, fax, Internet), campaign summary, historical context, target market, competition, marketing strategy, success in achieving goals, and suggestions for further reading. Nearly 150 reproductions of advertisements and over 500 sidebars enhance and expand the presentations. Over 40 advisors and contributors provided input to the editor. A table of contents, foreword, introduction, and an extensive index ease the search for specific topics or aspects. This unique encyclopedia could serve as a valuable source of insights and trends, as well as a reference to successful marketing campaigns.— **William C. Struning**

Directories

267. **The Directory of Mail Order Catalogs, 2013.** 27th ed. Millerton, N.Y., Grey House Publishing, 2013. 789p. index. $250.00pa.; $550.00 (online database). ISBN 13: 978-1-59237-878-4.

The *The Directory of Mail Order Catalogs* contains nearly 10,000 listings. Since the 2007 edition this directory has been combined with the publisher's title *The Directory of Business to Business Catalogs*. Not much has changed in the format of the directory since the last edition. The same 43 product categories are retained (most with 2 or more subcategories), although a bit more information is provided in each company's profile. In the 2013 edition the publisher decided to list only print catalogs (no online catalogs), which resulted in fewer listings than normal. On the plus side, hundreds of new print catalogs were discovered and added to the directory.

Currently, most listings contain the following information: name of company, address, telephone number, fax number, e-mail address, Website, a one-line description of the product(s), president's name, credit cards accepted, catalog cost, catalog circulation, printing information, type of press, type of binding, mailing list information, how long the company has been in business, and general sales figures. Of course, not every company in the directory provides all of these pieces of information, but the overall amount of data have improved since the previous editions. An online edition of this directory is provided from the publisher as well. Interestingly, *The Directory of Mail Order Catalogs* and *Business to Business Catalogs* have not been combined in the online editions. They can be purchased separately, with *The Directory of Mail Order Catalogs* costing $550 for single-user access and with *Business to Business Catalogs* costing $325 for single-user access. The site can be searched by product category, geographic location, sales volume, catalog printing information, number of employees, and more.

This kind of directory not only provides specific information on hard-to-locate companies, but is also a lot of fun to browse through. There is something for everyone. This directory is primarily recommended for public libraries that support small business entrepreneurs, although other libraries may have an interest in this kind of information.—**Thomas A. Karel**

268. **Plunkett's Advertising & Branding Industry Almanac 2014.** Jack W. Plunkett, ed. Houston, Tex., Plunkett Research, 2014. 540p. $349.99pa. ISBN 13: 978-1-60879-733-2.

Designed for those researching the advertising and branding industry, this reference guide is especially intended to assist with market research, strategic planning, employment searches, contact or prospect list creation and financial research, and as a data resource for executives and students of all types. *Plunkett's Advertising & Branding Industry Almanac* is arranged as follows: a glossary of advertising and branding industry terms; a look at major trends, statistics, and directory of contacts (e.g., trade associations, government agencies) in the advertising and branding industry; and the Advertising 400 (a directory of companies). Highlighted information includes advertising agency consolidations and mergers, consumer audience trends and viewing habits, search engine paid placement, and trends in branding private-label merchandising.

The largest section in the book concerns the Advertising 400. The companies were chosen by the editors for their dominance in the many facets of the advertising and branding industry in which they operate and these companies are based in the United States, Canada, Europe, and Asia. Companies are ranked within their specific industry group and sales figures are listed. Each company entry contains name, industry group code, ranks within the company's industry group; URL; brands/divisions/affiliates; contacts; financials; locations; and special features. Companies are also listed within categories, including Index of Firms Noted as Hot Spots for Advancement for Women and Minorities.

This source can provide a first stop for major research projects or it can provide statistics and directory information for one-stop research use. It is recommended for faculty and students of business and libraries supporting a business curricula.—**Lucy Heckman**

Handbooks and Yearbooks

269. **Consumer Americas 2013: Assessing the Risks.** Chicago, Euromonitor International, 2012. 336p. $600.00. ISBN 13: 978-1-84264-584-0.

Consumer Americas presents a detailed statistical look at several hundred consumer products with data covering 2006 to 2011 and providing forecasts up to the year 2017. It covers such industries as food and drink to toys and household products. This is the place to find out what industries are prospering under current market conditions and which are suffering.

The title covers 14 countries: Argentina, Bolivia, Brazil, Canada, Chile, Colombia, Costa Rica, Ecuador, Guatemala, Mexico, Peru, Uruguay, the United States, and Venezuela. Key socioeconomic indicators, such as economic indicators, population, household characteristics, income, consumer expenditure, travel and tourism, and information technology and communications, help to put market trends into context and the tables are presented in a way that it is easy to make comparisons across the different countries and industries. This title can be used to understand consumer trends in the Americas as well as to find contact information for further research. It would be a useful source for tracking the fastest growing markets and identifying those that are static or on the decline. The price of this resource was recently reduced by the publisher to make it more affordable to more types of libraries. This source is recommended for collections in research libraries and to academic libraries supporting advanced degrees in business.—**Lucy Heckman**

270.   **World Consumer Income and Expenditure Data.** 14th ed. Chicago, Euromonitor International, 2013. 582p. $400.00. ISBN 13: 978-1-84264-612-0; 978-1-84264-633-5 (e-book).

World Consumer Income and Expenditure Data provides hard-to-find information on how much people around the globe earn and how they spend their money. The book focuses on per capita spending on major products (e.g., food, leisure, housing) as well as per capita income. Statistics are presented in easy-to-read tables that date from 1990-2012. This volume is a cumulation of two previously published titles: *World Consumer Spending* and *World Income Distribution*.

In all, 75 types of household goods and services are presented for 71 countries. Key socioeconomic indicators help put income and spending statistics in perspective for readers. Income statistics researched include: annual household income, tax and social security contributions, annual disposable income by gender, consumer expenditure, and consumer expenditures by commodity and by purpose.

This work would be useful for those needing data on the similarities and differences in income and expenditure data on an international basis. It would also be an excellent starting point for understanding global income and spending trends. This is an expensive title that is best suited for large academic libraries with business and international business collections.—**Kay Stebbins Slattery**

271.   **World Consumer Lifestyle Databook 2013.** 12th ed. Chicago, Euromonitor International, 2013. 700p. $475.00. ISBN 13: 978-1-84264-591-8; 978-1-84264-610-6 (e-book).

The *World Consumer Lifestyles Databook 2013* is a treasure trove of useful, highly accessible international statistics on the lifestyles of consumers in 76 countries, including the United States. The volume is arranged in four sections: rankings, cross-country comparisons, country data, and sources. The statistical data are presented in tabular form in the rankings, cross-country comparisons, and country data sections. The data provided include statistics related to population, health, labor, income, consumer expenditures, education, eating, drinking, smoking, and leisure habits, as well as communications and more. While there is a fair amount of duplication of data among these three statistical sections, this duplication provides the user with a number of access points and ways to utilize the data. The data included cover the period 1997 through 2012 (although not each year), and is presented in U.S. dollars. The many years covered allows users to understand how lifestyles have changed in the last few decades. The final section is especially useful for its listing of sources and contacts by international organizations, regional organizations, and national organizations listed by country. There is no index to this volume, but the table of contents and list of tables are quite good and provide for easy access to the data. This book is highly recommended for any academic library that supports courses in international business or international studies.—**Martha Cooney**

Real Estate

272.   **Plunkett's Real Estate & Construction Industry Almanac.** 2014 ed. Jack W. Plunkett, ed. Houston, Tex., Plunkett Research, 2014. 590p. $349.99pa. ISBN 13: 978-1-60879-736-3.

The real estate industry has changed dramatically over the past five years. Not only has it been hit hard by the housing bubble and the economic hardships of Americans, there have also been dramatic changes in the way people look for housing, with some 80-90 percent of potential home buyers researching the housing market themselves online before even consulting a real estate professional. *Plunkett's Real Estate & Construction Industry Almanac* is intended to provide an overview of the more than 400 largest and most successful real estate and construction companies. Each entry has the company name, its NAICS codes, ranking within the industry group, the aggregate of the company's businesses, the officers of the company and their salaries, contact information (including Web addresses and toll-free telephone listings), a summary of the financial information from 2008-2013, and parent or subsidiary companies. There is a section of the entry for the company's plans for growth and special features, such as acquisitions, new services, and additions to employees' benefits. There is a business glossary, a chapter on major trends that affect the real estate and construction industry, industry statistics, and a discussion of the selection of the "Real Estate 400." There are two indexes for the listings of "Firms Noted as Hot Spots for Advancement for Women & Minorities" and "Subsidiaries, Brand Names, and Affiliations."

This publication is recommended for large public and corporate business libraries' collections for their business, investment, and corporate research about these real estate and construction companies.—**Kay Stebbins Slattery**

Taxation

273.   **Handbook of Research on Environmental Taxation.** Janet E. Milne and Mikael Skou Andersen, eds. Northhampton, Mass., Edward Elgar, 2013. 510p. index. $245.00. ISBN 13: 978-1-84844-997-8.

With contributions from leaders in environmental taxation from around the world, this title explores the elements for designing environmental tax measures, the factors that influence these measures, and how to successfully implement environmental tax. The work provides case studies on successful ways that taxes have been implemented around the world, and the significant policies dealing with environmental protection. The essays include case studies on the local level as well as on the broader international level. They are written from contributors all over the world. This work is not based solely on western ideals and philosophy; it includes scholarship from Latin America, Asia, and Africa as well. The ideas within will be useful for students just learning the role environmental taxation plays in environmental protection as well as for practitioners in the field.—**Shannon Graff Hysell**

5 Education

General Works

Almanacs

271. **The Almanac of American Education 2013.** 7th ed. Deirdre A. Gaquin and Gwenavere W. Dunn, eds. Lanham, Md., Bernan Press, 2013. 564p. index. $79.00pa.; $78.99 (e-book). ISBN 13: 978-1-59888-601-6; 978-1-59888-602-3 (e-book).

Education has always been a contentious public policy issue. Whether it is the role of the federal or state government in public education, the level of funding states should be obligated to provide for public education, the role of private charter schools in public schooling, the accountability of teachers and how to measure it, or outcomes assessment, schooling is under the microscope as never before. Policy debates rage on all of these fronts. To sensibly engage in these debates, one needs to be armed with objective data, and this almanac helps, in part, to meet that need. Data here are drawn primarily from government sources, including the Census and the National Center for Education Statistics, as well as some private sources like the College Board. Tables of data address national education statistics, state and region education statistics, and county education statistics. Within these broad geographic categories, there are data on enrollment, historical and current educational attainment, postsecondary education, and more. These categories are further broken down by such variables as state, age, race, sex, and ethnic origin. There are data on postsecondary enrollments, graduation rates, and earnings by race, level of education, or sex, to name but a few. For many tables, historical data back to the 1960s are presented. Source documents are identified at the end of each of the three major sections. Access to all of these tables is facilitated by a detailed table of contents and list of tables, as well as an extensive subject index. An annotated guide to education resources on the Internet is appended. While interested users can start here, they will no doubt appreciate the truism that, especially in this period where policy is often driven by ideology, data do not speak for themselves.—**Stephen H. Aby**

Dictionaries and Encyclopedias

275. **Asia for Educators. http://afe.easia.columbia.edu/.** [Website]. Columbia University. Free. Date reviewed: 2013.

This Columbia University site is a portal with lesson plans, timelines, images, and primary sources for all levels of instruction related to teaching about Asia across the disciplines. It also includes a searchable annotated bibliography of teaching materials. An initiative of the Weatherhead East Asian Institute at Columbia University, Asia for Educators (AFE) is designed to serve faculty and students

in world history, culture, geography, art, and literature at the undergraduate and pre-college levels.—
Noriko Asato

276.   **International Education: An Encyclopedia of Contemporary Issues and Systems.** Daniel
Ness and Chia-Ling Lin, eds. Armonk, N.Y., M. E. Sharpe, 2013. 2v. index. $249.00/set. ISBN 13: 978-
0-7656-2049-1.

Ness and Lin have led a team of over 50 contributors to this work meant to cover the intersection
of international education and human development. Part 1 is an encyclopedia arranged by topic, while
part 2 is a survey by region and individual country of the status of and issues faced by their educational
systems. Each part is divided into eight sections. Part 1 includes Sociopolitical and Cultural Issues in
Education; Gender and Education; Formal Education; Informal Education; Content, Curriculum, and
Resources; Intellectual and Motor Development; Technologies and Global Education; and Institutions of
Education Throughout the World. Part 2 covers Africa; East Asia; Australia, New Zealand, and Melanesia;
Europe; Middle East and South Central Asia; North American and Caribbean; South America; and Post-
Soviet Nations. Entries in the country sections include information on the Educational System, Teacher
Education, Informal Education, System Economics, and Future Prospects. The two major parts have
lengthy introductions with charts and references. References are also provided for major subdivisions
of each section. Tables and charts accompany some entries. The two parts of this work can be used in
tandem by moving from a particular topic to a country entry, or by reading a country entry and going
back to the general treatment of a topic.

The content is exactly what the title suggests, and the layout is easy on the eye, with plenty of white
space and the judicious use of bold type for headings. Entries are succinct, and there is a conscious effort
to provide world-wide perspectives on each topic. Not a comprehensive encyclopedia of education, this
is still an excellent addition to any academic library reference collection that supports teacher preparation
programs. This set is highly recommended.—**Rosanne M. Cordell**

Directories

277.   **Educators Resource Directory, 2013/2014.** 10th ed. Millerton, N.Y., Grey House Publishing,
2013. 716p. index. $145.00pa.; $275.00 (online edition; single user); $375.00 (print and online editions).
ISBN 13: 978-1-61925-113-7.

Few one-volume directories can claim to be fully comprehensive. But in the case of the *Educators
Resource Directory* it is a resource whose overall scope can satisfy the wide variety of information needs
germane to education and related pedagogic concerns. Information pertaining to education associations
and organizations are thoroughly covered along with listings of annual conferences and trade shows. For
school administrator and teachers this directory offers a by-state listing of financial resources, grants and
monies available through numerous educational foundations such as James Graham Brown Foundation
which offers grants in higher education as well as individuals seeking funding for projects related to
K-12 Education pursuits. In addition, the user is provided with hundreds of education statistical tables.
For example, statistics giving numerical data on high school drops outs, population and ethnic make-up
by-state and counties throughout the United States, as well as international comparisons on education
achievements in math and science. The text also includes a glossary of education terms followed by an
entry and publishers index. This resource is highly recommended for all educational personnel, students
and faculty. It would be a helpful addition in any library.—**Patrick Hall**

Handbooks and Yearbooks

278.　**Cases on Educational Technology Implementation for Facilitating Learning.** Albert D. Ritzhaupt and Swapna Kumar, eds. Hershey, Pa., Information Science Reference, 2013. 470p. index. $175.00; $265.00 (e-book); $350.00 (print and e-book editions). ISBN 13: 978-1-46663-676-7; 978-1-46663-677-4 (e-book).

Edited by an assistant professor and a clinical assistant professor at the School of Teaching and Learning at the University of Florida, this volume brings together 21 chapters authored by 48 international practitioners. While mostly U.S.-focused, there are also chapters on Ghana, Cyprus, Canada, and a cross between the United Kingdom and Portugal. The chapters address not only traditional educational technology usage, but also usage for nontraditional academic settings such as congregational religious schools and training in other instances. Offering teaching cases at all levels of education from K-12 to undergraduate and graduate, from general overviews of educational technology to usage in specific settings such as medical, STEM, or teaching, and from a specific technology to the integration of technology in a more general way, including technologies such as Twitter, mobile devices, online and hybrid courses, eportfolios, and more. Each chapter includes a description of the educational technology innovation or problem that is studied in the case, how learning was facilitated through the technology, and an analysis and/or discussion questions and/or a discussion of solutions and recommendations. The chapters each end with a list of references and a list of key terms and definitions. A lack in the volume is a comprehensive glossary, or list of key terms and definitions, to enable quick reference to terms and to ensure synonymous usage throughout the volume. This book is useful, as indicated in the purpose, for students and practitioners of disseminating information through educational technology tools at all levels of learning and in all settings, not just formal educational settings. The cases can be used individually for study and discussion, or for reference as to how others have dealt with a scenario similar to what one is facing, selected through the detailed table of contents or the brief index.—**Sara Marcus**

279.　**Cross-Cultural Considerations in the Education of Young Immigrant Learners.** Jared Keengwe and Grace Onchwari, eds. Hershey, Pa., Information Science Reference, 2014. 337p. index. (Advances in Educational Technologies and Instructional Design). $175.00; $265.00 (e-book); $350.00 (print and e-book editions). ISBN 13: 978-1-6664-928-6; 978-1-46664-929-3 (e-book).

Edited by a teacher educator with the College of Education and Human Development at the University of North Dakota and an associate professor in the Department of Teaching and Learning at the University of North Dakota, this volume presents 17 chapters that explore contemporary research on the learning styles and adaptation of young immigrant learners in the United States. The book addresses such topics as overcoming language barriers, cultural integration, and participation in curricular and extra-curricular activities. A theme throughout the volume is on new teaching pedagogies that have shown to be effective with this population of students. Written for K-12 educators, administrators, and teacher educators, this volume will be of interest to those working with or within school districts that are looking for enhanced methodologies in working with multinational students. The work begins with a basic table of contents, followed by a detailed table of contents containing abstracts of each chapter. An index enables location of desired information as well. Each chapter has a list of references, and the editors have also compiled all references into a single list at the end of the work. This work is a valuable addition to any education collection.—**Sara Marcus**

280.　**Debating the Issues in American Education.** Thousand Oaks, Calif., Sage, 2012. 10v. index. $680.00/set. ISBN 13: 978-1-4129-8978-7.

This title tackles a number of important issues in education today, including "should English-only curriculums be eliminated or expanded?" "Should all forms of ability groups be eliminated in schools?" and "Should corporal punishment in public schools be abolished?" Each debatable topic begins with an overview and a point and counterpoint argument. The tone is academic and the research that has been provided here ensures that the information is accurate. The entries include both a list of references for further information and a list of court cases to research for more information. With 150 issues covered, the range of topics is far reaching and includes: homeschooling, school safety, school funding, vouchers, and teacher certification. Each volume has an index to the entire set, making searching between volumes much easier. This work will be of interest to educators, policy makers, and involved parents. This set is highly recommended. [R: SLJ, June 13, p. 70]—**Shannon Graff Hysell**

281.   **ePedagogy in Online Learning: New Developments in Web Mediated Human Computer Interaction.** Elspeth McKay, ed. Hershey, Pa., Information Science Reference, 2013. 275p. index. $175.00; $265.00 (e-book); $350.00 (print and e-book editions). ISBN 13: 978-1-46663-649-1; 978-1-46663-650-7 (e-book).

Edited by an associate professor of business IT and logistics at RMIT University in Australia, this work brings together 14 chapters authored by 30 international scholars and practitioners. Organized into four sections, the work provides six chapters on technology and change management for the Web 2.0 environment, offering strategies to enhance eLearning in the Web 2.0 environment. Next, two chapters are presented that address social networking and collaborative learning through human computer interaction (HCI) for both synchronous and asynchronous learning. The third section presents four chapters focusing on epedagogy and students' use of HCI interactive learning environments, the performance measurement issues, and how can we tell that people have learned anything. The final section provides two chapters addressing rich Internet applications and HCI in educational practice, the educational and training design of these, including support systems, models, and cases. This volume is intended to build upon the 2007 title by Premier Reference Source, Enhancing Learning through Human Computer Interaction, expanding the ideas to today's technologies of Web 2.0. The preface sets the stage well, offering an overview and introduction to the topics presented, including a list of terminology. This list, however, does not exactly coincide with the key terms and definitions presented with each chapter in the volume; a better use would be to present a cumulative list of key terms and definitions that were used throughout the book. Each chapter includes as well a list of references and additional readings for further knowledge. This volume is of use to educators, instructional designers, and administrators who wish to integrate additional ways to reach learners.—**Sara Marcus**

282.   **Global Challenges and Perspectives in Blended and Distance Learning.** J. Willems, B. Tynan, and R. James, eds. Hershey, Pa., Information Science Reference, 2013. 297p. index. $175.00; $265.00 (e-book); $350.00 (print and e-book editions). ISBN 13: 978-1-46663-978-2; 978-1-46663-979-9 (e-book).

Edited by three seasoned practitioners in Australia, this volume brings together 21 chapters authored by 38 international scholars and practitioners, mainly located in Australia. Organized into three sections, the work addresses global issues and perspectives in distance and flexible education; provides seven case studies of global responses to distance and flexible education in Australia, Canada, and New Zealand; and ends with nine chapters on capacity development. Each of the chapters in this book were first presented at the DEHub and Open and Distance Learning Association of Australia (ODLAA) SUMMIT: Education 2011 to 2021—Global Challenges and Perspectives of Blended and Distance Learning held in Sydney on February 15-18, 2011. Each chapter has a list of references as well as a list of key terms and definitions. It would be beneficial if each list of key terms and definitions were alphabetized, and a compilation was provided at the end of the volume. The detailed table of contents, along with the compilation of references makes this work useful for the researcher, while the content of the chapters will guide users in their own uses and practices in blended and distance learning.—**Sara Marcus**

283.   **Literacy Enrichment and Technology Integration in Pre-Service Teacher Education.** Jared Keengwe, Grace Onchwari, and Darrell Hucks, eds. Hershey, Pa., Information Science Reference, 2014.

312p. index. (Advances in Higher Education and Professional Development). $175.00; $265.00 (e-book); $350.00 (print and e-book editions). ISBN 13: 978-1-46664-924-8; 978-1-46664-925-5 (e-book).

Three United States-based scholars and educators bring together 16 chapters by international scholars and practitioners that focus on the best practices in integrating technology into classroom instruction while continuing to offer an optimal environment for student learning. Although the focus is on teacher education, the seven sections are appropriate for an educator in any discipline seeking knowledge of online learning tools. Chapters address such topics as media-enhanced writing instruction, incorporating information literacy into instructional design, creating virtual field trips, implementing a problem-based technology learning environment to foster cultural literacy, and twenty-first century new literacies and digital tools. The contributors focus on the future of technology integration in education. This work includes both a basic table of contents, and a detailed table of contents that includes abstracts for each chapter. Each chapter includes examples and references as well as a discussion of what has been done in the situation. The editors provide a compiled list of references from all chapters, and an index to the work as a whole. This work will be useful to administrators, teachers, technology leaders, and technology staff.—**Shannon Graff Hysell**

284. **Practical Applications and Experiences in K-10 Blended Learning Environments.** Kyei-Blankson, Lydia and Esther Ntuli, eds. Hershey, Pa., Information Science Reference, 2014, 489p. index, $175.00; $265.00 (e-book); $350.00 (print and e-book editions). ISBN 13: 978-1-46664-912-5; 978-1-46664-913-2 (e-book).

Edited by an Associate Professor in the Department of Educational Administration and Foundations at Illinois State University and an Assistant Professor in the Department of Educational Foundations at Idaho State University, this work presents 26 chapters authored by 45 international practitioners of K-20 education in first world countries. Part of the Advances in Mobile and Distance Learning Book series, the volume offers ideas for researchers and practitioners at all levels of education through practical examples and student outcomes, as well was pedagogical and theoretical lenses. Each chapter includes a list of key terms and definitions, although a comprehensive glossary would lead to a valuable resource both for using the book and for a one-stop location to locate definitions of key terms found elsewhere. Organized into four sections, the work addresses trends, design and development in the first section, followed by six innovative strategies in blended education and three best practices in blended education. The final section offers 11 chapters on practical applications and student outcomes in K-20 blended education. While each chapter contains valuable references, which are also compiled into a single list at the end of the book, several of the chapters contain dated references and would benefit from reference to more recent literature on blended education. A detailed table of contents and index enables the user to find desired information, although due to the dated references some information might not be as valuable or timely as could be desired.—**Sara Marcus**

285. **Projections of Education Statistics to 2021.** By the National Center for Education Statistics. Lanham, Md., Bernan Press, 2013. 181p. $55.00pa. ISBN 13: 978-1-60175-890-3.

This report from the National Center for Education Statistics in the U.S. Department of Education includes statistics at the national level for elementary and secondary schools as well as institutes of higher education. Among these statistics are numbers for enrollment, graduates, classroom teachers, and expenditures beginning in 2000, along with projected numbers to the year 2021. From this report readers can learn, for example, the rate at which elementary and secondary enrollment is expected to increase. Statistics on enrollment, graduates, teachers, and expenditures are provided here. As well, users will find information on the expected enrollment and earned degrees of degree-granting institutions. Some information is also available for nonpublic schools.

Coverage of state-level statistics is not as comprehensive, being limited to projections of public elementary and secondary enrollment and high school graduates. Information is easy to access, being available in both narrative and tabular form and aided through a comprehensive table of contents. Appendixes explain methodologies used to develop projections.—**Barbara Delzell**

286.   **Research Perspectives and Best Practices in Educational Technology Integration.** Jared Keengwe, ed. Hershey, Pa., Information Science Reference, 2013. 358p. index. $175.00; $265.00 (e-book); $350.00 (print and e-book editions). ISBN 13: 978-1-46662-988-2; 978-1-46662-989-9 (e-book).

Edited by an associate professor of education in the department of teaching and learning at the University of North Dakota, this work brings together 16 chapters authored by 32 international scholars and practitioners in colleges and universities. The volume includes an annotated table of contents to assist with locating chapters of interest, while an index helps find specific areas within the book that can be of assistance in one's search for information and guidance. Offering case studies of technology integration at all levels of the educational process, from early childhood through higher education, the work focuses on teacher education programs, along with media literacy, librarian's roles, student engagement, and social media. This work will help educators of future educators as well as current educators to integrate technology into their curriculum and classrooms. References and key terms with definitions in each chapter assist in understanding the materials and finding additional resources. Lacking in this volume is a comprehensive list of key terms and definitions.—**Sara Marcus**

Elementary and Secondary Education

Bibliography

287.   Churches, Andrew, and Harry J. Dickens. **Apps for Learning—Elementary School Classrooms.** Thousand Oaks, Calif., Corwin Press, 2013. 151p. index. $24.95pa. ISBN 13: 978-1-4848-5670-3.

288.   Churches, Andrew, and Harry J. Dickens. **Apps for Learning for Middle School Classrooms.** Thousand Oaks, Calif., Corwin Press, 2013. 160p. index. $24.95pa. ISBN 13: 978-1-4791-6400-4.

289.   Churches, Andrew, and Harry J. Dickens. **Apps for Learning: 40 Best iPad, iPod Touch, iPhone Apps for High School Classrooms.** Thousand Oaks, Calif., Corwin Press, 2013. 160p. index. $24.95pa. ISBN 13: 978-1-4636-1285-6.

Designed by a team of authors who are serving on the 21st Century Fluency Project, these volumes will serve teachers of students in grades K-12 who are looking for reliable and well-regarded educational apps. The guides serve as annotated lists of both free and fee-based apps for iPads, the iPodTouch, and the iPhone. The elementary and middle school guides are organized in much the same way: they are first divided by curriculum (e.g., math, science, social studies) and then alphabetically by the name of the tool. The high school guide is organized alphabetically by tool name only. Each tool has an annotation describing the app, demonstrating ways in which teachers can utilize the app in their classroom, and provide an illustration of the screen.

Because many schools are beginning to incorporate iPads into their daily plan, these guides can serve as a starting off point in finding the right free and fee-based apps to include in the curriculum. The authors have attempted to select apps that will likely be around for longer than a nanosecond; however, it is likely these volumes will need to be updated regularly to ensure timeliness. [R: TL, Oct 2013, p. 44]—**ARBA Staff Reviewer**

Catalogs and Collections

290.   **Dig the Library. http://www.digthelibrary.com.** [Website]. Free. Date reviewed: 2013.

This site provides hundreds of online resources for the K-12 community reviewed and evaluated by teachers. Alongside online resources users will find recent reviews of apps, blogs, digital reference, digital libraries, e-book collection, ezines, podcasts, and video collections. Users can search the reviews by content type or by subject. Each review provides information on the content, the strengths and weaknesses, and a rating.—**ARBA Staff Reviewer**

291.   **Digital Literacy. http://digitalliteracy.rosendigital.com/.** [Website]. New York, Rosen Publishing. Price negotiated by site. Date reviewed: 2013.

The easily navigated content in this database focuses on issues to help students learn how to use digital resources successfully and safely. Topics include cyberbullying, social networking, privacy, research skills, tools, gaming, and career options. Within each of these main areas are subheadings with additional information. Five interactive activities correlate directly with provided lesson plans. The plans include supplemental materials like rubrics, videos, and reproducibles. Promotional materials, online training, curriculum correlations, and usage statistics are all also included. Due to its specific nature, budgetary concerns might be a purchasing consideration; however, for schools that purchase other online products from the publisher, including *Teen Health & Wellness* or *Financial Literacy* (see entry 181), special discounts are available.—**Elizabeth Kahn**

292.   **Federal Resources for Educational Excellence. http://www.free.ed.gov/.** [Website]. Free. Date reviewed: 2013.

This Web source is extremely useful and inclusive, containing such areas as the Arts, Educational Technology, Foreign Languages, Physical Education, Language Arts, Science, Mathematics, Social Studies, Vocational Education, and more. This site contains links to learning resources created and maintained by other public and private organizations. This information is provided for the visitor's convenience and is included as an example of the many resources that educators may find helpful and use at their option. Users can search by topic or can browse the content by subject or common core standards.—**ARBA Staff Reviewer**

293.   **Noodle Tools. http://www.noodletools.com.** [Website]. Palo Alto, Calif., Noodle Tools. Price negotiated by site. Date reviewed: 2013.

This Website is now a total program for citing, organizing, and presenting research. Students can set up a works cited list, write and organize notecards and an outline, and jump from NoodleTools into Google docs so their work can be shared. Moving back and forth from one task to another is smooth and it is easy to link notecards to sources. Helpful tips and extra information allow students to become ethical researchers. The Starter level, designed for elementary-age students, has the most support; it progressively lessens with Junior for middle school and Advanced for high school. To allow students to submit work, a teacher sets up an assignment drop box. Technical support is top-notch. The resource works well with an iPad. I have used it in my school for years, watched it grow and develop, and watched our students do the same. Definitely consider this tool for your school.—**Melinda W. Miller**

Handbooks and Yearbooks

294.   **Common Core Mathematics Standards and Implementing Digital Technologies.** Drew Polly, ed. Hershey, Pa., Information Science Reference, 2013. 422p. index. (Advances in Educational

Technologies and Instructional Design). $175.00; $265.00 (e-book); $350.00 (print and e-book editions). ISBN 13: 978-1-46664-086-3; 978-1-46664-087-0 (e-book).

Edited by an associate professor of Elementary Education at the University of North Carolina at Charlotte, this work brings 25 chapters by educators and scholars that provide context, case studies, and innovative approaches to educational standards in mathematics and describe how communication technologies can support the implementation of the Common Core. Traditionally states have set their own educational standards but the implementation of the Common Core requires a more integrated approach to educational standards. This book will supply math teachers and educational technology experts with a thorough definition of the Common Core State Standards in mathematics and it will provide examples, current research, and best practices for teach K-12 students using these new standards. The editor provides a compiled list of references from all chapters, and an index to the work as a whole. The work might benefit from cross-references between chapters, It will be useful for school administrators and teachers of mathematics interested in gaining a better understanding between implementing digital technologies while adhering to the Common Core Standards.—**Shannon Graff Hysell**

295.   **Critical Practice in P-12 Education: Transformative Teaching and Learning.** Salika A. Lawrence, ed. Hershey, Pa., Information Science Reference, 2014. 297p. index. (Advances in Early Childhood and K-12 Education). $175.00 $265.00 (e-book); $350.00 (print and e-book editions). ISBN 13: 978-1-46665-059-6; 978-1-46665-060-2 (e-book).

Edited by an associate professor of literacy and language arts at William Paterson University, this volume presents 11 chapters that explore new models of teaching that empower students, foster literacy development, and quip students to meet modern educational standards. A theme throughout the volume is on the rapid changes that technology has created in education and the need for teachers and administrators to ensure that all students, even those from lower socioeconomic backgrounds receive the same benefits for technology that other, more well off students receive. Written for P-12 educators, in-service teachers, administrators, and teacher educators, this volume is broken down into three key sections: Context of 21st Century Teaching and Learning, Crossing Boundaries and Redefining Learning Spaces, and Reconceptualizing the Curriculum. The work begins with a basic table of contents, followed by a detailed table of contents containing abstracts of each chapter. An index enables location of desired information as well. Each chapter has a list of references, and the editors have also compiled all references into a single list at the end of the work. This work is a valuable addition to any education collection where patrons have an interest in field-based educational research, specifically within the area of educational technology and its latest applications.—**Sara Marcus**

296.   Feber, Jane. **Engage Striving Students in the Common Core Classroom.** North Mankato, Minn., Maupin House/Capstone Professional, 2014. 144p. illus. index. $24.95pa. ISBN 13: 978-1-62521-510-9.

This book is designed for any teacher working with adolescent students who are struggling with reading in the Common Core classroom. The author, a middle school language arts teacher, provides users with 35 activities focused on phonemic awareness, phonics, fluency, vocabulary, and reading comprehension. Each activity is designed to align with the College and Career Readiness Anchor Standards from the Common Core State Standards that address literature, reading skills, and speaking and listening. For each activity users will find the objective clearly stated, the research that backs it up, Common Core Standard it addresses, materials needed, and step-by-step instructions. Any reproducibles needed for the activity are available as well. Each activity concludes with a reading list survey and student reading suggestions by genre. Examples of activities include poetry writing, readers' theater, and word pyramids. This title will inspire teachers and students as they work toward attaining Common Core Standards in the language arts.—**Janet Dagenais Brown**

297. Hagler, Kaye. **Inquire, Investigate, Integrate! Making Connections to the K-2 Science Standards and the Common Core.** North Mankato, Minn., Maupin House/Capstone Professional, 2014. 2010. $24.95pa. ISBN 13: 978-1-62521-516-1.

This book is designed for any teacher working with elementary students grades K-2 who are working on Common Core standards in the area of science. These thematic units also touch on literacy and math standards as well. The author, an educational consultant, provides units that are intended to engage students while they learn about landforms, forces and motion, weather, life cycles, and the food chain. Along with gaining knowledge on the scientific topic at hand students will practice their reading comprehension skills and writing skills as well. At the beginning of each unit the author provides information on the difficulty of the unit, its objective, and supplies needed. After instructional guidelines for the activity the author concludes with an "inspire" section that provides additional ideas to help students retain the information and encourage them to learn more. This title will inspire teachers and students as they work toward attaining Common Core Standards in the sciences.—**Janet Dagenais Brown**

298. Marcovitz, David M. **Digital Connections in the Classroom.** Eugene, Oreg., ISTE Publishing, 2012. 180p. index. $31.95pa. ISBN 13: 978-1-56484-316-6.

In the crowded field of technology books, ISTE is a trusted source for professional development. Written by a college professor, this book functions as a textbook on the basics, with a few lesson plan suggestions added in. Serving as a practical resource for the classroom, the book helps teachers to integrate technology into lesson plans and activities. It covers critical information literacy, collaborative projects, Web 2.0, search engines, digital citizenship, and how to use these resources to promote learning.—**Donna Reed**

299. Marcovitz, David M. **Powerful PowerPoint for Educators: Using Visual Basic for Applications to Make PowerPoint Interactive.** 2d ed. Santa Barbara, Calif., Libraries Unlimited/ABC-CLIO, 2013. 270p. index. $55.00pa. ISBN 13: 978-1-61069-136-9.

Written for those familiar with PowerPoint, this book teaches readers how to use Virtual Basic for Applications (VBA) scripting to make PPT more interactive. It takes users from the basics such as linking slides through creating multiple-choice tests and tutorials. Additional procedures include looping, conditionals, parameters, and creating communication between PPT and excel. Each chapter opens with a vocabulary list, but it would have been helpful if the words had been defined there. Each chapter concludes with a practice exercise. Directions are straightforward, easy-to-follow, and include screen shots. Since using VBA is a time-consuming process, the book will have limited appeal to busy teachers.—**Susan C. McNair**

300. Medea, Andra. **Safe Within These Walls: De-Escalating School Situations Before They Become Crises.** North Mankato, Minn., Maupin House/Capstone Professional, 2014. 176p. index. $24.95pa. ISBN 13: 978-1-62521-518-5.

This book will be a useful tool for school administrators, school counselors, and teachers. It covers a topic that is of upmost concern to most people in education today—the rise of violence in our schools. Creating a safe environment for children to learn is fundamental to the success of education, yet in the wake of recent school tragedies, it is oftentimes the hardest thing to ensure. This book, written by an expert in conflict management and the founder of Virtual Tranquilizer, a technique that calms and stabilizes aggressive people using finesse rather than force, provides readers with the tools to de-escalate aggression at the safest time—before it occurs. In 10 chapters the author addresses how to identify a volatile person, methods to de-escalate a situation, how to work with children grades K-2, 3-6, and at the middle school level to prevent future violence, and educating parents on the warning signs of possible violent behaviors. The work also discusses mental health issues in children and adolescents and how to recognize when outside help is necessary. This should be a must read for school administrators and counselors, and the title should be made available to educators as well.—**Shannon Graff Hysell**

301.   Polette, Nancy J. **Teaching Economic Concepts with Picture Books and Junior Novels.** Santa Barbara, Calif., Libraries Unlimited/ABC-CLIO, 2013. 311p. index. $50.00pa. ISBN 13: 978-1-61069-502-2; 978-1-61069-503-9 (e-book).

Authored by professor emeritus at Lindenwood University in Missouri, this work fills a niche of guiding librarians and educators in grades K-7 in the integration of reading and writing with economic and budgeting education. Covering 40 books, 20 for grades K-3 and 20 for grades 4-7, Polette presents the suggested grade level(s) for the book and activities, a brief summary of the book, a list of economic concepts that could be covered in the lesson, and a set of pre- and post-reading questions and activities. The pre- and post-reading activities not only include questions for discussion and worksheets such as fill-in-the-blank and short answer questions, but also activities such as similes, sequencing, predictions, proverbs, sentence starters, brainstorming, imagination, and more. The volume also includes a brief annotated bibliography at the end, along with selected sets of answers to activities, and a combined index of title, author, and illustrator.

The titles covered in this volume are both modern and classic, such as *Cloudy with a Chance of Meatballs*, *If You Give a Mouse a Cookie*, *Mike Mulligan and His Steam Shovel*, *Next Stop, Zanzibar Road*, *The Boxcar Children*, *Homer Price*, and *Charlotte's Web*. This book is a welcome addition to any K-8 professional collection, encouraging educators to bring writing across the curriculum, and to integrate economics into literature.—**Sara Marcus**

302.   Sampson, Victor, and Sharon Schleigh. **Scientific Argumentation in Biology: 30 Classroom Activities.** Arlington, Va., NSTA Press, 2013. 417p. index. $39.95pa. ISBN 13: 978-1-936137-27-5.

Building and defending arguments is one of the central themes of Common Core across all of the disciplines. Although this specific title focuses on activities that will help students learn how to defend arguments in biology, it can also serve as a useful model for other classroom curriculum. The work begins by giving a clear explanation of why student need to provide clear arguments when making research-related claims. It then goes on to provide 30 activities that students can use to learn how to propose and support their claims, validate (or refute) them based on scientific reasoning, and then compose a written argument. Notes for teachers can be found throughout the volume that provide examples of how these activities can be used in the classroom to supplement their current curriculum. It serves as a solid teaching tool to help students learn standards-based content.—**Craig A. Munsart**

303.   **The Social Classroom: Integrating Social Network Use in Education.** Gorg Mallia, ed. Hershey, Pa., Information Science Reference, 2014. 532p. index. (Advances in Educational Technologies and Instructional Design). $175.00; $265.00 (e-book); $350.00 (print and e-book editions). ISBN 13: 978-1-46664-904-0; 978-1-46664-905-7 (e-book).

Edited by a faculty member of the Media and Knowledge Sciences, at the University of Malta, this work brings together 22 chapters authored by more than 30 researchers, practitioners, and students in the fields of computer science, online education, and communications. The cases and examples in these chapters provide a unique role that social media can play in enhancing and motivating student learning. While the articles raise interesting points it is important to be aware that each of the countries represented has different educational systems and values which affect the way social media affects and is accepted within their education system. Separated into five sections, the work explores formal and informal uses of social media in the classroom, using social networks for specific teaching and learning exercises, ethical and psychological considerations when using social networks for educational use, individual social networks and their use in instruction, and specific case studies. Focusing on the benefits and challenges that social media represents in the world of education, this work is valuable to educators, practitioners, and students of education who want to know more about this changing impact and influences. The volume includes an annotated table of contents and an index as well as a compiled list of references at the end. This should not be the sole resource consulted when researching this topic, but it can be of value, particularly to those studying the impact of social media on education on a global scale.—**Shannon Graff Hysell**

304.   Suen, Anastasia, and Shirley Duke. **Teaching STEM and Common Core with Mentor Texts: Collaborative Lesson Plans, K-5.** Santa Barbara, Calif., Libraries Unlimited/ABC-CLIO, 2014. 237p. index. $48.00pa. ISBN 13: 978-1-61069-426-1; 978-1-61069-597-8 (e-book).

   School librarians can be a key resource for teachers when it comes to helping them find the right materials to use in the classroom to incorporate STEM resources in to the curriculum. This title, written by two teachers with knowledge and experience in teaching the science and technology in the classroom, provides librarians with the tools they need to guide teachers to the right books for their curriculum. The work offers more than 20 lesson plans (5 for each STEM subject) that can be used in the classroom. Additional lessons for classroom teachers are included as well as activities that can be done in either the library or the classroom. Lesson plans include an overview, step-by-step instructions, assessment options, and additional activities to expand learning. There is a grade range assigned to each lesson along with ideas for adapting it to other grades. This work will give librarians a wide range of ideas in how they can assist teachers with covering multiple Common Core State Standards and science standards.—**Janet Dagenais Brown**

305.   **Transforming K-12 Classrooms with Digital Technology.** Zongkai Yang, Harrison Hao Yang, Di Wu, and Sanya Liu, eds. Hershey, Pa., Information Science Reference, 2014. 386p. index. (Advances in Early Childhood and K-12 Education). $175.00. ISBN 13: 978-1-4666-4538-7.

   This volume presents 18 chapters authored by more than 35 international scholars and practitioners. Organized into two sections, each of these case studies presents the best research and practices regarding digital and social technology integration in the K-12 classroom. The contributors share both practical and conceptual ideas for using digital and social technologies as tools for implementing these new technologies into elementary and secondary learning environments. Chapters address such topics as fostering collaboration and digital literacy with mobile technologies, STEM in early childhood education, digital play, and promoting a balanced development of high-quality teacher resources with network technology. Those needing a collocated set of local and widespread case studies on e-learning tools use at the K-12 level around the world can benefit from this book.—**Shannon Graff Hysell**

Higher Education

Catalogs and Collections

306.   **Education About Asia. http://asian-studies.org/EAA/index.htm.** [Website]. Free; some subscription-based material available. Date reviewed: 2013.

   This site provides access to AAS's publication *Education about Asia* from 1996 to 2008. More recent issues are available by subscription. It contains much information for instructors, including reviews and lesson plans. The journal is a practical teaching resource for secondary school, college, and university instructors, as well as an invaluable source of information for students, scholars, libraries, and anyone with an interest in Asia. Teachers and students from a wide range of disciplines, including anthropology, Asian studies, business and economics, education, geography, government, history, language and literature, political science, religion, and sociology, among others will find this site useful. The site is a comprehensive guide to Asia-related print and digital resources, including movies, documentaries, books, curriculum guides, and Web resources.—**Noriko Asato**

Directories

307. **Fiske Guide to Colleges 2014.** 30th ed. By Edward B. Fiske. Naperville, Ill., Sourcebooks, 2013. 816p. index. $23.99pa. ISBN 13: 978-1-4022-6064-3.

Edward B. Fiske, the former *New York Times* Education Editor, has been compiling this excellent guide to colleges for over two decades. In this 30th edition, Fiske and his staff have produced a valuable resource for students and their parents to facilitate the important task of choosing the right college.

The process of choosing the more than 330 best and most interesting institutions involved statistical data combined with subjective interpretation of questionnaire results from administrators and students. Some hard decisions had to be made in order to select from more than 2,200 four-year colleges in the United States, Canada, and Great Britain. The editorial staff included the approximately 175 institutions considered to be the best academically, and rounded out the rest with engineering and technical schools, those with religious affiliations, and some located geographically in the Sunbelt of the United States, where costs were lower than those in the northern and eastern portions of the country. Other criteria revolved around colleges with an "unusual and fascinating brand of liberal arts," or institutions with unique focus.

The information from the questionnaires sent to administrators and students (the administrators were instructed to distribute surveys to a cross-section of their student population) was only one data point for the analysis. The writing staff visited many of the campuses, telephone interviews were held with some administrators and students, and more facts were gleaned from published materials about the colleges. All the information was incorporated into essays written by the staff under the editorial direction of Edward Fiske. The essays cover eight broad subject areas: academics, campus setting, student body, financial aid, housing, food, social life, and extracurricular activities.

The first part of the *Guide* contains several valuable indexes. Colleges are first listed by state and country. This is followed by an index by price and the best buys of the year. Other indexes provide a guide for pre-professionals (e.g., business, medicine, architecture, art) and colleges with excellent resources for the learning disabled.

At the beginning of each essay is a banner containing important facts to know before applying to the featured college. Each entry contains a sidebar with other valuable information such as location, enrollment, male/female ratio, and strongest programs. The *Fiske Guide* is readable, current, and informative. It is recommended for high school, public, community college, and academic libraries.—**Laura J. Bender**

308. **Higher Education Directory, 2013.** Reston, Va., Higher Education Publications; distr., Lanham, Md., Bernan Press, 2013. 1076p. index. $83.00pa. ISBN 13: 978-0-9149-2769-3.

This annual publication, which began in 1983, contains basic information on postsecondary, degree-granting institutions accredited by national, regional, professional, and specialized agencies recognized as accrediting bodies by the U.S. Secretary of Education and by the Council on Higher Education Accreditation. Descriptions are based on information gathered in 2012. It includes such institution changes as additions, deletions, mergers, and name changes. In order to get the most accurate information available the editors of the *Higher Education Directory* go directly to the universities themselves to verify information and claim to have a 99.9 percent participation rage among universities. For ease of use the work provides multiple indexes that are cross-referenced to the main institutional listings, which are arranged by state, territory, or possession of the United States. Information provided about each institution includes Carnegie Classification, contact information, size, calendar system, programs offered, accreditation, FICE number, and names of administrators. E-mail addresses have been added for most administrators. An academic reference librarian could need this type of information on a regular basis. Much of what is found here can be found for free with an Internet search; however, for people needing this information often it is nice to have it in one location.—**Lois Gilmer**

Handbooks and Yearbooks

309. **Activity Theory Perspectives on Technology in Higher Education.** Elizabeth Murphy and Maria Angeles Rodriguez-Manzanares, eds. Hershey, Pa., Information Science Reference, 2014. 307p. index. (Advances in Higher Education and Professional Development). $175.00; $265.00 (e-book); $350.00 (print and e-book editions). ISBN 13: 978-1-46664-590-5; 978-1-46664-591-2 (e-book).

Two international scholars bring together 11 chapters by scholars and practitioners that focus on activity theory, which is a tool that can be used to understand the complex changes that are occurring in higher education due to the changes and integration in technologies. The focus is on the social, cultural, and historical settings in which technology is used. After an introductory chapter on the theory itself, the book is arranged into two sections: Making Sense of the Complex World of Higher Education, and Activity Theory Applied to the Study of Higher Education international Students in Technology-Mediated Learning. Each chapter includes examples and references. The editors provide a compiled list of references from all chapters, and an index to the work as a whole. The work might benefit from cross-references between chapters, and a glossary either within each chapter or for the work as a whole. It will be useful for school administrators, teachers, academics, and policy makers interested in understanding and addressing the changes that occurring in education due to the swift changes in technology.—**Sara Marcus**

310. **Cases on Professional Distance Education Degree Programs and Practices: Successes, Challenges, and Issues.** Kirk P. H. Sullivan, Peter E. Czigler, and Jenny M. Sullivan Hellgren, eds. Hershey, Pa., Information Science Reference, 2013. 411p. index. $175.00; $265.00 (e-book); $350.00 (print and online editions). ISBN 13: 978-1-46664-486-1; 978-1-46664-487-8 (e-book).

This volume, part of the Advances in Mobile and Distance Learning Book series, offers 12 case studies regarding professional distance education degree programs around the world. Authored by 20 international scholars and practitioners, the collection has an international coverage from Western and Eastern countries, both technologically advanced and those not as advanced. Covering topics such as specific online programs including MBA and teacher education, plagiarism, creating online community and collaboration opportunities, interaction, and security, the authors offer reports from the field. Unfortunately, many of the references are dated, and a lack of consistency in format of the case studies makes it harder to follow from one study to another to find desired sections of information. A detailed table of contents and index will enable location of desired materials by subject and topic, while a compilation of references only serves to emphasize the dated nature of the literature reviewed for the case studies. While the topics discussed can be of value, the dated nature and lack of consistency lessen the value of this collection.—**Sara Marcus**

311. **Cases on Quality Teaching Practices in Higher Education.** Diane J. Salter, ed. Hershey, Pa., Information Science Reference, 2013. 426p. index. $175.00; $265.00 (e-book); $350.00 (print and e-book editions). ISBN 13: 978-1-46663-661-3; 978-1-46663-662-0 (e-book).

Edited by the Vice Provost, Teaching and Learning at Kwantlen Polytechnic-University in British Columbia, Canada, these 22 chapters authored by 33 scholars and practitioners in the field of higher education provide concrete examples of best practices in teaching and learning at individual and institutional levels. The authors provide materials that can inspire, and also that can be recreated, adapted, and excerpted for one's own classroom, department, or institution. Organized into three chapters, the work begins with an introduction and a chapter on background research, a lengthy and in-depth literature review on the topic of quality teaching practices in higher education. The second section provides eight case studies from award-winning teachers, while the third provides 12 institutional cases that support excellence in teaching. Ranging in both disciplines and sizes of institution, there is a chapter to suit each situation, easily identified through the detailed table of contents provided in the volume. A compilation of references enables further research on the topic as a whole, while references in each chapter offer topic-specific lists of readings. This book will assist any higher education educator, administrator, or instructional designer, as well as future educators, in identifying best practices for their own situations, as well as cases to study for professional development and class exercises.—**Sara Marcus**

312.   **E-Learning 2.0 Technologies and Web Applications in Higher Education.** Jean-Eric Pelet, ed. Hershey, Pa., Information Science Reference, 2014. 395p. index. (Advances in Higher Education and Professional Development). $175.00; $265.00 (e-book); $350.00 (print and e-book editions). ISBN 13: 978-1-46664-876-0; 978-1-46664-877-7 (e-book).

Edited by an assistant professor in management with a Ph.D. in marketing and an MBA in information systems, this volume brings together 15 chapters authored by over 30 international authors. The chapters range from narratives and case studies to analytical empirical works, sharing theory and practical writings, highlighting comparisons and practices of knowledge technologies in the higher education realm. Chapters focus on effective e-learning strategies, online learning communities, cultural issues in the adoption of e-learning, and effective implementation of an interuniversity e-learning initiative. Not for the novice to the field, these chapters all include ideas for further research or future work, references, and key terms and definitions. A detailed table of contents and index enables one to find specific areas of interest, while a compilation of references helps one to find additional information. What would be useful is a compilation of key terms and definitions to serve as a glossary for the field as not each author defined the terms for their own piece. This volume is geared for those in higher education and will be useful to academics who want to improve their understanding of the strategic role of e-learning.—**Shannon Graff Hysell**

313.   **Evolving Corporate Education Strategies for Developing Countries: The Role of Universities.** B. PanduRanga Narasimharao, S. Rangappa Kanchugarakoppal, and Tukaram U. Fulzele, eds. Hershey, Pa., Information Science Reference, 2013. 389p. index. $175.00; $265.00 (e-book); $350.00 (print and e-book editions). ISBN 13: 978-1-46662-845-8; 978-1-46662-846-5 (e-book).

This volume brings together 24 chapters authored by more than 30 international scholars, researchers, and practitioners on the area of corporate education. Separated into four sections—Corporate Education, Knowledge Economy, and Higher Education; Human Capital Development; Preparing Professionals; and Higher Education Institutions and Corporate Education—this volume provides theories and opportunities for integrating corporate education into traditional educational systems. It highlights the practice of developing countries putting academic theory into practice by integrating their cultural traditions with their intellectual higher education system. It is not a how-to book, but rather provides examples of how others have done it. This is good for those who wish examples of how other countries have grown to compete on the global scale by improving their corporate education. An index and detailed table of contents enables one to quickly find desired information. The work will be of use to policy makers, practitioners, and scholars.—**Sara Marcus**

314.   Gelb, Alan. **Conquering the College Admissions Essay in 10 Easy Steps.** 2d ed. Berkeley, Calif., Ten Speed Press, 2013. 224p. $11.99pa. ISBN 13: 978-1-60774-366-8.

Acknowledging that the personal essay can mean the difference between being accepted or rejected to a preferred university, the author of this work introduces readers to ways in which they can enhance their essay and provide it with enough professionalism and character to get the attention of college admission decision makers. Gelb notes that most public schools lack the necessary attention to college preparation that ensure success so he has set out to fill that gap with this instructional guide. The author's step-by-step approach will appeal to high school age students. He begins by helping students focus on a compelling topic that will catch the interest of admissions staff and then gives pointers on providing the right structure, tone, and point of view. The work provides several sample essays, which will be helpful for those needing extra assistance. With the addition of a teacher's guide at the end of the volume, this guide will work well in the classroom where composition teachers as well as guidance counselors can benefit from its expertise. [R: VOYA, Oct 2013, pp. 97-98]—**Sara Marcus**

315.   **International Education and the Next-Generation Workforce: Competition in the Global Economy.** Victor C. X. Wang, ed. Hershey, Pa., Information Science Reference, 2013. 288p. index. $180.00; $255.00 (e-book); $360.00 (print and online editions). ISBN 13: 978-1-46664-498-4; 978-1-46664-499-1 (e-book).

Edited by an associate professor at Florida Atlantic University, this work brings together 24 international scholars and practitioners to author 14 chapters that stand alone on the topic of international education and competing in the global economy. Offering an international coverage, including China, the Russian Federation, the European Union, Egypt, and Hong Kong, this volume is part of the Advances in Higher Education and Professional Development series. The chapters cover a range of topics, including collaboration, international education, the influence of andragogy, recruiting international students to a university in the United States, technology use, the role of professional organizations, open education, and more. Some of the chapters are case studies, offering insights on what has been done and how to improve or change what is currently occurring in one's own institution in any type of environment, while others offer a historical overview or an examination of the literature on a topic. While the range of topics and types of materials presented leads to a little bit for a lot of people, this very spread can lead to the lack of value for a specific purpose of the purchase. This book is good for larger collections, where there is a wider breadth of knowledge needed or desired.—**Sara Marcus**

316.   **The International Handbook on Social Innovation: Collective Action, Social Learning and Transdisciplinary Research.** 1st ed. Frank Moulaert, Diana MacCallum, Abid Mehmood, and Abdelillah Hamdouch, eds. Northhampton, Mass., Edward Elgar, 2013. 500p. index. $240.00. ISBN 13: 978-1-84980-998-6.

Some 61 scholars (including the 4 editors) from research institutes and universities in Europe, Canada and South America have contributed to this handbook. The chapters present not only theoretical discussions of social innovation, but also a thorough examination of the social, political, cultural, environmental, and economic drivers of innovative initiatives that are implemented in situations of social exclusion and inequality. As the editors state, they frame the book by three interrelated features of social innovation: "satisfaction of needs, reconfigured social relations and empowerment or political mobilization."

The handbook is divided into 6 parts and a total of 35 chapters. Each part begins with its own introduction and description of how the individual chapters relate to the topic at hand. Of particular interest are the questions for discussion at the end of each chapter as well as a conclusion to bring everything together. In addition, there are notes and lists of references, some in bold that signify a title recommended for further reading. Part 1 consists of seven chapters on social innovation from concept to theory and practice. Part 2 delves into the theory of social innovation, and part 3 provides 6 case studies in social innovation analysis. Part 4 showcases 7 methodologies and research strategies for social innovation analysis, and part 5 illustrates 6 examples of collective action. And finally, part 6 features an in-depth look at the frontiers in social innovation research. There are 13 figures (illustrations) and 13 tables to clarify concepts. A comprehensive index begins on page 481.

This handbook could serve as a textbook for upper-division and graduate sociology and public policy programs. It would be a good addition to large public, community, and academic library collections.—**Laura J. Bender**

317.   **Outlooks and Opportunities in Blended and Distance Learning.** B. Tynan, J. Willems, and R. James, eds. Hershey, Pa., Information Science Reference, 2013. 473p. index. $175.00; $265.00 (e-book); $350.00 (print and online edition). ISBN 13: 978-1-46664-205-8; 978-1-46664-206-5 (e-book).

Part of the Advances in Mobile and Distance Learning book series, this volume is organized into three sections: instructional design, interaction and communication in learning communities, and learner characteristics. These 29 chapters, authored by 53 international scholars and practitioners offer a strong emphasis on Australia, although the United States and South Africa are also represented. In the second section addressing interaction and communications, large emphasis is on the more advanced technologies, such as Second Life and virtual environments, simulations, and 3-D immersive virtual worlds, which is much needed, although there are still instances where lower-level technologies might also be suitable. The third section, which will be of most interest to the largest number of distance educators and administrators, addresses the learner and educator characteristics and shares ideas and insights on how to improve the learning experience from all sides. The volume includes a compilation of references and a detailed table of contents along with an informative introduction, which together enable the reader to find individual chapters of interest. An index enables location of specific pages of use to the individual user.

This book will assist any educator, administrator, or advanced student using any portion of distance learning in the educational experience, with an emphasis on the college and university level. However, all levels can benefit from learning about effective design for the current and future learning and educational experiences.—**Sara Marcus**

318.   **Social Media and the New Academic Environment: Pedagogical Challenges.** Bogdan Patrut, Monica Patrut, and Camelia Cmeciu, eds. Hershey, Pa., Information Science Reference, 2013. 487p. index. $175.00; $265.00 (e-book); $350.00 (print and e-book editions). ISBN 13: 978-1-46662-851-9; 978-1-46662-852-6 (e-book).

Edited by three faculty members representing the departments of computer science, political science, and communication studies at Vasile Alecsandri University of Bacau, Romania, this work brings together 20 chapters authored by more than 30 researchers, practitioners, and students in the fields of computer science, online education, and communications. The cases and examples in these chapters provide a unique overview of the role social media plays in the creation and exchange of user-generated content and social interaction in the educational realm. While the articles raise interesting points it is important to be aware that each of the countries represented has different educational systems and values which affect the way social media affects and is accepted within their education system. Separated into four sections, the work explores pedagogical challenges presented, social media as a means for current education, national practices of social media in higher education, and the impact of social media technologies. Focusing on the benefits and challenges that social media represents in the world of education, this work is valuable to educators, practitioners, and students of education who want to know more about this changing impact and influences. The volume includes an annotated table of contents and an index as well as a compiled list of references at the end. This should not be the sole resource consulted when researching this topic, but it can be of value, particularly to those studying the impact of social media on education on a global scale.—**Sara Marcus**

319.   **Social Media in Higher Education: Teaching in Web 2.0.** Monica Patrut and Bogdan Patrut, eds. Hershey, Pa., Information Science Reference, 2013. 448p. index. $175.00; $265.00 (e-book); $350.00 (print and e-book editions). ISBN 13: 978-1-46662-970-7; 978-1-46662-971-4 (e-book).

The predominant international authorship in *Social Media in Higher Education* illustrates the importance and increasing utilization of social media in higher education not only in the United States but also around the world. The editors, academics in the fields of political communication and computer science, present a snapshot of the current status and usage of social media tools, such as Facebook, Twitter, and Websites, by presenting case studies from 31 educators and researchers.

The 19 chapters are divided into 4 sections that reflect a logical division of significant issues that educators must address: teaching 2.0; student 2.0; tools and technological issues in Web 2.0; and educational and ethical issues in Web 2.0 Age. Topics addressing the implementation and integration of social media strategies in the classroom are presented in the first section. How students successfully engage in the learning environment using social media is covered in the next section. The third section focuses on Web technologies, Twitter, and Facebook concerns. The final section contains timely issues, such as subversive technologies, online anxiety, cyberbullying, and mobile learning. Each chapter begins with an abstract and introduction, and concludes with a list of References and Key Terms and Definitions. Some chapters contain figures, tables, additional reading lists, and endnotes. An index is included. Two features worth noting are: a detailed table of contents containing the chapter abstracts and a compilation of the individual chapter References.

The editors have compiled an impressive overview of the use of social media in higher education. This resource is an excellent starting point for educators who want and need to understand the valuable contributions that social media can make to the academic curriculum.—**Alice Crosetto**

320.   **Synergic Integration of Formal and Informal E-Learning Environments for Adult Lifelong Learners.** Sabrina Leone, ed. Hershey, Pa., Information Science Reference, 2014. 313p. index. (Advances in Higher Education and Professional Development). $175.00; $265.00 (e-book); $350.00 (print and e-book editions). ISBN 13: 978-1-46664-655-1; 978-1-46664-656-8 (e-book).

321.   **Technology Use and Research Approaches for Community Education and Professional Development.** Valerie Carson Bryan and Victor C. X. Wang, eds. Hershey, Pa., Information Science Reference, 2013. 338p. index. $175.00; $265.00 (e-book); $350.00 (print and e-book editions). ISBN 13: 978-1-46662-955-4; 978-1-46662-956-1 (e-book).

Drawing on the experiences of more than 20 international practitioners in higher education, *Synergic Integration of Formal and Informal E-Learning Environments for Adult Lifelong Learners* presents 12 chapters that present the issues and research from the study of adult education on developing, implanting, and evaluating formal and informal e-learning environments. Providing both content-based chapters and case studies, this work looks at the pedagogical potential of lifelong learning for adult students in a variety of academic subjects, cultures, and institutions. The work is organized into three sections: Infrastructural and Cultural Issues; Pedagogical Issues; and Technological Issues. The detailed table of contents and descriptive preface will help readers to locate desired chapters, while the index assists in locating pages on specific topics. A compilation of references serves as a bibliography for the topic.

Technology Use and Research Approaches for Community Education and Professional Development looks at how the rapid changes in information technology are affecting academic and professional environments. Specifically, it looks at the best practices for using technology to enhance professional development, the dissemination of information, and the future of professional development in the professional culture. The work has a detailed table of contents that will help readers discern where to go for the type of information they are looking for. There is also a compilation of references and an index that conclude the volume.

These books will be of use to any educator, instructional designer, administrator, or researcher interested in using the latest technologies in adult learning programs, or seeing how information and communication technologies can be implemented with adult learners who might be more resistant to the use of technology.—**Sara Marcus**

Nonprint Materials

322.   **The Digital Classroom. http://www.archives.gov/education.** [Website]. Free. Date reviewed: 2014.

This is NARA's gateway to resources about primary sources, activities, and training for educators and students. Links to the Summer Institute for Teachers, Presidential Libraries' Resources, and lesson plans can be found. Be sure to take a look at Regional Resources for Educators. The Digital Classroom is offering its newest online tool kit, DocsTeach, designed to let users use, modify, or create their own interactive lessons. Special model lessons will connect to themes like the "Bringing the Constitution to Life."—**Mary J. Johnson**

323.   **Primary Access. http://www.primaryaccess.org/.** [Website]. Free. Date reviewed: 2014.

     This Website offers a suite of free online tools with which students can use primary source documents to complete assignments. Using these tools, students can create digital movies, storyboards, or rebus stories. Teachers choose a variety of primary source resources to create the assignment online. Students then use a teacher-assigned user name and password and access the assignment where they use the documents and images in the folder to create their own finished product. Should the teacher not wish to create their own assignments, there are existing activities that they can use. Primary source documents are divided into two categories—U.S. history eras and world history eras—and they come from such well-known archives as PBS, the Smithsonian, and the Library of Congress. Although this reviewer did not find the use of the program intuitive, the Help section provides detailed, useful instructions. For schools with a low budget looking for ways to incorporate technology, this Website will provide a good resource.—**Ann M. G. Gray**

6 Ethnic Studies and Anthropology

Anthropology

324. **National Anthropological Archives and Human Studies Film Archives. http://www.nmnh. si.edu/naa/index.htm.** [Website]. Free and fee-based. Date reviewed: 2013.

The National Anthropological Archives and human Studies Film Archives has changed significantly since its inception and now is part of the Smithsonian Institution's National Museum of Natural History. As a result the number of collections it holds the resource has expanded significantly. Access to some of the site is fee-based; however, there are finding aids to about one-third of the collection plus online samples free of charge. In accomplishing their mission of collecting, preserving, and making accessible historical anthropological materials, the site provides an abundance of primary resources, including field notes, manuscripts, correspondence, maps, still images, sound recordings, maps, and journals. All of these have been collected from preeminent scholars in the field. Users will have access to hundreds of thousands of ethnological and archaeological photographs, thousands of works of native art, over 10,000 sound recordings, and original film and video. This source is a useful source of information for social scientists, scholars, and undergraduate students of anthropology.—**ARBA Staff Reviewer**

Ethnic Studies

General Works

Catalogs and Collections

325. **MIT Visualizing Cultures. http://ocw.mit.edu/ans7870/21f/21f.027/home/index.html.** [Website]. Massachusetts Institute of Technology. Free. Date reviewed: 2013.

This is a fantastic open-access collection of historical visual images emphasizing Japan and China's experience with modernity. It includes timelines and essays for educators. Topical units to date focus on Japan in the modern world and early-modern China. The concept of these explorations extends beyond Asia, however, to address "culture" in much broader ways—cultures of modernization, war and peace, consumerism, images of "Self" and "Others," and more.—**Noriko Asato**

Dictionaries and Encyclopedias

326.   **Encyclopedia of Race and Racism.** 2d ed. Patrick L. Mason, ed. Stamford, Conn., MacmillanGale/
Cengage Learning, 2013. 4v. illus. index. (Macmillan Library Reference). $595.00/set. ISBN 13: 978-0-
02-866174-2; 978-0-02-866195-7 (e-book).

This compilation examines racism and responses to racism through historical, cultural, political,
and biological perspectives, with an emphasis on developments in the United States and to a lesser
extent in Europe. However, race is analyzed as a factor in national and ethnic identity around the world,
including phenomena of racism in influential twenty-first century countries such as Russia, Brazil,
India, China, and Japan. Articles cover critical historical events such as the Voting Rights Act of 1965,
influential ideologies including Afrocentrism and Apartheid, significant individuals from Nat Turner to
Nelson Mandela, prominent organizations like the NAACP and SNCC, and cultural representations in
sports and the media. The selection of content reflects not only potential readership among students
and researchers in American colleges and universities, but also an approach that interprets racism as a
socially constructed system of controls tied to the expansion of Western societies on a global scale since
the sixteenth century.

A new editorial board has added substantial content since the 1st edition of 2008 (see ARBA 2008,
entry 302); over half of the material is new. Articles are arranged in alphabetic order, but information also
can be located through an index, cross-references, and a thematic list that ties each article to one of 22
topics such as African American culture, genocide, legal issues, genetics, and political economy. Close
to 500 entries are offered, including short sidebars, more than 60 biographical articles, and an appendix
of primary source texts drawn from speeches, manifestos, and court opinions. In addition to references at
the end of each signed article, there is an annotated bibliography, and an annotated filmography covering
both feature films and documentaries. Most of the contributors are American academics, but there is
substantial international representation, including some impressive names such as Richard J. Evans
writing about National Socialism in Germany.

The content does not shy away from potentially unpopular approaches to uncomfortable topics. The
concept of genocide is given a wide interpretation, one that extends to historical atrocities in Armenia,
Bosnia, and Rwanda, in addition to a long article on the Holocaust. A series of articles setting nationalism
and ethnicity in context around the globe replaces a controversial article in the first edition about Zionism.
Entries about biology and genetics relate principally to the employment of scientific evidence in social
science.

Among comparable publications, the *Encyclopedia of Racism in the United States* (see ARBA 2007,
entry 263) and the *Encyclopedia of Race, Ethnicity, and Society* (see ARBA 2009, entry 293) limit their
coverage narrowly to the United States. The current work takes a more global view, and also brings
coverage of events forward in time, including the reelection of President Barack Obama in 2012.—
Steven W. Sowards

327.   Minahan, James B. **Ethnic Groups in the Americas: An Encyclopedia.** Santa Barbara, Calif.,
ABC-CLIO, 2013. 411p. illus. index. (Ethnic Groups of the World). $89.00. ISBN 13: 978-1-61069-163-
5; 978-1-61069-164-2 (e-book).

Attitudes toward minority ethnic groups have varied over history. In the past, ethnic differences were
not valued and were often repressed. Now we better understand how ethnic groups enrich our society.
This reference provides an overview of the ethnic groups of North and South America from the Arctic
Circle to Tierra del Fuego—from well-known groups such as the Hopi and Navajo in the United States
to lesser-known peoples such as the Chatinos and Triques in Oaxaca, Mexico, the Aymaras in the central
Andes, the Chipewyans of the Canadian Arctic and the Kalaallits of Greenland. For example, we read
about the Guianans, the inhabitants of French Guiana, best known for the spice cayenne, Devil's Island
and the European Space Agency center at Kourou. During the French Revolution, political opponents

were sent to this French colony, now an overseas department of France. A penal colony since the time of Napoleon, this infamous prison was not closed until 1952. Entries cover the core populations of each country in the Americas as well as describing the rich tapestry that is created by the myriad ethnic groups of the two continents. For each group we learn the geographic location, languages spoken, and the highlights of its social, political, cultural, and historical development. Each entry is followed with suggestions for further reading. The author takes a broad definition of ethnic groups and includes people who self-identify as a separate entity on the basis of such factors as religious beliefs or language as well as those ethnically or racially differentiated. A useful feature is a geographic index to locate ethnic groups within a specific country. This reference demonstrates what an interesting and diverse world we live in and will be useful in high school and public libraries.—**Adrienne Antink**

328.   **Native Peoples of the World: An Encyclopedia of Groups, Cultures, and Contemporary Issues.** Steven Danver, ed. Armonk, N.Y., M. E. Sharpe, 2013. 3v. illus. index. $349.00/set. ISBN 13: 978-0-7656-8222-2.

This is an encyclopedia of the native peoples of each continent, their histories, and their connection to the ecosystem in which they live. Organized in three parts, "Groups" describes each indigenous group in terms of its culture, history, and current status. "Countries" gives the reader a sense of how these people have dealt with shifting populations. "Issues" discusses how issues are the same or different for various peoples across the globe. Unfortunately, it is very dry reading and it is doubtful that it will be used in a secondary school setting.—**Donna Reed**

Handbooks and Yearbooks

329.   **Cultures of the World: Afghanistan.** Tarrytown, N.Y., Marshall Cavendish, 2014. 144p. illus. maps. index. (Cultures of the World). $32.95/vol.; $197.70/set. ISBN 13: 978-1-60870-866-6.

330.   **Cultures of the World: France.** Tarrytown, N.Y., Marshall Cavendish, 2014. 144p. illus. maps. index. (Cultures of the World). $32.95/vol.; $197.70/set. ISBN 13: 978-1-60870-867-3.

331.   **Cultures of the World: Germany.** Tarrytown, N.Y., Marshall Cavendish, 2014. 144p. illus. maps. index. (Cultures of the World). $32.95/vol.; $197.70/set. ISBN 13: 978-1-60870-868-0.

332.   **Cultures of the World: Greece.** Tarrytown, N.Y., Marshall Cavendish, 2014. 144p. illus. maps. index. (Cultures of the World). $32.95/vol.; $197.70/set. ISBN 13: 978-1-60870-869-7.

333.   **Cultures of the World: Italy.** Tarrytown, N.Y., Marshall Cavendish, 2014. 144p. illus. maps. index. (Cultures of the World). $32.95/vol.; $197.70/set. ISBN 13: 978-1-60870-870-3.

334.   **Cultures of the World: Spain.** Tarrytown, N.Y., Marshall Cavendish, 2013. 144p. illus. maps. index. (Cultures of the World). $32.95/vol.; $197.70/set. ISBN 13: 978-1-60870-871-0.

This is the 3d edition of this popular award-winning series for middle and high school age students. Six new titles have recently been added on Afghanistan, Germany, France, Greece, Italy, and Spain. Each title provides information on the geography, early history, government, economy, environment, culture, lifestyle, religion, language, arts, leisure, festivals, and food. The focus is on the people of the culture and what makes them unique in their region of the world. The series provides several Common Core connections for researchers, including social studies words defined throughout the text and integrated visual information found throughout the text. The work is supplemented with maps, a historical timeline, a glossary, a bibliography, up-to-date statistics and fact, and resources for further information (including Websites for further information at the end of each chapter). This is an enjoyable series for students to use for research or for the lay reader to browse through. It continues to be a worthwhile series to add to most school and public libraries.—**Shannon Graff Hysell**

335.   **A History of Jewish-Muslim Relations: From the Origins to the Present Day.** Abdelwahab Medde and Benjamin Stora, eds. Princeton, N.J., Princeton University Press, 2013. 1145p. illus. maps. index. $75.00. ISBN 13: 978-0-691-15127-4.

This reference work of 14 centuries of shared history between Jews and Muslims is properly prescribed. Attempts at factual history and informed dialogue permeated the four parts of this illustrated and reader-friendly volume. The four parts are parsed into chapters and cover history, geography, culture, language, literature, personalities, philosophy, and religion. Primary and secondary sources are consulted. Part 1 surveys and medieval period. Part 2 discusses the Ottoman Empire, Asia, Africa, and Europe. Part 3 embraces twentieth-century nationalism, politics, and treatment of Jews and Muslims in the Arab states and the State of Israel, respectfully. Part 4 intersects origins, philosophy, beliefs, and scholarship.

Entries are well researched by an international team of Jewish, Christian, and Muslim scholars who write with fortitude and fairness. For the most part, the essays exhibit historiography, defining interrelating Jewish an Muslim issues of yore that are now in a state of disarray, and a wellspring of facts and tidbits that convey empathy not animosity between two monotheistic peoples bounded by history, defined by land, and guided by religion of law. Helpful to the nonspecialist are discussions of relevant belief claims and behavior patterns, and the effect of sacred tradition on the life of people. This work is highly recommended.—**Zev Garber**

African Americans

336.   Assensoh, A. B., and Yvette M. Alex-Assensoh. **Malcolm X: A Biography.** Santa Barbara, Calif., Greenwood Press/ABC-CLIO, 2014. 162p. illus. index. (Greenwood Biographies). $37.00. ISBN 13: 978-0-313-37849-2; 978-0-313-37850-8 (e-book).

Another in the Greenwood Biographies series aimed at high school students and the general reader, this biography offers nothing new in terms of scholarship but is packaged full of information for its intended audience. Attractively bound, illustrated with photographs, and reassuringly short, it lays out succinctly and in an engaging style the facts, life, and beliefs of Malcolm X in chronological order. Writing for a high school and young adult audience, the author provides plenty of examples of influences from his early childhood, his participation in illegal activity and time spent in prison, his conversion to the Muslim faith, and his relationship with other prominent African American civil rights leaders, including Martin Luther King Jr. In fact, students will learn about much more than just the life of Malcolm X; they will also get a better grasp on the struggle within the African American community during the Civil Rights movement of the 1960s. This emphasis on brevity and understandability does not do justice to the complexity of Malcolm X's life and role as a leader in the African American community, but it may gently lead otherwise reluctant readers to further study. A fairly extensive bibliography of print and electronic secondary sources support this effort. As is its intent, this book is appropriate for secondary school and public libraries.—**Nancy L. Van Atta**

337.   **Black Firsts: 4,000 Ground-Breaking and Pioneering Historical Events.** 3d ed. Jessie Carney Smith, ed. Canton, Mich., Visible Ink Press, 2013. 833p. illus. index. $24.95pa. ISBN 13: 978-1-57859-369-9.

Black Firsts is a record of black achievement, aimed to give readers a capsule view of the history of blacks worldwide. It is arranged chronologically under 16 broad chapter headings, such as "Civil

Rights and Protest," "Education," "Journalism," and "Science and Medicine." The broad headings are further divided into categories; for example, under "Arts and Entertainment" one finds "Comedy Shows," "Dance," "Drama, Dramatists, and Theater," "Festivals," and "Film," just to name a few. Under each category, entries begin with a date in bold type, followed by the person's name, his or her birth and death date (if applicable), and the person's "first" achievement. For inclusion in the book, entries had to be documented, using several sources of information whenever possible. Most entries are several sentences long, and some are more than one paragraph, not merely stating the person's "first" but giving something about the person's background and other accomplishments as well. Following each entry is the bibliographic information of the source or sources of information.

Sidebars provide additional information on items of interest, such as "The Supreme Court's First Black Justice," "The First Black Four-star Admiral," "The First Black Episcopal Bishop," or "The Oldest Surviving Black Medical School in the South." Interspersed throughout the text are black-and-white photographs or illustrations of subjects. A comprehensive index provides quick access to entries, and there is a complete bibliography of books and periodicals used as sources for the entries. Hundreds of new entries have been added since the publication of the 2d edition in 2003 and many more have been updated.

This is an authoritative reference work and a welcome addition to black history. It will be appreciated by researchers and browsers alike. Secondary schools, college and university libraries, and public libraries should all consider this an essential reference.—**ARBA Staff Reviewer**

338.   **Lucent Library of Black History Series.** Farmington Hills, Mich., Lucent Books/Gale/Cengage Learning, 2012. multivolume. illus. index. $34.80/vol.

This multivolume series on African American history is aimed at 6th through 10th grade students. Recently published volumes are on landmarks in black history, women civil rights leaders, and James Foreman and the Student Nonviolent Coordinating Committee. The series aims to provide young people with an accurate portrayal of the broad impact that African Americans have had on American history and how specific people have changed the course of history. All of these volumes achieve that aim through clear writing, comprehensive, age- and grade-level information, and attractive and colorful illustrations that bring each topic to life.

The authors are writers of books for young people. Each volume focuses on a type of unique period in time or person of influence. The series attempts to provide insight into the broad movements such as Black Nationalism as well as narrow topics such as Reconstruction. All volumes have sidebars describing historic people or historic events, numerous photographs and illustrations, documentation of quotations, and an annotated bibliography. This set is highly recommended for school and public libraries.—**Shannon Graff Hysell**

339.   Smith, Jessie Carney. **The Handy African American History Answer Book.** Canton, Mich., Visible Ink Press, 2014. 295p. illus. index. $21.95pa. ISBN 13: 978-1-57859-452-8.

Part of Visible Ink's Handy Answer Book Series, this new volume features answers to about 1,000 frequently asked questions about African American history and influential African American leaders and visionaries. It is organized into 14 chapters comprising broad areas such as religion, education, business and commerce, sports, literature, military, music, and science and invention. The chapters are subdivided into more specific categories; for example, the chapter on religion is broken down into specific eras such as African American Christians in the colonial era, racial segregation and the black church, early religious leaders and civil rights, and megachurches in the African American community. The responses vary in length from one to four paragraphs. Illustrations are in black and white, and there are sidebars highlighting interesting and relevant historical information. The index is adequate. An example of the questions answered, includes: What was the Black Arts Movement?; What Was the Impact of Negro Leagues Baseball on American Culture?; and What Is the Historical Role of the Barbershop in the African American Community? Given the scope and subject matter, the author has done an admirable job in crafting this work. It is recommended for public, school, and academic libraries.—**Lori D. Kranz**

Asian Americans

340.   **Asian Americans: An Encyclopedia of Social, Cultural, Economic, and Political History.** Xiaojian Zhao and Edward J. W. Park, eds. Santa Barbara, Calif., Greenwood Press/ABC-CLIO, 2014. 3v. illus. index. $310.00/set. ISBN 13: 978-1-59884-239-5; 978-1-59884-240-1(e-book).

This comprehensive three-volume work provides historical information on the social, cultural, economic, and political lives of Asian and Pacific Islander American groups from 1848 up to the present day. This work will serve as a one-stop resource for those looking for accurate information on important policies, events, and notable individuals from this population. Special attention has been placed on ensuring that women are well represented here as well as some of the lesser-known ethnic groups. While many of the expected topics appear here users will also find information on topics that will be difficult to find in other sources, such as transnationalism, gender and sexuality, and multiracial family units. Led by a professor of Asian American studies at the University of California, Santa Barbara, and a professor of Asian Pacific American studies at Loyola Marymount University, the volume has contributed entries by scholars, journalists, community activists, and other specialist of Asian American studies. The set is highly recommended.—**Seiko Mieczkowski**

Bengalis

341.   Chakrabarti, Kunal, and Shubhra Chakrabarti. **Historical Dictionary of the Bengalis.** Lanham, Md., Scarecrow, 2013. 571p. (Historical Dictionaries of Peoples and Cultures). $145.00; $139.99 (e-book). ISBN 13: 978-0-8108-5334-8; 978-0-8108-8024-5 (e-book).

This volume opens with a necessarily brief introduction to the history of the Bengalis who are located in the northeastern part of South Asia, more specifically Bangladesh, West Bengal, and Tripura. Its authors, a professor of ancient Indian history at the Jawaharlal Nehru University in New Delhi and an associate profess of history at Dayal Singh College in New Delhi, review the history, begin with an introductory essay discussing how the Bengalis have influenced culture within their region, particularly in the areas of political consciousness and cultural accomplishments. With sections on current political trends and economic mapping along with a discussion of the cultural fabric of the people, the reader gains a solid background for use of the dictionary itself with its hundreds of cross-referenced entries. These entries range from very short to several pages long and include discussions of many specific individuals from the full range of the history to consideration of movements and other topics, such as places, events, institutions, economy, politics, and culture. Of particular interest to some may be the many entries about the Bengali's contributions to the arts, political thought, and religious thought. The volume also includes a chronological outline, maps, and a very extensive topical bibliography. This historical dictionary can thus serve as an excellent starting point to learn about this people. Furthermore, its accessible language makes it easily comprehensible to the interested lay public. Ultimately, the volume will make an excellent addition to academic libraries, both colleges and larger high schools, as well as to general library systems.—**Susan Tower Hollis**

Indians of North America

Bibliography

342.   **Index of Native American Book Resources on the Internet. http://www.hanksville.org/ NAresources/indices/NAbooks.html.** [Website]. Free. Date reviewed: 2013.

Self-described as a "Virtual Library [for] American Indians," this site provides information resources to the Native American community, which comprises both the United States and Canada. The site provides a list of individual Native American authors; links to Native American playwrights, Native American women playwrights, and Native American storytellers; links to books available online; links to organizations; links to journals and online journals; links to Native American library collections; links to Native American presses; links to book reviews and excerpts; and a link to one Native American comic book Website. The site is maintained through the suggestions and updated information of both users and those listed on the site.—**Sharron Smith**

Dictionaries and Encyclopedias

343.   **Encyclopedia of American Indian Issues Today.** Russell M. Lawson, ed. Santa Barbara, Calif., Greenwood Press/ABC-CLIO, 2013. 2v. illus. index. $189.00/set. ISBN 13: 978-0-313-38144-7; 978-0-313-38145-4 (e-book).

This reference gives the reader an array of essays on the legal, political, economic, educational, cultural, environmental, artistic, religious, demographic, medical, and social issues affecting contemporary American Indians. As an example, we see how gaming, the "new buffalo," has spread across Indian lands and its financial impact on tribes. We learn that American Indians and Alaska Natives have the highest high school dropout rate of any ethnic group—as high as 45 percent. The Native American Higher Education Movement is described including the creation in 1977 of the Navajo Community College (now the Dine College), which was the first college established and controlled by an Indian tribe. Today, there are 37 tribal colleges and universities in the United States and 1 in Canada. The authors tell us about the difficulties in preserving Native American cultures and identities and the intricacies of determining ownership and repatriation of Indian remains and artifacts. Given the breadth of the topic to be covered in only two volumes, the information is by necessity fairly superficial. The use of multiple authors provides diverse viewpoints but also results in redundancy in the information conveyed. Interestingly, a section is included on Canadian First Nations and their relationship to the Canadian government.—**Adrienne Antink**

344.   Johansen, Bruce E. **Encyclopedia of the American Indian Movement.** Santa Barbara, Calif., Greenwood Press/ABC-CLIO, 2013. 362p. illus. index. (Movements of the American Mosaic). $89.00. ISBN 13: 978-1-4408-0317-8; 978-1-4408-0318-5 (e-book).

The American Indian, as has been the case with other racial minorities in America, has suffered a multitude of indignities. The *Encyclopedia of American Indian Movement* fill a gap in the literature for student interested in learning more about the people, events, and issues that affected the lives of American Indians during the 1960s and 1970s. Some of these events include the occupation of Alcatraz and problems with fishing rights contracts. The author makes comparisons between the American Indian to other repressed groups in our society, including African Americans, Latinos, and Asians. The author makes a point to connect how the treatment of Native Americans in prior decades has affected life for these people today. Numerous photographs and an extensive bibliography add to the usefulness of this work. This encyclopedia is recommended for undergraduate collections and for high school libraries.—**Lori D. Kranz**

345.   Keillor, Elaine, Tim Archambault, and John M. H. Kelly. **Encyclopedia of Native American Music of North America.** Santa Barbara, Calif., Greenwood Press/ABC-CLIO, 2013. 449p. illus. index. $89.00. ISBN 13: 978-0-313-33600-3; 978-0-313-05506-5 (e-book).

Although the bibliography of monographs on the Native American music of North America is replete, the number of reference sources on this topic is scant. The *Encyclopedia of Native American Music of North America*, therefore, is a welcome addition. In the introductory historical overview of the subject, the authors, Elaine Keillor, Timothy Archambault, and John M. H. Kelly (all proficient scholars and/or musicians), write that the *Handbook of North American Indians* (Smithsonian Institution, 1978-2008) had an editorial policy to include an essay on musical traditions in each volume, but that the results varied. Furthermore, the authors claim that researchers have documented to a significant degree only an estimated 200 of the 1,000 North American First People's cultures. The purpose of this encyclopedia is to give the reader an idea of the various types of music the Indians of North America (excluding Mexico) have used, mainly in social situations, through the twentieth century.

The *Encyclopedia* is essentially made up of two equal parts: regional essays and an A-Z listing of entries (often highlighted in the essays). The regional essays use the 10 North American culture areas of the Smithsonian multivolume set mentioned above: Arctic, Subarctic, Northwest Coast, Great Plateau, Plains, Northeastern, Southeastern, Great Basin, Southwest, and California. Each begins with a list of the main cultures (some bolded) in that geographical region; the bolded cultures get extensive treatment in the essay. Before the authors get to the main cultures, they write on broad topics related to that region. In the Plains region, for example, they include a section on "Sacred Dance Ceremonies with Their Many Songs" and "Major Changes in the 19th Century." These sections are often further divided into subsections, with a bibliography of readings and Websites at the end of the main section.

The second section is a collection of encyclopedia entries such as "Aerophones," "Ballard, Louis," "Chordophones," and "Drum Dance." Each entry concludes with Further Reading, while a few have photographs or sidebars that explore an aspect of the original entry. The user can consult a thorough index to learn the locations of terms or people throughout the book.

As mentioned above, encyclopedias of Native American music are few and far between. Although this title is clearly not intended to be the definitive source on the subject, it is a welcome supplement to the *Handbook of North American Indians*. The authors have culled from many monographs on Native American music to give the reader a historical overview, regional essays, and encyclopedia entries. This work is recommended for all public and academic libraries that focus on music or Native Americans.—**John P. Stierman**

346.   Stern, Pamela R. **Historical Dictionary of the Inuit.** 2d ed. Lanham, Md., Scarecrow, 2013. 245p. (Historical Dictionaries of People and Cultures). $100.00; $99.99 (e-book). ISBN 13: 978-0-8108-7911-9; 978-0-8108-7912-6 (e-book).

For those interested in studying the Inuit—in learning more about their history, their culture, and their contemporary people, lives, and issues—this is the basic reference that should be in their library. In this small, revised volume users will find an overview and more than 450 entries that address the social, political, and economic history of the Inuit. Special emphasis is given to the recent history of Inuit communities. This new edition has and updated chronology and the introduction provides a broader scope of the lives of the Inuit people.

Far from descriptions of snowhouses (in our childhood we called them igloos), parkas, and blubber, the reader is introduced to the educators, writers, environmentalists, politicians, and the associations and governmental agencies that have been or are influential as the Inuit continue to shape their future. The volume contains maps, an extensive chronology, a list of acronyms and special terms, an appendix that provides the dates and locations of Inuit Circumpolar Conference meetings, an appendix that lists Inuit Circumpolar leaders, Website addresses for Inuit and Arctic organizations, and an especially well-organized and comprehensive bibliography. The bibliography is organized to include reference works, ethnographies, thematic works, linguistically and geographically distinct groups, biographies, autobiographies, journals, and memoirs, and works by Inuit writers.

Of particular importance in a reference of this kind, is the experience and scholarship of the author. The reputation of the author, a recognized scholar in the field, brings credibility to the work.—**Karen D. Harvey**

Handbooks and Yearbooks

347. Akers, Donna L. **Culture and Customs of the Choctaw Indians.** Santa Barbara, Calif., Greenwood Press/ABC-CLIO, 2013. 176p. illus. index. (Culture and Customs of Native Peoples in America). $50.00. ISBN 13: 978-0-313-36401-3; 978-0-313-36402-0 (e-book).

In 2010, Greenwood Press introduced a series entitled Culture and Customs of Native Peoples in America; it is a collection of short, 150-plus page discussions of the culture, customs, contemporary issues, and history of a handful of Native American tribes. The focus of this review is *Culture and Customs of the Choctaw Indians* by Donna L. Akers.

The Choctaw Nation of Oklahoma, like the four other "Civilized Tribes" located in southeastern United States, was forced by President Andrew Jackson to leave its ancestral homeland in Mississippi and parts of Alabama in the 1830s. To help the reader understand how the Choctaw got to this tragic chapter in their history, Akers, professor of Native American History and Culture at the University of Nebraska, Lincoln, and author of *Living in the Land of Death: The Choctaw Nation, 1830-1860*, dedicates one-third of the pages to a historical overview, from the formative centuries in the Southwest to the present. These two chapters, like the other six, include helpful endnotes.

Although useful and succinct, the historical overview is not this reference book's primary selling point. A historical overview of the Choctaw is not difficult to find. But finding the information on culture and customs in the remaining chapters can tax the resources of online and print reference collections. Given the popularity of social history and ethnography, students routinely ask at the reference desk for an introduction to a "foreign" culture. Greenwood has published several series on this topic, such as Culture and Customs of Asia and Culture and Customs of Latin America and the Caribbean. Professor Akers draws from secondary sources and her personal experience as an enrolled citizen of the Choctaw Nation. She includes chapters on worldview and spiritual beliefs; social customs, gender roles, family life, and children; oral traditions; cuisine and agriculture; arts, ceremonies, and festivals; and contemporary issues. A chronology, selected bibliography, and index are also included.

Aimed at high school students and the general public, *Culture and Customs of the Choctaw Indians* will be a welcome addition to all public, school, and junior college and undergraduate libraries that serve students of Native American experience in the United States.—**John P. Stierman**

348. **American Indians at Risk.** Jeffrey Ian Ross, ed. Santa Barbara, Calif., Greenwood Press/ABC-CLIO, 2013. 2v. illus. index. $189.00/set. ISBN 13: 978-0-313-39764-6; 978-0-313-39765-3 (e-book).

What is the American Indian experience in the United States today? Although a relatively small percentage of the U.S. population (less than one percent), American Indians and Alaska Natives are more likely than other U.S. citizens to be victims of crime. This is just one example of the many problems facing contemporary indigenous peoples and therefore placing them at risk. There are many others, and Jeffrey Ian Ross, professor of criminal justice at Baltimore University, and his colleagues analyze them in *American Indians at Risk*, a two-volume handbook.

According to Ross's thorough introduction, the purpose of the text is to give readers a comprehensive understanding of the widespread controversies, policies, and practices affecting Native Americans in the United States. To do so, he has enlisted 37 scholars to tackle a variety of topics falling into one of five sections: crime/violence, culture, family, health, and work/society. The topics include, for example, gangs, victimization, hate crimes, child abuse, diabetes, substance abuse, border issues, the elderly, suicide, housing, and unemployment. Each section opens with Ross's introduction and an overview of the chapters within. The signed chapters include context, causes, current situation, and ideas for further investigation, to name a few, as well as references. Individual sections end with a selected bibliography. In addition, the handbook has a chronology, glossary, selected primary documents, and an index.

Bruce Johansen, a contributor to this title, also published a two-volume sociological examination of Indian life, *The Praeger Handbook on Contemporary Issues in Native America*, but he focuses more on current revitalization efforts within Native American society (see ARBA 2008, entry 329). Professor Ross and his colleagues are more concerned with problems or challenges: corruption, violence, delinquency, and gambling, for example. *American Indians at Risk* is a welcome addition to any undergraduate reference collection that serves students of the contemporary life of Native Americans.—**John P. Stierman**

349.   Clark, Blue. **Indian Tribes of Oklahoma: A Guide.** Norman, Okla., University of Oklahoma Press, 2013. 413p. illus. index. $19.95pa. ISBN 13: 978-0-8061-4061-2.

Long before Christopher Columbus sailed west to find a shorter route east, native peoples of the Americas inhabited what today is the state of Oklahoma. After California, Oklahoma has the largest Native American population. There are nearly 40 federally recognized tribes in the state, and Indians make up 12 percent of its population—its largest minority. To learn more about these tribes, students in the past have relied on Muriel H. Wright's *A Guide to the Indian Tribes of Oklahoma* (1951), which was reprinted as recently as 1986, but never updated. Blue Clark, professor and chair in American Indian Studies at Oklahoma City University and an enrolled member of the Muscogee Nation, has written *Indian Tribes of Oklahoma: A Guide* (see ARBA 2010, entry 299), which is now out in paper. Given shrinking book budgets, libraries of all kinds in Oklahoma and the south-central region will enjoy the 33 percent cost savings of this format.—**John P. Stierman**

350.   **The Native American Identity in Sports: Creating and Preserving a Culture.** Frank A. Salamone, ed. Lanham, Md., Scarecrow, 2013. 212p. index. $65.00; $64.99 (e-book). ISBN 13: 978-0-8108-8708-4; 978-0-8108-8709-1 (e-book).

This work provides a unique look at the impact Native Americans have had on American sports and explores the reasons why many of these achievements have gone unheralded in the sports history books. The work also explores sports that are special to the Native American culture, such as Native American tennis and the Seminole's custom of alligator wrestling, as well as the debate over using Native Americans images as sports mascots. Edited by a professor emeritus of sociology and anthropology at Iona College, New York, the volume takes an all encompassing look at how Native Americans are represented in the world of sports.—**Shannon Graff Hysell**

351.   **Voices of the American Indian Experience.** James E. Seelye Jr. and Steven A. Littleton, eds. Santa Barbara, Calif., Greenwood Press/ABC-CLIO, 2013. 2v. index. $189.00/set. ISBN 13: 978-0-313-38116-4; 978-0-313-38117-1 (e-book).

American Indian voices, throughout history, have often been erased, suppressed, or misinterpreted. In this two-volume collection of 224 documents, Native Americans, for the most part, are given the opportunity to speak for themselves.

The editors, James E. Seelye, Jr., an assistant professor of history at Kent State University, and Steven A. Littleton, a doctoral student at Northern Arizona University and former U.S. park ranger interpreter at the Little Bighorn Battlefield National Monument, have selected a wide variety of documents from creation myths to the Declaration on the Rights of Indigenous Peoples (2006). A majority are by Indian people themselves, and include myths, memoirs (e.g., war, disease, schooling), interviews, speeches, sermons, organizational records, songs, and more. The rest of the entries are either written by whites who had intimate association with Native peoples (e.g., captivity narratives, Jesuit priests' writings), or are official publications, such as pivotal Supreme Court cases, treaties, laws, resolutions, and other governmental/nongovernmental documents. Each entry has a brief description that usually includes the date of origin. Some are excerpts, so the reader may have to consult the original source (cited at the end of entry) for the complete text. A bibliography for further reading and a comprehensive index are included.

Although some of these documents are available online, many are reprinted from collections to which students may not have easy access. This work is recommended for libraries that support programs and curriculum that emphasize primary sources.—**John P. Stierman**

352.   Yasuda, Anita. **Explore Native American Cultures! With 25 Great Projects.** White River Junction, Vt., Nomad Press, 2013. 90p. Illus. $12.95pa. ISBN 13: 978-1-61930-160-3.

This book takes an interesting approach, pairing informational text with art projects that extend the learning. Pages are filled with "Words to Know" vocabulary builders, "Then and Now" comparisons, "Just for Laughs" connected jokes, and "Wow!" facts. Projects can be created from common classroom items and low cost/no cost supplies. Content include information about the five Native American cultures and their food, shelter, and clothing. Supplementary materials include a glossary and lists of additional Websites.—**Barbara Johnson**

Jews

353.   Adelman, Penina, Ali Feldman, and Shulamit Reinharz. **The Jgirl's Guide: The Young Jewish Woman's Handbook for Coming of Age.** Woodstock, Vt., Jewish Lights Publishing, 2012. 186p. $16.99. ISBN 13: 978-1-58023-215-9.

Began as a project by Ali Feldman when she was an intern at the Hadassah-Brandeis Institute it became a co-authored book along with Penina Adelman and Shulamit Reinharz. Originally published in 2005, this 2012 printing contains all of the same information and resources, leading some topics of the Internet age to be inadequately covered and some suggested resources to be omitted or needing of change. Regardless of the dated material, the content is still appropriate for all adolescent girls, particularly of the Jewish faith, who are on the cusp of becoming a teenager. Middle school and high school girls will benefit from the inspiring and interactive book that offers guidance based on Jewish beliefs and faith in areas such as school, home, friends, family, and one's own body and feelings.

Organized into 11 chapters, the work begins with an introduction that leads the reader to feel comfortable to have such confusing and questioning feelings. The following 11 chapters each discuss at least one mitzvah, or Torah commandment, related to the topic, followed by specific aspects the reader might have questions about, including opinions from other adolescents as well as adults and practitioners familiar with this age level. Some of the opinions might be conflicting, which enable the reader to make up her own mind based on her own family's and her own personal beliefs and traditions. This book is not geared for a Jewish girl of any one group, but rather offers insights and ideas for all, in a way that respects all opinions equally. Whether a girl has a question about friendship, family, eating, resting, health, self-esteem, body changes and sexuality, thinking before speaking, getting involved, or self-identity as a Jew, the book as a chapter to help. A glossary and information about the Jewish movement will help even the most estranged Jew, or non-Jew, to gain assistance and guidance from this book. Those working with this age group will also benefit from the book, as each chapter has clearly labeled parts for learning through background information and explanations, Jewish sources to base the concerns in the Jewish tradition and scriptures, discussion questions and ideas for the girl to consider alone or to use as a group discussion, stories of real-life to let the girl know she is not alone, journal writing prompts, quotes from Jewish women, activities that can be done alone or as a group, and additional points to consider as well as resources for further information.

Despite the Jewish orientation, others will also benefit from the materials and ideas presented, particularly professionals working with this age group.—**Sara Marcus**

354.   **Encyclopedia of Jewish Folklore and Traditions.** Raphael Patai and Haya Bar-Itzhak, eds. Armonk, N.Y., M. E. Sharpe, 2013. 2v. illus. index. $299.00/set. ISBN 13: 978-0-7656-2025-5.

This 2-volume set presents approximately 264 signed entries, ranging from half a page to several pages with subheadings in length on various aspects of Jewish folklore and traditions. Covering aspects including genres, authors, characters and people represented, themes, and ethnic and other groups, from biblical, historical, and contemporary times, this work will help any researcher who wants to know more about Jewish folklore. The traditions are addressed as found in the folklore, it is not a resource for in-depth information about the traditions as the title might mislead a user. The 100 contributors have performed research, and many entries include sources. The 18 color plates included, as well as the black-and-white illustrations throughout the set lend visual interest, while the layout and use of white space make this book approachable for younger readers than scholars. The cross-references and index enable finding additional and desired information, although the location of the index only in the second volume necessitates both volumes being available when researching. Two appendixes offer a list of sources, definitions, and abbreviations in the Hebrew Bible, Rabbinic literature and medieval compilations, and a list of anthologies of Jewish folklore. This is of use to Jewish collections where users are interested in folklore, as well as any folklore collection where readers want to know more than the stories themselves. [R: LJ, 15 June 13, p. 112]—**Sara Marcus**

355. **Jewish Responses to Persecution. Volume 3: 1941-1942.** Jurgen Matthaus, ed. Walnut Creek, Calif., Alta Mira Press, Inc., 2013. 551p. illus. index. (Documenting Life and Destruction: Holocaust Sources in Context). $55.00. ISBN 13: 978-0-7591-2258-1.

Authored by the director of the Applied Research Division at the Center for Advanced Holocaust Studies at the United States Holocaust Memorial Museum along with an applied research scholar at the USHMM, a historian, and a senior program office and applied research scholar at the USHMM, this third volume in the Documenting Life and Destruction: Holocaust Sources in Context series addresses the time period of 1941-1942. Organized into four parts consisting of three sections, each containing several essays each, the work embeds original historical documents in explanatory text written by the authors to place the documents into the context of history, community, and individual experiences. The first part addresses Jews and the expansion of the German Empire from January to June 1941, discussing facing increased pressure, struggling in the Lodz and Warsaw Ghettos, and confronting new challenges. The second part addresses the escalating violence from June 1941 to July 1942, discussing mass murder in the Occupied Soviet Union and deportations to the "East," the widening circles of persecution, and being in the grip of Germany's Allies. The third part addresses topics beyond compliance and resistance; the interactions after June 1941, including the elites and ordinary Jews; support networks; and the difference between deference, evasion, and revolt. The final part addresses patterns and perceptions of glimpsing of the abyss, organized into three sections on the role of religion, the limits of language, and making sense of the unthinkable. Intended for scholars and researchers of the Holocaust, the work opens with a list of abbreviations used, and ends with a list of documents, bibliography, glossary, chronology, and detailed index.—**Sara Marcus**

356. Rabbi Meszler, Joseph B., Dr. Shulamit Reinharz, Liz Suneby, and Diane Heiman. **The Jguy's Guide: The GPS for Jewish Teen Guys.** Woodstock, Vt., Jewish Lights Publishing, 2013. 186p. $16.99. ISBN 13: 978-1-58023-721-5.

Based in part on a need identified for boys after the publication of *The Jgirl's Guide* (see entry 353), this book is authored by the rabbi at Temple Sinai in Sharon, Massachusetts, the co-author of *The Jgirl's Guide*, and two authors of books for teens and children about mitzvoth and the bar/bat mitzvah. Organized into 10 chapters, the topics covered are not aligned to those in the volume for girls, but rather are geared specifically to what boys wonder about—courage, frenemies, being true to oneself, parents, questioning one's belief in God, the Torah (or Jewish tradition and law) of everything, stress, sex and love, whether what one does matters, and looking inside oneself at the person one wants to be and become. Based, as the female companion book, on interviews with teenage boys, Jewish wisdom, and Jewish texts, this book offers real-life, spiritual, and tradition-based advice and guidance to adolescent males in middle school and high school, and into college. Organized like the Talmud, the volume offers varying opinions on the topics in order for the reader to draw his own opinion and conclusions. Each chapter has the same sections –personal introduction with questions of life that teen guys face, voices of peers, did-you-know facts, lessons from historical and current role models, biblical and contemporary sources, discussion prompts, and Hebrew texts related to the topic. Whether observant, traditional, or even non-Jewish, the materials will help all boys to feel they are not alone. Jewish boys in particular will benefit, although any adolescent male who is questioning and needs real-life examples from contemporary peers, and Scripture support can find inspiration and guidance from the materials presented. This book will help adolescent and young adult males answer questions such as "who am I," "am I cool or a nerd," "do I fit in," "what kind of man will I become," "how does being Jewish work," "is my body okay," and more. Whether used by a boy alone, or by an adult working with this age group for inspiration and tips for workshops and one-on-one sessions.—**Sara Marcus**

Latin Americans

357.   **Chicano   Database.   http://www.oclc.org/support/documentation/firstsearch/databases/ dbdetails/details/ChicanoDatabase.htm.** [Website]. Dublin, Ohio, OCLC. Price negotiated by site. Date reviewed: 2013.

The *Chicano Database* (CDB) offers broad coverage of the Chicano experience from the late 1960s to the present. The original scope of CDB was Mexican American and Chicano studies; this sets it apart from a dataset like *Hispanic American Periodicals Index* (http://hapi.ucla.edu). The CDB now includes records that cover the broader Latino experience, including materials related to Puerto Ricans, Cuban Americans, and Central American immigrants. Some of the key areas are art, labor, bilingual education, literature, health, history, and politics. Updated quarterly and covering nearly 60,000 records, CDB offers citations for books and articles, rather than full text. CDB offers the *Spanish Speaking Mental Health Database*, which covers literature related to the psychological and sociological aspects of the Chicano experience. In addition to journal and book articles, users will find citations to specific works such as drawings, photographs, and poetry. The CDB is a focused, thorough database that will be particularly significant for schools with Chicano, Latino, and Latin American studies programs.—**ARBA Staff Reviewer**

358.   **Encyclopedia of Latino Culture: From Calaveras to Quinceaneras.** Charles M. Tatum, ed. Santa Barbara, Calif., Greenwood Press/ABC-CLIO, 2014. 3v. illus. index. $294.00/set. ISBN 13: 978-1-4408-0098-4; 978-1-4408-0099-3 (e-book).

Charles M. Tatum provides a concise three-volume reference source on the Latino culture for the Cultures of the American Mosaic series. *Encyclopedia of Latino Culture* examines the various Latino cultures as there are many cultural differences among the various ethnicities. The work examines the historical, regional, and ethnic diversity within specific traditions. Topics covered include food, art, film, music, literature, religious and secular traditions, and beliefs and practices. Interspersed throughout the volumes are sidebars with biographies of influential Latin American personalities and leaders. This encyclopedia provides interesting facts that are not found in other Latin American cultural histories. Therefore it makes for a very interesting read. This current set is recommended for public, school, and academic libraries, especially in areas serving Hispanic students and patrons.—**Kay Stebbins Slattery**

359.   Neumann, Caryn E., and Tammy S. Allen. **Latino History Day by Day: A Reference Guide to Events.** Santa Barbara, Calif., Greenwood Press/ABC-CLIO, 2013. 353p. index. $89.00. ISBN 13: 978-0-313-39641-0; 978-0-313-39642-7 (e-book).

This monograph is intended for middle school and high school media centers. The book is meant to be a day-by-day chronology of major historical events in Latino/Hispanic history. A glaring factual error in the introduction precludes me from recommending it to librarians. In the introduction it reads, "The interesting issue in this debate over Hispanic or Latino is that these are U.S. labels. Outside of the United States, people refer to themselves by their nationalities or nationality of origin. The singer Marc Anthony is not going to travel to London and introduce himself as a Latino or Hispanic. He is going to introduce himself as Cuban." The singer Marc Anthony is a well known singer of Puerto Rican descent. Until a fact checker goes through this book again it is not worth adding to a collection.—**Melissa M. Johnson**

7 Genealogy and Heraldry

Genealogy

360. Kemp, Thomas Jay. **International Vital Records Handbook.** 6th ed. Baltimore, Md., Genealogical Publishing, 2013. 697p. $69.95. ISBN 13: 978-0-8063-1981-0.

This book describes how to get vital records from around the world. It is divided into three parts based on geography. The first is the United States, the second U.S. Trust Territories and the third is International, which lists information for nearly 200 countries. In the U.S. section there are copies of forms needed to request the vital records along with the cost. In the other sections the forms are listed, if available, otherwise there is contact information. The idea for this work is that the user could photocopy or scan the forms, fill them in, and request the record. There are URLs for the various agencies, if available. There is also a warning in the introduction that the user should make sure to check the Website of the state vital records office to get the most current form and costs. That is good advice, since several of the forms now have incorrect information, especially about costs. Even though this work was published in 2013, prices have changed, and some of the forms have an expiration date. The author also mentions in the introduction that the Family History Library of Salt Lake City has microfilmed many of the original and published vital records and that these records can be obtained on microfilm from any Family History Center of the Church of Jesus Christ of Latter-Day Saints. In many of the entries there is a section that describes what information genealogist can obtain along with links to several databases for the area that have pertinent information, many of them free.

This will save much time and effort, avoiding needless delays because one does not know where to get the record needed or which form to use. It will be useful in most genealogical and reference collections.—**Robert L. Turner Jr.**

361. Phillips, Richard Hayes. **Without Indentures: Index to White Slave Children in Colonial Court Records (Maryland and Virginia).** Baltimore, Md., Genealogical Publishing, 2013. 283p. $29.95pa. ISBN 13: 978-0-8063-1979-7.

Occasionally a book comes along that breaks new ground. This is such a book. The author has collected the names of over 5,000 kidnapped white children that came to America. These were not indentured servants, who had contracts and had agreed to terms of their indenture. These were children taken from Ireland, Scotland, England and New England who were then transported to and sold in Maryland and Virginia from about 1660 to 1720.

The author did a systematic investigation of the surviving Court Order Books from the counties in Maryland and in Virginia. Most of those are available online. The author gives links to his sources. This is arranged by counties, arranged geographically beginning at the tip of the Delmarva Peninsula and ending at the James River. It follows the Chesapeake Bay in a counter clockwise manner. The information for each of the counties includes an alphabetic index of children without indentures, an alphabetic list of the judges that sentenced them to slavery, as well as a table arranged by year and listing the race of the people enslaved.

There is a lot of genealogical information in the Colonial Court Records that was not included since it was outside of the scope of this work. For example, indentured servants, Negro and Indian children, native born orphan children, and children given up for adoption are all not included in this index. After the individual county listings there is an alphabetic listing of the ship captains that brought these slaves to Maryland or Virginia. There is another index of the ships, the place that they arrived, and the years of the trips. That is followed by an alphabetic listing of the slaves. There is an interesting appendix. It is a listing of the 281 prisoners, called the Jacobite rebels, that were captured in the Battle of Preston in 1715 and sent to Maryland or Virginia. There were others that were sent to other areas, but they are not listed here. This work sheds light on a little-known history of America and should be very useful to most genealogy collections.—**Robert L. Turner Jr.**

Heraldry

362.   **World Flag Database. http://www.flags.net.** [Website]. Free. Date reviewed: 2013.

Descriptions and illustrations of flags for countries, territories, subnational regions, and international organizations can be found in this Website. It includes national and state flags, ensigns, and subnational flags. The Flag Institute created the original graphics found here. To date more than 260 entries covering hundreds of flag can be found on the pages of this site.—**ARBA Staff Reviewer**

8 Geography and Travel Guides

Geography

General Works

Bibliography

363. Rumney, Thomas A. **The Geography of Central America and Mexico: A Scholarly Guide and Bibliography.** Lanham, Md., Scarecrow, 2013. 185p. index. $95.00; $94.99 (e-book). ISBN 13: 978-0-8108-8636-0; 978-0-8108-8637-7 (e-book).

This comprehensive bibliography collection covers the scholarly historical and current titles of the geography of Central America and Mexico. The beginning chapter is a bibliography of the Mexico and Latin American region. The following chapters are about the specific countries in this region. The counties are Belize, Costa Rica, El Salvador, Guatemala, Honduras, Mexico, Nicaragua, and Panama. Each country's information is covered by atlases, books, monographs, chapters, scholarly articles, dissertations, and theses, under the subtitles of cultural and social geography, economic geography, historical geography, and urban geography. The dates for coverage begin as early as possible through current titles.

There is an author index and a list of periodicals used in this bibliography. This geographical bibliography is organized for easy reference, and I would highly recommend this bibliography for academic collections.—**Kay Stebbins Slattery**

364. Rumney, Thomas A. **The Geography of South America: A Scholarly Guide and Bibliography.** Lanham, Md., Scarecrow, 2013. 251p. index. $120.00; $119.99 (e-book). ISBN 13: 978-0-8108-8634-6; 978-0-8018-8635-3 (e-book).

This reference gives college-level students and professors a "one-stop shopping" place to find an exhaustive array of academic publications on the geography of South America. The publication begins with a chapter on the region as a whole followed by individual chapters covering each nation on the continent. Within each chapter resources are identified as general works and then categorized under the subfields of the discipline, such as cultural and social geography, economic geography, historical geography, physical and environmental geography, urban geography, and more. Within each subfield the entries are further classified by atlases, books, monographs, textbooks, book chapters, scholarly articles, master's theses, and doctoral dissertations. The citations are primarily in English, Spanish, and Portuguese but other languages are included. If you are looking for research on rainfall variation in

Chile, the relationship of street cars to popular protests in Rio de Janiero, or the settlement patterns on the Argentine Pampa, then this book is for you.—**Adrienne Antink**

Catalogs and Collections

365.   **Alexandria Digital Library. http://alexandria.ucsb.edu/.** [Website]. University of California. Free. Date reviewed: 2013.

Students and faculty increasingly want to utilize GIS data. This site has data files and software that allows such customized use. Its digital gazetteer has 5.9 million geographic names. ADL provides HTML clients to access its collections and gazetteer, and provides specific information management tools, such as the Feature Type Thesaurus for classing types of geographic features, as well as downloadable software code.—**Noriko Asato**

366.   **GEOnet Name Server. http://earth-info.nga.mil/gns/html/index.html.** [Website]. Free. Date reviewed: 2013.

The U.S. National Imagery and Mapping Agency's (NIMA) database of foreign geographic feature names as approved by the U.S. Board on Geographic Names. This site provides latitude, longitude, area, and UTM and JOG number. The database also contains variant spellings (cross-references), which are useful for finding purposes, as well as non-Roman script spellings of many of these names. All the geographic features in the database contain information about location, administrative division, and quality. The database can be used for a variety of purposes, including establishing official spellings of foreign place names, cartography, GIS, GEOINT, and finding places. There are currently more than 3.5 million entries, and the scope is worldwide, including the United States and Antarctica. Note: You must know the country in which the feature is located in order to utilize this site efficiently.—**ARBA Staff Reviewer**

Dictionaries and Encyclopedias

367.   Cybriwsky, Roman Adrian. **Capital Cities Around the World: An Encyclopedia of Geography, History, and Culture.** Santa Barbara, Calif., ABC-CLIO, 2013. 376p. illus. index. $89.00. ISBN 13: 978-1-61069-247-2.

Considering that the title purports to describe capital cities around the world, with regard to geography, history, and culture, one is a little surprised to see that the title is a single, relatively slim volume. First impression is that the entries in the title cannot be of any real depth, or offer any meaningful assessment of the development of said cities. Furthermore, such a title suggests that one may anticipate illustrations that will enhance the reader's understanding of same.

That first impression was correct—the entries, most of which barely take up two pages, offer broad descriptions of the cities, which give very little in the way of exposing the reader to the capital cities of the world and their geographies, histories, and cultures. Furthermore, the anticipated illustrations are merely black-and-white photographs of landmarks, but the use of these photographs seems uneven. Some alphabetic sections have several, such as the letter A. Some sections have none, such as G. The entries themselves contain brief descriptions of the city in question and include a historical

overview, major landmarks, culture and society (which requires further comment), and further reading. The content of these sections is written well and accessibly so, but it is brief (which could be said of the whole title). The Culture and Society section of the entries seem mostly focused on economics, rather than cultural, religious, or social practices or traditions. The same could be said of the whole title as well; it seems mostly focused on economics.

This reviewer's primary concern is that the kind of information provided in this title can more easily and effectively be located using the Internet, particularly the CIA's *The World Factbook*. Additionally, as quickly as politics and economies can change, a static print encyclopedia is likely to become outdated quite quickly; an electronic version would have been better, as it could be updated easily and quickly (like the *The World Factbook*). The title also contains a fascinating (but again, brief) appendix of Selected Historic Capital Cities Around the World. The work includes a selected bibliography of resources, an index, and a list of capitals by country. The introduction is full of data tables related to capital cities (e.g., largest capital city, most densely populated large capital city); while interesting, again, this kind of data can become outdated quite quickly, which again prompts this reviewer to wonder why the author chose a static format like print to create such a resource. While not a bad resource per se, this title is debatably useful. The information can more easily and still reliably be located on the Internet, where it will more up-to-date and more in-depth, as this title, while well written, is brief and does not provide significant coverage. Furthermore, it is rather focused on economics and does not adequately or meaningfully address or explore society or culture.—**Megan W. Lowe**

368. **Getty Thesaurus of Geographic Names** http://www.getty.edu/research/conducing_research/ **vocabularies/tgn/.** [Website]. Free. Date reviewed: 2013.

Created by the Getty Research Institute, this site provides a structural vocabulary with an emphasis on art and architecture, covering continents, nations, historical places, and physical features. Each record includes geographic coordinates, notes, sources for the data, and the role of the place (e.g., inhabited place, state capital). Names can include vernacular, English, other languages, historical names, natural order, and inverted order. Currently there are around one million entries, which are current, historical, and international in scope.—**ARBA Staff Reviewer**

369. Shelley, Fred M. **Nation Shapes: The Story Behind the World's Borders.** Santa Barbara, Calif., ABC-CLIO, 2013. 634p. maps. index. $100.00. ISBN 13: 978-1-61069-105-5; 978-1-61069-105-5 (e-book).

The purpose of this book is to explain how the almost 200 countries we know today obtained their geographic borders. Even though it starts with a discussion of the difference between states and nations, it confusingly has "nation shapes" as its title. It is actually about the boundaries of political entities, not nations. Nevertheless, it is systematic and well organized, so the reader can look up any country for a map and information about the history of its geographic limits.

There are seven chapters in this book, each a particular region of the world such as Europe, The Americas, Sub-Saharan Africa, and so on. Each chapter starts with a brief overview followed by what the author calls "vignettes" on the countries included in the region. Each country has a black-and-white map showing political boundaries and a discussion of the historical context and contemporary issues of those borders. Depending on their geographic and historical complexities, countries have from one to eight pages of text.

With such a vast project before the author, we should not be surprised to find a few errors. Unfortunately, in this book there are just enough that the reader begins to wonder how much to trust the text. For example, in the map of Israel the city of Qiryat Shemona is misspelled, and neither that map nor the map of Syria show the boundaries of the disputed Golan Heights. The value of drugs annually smuggled from Mexico into the United States is given as "between $15 million and $50 million," but these numbers are actually in the billions. The curious English Channel Islands of Guernsey and Jersey are not mentioned anywhere in the book, nor are they labeled on any map. Then again, the country descriptions are very fresh. Contemporary conflicts, including the ongoing revolution in Syria and unrest in Egypt, are mentioned, and the references for each section are up to date.

As always with this kind of encyclopedic volume, librarians must decide if they wish to purchase expensive paper copies or rely on far cheaper online sources. Will patrons look up this book, find it on a shelf, and open it up to read about the border history of, say, Kosovo? Or will they more likely use Web resources? I think the latter.—**Mark A. Wilson**

Handbooks and Yearbooks

370.   **Mountains of the World Series.** New York, Crabtree, 2012. 6v. illus. maps. index. $22.95/vol.; $9.95pa./vol.

This six-volume set from Crabtree Publishing, a company known for their multivolume, nonfiction series designed specifically for children, provides geographical and historical information on six of the world's most well-known mountain ranges. The volumes in the series discuss: the Rocky Mountains, the Urals, the Andes, the Alps, the Appalachians, and the Himalayas. The volumes focus on how these mountain ranges have shaped the course of human history by serving as the base of large civilizations, provide sources for mineral deposits for mining and trees for lumber, and form natural barriers to the movement of people and goods. Within each volume are plenty of color photographs and illustrations as well as sidebars full of additional information. Each volume has information on how the mountain range was formed, the climate of the region, plants and animals native to that region, and natural resources and tourism activities. Each volume ends with a timeline, a glossary, a list of resources for further research that includes both books and Internet sites, and a very short index, all of which can be used to teach young students basic researching skills. This series is recommended for elementary and middle school libraries and juvenile collections in public libraries. They provide a good introduction to the geography and history behind these mountain ranges and how they have shaped human civilization.—**Shannon Graff Hysell**

Place-Names

371.   Bright, William. **Native American Placenames of the Southwest: A Handbook for Travelers.** Norman, Okla., University of Oklahoma Press, 2013. 143p. $19.95pa. ISBN 13: 978-0-8061-4311-8.

Native American Placenames of the Southwest is a spin-off of *Native American Placenames of the United States* (see ARBA 2005, entry 389). Its author, William Bright, Professor Emeritus in Linguistics and Anthropology at UCLA, passed away before this slim volume could be published. The editors, Alice Anderton, a former Comanche language instructor, and Sean O'Neill, Associate Professor of Linguistics at University of Oklahoma, completed the project. Professor Bright added additional entries beyond the parent publication and the editors added a few more.

Native American Placenames of the Southwest is intended for travelers in the southwestern U.S. Organized alphabetically; the concise entries are for towns, cities, counties, parks, and geographic landmarks. They give the state and county, plus pronunciation information. The editors' introduction defines basic linguistic and common southwestern geographical terms. In addition, the book provides maps showing all counties in each of the four states: Texas, Oklahoma, New Mexico, and Arizona. At the conclusion the user finds lists of languages and language families mentioned in the guide, tribal contact information, and selected references.

The primary selling points for this title are its specificity and portability. The American southwest is a very popular travel destination, and it is replete with Native American placenames. We may never know if Professor Bright intended to publish other regional titles, but he was smart to begin with the southwest. And by making this book small enough to fit in a glove compartment, the publisher has made it easy for the user to stow it for effortless retrieval while taking road trips throughout the region. An essential tool for those who love to travel in the desert southwest and learn more about the places they go.—**John P. Stierman**

372.   Grumet, Robert S. **Manhattan to Minisink: American Indian Place Names in Greater New York and Vicinity.** Norman, Okla., University of Oklahoma Press, 2013. 259p. $34.95. ISBN 13: 978-0-8061-4336-1.

Anyone that has traveled in the Greater New York area (New York City, Long Island, Downstate New York, Eastern Pennsylvania, New Jersey, even Connecticut) owe ethnohistorian Robert S. Grumet a debt when he finally answers the many questions about the origin of many of the place-names that have Native American foundations. Divided into two parts, Colonial-Era Indian Place Names and Imports, Inventions, Invocations, and Imposters, the author explains why the Catskills are called the Catskills and why New Jersey has a Weehawken. Section 1 has 340 entries, each with the Indian name and where it was first recorded in colonial and American records. Each entry also has the native languages origin and a brief discussion of its etymology. The second section has over 200 place-names that people tend to think as having an Indian origin, but merely are "imports, inventions, invocations, or imposters." For example, the word Appalachian is in fact an import from Florida. Additionally, the author includes maps, a timeline, and a great set of sources.—**Scott R. DiMarco**

Travel Guides

373.   Andrews, Candice Gaukel. **Travel Wild Wisconsin: A Seasonal Guide to Wildlife Encounters in Natural Places.** Madison, Wis., University of Wisconsin Press, 2013. 246p. illus. maps. index. $24.95pa. ISBN 13: 978-0-29929-164-8.

For anyone who has traveled through Wisconsin it will come as no surprise that the state provides an array of bids, wildlife, fish, rivers, lakes, and national wildlife refuges that will please any nature lover. Wisconsin native, Candice Gaukel Andrews, shares her intimate knowledge of the bountiful natural history her home state has to offer. Organized first by season and then by month, Andrews provides an insider's view of the top places to visit, what to expect, what to bring, and how to plan ahead. The book is written in a very narrative style, rather than a typical travel guide; the words are meant to be read at a leisurely pace rather than in the quick reference style. Tips in sidebars will help users to find the most valuable information quickly. Black-and-white photographs and maps are interspersed throughout. This book will be a worthwhile purchase for public libraries in the Midwest region of the United States.—**Shannon Graff Hysell**

374.   Flynn, Sarah Wassner. **National Parks Guide U.S.A.** Washington, D.C., National Geographic Society, 2012. 160p. illus. maps. index. $14.95pa. ISBN 13: 978-1-4263-0931-1.

This "Kids' Companion to the Best-selling National Geographic Guide to the National Parks of the U.S." is like almost all *National Geographic* publications: delicious! Delicious because it has wonderful color pictures on every page and easy-to-read maps showing exciting experiences to be had at each national park. The book is divided into geographic regions: The East, Midwest, Southwest, West, and More. Two pages of "How to Use This Book" clearly describe the layout of 24 parks, which have 4 pages each of information, photographs and a map. This is followed by a few pages of "Other Must See Park Properties" in each region.

In the first region, The East, one finds Acadia, Everglades, Great Smoky Mountains, and Hot Springs National Parks. For each park, readers will find "Ranger Tips," "Take it Easy," "Be Extreme," "Best Views," "All About Animals," "Dare to Explore," and "My Checklist." Each of these helpful and fun sections has a couple sentences to entice the reader. Buddy Bison, the National Park Trust mascot appears

27 times throughout the book to keep kids hunting.

This is a sturdy paperback with yellow border all around, just like everyone is used to with *National Geographic* magazine. At $14.95, this is a real bargain for a high-quality guidebook to keep kids engaged and allow them to help plan amazing trips.—**Georgia Briscoe**

375.   **Outdoor Travel Guides. http://www.gorp.com/.** [Website]. Free. Date reviewed: 2013.

Away.com is a brand of The Away Network and is designed for travelers who want to choose their next vacation. Ideas and recommendations for trips are customized to specific travel interests. This database has more than two million pages of content covering nearly 50,000 destinations worldwide and offers a distinctive blend of expert and consumer advice. The Away Network itself includes Trip.com a travel research site that allows its consumers to quickly compare prices on multiple travel booking sites to find the best values. Another site, GORP.com, is the place for outdoor enthusiasts to plan hiking, camping, and visits to U.S. National Parks. It is focused on vacations both in the United States and worldwide. AdventureFinder.com is a directory of adventure vacations and outdoor-focused resorts while Outside Online is the Website of *Outside*, the leading active lifestyle magazine in the United States.—**William O. Scheeren**

376.   **UNESCO World Heritage Atlas.** By the United Nations Educational, Scientific and Cultural Organization. New York, United Nations, 2013. 278p. illus. maps. index. $80.00. ISBN 13: 978-92-31042-39-3.

377.   **World Heritage: Benefits Beyond Borders.** By the United Nations Educational, Scientific, and Cultural Organization. New York, United Nations, 2012. 384p. illus. $55.00pa. ISBN 13: 978-92-31042-42-3.

The year 2012 marked the 40th anniversary of the World Heritage Convention. To commemorate this milestone UNESCO and DeAgostini Libri have presented this first-time atlas featuring all of the World Heritage Sites, including those recently added in 2012 (e.g., the birth place of Jesus, the site of Xanadu). Color maps are presented for each region of the world. Also included are beautiful fold-out maps that feature detailed information and color images of the sites. An index concludes the volume with names of sites and descriptions.

World Heritage: Benefits Beyond Borders is a collection of essays that provide a thorough understanding of World Heritage sites and their value in sustainable development. They do this by discussing 26 of the sites and their value to local communities and ecosystems. The emphasis is on the role that the local community holds in managing and protecting the site and its importance in the ecosystem and in cultural heritage.

These are special edition volumes that will be of interest to most academic libraries. Many public libraries may want to purchase them as well.—**Shannon Graff Hysell**

9 History

American History

Biography

378.   **100 People Who Changed 20th-Century America.** Mary Cross, ed. Santa Barbara, Calif., ABC-CLIO, 2013. 2v. illus. index. $173.00/set. ISBN 13; 978-1-61069-085-0; 978-1-61069-086-7 (e-book).

This two-volume encyclopedia presents biographies of 100 people from a broad range of fields, all of whom had a significant impact on life in the United States in the twentieth century. Among them are those one would expect to see included: Martin Luther King, Jr., Elvis Presley, Walt Disney, Henry Luce, and Wilbur and Orville Wright, to name a few. But there are some unexpected names, or names that are not household names in every household, but names that contributed to the richness of the century. For example, Bart Simpson and Superman are listed. So is Joan Ganz Cooney, who proposed Sesame Street, and R. Crumb, the influential underground cartoonist.

Articles include portraits of the individuals, biographical information, and an overview of the person's impact and significance. The articles are written at a level accessible to the general public, making this a potentially useful starting point for research. Unfortunately, the lists of references at the end of the articles have some quality control issues. Some lists consistently lead readers to high-quality sources. Others, such as the article about George Gershwin, list only Websites. URLs are not uniformly included in references to online sources (one example is included in the list of references used in the entry on William J. Levitt).

Interestingly, the entries are presented chronologically by year of the person's birth, rather than alphabetically by last name. As a result, browsing the index or the table of contents is essential. While the Timeline of the American Century provides some context for the rest of the work, the organization is not particularly intuitive.

Finally, the definition of the twentieth century used here appears to be a loose one. Two of those included, Jimmy Wales and Mark Zuckerberg, created groundbreaking platforms in the early twenty-first century, not the twentieth. One has to wonder what twentieth-century people were left out in order to include these two twenty-first century entries.—**Amanda Izenstark**

Catalogs and Collections

379.   **FreedomFlix. http://freedomflix.scholastic.com.** [Website]. Danbury, Conn., Scholastic Library Publishing. Price negotiated by site. Date reviewed: 2013.

This site is a comprehensive resource focusing on American history from pre-Revolutionary America to the present day. Each historical division contains e-books, videos, and a Read It section that highlights the featured e-book. Each e-book contains a table of contents, glossary, informational text, an audio capability, and a bookmark feature. They also have a timeline and index, and a section that focuses on "influential individuals." There are open-ended questions for students to consider, and a multiple-choice quiz in each section. "Explore More" accesses Grolier Online for more information. There are related Websites, ideas for student projects, and a Resource section for teachers that contains lesson plans, a quiz, writing prompts, and whiteboard activities. This is a colorful, attractive collection that is wide-ranging in its scope and easily navigated. This resource will be utilized in myriad ways, limited only by the creativity of teachers and students, and is valuable on so many levels.—**Jennifer Welch**

380.   **The March of Time. http://moto.alexanderstreet.com/.** [Website]. Alexandria, Va., Alexander Street. Price negotiated by site. Date reviewed: 2013.

This resource is an engaging, accessible compilation of newsreels produced from 1935 through 1967 that students will not write off as dry historical documentaries. The complete archive totals over 400 films. The newsreels provide unique insight into American culture and current events, and cover topics such as anti-Semitism, the Dust Bowl, home life, and the wartime economy. Users can browse by subject, historical events, people, and place, and the advanced search feature is well-designed with thorough, thoughtful indexing. An especially helpful feature is the fully linked transcripts accompanying each film. Users simply click on a word in the transcript, and the video skips to that moment in the film. Film quality was excellent when not in full screen, and variable when maximized; audio quality showed similar variation. Users can compile and distribute playlists, allowing teachers to easily share films included in the class content. The varied content and ease of use make this an excellent choice for the high school classroom.—**Shanna Shadoan**

381.   **Mission-US: A Revolutionary Way to Learn History. http://www.mission.us.org/.** [Website]. Free. Date reviewed: 2013.

Sometimes a computer game is the perfect tool to excite students about subjects they deem boring. This first game in a planned series on U.S. history is about the Revolutionary War. "For Crown or Colony?" explores the reasons for revolution through the eyes of both loyalists and patriots in 1770 Boston. Users have two options: streaming video or downloading. It is loaded with resources for the teacher: instructions, tips, historical background, synopsis and activities, primary source documents, and more. The curriculum is well developed, including learning goals, historical understandings and skills, key related vocabulary, and classroom activities and materials. The games here are educational and addictive. A login/password is required although the site is free, and teachers and librarians can track student progress. Titles are also available in Spanish.— **Judyth Lessee**

382.   **ProQuest History Vault. http://www.proquest.com/.** [Website]. Bethesda, Md., ProQuest, 2012. Price negotiated by site. Date reviewed: 2013.

ProQuest History Vault is a U.S. history resource with thousands of documents, mostly primary sources. At the time of review it was made up of two modules: the Vietnam War and Black Freedom. Most documents in "Vietnam War" are scanned, although some were never published. Of the two volumes on "Black Freedom: Struggle in the 20th Century," the first deals mostly with blacks in the military. The second volume covers the Civil Rights Movement. Letters, essays, articles, and personal papers are included from the likes of Bayard Rustin and Mary McLeod Bethune. This source provides a lot of information, but working with the site can be tedious. Its use would probably be limited to teachers and students in advanced classes.—**Ron Marinucci** important people, politics, the economy, foreign relations, religion, and cultural of the times. Entries included the presidencies of Woodrow Wilson, Warren G. Harding, Calvin Coolidge, and Herbert Hoover, as well as the Harlem Renaissance, the Department of Labor, and the Sedition Act of 1918. Articles range in length from one sentence to several pages, and although the author did not attempt to write an encyclopedia, one wishes that in some instances there was more depth, especially for the lesser-known persons. Other features include cross-references, *see*, and *see also* references as well as two appendixes (presidents and their administrations and constitutional amendments). The 50-page bibliography is well chosen, including monographs and scholarly articles, and is arranged by broad subjects, subdivided by more specific topics. This work is a well-researched volume. Overall, this is a worthwhile reference source on this pivotal period of American history. Before purchasing this title, however, libraries should keep in mind that it has been minimally updated from the original 2003 title.—**Shannon Graff Hysell**

Handbooks and Yearbooks

390.   **American Decades. Primary Sources, 2000-2009.** Rebecca Valentine, ed. Stamford, Conn., Gale/Cengage Learning, 2013. 614p. illus. index. $184.00. ISBN 13: 978-1-4144-8602-4.

This is a treasure trove covering everything from world events, education, social trends, and media to the arts, business, science, and law and justice. And, fortunately, a sensible organization makes the information readily accessible. Each major topic begins with a useful chronology followed by primary sources that expand on the topic. For example, in the "Lifestyles and Social Trends" chapter there are primary source documents titled "TSA Ramps up Virtual 'Strip Searches,' " " *Harry Potter* is a Modern Phenomenon," "Guilty Verdict in Cyberbullying Case Provokes Many Questions over Online Identity," and "How MySpace Fell of the Pace." Of considerable help in sorting through the material is an exhaustive general index and number of photographs. This new volumes contains entries on many noteworthy events of the first 10 years of this century, including the U.S. Patriot Act, the fall of newspapers in the digital age, stem cell research, and hybrid vehicles. The entries span all subjects and the entries are written in a way that will encourage critical thinking and historical comprehension. This informative study will be a useful addition to the reference collections of high schools and universities.—**John W. Storey**

391.   **American Eras. Civil War and Reconstruction, 1860-1877: Primary Sources.** Stamford, Conn., Gale/Cengage Learning, 2013. 454p. illus. index. $160.00. ISBN 13: 978-1-4144-9825-6.

The American Eras Primary Sources series provides full text or excerpts of primary source material from a specific era in American history, highlighting trends, events, or personalities that will add to the reader's understanding of the era. They are designed to either work in tandem with the American Eras set. This volume on the Civil War era provides 10 chapter headings: the arts, business and the economy, communications, education, fashion and leisure, government and politics, law and justice, lifestyles and trends, religion, and science, medicine, and technology. Each chapter begins with an overview, which is followed by a brief chronological list of selected events unique to each subject. The text contains color and black-and-white photographs. The volume is convenient to use for beginning researchers. It gathers important information on the period in a single source. *Civil War and Reconstruction* is recommended for undergraduate libraries.—**ARBA Staff Reviewer**

392.   **American Eras: Industrial Development of the United States, 1878-1899. Primary Sources.** Stamford, Conn., Gale/Cengage Learning, 2013. 470p. illus. index. $160.00. ISBN 13: 978-1-4144-9824-9.

American Eras: Industrial Development of the United States, 1878-1899. Primary Sources vividly brings to life, through the use of primary sources, the period of U.S. history and culture during the l two decades of the nineteenth century. The volume is conveniently divided into chapters that encom

Dictionaries and Encyclopedias

383.   **American Immigration: An Encyclopedia of Political, Social, and Cultural Change.** James Ciment and John Radzilowski, eds. Armonk, N.Y., M. E. Sharpe, 2014. 4v. illus. index. $399.00/set. ISBN 13: 978-0-7656-8212-3.

Given the ongoing debate in Congress and across the nation on immigration reform, and with some conservative student groups on college campuses engaging in a controversial game called "Catch n Illegal Immigrant," this revised and updated encyclopedia, first released in 2001, is most timely. It highlights a conundrum in American society: pride in a country of diverse people from throughout the world united around shared ideals, yet periodically gripped by nativist fears of and hostility toward those "strangers in the land." For a nation of immigrants, diversity is simultaneously a fountain of strength and a source of mighty challenges over such issues as open or closed borders, bilingualism or English only, undocumented workers or illegal aliens, and multicultural or culturally unifying education. To use the common metaphors, is this nation a "melting pot" in which sundry peoples shed their differences and emerge as Americans, or a "mosaic" in which they all come together in a beautiful tapestry while retaining certain ethnic and cultural peculiarities? This superb study addresses such matters, and much more, while also putting them in historical perspective.

Based upon the research of some 130 scholars, this encyclopedia examines from the colonial era to the present why foreigners came to America, conditions they encountered once here, how they influenced their adopted land, and how subsequent generations of immigrants differed from previous ones (for example, changes in the 1960s to restrictive immigration laws of the 1920s opened the door to greater numbers of newcomers from Asian countries, thereby significantly increasing the flow of Muslims, Hindus, Buddhists, Sikhs, and others to these shores and making the U.S. far more religiously pluralistic). The co-editors organized their work into six logical parts. Part 1 explores the causes and motivations that prompted so many people to leave their native lands. Part 2 provides the historical context from the earliest Native American to the present, while part 3 looks at the economic, political, social, and cultural experiences of the new arrivals. Part 4 surveys the major groups of immigrants, citing 34 places of origin and listing principal U.S. destinations, from Chicago and Houston to New Orleans and rural America. Part 5 presents an international perspective, covering such topics as the global economy, law and politics, and human trafficking and slavery. And, finally, part 6 consists of documents from George Washington's revolutionary war correspondence and pertinent sections of the U.S. Constitution to the Supreme Court's 2012 decision on Arizona's controversial immigration law and the immigration planks of the Democratic and Republican parties from the mid-nineteenth century to 2012. Adding to this study's value are an extensive bibliography and a comprehensive 106-page index, affording easy access to a wealth of information. Scholars as well as general readers will find this an excellent contribution to the growing body of literature on immigration, and high school and college libraries should consider it for their reference collections.—**John W. Storey**

384.   Bruns, Roger. **Encyclopedia of Cesar Chavez: The Farm Workers' Fight for Rights and Justice.** Santa Barbara, Calif., Greenwood Press/ABC-CLIO, 2013. 344p. illus. index. (Movements of the American Mosaic). $89.00. ISBN 13: 978-1-4408-0380-2; 978-1-4408-0381-9 (e-book).

This informative and interesting volume begins with a biography of Cesar Chavez. This history tells the story of one migrant worker from Arizona who was profoundly influenced by experiencing the back-breaking labor and poverty of the migrant working family. At an early age he saw that alone, farm workers had no power of influence but together they could make their lives better. The introduction summarizes Chavez' efforts to improve working and living conditions, from organizing the first farm workers union (United Farm Workers) to banning the use of the short-handled hoe to winning fair wages and adequate housing for farm workers. The introduction concludes with a list of recommended reading.

The encyclopedic entries that follow the introduction are listed in alphabetic order. They include the most important people, places, and events of the story. In addition to the summaries for each entry, this volume includes interviews, letters, speeches, Congressional testimony, and proclamations relating to the many causes Chavez took on. Each entry is about three pages long and includes a short list of recommended readings. Many entries are accompanied by relevant photographs. An annotated bibliography and index complete the work.

This volume is both a tribute to the work of Cesar Chavez and a reminder of what that work has done to change the world. It is recommended for all libraries.—**Joanna M. Burkhardt**

385.   **Encyclopedia of American Studies. http://eas-ref.press.jhu.edu/.** [Website]. Baltimore, Md., Johns Hopkins University Press. Price negotiated by site. Date reviewed: 2014.

Johns Hopkins Press's online database the *Encyclopedia of American Studies* brings together over 750 online, searchable subject entries and biographical entries on American history and culture from pre-colonial days to the present. Each entry contains a bibliography for further reference. The content is suitable for high school students on up to undergraduates. It will aid those conducting research in American history as well as in sociology and ethnic studies. This is an ideal place for researchers to begin their research on a variety of American history topics. This site is sponsored by the American Studies Association and has a long list of well-respected contributors in the field of American studies and American history. It is updated quarterly ensuring it will provide users with up-to-date information.—**Shannon Graff Hysell**

386.   **Encyclopedia of Japanese American Internment.** Gary Y. Okihiro, ed. Santa Barbara, Calif., Greenwood Press/ABC-CLIO, 2013. 342p. illus. index. $89.00. ISBN 13: 978-0-313-39915-2; 978-0-313-39916-9 (e-book).

The encyclopedic volumes from ABC-CLIO are invariably good, and this one fits the mold. The editor and primary author, Gary Okihiro, professor of international and public affairs at Columbia University, begins with a useful essay on this shameful chapter in American history followed by an extensive bibliography and a complete chronology. The lengthy, solid entries, most of which were written by Okihiro, with the remaining ones by eight faculty and graduate students at Columbia University, comprise the bulk of the volume. Each includes several bibliography sources. Several pictures are included and the book concludes with a topical bibliography and an index. This is a fine piece of work, but its rather specialized nature means that it will have a relatively limited audience.—**Joe P. Dunn**

387.   Richter, William L. **Historical Dictionary of the Old South.** 2d ed. Lanham, Md., Scarecrow, 2013. 563p. (Historical Dictionaries of U.S. Politics and Political Eras). $130.00; $129.99 (e-book). ISBN 13: 978-0-8108-7914-0; 978-0-8108-7915-7 (e-book).

The Historical Dictionaries series by Scarecrow Press are universally excellent sources and this 2d edition is no exception. William L. Richter, professional historian and retired Arizona cowboy, starts with a definition of the Old South. To him it is geographical, chronological, and cultural—a particular section of the United States from the end of the American Revolutionary War through the Civil War that developed a unique culture largely defined by the institution of slavery. In the rest of a most useful introduction, the author outlines the various political, social, cultural, and economic questions that constitute the heart of the historiography of this region.

The alphabetically arranged dictionary is extensive, cross-listed, and well written; many entries have touches of humor. The chronology is valuable and the lengthy bibliographic essay that precedes an exhaustive topical listed bibliography is the single best feature of the volume. Appropriate appendixes include U.S. governments during the Antebellum Era, 1790-1861; U.S. and Confederate Governments during the Civil War, 1861-1865; the Articles of Confederation and Perpetual Union, 1781; and the Constitutions of the U.S. in 1860 and the Confederate States of American, 1861.

In sum, this volume, albeit a bit pricey, is a good addition to most university libraries. As with many reference sources, the e-book option may be most appropriate.—**Joe P. Dunn**

388.   **The 2000s in America.** Craig Belanger, ed. Millerton, N.Y., Salem Press/Grey Hous 2013. 3v. illus. index. $364.00/set. ISBN 13: 978-1-4298-3883-2.

Salem Press, now an imprint of Grey House Publishing, has for some time been produ volume sets of encyclopedias examining twentieth-century American history and popul. Progressing decade-by-decade, beginning with the 1920s, each set covers a broad spectrum, politics, fads and fashions, medicine, art, mass media, important individuals, and many other to "Publisher's Note" lists 30 separate areas examined within these pages).

The current volumes under review bring the series to the near present, taking an in-depth American life during the period 2000 to 2009 with about 400 alphabetically arranged signed There is a nice balance between the familiar and the obscure. As might be expected, famous are represented, such as erstwhile Presidential candidate and former Secretary of State Hillary Cli entertainment powerhouse Beyoncé Knowles and bodybuilder/actor Arnold Schwarzenegger. The s is true for well-known historic events, the September 11, 2001 terrorist attacks on New York Ci World Trade towers being but one example. Lesser-reported items or those overshadowed by mo dramatic events include entries for "Gun Control," the "Tea Party Movement," "Same-Sex Marriage and "Vaccinations." In all cases, the topics discussed helped to define this particular decade.

One of the outstanding features has been the consistency of format, with which experienced librarians will be well familiar. As with all previous sets, each signed entry begins with a boldfaced headword(s), followed by either a one-line definition (in the case of events or ideas) or a two-line "Identification" (in the case of individuals), that lists the person's significance, birth date, and place of birth. This is followed by a short paragraph of italicized text that summarizes the article itself. Entries run from one to six pages in length. The longer ones are broken down by subheads, making it much easier to zero in on specific passages of interest. An "Impact" paragraph places the person or event in the proper historical or cultural context, and serves as an epilogue, if you will, rounding out the discussion. All this is concluded with a further reading list of print and electronic sources providing additional information (the more substantial articles have annotated citations).

A number of special features are worth noting. Fifteen appendixes list major entertainment awards, best-selling book titles, a chronology of the decade, and overall bibliography, among others. Access points include a complete table of contents for all three volumes appearing in the front of each volume, a list of entries by category, a photograph index, and a subject index. The set is well illustrated with crisp black-and-white photographs, tables, charts, and other graphic material. Lastly, purchase of the print set entitles user to complementary access to the digital version, known as Salem Online.

Editor Belanger is a curious choice to helm such a project. Holding a Master of Science degree from the University of Advancing Technology (UAW) in Tempe, Arizona, where he is currently an associate professor, his biographical sketch on the university's Website lists his professional interests as the "philosophical/historical/sociological aspects of technology." He was previously editor-in-chief of *Journal of Advancing Technology* for about six years, which is published by UAW. This may help to explain the sometimes weak writing, compared to that of other sets in the series, and the diminished amount of material. Previous sets have averaged 1,100 pages, whereas current title has less than 800 pages.

Be that as it may, this set is recommended for purchase by all public and academic libraries. The writing level is appropriate for high school and undergraduate college students as well as members of the general public. Having said that, an entirely appropriate alternative to the American Decades series as a whole would be the *St. James Encyclopedia of Popular Culture* (2d ed.; see entry 973). As its focus is likewise the twentieth century in the United States, it covers much the same ground and is very solidly written and researched.—**Michael Francis Bemis**

389.   Wynn, Neil A. **Historical Dictionary from the Great War to the Great Depression.** 2d ec Lanham, Md., Scarecrow, 2014. 447p. (Historical Dictionaries of the U.S. Politics and Political Eras $120.00; $119.99 (e-book). ISBN 13: 978-0-8108-8033-7; 978-0-8108-8034-4 (e-book).

Beginning with a chronology from 1913 to 1933, Wynn focuses on the economic, social, and politic aspects of the period from the Great War to the Great Depression. There are nearly 700 entries, coveri

all major activities: the arts, business and the economy, communications, education, government and politics, fashion and leisure, law and justice, lifestyles and social trends, religion, and science, medicine, and technology. Within each chapter appears an overview and a basic chronology of important events during the period, a general overview, and a list of primary sources that provide a look into the hot topics of the time. Pictures are interspersed throughout the text, and they greatly enhance the volume's value and appeal. The chapter bibliographies are generally excellent, and a list of general references in the rear of the volume will alert readers to sources for further study. The index is exceptionally detailed and easy to use. Overall, this volume is a perceptive overview of the industrial epoch in the United States, and it is recommended for all types of libraries.—**ARBA Staff Reviewer**

393.   **The Articles of the Confederation.** By Blair Belton. Pleasantville, N.Y., Gareth Stevens, 2014. 32p. illus. index. (Documents that Shaped America). $26.60/vol.; $159.60/set. ISBN 13: 978-1-4339-8993-3.

394.   **The Declaration of Independence.** By John Shea. Pleasantville, N.Y., Gareth Stevens, 2014. 32p. illus. index. (Documents that Shaped America). $26.60/vol.; $159.60/set. ISBN 13: 978-1-4339-8997-1.

395.   **The Magna Carta.** By Janey Levy. Pleasantville, N.Y., Gareth Stevens, 2014. 32p. illus. maps. index. (Documents that Shaped America). $26.60/vol.; $159.60/set. ISBN 13: 978-1-4339-9001-4.

396.   **The Mayflower Compact.** By Kristen Rajczak. Pleasantville, N.Y., Gareth Stevens, 2014. 32p. illus. index. (Documents That Shaped America). $26.60/vol.; $159.60/set. ISBN 13: 978-1-4339-9005-2.

397.   **Thomas Paine's *Common Sense*.** By Ryan Nagelhout. Pleasantville, N.Y., Gareth Stevens, 2014. 32p. illus. index. (Documents that Shaped America). $26.60/vol.; $159.60/set. ISBN 13: 978-1-4339-9013-7.

398.   **The United States Constitution.** By Therese Shea. Pleasantville, N.Y., Gareth Stevens, 2014. 32p. illus. index. (Documents That Shaped America). $26.60/vol.; $159.60/set. ISBN 13: 978-1-4339-9009-0.
    These six volumes will help elementary-aged readers learn more about the key documents that have shaped American politics and law. Designed to align with social studies curriculum, the volumes go into more depth than most text books and explain in easy-to-understand terms the history behind each document, how it came to be, the viewpoints of those for and against it, and how it affects our lives today. The works are supplemented by colorful photographs, excerpts from primary documents, glossary definitions, and an index. There are For More Information sections that guide readers to more sources for further exploration of the topic. These volumes will be useful in elementary and middle school libraries.—**Shannon Graff Hysell**

399.   Becker, Peggy Daniels. **Japanese-American Internment During World War II.** Detroit, Omnigraphics, 2014. 223p. illus. index. (Defining Moments). $49.00. ISBN 13: 978-0-7808-1333-5.
    This volume provides a comprehensive overview designed for middle and high school students of the internment of Japanese Americans during World War II. This controversial episode during American history still serves as a black eye during what was otherwise thought of as a triumphant war for the American people. Fortunately, the author's engaging, simple style, combined with a visually enticing layout, will appeal to young readers, or to older readers who want a quick review. Like other works from this series, this title is arranged into three sections. It begins with a narrative overview that explains the

events leading up to the internment of Japanese American, provide details on their evacuation and living conditions, and discusses the emotional and physical toll it put on the people. Second, users will find biographies of key players in the decision to create this policy as well as biographies on the lives of some who lived through it. The third section includes primary sources of illuminating documents of this time. Excerpts from primary sources (a staple in recently published histories for teenagers) encourage young students to read these sources-when the full texts would otherwise be too daunting. A brief summary and analysis precedes each document. A bibliography gathers references suitable to the book's target audience-high school students but also sources that would be useful to college students. Other study tools include a glossary and a chronology. This book is recommended for public, school, and academic libraries.—**Nancy L. Van Atta**

400.   **The Causes of the American Revolution.** New York, Crabtree, 2014. 48p. illus. index. (Understanding the American Revolution). $26.60/vol.; $9.95pa./vol. ISBN 13: 978-0-7787-0804-9.

401.   **George Washington: Hero of the American Revolution.** New York, Crabtree, 2013. 48p. illus. index. (Understanding the American Revolution). $26.60/vol.; $9.95pa./vol. ISBN 13: 978-0-7787-0799-8.

402.   **King George III: England's Struggle to Keep America.** New York, Crabtree, 2013. 48p. illus. maps. index. (Understanding the American Revolution). $26.60/vol.; $9.95pa./vol. ISBN 13: 978-0-7787-0800-1.

403.   **Life on the Homefront During the American Revolution.** New York, Crabtree, 2013. 48p. illus. index. (Understanding the American Revolution). $26.60/vol.; $9.95pa./vol. ISBN 13: 978-0-7787-0801-8.

404.   **Marquis de Lafayett: Fighting for America's Freedom.** New York, Crabtree, 2013. 48p. illus. index. (Understanding the American Revolution). $26.60/vol.; $9.95pa./vol. ISBN 13: 978-0-7787-0802-5.

405.   **The Outcome of the American Revolution.** New York, Crabtree, 2013. 48p. illus. maps. index. (Understanding the American Revolution). $26.60/vol.; $9.95pa./vol. ISBN 13: 978-0-7787-0805-6.

406.   **Phillis Wheatley: Poet of the Revolutionary Era.** New York, Crabtree, 2013. 48p. illus. index. (Understanding the American Revolution). $26.60/vol.; $9.95pa./vol. ISBN 13: 978-0-7787-0803-2.

407.   **Significant Battles of the American Revolution.** New York, Crabtree, 2013. 48p. illus. maps. index. (Understanding the American Revolution). $26.60/vol.; $9.95pa./vol. ISBN 13: 978-0-7787-0806-3.

   This eight-volume set from Crabtree Publishing, a company known for their multivolume, nonfiction series designed specifically for children, provides a cursory introduction to the history behind the Revolutionary War written in a language that children will understand. The volumes in the series discuss a wide range of historical aspects of the war, including the causes of the war, the role of George Washington, the role of King Georg III, life on the home front, significant battles of the war, the outcome of the war, and influential poet Phillis Wheatley. This is a complex historical topic so the volumes in this series are for students in the middle school grades. Each two page spread covers a different aspect of the American Revolution. The author's writing is very descriptive and plenty of photographs, illustrations, maps, and sidebars are provided, which will appeal to the intended age group. Each volume ends with a glossary, a timeline, books and Websites for further reading, and a very short index, all of which can be used to teach young students basic researching skills. If library funds are available, this series is recommended for middle school libraries and juvenile collections in public libraries. They provide a good introduction to the American Revolution for both researchers and the general reader.—**Shannon Graff Hysell**

408.　**Cornerstones of Freedom Series.** Danbury, Conn., Scholastic Library Publishing, 2013. multivolume. illus. index. $30.00/vol.

Well-chosen cover illustrations accentuate interest in these high-priority topics for social studies, history, and science classes. Each book begins with encouragement for readers to become history investigators by examining primary and secondary sources, cross-examining witnesses, and taking a look at situations of that time period. All volumes include "Setting the Scene," influential individuals, a timeline, a map of events, boxed information to expand the text, future possibilities, a contents pages with pertinent illustrations, a glossary with pronunciations, resources, and primary and secondary sources.—**Ann Bryan Nelson**

409.　**The Great Depression.** San Diego, Calif., Reference Point Press, 2013. 96p. illus. index. (Understanding American History Series). $27.95/vol. ISBN 13: 978-1-60152-492-8.

410.　**The 1960s.** San Diego, Calif., Reference Point Press, 2013. 96p. illus. index. (Understanding American History Series). $27.95/vol. ISBN 13: 978-1-60152-494-2.

411.　**Prohibition.** San Diego, Calif., Reference Point Press, 2013. 96p. illus. index. (Understanding American History Series). $27.95/vol. ISBN 13: 978-1-60152-508-6.

Although these volumes are slim, they contain a wealth of information on these unique periods of American history for students in the upper middle grades or high school grades. Their purpose is to not only explain what occurred during these times in history but help readers explore how they continued to affect U.S. history and are still affecting our lives today. For example, prohibition of the 1920s saw an increase in organized crime that continues to this day; the Great Depression was an economic downturn that greatly affected the middle class, much like the economic recession our country recently experienced; and the 1960s marked a time of great distrust in our government, which can still be seen today. Each volume features a timeline and opening chapters describing the time frame being explored. Within the chapters users will find maps, photographs (most of which are from the era), and sidebars with interesting facts. Materials within the back matter include: a list of source notes, a biography of important people, further resources, and an index. These volumes will be worthwhile additions to most middle school libraries and public library collections.—**ARBA Staff Reviewer**

412.　Hendley, Nate. **The Mafia: A Guide to an American Subculture.** Santa Barbara, Calif., Greenwood Press/ABC-CLIO, 2013. 201p. illus. index. (Guides to Subcultures and Countercultures). $58.00. ISBN 13: 978-1-4408-0360-4; 978-1-4408-0361-1 (e-book).

How did an organization rooted in a distant, impoverished Mediterranean island come to dominate the American underworld for such a long time? That question gives continuity and structure to this brief but highly illuminating account of the Mafia, perhaps the most feared criminal organization in U.S. history. As a subculture, the Mafia represented a way of life at sharp odds with established society. Whereas most Americans saw hard work and honest-paying jobs as the road to success and the good life, Mafiosi, who lived in a subculture of greed, avarice, violence, and corruption, looked upon that as the dream of dimwitted weaklings. For the "wiseguys," illegal gambling, prostitution, labor racketeering, drug trafficking, extortion, loan sharking, bootleg booze, and, more recently, credit card fraud and online betting from offshore Websites were the route to "the American dream."

Hendley, a Toronto-based author who has written previously on crime and mobster's, covers the Mafia's historical background, organizational structure, geographical locales and key urban centers, significant leaders, specific criminal activities, and decline. Hendley attributed the Mafia's decline to several factors; Joseph Pistone, an FBI agent who infiltrated the organization in the 1970s; informers such as Joe Valachi and "Sammy the Bull" Gravano; tax laws, wiretaps, and the witness protection program; and the Racketeer Influenced and Corrupt Organizations Act (RICO). Thus, the major organized crime threat today comes from Mexican drug trafficking organizations rather than the Mafia. Even so, the Mafia remains strong, and in New York City the Five Families, the legacy of Salvatore Maranzano, who coined La Cosa Nostra, continue to thrive. Enhancing this study's appeal are a helpful timeline from 1880 to 2012, several photographs, an adequate index, and biographical sketches of mobsters from Charles "Lucky" Luciano to John Gotti. Particularly interesting is the appendix on the Mafia in popular culture, focusing on movies and television series from *Little Caesar* and *The Godfather* to the critically acclaimed *The Sopranos*. While this work offers nothing new for scholars, a general audience, along with students in history, sociology, and literature/film courses, will find it entertaining and informative.—**John W. Storey**

413. Hill, Jeff. **The WPA—Putting America to Work.** Detroit, Omnigraphics, 2014. 246p. illus. index. (Defining Moments). $49.00. ISBN 13: 978-0-7808-1331-1.

This slim volume on the Works Progress Administration, the key component of Roosevelt's New Deal program, is the latest installment in the Defining Moments series, designed for students grades 8-12, on pivotal events in U.S. history from the twentieth century forward. This volume, like others in the series, is divided into three primary sections: narrative overview, biographies, and primary sources. The narrative overview section provides a factual account of the topic, outlining origin, key players, major events, and impact. In *The WPA—Putting America to Work*, the timeline of events from its earliest inception to its legacy today is discussed. The author examines the different approaches the Hoover and Roosevelt administrations took to growing the American economy, the new agencies developed during this era, and the public reaction to this radical movement. The biographies section provides sketches of nine leading figures of the period, including Lyndon B. Johnson, Harry Hopkins, Orson Welles, and Ellen S. Woodward. Sources for further study accompany each sketch. Primary sources include 12 document. Additional useful materials include photographs, a chronology, a glossary, a bibliography that also includes Websites and videotapes, and a subject index.

The WPA—Putting America to Work is a well-organized, balanced, and approachable reference source for its intended audience, undoubtedly reflective of the composition of the series advisory board (public and school librarians and educators) and hopefully indicative of the quality of other titles in the series.—**Lisa Kay Speer**

414. Hillstrom, Kevin. **The Zoot Suit Riots.** Detroit, Omnigraphics, 2013. 214p. illus. index. (Defining Moments). $49.00. ISBN 13: 978-0-7808-1285-7.

The Zoot Suit Riots is a single-volume work consisting of three parts: a narrative overview, biographies of leading figures involved in the era, and primary sources consisting of essays, memoirs, and testimonials. It also includes a chronology, a glossary, photographs, and a bibliography.

The 107-page overview includes sidebars providing related information of events leading up to the zoot suit riots in Los Angeles in the 1930s. These will provide summaries, although not detailed reports, of hard-to-find events and people that students may need for assignments. The overview provides objective information on the events and people of the zoot suit riots, conveys its historical and cultural importance, and at the same time sheds light on his region's attitudes toward migrant worker from Mexico. Readers will find quality photography and maps that add context to the overviews.

The biographies focus on 10 leading social and cultural figures from this era. According to the book's preface, the biographies are on "leading figures associated with the event in question," but are not necessarily an authoritative list. People such as Fletcher Bowron (Los Angeles mayor), José Diaz

(Mexican far worker whose murder resulted in the Sleepy Lagoon Trial), Alice Greenfield (civil rights activist), and Henry "Hank" Leyvas (Mexican American defendant in the Sleepy Lagoon murder trial) have biographies.

The third part of this book consists of primary sources. The section starts with examples of Anti-Mexican discrimination in 1930s America and continues with primary documents associated with the Sleepy Lagoon trial, activist recounts of the zoot suit riots, and a landmark legal decision for Mexican Americans. These sources represent the writings of that time, although this section is not an exhaustive collection.

The Zoot Suit Riots succeeds in providing easy-to-read content without being overly simplified. Most teen readers and the general public will like this book's unpretentious organization and appearance. It lacks some details and expanded overviews, but compensates by providing bibliographies and recommended sources for additional information. The content provides some useful information for assigned papers, and for adults who want an introduction to this little-known controversy in America's history. This title is a good addition to a collection with other supporting books on this topic. Because Mexican immigration continues to be a hot button issue in today's society, some 80 years after the zoot suit riots, this book will have relevance in today's classrooms. *The Zoot Suit Riots* is recommended for middle and high school libraries, and public libraries.—**ARBA Staff Reviewer**

415.   Krawczynski, Keith. **Daily Life in the Colonial City.** Santa Barbara, Calif., Greenwood Press/ ABC-CLIO, 2013. 554p. illus. index. (The Greenwood Press Daily Life Through History Series: Daily Life in the United States). $68.00. ISBN 13: 978-0-313-33419-1; 978-0-313-04704-6 (e-book).

Krawczynski relates the history and explores the development and influence of cities in the colonization of North America. He organizes *Daily Life in the Colonial City* by broad themes, with chapters on such topics as education, religion, food and dining, health and medicine, and government. Krawczynski's thesis differs from the Frontier Thesis of Frederick Jackson Turner, maintaining that the greatest influence on the developing United States was not the ever-receding and always enticing frontier, with its promise of endless chances, but the cities. It was the cities that fostered interaction, conflict, and eventual grudging if not enthusiastic acceptance among different ethnic and economic groups; the cities that offered education and entertainment; the cities that through trade and commerce influenced their respective regions. Most of all, it was in cities that a diverse and growing population began to meld into Americans.

Krawczynski uses five cities as exemplars for developments in the different regions of the emerging county: New York/New Amsterdam; Boston; Philadelphia; Charles Town in Carolina, and Newport, Rhode Island. This allows the author to highlight regional differences in the various aspects of daily life he examines. As the developing country experimented with new ideas, the different regional centers, with populations from different areas of the world, all with different histories, traditions, and cultures, became testing grounds and crucibles for new ideas, new amusements, new industries, and new politics.

Supplemental material includes an introductory chronology, which begins in 1609 with Henry Hudson's exploration of what would be named the Hudson River near Manhattan, and ends in 1776 with the writing of the Declaration of Independence. Also included as supplementary material are notes to each chapter, providing further sources, a selected bibliography to the whole work, and a general index. *Daily Life in the Colonial City* is adequately, but not heavily illustrated. This volume would be useful as supplemental reading at the advanced high school or beginning college level.—**Terry Ann Mood**

416.   Sandler, Martin W. **Imprisoned: The Betrayal of Japanese Americans During World War II.** Walker and Company, 2013. 176p. Illus. index. $22.99. ISBN 13: 978-0-8027-2277-5.

This book explores the internment of Japanese Americans during World War II. By Executive Order 9066 American were stripped of their citizenship, their rights, their property, and livelihood, and shipped to live behind barded wire. At the same time, Japanese Americans made enormous contributions to the American war effort by valiantly serving in the Armed Forces. The final chapters discuss the national effort for redress, and the response of the Japanese community to September 11, 2011. Individuals, controversial issues, and items of particular interest relating to this time period are highlighted within each chapter. The text is copiously illustrated with photographs and other primary source documents. Readers will find the format inviting, which makes this an excellent choice for libraries to provide quality narrative nonfiction for Common Core reading material. Middle school students will find the work accessible; high school students will appreciate the primary documents. Further reading suggestions and sources are included.—**Karen Leon**

417.   Schlotterbeck, John T. **Daily Life in the Colonial South.** Santa Barbara, Calif., Greenwood Press/ ABC-CLIO, 2013. 419p. illus. index. (The Greenwood Press Daily Life Through History Series: Daily Life in the United States). $68.00. ISBN 13: 978-0-313-34069-7; 978-1-57356-743-5 (e-book).

In *Daily Life in the Colonial South*, historian John T. Schlotterbeck explores the tangible and intangible aspects of the daily lives of Africans, Europeans, and Native Americans in the American South between the sixteenth and mid-eighteenth centuries. Focusing on such topics as bodies, beliefs, material possessions, and identities, he depicts the colonial South as a crucible of terrific change and upheaval. Diseases, high mortality rates, migrations, and wars broke up old societies and caused new ones to take form. The deerskin trade, encroachment of European settlers on Indian lands, and widespread adoption of African slave labor forced a diversity of cultures to negotiate and renegotiate their identities in the face of changing economic and political realities. The cultural markers of Southern identity, then, were forged from the interactions between different ethnic, linguistic, racial, and religious groups over time and across regions.

Schlotterbeck covers a lot of intellectual ground, synthesizing many of the recent trends in the historical literature of the colonial South and incorporating insights from archaeological literature regarding its material culture. By examining the lives of ordinary people as well as elites, he identifies the ways families, food, labor, and leisure connected individuals and communities across class, ethnic, and racial lines. He likewise acknowledges the ways destructive forces like diseases and wars undermined attempts at promoting stability. Out of this environment of cultural exchange and disorder, he argues, the first stirrings of Southern consciousness emerged.

Schlotterbeck writes at a high academic level, which may ultimately limit this study's usefulness to those college students fluent with such abstract concepts as communities "negotiating cultural norms" and material objects "mediating cultural behavior." This minor criticism aside, *Daily Life in the Colonial South* is a solid synthesis of historical literature and a worthy addition to the Daily Life Through History Series.—**Craig Mury Keeney**

418.   Staples, Kathleen A., and Madelyn Shaw. **Clothing Through American History: The British Colonial Era.** Santa Barbara, Calif., Greenwood Press/ABC-CLIO, 2013. 444p. illus. index. $89.00. ISBN 13: 978-0-313-33593-8; 978-0-313-08460-7 (e-book).

Clothing Through American History: The British Colonial Era joins several other volumes in this series on American clothing. Like its predecessors on the Federal era through Antebellum era and the Civil War era through the Gilded age, this volume is more than a listing or a description of articles of clothing. It also places clothing in a larger context. Beginning chapters trace early settlement of the area surveyed, with some emphasis on different nationalities and ethnic groups; examine the role of clothing in establishing social class or indicating intentions, such as specific clothing for a wedding or the conventions of mourning; and include a lengthy chapter on the methods of clothes production. In this chapter, the authors present information on the fabrics used, the structure of various garments, the clothing trade, home manufacture, and the many and various trades associated with clothing, such as seamstress, hatter, wig maker, embroiderer, or dyer.

The bulk of the book is indeed on specific clothing and clothing styles, divided into chapters on men's clothing, women's clothing, and children's clothing. In these chapters, too the authors relate styles and developments of styles to sociological changes. For example, changes in children's clothing corresponded with changes in society toward more freedom and individuality. Children's clothing became looser, less cumbersome, and more comfortable as theories of child rearing began to recognize stages of child development, growing independence, and the necessity for movement and freedom.

This volume is rich in detail and information, with a thorough examination of the documentation used. Among the sources are portraits, probate records, letter, diaries, and newspaper accounts and advertisements. The authors also recognize that documentation for this topic is quite difficult. Portraits can be misleading, as attire in portraits may not be accurate. Portrait sitters might have wanted to appear more affluent than they were, or elected to be portrayed in the latest fashions whether or not they owned them. Probate documents might not include all items of clothing left by a deceased, particularly if certain items were given away before death. Letters or diaries might not mention clothing specifically, as being an unimportant detail. Complicating documentation is the obvious fact that most of the standard sources—the aforementioned portraits, wills, diaries, and letters—are more common to the wealthy than to the lower classes. Non-moneyed people seldom had their portraits painted, nor did they have enough worldly goods to bother with a will. Some were illiterate, or barely literate, and therefore left no letters or diaries. Of course, for many minorities populations, most especially those enslaved, there is almost no such documentation. To overcome this, the authors used newspaper accounts and advertisements. Often an advertisement for a runaway slave included a description of clothing worn, or an advertisement for a child sadly taken by a caretaker noted that information. Additionally, the clothing worn by the upper classes was of more sumptuous fabrics and might survive even to today, while the cotton and linen clothing of the masses wore out until the rags were sometimes used in paper production.

Supplementary material includes a glossary, a timeline of political events, a bibliography (and additionally a bibliography of costume museums), extensive chapter bibliographies, and an index. The index includes entries for various time spans to allow the reader to locate information on a specific span of years.

Uses for this volume are numerous. Students or historians researching the era would obviously be interested, as would those seeking information for a theatrical production or even a reenactment event. The volume would also be useful as a tool to introduce children not only to the clothing itself but to the many individuals and trades necessary to produce and supply it.—**Terry Ann Mood**

419. **This is Who We Were: In the 1960s.** Millerton, N.Y., Grey House Publishing, 2014. 607p. illus. index. $150.00. ISBN 13: 978-1-61925-248-6; 978-1-61925-249-3 (e-book).

Examining historical events by decade is one way of examining the history of a country, specific historical field, or other subject. This work attempts to examine personal, political, economic, and socio-cultural events in U.S. history during the 1960s. It is divided into five sections: Profiles, Historical Snapshots, Economy of the Times, All Around Us, and Census Data.

The Profiles section examines key life events from various individuals from different walks of life such as Chicago car salesman Wes Cameron describing key events from his life and work as well as significant socio-economic developments in the Chicago area. The historical snapshot section randomly lists what compilers consider as significant events during various parts of the 1960s such as the college students protesting the Vietnam War in New York's Time Square and San Francisco, the introduction of cereals with pre-packaged fruit, and the opening of St. Louis' Gateway Arch.

Economy of the Times features consumer expenditure statistics on specific items, including: how much consumers paid annually for clothing and utilities in 1961, 1966, and 1969; prices in these years for specific items such as hi-fi phonographs and an 8 mm camera; and the dollar's purchasing price value between 1860 and 2012. The All Around Us section features popular magazine and newspaper articles on various trends and developments including a September 10, 1960 *National Review* article with suggestions for improving school and college textbook quality, and a September 27, 1968 *Time* article on redwood forest conservation in northern California and Oregon.

The Census Data section features verbatim reprints from 1970 *Census of Population and Housing* volumes featuring state and country demographic trends and developments as well as age and racial backgrounds so readers can understand population settlement and migration patterns. A bibliography of secondary source works concludes the compilation.

This is a unique approach to documenting decadal history but it has problems. Poor to non-existent sourcing occurs in many sections of the work including the Economy of the Times and the This is Who We Were sections. The introduction, "America: The Rebellious Child," briefly describes key developments in the 1960s in areas such as immigration, sports, music, education, the Vietnam War, the space race, and the economy, but makes no attempt to provide deeper contextual analysis for these events and their significance in the 2010s. This work is most useful for high school students and public library readers. Except for the Census Bureau data, it has limited value for academic library users.—**Bert Chapman**

420.   **Voices for Freedom: Abolitionist Heroes Series.** New York, Crabtree, 2013. multivolume. illus. index. $23.95/vol.; $10.95pa./vol.

This multivolume set from Crabtree Publishing, a company known for their multivolume, nonfiction series designed specifically for children, provides biographical and historical information on leaders of the abolitionist movement in the United States during the Civil War era. New to this series are biographies on Abraham Lincoln and Theodore Weld. This is a complex topic so the volumes in this series are for students in the upper elementary to middle school grades. Within each volume are plenty of color photographs and illustrations as well as sidebars full of additional historical information. Each volume ends with a chronology of important events in the biographee's life, a list of resources for further research that includes both books and Internet sites, a glossary, and a very short index, all of which can be used to teach young students basic researching skills. This series is recommended for elementary and middle school libraries and juvenile collections in public libraries. They provide a good introduction to African American history and the abolitionist movement.—**Shannon Graff Hysell**

421.   Walters, Kerry. **Lincoln, the Rise of the Republicans, and the Coming of the Civil War: A Reference Guide.** Santa Barbara, Calif., ABC-CLIO, 2013. 281p. index. (Guides to Historical Events in America). $58.00. ISBN 13: 978-1-61069-204-5; 978-1-61069-205-2 (e-book).

Despite Abraham Lincoln's name in the title and cover illustration, the sixteenth president of the United States is not the primary subject of this book. Similarly, "Reference Guide" in the subtitle is perhaps an overstatement as it only minimally fits the definition of a reference work. Rather, this is primarily a narrative history of the impact of slavery on the rise and fall of political parties during the period between the Compromise of 1820 and Lincoln's first inaugural speech in 1861. While the volume includes brief biographical sketches, a chronology of the period, and a selection of pertinent documents, these tend to be secondary to the narrative history that is the heart of the work.

The author, Kerry Walters, a professor of philosophy at Gettysburg College, has a long list of publications in philosophy and several in American pre-Civil War history. He is credited with two of the four books published to date in ABC-CLIO's Guides to Historical Events in America series. The narrative of the present volume is written in an informal, at times almost storytelling manner that should appeal to students and the general public.

While this volume has value as a straight narrative history, it generally fails as a reference book. A key to any reference work is the ease with which users are able to access information, and this is the major failure of this volume. The index is woefully inadequate, covering only 180 of the books total 280 pages. Omitted from inclusion in the index are the biographical and appendix sections, both of which contain data essential to the book's subject. The table of contents similarly fails to list the contents of these two sections. Similarly, a bibliography of 84 titles is limited by failure to include pertinent sources listed in chapter endnotes. The book additionally contains a number of factual errors. These include failure to note that there were eight rather than seven slave states in 1787 (p. 2); the claim that the Whig Party name "harkened back to the heroes of 1776" when it was actually derived from the party in England that opposed the king (p 11); and an erroneous listing of the states, large "chunks" of which made up the Territory of Texas and that the Territory's border extended to Canada (p. 16).

As a historical narrative, this book may be recommended for general library collections and popular reading. It is not recommended, however for reference collections.—**Donald E. Collins**

422.   Wilson, Jamie J. **Civil Rights Movement.** Santa Barbara, Calif., Greenwood Press/ABC-CLIO, 2013. 232p. illus. index. (Landmarks of the American Mosaic). $58.00. ISBN 13: 978-1-4408-0426-7; 978-1-4408-0427-4 (e-book).

This latest entry into Greenwood's "Landmarks of the American Mosaic" reference series covers territory familiar to almost everyone cognizant of twentieth-century African American history—the Civil Rights Movement from the 1930s through the 1960s. As editor Wilson, who has an extensive publication history on the topic, notes, the coverage here is both telescopic and with "a bird's eye view"—narrative depth not found in larger resources yet broad enough to encompass the important campaigns and event of those years. Each of the eight chapters focuses on a narrower topic, such as the Movement in Alabama, with each chapter running roughly 15-20 pages long. Some black-and-white photographs are included, along with secondary bibliographies after each chapter. About 60 percent of the volume is devoted to primary documents, a glossary, annotated bibliography, biographical sketches, and the index. The writing and research overall are very good, and readers will find Staci M. Rubin's chapter on civil rights' court cases an excellent summary of the legal battles of the era. Although Wilson offers nothing especially new here, students in high school and undergraduate students in particular should use this volume as an entry point before deeper research into issues and events. This work is recommended for all African American history and culture collections.—**Anthony J. Adam**

African History

423.   Njoku, Raphael Chijioke. **The History of Somalia.** Santa Barbara, Calif., Greenwood Press/ABC-CLIO, 2013. 211p. illus. index. (The Greenwood Histories of the Modern Nations). $58.00. ISBN 13: 978-0-313-37857-7; 978-0-313-37858-4 (e-book).

The author of this work, the chair/director of the International Studies Program at Idaho State University, has written quite a nice monograph on Somali history in only about 200 pages. Given the complexity of the topic, this is no mean feat. Although it begins with the prehistoric period, it is current enough that it can discuss the dynamics of the state's collapse, democratization, terrorism, and piracy. As one might expect, however, the twentieth century garners half the book. This book is, of necessity, startlingly terse at times. Yet, that is not meant to be a criticism since it was written as an introductory text, especially for students, probably of high school or college age. It is also quite suitable as a reference work. It has a good index, a list of notable people in the history of Somalia (20 in all), and a brief bibliographic essay that probably could have been expanded somewhat. Also included are a timeline of historical events and a list of abbreviations.

There are few illustrations and the maps are limited and at best adequate. More maps, especially in the beginning of the text, would have been helpful. On the other hand, the initial chapter discusses Somalia today, its geography, population, economic conditions, mass media, and much more to set the stage for what follows. Overall, the text is well written, easy to follow, and a good place to start for readers who have no prior knowledge of Somali history. This work is recommended for most libraries, but especially high school, college, and public libraries.—**ARBA Staff Reviewer**

Asian History

General Works

424.   **Internet East Asian History Sourcebook. http://www.fordham.edu/halsall/eastasia/eastasiasbook.asp.** [Website]. Fordham University. Free. Date reviewed: 2013.

This site covers historical periods of China, Japan, and Korea. The contents include such themes as cultural origins, religious traditions, and "East Asian genders ad sexualities." This page is a subset of texts derived from the three major online Sourcebooks— Internet Ancient History Sourcebook, Internet Medieval Sourcebook, and Internet Modern History Sourcebook—along with added texts and web site indicators.—**Noriko Asato**

China

425.   Lew, Christopher R., and Edwin Pak-Wah Leung. **Historical Dictionary of the Chinese Civil War.** 2d ed. Lanham, Md., Scarecrow, 2013. 304p. (Historical Dictionaries of War, Revolution, and Civil Unrest). $100.00; $99.99 (e-book). ISBN 13: 978-0-8108-7873-0; 978-0-8108-7874-7 (e-book).

First published in 2002, and later reprinted as *The A-to-Z of the Chinese Civil War* (2010), this 2d edition has over 100 more pages of text. Lew, a U.S. Army veteran, has substantially revised and expanded the contents of 1st edition. The 12-page introduction provides the necessary background overview that one needs to understand this conflict, which is also a part of the Second World War and the Cold War. There are over 200 entries describing critical events, important personages, troop movements, proclamations, organizational structure, and foreign involvement. There are plentiful *see* and *see also* references, and highlighted words in the text indicate the cross-referencing to other entries, where one can look for more information. The 25-page bibliography is arranged by subject category, but there are no source notes at the end of the individual entries, which is standard for these dictionaries from this publisher. While there is a list of acronyms and abbreviations, along with a 13-page chronology (1919-1950), it is very disappointing that there are no maps to help one understand this important historical period. This sturdily bound work is the main English-language reference tool for this event, and is available online as well through EBRARY and EBSCO e-book collections. It complements Lawrence R. Sullivan's *Historical Dictionary of the Chinese Communist Party* (see ARBA 2013, entry 638). It is suitable for the reference collections of all academic and large public libraries, especially those lacking the 1st edition.—**Daniel K. Blewett**

Japan

426.   Henshall, Kenneth. **Historical Dictionary of Japan to 1945.** Lanham, Md., Scarecrow, 2014. 596p. (Historical Dictionaries to Ancient Civilizations and Historical Eras). $125.00; $119.99 (e-book). ISBN 13: 978-0-8108-7871-6; 978-0-8108-7872-3 (e-book).

This well-written collection of over 800 entries is a useful reference tool for those quick-answer questions about this long period of Japanese history and culture, which is not widely understood in the West. The entries vary in length, from a single paragraph to a few pages, and cover the important people, events, eras, themes, and issues that are the essential elements of Japan's history. Professor Henshall (Japanese Studies, University of Canterbury, Christchurch, New Zealand, and Fellow of the Royal Historical Society), is also an expert on the Japanese language and writing system, so in this book a word, phrase, or incident in the Japanese language is frequently followed by the Japanese writing characters, and entry titles in English are followed by a Japanese translation and writing characters. No index or photographs are provided, but there is a chronology (200,000 B.C.E. to 1945 C.E.), and an extensive 67-page bibliography arranged by topic, and including some appropriate Websites and journals. As is common in these types of reference books, there are numerous *see* and *see also* and in-text, cross-references, so that the reader can jump around inside the book to find related information. The appendixes have lists of the Emperors, Shoguns, and Prime Ministers, along with the texts of important documents, such as the Meiji Constitution of 1889, and items related to the Second World War. The single map is disappointing—it is of the country's administrative areas as of 2012, and because of the tiny print it is very hard to read. Surely there could have been more and clearer cartographic representations of this nation's history. Also lacking are historical statistical tables, charts, or graphs. But these are only minor quibbles. This thick book can be paired with the sister Scarecrow publications: *Historical Dictionary of Postwar Japan* (see ARBA 2012, entry 98); *Historical Dictionary of Tokyo* (2d ed.; see ARBA 2012, entry 97); and the *Historical Dictionary of Osaka and Kyoto* (see ARBA 2000, entry 438). The title under review is suitable for special collections, academic, and large public libraries. The work is also available as an e-book.—**Daniel K. Blewett**

427.   **Japan at War: An Encyclopedia.** Louis G. Perez, ed. Santa Barbara, Calif., ABC-CLIO, 2013. 615p. illus. index. $100.00. ISBN 13: 978-1-59884-741-3; 978-1-59884-742-0 (e-book).

The Japanese have a rich and legendary military history strife with codes, honor, and war. Yet the dichotomy exists between the way of the Samurai and as a country officially denouncing the right to declare war. This "fascinating reference explores the relationship between military values and Japanese society, and traces the evolution of war in this country from 700 CE to modern times." The editor of this ABC-CLIO encyclopedia, Louis G. Perez, has published several reference works on the Japanese culture and the numerous contributors are acknowledged experts. The roughly 300 entries, which are arranged alphabetically, bring the reader into the wider context of the Japanese people at war; each also contains a scholarly suggested reading list. A great preface and introduction are provided, as is a wonderful glossary, index, and bibliography. Additionally, the chronology and set of primary documents are very helpful. A few examples of the entries are: the Bataan Death March, Bushido, the Jokyu War of 1221, the 1918 Rice Riots, and Tomoyuki Yamashita (1885-1946). Overall, this encyclopedia is helpful; it is well organized and easy to use. It is a recommended purchase.—**Scott R. DiMarco**

Myanmar

428.   Topich, William J., and Keith A. Leitich. **The History of Myanmar.** Santa Barbara, Calif., Greenwood Press/ABC-CLIO, 2013. 173p. index. (The Greenwood Histories of The Modern Nations). $58.00. ISBN 13: 978-0-313-35724-4; 978-0-313-35725-1 (e-book).

One of the latest in The Greenwood Histories of the Modern Nations series, *The History of Myanmar* attempts to provide a comprehensive history of Myanmar (also known as Burma) from approximately 3000 B.C.E. to the present. While the majority of the book is devoted to the twentieth century, earlier periods are clearly delineated. Expository detail and quotations are used throughout the text to enliven the succinct and lucid narrative. The text is kept free of footnotes and references, rendering it easy to read. A supplementary timeline of significant events, list of important figures, a select bibliography, and index are extremely useful to both students and the layperson navigating the complex history of this lesser-known country.

While the entire book is organized chronologically, chapter titles such as "The British Conquest of Burma," "From Independence to Military Dictatorship," and "Political Turmoil and Natural Catastrophe, 1990-2007," attempt to provide some topical focus. However, there is little within the text itself or the brief conclusion that attempts to address or draw out persistent themes or patterns in Myanmar's history. A few references to subsequent academic interpretations of events are included, but the work generally avoids discussion of any scholarly debate surrounding events or topics in Myanmar's history. A bibliographic essay provides slightly more historiographical context, but further discussion would have rendered this book more valuable to academic audiences.

Survey histories must often compress expanses of time and complex scholarship and subject matter into concisely written, yet appealing, narratives catering to both the general public and students. In general, this work succeeds in presenting an introduction to Myanmar history suitable for both public and academic libraries.—**Hui Hua Chua**

European History

General Works

429.   Olson, Sherri. **Daily Life in a Medieval Monastery.** Santa Barbara, Calif., Greenwood Press/ ABC-CLIO, 2013. 211p. index. (The Greenwood Press Daily Life Through History Series). $58.00. ISBN 13: 978-0-313-33655-3; 978-0-313-05617-8 (e-book).

This book by Sherri Olson, associate professor of history and co-director of the medieval studies program at the University of Connecticut, belongs in the general collection with other books on medieval monasticism or medieval history. The book is very readable and informative. There are six maps, some of which shows where monasteries were. There are 16 black-and-white illustrations. The book has six chapters: the first is on St. Benedict and the early history of Christian monasticism. There are many quotes from the Rule of St. Benedict in this chapter. The second chapter is about the monasteries of St. Gall and Cluny. Chapter 3 is about child oblates and stories of various monks and nuns, like St. Hildegard. Chapter 4 is on visitation and inspections. The content for this chapter is from actual visitation reports. Chapter 5 is about a monastery of nuns from 1133 to 1540. Chapter 6 is on the relationships between monks and peasants. Many peasants were servants of monasteries. Each chapter has a bibliography. The book ends with a glossary, a bibliography, and an index. This book is highly recommended for the study of medieval monasticism.—**Benet Steven Exton**

430.   Willis, Jim. **Daily Life Behind the Iron Curtain.** Santa Barbara, Calif., Greenwood Press/ABC-CLIO, 2013. 243p. illus. index. (the greenwood Press Daily Life Through History Series). $58.00. ISBN 13: 978-0-313-39762-2; 978-0-313-39763-9 (e-book).

Nearly a quarter century has passed since the Iron Curtain's fall and most of that region's countries have experienced enhanced political freedom and varying degrees of economic success and failure. This work is a social history examining how Communism affected the daily lives of individuals living in these countries.

It describes how the rise of Communism, Fascism, and Nazism created the conditions bringing Eastern European countries under Soviet domination after World War II. Considerable emphasis is placed on the roles played by internal security organisations in these countries, particularly the Stasi in East Germany, in maintaining Communist Party dominance and squelching signs of political dissent. It also documents the role played by educational institutions in ideologically indoctrinating students into the Marxist-Leninist worldview to perpetuate Communist rule in these countries and throughout this region.

Additional content covers the attempts of some individuals and organizations to resist Communist rule and the heavy price that could be paid for such resistance. U.S. and western motion picture portrayals of life under Communism are also analyzed. These include romantic eulogies of communist rule such as *Reds* and more realistic portrayals such as *One Day in the Life of Ivan Denisovich*.

Particular emphasis is placed on media coverage of the Berlin Wall's collapse in 1989, subsequent German-Russian relations, and reunited Germany's problems in absorbing the former East Germany, including the higher levels of unemployment in the eastern part of Germany. This work will serve as a useful introduction for those desiring basic background on the lives of everyday individuals behind the Iron Curtain during the Cold war.—**Bert Chapman**

Great Britain

431. Murdoch, Lydia. **Daily Life of Victorian Women.** Santa Barbara, Calif., Greenwood Press/ABC-CLIO, 2014. 286p. illus. index. (The Greenwood Press Daily Life Through History Series). $58.00. ISBN 13: 978-0-313-38498-1; 978-0-313-38499-8 (e-book).

   In *Daily Life of Victorian Women*, Murdoch (Vassar College) examines the experiences and roles that women played during the Victorian era in England. Contrary to the image commonly shown in media and in books, women of this era were not all homemakers; many worked right alongside men as businesswomen, innkeepers, artisans, and fishmongers. This book addresses the lives of women from all socioeconomic classes, from high society to middle class to the working poor. Beginning with an introduction on the ideals of woman hood at the time, the book is then organized into eight chapters that address such topics as religion and death, family and home, health and sexuality, childrearing and education, wage labor and professional work, and urban life. The book contains chapter source notes, a chronology from 1828 through 1903, an extensive bibliography, historic black-and-white photographs, sidebars with interesting facts, and an index. The text provides worthwhile insights into what it was like to be a woman during Victorian England.—**William C. Struning**

432. Shepherd, Deborah J. **Daily Life in Arthurian Britain.** Santa Barbara, Calif., Greenwood Press/ABC-CLIO, 2013. 314p. index. (The Greenwood Press Daily Life Through History Series). $58.00. ISBN 13: 978-0-313-33295-1; 978-0-313-03852-5 (e-book).

   This book provides extensive information related to life in Britain in the fifth and sixth centuries, the period of time between the Roman withdrawal from Britain and the eventual Christianization of Britain by Rome. It is also the time period associated with Arthur and Arthurian legend, and the author spends quite a bit of time explaining the scholarship, resources, and history related to Arthur in Britain. Given that background, the book contains a detailed examination of the history, people, towns and countryside, social identities, agricultural lifestyle, city and town life, crafts and trade, political and social dimensions, and religious life in Britain during this time period. The book has many black-and-white photographs and drawings, including three very detailed maps of Britain during the period under discussion. There is a glossary and extensive bibliography. This book is part of the Greenwood Press Daily Life Through History series.—**Bradford Lee Eden**

Iceland

433. Johannesson, Gudni Thorlacius. **The History of Iceland.** Santa Barbara, Calif., Greenwood Press/ABC-CLIO, 2013. 172p. index. (The Greenwood Histories of The Modern Nations). $58.00. ISBN 13: 978-0-313-37620-7; 978-0-313-37621-4 (e-book).

   The "distinguished advisory board" of this series selects only those countries whose political, economic, and social affairs distinguish them as the most important at the beginning of the twenty-first century. Iceland was chosen because it is an interesting example of a nation that has gone from one of the wealthiest nations in the world to the fall of its economic system in 2008. The coverage of this work is heavily weighted on nineteenth and twentieth centuries. The pre-history and Norse period (for which Americans seem to have particular fascination) are dealt with in approximately 25 pages, while the same amount is devoted to years 999-1550. Invariably, many important facts have been left out; however, the author has provided a succinct overview of the countries history highlighting major political, economic, and social developments. Many developments of the period that would be helpful in understanding present-day Iceland have either been left out or dealt with inadequately. The twentieth century up to 2012, however, is covered more in-depth. The historical narrative is supplemented by a chronology of events, a chapter on biographical sketches, a bibliographic essay, and a subject index.— **Leena Siegelbaum**

Spain

434. Romero Salvadó, Francisco J. **Historical Dictionary of the Spanish Civil War.** Lanham, Md., Scarecrow, 2013. 411p. (Historical Dictionaries of War, Revolution, and Civil Unrest). $115.00; $109.99 (e-book). ISBN 13: 978-0-8108-5784-1; 978-0-8108-8009-2 (e-book).

The Spanish Civil War began in July 1936 when the country's military attempted a coup against Spain's Second Republic that proved partially successful. Their lack of total victory encouraged other factions to also revolt, thus plunging the country into vicious warfare that raged until April 1839. Although fought in Spain, the conflict impacted politics throughout Europe, to the extent that General Francisco Franco ultimately emerged victorious due in large measure to Germany's Adolf Hitler and Italy's Benito Mussolini.

Francisco J. Romero Salvadó, Reader in Modern Spanish History at the University of Bristol, United Kingdom and the author of such works as *The Spanish Civil War: Origins, Course and Outcomes* (Palgrave, 2005) and *Foundations of the Civil War: Revolution, Social Conflict and Reaction in Spain, 1916-1923* (Routledge, 2008), has produced an outstanding reference work that sheds valuable light on a conflict that has not been well represented in the reference literature. Like the other volumes in Scarecrow Press' series entitled Historical Dictionaries of War, Revolution, and Civil Unrest, this volume begins with an introductory section that includes maps, a chronology, and a general introduction to the topic. The bulk of the work is a dictionary with approximately 600 entries that are arranged alphabetically. The majority of the entries focus on key events, institutions, military campaigns, and people that were active within Spain's borders. Individuals, such as Hitler and Mussolini, who were important actors but whose activities took place outside of Spain's territorial borders apparently did not warrant their own entries. Instead, their actions are explored within the entries that are provided for each of the European countries impacted by Spain's turmoil. A major strength of this reference work is the bibliography, which is more than 40 pages long and includes bibliographic sources written in either English or Spanish. The excellent reference tool is highly recommended for academic libraries supporting programs in European History.—**John R. Burch Jr.**

Middle Eastern History

435. **Ancient Mesopotamia: This History, Our History. http://mesopotamia.lib.uchicago.edu/.** [Website]. Free. Date reviewed: 2014.

This site was developed under the assumption that "the story of ancient Mesopotamia is the story of humankind." It is based on the archaeological discoveries conducted by the University of Chicago over the past century and was developed in collaboration with a team of Chicago public school teachers who selected key artifacts from the Oriental Institute Museum's Mesopotamian collection to elucidate many aspects of the everyday lives of the ancient people who lived in what is now Iraq. The main menu offers options to explore topics about life in Mesopotamia. The essays are brief and informative and link to lesson and activities. Each page has a high resolution image that cannot, unfortunately, be rotated to view all angles of an artifact. There is also a smaller static image that illustrates the topic. One can also examine artifacts and view video clips from Oriental Institute scholars. One of these is a virtual archaeological dig in Iraq. Browsing the collection of teacher-selected artifacts by material, time period, or cultural themes shows the relationship between artifacts and helps students get a broader picture of ancient Mesopotamia. A section on teaching materials includes lesson plans and national standards.—**Norman Desmarais**

Latin America and the Caribbean

436.   **Conflict in the Early Americas: An Encyclopedia of the Spanish Empire's Aztec, Incan, and Mayan Conquests.** Rebecca M. Seaman, ed. Santa Barbara, Calif., ABC-CLIO, 2013. 485p. illus. index. $100.00. ISBN 13: 978-1-59884-776-5; 9-78-1-59884-777-2 (e-book).

As the 500th anniversary of Cortez's conquest of the Aztec Empire approaches (Summer 2020), readers can expect to see more references to this event. Spain's expeditious subjugation of the Aztec and Inca Empires stands out as one of the most fantastic events in world history and continues to captivate students. While there are several relatively recent reference books that include information on Spanish conquests of the Americas, such as the *Encyclopedia of Latin America* (see ARBA 2011, entry 107), *The Oxford History of Mexico* (see ARBA 2011, entry 410), *World and Its People: Mexico and Central America* (see ARBA 2010, entry 103), *Daily Life in the Inca Empire* (see ARBA 2010, entry 434), *The History of Peru* (see ARBA 2010, entry 435), *Daily Life in Maya Civilization* (see ARBA 2010, entry 436), the *Encyclopedia of Latin America History & Culture* (2d ed.; see ARBA 2009, entry 118), *Historical Dictionary of Ancient South America* (see ARBA 2009, entry 413), *Archaeology of Ancient Mexico and Central America* (see ARBA 2002, entry 407), and *The Oxford Encyclopedia of Mesoamerican Culture* (see ARBA 2002, entry 299), ABC-CLIO's *Conflict in the Early Americas: An Encyclopedia* of the Spanish Empire's Aztec, Incan, and Mayan Conquests is the only one to focus exclusively on the conquest.

As with most encyclopedias, *Conflict in the Early Americas* is a collective effort. The sole editor, Rebecca M. Seaman, is professor and chair of history and political science at Elizabeth City State University, North Carolina, but she does not appear to have published, until now, in this area. She wrote her dissertation on Native American enslavement in proprietary Carolina (Auburn, 2001), and has contributed entries to ABC-CLIO's *The Encyclopedia of North American Colonial Conflicts to 1775*. She appears to have written roughly half of the signed entries; she is joined by a team of more than 60 contributors, who include independent scholars, graduate students, fellows, librarians, professors, and college administrators from a wide variety of academic backgrounds.

As mentioned, each entry is signed and includes *see also* references and resources. They are arranged in alphabetic order, and include many historical personages, events, places, and practices. The writing reflects current research and does not appear to suffer for being written by many authors. The volume is sprinkled with illustrations, photographs, and maps. War timelines, an impressive bibliography, and an index round out the encyclopedia.

An encyclopedia as narrowly focused as *Conflict in the Early Americas* may not be a high priority for libraries in an era of flat acquisition budgets at best. Nevertheless, this encyclopedia touches on three very popular research topics in high schools, community colleges, colleges, and universities, and will find an appreciative and eager readership.—**John P. Stierman**

World History

Catalogs and Collections

437.   **A History of the Crusades. http://digicoll.library.wisc.edu/History/.** [Website]. Free. Date reviewed: 2013.

This digital library is part of the University of Wisconsin's digital history collection. The resource provides, in six volumes, the entire history of the crusades. Categories under which the collection can be browsed are the first hundred years; the later crusades, 1189-1311; the fourteenth and fifteenth centuries; art and architecture of crusader states; impact of the crusades on the Near East; and impact of the crusades on Europe. Boolean searching provides precise location of texts and illustrations.—**Anna H. Perrault**

Dictionaries and Encyclopedias

438.   **Atrocities, Massacres, and War Crimes: An Encyclopedia.** Alexander Mikaberidze, ed. Santa Barbara, Calif., ABC-CLIO, 2013. 2v. illus. index. $189.00/set. ISBN 13: 978-1-59884-925-7; 978-1-59884-926-4 (e-book).

Designed for a general audience, this encyclopedia offers a depressing yet informative overview of the horrors waged between humans. Each article is signed, includes a bibliography, and is generally one to three pages in length. They are relatively consistent and provide a good overview of the topic. The other consideration for this encyclopedia is coverage. It is important to note that it is not comprehensive, with the focus being on the twentieth century. One reason given is the issue of defining what constitutes a war crime from earlier periods. The example given in the introduction is that besieged cities were often an accepted practice of warfare. This difficulty with earlier periods makes it unclear why some events were chosen, but not others. Exacerbating this problem is the introduction, which provides a chronological overview of massacres, such as those by the Romans, but does not include any articles on the events described.

Other features of the encyclopedia include a substantial chronology going back to ancient times, a general bibliography that lists a few films and documentaries as well as books, and a glossary. Some black-and-white photographs are scattered throughout, but these are not indexed. Overall, a very good encyclopedia that provides fine overviews on a somber topic. This work is recommended for high school and university libraries.—**Allen Reichert**

439.   Frassetto, Michael. **The Early Medieval World: From the Fall of Rome to the Time of Charlemagne.** Santa Barbara, Calif., ABC-CLIO, 2013. 2v. illus. index. $189.00/set. ISBN 13: 978-1-59884-995-0; 978-1-59884-996-7 (e-book).

Michael Frassetto, university professor of medieval and world history at the University of Delaware, La Salle University, and Richard Stockton College of New Jersey, is author of this two-volume set, *The Early Medieval World: From the Fall of Rome to the Time of Charlemagne.* This set examines the early Middle Ages, explaining how the Western Roman Empire fell and how new civilization in Western Europe came to be, creating the Christian Church and the modern nation-state. After the table of contents, a list of entries (without page numbers), and guide to related topics (also without page numbers), the book's introduction explains the misnomer of "Dark Ages," provides an overview of the historiography of the Early Medieval World, and a brief history of late antiquity and the early middle ages. This introduction is an excellent starter for anyone new to the topic of the Early Medieval period, and has a fantastic selected bibliography. Next, a chronology is provided starting in 305 and ending in 1000; following this are a set of early maps before getting into the encyclopedic entries. The entries are well written, varying in length and depth, and include bibliographies. Covered in this set are barbarian peoples and dynasties; cultural and religious leaders; emperors, kings, and queens; events and documents; laws and government; military leaders and battles; places; popes; and social and religious history. The second book contains an index. I highly recommend this work for the public as well as undergraduates; this a good general reference to this time period.—**Michelle Martinez**

440.   **The Kingfisher History Encyclopedia.** 3d ed. Boston, Kingfisher/Houghton Mifflin, 2013. 496p. illus. maps. index. $32.99. ISBN 13: 978-0-75346-875-3.

This revised and updated edition is packed with facts, illustrations, photographs, and concise articles spanning the beginning of time to the present day. Organized chronologically then broken down thematically, each unit includes incredible photographs and illustrations, a running timeline across the top of the page, key dates, biographies, and features on art, architecture, and technology. Offering a great overview of history, its general appeal to readers of all ages will make this volume a wonderful asset to any library. Other features include a ready-reference section listing everything from ancient Egyptian dynasties to major wars dating back to the Trojan War.—**Laurie Balderson**

441.   Slack, Corliss K. **Historical Dictionary of the Crusades.** 2d ed. Lanham, Md., Scarecrow, 2013. 379p. (Historical Dictionaries of War, Revolution, and Civil Unrest). $100.00. ISBN 13: 978-0-8108-7830-3.

    This 2d edition expands upon the solid, original dictionary first published in 2003. The rationale for a 2d edition was to bring the bibliography up to date and to expand the number of entries. These new entries are either to expand coverage on specific crusades or events, such as the Baltic Crusades, or to reflect changes in current scholarship about the Crusades. The new edition admirably succeeds in strengthening this single volume source about the Crusades. The bibliography is helpfully divided into broad topics, such as specific crusades or geographic areas. Regrettably, there are no maps showing military details or regions. This updated work is recommended for academic libraries.—**Allen Reichert**

Handbooks and Yearbooks

442.   **The Civilization of Ancient China.** New York, Rosen Publishing, 2013. 232p. illus. maps. index. (The Illustrated History of the Ancient World Series). $53.25/vol. ISBN 13: 978-1-44888-502-2.

443.   **The Civilization of Ancient Egypt.** New York, Rosen Publishing, 2013. 232p. illus. maps. index. (The Illustrated History of the Ancient World Series). $53.25/vol. ISBN 13: 978-1-44888-500-8.

444.   **The Civilization of the Incas.** New York, Rosen Publishing, 2013. 232p. illus. maps. index. (The Illustrated History of the Ancient World Series). $53.25/vol. ISBN 13: 978-1-44888-499-5.

    Like the majority of Rosen Publishing's reference series for young students, these volumes are visually appealing with bright colors and ample photographs and maps. There are reproductions of artwork, tourist attractions, and monuments that will catch the interest of young readers. The text will help bring the day-to-day lives of the people of these civilizations to life and will encourage children to want to learn more about their inventions, many of which were behind the luxuries we have today. While these volumes are not true reference in the sense that kids will be able to look up quick facts, they do provide a lot of information that will be useful for research papers and projects. The supplemental material is rather skimpy compared to the rest of the text; for example, the glossaries provide very few words and no pronunciation guides, and the maps are not always sufficient. Criticism aside, however, these volumes will be fun additions to school and public libraries.—**ARBA Staff Reviewer**

445.   **Perspectives on Modern World History Series.** Farmington Hills, Mich., Greenhaven Press/ Gale/Cengage Learning, 2012. multivolume. illus. maps. index. $44.10/vol.

    Greenhaven's Perspectives on Modern World History discusses the more controversial aspects of each modern historical event covered, including background information leading up to the event, multinational perspectives, and long-lasting results. The series first explores the background leading up to each event and includes primary sources to do so. It then goes on to cover the various perspectives from people throughout the world as well as how it has affected different regions. The final section provides interviews and narrative text from people who survived the event and its aftermath on their lives. Supplementary materials include a glossary, further reading lists, a chronology, and other resources to consult for more information. Students will appreciate the full-color photographs and charts as well as the numerous sidebars that highlight factual information and quotes for key players. New topics covered in this series include: the *Challenger* disaster, the Bolshevik Revolution, Stalin's Great Purge, and the Haiti earthquake. This series publishes several new titles per year and is growing more quickly than most of Greenhaven's other series for youth. The series as a whole is more appropriate for high school age students with the critical thinking skills to understand the more complex language in the primary sources materials used.

In general, these books are excellent sources for high school readers to enhance their critical thinking skills. They could easily be used as jumping off points for research projects and debate topics. At $44.10 for the hardcover copies, these set as a whole is expensive. Many of the titles are also available in e-book versions. School librarians will most likely need to be selective if they choose to purchase books within this series.—**Shannon Graff Hysell**

446.   **World History Series.** Farmington Hills, Mich., Lucent Books/Gale/Cengage Learning, 2013. multivolume. illus. maps. index. $34.95/vol.

This multivolume series on world history is aimed at 6th through 10th grade students. Recently published volumes are on the history of the Alamo, the Japanese-American internment, and space exploration. The series aims to provide young people with information on the eras, events, civilizations, and movements that have shaped world history and the evolvement of human social history. All of these volumes achieve that aim through clear writing, comprehensive, age- and grade-level information, and attractive and colorful illustrations that bring each topic to life.

The authors are writers of books for young people. Each volume focuses on a type of unique period in time or person of influence. While attempting to make history interesting and relevant for this age group the goal of the series is also to make students aware that their unique historical era plays key role in a long string of important human events. All volumes have sidebars historic events, numerous photographs and illustrations, timelines, and an annotated bibliography. This set is recommended for school and public libraries.—**Shannon Graff Hysell**

10 Law

General Works

Biography

447. Greene, Meg. **Elena Kagan: A Biography.** Santa Barbara, Calif., Greenwood Press/ABC-CLIO, 2014. 172p. illus. index. (Greenwood Biographies). $37.00. ISBN 13: 978-1-4408-2897-3; 978-1-4408-2898-0 (e-book).

With *Elena Kagan: A Biography* Greene has provided a concise, fairly thorough, and well-written biography of this newly appointed Justice of the Supreme Court. She gives a complete view of the life of Kagan, from her birth and childhood through her college years at Princeton University, to her esteemed legal career that led her to a seat on the U.S. Supreme Court. Readers can follow Kagan's development through law and how she has risen through the ranks to be an inspiring role model for young people.

The book is well written, with little or no obvious bias. It includes a timeline of Kagan's life and career, an index, and a bibliography of sources cited and resources for further study. While this book, and the series as a whole, is not particularly valuable as a reference resource, it is a useful addition to the general collections of targeted libraries. The introduction to the series included with this book states that it (and the rest of the series) is intended for public and school libraries. It would be well suited for these libraries, and could be useful in academic libraries serving community and junior colleges, as well as those supporting lower-level baccalaureate students.—**ARBA Staff Reviewer**

448. **Justices of the United States Supreme Court: Their Lives and Major Opinions.** 4th ed. Leon Friedman and Fred L. Israel, eds. New York, Facts on File, 2013. 4v. illus. index. $375.00/set. ISBN 13: 978-0-8160-7015-2; 978-1-4381-4139-8 (e-book).

This four-volume set is a biographical encyclopedia of the men and women who have served on the United States Supreme Court. Each biographical essay includes portrait(s), a "factbox" of statistical data, the justice's major decisions/dissents, and a bibliography. Volume 1 contains a chronology of the Supreme Court, while volume 4 contains an essay by Roy Mersky on the compiled statistics of all the justices, followed by two charts and two tables. His essay summarizes the data for Court.

In the preface by Leon Friedman, the introduction by Louis Pollak, the biographical essays by distinguished contributors, and in Roy Mersky's essay, the Court is seen as a collective body that speaks as a whole, yet that voice is made from individual votes of the justices. The role of each justice in making that decision is very important, whether they voted with the majority or expressed dissent.

The essays are organized by the appointment number for that justice. The appointment number is not included in the essay itself. When we look at Chart II Alphabetical Chart of the Supreme Court Justices, the first column gives the justice's name in alphabetic order; and, the second column gives the appointment number of that justice. With this plan of organization, the table of contents and index become very important tools to finding a particular justice.

The essays are well written and easy for high school and college students as well as the general public to understand and use. The major decisions and dissents are discussed in considerable detail. Depending on the activity of the Court during their appointment and service, the length of the essays varies. This work is highly recommended for high school, college, law and public libraries.—**Ladyjane Hickey**

449.   **The Supreme Court Justices: Illustrated Biographies, 1789-2012.** 3d ed. Clare Cushman, ed. Washington, D.C., CQ Press, 2013. 562p. illus. index. $135.00. ISBN 13: 978-1-6087-1832-0.

The bulk of *The Supreme Court Justices* is devoted to biographical entries for the justices. The entries are arranged in chronological order by the date their service on the court began. Entries include birth and death dates, judicial title, beginning and ending dates of service, and the name of the president who appointed them. Each entry includes a handsome black-and-white portrait of the justice and a paragraph summarizing notable facts and achievements. The main text of each entry is two to three pages in length and gives a narrative of the justice's life and career, along with major highlights of their court service; their role in major cases; and the political, social, and religious philosophies that may have guided their decisions while on the bench. Each biographical entry provides valuable insight into their impact on American history and on the court. The entries are informative, concise, and easy and enjoyable to read, and will give the reader excellent background and insight into each of the justices and how they fit into the development of constitutional law and the American legal system. Each entry includes a brief reading list. A 22-page bibliography follows the biographical entries and is organized by subject, including general sources, sources on individual justices, books about the Supreme Court and the Court justices for young readers. The index is extensive and detailed, adding to the usefulness of the volume.

Supreme Court Justices is a useful and attractive volume that will be suitable for a wide range of audiences. The publisher indicates that it is intended for high school and college students and general readers. It would be an excellent addition to public, academic undergraduate, and school library collections, and the price is more than reasonable for the amount of information provided in the volume. It would also be a useful volume for law and government libraries to have on hand for ready-reference questions and to assist with questions from the lay public about the Supreme Court's history and function.—**Sara Anne Hook**

Dictionaries and Encyclopedias

450.   **Gale Encyclopedia of Everyday Law.** 3d ed. Stamford, Conn., Gale/Cengage Learning, 2013. 2v. index. $549.00/set. ISBN 13: 978-1-4144-9896-6; 978-1-4144-9899-7 (e-book).

The *Gale Encyclopedia of Everyday Law* covers legal issues affecting everyday life for most Americans. It is designed for ready-reference use, not as a self-help or "do-it-yourself" legal resource.

This 3d edition contains 276 articles of varying length arranged under 26 broad subject areas, such as consumer issues, education, estate planning, health care, real estate, and retirement, presented in alphabetic order. The articles included in each subject area are named by topic and also arranged alphabetically. For example, the broad subject area of education has 23 articles, such as competency testing, discipline and punishment, homeschooling, student loans, and teachers' rights. An index and glossary are included. The table of contents assists patrons in finding these articles. A list of Web addresses for state and federal agencies and national organizations assist patrons who want further information.

As in previous editions, each article includes brief background of the issue, important cases or statutes or provisions, profiles of the various federal laws and regulations on the topic, and variations of the laws in the different states. Each article includes a bibliography and a list of national and state organizations and agencies.

An Overview of the American Legal System explains the various components of the legal system in the United States. It is well written and can be easily understood by the average citizen. Also worth mention is the article The Patient Protection and Affordable Care Act, which attempts to provide real information about the act, popularly known as Obama-care. This work is highly recommended for all academic and public libraries.—**Ladyjane Hickey**

Directories

451. **Directory of State Court Clerks & County Courthouses.** 2014 ed. New York, Leadership Directories, 2013. 312p. index. $185.00. ISBN 13: 978-1-93965-325-3.

    Taken together with the *Federal-State Court Directory* (2014 ed.; see entry 452), these complementary directories provide a comprehensive and detailed guide to the courts of the United States and Canada. This directory focuses on the state courts. For each state, there is a one-page organizational chart of the court system (these are also in the *Federal-State* directory) followed by county-by-county listings of names, addresses, and telephone numbers of county courthouses and clerks. There is also a supplementary list of probate and recording offices that might have been better incorporated into the main directory, since users have to refer back to it for addresses and telephone numbers. Other state-by-state listings are for offices of vital statistics and offices that receive corporate and UCC filings.

    There are ample references to collective and individual Websites for updates or additional information. This directory also features useful auxiliary information, such as a list of state bar associations. This well-organized and thorough directory is recommended as a convenient references for legal professionals and law libraries.—**Jack Ray**

452. **Federal-State Court Directory 2014.** Linda Dziobek, ed. New York, Leadership Directories, 2013. 240p. index. $130.00. ISBN 13: 978-1-93965-324-6.

    Recently acquired by Leadership Directories from CQ Press, the 2014 edition of this work uses statistics compiled from April to August 2013. The *Federal-State Court Directory* is well known for its structure and current information about the court system from the U.S. Supreme Court, special courts, Federal Court of Appeals, and the district courts. This directory also contains a U.S. (Bankruptcy) Trustees list that contains all the regional office listings of all U.S. Trustee Offices in the country. The "State Court" section provides a diagram of the court system for each state along with all pertinent information for that state (e.g., Chief Justice, Justices of the Supreme Court, Clerk of Courts, the state judiciary homepage, court administration, governor of state, state Web page). It also includes the names and addresses of the State's Attorney General, Secretary of State, and Department of Vital Statistics. Listings for court Websites, places of holding court and counties in federal districts, and U.S. Attorneys' information can also be found here.

    This directory is a staple resource for any law firm library or any law school library. It is a basic guide to the federal district court system and will help anyone in need of understanding the litigation process and how it works. It is updated annually and this is necessary reference tool for a litigator.—**Sandhya D. Srivastava**

453. **FindLaw for Small Business. http://smallbusiness.findlaw.com.** [Website]. Free. Date reviewed: 2013.

    This handy Website is full of articles and guides on all aspects of business development. Legal information on business structure, finance, and intellectual property are covered thoroughly. The Closing a Business section discusses the closing of businesses with all types of business structure. FAQs and forms involved in closing a business are provided. Articles discuss lawsuits after you close your business, options to closing, and more. Information on a wide variety of small business legal issues is covered including forms and contracts and starting a business. Tax issues are also covered including help in preparing for an audit. A directory of lawyers by ZIP code is available. Links to relevant regulatory agencies are also provided.—**Susan C. Awe**

454.   **Judicial Yellow Book: Who's Who in Federal and State Courts. Fall 2013 ed.** New York, Leadership Directories, 2013. 1045p. illus. index. $445.00pa. (annual subscription); $423.00pa. (automatic renewal). ISSN 1082-3298.

455.   **Law Firms Yellow Book: Who's Who in the Management of the Leading U.S. Law Firms. Winter 2013 ed.** New York, Leadership Directories, 2013. 1275p. illus. index. $445.00pa. (annual subscription); $423.00pa. (automatic renewal). ISSN 1054-4054.

The *Yellow Book*'s from Leadership Directories includes 14 titles, most of which are common to library reference collections. The *Judicial Yellow Book* and the *Law Firms Yellow Book* are issued semiannually, in the Spring and Fall. The online version, *Leadership Online* is available via subscription and is updated daily at Leadership Directories' Website (http://www.leadershipdirectories.com).

The *Judicial Yellow Book* covers courts and agencies in both the federal and state judicial systems, including U.S. courts of limited jurisdiction (such as the U.S. Tax Court and the U.S. Court of Veterans Appeals), the Federal Judicial Center, the U.S. Sentencing Commission, and the Administrative Office of the U.S. Courts. Entries list name, title, addresses (including e-mail), telephone and fax numbers, birth year, year service began, by whom appointed, education, government and judicial positions held, type of legal practice, military service, and professional legal memberships. The names, telephone numbers, and education of staff follow each judge's entry. Among other things, this title will be useful to help users monitor transitions in the judicial system, including new judges, chief judges, and magistrates, as well as other judicial title changes, new state court appointees, and new law clerks. The federal appellate courts are organized by jurisdiction; the federal district courts by state, then jurisdiction. Only appellate courts are listed in the state courts section. A law school index, a name index, and an organization index aid the location of a particular judge's entry. State Supreme Court entries also list the state law librarian. Brief introductions to each state's court system describe the appointment or election of judges, the extent of jurisdiction, and retirement requirements. Occasionally a photograph accompanies an entry.

The *Law Firms Yellow Book* provides in-depth coverage of the organizational structure of the largest U.S. law firms practicing general corporate law and is published semiannually. The current edition profiles over 750 law firms, with emphasis on the personnel responsible for decision making and management. It includes more than 24,000 attorneys listed with their titles, functions, telephone numbers, and law schools they attended, as well as names, titles, and telephone numbers of the nation's top legal administrative personnel. It includes U.S. law firms and their foreign offices. The book also includes mergers, firm name changes, deletions, branch office openings and closings, managing partner changes, managing partners by law schools, firm locations, largest firms, and domestic and international law firm networks. It will also be useful for users looking for attorneys who make the business decisions for the firm as well as those in accounting, human resources, and information technology. There is also an excellent user's guide. The largest section of the book is devoted to an alphabetic list of law firms. There are numerous and useful indexes for departments, law schools, personnel, law firms, and subsidiaries and geographic indexes.

Academic libraries, large public libraries, and law firms will be most likely to purchase these publications. For larger libraries needing the directory-type information found in these two volumes as well as the other 12 volumes, the online directory is a good option.—**Nancy L. Van Atta**

456.   **Leadership Law Premium. http://www.leadershipdirectories.com/.** [Website]. New York, Leadership Directories. $1,3500.00 (annual subscription). Date reviewed: 2013.

Leadership Directories has long been providing a library of 14 directories that cover such topics as congress, state and municipal governments, associations, law firms, and nonprofits. They currently offer their legal directory online to subscribers through *Leadership Law Premium*. Much like the print volume, the online volume offers contact information for public and private law firms, lobby firms, federal courts, and state courts. It currently covers 84,000 U.S. legal professionals and provides name, title, addresses, telephone and fax numbers, and biographical and organization information. Users can also search individuals by the law school they attended, which will be useful for networking. For those in sales or even job-seeking, the site can be searched by specialty, including such topics as business, intellectual property, litigation, environmental law, and more. The site can be used to build lists specific to your users needs based on job titles, legal specialty, organization type, or region; those lists can then be exported into spreadsheets, mailing lists, or contact lists. (Users are limited to 5,000 records per year.) Users will also have access to Leadership Mobile, which will give them access to all of the information from their mobile telephone or mobile device.

This unique directory provides useful contact information on people within the legal industry that library patrons frequently request. The steep price, however, may limit the purchase to larger public and academic libraries or those specializing in law.—**Shannon Graff Hysell**

457.   **U.S. Patent and Trademark Office Patent Database. http://www.uspto.gov/.** [Website]. Free. Date reviewed: 2013.

These databases from the United States government allow users to search and view the full-text contents and bibliographic information of patents. Users can search by multiple elements of patent records such as patent numbers, titles, inventors, application dates, descriptions/specifications, and so on. The USPTO houses full text for patents issued from 1976 to the present and TIFF images for all patents from 1970 to the present.— **James E. Bobick**

Handbooks and Yearbooks

458.   Lurie, Jonathan. **The Supreme Court and Military Justice.** Washington, D.C., CQ Press, 2013. 256p. illus. index. (The Supreme Court's Power in American Politics). $135.00pa. ISBN 13: 978-0-8728-9974-2.

The Supreme Court and Military Justice examines the relationship between the U.S. Supreme Court and the U.S. military and explores how military law differs from civilian law. With the use of well-written essays and primary documents the text examines statutory and case law covering the military and military conduct. The work features key documents from the Supreme Court as well as articles from military journals (e.g., *Army Times, Armed Forces Journal*) and popular mass media, including *The New York Times* and *The Nation*. The work is separated into chronological sections that show how the Supreme Court has affected military justice throughout U.S. history. These sections are: the Civil War, World War II (1942-1946), Post-World War II (1956-1987), and Since 9/11. In all, this is an excellent resource, appropriate for libraries serving those interested in the American political process and those interested in the military justice system.—**Jack Ray**

459.   Novkov, Julie. **The Supreme Court and the Presidency: Struggles for Supremacy.** Washington, D.C., CQ Press, 2013. 441p. illus. index. (The Supreme Court's Power in American Politics). $125.00. ISBN 13: 978-0-8728-9525-6.

The Supreme Court and the Presidency: Struggles for Supremacy examines the relationship between the U.S. Supreme Court and the limitations and expectations it puts on the executive body of the President. With the use of well-written essays and primary documents the text examines the differing interpretations of what the President should be doing in a democratic society. Chapters focus on conflicts between these two branches of government, the presidents treaty-making and executive agreements with foreign governments, and presidential power in the time of war and national crisis, among others. In all, this is an excellent resource, appropriate for public and academic libraries.—**Jack Ray**

460.   **Research Handbook on International Conflict and Security Law.** Nigel D. White and Christian Henderson, eds. Northhampton, Mass., Edward Elgar, 2013. 685. index. (Research Handbooks in International Law). 265.50. ISBN 13: 9781849808569.

One interesting feature of the modern world system are attempts to rationally govern and restrain an activity that can easily blow up out of control, and harm so many people who are not directly involved with the fighting. Thus the book's Latin subtitle—"Jus ad Bellum, Jus in Bello, Jus post Bellum" (roughly, the right to war, limits and law in waging war, and law/justice/order after the war, respectively)—not only gives the book a little academic polish, but also indicates the intellectual orientation of the collection. These handbooks contain scholarly articles that give readers an overview of the current issues and important writings related to an emotional political topic, as well as noting the historical background for the development of international law. The 19 chapters were written by 21 experts, who are primarily based in Europe and Great Britain. Some of the topics covered include private military companies, the use of force for humanitarian purposes, disarmament, reparations, and the prohibition of threats of force. As one would expect, the entries are well documented with good source material, and return to the practice of having footnotes rather than endnotes. So the book is not something used to quickly look up answers to reference questions. The compilation is therefore useful for those undertaking a literature review of the subject, or as assigned readings for an advanced course. This particular series has companion research handbooks on the law of international organizations (2011), and the theory and history of international law (see ARBA 2012, entry 553). The expensive volume under review is most suited for the circulating collections of universities, law schools, and appropriate specialized institutions, or for consultation by faculty and graduate students undertaking research in human rights and conflict regulation.—**Daniel K. Blewett**

461.   **Social Security Handbook: Overview of Social Security Programs 2013.** Lanham, Md., Bernan Press, 2013. 703p. index. $60.00pa.; $59.99 (e-book). ISBN 13: 978-1-59888-624-5; 978-1-59888-625-2 (e-book).

The *Social Security Handbook: Overview of Social Security Programs* is a comprehensive and nicely organized volume that contains information about the benefit programs that are administered by the Social Security Administration. It includes the provisions of the Social Security Act, relevant sections from the *Code of Federal Regulations*, and rulings. This information is amended and updated by the *Federal Register*. Few readers may realize how many benefits programs are covered under the Social Security Act and related laws, such as retirement, survivors, medical and disability insurance, supplemental security income, veterans benefits, unemployment insurance, and public assistance and welfare services (including food stamps, energy assistance, and child support enforcement). A reference source that successfully condenses this material into one concise volume and presents the information in a readable language and format for the general public will fill an important niche in the literature. The *Social Security Handbook* is published by Bernan Press, which was founded to meet the demand of its customers for popular U.S. government statistical reference titles that were dropped by the U.S. Government Printing Office.

The *Handbook* is divided into 27 separate chapters on topics such as becoming insured, factors in evaluating disability, representative payees, and special veterans benefits. A special numbering system is used throughout the volume, making it especially easy to use. Within each chapter, the material is presented in a question-and-answer format. Each chapter has a separate table of contents and questions are numbered and printed in bold typeface. The organization of the volume is clever and effective; an overwhelming amount of important information for citizens has been distilled into a logical and readable format. For example, chapter 8 covers the question of who are employees, which has become an important issue with the trend of outsourcing duties and hiring more independent consultants and contractors. Through a series of questions and answers, the factors that are used to determine whether someone is an employee for Social Security purposes are itemized and explained. Chapter 1 provides an excellent overview of the Social Security system. The *Handbook* also contains an index.

Given the extent to which the programs that are part of the Social Security system impact the lives of all citizens, the *Social Security Handbook* would be an excellent addition to nearly any library collection. It would be particularly useful for reference collections in public libraries as well as for medical and law libraries and libraries that serve nonprofit, governmental, and advocacy organizations. The price is more than reasonable and it will be a more efficient source of information than the *Code of Federal Regulations* and other published federal government materials. The edition reviewed was the large print edition, which may be particularly valuable for those public libraries serving an aging population.—**Sara Anne Hook**

Copyright Law

462.   **Patent, Trademark, and Copyright Laws 2013.** Lanham, Md., Bernan Press, 2012. 970p. $175.00pa. ISBN 13: 978-1-61746-082-1.

This is a useful book containing the statutes enacted through the first session of Congress on March 1, 2012, on patents, trademarks, and copyrights. A shortcoming of any book of this type is its rapid obsolescence. However, the editor has provided the basic statutes and helpful finding lists so that the user may readily update statutes online.

The preface briefly explains the new developments, listing the important laws enacted in 2012. This reference work also contains a very useful popular name table that lists the public laws, the date, and the U.S. Code sections where the law was codified. Patent law saw sweeping changes in 2012 when President Obama signed into law the Leahy-Smith American Invents Act, and this volume makes note of the changes it will cause on behalf of attorneys and inventors. This book contains all the seemingly relevant provisions of patent, trademark, and copyright law under one cover that is user friendly.—**Bev Cummings Agnew**

Criminology and Criminal Justice

Dictionaries and Encyclopedias

463.   **Encyclopedia of Street Crime in America.** Jeffrey Ian Ross, ed. Thousand Oaks, Calif., Sage, 2013. 576p. illus. index. $125.00. ISBN 13: 978-1-4129-9957-1.

This single-volume encyclopedia will prove a valuable addition to any reference collection. There are more than 175 entries that are supported by photographs and illustrations. In addition, there is a reader's guide that groups all of the entries into general categories. The volume shows that due to the implementation of security cameras in many public places street crime has changed over the past several decades. The focus is on urban crime and some of the topics addressed include burglary, drug peddling, murder, and street scams. Also covered are terms associated with the police, courts, and other criminal justice sub-disciplines.

Each entry concludes with references (if any) to any related entries and recommendations for further reading. A chronology provides readers with a historical perspective of street crime in America, while the appendixes provide data and statistics on street crime. This work is highly recommended.—**David K. Frasier**

464.   **Encyclopedia of White-Collar & Corporate Crime.** Lawrence M. Salinger, ed. Thousand Oaks, Calif., Sage, 2013. 1216p. illus. index. $350.00; $438.00 (e-book). ISBN 13: 978-1-4522-2530-2; 978-1-4522-7617-5 (e-book).

"White-collar crime" is a phrase that conjures different definitions for different people. The 2d edition of the *Encyclopedia of White-Collar & Corporate Crime* begins by describing various attempts to define white-collar crime over the last century. The *Encyclopedia* adopts an expansive definition and includes articles that go beyond typical white-collar offenses, such as fraud and insider trading, to more tangential issues including war crimes and sexual harassment. This new edition has been updated to include some of the most notorious white-collar crime of the twentieth century including the Bernie Madoff Ponzi scheme and the Gulf Oil Spill caused by British Petroleum.

This work contains several aids for readers, including a fairly extensive index and a summary of relevant laws. Most articles are brief and all provide cross-references and a bibliography. There are black-and-white photographs included, but not many. Although the name and affiliation of each contributor is given, the educational background and current occupation of the authors should be added to advise readers of the qualifications of each author.

The *Encyclopedia* is aimed at public, high school, and college libraries and also seeks to be used by corporations, graduate schools, and law firms. Although it is an appropriate resource for the first set of libraries, it does not provide enough analysis to be more than a basic overview for patrons of law school or law firm libraries. These volumes do justice to a large and hard-to-define topic, but it is difficult to say how useful the material will be in the future. Perhaps this is why such a broad definition of white-collar crime was adopted. Although, because more material is included than the white-collar crimes in the headline today, these volumes may keep their relevance beyond the present day.—**Stefanie S. Pearlman**

Handbooks and Yearbooks

465.   **City Crime Rankings 2013: Crime in Metropolitan America.** Kathleen O'Leary Morgan and Scott Morgan, eds., with Rachel Boba Santos. Washington, D.C., CQ Press, 2013. 388p. index. $85.00pa. ISBN 13: 978-1-4522-2520-3.

City Crime Rankings 2013: Crime in Metropolitan America is an exhaustive set of statistics on offenses in locales of 70,000 people or greater in the United States. The reference work begins methodology used to gather data, and references. It continues with detailed statistics on crime in 2011 in the areas of violent crime, murder, forcible rape, robbery, aggravated assault, property crime, burglary, larceny-theft, and motor vehicle theft. The work concludes with an appendix of descriptions of metropolitan areas in 2011; a county index; national crime trends from 1992 to 2011; and national, metropolitan, and city crime statistics summary: 2011.

The work includes many interesting facts and figures; for example, the amount of police employed in New York was 34,542. Additionally, no killings occurred in 10 cities, including Logan, Utah. This work is crucial to academic and public libraries and fundamental for researchers of offenses in the United States.—**Melinda F. Matthews**

466.   **Crime in the United States, 2013.** 7th ed. Lanham, Md., Bernan Press, 2013. 618p. index. $105.00. ISBN 13: 978-1-59888-622-1; 978-1-59888-623-8 (e-book).

Although something of an anachronism because it appears in printed form, this 7th edition of *Crime in the United States* represents the most comprehensive, recent data available through 2011. Bernan Press now publishes these data since the Federal Bureau of Investigation, which began collection the data in 1930, ceased doing so some years ago. Most likely all useful government data will end up like this: published commercially because all government agencies find themselves on the budget chopping block.

The data come from the Uniform Crime Reporting (UCR) Program, the main intent of which is to make uniform crime data reported by law enforcement. The data are drawn from 18,000 city, college and university, county, tribal, and federal law enforcement agencies that voluntarily bring crimes to the attention of the program. This 2011 data from law enforcement agencies active in UCR represent more than 295 million inhabitants, over 90 percent of the total U.S. population, standard Metropolitan Statistical Areas, and population outside nonmetropolitan areas. In other words, it is unlikely that more comprehensive data can be found. Over the years, this data have been used to predict or benchmark social indicators for the country, though that was not its intent. While comprehensive, the data are not easily used for comparative purposes because they come from so many different agencies located in many different parts of the country. The FBI collects the data; it does not pass judgment on their various methodologies.

The volume is divided into five parts. The first part contains offenses known to police: violent crimes (e.g., murder, forcible rape, aggravated assault, robbery); and property crime offenses (e.g., burglary, larceny-theft, motor vehicle theft, arson). Part 2 contains offenses cleared, while part 3 lists the demography of arrested individuals (e.g., sex, age, race). Part 4 contains data about law enforcement personnel and part five lists hate crime.

Since all these data are available online and even in this very form, why the appearance of this volume, coming in at several pounds and $105? Convenience perhaps. In order to find certain tables online, one must click through three to five screens. Sounds easy enough, but in fact it is not if one is trying to follow through on a certain trend. Comparing several tables at once is also not as easy as one would expect with online access. Furthermore, the breakdown is so easily referenced and so very granular, online searches, while able, are not as malleable as one might wish. Even so, this tool is not long for this world as "digitals natives" continue to go "all native" on every printed matter. Enjoy this one while there is still time.—**Mark Y. Herring**

467.   **Genocide and Persecution Series.** Farmington Hills, Mich., Greenhaven Press/Gale/Cengage Learning, 2013. multivolume. illus. maps. index. $37.95/vol.

This new series from Greenhaven Press features eight volumes that discuss the inhumane events that have occurred in human history concerning genocide as well as why they have taken place, their impact on society as a whole and on specific groups in particular, and how they can be prevented in the future. The volumes are anthologies of previously published materials on genocide or crimes against humanity, with each volume focusing on a particular region. The newest title is on South Africa. Other titles in the series so far address Afghanistan, Cambodia, East Pakistan, El Salvador and Guatemala, Kosovo, the Kurds, The People's Republic of China, and Uganda. It is hoped that the larger genocides that are often studied in schools will be covered in the near future, including the Jewish Holocaust and Darfur. Material includes historical background, first-person narratives, and writings on current issues and controversies surrounding the subject. Useful for teachers are the analytical exercises and writing prompts that will help spur conversations from students and engage them in critical thinking around the topics. The works are supplemented with full-color photographs, maps, charts, and sidebars. A bibliography and a list of organizations at the back of each book points readers to other sources for further information.

These books are an excellent source for upper middle and high school readers to enhance their critical thinking skills. They could easily be used as jumping off points for research projects and debate topics. At $37.95 for the hardcover copies this set as a whole may be expensive to purchase as it expands to include new regions. School librarians will most likely need to be selective if they choose to purchase books within this series; however, for those that can afford the entire set, it will be worth having the collection.—**Shannon Graff Hysell**

468.   Newton, David E. **Marijuana: A Reference Handbook.** Santa Barbara, Calif., ABC-CLIO, 2013. 330p. index. (Contemporary World Issues). $58.00. ISBN 13: 978-1-61069-149-9; 978-1-61069-150-5 (e-book).

This latest addition to ABC-CLIO's Contemporary World Issues Series focuses on the historical and current issues surround the use of marijuana in American society. The book begins with a historical overview of the use of marijuana in the United States, including recreational, medicinal, and religious use. The volume also discusses the controversy surrounding marijuana and its uses, with an even-handed approach to the arguments for and against decriminalization and legalization of the substance. A list of issues and topics for research for high school and undergraduate students and a list of references featuring books, periodical articles, and Website articles is provided. A chronological listing of highlights in the history of marijuana is supplied as well as biographical sketches of key players in the fight for and against legalizing marijuana use. The largest chapter of the book reprints documents in the history of marijuana use in the United States. The remaining chapters give readers access to organizations; book, periodical, and pamphlet resources that discuss marijuana; and videos and Websites that feature information on marijuana. The book concludes with a list of abbreviations and acronyms used throughout the book and an index.

This handy reference work will be most useful in school and undergraduate libraries where students will be seeking information on marijuana and the controversy surrounding the legalizing of the substance. It is not a necessary purchase but can serve as a supplementary volume to current issues. [R: LJ, 15 June 13, p. 114]—**Stephen H. Aby**

469. Palmer, Louis J., Jr. **The Death Penalty in the United States: A Complete Guide to Federal and State Laws.** 2d ed. Jefferson, N.C., McFarland, 2014. 390p. index. $55.00pa. ISBN 13: 978-0-7864-7660-2; 978-1-4766-0679-1 (e-book).

Palmer's book provides a clear and coherent guide to the death penalty in the United States. To paraphrase Supreme Court Justice Thurgood Marshall's opinion in the 1972 Supreme Court capital punishment case *Furman v. Georgia*, the American public does not understand the reality of the death penalty. Palmer's book will help anyone come to understand the legal complexities that surround the capital punishment debate in today's society. There is no attempt to proselytize here. The material presents information relevant to the legal realities of the death penalty. The book is divided into six parts. Part 1 provides a brief background on the common-law influences on the death penalty, the position of the Eighth Amendment on the death penalty, and death-eligible offenses. Part 2 examines prosecutorial issues, such as the role of the prosecutor in criminal justice cases, the discretionary power prosecutors have in bringing a penalty case to trial, the indictment, and prosecuting a "nontriggerman." Part 3 offers information relating to the court proceedings, including the capital penalty phase of a capital trial, aggravating and mitigating circumstances relevant to a determination of sentence, and the appellate review of a death sentence. Part 4 discusses post-conviction proceedings, including automatic appellate review of the death sentence, the Innocence Protection Act, and challenging the death sentence under Racial Justice Acts. Part 5 explains related law, including barriers to execution, death row, witnessing an execution, and execution methods. The final section includes an explanation of other capital punishment laws: military death penalty laws, Native Americans and capital punishment, and opposition to capital punishment just to name a few. The chapter on the costs of capital punishment is particularly interesting. There are tables and boxes throughout the book that make points and issues dramatically clear. The book contains an appendix of federal death penalty laws, and concludes with a glossary, chapter notes, a bibliography (including death penalty sentencing statutes, books, articles, and cases), and an index. This work is highly recommended.—**Michael A. Foley**

470. **Research Handbook on Money Laundering.** Brigitte Unger and Daan van der Linde, eds. Northhampton, Mass., Edward Elgar, 2013. 502p. index. $240.00. ISBN 13: 978-0-85793-399-7.

On the day this book arrived in the mail a front page story appeared about JPMorgan Chase facing money laundering charges in relation to the Bernard Madoff Ponzi scheme (they served as his bank over a period of many years). Another current story addresses Pope Francis's initiatives in relation to the Vatican bank, which has been accused of money laundering, among other things. Money laundering is a significant phenomenon in our world today, but arguably one about which many questions arise. This handbook, edited by Brigitte Unger and Daan van der Linde, two economists associated with Utrecht University in the Netherlands, is designed to provide systematic answers to the core questions. As the editors remind us, although money laundering in some form has been in existence since time immemorial, it was only formally criminalized quite recently, in the early 1980s. The core meaning of the term itself—"the disguising of the illicit origin of money"—is reasonably well understood, but exactly how this is done and in what context is more complicated and sometimes a source of confusion.

Some countries have acquired reputations as havens for funds whose owners seek to evade taxes or inquiries about the sources of these funds. Prince Michael von and zu Liechtenstein, one such country, has contributed a chapter to this handbook defending the "long-term wealth preservation" practices of his country, at least as they relate to the alleged tax evasion strategies of nonresidents who deposit money in financial institutions in this country.

The notorious 1920s gangster and bootlegger Al Capone is credited with having provided a foundation for modern money laundering by running illegal funds through the cash-rich business of laundries. The term itself is sometimes attributed to the practice of casinos in literally washing money to protect female customers from the grime ingrained on coins. The very high-profile Watergate case of the early 1970s raised the public profile of money laundering through reports of how funds used by the Watergate burglars were "laundered" in an attempt to conceal their origins with political supporters of the Campaign to Re-elect President Nixon. In the contemporary era the term is quite commonly invoked. It continues to be especially associated with the activities of organized crime and related forms of criminal organizations, but since 9/11 the United States government in particular has directed much attention to money laundering involved in supporting terrorist groups.

Money laundering has a somewhat ambiguous moral status because it is not a predatory activity in a direct sense, and has accordingly sometimes been characterized as a "victimless" crime. This generates the first core question about money laundering: how and for whom does it pose a problem? The editors go on to identify some other core questions: who, specifically, is threatened by money laundering; what is the scale of the problem; what are the different ways in which money is laundered; and what are the specific legal measures that have been adopted in response to money laundering, how have these measures been implemented, and how effective is AML (anti-money laundering) policy? Following a survey of the history of money laundering by one of the editors, the six subsequent sections address these core questions. Altogether, there are a total of 34 different chapters, with the contributors (almost all Europeans) representing a range of disciplines and vantage points. Economists and law professors are especially well represented here. The level of sophistication in the different chapters is generally high, and at least some chapters incorporate rather technical information. An early chapter includes a series of complex mathematical formulas. This volume is likely to be most accessible and useful to graduate students, scholars, and practitioners (in the financial world, broadly defined) engaged with money-laundering issues. Certainly there is a wealth of information here for serious students of the money laundering phenomenon. In a world where finance plays an increasingly dominant role in the political economy it seems likely that the issues relating to money laundering will become more salient and perhaps more urgent, going forward. The chapters in this handbook are likely to provide a basic point of departure for much future research on money laundering.—**David O. Friedrichs**

Environmental Law

471.   **Clean Air Handbook.** 4th ed. Lanham, Md., Bernan Press, 2013. 350p. index. $115.00; $114.99 (e-book). ISBN 13: 978-1-59888-647-4; 978-1-59888-648-1 (e-book).

This handbook will help the user begin to understand the Clean Air Act (CAA), which is continuously described as the most complicated piece of environmental legislation ever established. The author is well versed in environmental law and heads the Hunton & Williams Environmental Team. Several members of this team contributed their expertise to help make this a more user-friendly reference source.

A researcher can find a variety of publications, both government and private, to look at the ever-changing issues involving clean air. For a person acquainted with the basic information, the *Clean Air Handbook* provides an enlightening overview of the Clean Air Act, giving the reader more insight into the enormous legal, health, and financial considerations related to this act and its amendments. Thankfully, the handbook helps to make these important issues more understandable; it also provides citations for those hardy souls who wish to delve deeper into the federal regulations, cases, and so forth.

This new edition examines the EPA's initiatives to impose emission reduction requirements through new air quality standards made more stringent in 2006, and the EPA's rules and guidance implementing the Title I nonattainment program and ongoing federal efforts to address interstate pollution issues.

The *Clean Air Act Handbook* gives a more in-depth and legalistic view of the Clean Air Act. This revised edition of the *Clean Air Handbook* is recommended for academic libraries with environmental science programs and large public libraries.—**Diane J. Turner**

472. **Environmental Law Handbook.** 22d ed. Thomas F. P. Sullivan, ed. Blue Ridge Summit, Pa., Government Institutes, 2014. 1068p. index. $105.00; $104.99 (e-book). ISBN 13: 978-1-59888-667-2; 978-1-59888-677-1 (e-book).

The 22d edition of this now classic reference handbook continues to meet its goal: "to give its users reliable, accurate and practical compliance information from some of the most respected experts in the field in each subject area." Previously published by Government Institutes, this new edition is published by Bernan Press. Because the writing is clear and concise with a minimum of legal jargon, this book is a great starting point to get a basic overview of the many complex compliance topics of environmental law.

The new edition follows the same format with the same chapter headings and chapter authors as previous editions. The first two chapters introduce the fundamentals, enforcement, and liability issues of environmental law. These are followed by chapters on each of the major environmental acts (e.g., Clean Air, Clean Water, CERCLA, NEPA, Toxic Substances, Pollution Prevention) and ends with a chapter on environmental management systems. All chapters have been updated a small amount and more than half have significant changes, which usually explain new regulatory changes, new case law, and what the future might bring. Coverage of new environmental events since the publication of the 22d edition include major changes to the law and enforcement in the areas of Clean Air, Clean Water, Climate Change, Oil Pollution, and Pollution Prevention. Each of the 17 chapters is nicely subdivided with all the chapter subunits recorded in the table of contents, creating a convenient outline of environmental compliance law and facilitating browsing—**Georgia Briscoe**

Human Rights

473. de la Vega, Connie. **Dictionary of International Human Rights Law.** Northhampton, Mass., Edward Elgar, 2013. 250p. index. $160.00. ISBN 13: 978-1-84980-377-9.

Just when you begin to think "everything is on the Internet" you are reminded once again just how rich and varied human ingenuity can be. The current slender volume fills a special niche: International Human Rights Law. But the niche is not only an important one, it is also very timely one. Author Connie de le Vega defines in succinct fashion the concepts, terms, organizations, charters, commission, committees, and more in the burgeoning discipline of international law.

It isn't so much that every library will want this book. But its accessibility and currency makes it certainly a volume every library will want to consider. If nothing else, the defined terms will help anyone who wants to investigate the subject matter a good, solid place to begin. For example, the Geneva conventions, the Atlantic Charter, International Bill of Rights, xenophobia, and World Food Conference are a smattering of terms that de le Vega defines. Cross-references, *see*, and *see also* terms make using this dictionary as thorough as possible. An appendix with the URLs for commissions, conventions, and declarations round out this helpful book. Many of the same terms can be found on the Web; however, they are not guaranteed to be found in one place or with such clear and meaningful definitions.—**Mark Y. Herring**

474. **Freedom in the World 2012: The Annual Survey of Political Rights and Civil Liberties.** Arch Puddington and others, eds. New York, Freedom House and Lanham, Md., Rowman & Littlefield, 2013. 864p. $55.00pa. ISBN 13: 978-1-4422-1795-9.

475.   **Freedom in the World 2013: The Annual Survey of Political Rights and Civil Liberties.** Arch Puddington, ed. Lanham, Md., Freedom House/Rowman & Littlefield, 2013. 887p. $55.00pa. ISBN 13: 978-1-4422-2566-4.

   You never know what you've got until it's gone, or so the familiar saying has it. Because we Americans have not known anything other than freedom, we are sometimes befuddled about it elsewhere in the world. We sniff when the slightest gnat of freedom is swatted here in these United States. Yet, we hardly bat an eye when political eruptions explode in places like Somalia, Syria, or the Arab world. The world may be too much with us, but while we luxuriate in it, freedom remains virtually absent in much of the rest of the world. And too often we forget that. Like an old and comfortable garment that fits so well, our freedom is a cloak we almost forget we have on. We are rightly shocked back to reality when we see how the rest of the world shivers in totalitarian winters.

   Freedom in the World helps us understand how few footholds freedom has gained in the 21st Century. Our once great hope in the democratization of the Internet has given way to it authoritarian uses when dictators censor it, black it out in places, or simply shutout down. This volume reminds us that yes, there are glimmers of hope for oppressed countries, but those glimmers are more like cooling embers than white hot fire raging toward enfranchisement.

   The 2012 volume opens with excellent summary on freedom the world over by broad regions (e.g., Asia-Pacific, Central and Eastern Europe/Eurasia, Sub-Saharan Africa). An arrow beside the name of the country tells readers at a glance if the country's freedom is trending upward or downward. There follows summaries of each country's freedom status that range in length from one page to a dozen, depending on that country's political or social unrest. A brief overview gives readers an idea of the main obstacles to freedom and why it may never get a strong foothold. This is followed by several pages discussing important events, uprisings, elections and so on. Each country section ends with a discussion of that country's political and civil rights. Graphs, tables, events, world leaders, and a detailed discussion of the rubric used to assign freedom scores are valuable additions to this important book.

   If anything, this volume, packed as it is with fascinating details about our world, underscores again just how important this land of the free and home of the brave remains for all those who are in chains.— **Mark Y. Herring**

476.   Hillstrom, Laurie Collier. **Plessy v. Ferguson.** Detroit, Omnigraphics, 2014. 226p. illus. index. (Defining Moments). $49.00. ISBN 13: 978-0-7808-1329-8.

   For many students today it may be hard to image a time when segregation was a fact of life and questioned by few. The book examines how the *Plessy v. Ferguson* case came to be and the legacy it left on race relations for decades after it was stated. Anecdotes, photographs, and biographies animate a shameful American story that is so familiar that students of any race often resist reading it. Fortunately, the author's engaging, simple style, combined with a visually enticing layout, will appeal to young readers, or to older readers who want a quick review. Excerpts from primary sources (a staple in recently published histories for teenagers) encourage young students to read these sources-when the full texts would otherwise be too daunting. A brief summary and analysis precedes each document. A bibliography gathers references suitable to the book's target audience-high school students-but also sources that would be useful to college students. Other study tools include a glossary and a chronology.

   Adult lay readers and college students looking for a more detailed discussion of the case and its context may also want to read this title to understand the political, social, and economic factors that led to this decision as well as how it promoted racial tension and social segregation for years to come. Hillstrom's book is recommended for public, school, and academic libraries.—**Nancy L. Van Atta**

477.   **Teen Rights and Freedoms Series.** Farmington Hills, Mich., Greenhaven Press/Gale/Cengage Learning, 2013. multivolume. illus. index. $38.45/vol.

   Greenhaven Press has several series available to young adults that deal with social issues, including the Opposing Viewpoints series and the At Issues series. This is yet another look at current social issues;

however, this series focuses on the legal rights and freedoms that impact the lives of American teens. It presents a collection key essays and articles as well as primary and secondary sources on the featured issue. For example, much of the material comes from journals, newspapers, nonfiction books, position papers, speeches, and Supreme Court and other court decisions. New titles added recently to the series include: *Labor and Employment*, *Dress*, *Privacy*, *Education*, and *Free Press* . The scope of the volumes includes right guaranteed under the Bill of Rights and how they can be interpreted in regard to the protection of children and teens. These titles would be especially useful in social studies and civics classes to support students writing reports on these important legal rights and social issues. The titles feature lists of organizations to contact for further information as well as lists of resources (mainly books and periodicals) for further research. These books provide a unique and personal perspective to today's social issues that will appeal to high school students. The series is highly recommended.—**Shannon Graff Hysell**

11 Library and Information Science and Publishing and Bookselling

Library and Information Science

Reference Works

478. Berman, Sanford. **Not in My Library!** Jefferson, N.C., McFarland, 2013. 197. index. $35.00pa. ISBN 13: 978-0-7864-7822-4.

In this collection of Sanford Berman's collection of his column "Berman's Bag" appearing in *The Unabashed Librarian* from 2000-2013, this work brings together many writings by one of the foremost scholars of subject headings in the United States, offering writings on censorship, subject cataloging, ethics, and intellectual freedom as found in the assigning of subject headings to materials in libraries. Including an index, this work collocates some of Berman's most popular or most currently applicable articles from this time span. For those who do not have access to *The Unabashed Librarian*, this book is of value, but for those with ready access to this periodical, the only worth of this book is the single volume of the best of the best. For students of subject cataloging, indexing, or access of any type to materials this book will be an excellent read, bringing together the cream of the crop of writings by Berman, and as such would be useful as an additional reading to a course on information access or as a gift to a diehard cataloger.—**Sara Marcus**

479. Greer, Roger C., Robert J. Grover, and Susan G. Fowler. **Introduction to the Library and Information Professions.** 2d ed. Santa Barbara, Calif., Libraries Unlimited/ABC-CLIO, 2013. 197p. index. $65.00pa. ISBN 13: 978-1-61069-157-4; 978-1-61069-158-1 (e-book).

It is difficult to keep up with the changes in the information professions. The three authors of this book, along with six of their professional colleagues from various institutions, attempt to keep students and practitioners of information science abreast of changes in their roles, in the cycle of information and the latest advances in technology. The discussion is client-centered and focuses on library and information professionals as change agents who plan and implement services. The authors present what they call a "toolbox of models," designed to guide information professionals in decision-making throughout their careers. In the book's introduction, one particularly valuable section features definitions of the information professions according to the authors. There is no consensus on the meaning of these categories among information professionals, and these definitions provide a consistent vocabulary for the following chapters in the book.

The book consists of 10 chapters, each containing several sections, and ending with a list of references for further study. Chapter 1 discusses the purpose and objective of the book. As mentioned above, it is a valuable guide for the reader, setting the direction and subject matter for the rest of the chapters. Chapter 2 examines and defines "data," "information," and "knowledge." Chapter 3 talks about the role of professionals as change agents; Chapter 4 explains the science that supports the information professions. Chapter 5 discusses information transfer and chapter 6 illustrates the cycle of professional service. Chapter 7 showcases models of information infrastructure, and chapter 8 goes deeper into the processes and functions of information professionals. Chapter 9 complements the section of information professional definitions by discussing the infrastructure of the professions themselves: professional associations, literature of the field, and the code of ethics, among others. Chapter 10 wraps up the content by providing trends and issues in information education and practice. There are two appendices, which list professional organizations and professional journals, respectively. A complete bibliography begins on page 189, and a comprehensive index on page 195.

There are many books about the topic of library and information professions. This volume is well written and delivers a compelling story about how the professions bring people and information together. It is recommended for public, community college, and university libraries.—**Laura J. Bender**

480.   Lipinski, Tomas A. **The Librarian's Legal Companion for Licensing Information Resources and Services.** Chicago, Neal-Schuman/American Library Association, 2013. 734p. index. $130.00pa. ISBN 13: 978-1-55570-610-4.

All librarians have some knowledge of copyright law and how it affects patrons' use of information. Yet, with libraries selecting more content and services controlled by license agreements librarians need some understanding of contract law. *The Librarian's Legal Companion for Licensing Information Resources and Services* is the fourth book in the American Library Association's series on legal topics in libraries.

This source provides librarians with both basic and advanced concepts in contract and licensing law. The content is divided into three parts. Part 1 discusses the essential concepts of contract law. Part 2 covers the general categories of licenses libraries are most likely to encounter, including those for music and media. Part 3 is the most practical section of the book, providing a "Basic Licensing Glossary" of numerous license terms; an analysis of four actual licenses (i.e., BioOne, NewspaperARCHIVE, Nature, and Amazon's Kindle); key clauses to look for in licenses; and questions and answers to ask when evaluating licenses. Content is accessible via a subject index and detailed table of contents. There is a separate index for referenced cases and laws.

Considering the complex nature of contract law, the author, Tomas A. Lipinski, makes this subject fairly accessible. This is likely due to his training as a lawyer and practical experience as a librarian, most recently Executive Associate Dean at Indiana School of Information and Library Science. Compared to Lesley Ellen Harris' *Licensing Digital Content: A Practical Guide for Librarians* (2d ed.; see ARBA 2010, entry 572), Lipinski's text is more complete, addressing background concepts in contract law, including numerous references to relevant cases and laws, and offering an extensive glossary. This book will give you the ability to play an active role when deciding the terms of a contract, or at the very least allow you to evaluate whether the terms are favorable or not. This work is highly recommended for all libraries.—**Kevin McDonough**

481.   **Planning Our Future Libraries: Blueprints for 2025.** Kim Leeder and Eric Frierson, eds. Chicago, American Library Association, 2014. 130p. index. $48.00pa. ISBN 13: 978-0-8389-1207-2.

Edited by director of library services at the College of Western Idaho and a Discovery Services at EBSCO Publishing, this work brings together eight chapters authored by eight practicing librarians on library planning and public services. Organized into four parts, the work addresses embracing participation, reimaging spaces, building new infrastructures, and the global future. Also included is an appendix by an additional author, which offers an abridged manifesto of redesigning library services. This book focuses on the most relevant and innovative qualities of today's libraries and librarians, offering predictions of where libraries are and where libraries should and will be heading by 2025. Written to be read alone, or cover to cover, these chapters will offer advice and guidance to any librarian looking to stay abreast and new in the future, embracing change without losing the current users and stakeholders who might be resistant to change. Each chapter has its own bibliography. The book lacks a comprehensive list of references, although a brief index is included.—**Sara Marcus**

482.   **The Whole Library Handbook 5: Current Data, Professional Advice, and Curiosa.** George M. Eberhart, ed. Chicago, American Library Association, 2013. 528p. illus. index. $50.00pa.; $45.00pa. (ALA members). ISBN 13: 978-0-8389-1090-0.

This new edition of *The Whole Library Handbook* does much more than update facts and figures since it was last published in 2006; 98% of the material is new or revised, and it includes discussions of the current state of libraries and issues librarians face. Each of the editions of this title has included essays or excerpts of lasting value, and the same can be expected of this one, perhaps in the essays on e-books or privacy. Trends, conditions, lists, statistics, guidelines, tips, and reflections are arranged in the following chapters: libraries, people, the profession, materials, operations, users, advocacy, technology, issues, and librariana. This last chapter includes items of whimsy that most professionals will appreciate as counterpoint to the weighty issues dealt with in other chapters. A general index concludes the volume.

The Whole Library Handbook is not a reference source, but it is a professional source invaluable to the busy librarian or library employee for keeping up to date on the state of libraries in the United States and abroad. This guide is highly recommended.—**Rosanne M. Cordell**

Libraries

College and Research Libraries

483.   **Challenges of Academic Library Management in Developing Countries.** S. Thanuskodi, ed. Hershey, Pa., Information Science Reference, 2013. 335p. index. $175.00; $265.00 (e-book); $350.00 (print and e-book versions). ISBN 13: 978-1-46664-070-2; 978-1-46664-071-9 (e-book).

Edited by an associate professor and head in the Department of Library and Information Science at Algappa University (India), this volume brings together 21 chapters authored by 32 international scholars and practitioners. Presented as a single unit, without sections, this work addresses through case studies and practical experiences the challenges faced by academic libraries in developing countries in terms of management. While geared toward and based in developing countries, the lessons learned can be of use in other nations as well, such as security challenges, social networking, access to and use of e-resources, and open-access initiatives. Best suited for those interested in working in developing nations and lower socioeconomic areas, these chapters will offer experience-based guidance on best serving and managing libraries for such areas, as well as for any library that might be facing budgetary cuts or a growing service to academics and college students living in such areas. Like others from this publisher, there is a detailed table of contents, although this volume is briefer than most, and there is a lack of topical organization into sections. Additionally, only some chapters include recommendations based on the findings or for further readings, while all contain a references list and well-documented research.—**Sara Marcus**

484.   Crumpton, Michael A., and Nora J. Bird. **Handbook for Community College Librarians.** Santa Barbara, Calif., Libraries Unlimited/ABC-CLIO, 2013. 172p. index. $50.00pa. ISBN 13: 978-1-61069-345-5; 978-1-61069-346-2 (e-book).

This is a very handy primer covering issues facing all librarians but specifically addressed to community and junior college librarians. It can be considered a textbook providing step-by-step guidelines. Covering functions and tasks such as administration, reference, collection development, and budgeting, the authors go beyond the basics to include more current topics like diversity, information literacy, assessment, and technology. Each chapter centers on an issue and addresses concerns and trends. For example, one chapter focuses on concerns specific to the community college, including language, racial, and gender diversity issues. Each chapter concludes with one of the authors' own words on how their experiences apply to the topic and "final words," a conclusion and advice often with useful references including Websites. An example is the chapter on supervision, which deals with skill sets, leadership, and planning. This last issue, planning, really deserves a chapter of its own, as does the most recent issue facing all librarians—branding (or marketing). A 2d edition should incorporate these ideas, but overall the volume is an excellent start or text for librarians in this evolving and essential field of librarianship. A list of references and brief index conclude the volume.—**Boyd Childress**

485.   **E-Learning in Libraries: Best Practices.** Charles Harmon and Michael Messina, eds. Lanham, Md., Scarecrow, 2013. 124p. index. $44.95pa. ISBN 13: 978-0-8108-8750-3.

Presenting nine case studies authored by practitioners in the library field across the United States, this volume will inspire and encourage other libraries who are seeking to enter, or expand, the use of e-learning in libraries. Whether at for-credit courses, integrating with existing courses, informational purposes, or workshops, this book will help all looking to serve the ever-growing users of e-learning. Including examples, steps, success and stumbling blocks, these case studies authored by those involved in the project offer real-world expertise in a down-to-earth manner for anyone seeking to learn more. As students at all levels experience and expect more and more online access to materials and training, libraries need to join this revolution, and this book offers ideas to jumpstart one's own projects. The only thing lacks is a compiled list of references for future research, rather than having to look chapter by chapter, as the topics often overlap between chapters.—**Sara Marcus**

486.   **Embedded Librarianship: What Every Academic Librarian Should Know.** Alice L. Daugherty and Michael F. Russo, eds. Santa Barbara, Calif., Libraries Unlimited/ABC-CLIO, 2013. 201p. index. $65.00pa. ISBN 13: 978-1-61069-413-1; 978-1-61069-414-8 (e-book).

Embedded Librarianship: What Every Academic Librarian Should Know does exactly what its title purports by serving as a sort of guidebook for librarians who want to learn more about embedded librarianship. This book has a very specific audience and purpose, which although very niche, makes it invaluable to those individuals it targets. Rather than a generic informational volume about embedded librarianship, the editors have created a guidebook to assist embedded librarians.

Embedded Librarianship gathers together 12 essays from different authors about all different aspects of embedded librarianship, starting with its history and including chapters on faculty and librarian collaboration, relationships and ethics, using a digital learning object repository, sustainability and scalability, and more. Each chapter is written by an authority in the field and concludes with a thorough bibliography. The articles are obviously written with a particular audience in mind, so as a result there is a certain amount of lingo and terminology the reader will encounter. Having said that, the essays are well written and full of great information.

The editors assert this book is not only for librarians, but also for professors interested in embedded librarianship. While that may be true to a certain extent, the real value of this volume lies in its ability to assist librarians in their embedded librarianship ventures. Those brand new to embedded librarianship, or even seasoned veterans, will find great value in this work.—**Tyler Manolovitz**

487.   **Higher Education Outcomes Assessment for the Twenty-First Century.** Peter Hernon, Robert E. Dugan, and Candy Schwartz, eds. Santa Barbara, Calif., Libraries Unlimited/ABC-CLIO, 2013. 258p. index. $50.00pa. ISBN 13: 978-1-61069-274-8; 978-1-61069-318-9 (e-book).

Authored by the editors and an additional professor at the GSLIS of Simmons College, this work offers updated and new information to what was presented in two prior volumes: *Outcomes Assessment in Higher Education* by Peter Hernon and Robert E. Dugan (Libraries Unlimited, 2004) and *Revisiting Outcomes Assessment in Higher Education* by Peter Hernon, Robert E. Dugan and Candy Schwartz (Libraries Unlimited, 2006). The editors of this edition, two professors at the GSLIS of Simmons College and the dean of libraries at the University of West Florida, offer 12 signed chapters organized into four sections. Each chapter ends with concluding thoughts and notes, and the volume itself ends with a bibliography and index. The first section, an introduction, offers two chapters of an overview of outcomes assessment today and literature on assessment for learning. The second section discusses some key stakeholders, including the U.S. government, higher education outcomes in the states and institutions, and outcomes and the National Party Platform in the 2012 Presidential election. The third and most lengthy section addresses selected issues of institutional effectiveness, information literacy as a student learning outcome and institutional accreditation, critical thinking and information literacy as related to accreditation and outcomes assessment, library engagement in outcomes assessment, some elements of study procedures, and evidence gathering. The final section is a conclusion discussing how to move forward. An appendix provides a list of higher education organizations, associations and centers with responsibilities, activities, and research related to outcomes. This book will help any academic library dealing with outcomes assessment, helping the library to build its place in the wider academic and institutional field of outcomes assessment. Offering practical and theory-based ideas and insights for implementation, activities, and advocating for the place of information literacy and libraries in outcomes assessment for the twenty-first century, this title is recommended for academic library professionals.— **Sara Marcus**

488.   Hollister, Christopher V. **Handbook of Academic Writing for Librarians.** Chicago, Association of College and Research Libraries/American Library Association, 2013. 248p. index. $56.00pa. ISBN 13: 978-0-8389-8648-6,

This useful guide for both professional academics and for students examines aspects of academic writing from getting started to getting published. The elements of good, well-crafted writing include the selection of ideas, content, structure, style, and mechanics. The special characteristics of scholarly papers and the criteria to be considered when selecting a journal for publication are presented followed by an examination of the publishing process. The final chapter gives an overview of the process for book publishing. Some chapters conclude with an appendix and notes or a brief bibliography with a more in-depth bibliography and an index after the last chapter. Several examples and diagrams serve to enhance the text. The information is well-researched, well-organized, and thorough, giving not only current information, but also some historical background, making it a good source, not only for librarians but anyone in academia.—**Martha Lawler**

489.   **Library Services for Multicultural Patrons: Strategies to Encourage Library Use.** Carol Smallwood and Kim Becnel, eds. Lanham, Md., Scarecrow, 2013. 338p. index. $65.00pa.; $64.99 (e-book). ISBN 13: 978-0-8108-8722-0; 978-0-8108-8723-7 (e-book).

This collection of 37 chapters authored by 48 diverse librarians from a range of geographic locales offers practical advice and strategies for encouraging library use by multicultural patrons in all types of libraries and library services. The first six chapters offer librarians in all types of libraries advice on getting organized and finding partners to collaborate to serve the growing multicultural population libraries are facing, whether a public, academic, or library of any type. The next seven chapters focus on reaching students, at the academic and school media levels, at large, multi-campus institutions that are face-to-face, as well as small local institutions. It also provides advice on reaching online and overseas students in their own languages and in the languages of instruction at the institution itself, whether part of a large group of staff in the library or a solo librarian. The third part, consisting of five chapters, focuses on creating community connections, not only with the community members visiting the library but those who do not visit the library for any reason, such as families of patrons or community groups. It examines effective collection development to meet the diverse populations. Part four focuses on applying technology in five chapters, whether collection development, virtual services, or technologies to help reach those who do not speak the language in use at the institution. Outreach initiatives are covered in five chapters in part five, addressing the community, oral history, promoting library resources, and attracting patrons to school libraries. The sixth part, consisting of five chapters, addresses programming and events that celebrate the diversity and multiculturalism within the communities served by the library. The final section presents four chapters focusing on reference services to multicultural patrons such as phone reference tips for this population, reference transaction instances that might be misconstrued due to differing standards of cultures, and genealogy reference for diverse customers. An index as well as a well-organized and descriptive table of contents enables one to find chapters and sections of need for one's particular situation at the time, while scanning the book as a whole will help one to find sections of interest when time is available. Despite its large size, the book will be valuable in any library where there is a growing diversity of patrons being served.—**Sara Marcus**

490.   **The New Digital Scholar: Exploring and Enriching the Research and Writing Practices of NextGen Students.** Randall McClure and James P. Purdy, eds. Medford, N.J., Information Today, 2013. 400p. index. $59.50pa. ISBN 13: 978-1-57387-475-5.

This edited volume provides evidence from writing instructors, librarians, and technical professions on the importance of their collaboration to ensure that the new generation of students succeed in their academic learning environment. The argument is that this generation of students are writing more than any other generation and it is essential for writing instructors and librarians to ensure that they have the research and technical skills to ensure success. All of the articles have been written by librarians working in the field and offer concrete suggestions for how to help improve the skills of students to ensure results. Topics discuss include new models for instruction on research, and examples of strong partnership ideas between writing programs and the library. This will be a useful instruction guide for libraries incorporating cooperative programs between first-year writing programs and the library. It will provide useful advice for instruction librarian and writing instructors. [R: LJ, 15 June 2013, p. 101]—**Shannon Graff Hysell**

491.   Stielow, Frederick. **Reinventing the Library for Online Education.** Chicago, American Library Association, 2014. 306p. illus. index. $75.00pa.; $67.50pa. (ALA members). ISBN 13: 978-0-8389-1208-9.

A relatively slim volume, *Reinventing the Library for Online Education* examines the place of the library-as-institution in the "teens of the twenty-first century" with the context of "redeeming and redefining roles from online education" (p. xi). Reinventing is divided into two parts: Part A, "Preparing Within a Revolution," and part B, "Virtual Campus Discourse." Part A begins with a history of libraries, starting with ancient history and moving to the modern day, as a foundation for how libraries have evolved already, which can serve as a tool for understanding how libraries may need to evolve as technology and information change. It also examines the dynamic between Web technology and libraries and how the two have influenced one another. Finally, it looks at how the economy, especially in the context of higher education, has affected libraries. It also outlines how all these things together will continue to affect libraries and how libraries might respond and use these factors to guide their responses.

Part B begins with a look at the factors related to libraries and higher education that impact the "virtual campus," or online education, including information literacy, digital preservation, the open access movement, and other information-oriented services. Another chapter in this section looks at services and roles and how they have been changed and will change by increasingly digital demands (such as bindery services or stacks browsing). This chapter is followed by another chapter which redefines existing library services and roles as they may fit with online education and in response to increasing demands that libraries define themselves in terms of ROI. It also examines such issues as copyright clearance and institutional repositories.

This chapter is followed by another which presents options for how all these factors may fit and work together; it includes sections on ADA compliance and intra-and internet applications. This section also contains a chapter on how librarians need to evolve and develop and change in order to better serve online populations, followed by a chapter on the role and functions of administration and managers, inside and outside the library. The title ends with an epilogue in which the author muses on the future of libraries in the twenty-first century.

Overall, this title is highly recommended. It provides a fresh perspective on the role of the library in the process of information acquisition, organization, creation, and processing and how the library might change and adapt as technology and information grow exponentially and as the needs and skills of users change. The title includes intriguing and relevant illustrations and graphics which make the title a pleasure to read. The content, although philosophical at times, is very concise and stripped-down and stays on target. This work is highly recommended for all academic and public libraries, especially at universities with LIS/MLIS programs.—**Megan W. Lowe**

492.   **Studying Students: A Second Look.** Nancy Fried Foster, ed. Chicago, Association of College and Research Libraries/American Library Association, 2014. 150p. illus. index. $44.00pa. ISBN 13: 978-0-8389-8680-6.

Edited by a senior anthropologist who works on participatory design of libraries, this work brings together 11 essays authored by 14 academic librarians in the United States. The work is a follow-up to ACRL's *Studying Students* (2007), which focused on ethnographic work done at the University of Rochester's River Campus Libraries. The work is a study on how students learn the technology needed to navigate through college today as well how they study for exams and research for term papers. Technology has created a change in how students use libraries today and this book brings to light what those changes are and how libraries can adapt with the times to best fit the needs of students today. The volume ends with a conclusion about the future of university libraries and serving the needs of today's and tomorrow's students. The inclusion of an index enables location of desired materials, although a lack of a cumulative bibliography or references list leads one to have to check each chapter's bibliography for potential readings of interest. With the growing interest and attention paid to how to best fit the needs of college students and ensuring that the library stays relevant in the age of technology, this work will benefit any academic librarian or library administrator.—**Sara Marcus**

493.   **Twenty-First-Century Access Services on the Front Line of Academic Librarianship.** Michael J. Krasulski and Trevor A. Dawes, eds. Chicago, Association of College and Research Libraries/American Library Association, 2013. 246p. index. $56.00pa. ISBN 13: 978-0-8389-8666-0.

Edited by an Assistant Professor of Information Science and Coordinator of Access Services at the University of the Sciences in Philadelphia and an Associate University librarian at Washington University in St. Louis, this volume is geared to leaders of access services and those wishing to lead such areas in academic library settings. While the content is of value, it is hard to find specific information without an index or detailed table of contents; and the author biographies being hidden in the introduction to the volume leads one to question the authority of each author until this information is encountered. The 11 chapters are authored by 11 U.S. contributors along with the two editors, and are organized into three sections: core access services, access services beyond circulation (such as interlibrary loan and course reserves), and special topics in access services (such as department organization and assessment of access services). This technical and well-documented volume would be appropriate for practicing librarians in access services, and for those wishing to study the field in depth, but is not for the novice or tangentially interested reader.—**Sara Marcus**

Public Libraries

494.   **Public Libraries and Resilient Cities.** Michael Dudley, ed. Chicago, American Library Association, 2013. index. $65.00pa. ISBN 13: 978-0-8389-1136-5.

Authored by an indigenous and urban services librarian at the University of Winnipeg these 14 chapters authored by 17 international scholars, librarians, practitioners, and experts in other fields focus on urban public libraries. Exploring the roles that public libraries can play in urban settings promoting ecologically, economically, and socially resilient communities in the midst of economic and technological turmoil, this book is of use to a limited audience. The success stories and case studies of success in resiliency from library and planning practitioners from urban public libraries of various sizes and locations offer innovation in public library design, management, collaboration, and public services. While this topic is timely and important, only those in similar situations can implement many of the ideas or understand the situations posed, although some of the material might be of assistance to other library types and settings.—**Sara Marcus**

495.   Schull, Diantha Dow. **50+ Library Services: Innovation in Action.** Chicago, American Library Association, 2013. 335p. index. $55.00pa.; $49.50pa. (ALA members). ISBN 13: 978-0-8389-1119-8.

Authored by an advisor to libraries, museums and foundations on organizational and program development, this work provides 12 chapters on innovative services to patrons ages 50 and over, which can also be of use for others working with this population as well. Whether in a public, academic, or special library serving this population, one will benefit from the inspiration offered in this book to adapt the library services and offerings to best serve this population. Drawing on experiences and examples from Leading-Edge States and Beacon Libraries across the United States, the author also offers chapters on work, careers, and service; reflections and transitions; health and wellness; information technology and social media; creativity; information, and community connections; lifelong learning; intergenerational programs and services; financial planning and business development; and the 50-plus place. Written to be read cover-to-cover, or by individual chapter, this book will help all types of libraries serving the growing population of over 50 to ensure these patrons are included in all offerings of the library and have their particular needs addressed and met.—**Sara Marcus**

School Libraries

496.   Baumann, Nancy L. **For the Love of Reading: Guide to K-8 Reading Promotions.** Santa Barbara, Calif., Libraries Unlimited/ABC-CLIO, 2013. 161p. illus. index. $45.00pa. ISBN 13: 978-1-61069-189-5; 978-1-61069-190-1 (e-book).

Baumann points out in her introduction to this illustrated volume that reading promotional programs can be used in association with the standards of both the American Association of School Librarians (AASL) and the Common Core. Baumann concentrates on approximately nine different programs to promote reading in schools by either school librarians or reading teachers. These activities promote Sustained Silent Reading (otherwise known as SSR, in the literature).

Each chapter details the implementation of the program that the chapter covers. It provides the purpose, goals, materials needed, results of what a specific implementation of the program achieved, and a step-by-step timeline of how to prepare for and to effectuate the program covered. Baumann also discusses how to use volunteers, such as parents, to run the program. The names of the programs covered in the book, and the titles of each of eight of the nine chapters in the volume are: "Beary Special Readers"; "Early Bird Readers"; "Reading Lunch"; "Mock Newbery Book Club"; "Book Swap"; "One Book One School Community Read"; "Battle of the Books"; and "Reading Millionaires Project." Chapter nine covers two additional reading ideas. These are a "Newbery Book Club" where, instead of choosing of a book to win the Newbery as in the aforementioned Mock Newbery Book Club, participants read Newbery award winners; and a "State Award Book Club," where participants read winners of state book awards. The book is rounded out by four appendixes, which contain resources for the implementer: "Vendors, Journals, and Further Reading," "Websites," "Sample Booktalks for Reading Lunch," and "Common Core State Standards/AASL Standards for 21st-Century Learners and Reading Promotional Programs Charts."

This book is clearly written and meant to be a do-it-yourself manual for K-8 school librarians or reading teachers hoping to promote reading in their institution. As such it is strongly recommended if that is the need of the intended library.—**Scott Alan Sheidlower**

497.   Bell, Mary Ann, Holly Weimar, and James Van Roekel. **School Librarians and the Technology Department: A Practical Guide to Successful Collaboration.** Santa Barbara, Calif., Linworth/ABC-CLIO, 2013. 117p. index. $40.00pa. ISBN 13: 978-1-58683-539-2; 978-1-58683-540-8 (e-book).

Authored by a professor in the Department of Library Science at Sam Houston State University (Huntsville, Texas), along with an associate professor and the associate director of Lowman Student Center at the same school, this work provides a practical approach and guide for school librarians and other librarians to collaborate effectively with the technology department. Organized into six standalone chapters with individual introductions, summaries, and works cited lists, the work begins with a chapter on the past and the current state of technology use in libraries. Next addressed is the effective working of school librarians in their environment, with a strong emphasis on the use of technology, working collaboratively, and using and evaluating technology applications. The third chapter focuses on the technology department's current responsibilities and challenges, while the fourth focuses on students and teachers. The fifth chapter discusses building bridges between the school library, the technology department, and the intended users (the teachers and students). The final chapter looks forward, to what can be done now that the issue has been explored and includes such topics as shared spaces and planning, staff developments, and evaluating what is implemented. The authors also include five appendixes: a library use survey, two technical evaluation checklists, a discussion of "techheads," and a technology implementation request.

While each chapter ends with a works cited list, there is no compilation of references at the end of the book, a lack that could easily be rectified. Otherwise, this is a valuable book for any school librarian, or other librarian seeking to, or forced to, collaborate with the technology department to offer services to the intended users of the library. The down-to-earth and practical advice offered will help all who are approaching this situation for the first time or who have been doing this for a while and need new inspiration. [R: TL, Oct 2013, p. 44]—**Sara Marcus**

498.   **Collaborative Models for Librarian and Teacher Partnerships.** Kathryn Kennedy and Lucy Santos Green, eds. Hershey, Pa., Information Science Reference, 2013. 260p. index. $175.00; $265.00 (e-book); $350.00 (print and e-book editions). ISBN 13: 978-1-46664-361-1; 978-1-46664-362-8 (e-book).

Collaboration increasingly seems an integral element of school librarianship. As part of the Advances in Library and Information Science series, *Collaborative Models for Librarian and Teacher Partnerships* demonstrates the value and importance of the librarian being viewed as an instructional partner within the education environment. Using their knowledge and experience in instruction, research, and librarianship, editors Kathryn Kennedy and Lucy Santos Green have compiled an anthology of 19 chapters authored by 30 individuals who provide first-hand research-based evidence and field-based examples of essential topics and concerns being addressed in the K-12 classroom and library.

The first section, Research, contains nine chapters that provide substantial background for supporting collaborative endeavors between classroom instructors and school librarians. Multiple literacies, online professional learning communities, special education, and music education are some of the topics discussed. The next five chapters in the second section, Case Studies and Models, contain specific examples of successful partnerships. Learning design, media-rich projects, and technology use are explored. The last section, School Library Voices, includes five chapters that identify the integral elements within a school that must be addressed in order to ensure successful partnerships. Securing administrative support and the exponential impact on the school library are two of the areas covered. A chapter abstract is located at the beginning of each of the chapters as well as in the contents. Most chapters provide a list of references and a section of key terms and definitions. Additional reading lists, figures, and tables are included in some chapters. A compilation of the individual chapter references, an About the Contributors section, and an index conclude the work.

Sharing the research and practice of successful collaborations between classroom instructors and school librarians not only reveals the impact that librarians have on student learning, but also encourages others to promote and engage in comparable activities. Kennedy and Green's compilation of successful partnerships will appeal to new as well as veteran professionals, both in the classroom and the library. This compilation of worthwhile collaborations will assist those professionals who encounter challenges in establishing instructional partnerships. This volume is strongly recommended to be included on the shelf of every school library.—**Alice Crosetto**

499.   Copeland, Brenda S., and Patricia A. Messner. **School Library Storytime: Just the Basics.** Santa Barbara, Calif., Libraries Unlimited/ABC-CLIO, 2013. 194p. illus. index. (Just the Basics). $40.00pa. ISBN 13: 978-1-61069-202-1; 978-1-61069-203-8 (e-book).

Co-authored by an elementary media specialist in Lebanon City School District, Ohio, and an elementary librarian in Palmyra School District, Pennsylvania, this work organizes the knowledge needed to plan and deliver a school storytime with little to no experience. Focusing on the school media center, the work is also applicable to any children's library area, and the focus of the work itself is geared for the elementary school media center. Drawing on their combined experience, the authors provide tips for selecting just the right story as well as suggest supply materials and lesson plans that can be used for each month of the school year. Part of the Just the Basics series, this book provides just that—enough to get started and have a wonderful library, with a few tips an experienced librarian might not be aware of. Arranged according to month, the volume provides detailed instructions, tips, and templates and handouts for each storytime. The authors share their years of experience for those new to storytime in the elementary library. This work will be a useful addition to the school library professional development library as well as a useful tool in many public libraries.—**Sara Marcus**

500.   Harvey, Carl A., II. **Adult Learners: Professional Development and the School Librarian.** Santa Barbara, Calif., Libraries Unlimited/ABC-CLIO, 2012. 77p. illus. index. $40.00pa. ISBN 13: 978-1-61069-039-3; 978-1-61069-040-9 (e-book).

Authored by a school librarian at North Elementary School in Noblesville, Indiana and past president of AASL, this volume guides school media specialists at all levels and in all environments in offering professional development opportunities as a way to prove the worth of a school media specialist to the administration and stakeholders of the school. Using a down-to-earth and practical writing style, Harvey presents ideas, tips, scenarios, and tools that can assist in determining the best way to present the indispensible nature of the licensed school media specialist to the school environment. Organized into six chapters, the work begins by discussing what professional development is, and how librarians can be leaders and providers of professional development. Next, Harvey guides the reader in aligning the school library program and professional development to the school improvement program, followed by chapters on designing and delivering professional development from the library media center. The final chapter gives a detailed example of a professional development of 21st Century Tools with sufficient information to guide the user in creating other professional development sessions geared to the specific situation, whether face-to-face or online, whether on the tools or other aspects in which the school media specialist is to be considered an irreplaceable specialist. Each chapter includes a list of resources, and the book has an index to help located desired information that cannot be found using the in-depth table of contents. The volume lacks a compilation of resources used throughout. This volume is an excellent resource for current and future school media specialists, who must at some point join the fight in proving the worth and value of a school media specialist on the faculty of the school.—**Sara Marcus**

501.   Johnson, Doug. **The Indispensable Librarian: Surviving and Thriving in School Libraries in the Information Age.** 2d ed. Santa Barbara, Calif., Linworth/ABC-CLIO, 2013. 207p. index. $40.00pa. ISBN 13: 978-1-61069-239-7; 978-1-61069-240-3 (e-book).

Authored by the Director of Media and Technology for the Mankato Public Schools and adjunct faculty member at Minnesota State University, this update of the 1997 book by the same title offers new ideas for implementing techniques in one's own library and school as well as tips for advocacy. While some basics have not changed, growth in technologies and changing standards has led to a need for a new book to support new and experienced K-12 librarians in their work in the information age. Organized into 15 chapters, this work addresses the roles and missions of the librarian, program assessment, planning, communications and advocacy, managing others and collaboration, managing digital resources, curriculum, budget, facilities, digital intellectual freedom, ethics and technology, copyright and creative commons, the librarian's role in effective staff development, surviving professional transitions, and libraries and the future. Including tips and ideas that can be adapted for any setting, all K-12 school media specialists will benefit from the insights and knowledge written specific for this volume as well as reprinted from prior works published by the author.—**Sara Marcus**

502.   Kay, Linda. **Read It Forward.** Santa Barbara, Calif., Libraries Unlimited/ABC-CLIO, 2014. 120p. index. $35.00pa. ISBN 13: 978-1-59884-808-3; 978-1-59884-809-0 (e-book).

Authored by a middle school librarian in collaboration with 6 contributors, this work presents 10 chapters, 8 of which are co-authored, based on a Read it Forward program launched in Texas and presented at the Texas Library Association meeting in 2009. The program shared is collaborative and student-led, focusing on middle school students, although it can be used, according to the author, with students in grades 1 through college. Encouraging students to collaborate, and create a sense of belonging for all, not only in the school but across the district, this work will guide librarians and educators in creating a one book for one setting program that uses not only face-to-face interactions but also Web 2.0-enhanced communications such as wikis, blogs, and video conferencing. Serving as a step-by-step guide, with examples drawn from the middle school program instituted by the authors, this work begins with choosing a great book, obtaining buy-in, and obtaining copies of the book, followed by promoting excitement, distributing the books, and programming ideas. The volume ends with keeping track, a culminating event, and follow-up in years two and three. This volume will inspire widespread reading for pleasure programming at any level, both in schools or other community groups.—**Sara Marcus**

503.   McCord, Gretchen. **What You Need to Know About Privacy Law: A Guide for Librarians and Educators.** Santa Barbara, Calif., Libraries Unlimited/ABC-CLIO, 2013. 134p. index. $45.00pa. ISBN 13: 978-1-61069-081-2; 978-1-61069-082-9 (e-book).

As technology has infiltrated our school and public libraries it has become increasingly important to ensure that our youngest technology users are using resources with secure privacy settings to help protect their privacy. This is no easy task as U.S. privacy laws are difficult to understand and to enforce. This work, written by a licensed attorney specializing in copyright and privacy laws, provides a thorough overview of the laws most pertinent to educators. She provides tips on how to recognize and analyze privacy issues in the educational context. The work is written in an easy-to-understand style that will make it easy for librarians to decide what information is critical for their library and their patrons. The work provides lists of resources to help educators and librarians stay current. It will be a valuable addition to school library professional collections as well as for teachers, school administrators, and even parents.—**ARBA Staff Reviewer**

504.   Preddy, Leslie B. **School Library Makerspaces: Grades 6-12.** Santa Barbara, Calif., Libraries Unlimited/ABC-CLIO, 2013. 192p. illus. index. $45.00pa. ISBN 13: 978-1-61069-494-0; 978-1-61069-495-7 (e-book).

Authored by a school librarian at Perry Meridian Middle School in Indianapolis, this work focuses, as the title indicates, on school library makerspaces, although children's and young adult librarians in public libraries, and others working with those in grades 6 to 12, and possibly older or younger, will also benefit from the ideas presented in this book. Organized into three chapters, the work begins with an introduction to the school library makerspace, including topics such as the faculty, money and budgets, guided instruction, Pathfinders, learning standards, safety, rules, instruction, participation recognition, and supplies. This first chapter will help the reader to understand what a makerspace is, and to plan as well as support their desire to implement one in their organization. The second and third chapters provide suggested activities and projects, each idea clearly laid out in a lesson plan format, including materials, objectives, and photographs for guidance in creating the craft or takeaway. Chapter 2 focuses on programming and activities, beginning with a discussion of creative commons followed ten suggested projects and 18 activities. The third chapter offers 17 make and take activities such as bookmarks and deskblotters. The volume ends with four appendixes: a glossary; a listing of national and local events and contests; ideas and inspirations; and maker communities and resources. An index and bibliography enable one to use this book as a resource and to find additional information.—**Sara Marcus**

505.   **School Libraries Matter: Views from the Research.** Mirah J. Dow, ed. Santa Barbara, Calif., Libraries Unlimited/ABC-CLIO, 2013. 173p. index. $50.00pa. ISBN 13: 978-1-61069-161-1; 978-1-61069-162-8 (e-book).

Edited by an associate professor in the School of Library and Information Management at Emporia State University and director of the doctoral program, this work offers 11 chapters authored by 16 scholars and practitioners in the United States. Each chapter summarizes research on a specific topic, such as professional dispositions of school librarians; school librarians in Vygotsky's zone of proximal development; influencing instructional partnerships in pre-service; everyday life information seeking practices of upper-income high school students; the impact of school libraries on academic achievement; the role of the school library in building collaborations to support school improvement; perspectives of school administrators related to school libraries; empowering professional development at school librarian conferences; school-based technology integration and school librarian leadership; and the potential for school librarians in facilitating cross-cultural teaching and learning in the school library. The work ends with a chapter by the editor that offers views from the research, from ideology to action. Each chapter has an introduction and conclusion, along with references. Although the volume does not have a cumulative bibliography, this is not necessary as each chapter's bibliography serves as a subject-oriented listing of research on the specific topic. Much of the research summarized, however, is older and dated, there is limited reference to research after 2010. Despite this lack of newer material, the summaries are well written and offer not only valuable research for librarians, but also examples of literature reviews for students of library science.—**Sara Marcus**

506.   Wadham, Rachel L., and Jonathan W. Ostenson. **Integrating Young Adult Literature Through the Common Core Standards.** Santa Barbara, Calif., Libraries Unlimited/ABC-CLIO, 2013. 260p. index. $45.00pa. ISBN 13: 978-1-61069-118-5; 978-1-61069-119-2 (e-book).

Authored by a librarian and professor of adolescent literature at Brigham Young University and a professor in the English education program at Brigham Young University, this book will help school professionals working with young adults in particular implement the common core standards through young adult literature and inquiry learning. While examples are drawn from young adult literature, those in other levels of education will benefit from ideas and techniques presented in this volume on a relatively new concept of the Common Core Standards.

Organized into two parts, the first six chapters define the complexity of young adult titles using the Common Core Standards, including defining young adult literature and the Common Core Standards, and offer a discussion of quantitative, qualitative, and reader and task dimensions of text complexity. The section ends with a discussion of how to apply the three-tiered model of text complexity. The second part addresses planning instruction using young adult literature and the Common Core Standards. It begins by discussing inquiry learning, followed by a model unit plan. Also provided are raw materials for unit planning and textual connections. The volume ends with three appendixes to help the educator implement the ideas presented in the volume—a blank analysis form, a blank raw materials planning sheet, and a model unit materials sheet. This volume is a must-have for any professional development and school media collection at the high school level, and a strongly suggested addition for other levels due to the lack of materials currently available on integrating literature through the common core standards at any or all levels.—**Sara Marcus**

507.   Woolls, Blanche, Ann C. Weeks, and Sharon Coatney. **The School Library Manager.** 5th ed. Santa Barbara, Calif., Libraries Unlimited/ABC-CLIO, 2014. 277p. index. (Library and Information Science Text Series). $55.00; $50.00pa. ISBN 13: 978-1-61069-132-1; 978-1-61069-133-8 (e-book).

The world of librarianship has many outstanding individuals who champion issues, blaze new trails, and set the standards for us all. Librarian and educator Blanche Woolls, whose career spans almost 50 years, is such an individual. *The School Library Media Manager*, now in its 5th edition, represents the author's lifetime dedication to the field of school librarianship. With this new edition two new editors join her in author this volume: Ann Weeks is the associate dean for academic programs at the University of Maryland's College of Information Studies, and Sharon Coatney, an acquisitions editor for Libraries Unlimited (the publisher of this book) and past president of the American Association of School Librarians.

Starting with the role of the school library media center, Woolls details the process of becoming a school library media specialist, including how to choose the appropriate program, how to obtain certification, and how to locate a job. Included is a first-week "survival guide" for excelling in a new position, including how to manage collections, facilities, personnel, and technology. The logically laid out chapters read as guidelines for the various responsibilities encountered throughout the school year and throughout the lifetime of a school library media specialist. In most of the chapters Woolls includes checklists, how-to projects, and exercises for hands-on activities. Writing grants, working with the administration, and weathering the challenges of networking and of the political process are but a few of the practical topics covered. New to this edition is updated coverage of student learning assessment, managing digital and virtual libraries and collections, and key strategies for meeting AASL and Common Core standards.

This book will enlighten the student interested in this field as well as provide benchmarks for the seasoned veteran. Woolls's thorough blueprints should be used as the textbook in every school media library course and be on the professional shelf of every K-12 school library media center.—**Alice Crosetto**

Special Libraries

508.   Gil, Esther L., and Awilda Reyes. **International Business Research: Strategies and Resources.** Lanham, Md., Scarecrow, 2013. 195p. index. $60.00pa.; $59.99 (e-book). ISBN 13: 978-0-8108-8726-8; 978-0-8108-8727-5 (e-book).

Although we live in a global economy, conducting international business research is still a daunting task due to its complexity and the growing number of information resources from which to choose. The authors, Ester L. Gil and Awilda Reyes, both academic librarians, provide an excellent overview of the international business research process in *International Business Research: Strategies and Resources*. Rather than focusing on individual resources, the book provides strategies to guide users through the research process for different aspects of international business. The nine chapters cover: basic tools and sources, international monetary system and financial markets, resources with world coverage, regional economic organizations and trade blocs, international company research, industry classification systems, international industry research, international market research and global investing. Chapters begin with general strategies on how to locate various types of information for that sector with suggested resources briefly described. As the book is aimed at all types of users, resources range from freely available U.S., foreign, and international resources to subscription-based resources only available at academic or large research libraries. The work suffers from some minor editorial issues and the addition of boldfaced headings may have helped to break up text and better delineate sections but overall this is a very solid reference work that will be useful to any collection.—**Colleen Seale**

509.   **Law Librarianship in the Digital Age.** Ellyssa Kroski, ed. Lanham, Md., Scarecrow, 2014. 515p. index. $75.00pa.; $74.99 (e-book). ISBN 13: 978-0-8108-8806-7; 978-0-8108-8807-4 (e-book).

Written by the director of information technology for the New York Law Institute and the esteemed editor of Neal-Schuman's Tech Set series, this book explores the issues that are most relevant to law librarians and that are at the forefront at law library conferences and events. The work is arranged into eight sections: Major Introductory Concepts (e.g., copyright in the digital age, law library management), Technologies (e.g., e-books in law libraries, the cloud), Reference Services (e.g., online information sources, major legal databases), Instruction (e.g., educational technologies), Technical Services (e.g., collection development, electronic resources management), Knowledge Management (e.g., the law library intranet), Marketing (e.g., digital age marketing, competitive intelligence), and Professional Development and the Future (e.g., associations and conferences, the future of law librarianship). Articles have been contributed by well-known law librarians from academic, government, and private law libraries. This book is a great overall handbook for anyone in the area of law librarianship. Its combination of scholarship and practical application make it a must-read for those in this industry.— **ARBA Staff Reviewer**

510.   Matarazzo, James M., and Toby Pearlstein, with Sylvia James. **Special Libraries: A Survival Guide.** Santa Barbara, Calif., Libraries Unlimited/ABC-CLIO, 2013. 167p. index. $55.00pa. ISBN 13: 978-1-61069-267-0; 978-1-61069-268-7 (e-book).

Three of the most prestigious names in the special library world—Matarazzo and Pearlstein from the United States, and James from England—have contributed to this very useful book about survival. As we well know, the landscape for libraries is changing rapidly. Survival of some academic and public libraries is questionable. However, it is the special library that has faced huge challenges to prove individual worth and value to parent institutions. It is the librarian and the information center that keep ignorance at bay in these organizations and it is crucial to keep librarians in the corporate mix, as self-serving as that sounds.

The book consists of 3 parts and a total of 15 chapters. Part 1 is the discussion of data measurement as a survival tool, and has three chapters describing specific tools to use, a case study of AT&T Bell Labs, and a review of research related to the management of corporate libraries. Part 2 provides actual strategies and tactics for survival, including case studies and models for teaching special librarians now and in the future. It also demonstrates the universality of today's challenges by taking a look at corporate libraries in New Zealand and Australia. Part 3 is entitled, "So What Does Your Manager Think?" and features what special libraries must do to be successful in adding value to their organizations. Chapter 14 in this section showcases Bain & Co., and chapter 15 reviews how Putnam Investments successfully interfaces with its clients to prove its value. The book's index begins on page 165.

Readers will gain insight into closure avoidance strategies by digesting the content of this well-written, straightforward book. The writers do emphasize special libraries, but the strategies and models could easily be adapted to academic and public library situations. The book is highly recommended for special/corporate libraries and academic libraries that support schools of library and information science.— **Laura J. Bender**

511.   **Public Law Librarianship: Objectives, Challenges, and Solutions.** Laurie Selwyn and Virginia Eldridge, eds. Hershey, Pa., Information Science Reference, 2013. 319p. index. $175.00; $265.00 (e-book): $350.00 (print and e-book edition). ISBN 13: 978-1-46662-184-8; 978-1-46662-185-5 (e-book).

Consisting of 10 chapters authored by two law librarians working as county law librarians, this work provides a comprehensive overview of the funding, organization, and governance related to serving in a public law library. With years of practical experience behind them the authors try to be as comprehensive as possible, including chapters on the patron base, how to organize the library, library management, hiring and staffing personnel, public relations, collection development, technology and electronic resources, technical services, and public services. Several appendixes have been included that provide sample forms and surveys for such things as collection development, funding and governance grid, jail services procedure, job descriptions, and a bibliography of professional resources. It will be useful for new law librarians needing up to date administrative guidance and professional resources for running or reviving a public law library.— **Sara Marcus**

Special Topics

Archives

512.   Beredo, Cheryl. **Import of the Archive: U.S. Colonial Rule of the Philippines and the Making of American Archival History.** Sacramento, Calif., Litwin Books, 2013. 157p. index. $25.00pa. ISBN 13: 978-1-936117-72-7.

Based on the dissertation of Cheryl Beredo, this book examines the role of archives in the United States' colonization of the Philippines between 1898 and 1916. Organized as a bibliography, with the inclusion of an index, this work looks at archives and war, archives and anti-imperialism, and archives and land, along with a chapter of introduction and a concluding chapter. Intended to attempt an understanding of the colonial project both as strong and weak, beneficial and harmful, Beredo aims to demonstrate that the archives of the "Other," or nonmajority, can offer additional insights and knowledge regarding any situation or time period, using this specific time period in the Philippines to illustrate her case. Well researched and documented, this book offers support for researchers studying the histories and impacts of minorities as well as data to support the use of alternative archives and views, rather than solely the mainstream materials made more readily available.—**Sara Marcus**

513.   **Make Your Own History: Documenting Feminist and Queer Activism in the 21st Century.** Lyz Bly and Kelly Wooten, eds. Sacramento, Calif., Library Juice Press, 2012. 180p. illus. index. $30.00pa. ISBN 13: 978-1-936117-13-0.

Edited by a history and gender study scholar and a librarian at the Sallie Bingham Center for Women's History and Culture and Librarian for Sexuality Studies at Duke University, this work brings together 16 scholars and practitioners in feminism, queer, and zine fields to discuss the documenting of non-mainstream cultures' histories using the technologies of today and yesterday. The 12 chapters are organized into 4 sections—Zines and Riot Grrrl, LGBT Archives, Electronic Records, and Second Wave—offering personal stories, reaching out and instructing in the use of materials, and collecting materials that are not traditional in content or format. Whether looking to archive a movement or the underground, to explore accessibility and accountability, to explore electronic and born digital materials, there are chapters to support any reader's needs and interests. This book will assist any scholar or researcher of nontraditional or non-majority groups in finding alternative resources to locate resources, and to determine the types of materials that might be of use. This book should be read by any public history scholar or practitioner, to assist in determining types of materials to consider.—**Sara Marcus**

514.   **Preserving Local Writers, Genealogy, Photographs, Newspapers, and Related Materials.** Carol Smallwood and Williams Elaine, eds. Lanham, Md., Scarecrow, 2012. 344p. index. $55.00; $49.99 (e-book). ISBN 13: 978-0-8108-8358-1; 978-0-8108-8359-8 (e-book).

Edited by a former public library systems administrator and consultant and former school, academic and special librarian, along with the branch manager and youth librarian at the Lynchburg (Ohio) Branch of the Highland County District Library, this work presents 31 chapters organized into 9 sections. Whether one is interested in the basics of special collections of local history materials, specific materials (such as newspapers, scrapbooks, photographs, or oral histories), types of services and sources (such as local history and digital), or preservation there is a chapter of use for any type of collection. The writings include case studies of specific situations and more general topics, such as affiliation agreements, organizing and indexing photograph collections, copyright, and indexing local newspapers. Students of public history, archives, and preservation will all benefit from this knowledge, as will practicing archivists and preservationists as well as librarians working with special collections of nonprint materials used for genealogy such as photographs, newspapers, and related materials. The 33 contributors from around the world, including Nigeria and Canada, bring experience from academic, public, and special libraries, and offer their expertise and knowledge in an approachable manner for any researcher or practitioner of public history in any form that requires looking beyond the traditional print materials.—**Sara Marcus**

Careers

515.   Hicks, Deborah. **Technology and Professional Identity of Librarians: The Making of the Cybrarian.** Hershey, Pa., Information Science Reference, 2014. 260p. index. $175.00; $265.00 (e-book); $350.00 (print and e-book editions). ISBN 13: 978-1-46664-735-0; 978-1-46664-736-7 (e-book).

Authored by a doctoral candidate with the Department of Education Policy Studies at the University of Alberta, this volume brings together 11 chapters on the role of librarians in the wake of rapidly changing technology. Presented as a single unit, without sections, this work addresses through case studies and practical experiences the challenges faced by librarians as technology changes the way society wants and retrieves information. The book highlights new methods involved in data management, library information education, research, and communication. Topics covered include: Internet communities, modern library technologies, professional identity, Web 2.0 applications, and core values and ethical standards. The focus of the work is positive—the goal being to help librarians find new ways to remain current and relevant in this ever-changing society.—**Sara Marcus**

516.   **Jump-Start Your Career as a Digital Librarian: A LITA Guide.** Jane Monson, ed. Chicago, American Library Association, 2013. 235p. index. $47.00pa.; $42.30pa. (ALA members). ISBN 13: 978-1-55570-877-1.

This is a very well-done book on both starting and renewing a career in digital librarianship. It takes the reader step-by-step through the career planning process and things one needs to know once in the career field.

The book begins with a section titled "Planning Your Career," which provides a clear definition of what digital librarianship is and the tasks it entails, how to get the most out of library school to launch your career in that direction, and landing your first job. There is also a chapter on making a career shift into digital librarianship that includes a case study of one librarian's transition from interlibrary loan to digitization. The final section in this chapter discusses how to further your career. Part 2 discusses the nuts and bolts of a career in digital librarianship. It includes chapters on key technological concepts, learning about metadata, and putting metadata into practice. There is a very useful chapter on managing digital projects that includes two case studies: one on digitizing university archive photographs, and the second on Web page auditing and site migration. The final three chapters discuss the digital librarian's role in the new scholarly publishing landscape, collaborating on digital projects, and preserving digital content. The work concludes with a glossary and an index.

This book is an excellent and welcome addition to this genre. It is the kind of book all librarians should have had when they entered the profession. It codifies all the knowledge, common sense, and wisdom we acquire in our years in the profession. This work is an excellent choice for special and academic libraries. It will do well in most public libraries as well. For those who are thinking about a career in library science or are already in a career, this book gets the highest recommendation.—**Gary L. Parsons**

517.   **Library 2020: Today's Leading Visionaries Describe Tomorrow's Library.** Joseph Janes, ed. Lanham, Md., Scarecrow, 2013. 161p. index. $45.00pa.; $44.99 (e-book). ISBN 13: 978-0-8108-8714-5; 978-0-8108-8715-2 (e-book).

Edited by associate professor and chair of the MLIS program at the University of Washington Information School, this work brings together 23 chapters answering the question "The library in 2020 will be ...." Authored by 24 invited librarians, professors, and practitioners, and organized into 5 sections, the work discusses the future of libraries in terms of "stuff," people, community, place, and leadership and vision. Interestingly, while the materials come from various backgrounds and environments, they share similar messages. A lack of organization by title makes this hard to follow, as the only locator provided is a table of contents by contributor. The individual essays are poignant, ranging from personal ideas to well-researched and documented essays. For anyone considering the future of libraries and librarianship of any type, this book is a welcomed read, as ideas seen on blogs, at conferences, in professional readings all come together and can be shared in a way that one does not feel so isolated. Whether reading the thoughts of "The Annoyed Librarian," Marie Radford, Stephen Abram, Michael Crandall, or Daniel Chudnov, the reader will gain an understanding from the inside of what the future of the library may become.—**Sara Marcus**

Cataloging and Classification

518.   Cole, Timothy W., and Myung-Ja K. Han. **XML for Catalogers and Metadata Librarians.** Santa Barbara, Calif., Libraries Unlimited/ABC-CLIO, 2013. 388p. index. $60.00pa. ISBN 13: 978-1-59884-519-8; 978-1-61069-291-5 (e-book).

XML is a tool used to enforce metadata quality and enable the reuse and repurposing of metadata. This text, when studied well and thoroughly, provides a good foundation for implementing XML technologies. The authors intend the text to be accessible to readers with little or no prior practical knowledge of or experience with XML. However, the text is daunting for the casual reader. Chapters 1, 2, and 13 do provide an excellent overview of why XML is relevant in today's library and why catalogers need to be conversant with XML. The included case studies may very well inspire readers to investigate potential projects that expand library services. The rest of the book is dense with programming vocabulary and syntax.

The book is organized into four parts: introduction and overview, structured metadata in XML, authoring and validating XML, and metadata crosswalks with XML transformations, and RDF XML. A glossary and index are also included. The text is illustrated with screen shots, sample XML records, and tables.

Each of the 13 chapters is followed by a summary, questions and topics for discussion, suggestions for exercises, notes, and references. Several case studies of XML implementations are described that illustrate by example the power of XML technologies. The inclusion of exercises, topics for discussion, and working examples can be used in a classroom setting. Readers may also use the text for personal study to gain a working knowledge of XML technologies.—**Linda M. Turney**

Children's and Young Adult Services

519.   Adams, Suellen S. **Crash Course in Gaming.** Santa Barbara, Calif., Libraries Unlimited/ABC-CLIO, 2014. 125p. index. (Crash Course). $45.00pa. ISBN 13: 978-1-61069-046-1; 978-1-61069-047-8 (e-book).

Written for the new librarian or one who has no training in creating a gaming program into their library, *Crash Course in Gaming* truly presents the reader with a comprehensive overview of how to build a gaming program into their library—one that will not only be a hit with young adults but also with adults, seniors, and other special populations. The chapters are clearly defined and arranged to take the reader from the beginning steps of planning through implementation. The book begins by providing a thorough explanation of why including gaming programming into your library is beneficial. It then goes on to discuss the various types of games as well as how to go about building your collection with the help of reviewing sources and scanning awards. Developing a circulation policy is also discussed in this section. The main focus on the volume follows—developing in-library gaming programs. The author provides planning ideas and tips for creating gaming programs for young adults, adults, seniors, and intergenerational programming. Video gaming has its own chapter. The final chapter discusses how to start gaming programs on a budget, marketing your program, and the evaluation process. The work concludes with appendixes listing notable games, game-related movies, books for games, a sample gaming budget, and a sample evaluation. This text could easily be used by the inexperienced librarian starting their first gaming program and at $35 is a great deal.—**Sara Marcus**

520.   Behen, Linda D. **Recharge Your Library Programs with Pop Culture and Technology: Connect with Today's Teens.** Santa Barbara, Calif., Libraries Unlimited/ABC-CLIO, 2013. 179p. illus. index. $45.00pa. ISBN 13: 978-1-61-69-369-1; 978-1-61069-370-7 (e-book).

One of the issues facing school library media specialists these days is discovering ways to get this "plugged-in" generation of students to be "plugged-into" not only technology but also the library and what it can do for them. Behen has presented her way of successfully doing this. Behen is an school library media specialist in Cincinnati, Ohio. She seems to lead her students to what she feels they must know, meaning good research techniques by meeting them in two areas they enjoy: technology and pop culture. The title of the book lays this thesis out very clearly. That is to say: "How do you teach today's students in the library? You must recharge your library programs with pop culture and technology [in order to] connect with today's teens."

Behen, writing in a lively style, explains how to do this in seven chapters and a preface. The preface discusses "Why We Do What We Do?" The chapters are entitled: "Schools and Libraries in Transition: So Much More than Materials, Reference, and a Reading Room;" "Lead the Change;" "Things We Can Control;" "Engaging Today's Teens;" "Connect to Today's Teens Through Media and Technology Tools;" "There Is an App for That and That and That;" and "Discover Your Favorite Power Tools." The titles of these chapters are self-evident. The only one that might not be clear is: "Things We Can Control." That chapter concentrates on some fairly standard library practices that Behen believes can be jettisoned in order to create more time to both grow and empower the reader's library program. An example of what we can control from that chapter is "Don't worry about beautiful shelves." This book is highly recommended for school library media specialists who wish to make their programs more relevant to today's teens. It is full of useful and detailed suggestions. [R: TL, Oct 2013, p. 44]—**Scott Alan Sheidlower**

521.   Bromann-Bender, Jennifer. **Booktalking Nonfiction: 200 Surfire Winners for Middle and High School Readers.** Lanham, Md., Scarecrow, 2014. 153p. index. $45.00pa.; $44.99 (e-book). ISBN 13: 978-0-8108-8808-1; 978-0-8108-8809-8 (e-book).

According to her biography in *Booktalking Nonfiction*, Bromann-Bender is a librarian at Lincoln-Way West High School in Illinois and has authored several other books on booktalking. From reading this book one can see that she is also a thoughtful, experienced professional. This book contains everything the reader needs in order to begin booktalking nonfiction titles for teens. Nonfiction is the focus on the volume mainly because the Common Core Standards Initiative requires that 70 percent of the materials students read be information texts. Broken into four chapters, the book outlines all the skills and steps necessary to booktalk. The author begins by giving instruction on how to select, write, prepare, and present booktalks. She then goes on to discuss incorporating quick talks into library services. Using nonfiction in the library and classroom is the focus of chapter 3. The final chapter presents booktalks by theme, including animals, crime and serial killers, overcoming the odds, history and war, science and inventions, and sports, just to name a few. The author provides the user with ready-made booktalks; however, the librarian can expand on them by using tips provided at the beginning of the book. This book is recommended for young adult librarians in school and public libraries.—**Scott Alan Sheidlower**

522.   Craig, Angela, and Chantell L. McDowell. **Serving At-Risk Teens: Proven Strategies and Programs for Bridging the Gap.** Chicago, American Library Association, 2013. 220p. index. $60.00pa.; $54.00pa. (ALA members). ISBN 13: 978-1-55570-760-5.

Like every other teen in your community, at-risk teens will either use library services or they will not. However, as Craig and McDowell emphasize these teens are not throwaway people. They need our services as much as anyone else in the community. The problem is how to work with them successfully. Craig and McDowell have written a book of strategies that deals with the question of how librarians can best work with at-risk teens and help them to use the library.

The authors, who cover a wide range of topics, such as collection development and technology programs, as well as assessment of your program(s) for at-risk teens do not concentrate on one group of at-risk teens alone. Among other groups they look at incarcerated teens, LGBTQ teens, pregnant teens, and gang members. They also are very sensitive to how the community might see these patrons and devote large sections to how to convince a library to work with them, and working with "reluctant fellow employees."

Craig and McDowell also shine their spotlight on our profession and discuss how a lack of librarian diversity affects services to these teens. Their suggestions are very practical, for example they discuss some of the rules that a librarian might run into in a juvenile detention facility as well as how these rules could have an impact on what we do. The book includes multiple case studies of successful library programs for at-risk teens from around the country. The authors analyze these and find the lessons to be learned from them so one could replicate the program at their library if they so desired.

The book is definitely worth reading if you deal with at-risk teens or want to deal with at-risk teens. It is recommended for the professional shelf of any young adult librarians who wish to work with at-risk teens or who are already working with them.—**Scott Alan Sheidlower**

523.   Gough, Sarah, Pat Feehan, and Denise Lyons. **Serving Grandfamilies in Libraries: A Handbook and Programming Guide.** Lanham, Md., Scarecrow, 2014. 147p. illus. index. $45.00pa.; $44.99 (e-book). ISBN 13: 978-0-8108-8763-3; 978-0-8108-8764-0 (e-book).

Written for the librarian looking for inspiration on how to provide outreach and programming ideas for the growing number of grandparents raising their grandchildren, *Serving Grandfamilies in Libraries: A Handbook and Programming Guide* truly presents the reader with a comprehensive overview of how to develop an outreach program to this special population. This book provides insider advice from other libraries that have implemented these types of programs into their libraries, highlighting both the successes and the failures they experienced. Beginning chapters provide an overview of this demographic and their needs, the benefits to having a grandfamily resource center in your library, the challenges in developing a program for this population, and a sample of model programs. Appendixes include a bibliography of resources for more information on the subject, planning and curriculum resources, online resources, and promotion and publicity resources. Special topics covered include some information on grants and funding opportunities and ideas for potential community partnerships. This text could easily be used by the new librarian put in charge of heading or creating a program for this population as well as the seasoned professional who is new to this role. The work is a great review as well as introduction to the life of a librarian, illustrating both the positive and the challenging situations.—**ARBA Staff Reviewer**

524.   **How to STEM: Science, Technology, Engineering, and Math Education in Libraries.** Vera Gubnitskaia and Carol Smallwood, eds. Lanham, Md., Scarecrow, 2014. 280p. index. $55.00; $54.99 (e-book). ISBN 13: 978-0-8108-9273-6; 978-0-8108-9274-3 (e-book).

Edited by Carol Smallwood, a prolific editor of works, in conjunction with Vera Gubnitskaia, a manager at the Orange County Library System, Florida, this work brings together 25 chapters organized into 8 sections: Range and Scope; Teaching; Information Literacy and Educational Support; Collection Development; Research and Publishing; Outreach; Partnerships; and Funding. Thirty-four public and academic librarians from the United States share their experiences and knowledge on how libraries can engage youth in science, technology, engineering, and math. The work provides exciting ideas to encourage engagement from preschoolers to college students. The chapters provides practical ideas that are completed with instructions, supply lists, related educational standards, and reading lists. Activity ideas include science activities for preschoolers, partnership programs featuring LEGO, and animation workshops for teens. Students and practitioners alike will benefit from these tips and tales from the trenches.—**ARBA Staff Reviewer**

525.   Kemp, Adam. **The Makerspace Workbench: Tools, Technologies, and Techniques for Making.** Sebastopol, Calif., Maker Media, 2013. 282p. Illus. index. $29.99pa. ISBN 13: 978-1-4493-5567-8.

Makerspaces are all the rage right now in libraries across the nation. While it can be fairly simple to create a simple creative space in public and school libraries, more in-depth planning and budgeting need to be used when incorporating new technologies, new tools, and larger work spaces. *The Makerspace Workbench* will provide guidance on planning just what you would like your makerspace to be used for, the patrons you plan on serving there, and the budgetary needs you will need to keep it relevant for years to come. The only problem with a title such as this is that makerspaces are evolving quickly and the information here may become outdated as new technologies take off. Users should not let that deter them from utilizing the advice in this book. This title can serve as a benchmark for building the infrastructure needed when adding makerspace areas to your library.—**Shannon Graff Hysell**

526.   Lang, David. **Zero to Maker: Learn (Just Enough) to Make (Just About) Anything.** Sebastopol, Calif., Maker Media, 2013. 204p. Illus. index. $199.99pa. ISBN 13: 978-1-4493-5643-9.

Zero to Maker will be a useful guide for any librarian who is intimidated by the idea of having to come up with ideas, projects, and "inventions" for children and young adults to create in the library's makerspace. Lang discusses the importance of adopting an appreciation for less formal learning and how the library can be an ideal place to bridge the formal learning of the classroom with the informal learning that leads to creativity and problem solving. Children have a natural attraction to these types of activities and will benefit from having the library or media center serve as a place where informal learning, creating, inventing, and hands-on activities are the objective.—**Shannon Graff Hysell**

527.   Nichols, Joel A. **iPads in the Library: Using Tablet Technology to Enhance Programs for All Ages.** Santa Barbara, Calif., Libraries Unlimited/ABC-CLIO, 2013. 136p. illus. index. $45.00pa. ISBN 13: 978-1-61069-347-9; 978-1-61069-348-6 (e-book).

Authored by the manager of the Free Library Techmobile, a digital literacy outreach vehicle at the Free Library of Philadelphia, this work offers 50 programming scenarios to integrate iPads or other tablets into their programming for all age levels. Each easily adapted plan offers step-by-step instructions so that the specific audience at the individual library can be served most effectively. This book is focused on the iPad for examples, but most plans can be tweaked for other tablet platforms. Organized into seven chapters, the work begins with an introduction to device management best practices for the iPad followed by a discussion of how to select apps for the iPad, including tips for the iTunes Store and essential review sources. The next four chapters focus on specific age groups—birth to five, school-aged, teens, and adults. The final chapter offers program evaluation tips for media created, attendance and circulation, and surveys. The work ends with a list of 85 essential apps for library programming organized alphabetically and then by subject, followed by an index.

Teachers and librarians in schools, public libraries, and academic libraries will benefit from the ideas presented in this book, although without access to iPads the plans need much more research and redesigning. Each plan offers a goal, required apps, planning notes, books and other materials, and instructions for the actual program. The only drawback of this book being that the apps are for the iPad only.—**Sara Marcus**

528.   Pandora, Cherie P., and Stacey Hayman. **Better Serving Teens Through School Library— Public Library Collaborations.** Santa Barbara, Calif., Libraries Unlimited/ABC-CLIO, 2013. 256p.

index. (Libraries Unlimited Professional Guides for Young Adult Librarians Series). $40.00pa. ISBN 13: 978-1-59884-970-7.

Cherie P. Pandora and Stacey Hayman, this book's co-authors, both have different backgrounds and both have approached the topic of young adult services through school library-public library collaboration from different viewpoints. Pandora had been a school librarian in Rocky River, Ohio, and Hayman had been her counterpart in the public library there. According to the introduction they wrote the chapters together and, occasionally, one can individually discern one of their voices in the writing. However, usually it is impossible to identify who is writing and when in a chapter.

The book is divided into an introduction, 15 additional chapters, and 2 appendixes. The authors encourage the reader to read each chapter as they need it or when it interests them rather than necessarily reading them sequentially as is traditional. The chapter's titles are: "What is Collaboration, Why We Should Do It, and How To Get Started"; "Professional Projects"; "Programs"; "Celebrate Reading!"; "Summer Reading"; "Author Visits"; "Poetry Slams"; "Technology and Social Networking"; "Homework Help"; "Teen Advisory Boards"; "Budget/Finance"; "Grants"; "Resource Sharing"; "Professional Development"; and "Reporting Your Success." The appendixes consist of a Reading Calendar Month-by-Month and a Listing of State and Provincial Library Associations. The text is completed with an extensive bibliography, an index, and, embedded within the chapters, short one- or two-paragraph Notes from the Field (short statements from librarians besides Pandora and Hayman on what worked) and In our Experience sections (equally short asides by Pandora and Hayman).

Pandora and Hayman seem to work together very well as collaborators both in their professional life in their various libraries and as co-authors. This book is recommended for the professional reading shelf of any school librarian or public librarian who is looking for a way to make an impression in their community and is not sure where to begin.—**Scott Alan Sheidlower**

529.   Poe, Elizabeth A. **From Children's Literature to Readers Theatre.** Chicago, American Library Association, 2013. 190p. index. $40.00pa.; $36.00pa. (ALA members). ISBN 13: 978-0-8389-1049-8.

Author Poe puts a new twist on traditional readers' theatre with her book *From Children's Literature to Readers Theatre*. The author encourages librarians and students to create their own readers' theatre scripts from literary pieces found right in the library. She demonstrates how to create a readers' theater script, suggests titles that children and young adults can use, and gives suggestions for how to prepare children to present readers' theatre. The work includes a bibliography of more than 100 books that will work well for these projects. By encouraging students to create the scripts it will promote comprehension skills, writing skills, and performance skills on the part of the children. Most importantly it will engage them in the learning process. If the school librarian wants to take the project further they could encourage their students to film their performances and share them with each other. This book provides a wealth of inspiration for both school librarians and children and youth librarians in public libraries.—**Sara Marcus**

530.   Polette, Nancy J. **Gateway to Reading: 250+ Author Games and Booktalks to Motivate Middle Readers.** Santa Barbara, Calif., Libraries Unlimited/ABC-CLIO, 2013. 261p. index. $45.00pa. ISBN 13: 978-1-61069-423-0; 978-1-61069-424-7 (e-book).

Authored by professor emeritus at Lindenwood University and author of more than 150 professional books, this book offers over 250 author games and booktalks to motivate middle school readers to read junior novels. Organized alphabetically by the author's last name, the volume covers 40 classic and contemporary authors such as Laurence Yep, Bill Wallace, Jon Scieszka, Zilpha Keatley Snyder, Paula Fox, Neil Gaiman, Sharon Creech, Avi, and Lloyd Alexander. Each author, or chapter, offers four games to be used: "The I Have / Who Has Game," "Mystery Titles," "Name That Book!," and "Circle the Hidden Titles," as well as the keys to the activities. Of more value to some librarians and educators is a list of authors and titles with publishing information organized by author, offering a bibliography of books written by each author with year of publication. The activities might be of use to some educators, but the repetitive nature and lack of focus on specific titles leads the child to have knowledge of multiple books by the same author. This book does not offer booktalks, but rather repetitive activities to use with studies of a particular author.—**Sara Marcus**

531.   Schall, Lucy. **Teen Talkback with Interactive Booktalks!** Santa Barbara, Calif., Libraries Unlimited/ABC-CLIO, 2013. 305p. index. $45.00pa. ISBN 13: 978-1-61069-289-2; 978-1-61069-290-8 (e-book).

This professional guide is intended to help librarians, teachers, and home school instructors motivate teenagers to read. The author has selected more than 100 books published between 2008 and 2012 to present as short, ready-to-use booktalks that will involve teens in the presentation rather than having them just passively listen. The booktalks are divided into seven categories that reflect topics in which teenagers can look at various issues and discuss their beliefs: "Issues," "Contemporary," "Action/ Adventure/Survival," "Fantasy," "Heritage," and "Multiple Cultures." Each category is further divided into topics that can provide the focus of an individual booktalk program. Each theme includes four to five booktalks. To encourage interaction the booktalks include talkback questions.

Overall, the book is written in a clear and effective manner and organized for easy use. Each booktalk segment includes a comprehensive citation, a summary/description, a booktalk (many of which begin with suggestions for presentation), a list of related activities for group or individual projects, and a list of related works with annotations. Also included are general grade ranges, notes on which gender the book will appeal to, and a list of similar works. The book includes a combined author/title and subject index. The author has selected a wide range of books, many of which will be new to readers and broaden their reading scope. This booktalk guide should prove invaluable to the audience for which it was designed.— **Sara Marcus**

532.   **Teen Games Rule! A Librarian's Guide to Platforms and Programs.** Julie Scordato and Ellen Forsyth, eds. Santa Barbara, Calif., Libraries Unlimited/ABC-CLIO, 2014. 144p. index. (Libraries Unlimited Professional Guides for Young Adult Librarians Series). $45.00pa. ISBN 13: 978-1-59884-704-8; 978-1-59884-705-5 (e-book).

There is no doubt that games and gaming are hot topics for young adults. Gaming offers young adults a way to reach out to their teen population and find new and creative ways to develop programming that will keep them coming back to the library. This interest provides young adult librarians with a creative way to incorporate after-school programs for the teens in their library. This book will serve librarians in both public and high school libraries that are looking for innovative ways to incorporate gaming into their library programming. The authors present a comprehensive overview of the topic, supplying good practice examples from successful libraries, providing necessary details on format and implementation within a library program for teens, and covering different game formats ranging from live action role-playing and Dungeons & Dragons to Minecraft and traditional board games. The work is divided into two parts. Part 1 provides specific examples of how libraries have incorporated gaming into their library. Part 2 provides specific example of games that readers can use to inspire their programming ideas. Useful for both high school and public library programs, this work should be considered by both to supplement their professional programming library.—**Scott Alan Sheidlower**

533.   **Transforming Young Adult Services.** Anthony Bernier, ed. Chicago, American Library Association, 2013. 254p. index. $65.00pa.; $58.50pa. (ALA members). ISBN 13: 978-1-55570-907-5.

Bernier, associate professor at San Jose State's School of Library and Information Science, has posed an interesting and provocative question in this book of edited essays. He notes that many of the theories that the field of library sciences uses to study and to think about young adults, come from other discipline's epistemology, some theories dating back as far as the nineteenth century and some created in the twentieth century. While it is true that until this point in time this strategy has worked well for library and information science (LIS), Bernier observes, nonetheless, that we need to begin to work on an understanding of youths that add to a discussion of what young adulthood is from an LIS point-of-view.

This book is Bernier's attempt to begin a discussion of young adults as seen through the lens of LIS in the twenty-first century.

This book is laid out in an introduction, a conclusion, and nine thoughtful, well-written essays ranging in length from 12 pages to 24 pages. These essay are placed in one of three parts. These parts are: "Part I: What Is in an Age?;" "Part II: From White and Marginal to Civic Partners;" and "Part III: Beyond Youth Development and Intellectual Freedom." While the chapters are written from an LIS viewpoint, they include concepts from the fields of education, history, sociology, cultural diversity, and civil rights, among others to create new ideas.

Transforming Young Adult Services is both readable and interesting. The book is highly recommended for junior and senior young adult librarians as well as young adult librarian wannabes. It additionally could be used by school library media specialists at any stage of their career. This reviewer expects that this book will help drive discussion in the field of YA librarianship for many years to came.—**Scott Alan Sheidlower**

Collection Development

531. Dandy, H. Anthony. **E-Booked! Integrating Free Online Book Sites into Your Library Collection.** Santa Barbara, Calif., Libraries Unlimited/ABC-CLIO, 2013. 209p. illus. index. $45.00pa. ISBN 13: 978-1-59884-890-8; 978-1-59884-891-5 (e-book).

Integrating free online book sites into the public library collection sounds like a no brainer for most library personnel. Unfortunately, the staff of public libraries are oftentimes pressed to the limit when it comes to time and budgets. While the worthwhile e-book collections from Google Books, the Open Library, and HathiTrust are user friendly (and free) it takes valuable time for staff member to research the right collection for their needs and to implement it into their collection. This guide from author Bandy, founder of Library Knowledge, explains four of the largest free e-book collections available on the market and discusses how libraries can make effective use of their resources. He begins by profiling each site and its collection, giving insight into its origin, and explaining its organization. The work provides useful screenshots and provides example scenarios that demonstrate user needs that are applicable to this site. This is a practical guide giving librarians insight into how they can best integrate these site offerings into their library collection. It will be useful to public libraries looking to broaden their collection, especially smaller libraries with limited budgets.—**ARBA Staff Reviewer**

535. Bishop, Kay. **The Collection Programs in Schools: Concepts and Practices.** 5th ed. Santa Barbara, Calif., Libraries Unlimited/ABC-CLIO, 2013. 263p. index. (Library and Information Science Text Series). $50.00pa. ISBN 13: 978-1-61069-022-5.

This work is the newest edition of a title that examines the role of the media collection in the school library and presents information about the concepts, practices, and information sources that are basic to this issue. The book focuses on the setting, including sections on the environment of the media program, issues surrounding the collection, professional functions (such as selecting), issues and responsibilities pertaining to the collection, the external environment, and policies and procedures. Following chapters deal with selection, with chapters on knowing the community, assessing needs, selecting materials, acquiring and processing materials, evaluating the collection, and the consideration needed for specific individuals and groups (e.g., ethnic minorities and ESL students). The final chapters contain information about administrative concerns, and covers acquisition of materials, fiscal and electronic access issues, and collection maintenance.

Because it does indeed provide coverage of many commonly recognized aspects of the school library medial collection program this book has almost become a classic in its field. In this 5th edition, Bishop has incorporated pertinent Websites throughout the bibliographies and suggested additional readings. Issues surrounding electronic access to information are incorporated into the section on fiscal and access concerns. Acceptable use policies and Internet filtering are included. The work includes the advantages, disadvantages, and copyright concerns of various formats. It provides guidance on how to write policy and procedure manuals for school libraries, explores ethical and fiscal concerns, and discusses the best way to promote the collection. It is also important to note that entries in the additional readings at the end of each chapter have been annotated, thus giving the reader helpful information about each title. Each chapter concludes with a helpful conclusion, list of references, additional readings, and list of helpful Websites.

Overall, this work remains a useful title, and there are sufficient changes to justify purchase of this new version. It could also serve as supplemental material in school library media management or general collection development courses.—**ARBA Staff Reviewer**

536.   Johnson, Peggy. **Developing and Managing Electronic Collections.** Chicago, American Library Association, 2013. 186p. index. $65.00pa.; $58,50pa. (ALA members). ISBN 13: 978-0-8389-1190-7.

Authored by the former associate university librarian at the University of Minnesota Libraries and past president of the Association for Library Collections and Technical Services, this work draws on Johnson's extensive experiences working and researching in the area of collection development and management. Organized into eight chapters, the work begins with an overview of the evolving electronic collections environment, followed by chapters focusing on specific aspects of collections development and management such as selecting and evaluating, order placement, licenses, working with e-content and service suppliers, working across organizational units to acquire and manage e-resources, and budgeting and financial considerations. The work ends with a chapter on the future of e-content in libraries. A glossary and an index enable novice readers to appreciate and use this book as a guide, while the detailed explanations will help even the more experienced librarian to better understand and improve their own electronic collections. This book's scope encompasses any electronic content selected by librarians from any source, managed by the library, and made available for users; the materials can be obtained for free, purchase, or lease. This wide range enables the volume to be a concise source of information for all types of electronic materials that a library might offer, and thus is appropriate for any type and size of library.

This book will help practicing librarians. It would also serve as a wonderful text for future librarians wanting to know more about collection development and management of electronic materials in general.—**Sara Marcus**

537.   Pattee, Amy S. **Developing Library Collections for Today's Young Adults.** Lanham, Md., Scarecrow, 2014. 267p. index. $55.00pa.; $54.99 (e-book). ISBN 13: 978-0-8108-8734-3; 978-0-8108-8735-0 (e-book).

This handbook, written by an associate professor at Simmons College in Boston, provides advice on building a teen collection from the assessment phase through to the evaluation phase of the process. The author takes a close look at library policies to ensure that there is a respect for intellectual freedom for this population, recognizing that they have diverse needs and a need to be challenged by their selections. The book begins with an overview of the topic and then a discussion on the various perspectives shared by leaders in the field. It then goes into more focused chapters on the process of collection development for young adult collections. Topics covered include: collection development policies, needs assessment, selecting materials, acquiring materials, collection assessment and weeding, and maintaining a worthwhile collection. Not limited to the collection of print materials the work also looks at the selection and acquisition of e-books, databases, and computer games. This work provides a thorough overview of collection development for young adult collections and will be useful to both novice and veteran librarians.—**Rosanne M. Cordell**

538.   **Progressive Trends in Electronic Resource Management in Libraries.** Nihar K. Patra, Bharat Kumar, and Ashis K. Pani, eds. Hershey, Pa., Information Science Reference, 2014. 260p. index. $175.00; $265.00 (e-book); $350.00 (print and e-book editions). ISBN 13: 978-1-46664-761-9; 978-1-46664-762-6 (e-book).

Edited by two library professionals and one information systems professional, all at the academic level, this work brings together 12 chapters authored by 15 international scholars and practitioners about the current landscape of e-resources management, including history and scope, collection development considerations, patron-driven acquisition, e-journal subscription cost benefit analysis, copyright and licensing, electronic resources management systems, open resources, and three case studies at different types of libraries. Part of the Advances in Library and Information book series, this work offers theoretical frameworks and empirical research to help those working in or studying the field of electronic resources. Not intended for the novice, the chapters are presented as a single section, although a detailed table of contents will guide the reader to desired chapters, while the index will help the user to find specific areas of need in any type of library.—**Sara Marcus**

Evaluation and Assessment

539.   Dando, Priscille. **Say It with Data: A Concise Guide to Making Your Case and Getting Results.** Chicago, American Library Association, 2014. 132p. index. $40.00pa.; $36.00pa. (ALA members). ISBN 13: 978-0-8389-1194-5.

Authored by a library information services educational specialist supporting the secondary library programs of Fairfax County Public Schools in Virginia, this work is written as if one were attending a professional development session, or talking to Dando one-on-one about how to make your case and get results using quantitative and qualitative data gathered through surveys and focus groups, among other methods. Organized into six linear chapters, the work begins by helping the reader to determine the need, message and audience for the data, followed by Dando's identified secrets of effective communication, focusing on communicating data to support one's case. Next, the volume explores working with the power of statistics and how to best gather, interpret, and share the findings from statistics. The following two chapters address surveys and focus groups, followed by a chapter on presenting data to get results. Drawing on personal experience and written in a nontechnical manner, this book will help any librarian or other leader to effectively gather and use data to support one's arguments to boards, government, and other decision-makers. Whether a seasoned leader or a student aspiring for a leadership role, or a librarian seeking to prove to others the importance of a new idea or change, or a student learning how to use surveys and focus groups to support decision-making, this book will be of value. Eight appendixes provide checklists for surveys, focus groups, and data presentation, along with four sample surveys (public library patrons, high school students and teachers, and school library survey of faculty), and a sample survey results for data presentation.—**Sara Marcus**

540.   Hernon, Peter, Robert E. Dugan, and Joseph R. Matthews. **Getting Started with Evaluation.** Chicago, American Library Association, 2014. 242p. index. $65.00pa.; $58.50pa. (ALA members). ISBN 13: 978-0-8389-1195-2.

Authored by the dean of libraries at the University of West Florida, a professor at the Graduate School of Library and Information Science at Simmons College as well as the principal faculty member for the doctoral program, Managerial Leadership in the Information Professions at the same school, and a former instructor at the San Jose State University School of Library and Information Science and current consultant, this work draws on the experience and research of the authors to help readers in performing evaluations as part of their workload. Geared for the library manager, particularly in smaller libraries, this work is intended to guide current and future library managers and leaders through assorted topics related to evaluation such as evidence-based planning and decision making, library metrics, internal evaluation for planning and decision making, external evaluation to inform stakeholders and to guide continuous improvement, measuring satisfaction, measuring service quality, measuring return on investment, measuring the value of the library and its services, using and communicating the results of evaluation, and positive organizational change. What makes this valuable especially for an educational setting is the inclusion of chapter exercises, enabling the reader to put into practice the techniques and concepts covered in each of the 11 chapters. Whether a seasoned leader or one just starting out, the down-to-earth and user-friendly language brings to life concepts related to evaluation in a way that anyone can understand, but at the same time offers sufficient new ways of looking to enable those already familiar with the concepts to learn more. A list of suggested readings at the end of the book enables the user to find out more about specific topics of personal interest and use.—**Sara Marcus**

541.   Matthews, Joseph R. **Research-Based Planning for Public Libraries: Increasing Relevance in the Digital Age.** Santa Barbara, Calif., Libraries Unlimited/ABC-CLIO, 2013. 207p. index. $50.00pa. ISBN 13: 978-1-61069-007-2; 978-1-61069-008-9 (e-book).

Authored by a consultant who has assisted numerous libraries in a range of projects and former instructor at the San José State University School of Library and Information Science, this volume serves as a guide that focuses on the evolving nature of the collection in the public library. Matthews offers his expertise as a consultant in his writing style and content to guide the public library access services administrator to best utilize and market the collection, both print and online, in order to keep the library relevant in today's technology-driven age. Separated into nine chapters that are best read in order, but can be read individually, the work begins with an introduction about how the process is "Going to be a Wild Ride," addressing the need to change strategies and the challenges one will face. The remaining nine chapters all end with a summary of findings and a "take action" section that offers activities a library can act upon to gather information to help improve services in the area covered by the chapter. The second chapter focuses on understanding your market, followed by developing a plan, the physical collection, and the virtual library. Next addressed are selection policies, evaluating the collection, providing access, and evaluating the library. The volume ends with a list of references and an index. The detailed table of contents, with descriptive subheadings, and an in-depth index enable the user to focus in on desired areas, while the writing style encourages one to treat the book as a discussion with a consultant regarding how to increase the relevance in the digital age of the collections in the public library. Public library administrators and leaders of access services will benefit from this volume, as will students of access services. Those working in access services in other types of libraries may also benefit from this volume, although the specifics are focused on the public library patron and practice.—**Sara Marcus**

542.   **The Quality Infrastructure: Measuring, Analyzing, and Improving Library Services.** Sarah Anne Murphy, ed. Chicago, American Library Association, 2014. 186p. index. $60.00pa. ISBN 13: 978-0-8389-1173-0.

Edited by the coordinator of assessment at the Ohio State University Libraries this work brings together 11 chapters authored by 19 practicing librarians and information science professionals in the United States and Canada. Focusing on academic libraries, with a single chapter devoted to the NIST Information Services Office's Baldrige journey, this work will help academic, college, and university libraries and consortia to develop evaluation and assessment programs and processes in their own settings. Each case study focuses on a specific setting, such as 20 years of assessment at the University of Washington Libraries, or tracking performance at the University of Virginia Library. Also shared are how the University of Arizona Libraries implemented and evolved quality management, and the Syracuse University Library's Program Management Center. Emory University librarians share their journey towards organizational performance excellence, while the single Canadian-based chapter focuses on the development of an evaluation and assessment program for the Ontario Council of University Libraries. The University of California—San Diego shares how they created analyst positions, while Kansas State University Libraries Office of Library Planning and Assessment is explored next, followed by the building of an assessment program in a liberal arts college library and the development of a library assessment program at Washington University in St. Louis.

Combined or alone, the chapters will guide a library's administration to promote the benefits of developing a quality infrastructure within the library organization, to insiders and outsiders. Expanding the reader's eyes to assessment beyond customer perceptions of service quality, learning outcomes, and Website usability, these chapters will help to broaden the definition of assessment and areas to assess within libraries to demonstrate the true worth. Each chapter has references, and the work itself includes an index, making this volume valuable not only for reading cover to cover for inspiration, but also as a reference, and to find chapters of use and interest to one's own particular situation.—**Sara Marcus**

Fundraising

543.   **Beyond Book Sales: The Complete Guide to Raising Real Money for Your Library.** Susan Dowd, ed. Chicago, American Library Association, 2014. 286p. illus. index. $75.00pa.; $67.50pa. (ALA members). ISBN 13: 978-1-55570-912-9.

Edited by the capital campaign coordinator and special projects coordinator for the Friends of the Saint Paul Public Library, along with 5 fellow Friends' staff members, all 6 of whom are consultants for Library Strategies, this work presents 19 chapters about how to raise money for your library. Focusing on public libraries, the ideas will also work for school, special, academic, and other libraries where fundraising is a necessity, with or without an organized Friends committee. Organized into two parts, the first focuses on fundraising fundamentals, while the second offers types of fundraising activities one might implement as is or adapt for specific environments. A detailed table of contents, along with an index, enables one to quickly find information of use, whether on the need for fundraising, ways to connect with donors, private fundraising, facts about library fundraising, places and people to help with fundraising, thanking donors, marketing and public relations related to fundraising, or specific types of fundraising such as membership programs, annual and special appeals, tributes and memorials, major gifts, legacies and planned giving, fundraising events, online giving, businesses, grants, and capital campaigns. This book is of great use to any library seeking to raise money for any purpose or need, not just the publicly visible ones.—**Sara Marcus**

Indexing and Abstracting

544.   Cleveland, Donald B., and Ana D. Cleveland. **Introduction to Indexing and Abstracting.** 4th ed. Santa Barbara, Calif., Libraries Unlimited/ABC-CLIO, 2013. 384p. index. $55.00pa. ISBN 13: 978-1-59884-976-9.

As in its previous three editions, this book provides practical and procedural guidance for indexing and abstracting. Section 1, chapters 1-4, introduces the basics of indexing and abstracting. The second section covers such topics as the organization of information (e.g., thesaurus construction, vocabulary control), information access and retrieval (e.g., information retrieval systems, user-focused systems), information-seeking behavior (e.g., theories of information-seeking behavior, information behavior in subject areas), and types of indexes (e.g., author, classified, database, hypermedia). Section 3 covers a variety of techniques used in indexing in abstracting including, abstracts, journal indexing, book indexing, image indexing, the abstracting process, and computer tools and applications. This final section provides useful information on guidelines for professional practice, including ethics, copyright, resources and aids, and a final chapter on careers and the future for this type of work.

The book, as stated by its authors, no doubt can serve as a guide for the neophyte indexer and practitioner to the fundamentals of indexing and abstracting. It would also be an excellent textbook for the subject. As the field of publishing has changed greatly with the explosion of new technologies available since the 3d edition was published in 2000, this updated edition will be a welcome addition to practicing librarians, students of library and information science, and educators in the area of information organization.—**ARBA Staff Reviewer**

Information Literacy

545.   Burns, Christa, and Michael P. Sauers. **Google Search Secrets.** Chicago, American Library Association, 2014. 211p. illus. index. $48.00pa.; $43.20pa. (ALA members). ISBN 13: 978-1-55570-923-5.

Authored by a Special Projects Librarian, Technology and Access Services and a Technology Innovation Librarian at the Nebraska Library Commission, this work is a follow-up book to *Searching 2.0* (see ARBA 2010, entry 589). This book offers tips and tricks for effective Google searching, written for librarians, educators, students, and any user of Google wishing to enhance and expand their searching skills beyond the basic search, such as searching collections including images, blogs, maps, or filtering searches by date. The authors also offer tips for configuring Safe Search and using the bibliography manager feature of Google Scholar. Organized into 12 chapters, the book begins with an introduction to Google. Next are chapters devoted to tips and tricks for specific Google features such as Web search, Google Images, news, videos, maps, blog search, scholar, patents, and books. The volume ends with a chapter on Google Alerts and one on Google Search Tips and Tricks in general. This book is a welcome addition to any collection serving those who use Google to find information of any type or format.— **Sara Marcus**

546.   **Common Ground at the Nexus of Information Literacy & Scholarly Communication.** Stephanie Davis-Kahl and Merinda Kay Hensley, eds. Chicago, Association of College and Research Libraries/American Library Association, 2013. 340p. index. $54.00pa. ISBN 13: 978-0-8389-8621-9.

Edited by the Scholarly Communications Librarian at Illinois Wesleyan University and the Instructional Services Librarian and Assistant Professor at the University of Illinois at Urbana-Champaign, this work brings together 17 chapters authored by 28 librarians, scholars, and practitioners of librarianship in the United States and Canada on the intersection of information literacy and scholarly communication in academic libraries. Addressing undergraduate, graduate, and specialized programs, as well as faculty concerns, this work demonstrates the interrelatedness of two vital areas of academic librarianship—teaching information literacy and the concept of scholarly communication. The authors offer chapters that will guide and inspire readers in opening dialogues grounded in information literacy with students and faculty on areas such as open access, copyright, fair use, publishing models, and the social and economic aspects of scholarship and publishing. Drawing on research and experience, this volume will serve as the groundwork for future work in these areas, whether as a scholar or a practitioner. With the growing emphasis on open access, information literacy, and the need to publish or perish, this work will provide the basis for many informative sessions for students and faculty alike at any academic institution.—**Sara Marcus**

547.   Devine, Jane, and Francine Egger-Sider. **Going Beyond Google Again: Strategies for Using and Teaching the Invisible Web.** Chicago, Neal-Schuman/American Library Association, 2014. 180p. index. $70.00pa.; $63.00pa. (ALA members). ISBN 13: 978-1-55570-898-6.

Co-written by the Chief Librarian/Department Chair and Coordinator of Technical Services at LaGuardia Community College, *Going Beyond Google* is separated into three parts to assist the reader in examining the invisible Web in learning and teaching. Beginning with a part on understanding the division between the visible and invisible Web, the authors next focus on teaching students how to use the invisible Web in their research, and end with a section on tools for mining the invisible Web and looking into its future. The first part defines the characteristics of the invisible Web and the use of the Web for research. The second part addresses introducing students to the invisible Web, furthering exploration of the invisible Web, and provides examples of Internet research strategies and tools for mining the invisible Web. The final section examines the shifting boundaries between the visible and invisible Web. An appendix provides a Survey Monkey survey for students to assess their knowledge of how to use the invisible Web. Written to assist the novice, the work nevertheless is advanced enough to teach the experienced user something new. With many figures and tables, the reader's interest is kept, while the material itself is understandable and informative. Useful for any librarian working with the Web as well as for any researcher seeking to find more on the Internet, this book is a valuable addition to any academic, public, or school library.—**Sara Marcus**

548.   Heine, Carl, and Dennis O'Connor. **Teaching Information Fluency: How to Teach Students to be Efficient, Ethical, and Critical Information Consumers.** Lanham, Md., Scarecrow, 2014. 214p. index. $55.00pa.; $54.99 (e-book). ISBN 13: 978-0-8108-9062-6; 978-0-8108-9063-3 (e-book).

We live in an era where much of the information we gather and share comes from digital sources and most young people today have grown up using electronic devises for their research needs. Research has shown, however, that just because they are skilled Web users does not mean that they are information fluent—meaning that they have the knowledge, skills, and attitudes essential to using this newfound wealth of information to make a difference in our world. This book, written by a Ph.D. in education who has worked with the 21st Century Information Fluency Project and a teacher at the University of Wisconsin-Stout, examines the abilities of students today in finding online information, evaluating it, and using it ethically to determine how information fluent they truly are. The book addresses information fluency in five areas: digital information fluency, speculative searching, investigative searching, ethical and fair use, and instructional applications. Along the way the authors provide tips to teachers to devise methods of integrate information fluency into their teaching, particularly in the areas of language arts, history, and science. For anyone interested in information literacy and information fluency this is a must read.—**ARBA Staff Reviewer**

549.   Hider, Philip. **Information Resource Description: Creating and Managing Metadata.** Chicago, American Library Association, 2013. 220p. index. $99.95pa.; $89.96pa. (ALA members). ISBN 13: 978-0-8389-1201-0.

Authored by head of the School of Information Studies at Charles Sturt University in Australia, this book serves as a primer on information resource description in today's growing digital environments. Organized into nine chapters, the work begins with a definition and scope of the book, followed by a discussion of information resource attributes and then a chapter on tools and systems for organizations that will use information resource description, such as libraries, indexes, databases, library catalogs, federated search systems, archives, museums, digital collections, and search engines. The fourth chapter focuses on metadata sources, followed by a chapter on metadata quality and sharing metadata. Chapter 7 addresses metadata standards for Web publishing, libraries and digital libraries, archives, museums, book publishing and indexing, database indexing, e-research, education, audiovisual industries, business, government, and registries. Next addressed are types of vocabularies. The final chapter focuses on the future of metadata. Including numerous figures and tables to present examples, along with an in-depth index and a list of further readings to supplement the chapter-by-chapter references, this work is approachable to even the most novice reader, while including enough materials to reinforce and add to the knowledgebase of experienced workers with information resource description. An appendix of sources for metadata standards organized by type will help all to find, and select, the most appropriate tools for their own particular situation.—**Sara Marcus**

550.   Kaplowitz, Joan R. **Transforming Information Literacy Instruction Using Learner-Centered Teaching.** Chicago, Neal-Schuman/American Library Association, 2012. 326p. index. $75.00pa. ISBN 13: 978-1-55570-765-1.

Learner-centered teaching is not a new idea, and this handbook does an excellent job of giving the reader the theory and history of it as well as practical ideas for using it to teach information literacy. The book explains learner-centered teaching; discusses planning for learner-centered teaching; contains ideas for applying leaner-centered theory to information literacy instruction; and gives conclusions as well as suggestions for implementing the ideas in the book. The writing is clear and concise, the theory of learner-centered teaching lends itself to information literacy instruction, and the advice is sound. As with any teaching method, one should use those ideas and theories that will work for you and your learners. This is an excellent addition to a professional librarian's library.— **Robin Henry**

551.   **Library Reference Services and Information Literacy: Models for Academic Institutions.** Rosanne M. Cordell, ed. Hershey, Pa., Information Science Reference, 2013. 240p. index. $175.00; $265.00 (e-book edition); $350.00 (print and e-book editions). ISBN 13: 978-1-46664-241-6; 978-1-46664-242-3 (e-book).

Cordell advocates that reference and instruction are the core services in academic libraries with a single purpose of integrating information literacy (IL) with the institutional curriculum. In section one, she examines the history of reference and instruction services in academic libraries and explores reference services today that use a variety of technologies.

Section two includes detailed descriptions of reference and instruction services authored by seven academic librarians in various regions of the states. Each provides the respective institution's background, current state of the reference and instruction services, the relationship between the two services, assessment of their services, the challenges and future directions. Academic librarians can identify with the array of services presented and find familiar grounds on the services they also offer in their institutions. Other libraries can aspire towards the different service models presented in the chapters. For example, librarians at the Utah State University library link the chat widget on their LibGuide to the reference desk for students to get immediate help during reference hours. The California state University, East Bay's IL program includes credit courses, one- and two-time library sessions, and embedded librarianship. Skype is identified as a technology to be used for future reference and instruction.

Despite the challenges most institutions face in technology, assessment, space, budget and staff, the libraries in the volume tried various current technologies to provide services that meet the needs of their users. References follow each chapter. This volume provides current and future trends of the core library instruction services and is recommended for academic libraries.—**Ma Lei Hsieh**

552.   **Using LibGuides to Enhance Library Services.** Aaron W. Dobbs, Ryan L. Sittler, and Douglas Cook, eds. Chicago, American Library Association, 2013. 307p. index. (A LITA Guide). $65.00pa.; $58.50pa. (ALA members). ISBN 13: 978-1-55570-880-1.

The purpose of these essays by several individuals is to examine various aspects of using the LibGuides software. It begins with a short history of library guides and their usefulness, followed by sections on administering, maintaining, creating, and using guides. The last section presents some outstanding examples of LibGuides that are in actual use. Each essay includes useful information that is thoroughly and logically presented. There is a lot of information that gives step-by-step instructions along with a series of items of interest or things to consider. There are several excellent illustrations that serve to make the instructions clear by presenting examples. Some of the essays include a brief bibliography and there are appendixes that offer further information. At the end are a list of editors and contributors with brief biographies and an index. For anyone who is interested in making the most use our of the LibGuides software, this source would be a good place to start.—**Martha Lawler**

Information Technology

553.   **The Handheld Library: Mobile Technology and the Librarian.** Thomas A. Peters and Lori Bell, eds. Santa Barbara, Calif., Libraries Unlimited/ABC-CLIO, 2013. 218p. illus. index. $65.00pa. ISBN 13: 978-1-61069-300-4; 978-1-61069-301-1 (e-book).

Edited by the dean of library services at Missouri State University and an instructional technology support at Graham Hospital School of Nursing Library, this book offers 19 articles on handheld and mobile technologies in libraries. Organized into 5 sections, the essays, authored by 20 scholars and practitioners in public and academic library settings throughout the United States, address mobile tech trends in libraries, mobile library users, mobile access to content, mobile reference, and mobile professional development and new opportunities. While focused on library services, chapters can also appeal to those in museums, such as the article entitled "Mobile Tours for the Library with Historic Photos and Podcasts," and educators, such as the article "Smartphones, QR Codes and Augmented Reality in the Library." Each chapter is well documented and includes both references and further readings. Written so the novice can understand, while packed with ideas and concepts for the more advanced user, this book will assist any library or media center worker with adding mobile technology into the offerings, whether as an enhancement or new addition.—**Sara Marcus**

554.   Hastings, Robin. **Making the Most of the Cloud: How to Choose and Implement the Best Services for Your Library.** Lanham, Md., Scarecrow, 2014. 95p. index. $40.00pa.; $39.99 (e-book). ISBN 13: 978-0-8108-9109-8; 978-0-8108-9110-4 (e-book).

Written by the director of technology services at the Northeast Kansas Library System in Lawrence, Kansas, this book takes the reader through the most popular cloud services being used in libraries and breaks them down so that the user can know how to pick the best one for their particular library's needs. This is a fast-changing industry right now with new types of services being added to the cloud daily. While the overview of services will be useful to those new to using cloud technology in the library, much of the information in this volume may become dated quickly due to the ever-changing industry. Arranged into chapters that build upon each other, this volume discusses the use of the cloud in libraries, Web hosting in the cloud, cloud backups, managing computers from the cloud, project management, social media, security, and training. The author does a good job at demystifying the concept of the cloud and at helping the reader make a more informed decision for their library.—**Sara Marcus**

555.   Krier, Laura, and Carly A. Strasser. **Data Management for Libraries.** Chicago, American Library Association, 2014. 104p. index. $58.00. ISBN 13: 978-1-55570-969-3.

Data Management for Libraries is a new publication from the American Library Association focused on helping libraries build and support a data management service. Because data management in libraries is still very new, and librarians across the country are struggling to learn everything they need to know, the authors felt some guidance in the form of this book would be appropriate.

This book is straight forward and includes what one would expect in a book about this topic. It begins with an introduction to data management and continues into chapters about its various aspects, such as starting a new data management service, metadata, data preservation, access, and more. Three appendixes are also included that provide resources for institutional repositories, sample job descriptions for data librarians, and sample data management plans. Each chapter includes footnotes about the text, and is well written, easy to understand, and flows nicely. Having said that, one must keep in mind this is intended for a very specific audience, so an understanding of librarian jargon and lingo is expected when reading this book.

Data Management for Libraries provides some good information for librarians interested in learning more about the field. The text is somewhat brief at 104 pages, but this could just be a reflection of the topic's recent rise and relevance to libraries. This book does not pretend to be anything it is not, and as a result, will provide great information for its intended audience.—**Tyler Manolovitz**

556.   **Mobile Library Services: Best Practices.** Charles Harmon and Michael Messina, eds. Lanham, Md., Scarecrow, 2013. 153p. index. $44.99pa. ISBN 13: 978-0-8108-8752-7.

Presenting 11 case studies from academic and public libraries in the United States, this volume will inspire and encourage other libraries who are seeking to enter, or expand, the world of mobile library services. Whether looking for a full-service mobile app, or to offer select services in a mobile format, this book will help all looking to serve the ever-growing population using smartphones and tablets to access the Internet. Including examples, steps, success, and stumbling blocks, these case studies authored by those involved in the project offer real-world expertise in a down-to-earth manner for anyone seeking to learn more. Whether looking at apps, a scavenger hunt, Web design, or the use of iPads for library tours, this book will help those in any type of library, on any budget, to expand their reach. The only lack is a compiled list of references for future research, rather than having to look chapter by chapter, as the topics often overlap between chapters.—**Sara Marcus**

557.   Tu, Chih-Hsiung. **Strategies for Building a Web 2.0 Learning Environment.** Santa Barbara, Calif., Libraries Unlimited/ABC-CLIO, 2014. 169p. index. $50.00pa. ISBN 13: 978-1-59884-686-7; 978-1-59884-687-4 (e-book).

While online education has been around for years now, the concept of integrating Web 2.0 tools into that environment and essentially making it open network learning is still a relatively new concept. This volume provides librarians and educators with design models, guidelines, and activities for making the shift into the Web 2.0 learning environment. The author, a professor at Northern Arizona University in Flagstaff and an educational and instructional technology consultant, shares his personal experiences in working in this environment as well as his personal research in this area. The work is organized into six parts: Background and Concepts; Social Dimension; Network Dimension; Integration Dimension; Cognitive Dimension; and Comprehensive Integration. While the book does share some theoretical concepts it also provides users with a lot of practical advice, including learning activities, interactive links and templates, and resources for educators and trainers. It will be useful to library professionals beginning the process of integrating a open network learning environment.—**Sara Marcus**

Intellectual Freedom

558.   Adams, Helen R. **Protecting Intellectual Freedom and Privacy in Your School Library.** Santa Barbara, Calif., Libraries Unlimited/ABC-CLIO, 2013. 263p. index. $55.00pa. ISBN 13: 978-1-61069-138-3; 978-1-61069-139-0 (e-book).

Protecting Intellectual Freedom and Privacy in Your School Library is a collection of short essays providing information, guidance, and background for school librarians about issues related to intellectual freedom and privacy. For the most part the essays have been collected from a series of columns Helen R. Adams wrote and published between 2006 and 2012 for *School Library Monthly*.

Organized into nine broad chapters, this volume covers such topics as basic intellectual freedom and privacy information, the challenging of library materials, special needs students, and advocating for intellectual freedom. Each chapter begins with an introduction that flows into approximately five of the reprinted columns, and concludes with some key ideas from the chapter, a concise annotated bibliography of relevant resources, and discussion questions. Scattered throughout each chapter are numerous sidebars with information gathered since the original publication of each column. The book concludes with an index and two appendixes with information from the American Library Association and a list of supportive organizations.

Adams provides wonderful information about intellectual freedom and privacy in our school libraries. Having written and researched this issue since at least 2006, Adams has proven her knowledge about these issues, which comes through in her writing. One could argue that instead of reprinting the original columns with updated sidebars, the columns could have been rewritten with current information, but this format does provide insight into the topic as it has moved through time. This is a great resource and will be of particular value to school librarians or other interested parties.—**Tyler Manolovitz**

International Librarianship

559.   Bordonaro, Karen. **Internationalization and the North American University Library.** Lanham, Md., Scarecrow, 2013. 161p. index. $75.00; $74.99 (e-book). ISBN 13: 978-0-8108-9183-8; 978-0-8108-9184-5 (e-book).

The number of foreign students enrolled in the North American Universities has increased tremendously since 1945. During 2011-2012, over 630,000 foreign students were enrolled in the United States. A majority of these students have come from non-speaking English countries of Africa, Asia, Europe, and Latin America. Due to the cultural and language differences, their library needs are different as compared to the American and Canadian Universities, where the medium of instruction is English. Many articles and books have been published on the topic but the book under review is different because it includes views of foreign students and scholars as well as academic librarians on the topic.

This book is the result of an online survey done with a limited number of foreign students and scholars enrolled in two border universities of Canada and the United States in Ontario and New York, respectively. It was followed by in-depth interviews with 10 librarians of two universities, as well as a few foreign students and scholars. The results show that there is a need of internationalization of academic library services due to the changing impact of the introduction of technology in libraries, including databases and the internet. Views of three parties who participated in the survey are important and can help to define the roles foreign students, international scholars of various universities, and academic librarians working with them can play in internationalization of libraries in higher education. There are seven well-written chapters in the book and a good selected bibliography. There is an urgent need to do a more in-depth and detailed study of the subject for the benefit of all parties in Canada and the United States. This book is recommended for all academic libraries with a large foreign student population and international visiting scholars.—**Ravindra Nath Sharma**

560.   **Information Access and Library User Needs in Developing Countries.** Mohammed Nasser Al-Suqri, Linda L. Lillard, and Naifa Eid Al-Saleem, eds. Hershey, Pa., Information Science Reference, 2014. 259p. index. (Advances in Library and Information Science Series). $175.00; $265.00 (e-book); $350.00 (print and e-book editions). ISBN 13: 978-1-46664-353-6; 978-1-46664-354-3 (e-book).

561.   **Rural Community Libraries in Africa: Challenges and Impacts.** Valeda F. Dent, Geoff Goodman, and Michael Kevane, eds. Hershey, Pa., Information Science Reference, 2014. 309p. index. (Advances in Library and Information Science). $175.00. ISBN 13: 978-1-4666-5043-5.

These two volumes in Information Science Reference's Advances in Library and Information Science series provide a detailed look at the history and the possible futures of the evolution of library services in developing countries and in rural communities in Africa specifically. The editors all hold advanced degrees of Library Science from respected schools and each contributed chapters to these books along with their authoritative contributors. The basis of these books is on the acknowledgement that high-quality library services can help strengthen economic and social development in developing countries; however, most of the research and knowledge that exists on these findings have been based on the needs and user behaviors of English-speaking, western countries. These books focus on the needs specific to library customers in developing countries and the gaps in information and accessibility that need to be addressed to ensure success.

Information Access and Library User Needs in Developing Countries highlights ways in which users in these countries can benefit from LIS services being implemented with their skills and needs in mind. *Rural Community Libraries in Africa* looks at the relationship between local libraries and community development and its success. It examines how libraries contribute directly to literacy rates and economic gains in rural African communities. These titles will be of interest to librarians interested in international librarianship as well as those interested in the design and delivery of information services and their impact on the community and customers.—**Shannon Graff Hysell**

Library Education

562. **Advancing Library Education: Technological Innovation and Instructional Design.** Ari Sigal, ed. Hershey, Pa., Information Science Reference, 2014. 318p. index. $175.00; $265.00 (e-book); $350.00 (print and e-book editions). ISBN 13: 978-1-46663-688-0; 978-1-46663-689-7 (e-book).

Edited by a library director at Catawba Valley Community College, Hickory, North Carolina, this work brings together 20 chapters authored by more than 30 researchers, practitioners, and students in the fields of academic librarianship and information studies. This work offers theoretical frameworks, empirical research, and new examples for those teaching and developing courses for library and information science. The cases and examples in these chapters provide a unique overview of the role new technologies are having in library education. Individual chapters address such topics as online teaching, the role of social media in high education, professional development in the virtual world, evolving technologies being used in distance education, and the use of e-resources among library and information science distance learners. The volume includes an annotated table of contents and an index as well as a compiled list of references at the end. This should not be the sole resource consulted when researching this topic, but it can be of value, particularly to those studying the future of library education and the role new technologies play in education and the advancement of library science education.—**Sara Marcus**

563. **Revolutionizing the Development of Library and Information Professionals: Planning for the Future.** Samantha Schmehl Hines, ed. Hershey, Pa., Information Science Reference, 2014. 319p. index. $175.00; $265.00 (e-book); $350.00 (print and e-book editions). ISBN 13: 978-1-46664-675-9; 978-1-46664-676-6 (e-book).

Revolutionizing the Development of Library and Information Professionals provides a resource for a very important, but often overlooked, aspect of the library and information science profession: professional development. In a field that must maintain its relevance by moving with, or even ahead, of cultural and technological trends, the professional development of library and information professionals is an important investment by both the professionals and their supervisors. This resources provides information to help everyone involved in the profession understand the future trends in this area.

This book is organized into 17 chapters, or research articles, investigating and discussing different aspects of the subject at hand. Topics include looking at what library personnel desire from professional conferences, providing professional development to staff in tough economic times, partnering with educational faculty for pedagogical professional development, and more. Each chapter includes its own references, but the volume also compiles all of the references at the end of the book. This is followed by some related references, an index, and brief biographies for each of the authors.

The articles are all very well written and contain a wealth of helpful information. One must keep in mind this is more or less a collection of essays rather than a series of sequentially written chapters, so although topics are all related, they do not necessarily flow into one another. This does, however, provide the benefit of being able to read any individual chapter without worrying about its context within the volume.

Different chapters will definitely appeal to different audiences, but as a whole, this is an excellent resource for those interested in the future of professional development of library and information professionals.—**Tyler Manolovitz**

Library History

564. Libraries and the Reading Public in Twentieth-Century America. Christine Pawley and Louise S. Robbins, eds. Madison, Wis., University of Wisconsin Press, 2013. 281p. index. $39.95pa. ISBN 13: 978-0-299-29324-6.

This edited volume is a tribute to the role that libraries have played in educating the public, providing access to literature, and protecting the public from censorship. Rather than looking at librarianship from the managerial point of view it looks at it from the historical point of view, focusing on the diverse role it has played in modern history and the role it continues to play in the twenty-first century. In this book users will see libraries as social spaces that serve the needs of a diverse population and serve as a hub for their communities. The work is organized into four parts: "Methods and Evidence," "Public Libraries, Readers, and Localities," "Intellectual Freedom," and "Librarians and the Alternative Press." Essays have been written by scholars in the field and are scholarly in tone and presentation. Library history buff will enjoy this tribute to the profession.—**Shannon Graff Hysell**

Library Instruction

565. Accardi, Maria T. **Feminist Pedagogy for Library Instruction.** Duluth, Minn., Library Juice Press, 2013. 148p. index. $22.00pa. ISBN 13: 978-1-936117-55-0.

Authored by the associate librarian and coordinator of instruction at Indiana University Southeast in New Albany, Indiana and co-editor of *Critical Library Instruction: Theories and Methods* (Library Juice Press, 2010) this first-person narrative explores the pedagogy of effective library instruction, and other teaching, from a feminist perspective. Accardi demonstrates through this book how an effective library instruction provider can benefit from feminist pedagogue, beginning with a discussion of feminism in terms of narrative, intuition, and experiential knowledge; this is followed by a discussion of what feminist pedagogy is. Chapter 3 focuses on feminist teaching specifically in the library instruction classroom, although this discussion can be applied to other educational settings as well. The final chapter discusses feminist assessment. After a heartfelt and informative conclusion appears a lengthy list of references, followed by a list of further readings. The work ends with three appendixes: five sample lessons; sample worksheets for the lessons; and sample classroom assessment techniques. This volume is of great use to any pedagogical or teaching collection, whether for the library or other teaching settings in formal or informal environments. It will also be useful for all types of educators who wish to find other ways to reach students and learners.—**Sara Marcus**

566. Crane, Beverley E. **How to Teach: A Practical Guide for Librarians.** Lanham, Md., Scarecrow, 2014. 177p. index. (Practical Guides for Librarians, no.1). $65.00pa.; $64.99 (e-book). ISBN 13: 978-0-8108-9106-7; 978-0-8108-9106-7 (e-book).

The Practical Guide for Librarians series, of which this title belongs to, is designed to give librarians practical and innovative solutions to the everyday problems they face that can drain them of time and resources. The guides provide step-by-step plans for librarians brand new to the role of teaching customers how to access, evaluate, and use information. *How to Teach* explains to readers the theory behind delivering good instruction; helps them identify whether face-to-face or online instruction will be more effective for their users; shows them how to develop successful instruction; demonstrates ways to use individualized instruction; and provides advice on how to create objectives, present activities, and evaluate instruction. The work takes the reader through the steps of effective teaching. Library instruction is becoming a basic component of many library positions these days and this book will greatly assist those that are new to teaching and instruction. The suggestions can be adapted to fit face-to-face instruction as well as online instruction, making this volume a useful tool for any library manager looking to provide assistance to their staff in the area of teaching.—**ARBA Staff Reviewer**

Library Management

567. Applegate, Rachel. **Practical Evaluation Techniques for Librarians.** Santa Barbara, Calif., Libraries Unlimited/ABC-CLIO, 2013. 232p. index. $50.00pa. ISBN 13: 978-1-61069-159-8; 978-1-61069-160-4 (e-book).

Authored by an associate professor of library and information science at Indiana University, this work is organized into five sections to guide the reader through evaluation techniques in the library. From personal techniques such as surveys, interviews, focus groups, instructional evaluation, observations, and mystery shopping, to impersonal techniques such as list-checking, citation analysis, collection mapping, use analysis, process evaluation, and transaction log analysis, Applegate offers suggestions for all areas of service and preferred evaluation methods. She next addresses how to select a technique and sample the population to be studied through sections on decision factors, summarizing and analyzing data, using technology, and using consultants. The fourth chapter deals solely with planning for evaluation through library operations evaluation plans. The final chapter guides the user through reporting about the evaluation through targeted evaluation reports, periodic organizational reports, and reporting and organizational communication. Two appendixes offer a study question answer key and a guide for formatting data. This book can be used as a reference, as a guide, or as a text to help librarians, administrators, and future librarians and administrators evaluate libraries for managerial decision making and research purposes. This book is also of use as a guide for graduate students in library and information science who are seeking to perform evaluation studies on libraries. This book is not a theoretical book but rather a practical guide to performing the evaluations necessary to improve library services, and to demonstrate effectiveness of current services. [R: TL, Oct 2013, p. 44]—**Sara Marcus**

568. Evans, G. Edward, and Camila A. Alire. **Management Basics for Information Professionals.** 3d ed. Chicago, American Library Association, 2013. 577p. index. $75.00pa.; $67.50pa. (ALA members). ISBN 13: 978-1-55570-909-9.

Libraries and information centers are an important part of the present world. Many changes have been introduced in them in the information age that have affected their operation, management, storage facilities, and services. Two well-known library educators and management experts from the United Kingdom, and the United States have updated this excellent book to help professionals manage libraries and information centers in the twenty-first century. The book has 21 chapters, one of which are new to this edition ("Building Teams"), and has been divided into 5 parts under different broad headings. Part 1 has 3 chapters and deals with the background of management concepts, the operating environment, and legal issues. Part 2, under the heading "Managerial Skill Sets," has 8 chapters and discusses various issues, such as power and responsibility, delegating, decision making, communicating, and marketing and advocacy. Part 3 has 5 chapters and deals with issues of managing people. It provides chapters on motivating, leading, addressing diversity, and staffing. Part 4 deals with managing resources, and addresses such issues as budgeting, technology, and managing the physical plant. The final section discusses managing yourself and your career, and includes the topics of ethics and career building. There is a combined name and subject index, and a list of figures and tables to help professionals use the book more effectively.

All chapters are written in a scholarly manner. They include an introduction, discussion of the topic, case studies, excellent examples of library and information centers from different countries, many questions for further research and practice, references, and a list for general reading as well as a list for further research in library and information services. A new addition to this edition is an advisory board with members who have contributed advice and tip throughout the volume. This is an excellent addition to the volume and provides the real-life experience that managers will be seeking from a book like this. This work is an excellent addition to the library literature and an authoritative guide to all information library managers and future administrators. It will teach them how to communicate; make decisions; lead; and manage staff, budgets, and facilities. It is highly recommended for all libraries, library schools, and library administrators of the twenty-first century.—**Ravindra Nath Sharma**

569.   Holt, Leslie E., and Glen E. Holt. **Success with Library Volunteers.** Santa Barbara, Calif., Libraries Unlimited/ABC-CLIO, 2014. 156p. index. $45.00pa. ISBN 13: 978-1-61069-048-5; 978-1-61069-049-2 (e-book).

Authored two library consultants that work with public and school libraries as well as museums and historical societies, this work reflects covers the principles and best practices for establishing and operating a library volunteer program in any type of library. Presented in nine chapters, the work addresses the basics of managing volunteers, finding volunteers within your community, popular types of library volunteers, planning, recruitment and retention, evaluating your program, volunteers that require special attention, volunteers that work with information systems, and the future of volunteerism. Whether a newly appointed volunteer manager, a seasoned volunteer director, or a librarian who is just trying to get and manage volunteers, this volume will be of benefit with its ideas, underlying support for existing procedures, samples, policies, and practical discussions. The appendix provides a "success model" from the King County Library that includes highlights and advice from establishing the program to creating policies to evaluating the volunteer program's effectiveness. Any type of library will benefit from this book, as will others working with volunteers such as schools and other organizations.—**Sara Marcus**

570.   Matthews, Stephen A., and Kimberly D. Matthews. **Crash Course in Strategic Planning.** Santa Barbara, Calif., Libraries Unlimited/ABC-CLIO, 2013. 101p. index. (Crash Course). $35.00pa. ISBN 13: 978-1-59884-482-5.

Written for the new librarian or one who has no training in public library administration, *Crash Course in Strategic Planning* truly presents the reader with a comprehensive overview of how to step into the role of the library administrator in charge of creating a vision and mission for the library. The chapters are clearly defined and arranged to take the reader from the beginning steps of planning through the strategic plan ending. In between are chapters on creating a mission statement, creating a vision statement, forecasting, creating goals and objectives, assessing measures and outcomes, and allocating resources. The work concludes with a chapter on advice on dealing with change within your library, executing your plan, and the road to becoming a twenty-first century library. This text could easily be used by the inexperienced librarian thrown into the role of library management and administration, either by choice of by necessity. The work is a great review as well as introduction to the life of a librarian, illustrating both the positive and the challenging situations.—**Sara Marcus**

571.   Moran, Barbara B., Robert D. Stueart, and Claudia J. Morner. **Library and Information Center Management.** 8th ed. Santa Barbara, Calif., Libraries Unlimited/ABC-CLIO, 2013. 470p. index. (Library and Information Science Text Series). $70.00; $55.00pa. ISBN 13: 978-1-59884-988-2; 978-1-59884-989-9pa.

This revision of the standard textbook in library management builds on the solid foundation laid by previous editions. Although the main topics covered and the sequence of the chapters remain the same, the size of the text has been increased by 25 percent over the 8th edition. This increase has been achieved by adding a few new sections dealing with recent topics, updating the lists of readings, and by increasing the number of illustrative quotations and examples that are embedded in the text. In this edition, the authors appear to have paid special attention to new changes brought about by the digital revolution as well as the skills needed by library managers as libraries are facing severe budget cuts due to the recent recession. Users will also find examples of organization charts, evaluation forms, and similar management documents from a variety of libraries.

Introductory chapters address such issues as the ever-changing role of library staff and how they must be continually encouraged to rethink their role. There is also a strong emphasis on new approaches to management techniques and how some of the most respected techniques of the past are now outdated and no longer apply to today's changing industry. In this time of stressed budgets managers will appreciate the chapters on fundraising, facilities management, and marketing for today's library. This textbook remains the best introductory source on library management, and this revision is welcome.—**ARBA Staff Reviewer**

572. Munde, Gail. **Everyday HR: A Human Resources Handbook for Academic Library Staff.** Chicago, Neal-Schuman/American Library Association, 2013. 183p. index. $65.00pa.; $58.50pa. (ALA members). ISBN 13: 978-1-55570-798-9.

If you are lucky enough to be employed, then you are lucky enough to be subject to oftentimes complicated or confusing employment policies. As the author of this book acknowledges, it can be even more complicated for employees in the academic setting. Written by an assistant professor of library science at East Carolina University in Greenville, North Carolina, who is also a certified professional in human resources, this volume addresses the specific policies that academic libraries are likely to encounter. She provides clear explanations for the most common HR applications in university libraries. Chapters include: "Positions and Position Management," "Basic Employment Law," "Working with Others," "Supervising Others," "Recruitments and Search Committees," and "Tenure and Continuous Employment." The work also provides an overview of the recruitment process, including a look at the roles of search and tenure committees.—**Gary L. Parsons**

573. **Staff Development: A Practical Guide.** 4th ed. Andrea Wigbels Stewart, Carlette Washington-Hoagland, and Carol T. Zsulya, eds. Chicago, American Library Association, 2013. 219p. index. $55.00pa.; $49.50pa. (ALA members). ISBN 13: 978-0-8389-1149-5.

Most library environments are finding that they are having to do more with less—and that oftentimes means less staff as well. For this reason it is all the more important that staff members are retained and are well-utilized so that they are both fulfilled in their career and an asset to the library. From the great variety of information found within the covers of this small volume, library administrators can learn how to assess library needs, set goals, and plan a proactive staff development program using such current trends as online tutorials, technical training, mentoring, and developing a customer service attitude. In this 4th edition, chapters begin with introductory material and are then divided into discussion topics. Most chapters contain conclusions and references. Some chapters end with appendixes. The appendixes are mostly survey instruments developed at various libraries of different types for different purposes. Biographical information about the contributors, most of them practicing librarians, and an index complete the book.—**ARBA Staff Reviewer**

574. **Time and Project Management Strategies for Librarians.** Carol Smallwood, Jason Kuhl, and Lisa Fraser, eds. Lanham, Md., Scarecrow, 2013. 295p. index. $55.00pa.; $54.95 (e-book). ISBN 13: 978-0-8108-9052-7; 978-0-8108-9053-4 (e-book).

Edited by a prolific editor of works in conjunction with the executive director of the Arlington Heights Memorial Library in Illinois and the services implementation coordinator for the King County Library System in Washington, this work brings together 33 chapters organized into 8 sections: management strategies; working with staff; students, volunteers, and interns; monitoring time and projects; getting organized; using technology; work-life balance; and professional development. Thirty-three public and academic librarians from the United States and Canada share their experiences and knowledge on time and project management to assist others. Ranging from the macro level of library systems to the micro level of personal time and project management, chapters will be found to support and guide librarians at all levels with their needs. Offering tips drawn from personal experiences, the chapters will enhance any librarian's practices through narrative, takeaways, and step-by-step guidelines to building one's own abilities in time and project management. This is a valuable tool for any librarian's arsenal as the tasks grow in number and complexity and the budget and manpower shrink. Students and practitioners alike will benefit from these tips and tales from the trenches.—**Sara Marcus**

Library Outreach

575.   Maddigan, Beth, and Susan Bloos. **Community Library Programs that Work: Building Youth and Family Literacy.** Santa Barbara, Calif., Libraries Unlimited/ABC-CLIO, 2014. 215p. illus. index. $45.00pa. ISBN 13: 978-1-61-69-263-2; 978-1-61069-264-9 (e-book).

Creating a culture of community within your library and for your library patrons is an important element to any public library, whether in a large city or in a small rural community. This volume, co-authored by an education librarian at Memorial University Libraries in Newfoundland, Canada, and a manager of the Forest Heights Community Library in Kitchener, Ontario, this work presents ideas and guidelines for creating library literacy programs for children, teens, and families. The work is organized into thematic chapters that each provide three to eight community-focused programs that public libraries can incorporate into their programming. The chapters address such topics as: "Programs to Explore Your Roots," "Programs for Reaching Out to Everyone," "Programs to Connect Globally," and "Programs that Encourage Personal Growth." Most of the programs can be adapted to fit within smaller community settings to very large public library settings, and most can be adapted to fit the budgetary guidelines of the library incorporating the program. There are programs featured in this volume that match early literacy research and the Every Child Ready to Read model. This practical guide will be a useful addition to any public library looking to add innovative programming into their library that will appeal to a wide range of users and will focus on the values and identity of their community.—**Sara Marcus**

Public Relations

576.   **Bringing the Arts into the Library.** Carol Smallwood, ed. Chicago, American Library Association, 2014. 233p. index. $50.00pa.; $45.00pa. (ALA members). ISBN 13: 978-0-8389-1175-4.

As centers for cultural preservation, it is important for libraries to collaborate with arts communities. Approaches and ideas that were actually used by a cross-section of libraries are presented highlighting the techniques used and what did or did not work. A foreword and introduction give an overview and are followed by a list of arts contributors who assisted with the projects. The main text is divided into categories of aspects of artistic endeavors: literary arts, visual arts, performing arts, and mixed arts. There is also a section on the management and administration of arts collaborations that includes the practical side of things. Each presentation gives a background on the motivation for the arts project, the process and problems/successes of creating programs, and an examination of the results or aftermath. This is followed by a brief bibliography. Some illustrations are included. A list of contributors with brief biographies and an index conclude the work.—**Martha Lawler**

577.   Crawford, Walt. **Successful Social Networking in Public Libraries.** Chicago, American Library Association, 2014. 167p. index. $55.00pa.; $49.50pa. (ALA members). ISBN 13: 978-0-8389-1167-9.

Examining nearly 6,000 libraries across the United States, the author of this work presents information on how public libraries of all sizes and with all types of budgets are using social networking sites to market their services, connect with the community, and better service their patrons' needs. The examples provided in the book show the diversity of ways that libraries can use social networking sites, including Facebook, Twitter, Instagram, and Tumblr, based on their user's needs and styles of communication. The work provides guidelines for setting up social networking sites, establishing goals for what they would like to accomplish through social networking, and conducting effective evaluations of the program. While not a how-to guide, this work will provide users with a lot of practical advice from others in the field as well as provide ideas for how to best implement the social networking campaign that will best fit their library's needs.—**ARBA Staff Reviewer**

578.   Edwards, Julie Biando, Melissa S. Robinson, and Kelley Rae Unger. **Transforming Libraries, Building Communities: The Community-Centered Library.** Lanham, Md., Scarecrow, 2013. 230p. index. $55.00pa.; $54.99 (e-book). ISBN 13: 978-0-8108-9181-4; 978-0-8108-9182-1 (e-book).

Authored by the ethnic studies librarian and multicultural coordinator at the Mansfield Library at the University of Montana in Missoula, the teen librarian at the Peabody Institute Library in Peabody, Massachusetts, and the adult services librarian at the Peabody Institute Library, this work offers 15 chapters organized into 3 parts: the what and why of community-centered libraries, how to create community-centered libraries, and inspiration for community-centered libraries. Intended for the public librarian, this work demonstrates how public libraries can position themselves as active and vibrant centers of community life in the twenty-first century" (p. vii). Drawing on real-life examples, the co-authors demonstrate through case studies how libraries of all sizes, demographics, and budgets in the United States can and do work to become community-centered. Drawing on what has already been done, sharing tips, tricks, inspiration, what to do, and what not to do, this book will encourage and enable any public library to become more community-centered. Librarians in other types of libraries can also benefit from selected chapters, based on the community needs, whether looking to find the importance and relevance of being community-centered; how to allocate the resources, collaborate, and obtain grants; or determining how to focus on civic action, sustainability, the arts, or other purposes. Down-to-earth and practical, yet packed with ideas and inspiration, this work is beneficial to any public library's professional collection.—**Sara Marcus**

579.   Kennedy, Marie R., and Cheryl LaGuardia. **Marketing Your Library's Electronic Resources: A How-To-Do-It Manual for Libraries.** Chicago, Neal-Schuman/American Library Association, 2013. 177p. index. (How-To-Do-It Manuals). $60.00pa.; $54.00pa. (ALA members). ISBN 13: 978-1-55570-889-4.

Front line library staff usually have limited marketing expertise that would enable them to improve customer awareness of under-utilized resources in their libraries. A well-designed marketing plan would not only complement existing discovery systems for customers; the increased awareness resulting from the plan would generate demand for more and better resources and likely produce increased funding for today's economically strapped libraries.

Kennedy and LaGuardia provide the steps needed to design a plan for public and academic libraries offering advanced electronic resources that would communicate their importance in a world where customers believe all information can be found via Google. They illustrate a circular process of assessment (feedback from customers), advertisement (communication strategies about available resources), staff training, instruction for customers/researchers, assessment, advertisement, and more. Even though this volume deals with e-resources, the authors also make it clear that their basic marketing strategies can be used for many other library services.

The book consists of two parts. Part 1 is the guide to designing a successful marketing plan, and has six chapters outlining practical steps toward that goal. Chapter 1 sets the tone and roadmap for all the other steps. It requires a definition of purpose including an assessment of current e-resources (e.g., usage statistics, cost, cost-per-use). Chapter 2 identifies the components of the marketing plan. Chapter 3 deals with plan

implementation and chapter 4 illustrates how to construct a report about the plan. Chapter 5 demonstrates how to assess the plan and chapter 6 teaches staff how to revise and update the plan based on their assessment.

Part 2 contains four sample, well-executed marketing plan reports: Example 1 is a report from an all-electronic library. The second and third examples showcase plans from two different public libraries. And the fourth example features a plan from an academic library. A comprehensive index begins on page 173.

The goal of the authors was to reach the entire library community with this book. It is written in a clear style with easy-to-understand examples, including outcomes. It is highly recommended for academic, community college, and large public libraries.—**Laura J. Bender**

580.   Solomon, Laura. **The Librarian's Nitty-Gritty Guide to Social Media.** Chicago, American Library Association, 2013. 211p. index. $52.00pa.; $46.80pa. (ALA members). ISBN 13: 978-0-8389-1160-0.

Facebook, Twitter, and LinkedIn, are three of the latest social media tools used by libraries to communicate with their patrons. *The Librarian's Nitty-Gritty Guide to Social Media* by Laura Solomon, a terrific social media reference for both novices and veterans alike, offers the most effective social media approaches for communicating with your library patrons. Chapters include "Strategies for Social Media Success"; "Rethinking Status Updates"; "What Can We Count? Measuring Success; and Social Media in the Long Term."

Today, many libraries are using social media as a one way tool to broadcast information, however, as the author notes, "social media is not about numbers or coverage it is about connections." Examples and explanations provided for improving your library's connections with its patrons include providing posts that have relevance to the reader, providing a link, requesting engagement from users, monitoring your social media, encouraging staff to participate, and re-tweeting your patrons and employees. This reviewer recommends this book for any library, whether it is K-12, academic or public, wanting to start or improve their social media efforts.—**Linda W. Hacker**

581.   Woodward, Jeannette. **The Transformed Library: E-books, Expertise, and Evolution.** Chicago, American Library Association, 2013. 131p. index. $55.00pa.; $49.50pa. (ALA members). ISBN 13: 978-0-8389-1164-8.

Authored by a principal of Wind River Library and Nonprofit Consulting and prior academic library administrator and public librarian, Woodward draws on her extensive experiences and knowledge of librarianship to offer a first-person account of the impact of technology, in particular e-books, on librarianship and society. Approachable and down-to-earth, the writing style encourages reading cover to cover from chapters 1 through 6, while the last three chapters offer survival strategies for public, academic, and school libraries respectively. This unbiased discussion of the transformation and evolution of libraries, not only in terms of e-books but technology in general, presents all views equally and includes a history of technologies and their impacts not only on libraries but on society as a whole. Each chapter includes clearly labeled personal experiences, and lists of references. Lacking in the volume is a comprehensive list of references, although this lack does not detract from the value of this book to those wishing to gain a personal understanding of the transformations over time. This is not a reference book, nor are there ideas or inspirations abounding for implementing in one's own library. However, for background and a better understanding of where we have been and where we are going, this book is invaluable.—**Sara Marcus**

Reference

582.   Nims, Julia K., Paula Storm, and Robert Stevens. **Implementing an Inclusive Staffing Model for Today's Reference Services: A Practical Guide for Librarians.** Lanham, Md., Scarecrow, 2014. 143p. index. (Practical Guides for Librarians, no.2). $65.00pa.; $64.99 (e-book). ISBN 13: 978-0-8108-9128-9; 978-0-8108-9128-9 (e-book).

Reference services have changed dramatically over the past several years due to technology and the ways in which user needs have changed. This also means that the way that reference services are managed is changing as well. One way that libraries have found to keep up with the needs of users is to switch to an on-demand, in-person approach to managing the reference needs of their patrons. That oftentimes means that more staff is trained at handling reference questions and more reference service points are offered. This book provides practical suggestions for implementing these changes in your references services department. It address such issues as the best approach to getting staff on board with the new model (both those with an MLS and those without), determining optimal staff numbers to have on hand, creating training materials, evaluating the quality of reference service once the switch has been made, and staff supervision considerations. The book provides sample forms, checklists, and sample materials that will save you time while implementing changes to your reference department and provide you with ideas that you may not have considered beforehand. This is a useful and worthwhile guide for any library looking to revamp their reference services department.—**Sara Marcus**

Research

583.   Pickard, Alison Jane. **Research Methods in Information.** 2d ed. Chicago, American Library Association, 2013. 361p. index. $85.00pa.; $76.50pa. (ALA members). ISBN 13: 978-1-55570-936-5.

No doubt many of us remember the dry textbooks assigned to us in college that dealt with the theory and philosophy of research and the research process. This resource by Alison Jane Pickard is a departure from those hard-to-get-through models and presents the philosophical framework as context for a very practical, clearly written tome.

This 2d edition includes two guest chapters that did not appear in the 1st edition. One chapter presents results from a Joint Information Systems Committee (JISC in the UK) funded "DATUM" project that focuses on research data management, and the other is an analysis of existing research documents that complements the content of the text. As Pickard states, "These are very practical, 'real' benefits of research but there is also the need to increase the body of knowledge that makes up the profession, to continue to engage in the questioning process that allows the professional to grow." In short, researchers must also be good consumers of research.

The emphasis is on the "doing" of research. To that end, the book is divided into five parts consisting of 25 chapters. Part 1 is starting the research process. Part 2 is research methods. Part 3 is data collection techniques. Part 4 is data analysis and research presentation, and Part 5 is the glossary and references. There are tables throughout to illustrate differences between concepts, quantitative, qualitative, and mixed methodological research design. Some of the chapters cover surveys, usability studies, case studies, observation, and diaries, to mention just a few topics. Each chapter contains practical exercises and suggestions for further reading to instill confidence in any student embarking on a research project. A complete list of references and further reading begins on page 329, and an index begins on page 347.

This resource is highly recommended for students and practitioners of information science, communications, records management, knowledge management, and the pedagogy of research methods. It is highly recommended for academic, community college, and large public libraries.—**Laura J. Bender**

584.   **Successful Strategies for Teaching Undergraduate Research.** Marta Deyrup and Beth Bloom, eds. Lanham, Md., Scarecrow, 2013. 192p. index. $65.00pa. ISBN 13: 978-0-8108-8716-9; 978-0-8108-8717-6 (e-book).

Co-edited by the Catalog Coordinator and the Information Literacy Coordinator at Seton Hall University Libraries, this work offers 11 chapters organized in 2 sections. Seven chapters focus on the state of teaching today, with an emphasis on teaching research skills and methodologies, whether as a separate research class or as part of a subject or content course. This first part addresses research questions, the relationship between good research and good writing, what is a "good" research assignment as determined by a librarian and by an academic, new media as a form of writing, information ethics, and more. The final four chapters offer four ideas that work, presenting strategies that have worked in case study format: scaffolding, RAIDS, Wikipedia editing, and training. This unique volume offers a focus on the research question itself, rather than information literacy as a whole, or research as separate from the library. This focus on information literacy as related to research, specifically at the undergraduate level is something that is of great importance but can be hard to find, and the way it is covered enables librarians in high schools and working with graduate students to also benefit from the information provided in the volume to successfully teach students and others about how to perform research, starting with the base of a strong research question.—**Sara Marcus**

Publishing and Bookselling

585. **Big Universe. http://www.biguniverse.com.** [Website]. Reston, Va., Big Universe Learning. Price negotiated by site. Date reviewed: 2013.

Big Universe is an online "bookshelf" in which participants can read published books from selected publishers, read books that other members of *Big Universe* have created and shared within the site, or create their own book to share. The site contains nearly 5,000 "self-published" books, as well as over 900 print resources from such publishers as Weekly Reader, Lobster Press, and Teacher Created Materials. There are a variety of subscription options, from a "personal" membership to memberships for classes within schools. A wonderful way for teachers and librarians to share published books on interactive whiteboards and projected screens with their students, individual students can explore various concepts about bookmaking and publishing on a self-directed project. While the majority of the books found within *Big Universe* are written in English, there are books written in other languages, ranging from Albanian to Ukrainian, with 11 languages featured. *Big Universe* has a search capability that allows users to browse by subject, age levels, publisher house, and popularity. While bibliophiles will always love their printed word, today's tech-savvy student will thoroughly enjoy the journey they will be able to take within *Big Universe*'s cybershelves.—**Beth Green**

586. **Lerner Interactive Books. http://www.lernerbooks.com/Pages/Home.aspx.** [Website]. Minneapolis, Minn., Lerner Books. Price negotiated by site. Date reviewed: 2013.

Lerner's e-book platform offers an interactive component that is available on both computer and iPad. Once a book is purchased, many students can log in at the same time. Students will enjoy reading book on the iPad. Users can search for a book by topic, title, and author or by scrolling through options. Once a book is found, students can control the reading speed, watch highlighted words, and turn off the sound to practice reading on their own. After reading, students can play a game or take a quiz for comprehension. Lerner Interactive Books will be helpful for students who are learning to read or struggling to read on their own. If a school is looking to add interactive e-books, especially for struggling readers, this product would be a good start.—**LJ Martin**

12 Military Studies

General Works

Biography

587. Hunt, Roger D. **Colonels in Blue—Indiana, Kentucky and Tennessee.** Jefferson, N.C., McFarland, 2013, 260p. illus. index. $39.95pa. ISBN 13, 978-0-7864-7318-2.

Roger D. Hunt continues to fill a need in our knowledge of the Civil War with this, his fifth in a biographical series on men who at one time or another attained the rank of colonel in regiments in the Union army. His several preceding volumes covered of officers of that rank in the states of New England, the Mid-Atlantic, Ohio, and West Virginia. The current work adds the colonels who led regiments from the states of Indiana, Kentucky, and Tennessee. Those who rose to the rank of general are included in two earlier volumes.

Although the author appears to have no formal background in history other than an intense interest in the American Civil War, his research is impeccable and the work is well done. The organization is logical and easy to follow. Biographies are grouped by state, first Indiana, followed by Kentucky and Tennessee. The biographical sections are preceded by a list of regiments for that state and the colonels who served in those units. These are followed by the alphabetically arranged biographies, which are brief and follow a standard format: name; a brief history of his military ranks and service; birth date and place; death date, place, and cause of death; other offices held or honors bestowed; miscellaneous (generally where they resided); place of burial; and a list of references of sources used for that individual. Pictures are included for a great many. The volume concludes with an extensive bibliography and name index.

For what this book contains, this reviewer finds no fault. The inclusion of narrative sections, however, would make this a better, and from a reader's standpoint, a more interesting volume. This is particularly the case for Kentucky and Tennessee, unique in that those two states were sharply divided between support for the Union and Confederacy and had regiments in both armies. Such is the case for the colonels themselves, many of whom were connected by family and friendship to well-known political and military leaders on the other side. A survey of the biographical entries reveals the gross incompetence of a great many men who were appointed to leadership positions. A discussion of this would be a welcome addition. Hopefully, a sixth volume is planned to provide similar information for colonels in the numerous Union army regiments recruited in the Confederate states. This is an important series and is highly recommended for libraries with Civil War collections.—**Donald E. Collins**

Dictionaries and Encyclopedias

588.   **American Civil War: The Definitive Encyclopedia and Document Collection.** Spencer C. Tucker, ed. Santa Barbara, Calif., ABC-CLIO, 2014. 6v. illus. maps. index. $625.00/set. ISBN 13: 978-1-85109-677-0; 978-1-85109-682-4 (e-book).

This is another in a series of encyclopedias on major wars published by ABC-CLIO and edited by Spencer Tucker, and a fine addition it is. It is rich in features: six volumes of A-Z entries covering both battlefronts and homefronts as well as individual biographies and art and literature; several sidebars examining historical controversies; a volume providing the texts of several hundred documents; numerous photographs and black-and-white maps; an overview essays on the origins, conduct, and legacy of the war; an extensive general bibliography; a chronology; a glossary; an index; and a list of medals, decorations, and military honors. The list of contributors and the entries reflect a comprehensive scope. There are entries on subjects not well covered in more traditional surveys. Although, of necessity, some of the entries are short, they are supplemented by *see also* references and suggestions for further reading. This encyclopedia is not only an excellent reference source for secondary and undergraduate students and the general reader but its many special features make it a useful starting point for advanced researchers. It is highly recommended for public and academic libraries.—**John Howard Oxley**

589.   **Encyclopedia of American Women at War: From the Home Front to the Battlefields.** Lisa Tendrich Frank, ed. Santa Barbara, Calif., ABC-CLIO, 2013. 2v. illus. index. $189.00/set. ISBN 13: 978-1-59884-443-6; 978-1-59884-444-3 (e-book).

The editor of this work, Lisa Tendrich Frank, has compiled in a two volumes, the most informative and thorough treatment of the role American women during wartime. Through a series of synoptic biographies, topical essays, and historical overviews of public laws that increase women's role in military operations during protracted conflicts, the reader is presented with an extraordinary amount of information that debunks many of the popular misconceptions surrounding the role of women in wartime. Stories of the important roles women have played in American wars include Molly Pittcher who served as an artillery specialist during the Revolutionary War and Marguerite Higgins who was a frontline army war correspondent in the European theatres during World War II. The history of the Women's Army Corps or WAC is also given ample explanation and was the leading military organization that gave birth to Public Law 90-130 in 1967. This law was the ground breaking legislation that eliminated many of the inequities for women serving in the Armed Forces. Each article in this encyclopedia is follow by a bibliography for further study of any issues or historical event. A comprehensive bibliography also appends this set along with a Categorical Index highlighting individuals, conflicts and war theatres, court and legal legislation, organizations, and information about the role of various women minorities who served in our nation's wars. This text is highly recommended for both high school and college libraries. Universities offering a Reserve Officer Training Corps Program will also find this work a valuable asset within their collection—**Patrick Hall**

590.   **Encyclopedia of Insurgency and Counterinsurgency: A New Era of Modern Warfare.** Spencer C. Tucker, ed. Santa Barbara, Calif., ABC-CLIO, 2013. 683p. illus. index. $100.00. ISBN 13: 978-1-61069-279-3; 978-1-61069-280-9 (e-book).

Reference sources on terrorism, insurgency, and counterinsurgency are in vogue. However, few publishers do encyclopedias better than ABC–CLIO and no editor is more prolific than Spencer C. Tucker, who has completed references works on most of America's wars. All his products are excellent and this is no exception. The volume is both historical and contemporary and it is global in scale. With this vast scope, it must of necessity be highly selective. Although it includes citations from antiquity and the medieval eras and it spans the globe, its focus is the modern period and it emphasizes the American experience. The alphabetically arranged, individually authored entries are generally from one to three pages and each includes two are three major sources for further reference. Other important features include several valuable maps, a chronology of selected insurgencies through history, a few pictures, an index, a listing of the contributors, and a relatively brief but good bibliography. All the ABC-CLIO encyclopedias are attractive volumes and are worthy acquisitions for libraries that seek such a resource.—**Joe P. Dunn**

591.   **Encyclopedia of U.S. Military Interventions in Latin America.** Alan McPherson, ed. Santa Barbara, Calif., ABC-CLIO, 2013. 2v. illus. index. $189.00/set. ISBN 13: 978-1-59884-259-3; 978-1-59884-260-9 (e-book).

Anyone that knows American history surely can tell of the numerous incidents of American political and military involvement in Latin America. Beginning in 1811 and continuing to the present, Central America, Latin America, and the Caribbean have all played a role in American foreign policy from tariffs and other legislation to outright war. McPherson provides the reader with a compelling and detailed analysis of everything on this topic, including people, places, events, strategies, and adventurers and misadventures. The entries, most written by acknowledged experts, are arranged alphabetically, ranging from a few sentences to several pages, and include associated entries and short list of references. Yet, to make this 2-volume even better, 13 primary documents that range from 1811 to 1965 are included. A solid bibliography and glossary is present as well.

The range of entries include: the Windward Passage, Venezuela, the Sugar Quota, Cuba, Sandinistas, Daniel Ortega, The Monroe Doctrine, and Americo Lugo. A typical entry is Caracas Conference of 1954. It contains several paragraphs over two pages, a black-and-white photograph, a list of associated entries, and a short bibliography.—**Scott R. DiMarco**

592.   **Ethnic and Racial Minorities in the U.S. Military: An Encyclopedia.** Alexander M. Bielakowksi, ed. Santa Barbara, Calif., ABC-CLIO, 2013. 2v. illus. index. $189.00/set. ISBN 13: 978-1-59884-427-6; 978-1-59884-428-3 (e-book).

Racial and ethnic minorities have been a significant part of our nation's military heritage since before the American Revolution and this two-volume set documents much of that rich history. People (e.g., Chappie James), places (e.g., Camp Shelby), and things (e.g., Executive order 9981) are included in well-written essays ranging from two to three pages to longer entries on topics such as Filipino Americans and Puerto Ricans in various wars. The definition of minorities is broad enough to include Civil War Admiral David Farragut (born of a Spanish father) and World War II hero Audie Murphy (born of Irish parents). Another entry details the Civil War Battle of the Crater where nearly 500 African American Union troops were killed and massacred—during the battle and while attempting to escape. Entries on the Tuskegee Airmen and the Navajo Code Breakers document minority troops whose contributions in World War II have been recently memorialized in museums and film. In all the volumes include over 300 entries by more than 100 contributors. Entries include *see also* references and further reading suggestions. An extensive chronology, bibliography, and a detailed index conclude the set. Although a specialized reference work, the set is another solid contribution to ABC-CLIO's ongoing project of historical reference volumes. This work is recommended for academic and larger public libraries.—**Boyd Childress**

593.   **The Iraq War Encyclopedia.** Thomas R. Mockaitis, ed. Santa Barbara, Calif., ABC-CLIO, 2013. 542p. illus. index. $100.00. ISBN 13: 978-0-313-38062-4; 978-0-313-38063-1 (e-book).

With the Middle East once again on the precipice of war, this is a timely comprehensive book on the Iraq War (2003-2011). In over 200 alphabetically arranged entries by in excess of 80 contributors, the typical who, what, where, and when are detailed in readable entries ranging from a page to 3-4 pages. The volume includes brief essays on the causes and consequences of the war, eight maps (a detailed Baghdad map would have been a nice inclusion), an extensive index, bibliography, a useful chronology, and a handful of black-and-whites photographs. The signed entries include *see also* references and suggested readings. Several entries stand out such as those on Blackwater, suicide bombings, and religious aspects of the war so often overlooked for military actions. The entry on Tariq Aziz points out he was the only Christian in a position of power under the Saddam Hussein regime—one of the many interesting facts revealed. Curiously absent is Baghdad Bob (Muhammad Saeed al-Sahhaf), the comical information minister under Hussein. Mockaitis (history, Depaul) is highly qualified to organize and edit this excellent ABC-CLIO reference work.—**Boyd Childress**

594. Wells, Anne Sharp. **Historical Dictionary of World War II: The War Against Germany and Italy.** Lanham, Md., Scarecrow, 2014. 535p. (Historical Dictionaries of War, Revolution, and Civil Unrest). $130.00; $129.99 (e-book). ISBN 13: 978-0-8108-5457-4; 978-0-8108-7944-7 (e-book).

With more than 300 entries, this dictionary is not intended as a comprehensive guide but rather as an introductory work for students with little or no knowledge of the conflict between the "Grand Alliance" of Great Britain, the United States, and the Union of Soviet Socialist Republics and the European Axis, which was led by Germany and Italy and their notorious leaders. Brief battle summaries, biographical sketches, and entries on related topics are included as well as a lengthy introductory essay on the conflict. A chronology of events, a topically arranged bibliography of further readings, and a list of acronyms and abbreviations also are included. The dictionary section of the volume provides cross-referenced entries on the countries and geographical areas involved in the war. Countries that remained neutral as well as wartime alliances, significant civilian and military leaders, and major ground and naval operations are featured. This will be a useful supplemental volume for students and researchers studying World War II and the European theater.—**ARBA Staff Reviewer**

595. West, Nigel. **Historical Dictionary of World War I Intelligence.** Lanham, Md., Scarecrow, 2014. 444p. (Historical Dictionaries of Intelligence and Counterintelligence). $120.00; $119.99 (e-book). ISBN 13: 978-0-8108-8001-6; 978-0-8108-8002-3 (e-book).

West has created a handy one-volume dictionary of intelligence activities during World War I. World War I saw the introduction of many technological advances in the area of military intelligence, including submarines, sea mines, torpedoes armored tanks, and mechanized cavalry, just to name a few. Also influential were the use of train watching, bridge watching air-bone reconnaissance, and radio interception, which all had a profound impact on the war. Most nations today engage in this sort of intelligence gathering activity. This dictionary is number 17 of a publisher's series on Historical Dictionaries of Intelligence and Counterintelligence. The author covers a variety of topics in the dictionary, from large agencies to specific operatives. Also covered are locations, projects, and devices used in World War I intelligence. West includes in the volume a chronology, list of acronyms and abbreviations, a bibliography, and an index. The bibliography is classified into topics (e.g., allies, Central Powers, espionage, naval intelligence) and consists primarily of basic additional readings. The dictionary is well done and will provide a handy and informative addition to reference shelves dealing with World War I.—**Ralph Lee Scott**

Handbooks and Yearbooks

596. **Graphic Modern History: Cold War Conflicts.** New York, Crabtree, 2013. 4v. illus. index. $23.49/vol.; $10.95pa./vol.

597. **Graphic Modern History: World War I.** New York, Crabtree, 2013. 6v. illus. index. $23.49/vol.; $10.95pa./set.

These two new series from Crabtree Publishing take a departure from their standard children's reference format. In the first series they introduce the individual wars of the Cold War in a graphic novel style that will appeal to middle and high school age students. The four volumes in the series include: The Cuban Missile Crisis, The Korean War, The Soviet War in Afghanistan, and the Vietnam War. The second series explores the battles of World War I and includes volumes on: the Western Front, Gallipoli and the Southern Theaters, Lawrence of Arabia and the Middle East and Africa, War at Sea, War in the Air, and war on the Eastern Front.

Each book begins with about six pages of introduction to the war, including the historical factors leading up to the war, an introduction to key leaders and figures, and new tactics used in warfare. The remainder of the title consists of graphic novel type re-enactments of battle scenes that include an up-close look at troops on the ground and in the sky, the government officials at home making decisions, and the attitude of Americans on the home front. This volume will be useful in middle and high school library collections and may be more useful in the circulating collection. This is an interesting way for lovers of graphic novels to find an interest in military history.—**Shannon Graff Hysell**

598. Hillstrom, Kevin. **The Battle of Gettysburg.** Detroit, Omnigraphics, 2013. 229p. illus. index. (Defining Moments). $49.00. ISBN 13: 978-0-7808-1323-6.

This book is an excellent portable archive on the Battle of Gettysburg, and is divided into three main parts. The first section, which covers about 55 percent of the book, is a narrative description of the battle and the events that led up to the battle. The second section contains biographies of between four and five pages each of important persons connected with the battle. The final portion of the book is devoted to primary sources about the battle of Gettysburg. Typical primary sources provided include: a first-hand account of the battle by an English observer, Lincoln's Gettysburg Address, contemporary newspaper accounts, two first hand-accounts of Pickett's charge, and a 2000 address by historian James McPherson (not exactly a primary source on the battle). Appendixes include: a list of important people, places and terms; a chronology; sources for further study; and a bibliography.

The work is written primarily for students of the Civil War who need a one-volume book to carry. The book seems to be aimed at high school and lower division college students who do not have ready access to large libraries with primary sources. It is not clear what the difference is between the "sources for further study" section and the bibliography section. The bibliography section is longer (both sections are two pages in length), while the "sources" section contains fewer entries and is annotated.

Overall, the book is an easy read and when combined with the primary sources the text gives the reader a real feel for the period in which the battle took place. In the front matter of the book the author has provided a handy list of research topics for students to contemplate. There are occasional black-and-white illustrations scattered throughout the volume. The cover is attractive and book is well bound; however, there is an error. The back cover makes reference to materials contained on pages xv-xvi, but the front matter in the book stops at xiv. The 2000 McPherson address, while interesting and important, hardly qualifies as a primary source for the period 1860-1865. The author has also included an essay by Woodrow Wilson on the battle, again not exactly primary source material. When it comes to primary sources this book may actually confuse students as to what primary sources are. This is unfortunate because the book is actually a good place for a young reader to start their research on the battle.—**Ralph Lee Scott**

599. Hillstrom, Kevin. **World War I and the Age of Modern Warfare.** Detroit, Omnigraphics, 2013. 234p. illus. index. (Defining Moments). $49.00. ISBN 13: 978-0-7808-1325-0.

In reviewing several of the volumes in the Defining Moments series, which is written for middle school and high school students, I have found that if I have strong expertise on a particular topic, I tend to be less favorable about the individual book. However, if it is not an area of my particular strength, I tend to find the volume more acceptable. The fact is that the more one knows about a subject, the more critical one is of the difficult effort to summarize complex events to a very novice audience in a few brief pages. World War I is not one of my primary areas of study so I give this volume more latitude.

The series follows a common pattern of narrative, biographies, documents, terms, chronology, sources for further study, bibliography, and index. The latest addition to the series is a brief list of potential research topics, which is not anything more than possible discussion questions touched on in the volume. The writing is appropriate for the target audience and the volumes are attractive and appealing. The pictures are one of the best features. With photographs from most of the adversaries as well as affected populations such as Serbian and Armenian refugees, the author has done a good job of demonstrating that indeed the conflict touched the entire European community.—**Joe P. Dunn**

600.   Mahoney, Kevin A. **Fifteenth Air Force Against the Axis: Combat Missions over Europe During World War II.** Lanham, Md., Scarecrow, 2013. 485p. index. $95.00; $94.95 (e-book). ISBN 13: 978-0-8108-8494-6; 978-0-8108-8495-3 (e-book).

The Strategic Bombing Campaign of World War II played a critical role in defeating the Axis powers. The Fifteenth Air Force played a significant role in that campaign. Twentieth-century military historian, Kevin A Mahoney, gives the reader the *Fifteenth Air Force Against the Axis: Combat Mission over Europe in World War II* by providing a "detailed combat history of the crucial role played by this air force from November 1943 through May 1945. Presented by month in chronological order, Mahoney describes all the major bombing and fighter missions ... it highlights the purpose and importance of the month's operations, and reviews the Luftwaffe's resistance and changes in tactics and important developments in the Fifteenth Air Force's organization."

Each chapter includes: an introduction; the evaluation of the strategic campaign; the purpose and highlights of that month's operations; the Luftwaffe's resistance and changes in tactics; and alterations in the overall makeup of the Fifteenth Air Force's organization. We see the day-by-day, month-by-month, and year-by-year losses to the crews and aircraft, the shifts in targets, and an overview of how the general war was progressing. In addition to the usual notes and table of contents, the sources and bibliography is simply marvelous as are the four appendixes and list of individual targets.

A sample of a typical entry is on page 170: July 6 1944. We learn of attacks in Verona, Italy by fifty-three B-17's with an escort of thirty-six P-51s by parts of two Bomb Groups on railroad marshaling yards. The flak was intense and a smoke screen was present, in addition to being attacked by four German fighters (which they confirmed one shot down), they lost one bomber and one fighter themselves. Details like this extend for several more paragraphs. This work is highly recommended.—**Scott R. DiMarco**

601.   **Nam: The Vietnam War.** Tim Cooke, ed. Mankato, Minn., Black Rabbit Books, 2013. 6v. Illus. index. $213.90/set. ISBN 13: 978-1-78121-042-0.

This six-volume set on the Vietnam War is written with elementary and middle school students in mind. This is a complex topic for children this age and, while the publisher does a good job of relaying information, many of the complexities of the war and its after affects are lost due to the brevity of the text. Still, students will get a better understanding of this war from this set, which uses photographs, eyewitness reports, key moments and themes, and personalities to supplement the text. The volumes conclude with a very brief glossary (which provides no indication in which volume the term is used), a further resources section listing books and Websites, and a brief index. A pronunciation guide would have been a helpful addition to a book such as this.—**Shannon Graff Hysell**

602.   Springer, Paul J. **Military Robots and Drones.** Santa Barbara, Calif., ABC-CLIO, 2013. 297p. index. (Contemporary World Issues). ISBN 13: 978-1-59884-732-1; 978-1-59884-733-8 (e-book).

The history of warfare has been to a large extent a chronicle of the application and employment of new technology to the art of war. This latest contribution in the ABC-Clio Contemporary World Issues reference book series, by Paul Springer of Air University and formerly the U.S. Military Academy, makes a significant contribution as it addresses one element of present military technology. Electronics, robotics, and drones are decisive elements in contemporary conflict and some of the systems raise the same kinds of philosophical and moral issues about their usage that technological advances have often engendered in the past.

The volume's contents include essays on background and history, problems and controversies, and worldwide perspectives. A good chronology, biographical sketches of key figures in the history of this technology, and definitions of the various robots and drones provide a vast amount of information not easily accessible elsewhere. The inclusion of several important documents that deal with policy and procedures and a directory of organizations involved with these technologies are useful. The book concludes with a good annotated bibliography and a glossary.

This is a fine collection on a subject where available sources are scarce. However, the number of libraries with significant demand for this information may also be limited.—**Joe P. Dunn**

603.   **Vietnam War.** By Martin Gitlin. Minneapolis, Minn., ABDO Publishing, 2013. 112p. illus. maps. index. (Essential Library of American Wars Series). $34.22/vol. ISBN 13: 9781-617838-80-4.

604.   **World War I.** By Mary K. Pratt. Minneapolis, Minn., ABDO Publishing, 2013. 112p. illus. maps. index. (Essential Library of American Wars Series). $34.22/vol. ISBN 13: 978-1-617838-81-1.

605.   **World War II.** By Susan E. Hamen. Minneapolis, Minn., ABDO Publishing, 2013. 112p. illus. maps. index. (Essential Library of American Wars Series). $34.22/vol. ISBN 13: 978-1-617838-82-8.

These three volumes on twentieth century wars provide good information for students in the middle grades. The text provides information in enough detail that this age group will be able to understand the reasons behind the war and the United States' role in it. Photographs are scattered throughout the text, many of which are archival in nature and depict real-life scenes from the war front. The volume on the Vietnam War even has a few full-color photographs. Information boxes are provided on most pages to give more in-depth information on topics that students will find interesting. Each volume includes the following back matter: a timeline, a glossary, additional resources, source notes, and a graphic depiction of the scope of the war. These volumes will be a solid addition to most school and public library collections as supplemental materials to more inclusive military history resources.—**ARBA Staff Reviewer**

Army

606.   **The U.S. Army Center of Military History. http://www.history.army.mil/.** [Website]. Free. Date reviewed: 2013.

The Center of Military History, headquartered in Washington, D.C., is responsible for "the appropriate use of History throughout the U.S. Army." The site contains an extensive range of material including changing exhibits. Some topics have been "Native Americans in the U.S. Army," "Remembering Desert Shield/Desert Storm 10 Years Later," and "Remembering the Korean War." There is helpful information for researching service records and unit histories. There is a chronologically arranged list of Medal of Honor recipients from all services with the history of the medal and a list of Black World War II recipients. Of recent interest is a bibliography on Afghanistan with primary and secondary resources including online publications and Websites as well as print materials. The site is extensive and anyone researching U.S. military history should visit it.

Another U.S. Army history site is maintained at the U.S. Army Military History Institute at Carlisle Barracks, Pennsylvania. The Website provides access to the electronic catalog, reference bibliographies, unit history bibliographies, Civil War biographical bibliographies, and more. There are a number of digitized historical materials on the site, but it mainly provides information on the extensive collections available for use on site. The online finding aids are continually being added to. *A Guide to the Study and Use of Military History* by John E. Jessup Jr. and Robert W. Coakley was published by the Center of Military History (1979). This bibliography is based on the extensive holdings of the U.S. Military Institute Library. The first section of the work is a general one on military history and sources. The major portion of the work is part 2, which contains seven bibliographic essays on U.S. military history by period from 1607 to the early 1970s. The remaining two sections are devoted to the U.S. Army. The work is indexed. Anyone researching U.S. military history should not overlook the fine collections at the U.S. Army Military History Institute (available at http://carlisle-www.army.mil/usamhi/).—**Anna H. Perrault**

Navy

607.   Williams, Greg H. **World War II U.S. Navy Vessels in Private Hands.** Jefferson, N.C., McFarland, 2013. 358p. index. $55.00pa. ISBN 13: 978-0-7864-6645-0.

The Second World War saw the U.S. Navy become the largest in world history. The sheer number and variety of ships and boats serving in the war is astounding. In the years following the conflict, many vessels were eventually sold or transferred to individuals or organizations, where they continued to perform yeoman commercial or recreational service for their new owners. The book is first of all arranged alphabetically by naval craft type categories (e.g., LST, YOL), and then alphabetically within those categories by ship name, although some vessels have a very generic designation (e.g., PCE-843). Each individual entry has the official designation, when and where built, building company, where it operated during the war, who owned it after the war, and what was/is the final known status of the vessel. Some entries are very short, while others are much longer, reflecting a varied work career for different owners. This specialized directory is the result of an impressive amount of tedious research in a multitude of administrative records. It is a great time saver for others trying to track down old naval craft. The work includes a bibliography, glossary, and impressive index. Electronic versions of this book are also available in EBSCO e-book and EBLIB formats. Williams, a Navy veteran, is an authority on researching naval topics, and had previously compiled other reference works, such as *World War II Naval and Maritime Claims against the United States: Cases in the Federal Court of Claims, 1937-1948* (see ARBA 2007, entry 569). He gratefully acknowledges all of the courteous help that he received from numerous archives, government agencies, and online Ask A Librarian services around the country. This unique compilation is suitable for academic, large public, and special collections.—**Daniel K. Blewett**

Weapons and Warfare

608.   DeVries, Kelly, and Robert Douglas Smith. **Medieval Military Technology.** 2d ed. Toronto, University of Toronto Press, 2012. 356p. illus. index. $34.95. ISBN 13: 978-1-4426-0497-1.

This historical reference title substantially updates the previous edition, and is written by a pair of recognized experts in this field. The clearly written text not only covers the range of medieval military technologies (both land and sea) but also provides a balanced presentation of the many controversies in this area. Particular strengths are the careful explanations of how Roman technology and systems formed the basis of military technology in the early Middle Ages, along with exact descriptions of changes occurring throughout the era. The monochrome illustrations mix period reproductions and modern images, effectively complementing the text. An extensive bibliography provides a wealth of additional research resources, while finding aids are limited to the table of contents and a detailed index.

Apart from a couple of minor typographical errors ("inconsisten" for "inconsistent" on p. 126 and "flounder" for "founder" on p. 300), the book appears free from error. Prospective purchasers in the United States should note, however, that the authors list all measurements in metric values.

The book is well-bound and clearly printed on high-quality paper. The subject's treatment makes it a good candidate for collections serving both general and military history interests.—**John Howard Oxley**

609.   Johnson, E. R. **American Military Transport Aircraft Since 1925.** Jefferson, N.C., McFarland, 2013. 480p. illus. index. $45.00pa. ISBN 13: 978-0-7864-6269-8; 978-1-4766-0155-7 (e-book).

Far too often when we think about airpower our minds go to the vision of the dogfighting fighter of the bomber making a critical strike. How often do we remember that without the workhorse transportation aircraft providing the necessary logistics or personnel neither the fighter nor the bomber would be airborne? In fact, the need for transport aircraft to support military operations, anywhere in the world, at any time is crucial to the projecting of U.S. foreign policy.

Johnson and Jones have written a nice companion piece entitled *American Military Transportation Aircraft Since 1925.* By breaking down the book chronologically (1925-1962 – Series I; 1962-Present – Series II; and 1962-Present – Utility and Miscellaneous Transport) the reader is given a nice guided tour of the subject that crosses individual branches of military service. A helpful appendix (Military Transportation Aircraft and Unit Designations, Nomenclature and Abbreviations) is present, as is a solid glossary and bibliography. Yet, the best aspect of this book is the illustrations and pictures. They are ideal in understanding each type of aircraft.

A typical entry is Cessna C/UC-78 (JRC)-1942 that is on pages 133-135. A great illustration accompanies the technical specifications and a 1/3 page narration. Compact, but informative in nature, this entry will start your research or give you all the information one needs.—**Scott R. DiMarco**

13 Political Science

General Works

Catalogs and Collections

610. **CQ Global Researcher. http://www.cqpress.com/.** [Website]. Washington, D.C., CQ Press, 2013. Price negotiated by site. Date reviewed: 2013.

Students looking for international perspectives on global events will find this database a very useful research tool. It contains reports that are written by scholars and experts. Students can search for entire articles, or narrow down the search to specific report sections. Students can also browse the reports by topic, date, or country. Each article includes a pros/cons section, chronology, and Voices from Abroad (a section with international quotes that relate to the topic), all of which are accessible via a sidebar of shortcuts. Topics range from Conflicts in Africa, to the Elderly, to Water Pollution. The interface is well organized with sidebars and the current report on the home page, and utilizing the database is intuitive. How to cite information is also included. The ease of use, coupled with the large amount of information available make this a valuable addition to the reference collections of high school and undergraduate libraries.—**Allison L. Bernstein**

611. **PAIS International. http://www.proquest.com/en-US/catalogs/databases/detail/pais-set-c. shtml.** [Website]. Bethesda, Md., ProQuest. Price negotiated by site. Date reviewed: 2013.

With files going back to almost 1900, PAIS International is a respected index that provides access to citations to over 3,600 journals dealing with public and private sector policies. It also indexes gray literature government and NGO reports that are invaluable for researchers. It has little in Chinese, Japanese, and Korean languages, but contains data on East Asia. For example, a simple keyword search "Japan" netted citations to nearly 19,000 scholarly articles and 8,000 books.—**Noriko Asato**

612. **Worldwide Political Science Abstracts. http://www.proquest.com/en-US/catalogs/databases/ detail/polsci-set-c.shtml.** [Website]. Ann Arbor, Mich., ProQuest. Price negotiated by site. Date reviewed: 2013.

This ProQuest database abstracts and indexes over 1,500 international journals on political science, international relations, and international law from 1975 to the present. Since 2000, development of the serials list has focused on expanding international coverage. As of November 2005 approximately 1,500-plus titles are being monitored for coverage; of these, 67 percent are published outside the United States. The references cited in the bibliography of the source article have been included for citations to core journals in political science, added to the database since 2001, and for all journals added since 2004. Each individual reference may also have links to an abstract and/or to other papers that cite that reference; these references are linked both within Worldwide Political Science Abstracts and across other social science databases available on Illumina. Subject coverage includes comparative politics, economic policy, military policy, politics and law, public administration, and security and defense.—**Noriko Asato**

Dictionaries and Encyclopedias

613.   **The Wiley-Blackwell Encyclopedia of Social & Political Movements.** David A. Snow, Donatella Della Porta, Bert Klandermans, and Doug McAdam, eds. Hoboken, N.J., Wiley-Blackwell, 2013. 3v. index. $595.00/set. ISBN 13: 978-1-4051-9773-1.

These volumes provide expanded entries on the social movements that have shaped the history of the world over the last three centuries. The essays cover specific social movements, individuals associated with social movements, and the methodologies and theories used in the study of social movements. As a sampling of what the student will find in this encyclopedia, topics range from Otpor (the Serbian social movement that ousted Milosevic from power in 2000), the Zapatistas in Mexico, to the French Revolution, agrarian movements in the United States, Solidarity, animal rights, the slow food movement, Saul Alinsky, Occupy Wall Street, fuzzy-set qualitative comparative analysis, contagion theory, and much more. Each entry concludes with suggestions for further reading. Features include a lexicon that helps the reader find appropriate entries under broad categories such as class, identity, race and ethnicity, politics, research methods, and more. There is also a timeline listing influential events and figures in the study of social movements from 1715 to the present.—**Adrienne Antink**

Handbooks and Yearbooks

614.   **The Oxford Companion to Comparative Politics.** Joel Krieger, ed. New York, Oxford University Press, 2013. 2v. index. $295.00/set. ISBN 13: 978-0-19-973859-9; 978-0-19-973859-5 (e-book).

Originally published in 2001, *The Oxford Companion to Comparative Politics* has been updated and expanded, and the publisher claims that over 40 percent of the 350 articles in the present edition are new, with the remaining being revised. Entries are arranged into seven categories: countries and regions, biographies, interpretive essays, concepts, government and institutions, historical events, and political, economic, and social issues. Entries typically range from a paragraph in length to full 4,000-word essays. Included are great thinkers of politics, political events, contemporary leaders, and social issues. All entries include cross-references to relevant entries, bibliographies, and a byline of the contributor. The work concludes with useful appendixes and an index. *The Oxford Companion to Comparative Politics* remains a valuable compendium for political inquiry and reference. While useful alone, it would be even more helpful used in conjunction with other scholarly resources, such as *The Oxford Handbook of Comparative Politics* (Oxford University Press, 2007). [R: Choice, June 13, p. 1813]—**Shannon Graff Hysell**

615.   **What is a Democracy?** New York, Crabtree, 2013. 48p. illus. index. (Forms of Government). $22.95/vol.; $9.95pa./set. ISBN 13: 978-0-7787-5316-2.

616.   **What is a Dictatorship?** New York, Crabtree, 2013. 48p. illus. index. (Forms of Government). $22.95/vol.; $9.95pa./set. ISBN 13: 978-0-7787-5317-9.

617.   **What is a Monarchy?** New York, Crabtree, 2013. 48p. illus. index. (Forms of Government). $22.95/vol.; $9.95pa./vol. ISBN 13: 978-0-7787-5318-6.

618.   **What is a Theocracy?** New York, Crabtree, 2013. 48p. illus. index. (Forms of Government). $22.95/vol.; $9.95pa./vol. ISBN 13: 978-0-7787-5319-3.

619.   **What is an Oligarchy?** New York, Crabtree, 2013. 48p. illus. index. (Forms of Government). $22.95/vol.; $9.95pa./vol. ISBN 13: 978-0-7787-5320-9.

This new five-volume series from Crabtree Publishing, a company known for their multivolume, nonfiction series designed specifically for children and middle school students, provides an introduction to the major forms of government found throughout the world. The work focuses the history of how the government is formed, how they function, what right and responsibilities the citizens have, and the effects that the government has on the culture and economic life of the people. The volumes in the series discuss democracy, theocracy, oligarchy, monarchy, and dictatorship. The books are written at a level appropriate for middle school and even high school students. Within each volume are plenty of color photographs, illustrations, and maps as well as sidebars full of additional information. Each volume ends with a list of resources, a glossary, and a very short index, all of which can be used to teach young students basic researching skills. This series is recommended for middle school and high school libraries and young adult collections in public libraries.—**Shannon Graff Hysell**

Politics and Government

United States

Biography

620.   **The Almanac of the Unelected 2013: Staff of the U.S. Congress.** 24th ed. Suzanne Struglinski and Samantha Young, eds. Lanham, Md., Bernan Press, 2013. 690p. illus. index. $299.00; $289.99 (e-book). ISBN 13: 978-1-59888-631-3; 978-1-59888-632-0 (e-book).

Now in its 24th edition, *The Almanac of the Unelected* is a unique reference directory that profiles more than 600 directors, counsel members, and other staff who support the administrative work and policy-making efforts of the 112th Congress. Profiles are divided into four parts: committee staff of the House of Representatives, committee staff of the Senate, staff working for select and special committees, and staff on joint Congressional committees. Each set of committee profiles begins with a brief essay reviewing the current political activities and insider bargaining that have taken place on the committee. This helps the reader understand how the staff was appointed to the positions that they are in. The profiles contain a variety of information, with most accompanied by a photograph. Each individual's professional history and experience is described in detail, including prior work, a list of specific areas of expertise, educational background, and their current telephone number and e-mail address. The profiles also contain a description of the specific legislative contributions an individual has made in support of the mission of a particular committee. This aspect of the profiles is particularly helpful in identifying and comparing staff responsibilities throughout Congress. For example, both houses of Congress have a Committee on Veteran Affairs. Easy comparisons and contrasts can be made by examining the roles and responsibilities of subcommittee directors in the House and the less structured administrative organization of the Senate's committee. For scholars, the *Almanac* helps to illuminate these hidden areas of analysis. A retrospective online version of this resource would create a powerful research tool for scholars of all types. End matter includes a name index. The *Almanac* remains a useful tool for researchers, students, and anyone interested in understanding the support personnel of Congress. At $299.00, the hardcover edition may be considered a luxury for most libraries; however, those that can make do with the lower-priced paperback edition would do well to purchase this title.—**Robert V. Labaree**

621.   **American Presidents: Life Portraits. http://www.americanpresidents.org.** [Website]. Free. Date reviewed: 2013.

This site contains a complete video archive of all American Presidents: Life Portraits programming. It also provides the following resources: Biographical Facts, Key Evens of each presidency, Presidential Places, and Reference Materials. The award-winning series provides an in-depth look at each of the presidents, their lives, families, and administrations. There is a useful Teachers section that includes curriculum links for lesson plans and related activities that will engage students. The series was included among the 59th Annual Peabody Award winners in 2000.—**ARBA Staff Reviewer**

622.   McKenney, Janice E. **Women of the Constitution: Wives of the Signers.** Lanham, Md., Scarecrow, 2013. 241p. illus. index. $50.00; $49.99 (e-book). ISBN 13: 978-0-8108-8498-4; 978-0-8108-8499-1 (e-book).

This title, a project of the District of Columbia Daughters of the American Revolution, provides concise details on the wives of the signers of the U.S. Constitution. Research for the title was done primarily from primary sources and entries include such information as place of birth and death, details of their marriage and children, education, and family. Many of the entries are accompanied by a photograph or illustration and all include a useful bibliography. The work includes an appendix that lists historic homes of the women mentioned in the book. Useful for academic and high school libraries, this title will be of interested to anyone researching Colonial American history as well as historical women's studies. While the information is too concise for the serious researcher it will serve well as a jumping-off point to more detailed research. [R: LJ, 1 June 13, p. 132]—**ARBA Staff Reviewer**

623.   Nowlan, Robert. **The American Presidents, Washington to Tyler: What They Did, What They Said, What Was Said About Them, with Full Source Notes.** Jefferson, N.C., McFarland, 2013. 450p. illus. index. $55.00pa. ISBN 13: 978-07864-6336-8; 978-0-7864-6336-7 (e-book).

This book provides a wide range of detailed information on the first 10 presidents of the United States, including little-known information that may be difficult to find in standard reference sources. Information provided includes: a detailed description of their physical appearance, family backgrounds, their personal likes and dislikes, and the rationale behind many of their policies. One of the interesting aspects of this resource is that it forces the reader to look at the policies of the president in the context of the time in which they lived and according to the political and social climate of the United States at the time. For instance, while many people today are appalled at our country's history of slavery and the fact that many of our presidents were slave owners, it was the standard of the time and for many years within this country it was very difficult for the African American to live, work, and survive outside of slavery. It also takes a hard look at the view of Native American people during America's early years and the incongruence of both cultures trying to share the same land. These realities strongly affected the policies of such early presidents as Thomas Jefferson, William Henry Harrison, and Andrew Jackson. This will be an interesting and valuable read for anyone interested in the early presidents of the United States. [R: Choice, June 13, p. 1812]—**Shannon Graff Hysell**

624.   Rubel, David. **Encyclopedia of Presidents and Their Times.** rev. ed. Danbury, Conn., Scholastic Library Publishing, 2013. 256p. illus. index. $24.99. ISBN 13: 978-0-545-49985-9.

The *Encyclopedia of Presidents and Their Times* is another quality Scholastic publication. The texts are well written at a middle school level by notable authors in both children's and adult literature. In addition to the main narrative, there are randomly placed boxes throughout the text, which provide timelines, commentary on world events, and trivia concerning the president in question. The main text ends with presidential facts, which summarize the milestones of the president's life with an accompanying list of facts on the First Lady. This is followed by a timeline of the president's life, a glossary, suggestions for further reading, the addresses of related visitors centers around the United States, a list of online sites, a table of all of the presidents through President Obama, and a subject index. Each volume is copiously illustrated with both black-and-white and color illustrations. However, while the content is commendable, these illustrations, combined with a relatively large font and a great deal of white space around the text, give the series the look of children's books. This reviewer would recommend this title as a solid addition to American history collections in elementary and middle school libraries. [R: SLJ, June 13, p. 69]—**Philip G. Swan**

625.   **The United States Presidents. http://www.abdodigital.com/.** [Website]. Edina, Minn., Abdo Digital. Price negotiated by site. Date reviewed: 2013.

The United States Presidents database includes everything one needs to know about the presidency. Portraits of each president provide an access point to the information. "Fast Facts," a timeline, and a "Did You Know?" section cover childhood, marriage, political careers, elections, and important events during the presidency. Unfamiliar words are highlighted and are hyperlinked to a glossary. For those who wonder about the line of succession to the presidency, it is included all the way down to the eighteenth place—Secretary of Homeland Security. A video with President Obama discusses the letters he receives. Games, on topics such as presidential hobbies and which president is on which monetary denomination, will enhance learning and will be fascinating to young researchers. This site is recommended for school research as well as for independent interest.—**Ellen Spring**

626.   Vile, John R. **The Men Who Made the Constitution: Lives of the Delegates to the Constitutional Convention.** Lanham, Md., Scarecrow, 2013. 447p. index. $60.00. ISBN 13: 978-0-8108-8864-7.

Nothing should be more politically precious to us than our own Constitution. And yet nothing is less well known than this document that undergirds the very existence of these Untied States. This is a puzzling paradox, both about us as Americans, and about our educational system. Perhaps this is what Franklin meant when he responded to Mrs. Powel [sic] of Philadelphia that we have a republic "if we can keep it."

One way to remedy this gross deficiency would be to make required reading this volume of John Vile for all citizens, new and old. Not only would it provide valuable insights about the men—they were all men—who made the Constitution, but it also would help us understand that political disagreement was the midwife who delivered our Republic.

As a kind of companion volume to his *The Constitutional Convention 1787: A Comprehensive Encyclopedia of American's Founding* (see ARBA 2006, entry 446), Vile regales us with more of his encyclopedic knowledge and lucubration in this volume about the delegates who debated our founding and signed, or refused to sign, the final draft. The arrangement is simple. Following a 20-page informative introduction about the conditions that provided the setting for this famous historical moment, the delegates are listed alphabetically. The entries are uniform as to content but the length varies with respect to the individual's importance at the debate. Thus, while most entries are 3-5 pages in length, Hamilton's runs 10 pages, Gerry's (of Massachusetts) runs 15. Gerry, by the way, refused to not sign (one of three) although he had already signed both the Declaration and the Articles. The content of each entry is also uniform: biographical sketch, life in congress, life after the convention, and a brief "further reading" bibliography.

The introduction alone is worth reading, but the entries, too, are most entertaining and illuminating. Brief excursions in this tome will reward readers with not only valuable information about our country's founding document, but also a better grasp about how debate was once really a contact sport.—**Mark Y. Herring**

Catalogs and Collections

627.   **History and Politics Out Loud (HPOL). http://www.hpol.org/.** [Website]. Free. Date reviewed: 2013.

This searchable multimedia database documents and delivers authoritative audio relevant to U.S. history and politics. This project, supported by a major grant from the National Endowment for the

Humanities Teaching with Technology Program, in collaboration with Michigan State University and the National Gallery of the Spoken Word, has additional Website support from Northwestern University Library, School of Communication; Office of the Provost, Weinberg College of Arts and Sciences; and the Department of Political Science. This archive includes audio files dating back to the 1930s. Students who are preparing a U.S. history report may wish to add the actual voice(s) of persons in their reports.—**William O. Scheerer**

Dictionaries and Encyclopedias

628.   **Encyclopedia of the U.S. Presidency: A Historical Reference.** Nancy Beck Young, ed. New York, Facts on File, 2013. 6v. illus. maps. index. $550.00/set. ISBN 13: 978-0-8160-6744-2; 978-1-4381-4140-4 (e-book).

The publisher's press release for the *Encyclopedia of the U.S. Presidency: A Historical Reference* asserts that "[n]o subject in American history has wider universal appeal than the presidency" and that may very well be true. The president and his administration are at the center of the decisions that create domestic and foreign policy and formulate the country's actions (and reactions) related to major events that occur during a president's term in office. The presidency is a tangible, even personal, entry point into understanding the essential issues and themes in our country's history. This six-volume set is a massive undertaking, both deep and broad, and attempts to describe each president in the context of his time by providing articles on every significant law, action, incident, and event—political and societal—occurring in that era. The first volume is devoted to 19 Thematic Articles on a variety of critical topics that illustrate both change and continuity in the office of the president including origins of the presidency, presidential powers, the election process, political parties, the presidency and the three branches of government, policies of race, first ladies and women's history, and the presidency and popular culture. The thematic essays, written by academic experts, are in-depth and thorough and often reveal unique information about which the reader may not have been previously aware. Volumes 2 through 6 contain the presidential chapters. Each of these chapters features biographies of the president, the first lady, and vice president; an article about the presidential election and campaign for each term served, with an electoral vote map and election statistics by state and party; a discussion of the president's administration, his cabinet, Supreme Court appointments, and congressional leaders; a social history essay on a key event or personal aspect of that presidency; a series of essays on the major events and issues of the time, arranged alphabetically; a lengthy bibliography of further reading; and documents of note from the president, such as personal letters, proclamations, and speeches. To assist the reader in navigating through this detailed, multi-volume reference work, each volume begins with three tables of contents: the overall Contents in that volume (in volume 1 this includes contents for each of the six volumes), Major Events and Issues, and Documents. At the end of volume 6 are an extensive master bibliography and a cumulative index. There are many illustrations spread throughout the six volumes: tables, maps, portraits, document reproductions, and more. Unfortunately, the illustrations are not indexed separately, but the cumulative index does denote illustrations using italics so that those may be located. This comprehensive historical reference will be useful for students, researchers, and the general public and is highly recommended for high school, college, and public libraries.—**Polly D. Boruff-Jones**

629.   Kaufman, Diane, and Scott Kaufman. **Historical Dictionary of the Carter Era.** Lanham, Md., Scarecrow, 2013. 301p. (Historical Dictionaries of U.S. Politics and Political Eras). $95.00; $94.99 (e-book). ISBN 13: 978-0-8108-7822-8; 978-0-8108-7968-3 (e-book).

American Presidents are a never-ending source of fascination and research. They set the tone for the country and the world during their tenures and American history are often discussed around presidential terms. In the newest addition to their Historical Dictionaries of U.S. Politics and Political Eras series, Scarecrow Press has tackled the four years of Jimmy Carter's presidency.

Similar to their other Historical Dictionaries, this one aims to provide short entries on more subjects rather than treating any single idea or item in depth. But the coverage of their entries is broad, reaching from events that occurred during his presidency (e.g., Love Canal) to the people central to it (e.g., Ayatollah Khomeini, Tip O'Neill) to more broad entries on issues (e.g., Abortion, Environment). But the short alphabetic entries are only about half of the book. The rest is taken up by very valuable bibliography of data and primary source material. A well-organized introductory essay, a chronology of his presidency, a list of all presidential vetoes, all State of the Union addresses, approval ratings for each month he was in office, and a very thorough bibliography all make this dictionary more valuable than it would be otherwise. Libraries supporting high school and undergraduate students who research American history and politics would be well served adding this to their collection if they are looking to provide basic context for the Carter presidency.—**Rosalind Tedford**

630.   **MyGovernment. http://www.gale.cengage.com/.** [Website]. Stamford, Conn., Gale/Cengage Learning. Price negotiated by site. Date reviewed: 2013.

MyGovernment provides users with up-to-date information about local, state, and federal representatives. Users can research issues and platforms of elected officials. Information on how to contract a local legislator or for research can be found in one, easy-to-use database. Users can locate information by using one of three tabs: Who (searching by representative name); Where (find out who the representatives are); and What (who sits on a particular committee or deals with specific issues). Government teachers will like the Tips and Resources box as it gives basic information about the government, how laws are made in Congress, how to become a U.S. citizen, voter information, as well as other useful links and Websites.—**Karen Alexander**

631.   O'Dea, Suzanne. **From Suffrage to the Senate: Americas Political Women. An Encyclopedia of Leaders, Causes & Issues.** 3d ed. Millerton, N.Y., Grey House Publishing, 2013. 2v. illus. index. $225.00/set. ISBN 13: 978-1-61925-101-9; 978-1-61925-104-5 (e-book).

This 3d edition of *From Suffrage to the Senate: American Political Women: An Encyclopedia of Leaders, Causes & Issues* was planned to capture the results of the 2012 elections, which resulted in the highest number of freshmen congresswomen ever in United States history. The content includes not only biographical information about women serving in the house and senate, but also material about female judges in the federal court of appeals, women in presidential cabinets, women in the military, and many other significant women (both contemporary and historical), plus essays about laws, court cases, and organizations that influenced, established, or altered American women's relationships within their families, communities, and political structures. Selection criteria for inclusion in this title are women who have served or are serving as governors, mayors of cities with more than one million people, women in the U.S. House of Representatives and the U.S. Senate, presidential cabinet members, and U.S. Supreme Court justices. Also included are the female leaders of national organizations with a political agenda to influence policies affecting women, women in the national media who focus on national politics, women in leadership positions in political campaigns, and other women who have influenced and shaped national policies and changes in societal norms through their scholarship and activism.

This reviewer is always pleasantly surprised to find a reference resource that contains new information or little known facts on a subject that may be covered in a variety of other sources. This two-volume set is one of those reference resources. Did you know, for example, that when Luci Baines Johnson, daughter of President Lyndon Johnson, applied for readmission to Georgetown University in 1966 (after she was married), she was denied because married female students were not accepted? The 3d edition of *From Suffrage to the Senate* contains 937 entries: 636 biographies, 89 court cases, 42 pieces of legislation, 122 organizations, and 48 social issues. Each volume begins with an alphabetic list of entries with a preface and introduction in volume 1 and appendixes (topical and statistical), a chronology, a lengthy bibliography to assist with further research, and a complete index in volume 2. The essay entries conclude with cross-references to related entries and source references for that specific essay. This set is highly recommended for public libraries, high school libraries and media centers, and undergraduate college and university libraries. [R: LJ, 15 June 13, p. 112]—**Polly D. Boruff-Jones**

Directories

632. **Congressional Yellow Book: Who's Who in Congress, Including Committees and Key Staff. Winter 2013 ed.** New York, Leadership Directories, 2013. 1500p. illus. index. $595.00pa. (annual subscription); $566.00pa. (automatic renewal). ISSN 0191-1422.

Herein is everything readers always wanted to know about Congress, but just could not bring themselves to ask. The section, "Action on the Hill" outlines all sorts of new information. It highlights changes that have occurred since the previous edition. These changes range from new members elected in special elections to deaths of congresspersons, changes in committees, resignations, and the upcoming schedule.

As for the bulk of the *Yellow Book*, after its plethora of useful numbers, users will find each entry with the following information: member's name, contact information, photograph, key aides, committee assignments, organizations and state and district offices, and more. Users will find information on committee and subcommittee listings, Congressional leadership offices, information on each listee's responsibilities, district maps and state delegations with counties, and expanded biographical and education information Subject, staff, and organization indexes allow access in other ways beyond the obvious. It is hard to imagine a more comprehensive guide to those who lead us by representation. Surely, this government is a government by the people, and such books as this one helpfully remind us of this central, enduring, and, we hope, eternal truth.—**Mark Y. Herring**

633. **Federal Regional Yellow Book: Who's Who in the Federal Government's Departments, Agencies, Diplomatic Missions . . . Winter 2013 ed.** New York, Leadership Directories, 2013. 1270p. index. $445.00pa. (annual subscription); $423.00pa. (automatic renewal). ISSN 1061-3153.

634. **Federal Yellow Book: Who's Who in Federal Departments and Agencies. Winter 2013 ed.** New York, Leadership Directories, 2013. 1415p. index. $595.00pa. (annual subscription); $566.00pa. (automatic renewal). ISSN 0145-6202.

The *Federal Regional Yellow Book* helps one find who is working in what position in federal offices outside of the nation's capital. The main government directories seem to focus mostly on the headquarters in Washington, D.C. Not every library wants to have copies of all of the individual department directories, so this series is a good source to turn to; it is certainly updated more frequently than the government publications, which suffer from staff and funding limitations. The book starts out with a regional review of personnel changes, nominations, and senate confirmations that have taken place since the previous edition. A user's guide and a thoughtful section of helpful maps showing the administrative subdivisions as established by the various government bureaucracies follows. Then comes the real meat of the book: listings for the departments of the executive branch and the multitude of independent agencies. There are sections for two congressional support agencies that have outlying branch offices: the General Accounting Office (GAO) and the Government Printing Office (GPO). This is followed by over 100 pages listing the personnel at some 170 U.S. Embassies and Foreign Service Posts. There is no section for the federal courts system; the company wants users to use their *Judicial Yellow Book* instead. The listings on all of these pages have the address, telephone and fax numbers, and Website addresses of the offices, the official titles and the names of the 40,000-plus individuals who have that responsibility (with their telephone numbers and e-mail addresses). The printing is clear and bold typeface is used for individual names. There are three separate indexes for geographic locations, names, and organizations.

Listed in this updated edition of the *Federal Yellow Book* are the names and addresses of 45,000 individuals in the executive branch of the federal government. Coverage of this volume extends to federal departments, their subdivisions, and independent agencies. The updated included at the beginning of the volume reflect new appointees to head agencies, nominations requiring senate confirmation, and presidential appointments. Following the updates are the three main sections: "Executive Office of the President and Office of the Vice President," "The Departments," and "Independent Agencies." Within these three sections, the listings begin with the name of the department or agency, its address, and a photograph, along with biographical information of the department or agency head. Offices are listed according to hierarchy and include the mailing address, fax number, and Web address. As with previous editions, this volume contains many access points for its readers. In addition to the main table of contents, a table of contents is supplied before each department or agency whose listing spans more than four pages. Equally important are the useful subject, organization, and name indexes at the end of the volume that also assist the reader in locating people and agencies.

This is a lot of information packed into these volumes. Readers desiring the latest information can check out the company's Website (http://www.leadershipdirectories.com/) for free highlights of the daily changes to the directory database. One may question the need for this kind of printed publication in this age of Web-based directories and telephone listings, but sometimes it is actually more frustrating and time-consuming to try to find the correct office and telephone number using the computer than by looking something up in a printed directory. These serial publications are expensive, but it does take a lot of work to produce them. These directories are suitable for the reference collections of academic and large public libraries that get a lot of these kinds of requests.—**Daniel K. Blewett**

635.   **Foreign Representatives in the U.S. Yellow Book: Who's Who in the U.S. Offices of Foreign Corporations, Foreign Nations, the Foreign Press, Winter 2013 ed.** New York, Leadership Directories, 2012. 775p. index. $445.00pa. (annual subscription); $423.00pa. (automatic renewal). ISSN 1089-5833.

636.   **Government Affairs Yellow Book: Who's Who in Government Affairs. Winter 2013 ed.** New York, Leadership Directories, 2013. 1510p. index. $445.00pa. (annual subscription); $423.00pa. (automatic renewal). ISSN 1078-9812.

As part of the series of directories produced by Leadership Directories, *Foreign Representatives in the U.S. Yellow Book* provides information on foreign leaders located in the United States— representative of non-U.S. corporations and financial institutions, foreign nations, intergovernmental organizations, and foreign media and law firms. The Winter 2011 edition profiles more than 1,000 foreign corporations and financial institutions, 192 nations, 16 intergovernmental organizations, 173 foreign media, and 29 law firms. Together these listings cover over 19,000 executives managing the U.S. offices of leading foreign companies and organizations. Each entry contains the name of the company or organization, a brief description, communication information, a list of executives, and lists of other related organizations or subsidiaries active in the United States. The directory provides an authoritative way to keep track of government and business transitions (mergers, new heads of state), discover newly appointed ambassadors, and get the contact information for those in charge of such things as tourism, military affairs, press, and legal affairs. To assist finding specific information, this directory contains four indexes: industry (organizations arranged by principal fields of operation), geographic (by U.S. location), name (by all individuals), and organization.

The *Government Affairs Yellow Book* provides contact information for a wide variety of corporations, financial institutions, associations, labor unions, interest groups, and lobbying firms that have dealings with government at the state or federal level. Each entry includes the address, telephone number, and names of key members of the office. Entries focus on varying aspects of the organization, including its annual revenue, assets, budget, and association memberships. Each entry also lists any representation the agency may have in Washington, D.C., or individual state offices, and cites lobbying firms the agency patronizes as outside counsel. Government departments at the federal, state, city, and county levels are also covered in some detail, with the names, e-mail addresses, and fax numbers of key individuals listed and with particular attention paid to the unique structuring of each individual agency. The *Government Affairs Yellow Book* contains four indexes. The subject index lists groups by their field of concentration; the geographical index is arranged by state and, within states, by city. The name index lists every person mentioned in the book. The organization index lists organizations alphabetically by their names. The publisher has made the information in these directories available (along with the other 12 Yellow Book Directories) on the Leadership Library Internet site (http://www.leadershipdirectories.com), which is updated daily.—**Philip G. Swan**

637.   **Municipal Yellow Book: Who's Who in the Leading City and County Governments and Local Authorities. Winter 2013 ed.** New York, Leadership Directories, 2013. 1090p. index. $445.00pa. (annual subscription); $423.00pa. (automatic renewal). ISSN 1054-4062.

638.   **State Yellow Book: Who's Who in the Executive and Legislative Branches of the 50 State Governments. Winter 2013 ed.** New York, Leadership Directories, 2013. 1570p. index. $595.00pa. (annual subscription); $566.00pa. (automatic renewal). ISSN 0899-2207.

The *State Yellow Book* contains listings for senior personnel and organizational contact information and changes in all 50 states, the District of Columbia, American Samoa, Guam, Puerto Rico, and the Virgin Islands from September to November 2012. The executive and legislative branch information and contacts, the state profiles, and the intergovernmental organization material are all useful for researchers and students. A helpful state capitol spotlight provides highlights such as new state legislative members, state government party control, and a listing of those states with term limits. This title gives users access to 7,000 state legislators, helps them find the names of the decision makers in areas such as budgets and purchasing, and provides up-to-date information on the legislative calendar and reelection years for state officials. The subject index alphabetically lists departments, agencies, and offices. The name index contains an alphabetic listing of every name in the *State Yellow Book*.

According to the prefatory matter, the *Municipal Yellow Book* covers more than 38,000 elected and administrative officials in U.S. cities, counties, and local authorities. The organization is consistent throughout, with contact information included for each mayor/county executive. Other city/county offices follow, with names and contact information (address, telephone number, and e-mail address) for each official or administrator. Name, geographical, and organization indexes close the volume.

The Websites prepared and maintained by the state governments, municipalities, and counties themselves are the real competition for these directories. When this reviewer checked her own local state, city, and county sites, they were more up-to-date and in most cases (although not all) provided much more information than the directory does. However, these volumes do offer some advantages: they provide information for all administrations included using a consistent and clear organization and a handy format, and provide a historical record for future researchers.—**Denise A. Garofalo**

639.   **State and Local Government on the Net. http://www.statelocalgov.net/.** [Website]. Free. Date reviewed: 2013.

This site provides convenient access to all state and local government sites by listing the states alphabetically. Frequently updated, this directory of official state, county, and city government Websites also provides a list of topics to choose from plus listings of government grants, with applications. Links are provided to even the smallest counties or state agencies in the nation if they have a Web presence. The directory lists 10,792 Websites, and can be searched by state, topic, or local government name.—**Susan C. Awe**

640.   **The United States Government Internet Directory 2013.** 10th ed. Shana Hertz Hattis, ed. Lanham, Md., Bernan Press, 2013. 553p. index. $72.00pa. ISBN 13: 978-1-59888-628-3.

Edited by Shana Hertz Hattis, the *United States Government Internet Directory* (formerly titled the *e-Government and Web Directory: U.S. Federal Government Online*) is an all-encompassing list of government Internet addresses presented in one volume. Along with a quick guide to primary government Websites, government and social media online, information on what to watch for in 2013-2014, Freedom of Information Act Websites, and organizational charts, users have access to 21 topically arranged chapters: Finding Aids; Agriculture, Fishing, and Forestry; Business and Economics; Culture and Recreation; Defense and Intelligence; Demographics and Sociology; Education; Employment; Energy; Engineering and Technology; Environment and Nature; Government and Politics; Health and Safety; International Relations; Law and Law Enforcement; Legislative Branch; Presidency; Science and Space; Social Welfare; Transportation; and Beyond the Federal Web—Nongovernmental Web Sites. The work concludes with two appendixes listing members of congress and congressional committees, and a master index.

The records on the greater than 1,700 addresses in each volume cover details on the promoters, how to use the addresses, and any published works. Anyone needing knowledge from the government on all subjects will benefit from this convenient government Internet directory.—**Melinda F. Matthews**

641.   **United States Government Policy and Supporting Positions (Plum Book).** Lanham, Md., Bernan Press, 2012. 224p. $38.00pa. ISBN 13: 978-0-16091-519-2.

Commonly known as the "plum book," *United States Government Policy and Supporting Positions* is published every four years just after the presidential election. It provides a listing of more than 9,000 filled and vacant civil service leadership and support positions in the Legislative and Executive branches of the government. Many of these are strictly granted by direct appointment. These positions include agency heads and their immediate subordinates, policy advisors and executives, and even aide positions. Some of the positions listed here provide support to administration programs. This book is known as the "plum book" due to the fact that all positions listed here are known to have a close and oftentimes confidential relationship with the agency head or with other related key officials. This title will have a selective audience due to the fact that very few people will be qualified to hold the positions it details.—**ARBA Staff Reviewer**

642.   **Washington Representatives 2013.** Bethesda, Md., Columbia Books, 2013. 1v. (various paging). index. $269.00pa.; $399.00pa. (Spring and Fall editions); $799.00 (online edition). ISBN 13: 978-1-93893-908-2.

643.   **Lobbyists.info.   https://www.columbiabooks.com/ProductDetail/the-2-0-115/Lobbyists_Product_Suite.** [Website]. Bethesda, Md., Columbia Books. $99.00 (monthly subscription); $1487.00 (practitioner's package). Date reviewed: 2013.

This work is a compilation of Washington representatives of the major national associations, labor unions, governments, and U.S. and foreign companies; registered foreign agents; lobbyists; lawyers; law firms; and special interest groups, together with their clients and areas of legislative and regulatory concern. It is a comprehensive directory on lobbying and government affairs in Washington, D.C., consisting of approximately 18,000 individuals and 12,000 organizations and firms, mostly registered under the Lobbying Disclosure Act and the Foreign Agent Registration Act.

The main body of information is organized into three sections. "The Firms" section is an alphabetic list of the law firms, lobbying, and public relations firms. A firm that is registered to lobby under the Lobby Disclosure Act or the Foreign Agents Registration Act has a LDA and/or FARA notation. The following information for each firm is provided: address, telephone numbers, registered notation (LDA and/or FARA), URL, e-mail, Political Action Committee (PAC), DC-area employees representing listed clients, and clients. "The Clients" section lists alphabetically the companies, associations, interest groups, and government entities. It provides for each client, whenever possible, address, telephone numbers, registered notation, URL, e-mail, and legislative issues in three-letter codes, Political Action Committee, in-house DC-area employees, and outside counsel/consultants. "The People" section gives in alphabetic order all the lobbyists who work for the firms and organizations listed in the preceding two sections. It provides for each person address, telephone numbers, registered notation, e-mail, background, employers, and client represented. There are four indexes: client index by subject/industry, foreign clients index by country, PAC index, and legislative area index.

Washington Representatives is also available online via Lobbyists.info, for speedy access and use. The online version lists more than 28,000 advocacy, policy and government relations professionals including registered lobbyists. This work has grown in excellence and is highly recommended.—**Tze-chung Li**

Handbooks and Yearbooks

644.   Barone, Michael, and Chuck McCutcheon. **The Almanac of American Politics, 2014.** Chicago, University of Chicago Press, 2013. 1883p. index. $90.00pa. ISBN 13: 978-0-226-10544-4.

For decades, *National Journal's Almanac of American Politics* has been a standard on the shelves of academic and public libraries. The subtitle perhaps provides the best description of what the Almanac contains—*The Senators, The Representatives and the Governors: Their Records and Election Results, Their States and Districts.* Arranged by state, the Almanac provides not only detailed information about each representative and state chief executive, but also portraits of the states and districts they represent. Group ratings from the ADA, ACLU and more are presented for each person, along with *National Journal* ratings. Key votes and election results are also presented. The strength of the *Almanac* is not in any unique content but rather in great amounts of important information presented all in one place. For researchers looking into particular districts, congress people or governors, this resource provides the perfect starting place for the background and context so important in understanding the larger workings of our governments.—**Rosalind Tedford**

645.   Dubin, Michael J. **United States Gubernatorial Elections: 1912-1931: The Official Results by State and County.** Jefferson, N.C., McFarland, 2013. 295p. index. $125.00pa. ISBN 13: 978-0-7864-7033-4.

This is a comprehensive statistical compendium documenting election results in every gubernatorial race from 1912 to 1931, effectively covering a period of time from the emerging Progressive Era to the early depths of the Great Depression. Based on primary documents and online archives, the election results are presented in two parts. Part 1 of the book contains annual summaries of statewide votes by year for every candidate receiving at least one percent of the total vote. Arranged alphabetically, information is presented clearly and with bold type used to highlight the winner of each election and an asterisk used to indicate incumbents. Part 2 contains detailed county election returns. Basic information, including 1910, 1920, and 1930 population data, are included at the beginning of each state chapter. Also arranged alphabetically by state, the statistics are presented consistently throughout and assist the reader in comparing and contrasting, for example, elections results by party affiliation in the same county over the three decades. Front matter includes a preface about the book, a list of counties whose names have been changed or abolished, and a list of party abbreviations. End matter includes a bibliography and an alphabetic index of each candidate's name and the year or years they ran for office. Bold text is used to indicate candidates who were elected governor. This work is an essential source of gubernatorial data for the time period covered. As such, this reviewer hopes additional volumes are planned documenting gubernatorial elections for other periods of modern American history.—**Robert V. Labaree**

646.   **How Congress Works.** 5th ed. Washington, D.C., CQ Press, 2013. 250p. illus. index. $50.00pa. ISBN 13: 978-1-6087-1911-2.

The 5th edition of CQ Press's *How Congress Works* continues to be an excellent resource for all collections. While the chapters are unsigned and there is no list of contributors the monograph provides a comprehensive introduction into the workings of Congress. The text covers the hierarchy of both the House and Senate and depicts the distinct personalities of each. The monograph also outlines the legislative process, demystifying the procedures for students and the general public. Written in four chapters, this is a dense monograph for such a slim volume that packs a lot of useful information. The chapters conclude with a notes section as well as a selected bibliography section that will point researchers toward other helpful sources. Updates to this 5th edition include the legislative successes and defeats of House Leaders John Boehner, Eric Cantor, Nancy Pelosi, and Steny Hoyer as well as Senate leaders Harry Reid and Mitch McConnell. There is also discussion of the relationship between procedural rules and partisanship. Recent trends among congressional staff are provided, including the emerging trend of Congress using social media as a means to communicate with constituents. Its structure precludes it from being a ready-reference type resource, but its versatility will help high school students needing to understand how laws are made to researchers tracking the history of Congress. Educators, including librarians, will find the reference materials at the end of the book very valuable. This section contains a nice graphic on how a bill becomes a law. The section also includes where to find congressional information online. The text concludes with a functional index. While made with a simple binding and thin paper that may not stand up to heavy use, this work is an excellent reference source for media centers, public, and academic libraries.—**Melissa M. Johnson**

647. Shea, Daniel M., and Brian M. Harward. **Presidential Campaigns.** Santa Barbara, Calif., ABC CLIO, 2013. 303p. index. (Documents Decoded). $79.00. ISBN 13: 978-1-61069-192-5; 978-1-61069-193-2 (e-book).

This work has a unique focus in that it pulls together primary source documents that have played a critical role in the outcome of U.S. presidential elections. While we like to think that the outcome of elections are based off the thorough reflection and contemplation of our citizens, the reality is that the slightest change in press can shift the focus of the nation—either for or against a candidate. Beginning with the election of 1952 and concluding with the election of 2012, primary source documents that have had a role in the outcome of elections are listed chronologically. They include a controversial answer during a publicized debate, or an allegation that arises mid-campaign, or the handling of a critical crisis just in time for the election, among others. Each primary source document is introduced with several paragraphs from the authors describing the circumstances around the event and why it was important. The document is then presented, allowing students to experience firsthand what voters at the time may have been experiencing. Side notes are provided to explain difficult concepts or to provide context to what is being discussed.

This work will provide students with a deeper understanding of why each president was elected and what obstacles they or their opponent had to face during their candidacy. This will be a particularly useful book in high school libraries and undergraduate libraries.—**ARBA Staff Reviewer**

648. **Sourcebook of United States Executive Agencies 2012.** By Executive Office of the President. Lanham, Md., Bernan Press, 2013. 186p. $16.00pa. ISBN 13: 978-0-16091-706-6.

This sourcebook is a guide to the agencies and organizational entities of the executive branch of the U.S. government. Created by the Administrative Conference of the United States (ACUS), this volume was created to provide a comprehensive overview of this organization in an effort to ensure that any problems within the agency will be identified and easily corrected. It also provides insight into the inner workings of this organization for anyone unfamiliar with how it is run. Independent agencies are included alongside governmental agencies so that users can see how all work together. The work describes all of the United States Executive Branch agencies, including their unique characteristics, their place in the organization, and how they influence political control and performance. Any emerging trends are noted and the evolution of agencies within the Branch are explained.—**Shannon Graff Hysell**

649. **The United States Government Manual 2012.** By the National Archives and Records Administration. Lanham, Md., Bernan Press, 2013. 620p. $34.00pa. ISBN 13: 978-0-16090-014-3.

The standard way to obtain information about the federal government is to consult its official handbook, *The United States Government Manual*, which has been published annually since 1935 and which is online. Normally, a new edition is released in late summer. The *Manual* describes the federal government and provides mission statements, descriptive information, organizational charts, and director information for legislative, judicial, and executive agencies and offices, as well as for independent boards, commissions, committees, and quasi-official agencies. Entries cover dates of establishment, key personnel, major sub-agencies, and programs and services. It is a convenient source for locating contacts, including those for public information inquiries and regional offices.—**Shannon Graff Hysell**

650. Vile, John R. **The United States Constitution: Questions and Answers.** 2d ed. Santa Barbara, Calif., ABC-CLIO, 2014. 308p. illus. $68.00. ISBN 13: 978-1-61069-571-8; 978-1-61069-572-5 (e-book).

Intended to help high school students understand the constitutional dimensions of U.S. government, this guide uses a question-and-answer format to present detailed information about the U.S. Constitution (i.e., How many times has the U.S. House of Representatives impeached a U.S. president?). Each chapter covers a specific issue or set of amendments. The final chapter focuses on key dates and events in U.S. constitutional history. The answers given vary in length from a simple sentence to a short paragraph. Following the question-and-answer chapters are eight appendixes that contain the text of the U.S. Constitution, the Declaration of Independence, and the Articles of Confederation; and lists of the speakers of the House, the U.S. presidents, the U.S. Supreme Court justices, and the 50 states with their dates of admission to the union and the number of representatives. The work concludes with a comprehensive subject/name index.

Given its intended audience, this is a somewhat useful supplement to general encyclopedias and specialized guides and handbooks. It is important to note that the questions and answers are not placed in any historical, political, or social context. It will be most useful for students researching specific constitutional topics or engaged in academic competitions regarding the Constitution as well as general readers interested in following and better understanding contemporary political issues.—**Robert V. Labaree**

651. Warshaw, Shirley Anne. **CQ Press Guide to the White House Staff.** Washington, D.C., CQ Press, 2013. 488p. illus. index. $170.00. ISBN 13: 978-1-602-6604-7.

CQ Press has long been the go-to resource for school, public, and academic libraries for information about our government, and their Guide series has proven to be a critical series for many libraries. This newest addition to the series covers an area of the American political system that is often overlooked in other sources of information. While there is a fair amount of research covering the White House from the President's perspective, the research on the staff of the White House from a historical perspective is not as readily available. This volume looks at how the White House staff has evolved historically from a group with limited powers into to a formidable force in shaping policy and national discourse. The entry for each president discusses the role the staff played in various policy roles—domestic, security, foreign and others—and the broader ways the presidents used their staff to advance their agendas. Other important elements include a full list of staffers by president by year, a look at the role of staff in transition planning, their role in policy making and what becomes of these critical public servants after they leave Pennsylvania Avenue. Well organized and indexed, this book is a welcome addition to the series. [R: LJ, 1 June 13, p. 140]—**Rosalind Tedford**

652. **What is the Executive Branch?** New York, Crabtree, 2013. 32p. illus. index. (Your Guide to Government). $19.95/vol.; $8.95pa./vol. ISBN 13: 978-0-7787-0902-2.

653. **What is the Judicial Branch?** New York, Crabtree, 2013. 32p. illus. index. (Your Guide to Government). $19.95/vol.; $8.95pa./vol. ISBN 13: 978-0-7787-0880-3.

654. **What is the Legislative Branch?** New York, Crabtree, 2013. 32p. illus. index. (Your Guide to Government). $19.95/vol.; $8.95pa./vol. ISBN 13: 978-0-7787-0879-7.

655. **How Does the Canadian Government Work?** New York, Crabtree, 2013. 32p. illus. index. (Your Guide to Government). $19.95/vol.; $8.95pa./vol. ISBN 13: 978-0-7787-0903-9.

The four new volumes in this series from Crabtree Publishing, a company known for their multivolume, nonfiction series specifically deigned for children, offer straightforward, easy-to-understand information on the United States government as well as one title on the Canadian government. The titles address the election process, how laws are passed, the levels of government, and the three branches. Each key topic is covered in a two-page spread and discusses such things as the key positions in that area of government, how the systems work together, the process of getting work done, and how our system compares to other countries. The chapters have vivid color photographs and sidebars with highlighted information. Each volume concludes with a glossary, a list of further resources, and a very short index, all of which can be used to teach young students basic researching skills. This series is recommended for elementary school libraries and juvenile collections in public libraries. They provide a good introduction to our government system and how the different branches work together. In future volumes it is hoped that the publisher will expand on the Canadian government.—**Shannon Graff Hysell**

Africa

656. Badru, Pade, and Brigid Maa Sackey. **Islam in Africa South of the Sahara: Essays in Gender Relations and Political Reform.** Lanham, Md., Scarecrow, 2013. 416p. index. $85.00; $84.99 (e-book). ISBN 13: 978-0-8108-8469-4; 978-0-8108-8470-0 (e-book).

Recent times have witnessed greater Islamic political expression and sub-Saharan Africa has also experienced its version of greater political Islamic influence. This book's intent is to focus on gender relations and Sharia law in sub-Saharan Africa through a collection of essays.

The first part consists of four essays that explore the historical spread of Islam in sub-Saharan Africa, including one that traces the multiple views on slavery in Africa. The second part has five essays that focus on the status of women and the role some of the women organizations are playing in politics and religion. The next four essays explore the intersection between gender and Sharia law. The last section has three essays that are case studies of Islamism in Somalia, South Africa, and one on the Nation of Islam in the United States. Each of the 16 essays has extensive notes, and some have a bibliography. However, there is a selected bibliography section at the end as well as a glossary of common Islamic words. The addition of an index is helpful to find areas of interest quickly.

This book covers primarily Central and Western sub-Saharan Africa (although there are a small number of essays that cover other areas). Interestingly Mali, with its recent political clashes, is not a main focus in any of the essays. While each essay is good as a stand-alone piece, seeing how each of the essays fit into a coherent unifying theme is not always apparent. The essays are useful for students interested in case studies of women organizing to reinterpret traditional Islamic customs and renegotiate their space in sub-Saharan society.—**Muhammed Hassanali**

Europe

657.   **The Handbook of Political Change in Eastern Europe.** 3rd ed. Sten Berglund, Joakim Ekman, Deegan-Krause Kevin, and Terje Knutsen, eds. Northhampton, Mass., Edward Elgar, 2013. 840p. index. $325.00. ISBN 13: 978-0-85793-537-3.

Eastern European countries have experienced multiple political, economic, and social changes since the collapse of the Soviet bloc between 1989 and 1991. These countries have developed, with varying degrees of success, political democracies and free-market economies and this handbook represents an opportunity to assess the economic, legal, and political development of these countries during the past two decades.

Initial essays describe the variety of political regimes that have developed in these countries; how historical resilience has shaped and continues shaping the political culture of these countries; and how societal cleavages, including church versus state, urban versus rural, owner versus worker, and global versus local, continue affecting the political culture within these countries.

Examples of counties whose political developments are described in this compilation include Baltic republics such as Estonia and Lithuania; Central European counties including Poland, the Czech Republic, and Hungary; former Yugoslav republics such as Croatia, Bosnia, and Serbia; and the former Soviet republics of Georgia and Ukraine.

Chapters for individual countries include their electoral histories since their independence since post-Soviet independence, featuring the names of political parties and significant leaders, election results and parliamentary representation for individual parties, national electoral system descriptions, national constitutional framework descriptions, analysis of the role played by corruption and ethnic cleavages in domestic political debate, detailed bibliographic references, and relationships between these counties and their geographic neighbors and with transnational institutions like the European Union and North Atlantic Treaty Organization.

This is a very useful resource for students desirous of gaining an overview of recent and contemporary Eastern European political developments. It includes some maps and charts along with detailed bibliographic citations for further reading. A serious weakness with this work, given its high price, is the poor and barely legible typeface and font with which it was printed. This makes it particularly difficult to use for older readers, with this problem being particularly egregious in the notes and references section of individual chapters. This work is recommended for libraries desirous of having comprehensive Eastern European political science and history collections.—**Bert Chapman**

658.   Kimmich, Christoph M. **German Foreign Policy, 1918-1945: A Guide to Current Research and Resources.** 3d ed. Lanham, Md., Scarecrow, 2013. 329p. index. $85.00; $84.99 (e-book). ISBN 13: 978-0-8108-8445-8; 978-0-8108-8446-5 (e-book).

The approaching centennial of World War I will turn public and academic attention to this conflict and World War II as well as the period between these conflagrations. This work will be very beneficial to users desirous of conducting substantive research on German foreign policy over the period from the end of World War I through World War II's conclusion.

It provides detailed overviews and descriptions of the organizations, contributing documentation on German foreign policy including the Foreign Ministry and competing agencies including the Abwehr, Reichstag, and the German Chancellor's office. This same introductory section also includes the names and positions held by major German foreign policymakers during this time period.

A subsequent section covers archives and libraries in Germany and other countries holding significant primary source documentary material for events such as the Nuremberg War crimes. The third section includes an exhaustive bibliography covering primary and secondary source material in English, French, and German. The fourth and final section places acute emphasis on the expanded access to these resources provided by the Internet including online guides to libraries and archives including resources such as the Hathitrust Digital Library and listservs and discussion groups including H-German and H-Diplo.

This work is highly recommended for upper division undergraduates, graduate students, and faculty desirous of conducting primary source and archival research on this time period in German history.—**Bert Chapman**

International Organizations

659.   Dent, David W., and Larman C. Wilson. **Historical Dictionary of Inter-American Organizations.** 2d ed. Lanham, Md., Scarecrow, 2014. 461p. (Historical Dictionaries of International Organizations). $125.00; $119.99 (e-book). ISBN 13: 978-0-8108-7860-0; 978-0-8108-7861-7 (e-book).

This text starts out with a list of abbreviations and acronyms, followed by a chronological listing of inter-American organizations, an introduction that gives general information on the roles of inter-American organizations in the twenty-first century, and then the main portion of the book—a dictionary listing organization, significant leaders, founders, and key members. Inter-American organizations have played a key role in bilateral and multilateral efforts to solve a range of problems in the Americas, including those of drugs, terrorism, human rights, migration, border conflicts, and political corruption. Definitions run from a few lines to a couple of pages in length. The dictionary is followed by a detailed bibliography arranged alphabetically by subject. This type of information is often scattered and difficult to find. Therefore, this publication will be essential for anyone interested in inter-American organizations. This new edition provides more than 400 entries. The book is of average paper, font size, and binding quality. It will be useful to students and researchers. It should be in all political and international libraries.—**Herbert W. Ockerman**

660.   **United Nations at a Glance.** New York, United Nations, 2012. 224p. illus. $20.00pa. ISBN 13: 978-92-11012-52-1.

United Nations at a Glance provides an overview of this powerful and respected international organization. In easy-to-understand language the book explains the mission of the UN, who the key actors are, how they accomplish their mission, and the historical milestones that they have helped instigate and played a major role in. The volume discusses in depth the role that the UN has played in helping the world through international peace and security, economic and social development, human rights, and humanitarian action. The book provides rich photographs of the United Nation's key members as well as statistics, glossary words, and frequently asked questions. This is a worthwhile place to start for those new to the United Nations who would like to learn more about its organization, members, and mission.—**Shannon Graff Hysell**

International Relations

661.   Neville, Peter. **Historical Dictionary of British Foreign Policy.** Lanham, Md., Scarecrow, 2013. 357p. (Historical Dictionaries of Diplomacy and Foreign Relations). $105.00; $99.99 (e-book). ISBN 13: 978-0-8108-7173-1; 978-0-8108-7371-1 (e-book).

The recent death of former British Prime Minister Margaret Thatcher produced significant analysis of her domestic and international political significance including the foreign policies pursued by her government between 1979-1990. British foreign policy has been a significant force in historical and even contemporary international history and this historical dictionary helps introduce readers to the events, individuals, and institutions characterizing British diplomatic history.

A chronology covers events from the beginning of the War of Spanish Succession in 1702 until the May 2012 expulsion of Syrian diplomats from London following a massacre during the ongoing Syrian civil war. An introductory contextual essay begins with the 1782 establishment of the Foreign Office and stresses this institution's preeminent foreign policy objective as maintaining a European balance of power to prevent any single European power from dominating Europe including countries such as Belgium and Holland bordering the North Sea. This introduction also details Britain's rise to global power through its colonial empire, the influence of World War I, the interwar period, World War II in weakening British global preeminence, and post-World War II developments including decolonization, the rise of the European Union and London's complicated relationship with that entity, the post-Cold War policy developments including Britain's relationship with the United States and its participation in controversial military operations in Afghanistan and Iraq.

The dictionary section includes detailed but succinctly written entries on topics such as American Bases in Britain, the British Commonwealth, Eton College, Foreign Secretary Ernest Bevin, India, Chancellor of the Exchequer Niger Lawson, Russia, Margaret Thatcher, and the 1921-1922 Washington Naval Conference. Appendixes include a list of Foreign Secretaries and Permanent Undersecretaries at the Foreign Office. A bibliography of scholarly secondary sources covering various periods of British diplomatic history concludes the work.

There are errors as is to be expected in a work of this size. Nineteenth-century Prime Minister Benjamin Disrael's birth is incorrectly listed as being in 1807 when it should be in 1804 and his German contemporary Chancellor Otto von Bismarck's birth is incorrectly listed as being in 1809 instead of 1815. There should also be entries on the role played by British Parliament in British foreign policy and the importance of the 1909 Official Secrets Act in influencing historical research on this topic. The bibliography should also list important online primary source materials including parliamentary debates, committee hearings and reports, and Cabinet Office papers. Despite these weaknesses, this will serve as a useful introduction to those desiring to study British diplomatic history. [R: LJ, 15 June 13, p. 115]— **Bert Chapman**

662.   **Treaties in Force: A List of Treaties and Other International Agreements of the United States in Force on January 1, 2012.** Lanham, Md., Bernan Press, 2013. 500p. $55.00pa. ISBN 13: 978-0-1609-1710-3.

This work by the U.S. Department of State provides an up-to-date list (as of January 2012) of treaties and other international agreements that the United States has signed and is a party to. The treaty subjects cover a wide range, including economic, technical, defense, education, relief supplies and packages, extradition, agriculture, and more. The book is arranged by countries between the United States and a single country (listed by the other countries name), as well as by treaties in which there are multiple countries involved (listed by the subject of the treaty). An appendix provides a consolidated tabulation of documents affecting copyright relations of the United States concludes the volume.—**Henry E. York**

Peace Studies

663.   **Annual Review of Global Peace Operations 2013.** By the Center on International Cooperation. Boulder, Colo., Lynne Rienner Publishers, Inc., 2013. 474p. index. $27.50pa. ISBN 13: 978-1-58826-902-7.

The *Annual Review of Global Peace Operations 2013* comes at an appropriate time in U.S. history since the country is divided on U.S. policies in this area and also divided on the effectiveness of the U.N. peace operations as well as being suspicious of the ability of all news media to be fair and honest in their evaluation. Since the annual review is editorially independent but produced with the support of the U.N. Development of Peace Keeping Operations and the African Union Peace and Security Department the first thing this reviewer wanted to know is who published it and why. I checked out the Center for International Cooperation and they appear to be a credible organization. I also checked out their funding and it also passed this reviewer's scrutiny. The book is primarily based on company operations that are authorized by multilateral bodies that are multinational in their composition, have a substantial military component, and are deployed principally in support of a peace process or conflict management objective. This, of course, leaves out the U.S. operations in Afghanistan and concentrates primarily on U.N.-type operations. The book is divided into chapters that include reviews of missions in Chad and the Central African Republic, Haiti, Liberia, and Sudan; mission notes in Bosnia and Herzegovina, Cyprus, Georgia, Kosovo, Somalia, and the Solomon Islands; global statistics on U.N. missions and non-U.N. missions; statistics; and statistics on the African union mission in Sudan. The manuscript contains many tables and charts, most of which are referenced; much of the information is difficult to find from other sources. It is well written and easy to read and the paper quality, font size, and soft cover binding are appropriate for an annual review. The maps and color photographs, tables, and charts are abundant and helpful in understanding this book. This should be one of the sources of information for policy-makers and practitioners that are interested in global peace operations.—**Herbert W. Ockerman**

664.   Harris, Ian M., and Mary Lee Morrison. **Peace Education.** 3d ed. Jefferson, N.C., McFarland, 2013. 284p. index. $39.95pa. ISBN 13: 978-0-7864-7246-8.

This 3d edition of *Peace Education* builds upon the 1st and 2d editions of this title. The 1st edition, published in 1988, focused heavily on the effects of the Cold War and the threat of nuclear war, while the 2d edition, published in 2003, focused more on school violence and the after effects of Columbine. The 3d edition focuses on the growing field of literature in peace studies and the cultural and global aspects of peace. It provides insight into how education, citizenship, environmental and sustainability education, and violence prevention can help lead nations to peaceful resolutions. The nine chapters discuss such topics as: "Religious and Historical Concepts of War, Peace and Peace Education," "Peace Education as Transformative and Empowering," "Getting Started: First Steps in Educating for Peace," "Foundations for Educating for Peace: Human Development, Families and the Contributions of Feminist Educators," and "Some Challenges and Effective Responses." The work has a concluding chapter on the values and visions for a more hopeful and interdependent world as well as an appendix of standards for peace education.—**Shannon Graff Hysell**

Public Policy and Administration

665.   **A Handbook of Comparative Social Policy.** 2nd ed. Patricia Kennett, ed. Northhampton, Mass., Edward Elgar, 2013. 406p. index. $225.00. ISBN 13: 978-1-8498-0366-3.

This collection of 18 chapters by 21 experienced contributors provides scholarly discussion of the various theoretical concepts (e.g., state and society), important definitions, and current themes and debates (e.g., crime, poverty, housing) in cross-cultural policy studies. There are chapters on the comparative research process, and how the disruptive phenomena of globalization affects analysis of national conditions. The chapters are well documented, and reference notes are found at the end of the essays. The 1st edition, also edited by Kennett (Comparative Policy Studies, University of Bristol), was published in 2004, and had 22 chapters. Both editions are available online as well from various vendors. The item under review is not a reference book in the traditional sense, and is recommended for the circulating collections of university and research institutions, for the graduate students and professionals working in this expanding field.—**Daniel K. Blewett**

666.   **Research Handbook on Environment, Health, and the WTO.** Geert Van Calster and Denise Prevost, eds. Northhampton, Mass., Edward Elgar, 2013. 857p. index. $310.00. ISBN 13: 978-1-84720-897-2.

This book provides a dense but thorough examination of the complex relationships between the World Trade Organization (WTO) and international concerns over health and the environment. The chapters are written by an impressive array of international experts, primarily from the field of law.

Considered collectively, the chapters provide detailed analysis of free trade agreements and the role that the WTO plays in overseeing and regulating issues of climate change, food safety, animal welfare, disease prevention, health insurance, public health care services, and access to preventive medicines.

The work is divided into five parts. Chapters in part 1 examine general issues of trade law and regulation, and provide important background information. The six chapters in part 2 focus on trade law and the regulation of health services. Part 3 explores trade law and environmental regulation. It is divided into two sections: five chapters that cover the legal aspects of climate change mitigation and adaption and two chapters that examine the liberalization of trade in climate-friendly technologies and that study the regulation of emerging bio- and nano-technologies. Part 4 consists of a single chapter devoted to WTO dispute settlement processes The single chapter of part 5 applies the case study of WTO Agreement on the Application of Sanitary and Phytosanitary Measure's impact on India's select product-specific export efforts to understand the effect of nontariff trade measures on emerging economies. Each chapter includes a bibliography of sources cited in the footnotes. The book concludes with an index that serves as an essential tool for locating references to specific topics—a critical feature in such a comprehensive volume.

This work not only provides a comprehensive study of the WTO's role in area of dispute resolution and trade regulation in health and the environment, but succeeds in fulfilling the editor's aim of humanizing the impact of the organization's role in world affairs. The *Handbook* is highly recommended for scholars, professionals, and international law experts.—**Robert V. Labaree**

14 Psychology, Parapsychology, and Occultism

Psychology

Bibliography

667. **Dream Gate and Electric Dreams. http://dreamgate.com/dream/bibs/.** [Website]. Free. Date reviewed: 2013.

This Web site offers a collection of bibliographies of dream researchers, clinicians, dream workers, anthropologists, and other dream-concerned individuals and groups. Users will find a bibliography of dream tests that have been prepared by experts in the field that cover a wide range of dream-related topics. Users will also have access to articles from the ASD Journal Bibliography published by Human Sciences Press, which extends back to 1991. Dream-related film reviews and newsletter reviews are also available here.—**Shannon Graff Hysell**

Dictionaries and Encyclopedias

668. **AllPsych Online. http://allpsych.com/.** [Website]. Free. Date reviewed: 2014.

The roots of *AllPsych* go back to 1992 when Dr. Chris Heffner, as a graduate student in psychology, started a small Website to assist with data collection for research purposes and dissemination of academic material. The site began to grow as the Internet became more widely used and soon the site was getting requests for information in many different areas of psychology and mental health. As such, new articles and features were added to the site over the years. Since 1999 the site has been revised several times and new material is continually being added. Today it is one of the most comprehensive psychology Websites on the Internet. It is regularly referenced by universities internationally and cited by professional organizations and college textbooks. There are a variety of things to search within this site: psychiatric disorders, journal indexes, career opportunities, research projects, psychology resources, and even online quizzes and games. Newly added material is highlighted at the top of the page and the most searched areas of the site are highlighted as well.—**Shannon Graff Hysell**

669. **Encyclopedia of Body Image and Human Appearance.** Thomas Cash, ed. San Diego, Calif., Academic Press, 2012. 2v. illus. index. $500.00/set. ISBN 13: 978-0-1238-4925-0.

This two-volume set from Academic Press is presented by well-qualified editors and a team of contributing authors. The focus of the set is on the physical and psychosocial aspects of body image and appearance. The 117 well-written articles cover a wide range of topics including prosthetic devices, appearance discrimination and the law, weight-loss programs, and teasing based on appearance. Many are accompanied by color illustrations and photographs, graphs, and charts. The entries are several pages in length and each begins with an introduction, includes cross-references to related entries, has a list of further readings and Websites, and includes a glossary. Volume 2 includes subject and subject classification indexes. Overall, this is a fascinating compilation of topics related to body image and human appearance that will be useful in psychology, mental health, health care, and counseling and social work libraries. It is highly recommended. [R: Choice, June 13, p. 1809]—**Shannon Graff Hysell**

670.   **Encyclopedia of the Mind.** Harold Pashler, ed. Thousand Oaks, Calif., Sage, 2013. 2v. illus. index. $!75.00/set; $219.00 (e-book). ISBN 13: 978-1-4129-5057-2; 978-1-4129-5057-2 (e-book).

The *Encyclopedia of the Mind* is a multivolume set that brings together the work of experts from a range of fields. The volumes contain a table of contents, an alphabetic list of entries, and a reader's guide of topical entries. The first volume contains a list of contributors with names and affiliations. There are over 300 signed entries covering topics ranging from consciousness, decision making, and attention to genetics, epistemology, and language and communication. The entries range in length from 400 to 5,000 words. All entries are followed by citations for further readings and references. Because of the broad coverage, the reader's guide is essential. The category names in the reader's guide are accessible to the general public. This is a cross-disciplinary tool that pulls from the fields of philosophy, psychology, neuroscience, anthropology, education, and molecular biology, just to name a few. The contributors have strived to cover the latest information from these fields to make the set as up to date as possible. Overall, this is a very good resource for the general public and undergraduate students. This work is recommended for public and academic libraries.—**ARBA Staff Reviewer**

671.   **Mental Health Care Issues in America: An Encyclopedia.** Michael Shally-Jensen, ed. Santa Barbara, Calif., ABC-CLIO, 2013. 2v. index. $189.00/set. ISBN 13: 978-1-61069-013-3; 978-1-61069-014-0 (e-book).

With the purpose of examining the concept of institutional vs. community-based care, these articles were written by a variety of researchers in the field of mental health. It begins with an alphabetic listing of the entries and another with the entries arranged within broader topics. An introduction gives an overview of the current state of mental health, including an explanation of the problems and trends associated with mental health issues, as well as an explanation of the format and content of the material included and a bibliography. The entries are arranged alphabetically and include the name of the person who wrote the entry, a brief history of the topic, an examination of different aspects of the topic (e.g., different causes, variations in progression or severity of a disorder, different therapeutic techniques). Each entry ends with a brief bibliography of additional resources and sidebars placed throughout the text serve to enhance the information. At the end of volume 2 is a list of contributors with background information on each of them, followed by an index. Since the entries are written by different authors, each has a different style; however, each provides a wealth of information that is well organized and thoroughly researched.—**Martha Lawler**

Handbooks and Yearbooks

672.   **Anti-Bullying Basics.** Chicago, World Book, 2014. 8v. illus. index. $179.00/set. ISBN 13: 978-0-7166-2070-9.

While bullying has always been a problem in schools, it has garnered the attention of school administrators as a national problem due to the long-term psychological effects it can render and the safety issues it can cause in the school environment. The statistics are startling: 71 percent of students report bullying as an ongoing problem; one-half of teens have been a victim of cyberbullying; and 1 out of every 10 students drops out or changes schools due to bullying. The book is designed with middle school and high school students in mind. Each volume addresses a different aspect of bullying: bullied by girls, bullied by boys, bullied by friends, bullied by groups, bullied in cyberspace, and bullied to belong. Librarians and teachers can refer students to this work to help them find advice on how to find relief from bullying as well as how to stop it within their school. Supplementary materials include additional online and print resources, difficult vocabulary defined, question-and-answer segments, and color photographs and illustrations. This series can provide a way for library and teaching staff to connect with students who are experiencing this problem firsthand. This new set from World Book will be a welcome addition in middle and high school libraries.—**Shannon Graff Hysell**

673.   **Anxiety and Phobias.** By Carrie Iorizzo. New York, Crabtree, 2014. 48p. illus. index. (Understanding Mental Health). $23.95/vol.; $10.95pa./vol. ISBN 13: 978-0-7787-0082-1.

674.   **Attention Deficit Hyperactivity Disorder.** By Harry Tournemille. New York, Crabtree, 2014. 48p. illus. index. (Understanding Mental Health). $23.95/vol.; $10.95pa./vol. ISBN 13: 978-0-7787-0069-2.

675.   **Autism Spectrum Disorder** New York, Crabtree, 2014. 48p. illus. index. (Understanding Mental Health). $23.95/vol.; $10.95pa./vol. ISBN 13: 978-0-7787-0081-4.

676.   **Depression and Other Mood Disorders.** New York, Crabtree, 2014. 48p. illus. index. (Understanding Mental Health). $23.95/vol.; $10.95pa./vol. ISBN 13: 978-0-7787-0084-5.

677.   **Fetal Alcohol Spectrum Disorder.** New York, Crabtree, 2014. 48p. illus. index. (Understanding Mental Health). $23.95/vol.; $10.95pa./vol. ISBN 13: 978-0-7787-0083-8.

678.   **Schizophrenia and Psychotic Disorders.** New York, Crabtree, 2014. 48p. illus. index. (Understanding Mental Health). $23.95/vol.; $10.95pa./vol. ISBN 13: 978-0-7787-0085-2.

This new six-volume set from Crabtree Publishing, a company known for their multivolume, nonfiction series designed specifically for children and middle school students, discusses the importance of maintaining healthy social and emotional health. It covers several major mental health disorders and discusses the symptoms of each and how they are can be treated with medication and with therapeutic interventions. The volumes in the series discuss anxiety and phobias, attention deficit hyperactivity disorder, autism spectrum disorder, depression and other mood disorders, fetal alcohol spectrum disorder, and schizophrenia and psychotic disorders. The volumes cover the symptoms of each disorder, diagnosis and treatment, managing behavior, family ties, and dealing with the stigma. Within each volume are plenty of color photographs and illustrations as well as sidebars full of additional information. Each volume ends with a "toolbox" that provides helpful tips for living with the disorder; for example in the title on attention deficit hyperactivity disorder there are tips provided on avoiding distractions, remembering things, setting goals for your day, honing your social skills, and how to control frustration. Also included is a list of other resources (e.g., hotlines, Websites), a glossary, and a very short index, all of which can be used to teach young students basic researching skills. This series is recommended for middle school and high school libraries and young adult collections in public libraries. A series like this will be popular among this age group as it is something they hear about or face in their daily life and is a popular research topic.—**Shannon Graff Hysell**

679.   **Cyber Bullying.** By Rachel Stuckey. New York, Crabtree, 2013. 48p. illus. index. (Take a Stand Against Bullying). $22.95/vol.; $10.95pa./set. ISBN 13: 978-0-7787-7913-1.

680. **Physical Bullying.** Jennifer Rivkin, comp. New York, Crabtree, 2013. 48p. illus. index. (Take a Stand Against Bullying). $22.95/vol.; $10.95pa./vol. ISBN 13: 978-0-7787-7914-8.

681. **Social Bullying.** By Margaret Webb. New York, Crabtree, 2013. 48p. illus. index. (Take a Stand Against Bullying). $22.95/vol.; $10.95pa./vol. ISBN 13: 978-0-7787-7915-9.

682. **Verbal Bullying.** By Jennifer Rivkin. New York, Crabtree, 2014. 48p. illus. index. (Take a Stand Against Bullying). $22.95/vol.; $10.95pa./set. ISBN 13: 978-0-7787-7916-2.

This four-volume set from Crabtree Publishing, a company known for their multivolume, nonfiction series designed specifically for children and middle school students, discusses the psychological, social, and physical problems that pre-teens and teenagers experience when bullied by their peers. The volumes in the series discuss cyber bullying, physical bullying, social bullying, and verbal bullying. The volumes discuss the nature of bullying, what bullying is, the psychological and physical issues associated with it, why it needs to be prevented, and how teens can work together to diminish it or abolish it in their school. Within each volume are plenty of color photographs and illustrations as well as sidebars full of additional information. Each volume ends with a quiz to discover if you are a bully, a glossary, a list of resources, and a very short index, all of which can be used to teach young students basic researching skills. This series is recommended for middle school and high school libraries and young adult collections in public libraries. A series like this will be popular among this age group as it is something they hear about or face in their daily life and is a popular research topic.—**Shannon Graff Hysell**

683. Lawhorne, Cheryl. **Military Mental Health Care: A Guide for Service Members, Veterans, Families, and Community.** Lanham, Md., Rowman & Littlefield, 2013. 228p. index. $34.95pa. ISBN 13: 978-1-4422-2093-5; 978-1-4422-2094-2 (e-book).

Military members returning home from combat face stressors and trials that those in the civilian world rarely experience due to their choice of career. These can oftentimes include depression, disconnect, post-traumatic stress disorder, grief, and unemployment. Unfortunately, mental illness still comes with a stigma in many sectors within the military and this population oftentimes has a difficult time reaching out for the help that they understandably need. Since the United States has been more than 10 years at war the country is more alert to the problems that these young men and woman are facing making this is a timely resource. The work is divided into chapters that deal with specific mental issues with subsections used to further breakdown the topics. It is written in a ways that will make it accessible to service member, their families and community members; however, the content will be especially valuable to mental health care providers and social workers working with this population.—**Shannon Graff Hysell**

684. Sajatovic, Martha, and Luis F. Ramirez. **Rating Scales in Mental Health.** 3d ed. Baltimore, Md., Johns Hopkins University Press, 2012. 502p. index. $60.00. ISBN 13: 978-1-4214-0666-4.

This concise volume provides a single, high-quality source for information on common rating scales used in the mental health fields. The volume begins with several short articles that provide context for the use of rating scales, including a broad discussion of the history and use of rating scales and rating scale data. The section that includes the information about the scales themselves starts with coverage of general diagnostic scales, and then moves to thematically grouped scales, such as anxiety scales, general health scales, substance abuse scales, and others. Scales that apply specifically to children are listed separately at the end of this section. Each entry includes an overview of the purpose and use of the specific scale, references, information on copyright and purchase, estimated time needed to use the instrument, and a citation to a sample research article that used the scale in research. This last element, along with the inclusion of actual instruments as copyright allows, makes this very useful for students. Appendixes include tables that list common terminology and rating scales by disorder. The indexes list rating scales by name and by acronym or abbreviation. Overall, this is highly recommended for academic and research libraries supporting students and researchers in mental health. [R: Choice, June 13, p. 1804]—**Amanda Izenstark**

685.   **Stress Information for Teens.** 2d ed. Lisa Bakewell, ed. Detroit, Omnigraphics, 2013. 399p. index. (Teen Health Series). $69.00. ISBN 13: 978-0-7808-1315-1.

This title, one in the Teen Health Series from Omnigraphics, addresses health and hygiene issues that teens face during the adolescent years. Much like Omnigraphics' Health Reference Series, this series pulls together excerpts from government organizations such as the Centers for Disease Control and Prevention, the National Center for Complementary and Alternative Medicine, the National Center for Posttraumatic Stress Disorder, and the Substance Abuse and Mental Health Services Administration. The articles selected will specifically appeal to young adults and are designed to answer their most common questions.

Part 1 is a short section designed to help teens understand the concept of stress and how it is experienced. Part 2 covers the common causes of stress, including school violence, bullying, test anxiety, family violence, stepfamily issues, and sleep deprivation. Part 3 discusses how stress affects the body, including chapters on its effects on the brain, its role in eating disorders and body dysmorphic disorder, and how it relates to loss and grief. Part 4 provides chapters on diseases and disorders with a possible stress component, which include fibromyalgia, lupus, eczema, and hair loss. And finally, chapter 5 provides chapters on managing stress, including seeing a therapist, the benefits of exercise, and relaxation techniques. The work concludes with Websites that discuss stress management and addition reading materials that cover the topic.

This work is an optional purchase for high school libraries and many larger public libraries. This title is recommended.—**Shannon Graff Hysell**

Occultism

686.   **The Ashgate Research Companion to Nineteenth-Century Spiritualism and the Occult.** Tatiana Kontou and Sarah Willburn, eds. Burlington, Vt., Ashgate Publishing, 2012. 436p. illus. index. $134.96. ISBN 13: 978-0-7546-6912-8.

Edited by a Senior Lecturer in Nineteenth-Century Literature at Oxford Brookes University, and an independent scholar living in Amherst, Massachusetts, this work brings together 17 chapters on nineteenth-century mysticism organized into three parts. Intended for seasoned scholars and new researchers, this work offers insights by international scholars on areas of spiritualism, science, and technology; sex, politics, philosophy and poetics; and the Victorian afterlife in magic shows and dinner parties and more. The volume offers essays on such topics as the undead author, the nature of evidence and the matter of writing, recent scholarship on spiritualism and science, the evolution of occult spirituality in Victorian England and the representative case of Edward Bulwer-Lytton, sexuality and spirituality in the work of Edward Carpenter, the conflict between magicians and spirit mediums in the United States and England, food in Victorian Spiritualism, and viewing history and fantasy through Victorian spirit photography, among other topics. There are numerous illustrations, and each chapter is well researched and documented, with a compiled bibliography at the end of the volume. The detailed titles and index enable one to quickly find areas or articles of interest. This work will suit any collection of literature of the Victorian era, the occult, or history of the Victorian era, for both scholars and pleasure readers.—**Sara Marcus**

Parapsychology

687.   Randle, Kevin D. **Alien Mysteries, Conspiracies and Cover-Ups.** Canton, Mich., Visible Ink Press, 2012. 340p. illus. index. $19.95pa. ISBN 13: 978-1-578594-18-4.

For those with an interest in the unknown world of aliens and extraterrestrial life, this book is a treasure trove of stories and encounters that will entertain and well as inform. Randle, a retired U.S. Army Lieutenant Colonel who has interviewed hundreds of witnesses to mysterious sightings, shares more than 100 investigations into sightings, events, and discoveries of alien encounters and government conspiracies. The work is arranged into 14 topical chapters covering a variety of themes, including great airships, alien bodies, suspiciously out of place things, and conspiracies. The work investigates claims of aliens living among us, abductions of humans, and accounts of interstellar cooperation since the UFO crash in Roswell. This is a well-researched and well-written book that will appeal to a broad range of people in the general public. It is recommended for high school and public library collections.—**Shannon Graff Hysell**

15 Recreation and Sports

General Works

Catalogs and Collections

688. **Inside MLB. http://www.abdodigital.com/.** [Website]. Edina, Minn., Abdo Digital. Price negotiated by site. Date reviewed. 2013

689. **Inside the NFL. http://www.abdodigital.com/.** [Website]. Edina, Minn., Abdo Digital. Price negotiated by site. Date reviewed: 2013.

Inside the NFL and *Inside MLB* will give young sports fans information and an all-encompassing experience. Each begins with a map of the United States that appears with symbols indicating the location of a team. These are clickable links to a timeline, history, quotations, photographs, and Quick Stats. There is a Hall of Fame section where players who have been inducted are listed with many links to biographical information. However, when I tried to click the links in *Inside MLB*, they would not work but were fine in *Inside the NFL*. The games section will let fans test their knowledge and skills. At the time of this review there was no information on the 2011 Super Bowl, so it was not as current as I would have wished. Statistics for each team are updated through 2009 season. In spite of these few minor problems, these databases are each worth consideration for purchase.—**Ellen Spring**

Dictionaries and Encyclopedias

690. **American Sports: A History of Icons, Idols, and Ideas.** Murry R. Nelson, ed. Santa Barbara, Calif., Greenwood Press/ABC-CLIO, 2013. 4v. illus. index. $415.00/set. ISBN 13: 978-0-313-39752-3; 978-0-313-39753-0 (e-book).

This four-volume set attempts to "convey the importance and ubiquitous nature of sport in American Culture" (p. xvi). As such, the focus is not purely on history, but more on cultural impact as defined by the editorial board. People, organizations, and events that had ample social significance and have retained their recognizability with the passage of time are included, while those whose importance and familiarity have faded are not.

What is most impressive about the set is the breadth of the entries. As expected, there are entries on players, officials, teams, leagues, and events. In addition, though, users will also find essays on products, clothing, dramatic plays, novels, films, ideas, movements, substances, awards, and places. For example, there are entries on Adidas, Nike, Chest Bumps, Tailgating, the Rooney Rule, Soccer Moms, Steroids, Caddyshack, Moneyball, Death of a Salesman, Lake Placid, and Saratoga Springs, to name just a few of the more interesting pieces. These are all classified in the Guide to Related Topics contained in volume1.

The 480 entries generally consist of a good-sized narrative that sometimes runs to several pages, a list of *see also* references, a short bibliography of additional resources, and a sidebar of tangential interest. At times there are inconsistencies with the *see also* references. For example, The Green Bay Packers entry has *see also* references to ESPN Channels for no clear reason but not one for Cheeseheads. There is also one to the Chicago Bears, but the Bears' entry does not reciprocate that.

A good illustration of this set at its best is the entry on one-time blackballed basketball star Connie Hawkins where the text clarifies Hawkins' cultural significance in several ways: showing basketball as an escape route from the ghetto; leading the evolution in the style of play; detailing the interaction of money and the game; and depicting the competition among various pro leagues and the independent cultural relic of the Harlem Globetrotters.

Some of the selections beg obvious questions. Why is there an entry for the NBA Draft, but not for the much more culturally visible NFL draft? Why entries for the NFL coaches Bill Belichick, Vince Lombardi, and George Halas, but not for the equally significant and celebrated Paul Brown, Don Shula, and Bill Walsh? Why current quarterbacks Peyton Manning and Ben Roethlisberger and not Tom Brady? Why Woody Strode but not the other three players who broke the pro football color line in 1946 and who are more memorable (e.g., Kenny Washington, Marion Motleyk, Bill Willis)? Why the Lingerie Bowl and not Competitive Eating?

There are black-and-white photographs throughout as well as an overall bibliography and an index to the set. Aimed at high school and college students, this reference set that is applicable to contemporary American culture would be of use in school and college libraries that can afford it.—**John Maxymuk**

Directories

691.   **Sports Market Place Directory, 2013.** Millerton, N.Y., Grey House Publishing, 2013. 2301p. index. $250.00pa.; $550.00 (online database; single user); $700.00 (print and online editions). ISBN 13: 978-1-61926-119-9.

This well written directory is a valuable resource for anyone who is interested sports. The content of the directory is comprehensive. It begins with a table of contents that lists the book's sections: Single Sports; Multi Sports; College Sports; Events, Meetings, and Trade Shows; Media; Sport Sponsors; Professional Sponsors; Facilities; Manufacturers and Retailers; Statistics; and an index. Tabbed pages are located throughout the directory and correspond with their respective section. This is a useful design and clearly identifies each section. Within users will find information on 103 sports, from the expected (e.g., baseball, basketball, golf) to the unexpected (e.g., billiards, tug-of-war).

This directory includes more than 2,300 pages. It is comprehensive and detailed. A variety of industry contact information, including Websites, e-mail addresses, and mailing addresses are included. The text is easy to read and comprehend. Sections are cross-referenced and clearly identified. *Sports Market Place Directory, 2013* would complement any library. This directory is also available in an online format from the publisher's GOLD database (Grey House Online Databases; http://gold.greyhouse.com). Users can search the database in a variety of ways, including by organization name, personal names, geographic area, and keyword. It is likely to be a useful resource for athletes, companies, and the general public.—**Paul M. Murphy III**

Handbooks and Yearbooks

692.   Beck, Stan, and Jack Wilkinson. **College Sports Traditions.** Lanham, Md., Scarecrow, 2013. 415p. index. $40.00. ISBN 13: 978-0-8108-9120-3.

Some books are really good, some are fun, and a very few are both—this is one of those. From Virginia Tech football's entrance "Enter Sandman" music to burning couches after a loss or win at West Virginia, traditions are a major aspect of college sports. In 22 chapters spanning pre- and post-game traditions, to music, to mascots and trophies, the authors list some 1,200 traditional practices at colleges across America, both large and small institutions. A few examples range from the well-known band at Stanford or rolling Toomer's Corner at Auburn to the less familiar super fan rewards at Boston College, to streaking at Bucknell lacrosse matches, to ugly sweater Mondays at Albion College. Readers find the good, bad, and downright ugly of American college sports—and not just football and basketball. Included are a list of sources and an index, although the latter could benefit from a more careful editing. Although impossible to include every tradition—absent are victory cigars for the winning team in the Alabama-Tennessee football rivalry and Iowa State's unforgettable introduction for basketball coach Johnny Orr at home games, "Here's Johnny" mimicking Johnny Carson's intro on The Tonight Show—the authors include an array of and interesting insights into college sports traditions. This work is recommended for all libraries.—**Boyd Childress**

693.   Gavin, Michael. **Sports in the Aftermath of Tragedy: From Kennedy to Katrina.** Lanham, Md., Scarecrow, 2013. 159p. index. $65.00; $64.99 (e-book). ISBN 13: 978-0-8108-8700-8; 978-0-8108-8701-5 (e-book).

This volume is an interesting look at two seemingly unrelated topics—sports and American historical tragedies—and the ways in which they coincide and how the world of sports responds to national tragedies. The author has observed that after a national tragedy many sports columnists write articles or commentaries on the role that sports plays in national recovery. The author provides chapters on how American athletes, sports teams, and sports fans have reacted to such historic tragedies as John F. Kennedy's assassination, Hurricane Katrina, the 9/11 terrorist attacks, the assassination of Martin Luther King Jr., the bombing of the 1996 Olympics, and the 2011 Japanese tsunami in which the American and Japanese women's soccer teams competed soon after in the final round of the World Cup. The American public has strong ties to its sports teams and this book provides a unique perspective on how the American public copes with adversity and loss through sports in the aftermath of tragedy.—**Shannon Graff Hysell**

694.   Newton, David E. **Steroids and Doping in Sports: A Reference Handbook.** Santa Barbara, Calif., ABC-CLIO, 2014. 320p. index. (Contemporary World Issues). $58.00. ISBN 13: 978-1-61069-313-4; 978-1-61069-314-1 (e-book).

Educator and prolific author David E. Newton's experience in teaching science in secondary and higher education is evident in his latest contribution to the Contemporary World Issues series. By following the format of his previous titles in the series, Newton provides a commendable overview of the controversy over performance-enhancing drugs in sports today.

The first three chapters cover the background, problems, and perspectives of steroid use as well as the role this abuse has played in amateur and professional sports throughout history. Chapter 5 includes biographical sketches of about 25 men, woman, and organizations that have either spoken out against the use of anabolic steroids or who have fallen from grace due to their use of the drugs. Data and documents such as historical documents and court cases comprise chapter 6. The directory of organizations in chapter 7 is a selective list of governmental, professional, academic, and private groups that address steroid use. The print and nonprint resources listed in chapter 8 are divided into the three topics—books, articles, reports, and the Internet—for easy locating. Newton provides substantial annotations for the entries in chapters 7 and 8, especially noting Website features and organizational publications. A glossary and index conclude the work.

While most would believe that steroid use is a relatively recent culture phenomenon, Newton's work documents its existence since the beginning of civilization and its current status. Secondary and higher education students as well as the public will benefit from this authoritative volume. All libraries need Newton's latest work on their shelves.—**Alice Crosetto**

695.   Science Behind Sports Series. Farmington Hills, Mich., Lucent Books/Gale/Cengage Learning, 2012. 11v. illus. index. $34.10/vol.

This multivolume series on the scientific principles behind many popular sports is aimed at 6th through 10th grade students. Recently published volumes are on cycling, taekwondo, and tennis. The series aims to provide basic scientific concepts, such as kinetics, acceleration, and velocity, by describing how these principles work in athletics. All of these volumes achieve that aim through clear writing, comprehensive, age- and grade-level information, and attractive and colorful illustrations that bring each topic to life.

The authors are writers of books for young people. Each volume provides an overview of the sport, its history, changes to its rules over time, equipment needed, and techniques. Throughout users will find information on the biomechanics and physiology of playing the sport and well as common injuries and medical conditions associated with the sport. All volumes have sidebars, numerous photographs and illustrations, a glossary, and resources to consult for further information. Because young adults have a natural interest in sports that at times supersedes their interest in science, this set will provide a good link between the two subjects.—**Shannon Graff Hysell**

Baseball

696.   Cohen, Robert W. The 50 Greatest Players in St. Louis Cardinals History. Lanham, Md., Scarecrow, 2013. 361p. index. $45.00; $44.99 (e-book). ISBN 13: 978-0-8108-9215-6; 978-0-8108-9216-3 (e-book).

In 2012 sports historian Robert Cohen published *The 50 Greatest Players in New York Yankees History* (see ARBA 2013, entry 675), portraits of stars from the American League's historically most dominant team. This new book features distinguished players from the historically most prominent National League team with 11 World Series victories and 18 National League pennants. As Cohen notes, by the 1930s, "all cities west of the Mississippi and south of the Mason-Dixon Line broadcasted cardinals games over the radio," thereby "making the redbirds 'America's Team' in many ways" (p. x).

Cohen first chose his top 50 St. Louis Cardinals players since 1892 based solely on their performance during their careers with the Cardinals, no easy task. He then applied his ranking criteria: the player's "level of dominance" on the team, the player's statistics, the player within the baseball era, the player's contributions to team success, how the player influenced the team both on and off the diamond, and how much the player contributed to the team's winning records. Individual player entries include a biographical sketch with comparisons to other players, together with "Cardinal Career Highlights" divided into "Best Season," "Memorable Moments and Greatest Performances," and "Notable Achievements." Brief notes at the end of ach entry cite articles, books, and Websites. Cohen uses his rankings to define the All-Time Cardinals First and Second Teams plus pitching staffs for each of these hypothetical teams. He also included in the book a glossary of relevant baseball terms and a bibliography citing mainly baseball statistical and player biographical Websites.

Written in a lively, entertaining manner, this book belongs in most public and school libraries. Cohen's choice of players and his rankings will generate plenty of controversy among long-time Cardinals fans, but the book will appeal to both old and new baseball fans of all ages who admire brilliant individual player careers summarized in crisp biographical sketches and statistics. Twenty black-and-white photographs enhance the text.—**Julienne L. Wood**

697.   Hillstrom, Laurie Collier. Jackie Robinson and the Integration of Baseball. Detroit, Omnigraphics, 2013. 221p. illus. index. (Defining Moments). $49.00pa. ISBN 13: 978-0-7808-1327-4.

This work provides a detailed account of the events that occurred leading up to April 15, 1947 when Major League Baseball's longstanding color barrier was in place and the role that Jackie Robinson played in that monumental occasion. For young people today who did not grow up during the era of segregation in sports, this work may be particularly shocking and disturbing. The work discusses the rise of the Negro League baseball, the selection of Jackie Robinson as the first black player in the major leagues, and chronicles the verbal and physical abuse he survived his rookie season. Moreover, however, it shows the influential role he played as an African American leader in baseball's legacy and America's struggle toward civil rights. The author, Laurie Collier Hillstrom, succeed in her effort to provide an objective and balanced account of a shameful period in American history.

Like other volumes in this series, *Jackie Robinson and the Integration of Baseball* is divided into three sections: narrative overview, biographies, and primary sources. The narrative overviews do what reference books should do: provide context quickly. The authors strategically add sidebars within the overviews, some from primary documents, that have the capacity to capture the reader's attention and perhaps give them ideas for further research. Over six chapters the author proceeds chronologically from segregation in baseball to the selection of Robinson in the major leagues to the stardom and death threats that followed. The biographies take students deeper into the influential characters who participated in this drama. The primary sources are a mix of documents from all perspectives.

Additional features are a glossary of important people, places, and terms; a chronology; sources for further study; and a bibliography. Overall, however, the Hillstrom succeeds in packing a lot of easily accessible and useful information into only 221 pages. Young students interested in baseball, the history of sports in America, and racial relations in America could benefit from more titles in a series that is heavily weighted in favor of the twentieth century and beyond.—**John P. Stierman**

698.   Pahigian, Josh. **Spring Training Handbook: A Comprehensive Guide to the Grapefruit and Cactus League Ballparks.** Jefferson, N.C., McFarland, 2013. 252p. illus. index. $39.95pa. ISBN 13: 978-0-7864-7195-9; 978-1-4766-0198-4 (e-book).

All baseball fans owe a debt of gratitude to Josh Pahigian, author of *The Ultimate Baseball Road Trip: A Fan's Guide to Major League Stadiums* (2d ed., 2012) and *101 Baseball Places to See Before You Strike Out* (2010), as well as the 1st edition of this delightful book about spring training baseball stadiums (see ARBA 2005, entry 769). This comprehensive new edition features updated chapters, deletes no longer used ballparks, and includes the five minor league parks opened since 2004. Fans planning a trip to Florida or Arizona will enjoy reading about these family-friendly destinations and fans unable to actually travel to these states will appreciate the author's engaging writing style and his success in portraying "a unique baseball atmosphere that the game's players and fans treasure" as well as the historical detail about each stadium and city. Pahigian's hope is that after reading this book "every fan will agree that he or she deserves to spend at least one March in Florida, Arizona, or both" (p. 3).

Arizona's Cactus League now includes 15 teams while Florida's older Citrus League retains that same number of teams. The books 24 chapters cover all of the current spring training sites, includes a substantial historical sketch of the current and past stadiums in each place as well as individual team spring training history, fan traditions and stadium food, and information about areas attractions outside the ballparks. Black-and-white photographs enhance the text. The entry for each ballpark yields an address, telephone number, Website, dates opened/renovated, seating capacity, distance to other nearby spring training stadiums, instructions for getting to the park, detailed seating advice, a description of the particular ballpark experience, and places in the surrounding community such as sports bars, restaurants, golf courses, and beaches. Fans will learn where to park, which seats are less sunny, and what to eat, as well as where Michal Jordan and Garth Brooks tried spring baseball. Pahigian also provides a complete list of team training sites since 1914; a bibliography featuring periodicals, books, and Websites; and an index.

The e-book version of this title will be of special value to traveling fans. The book is essential for baseball collections in all public and many academic libraries.—**Julienne L. Wood**

699.   Spatz, Lyle. **Historical Dictionary of Baseball.** Lanham, Md., Scarecrow, 2013. 467p. (Historical Dictionaries of Sports). $115.00; $109.95 (e-book). ISBN 13: 978-0-8108-7812-9; 978-0-8108-7954-6 (e-book).

To the casual fan names such as Babe Ruth and terms like *no-hitter* are part of the language of baseball. For those more interested and experienced, this 11th volume in Scarecrow's new historical sports dictionaries is a welcome addition to reference literature. Arranged in alphabetic order, more than 900 names, places, terms, organizations, leagues and conferences, teams and schools, and events chronicle the history of the game. Included are players, teams, and the game's rules and statistical categories. Both players and nonplayers (e.g., general managers, coaches, umpires) are given biographical entries. An interesting chronology and introduction precede the well-written entries and 12 appendixes trace professional and college baseball, World Series results, and statistical information (e.g., career leaders in games played, batting average, home runs, games pitched). Cross-references in bold lead the user to other relevant entries. Nearly 40 pages of bibliography conclude this useful ready-reference book.—**Boyd Childress**

700.   Worth, Richard. **Baseball Team Names: A Worldwide Dictionary, 1869-2011.** Jefferson, N.C., McFarland, 2013. 408p. index. $55.00pa. ISBN 13: 978-0-7864-6844-7.

The title of this volume is something of a misnomer; this delightful reference contains not only team names, but team nicknames as well. So, in addition to getting an explanation of why the New York American League team has been known as the Yankees since 1903 (officially since 1913), we also get the origins of such popular nicknames as Murderer's Row and the Bronx Bombers as well as such short-lived lesser monikers as Steinbrenner's Brownshirts and the Skankees. When one considers that Worth is providing that level of detail for all professional teams in all leagues worldwide since 1869, the impressive bit of research this work represents becomes clear.

The book's 7,348 entries are listed by team city, with the cities arranged alphabetically and the entries under each place recorded chronologically. There is just one listing for all cities into which all countries, all leagues, and all levels of professional baseball are interfiled so following one team's name variations can be daunting at times.

The entries make for some fascinating reading. Many baseball fans might know that New York began to be called the Yankees because their prior name, the Highlanders, sounded too British. However, how many people are aware that the Omaha team in the Western League was known as the Kidnappers from 1900-1903 because career criminal and folk hero Pat Crowe kidnapped the son of a local meat packing magnate in 1900 and fans equated the team's rowdy players with hooligans?

In these pages, we learn that the Washington Senators were officially the Nationals until 1957, and while the Dodgers' name dates to 1884, it did not become the Brooklyn team's official name until 1932. As a matter of fact, Brooklyn did not have an official name until then. It should also be noted that to fully explore the Dodgers' history, the user needs to consult entries under both Brooklyn and Los Angeles. What other source will provide all of the above information as well as the origins and extent of Osaka, Japan's Kintetsu Buffalo and Hanshin Tigers? How about the Beijing Fierce Tigers? Or the Veracruz Aguilas Rojas? Or the Roma Café Danesi Nettuno? Or the Saginaw Wa-was? All are elucidated here.

Two useful appendixes track both official names and nicknames for all major league teams on an annual basis. A team index offers a useful additional access point. However, the lack of access points by foreign country and by league is a shortcoming. That said, this remarkably thorough work would be welcome in any sports reference collection.—**John Maxymuk**

Basketball

701.   Bradley, Robert D. **The Basketball Draft Fact Book: A History of Professional Basketball's College Drafts.** Lanham, Md., Scarecrow, 2013. 641p. index. $125.00; $124.99 (e-book). ISBN 13: 978-0-8108-9068-8; 978-0-8108-9069-5 (e-book).

Massive book, hefty price, and highly specialized are terms that all describe *The Basketball Draft Fact Book.* Yet this is an impressive array of research that provides year-by-year listings of professional basketball player drafts of both men and women since 1996. Author Bradley includes all four major men's leagues and two women's leagues, and clearly the bulk of the book (over 400 pages) covers the now well-established NBA. Beginning with the initial Basketball Association of America draft in 1947, the volume lists draft rounds, teams, and players selected. Although the now popularly televised NBA draft includes only two rounds, in 1968 the NBA draft went into a twenty-first round with 214 players selected. Especially interesting are the American Basketball Association (ABA) drafts with an intriguing cast of characters who made up the original ABA. Each draft is introduced by a brief synopsis where users will find interesting facts such as only one player from the 2.00 draft ever made an All-Star team (Michael Redd, the 43d choice). Additional chapters cover draft order, eligibility, draft facts, and the women's draft. Other features include television draft coverage, site and dates of drafts, a glossary, resources, and an incomplete index. This is an excellent reference volume for academic and larger public libraries.—**Boyd Childress**

702.   Cohen, Robert W. **Pro Basketballs All-Time All-Stars Across the Eras.** Lanham, Md., Scarecrow, 2013. 467p. index. $95.00; $94.99 (e-book). ISBN 13: 978-0-8108-8744-2; 978-0-8108-8745-9 (e-book).

Say it isn't so—the Big O on the second team and the incomparable Dr J on the fifth team? That may be hard to swallow but that is where we'll find Oscar Robertson and Julius Erving in Cohen's all time all-star basketball volume. Spanning six pro eras from the set shot age to the advent of free agents, Cohen selects an all-star team from each period—first and second teams. Cohen, author of numerous sports books, uses statistics (offensive and defensive), sustained excellence, and input from writers, coaches, and players to compare players at each of five positions from each era. A daunting task indeed but Cohen pulls it off and the result is a highly entertaining reference volume. He includes a preface and introduction to explain his objective and criteria. A brief bibliography and index add little to the volume but his all star teams are the book's features. Not quite a sports fantasy book, the volume is rather expensive considering the content. And in case you are wondering, the all time all-star starting five is as follows: Bill Russell, Karl Malone, Larry Bird, Magic Johnson, and Michael Jordan. Let the debate begin.—**Boyd Childress**

703.   Malolepszy, Tomasz. **European Basketball Championship Results Since 1935.** Lanham, Md., Scarecrow, 2013. 251p. $105.00. ISBN 13: 978-0-8108-8783-1.

This book charts the growth and history of basketball in Europe. It is largely a statistical recap of men's and women's competitions dating from the inception of the sport in Europe in 1935 through 2012. The work begins with a two-page introduction to the history of the sport. As expected, two pages does not give much space to give a thorough overview of nearly 80 years of sports history. It does show, however, how Europe's inaugural championship competition has grown from 10 teams in 1932 to 24 teams competing today. The bulk of the volume consists of statistics on game results, team rosters, medalists, and standings for European championship games. Many of these records are difficult to come by and many have never before been published. While it is difficult to say how much use a volume like this will have on the shelves of university and public libraries in the United States, those libraries with avid international sports fans or comprehensive sports collections may want to consider its purchase.—**Shannon Graff Hysell**

Boxing

704.   Grasso, John. **Historical Dictionary of Boxing.** Lanham, Md., Scarecrow, 2014. 551p. (Historical Dictionaries of Sports). $125.00; $119.99 (e-book). ISBN 13: 978-0-8108-6800-7; 978-0-8108-7867-9 (e-book).

Although many of the basic facts regarding the game of tennis, such as who won major matches, are accessible online, the boxing enthusiast will enjoy simply sitting down and thumbing through pages that reflect a love for the sport. The bulk of the dictionary is the hundreds of cross-referenced, A-Z entries on important boxers, rules, organizations, and technical terminology. John Grasso, a historian of the Olympics and author of the *Historical Dictionary of Basketball* (see ARBA 2012, entry 798) as well as other titles in this series, writes these in an accessible, conversational style. The entries are accompanied by a historical overview of boxing from its origins in Ancient Greece, a list of acronyms used throughout, a chronology, appendixes (winners/champions of the major events), and a bibliography subdivided by topic. Although academic librarians may not consider this an essential purchase, public librarians and boxing historians will want to add the *Historical Dictionary of Boxing* to their collections.—**John P. Stierman**

Chess

705.   Di Felice, Gino. **Chess Results 1961-1963: A Comprehensive Record with 938 Tournament Crosstables and 108 Match Scores, with Sources.** Jefferson, N.C., McFarland, 2013. 438p. illus. index. $49.95pa. ISBN 13: 978-0-7864-7572-8; 978-1-4766-0372-8 (e-book).

706.   Di Felice, Gino. **Chess Results 1964-1967: A Comprehensive Record with 1,204 Tournament Crosstables and 158 Match Scores, with Sources.** Jefferson, N.C., McFarland, 2013. 549p. illus. index. $49.95pa. ISBN 13: 978-0-7864-7573-5; 978-1-4766-0373-5 (e-book).

707.   Di Felice, Gino. **Chess Results 1968-1970: A Comprehensive Record with 854 Tournament Crosstables and 161 Match Scores, with Sources.** Jefferson, N.C., McFarland, 2013. 436p. index. $49.95pa. ISBN 13: 978-0-7864-7574-2; 978-1-4766-0371-1 (e-book).

Written by Gino Di Felice, an author of several other volumes in the Chess Results series from McFarland, these volumes are comprehensive, chronological list of the results of men's chess competitions from all over the world from the years 1961-1963, 1964-1967, and 1968-1970, respectively. Both individual and team matches are recorded, including the lesser-known competitions and players. Compiled from contemporary sources (e.g., newspapers, periodicals, tournament records, match books), the volume covering the years 1961-1963 contains 938 tournament tables and 108 match scores, the volume covering the years 1964-1967 covers 1,204 tournament tables and 158 match scores, and the volume covering 1968-1970 contains 854 tournament tables and 161 match scores. They are indexed by events and players. First and last names of players are included whenever possible. Entries note the location and, when available, the group that sponsored the event. Published sources are cited.—**Shannon Graff Hysell**

Cycling

708.   Laurita, Jennifer. **Anatomy of Cycling: A Trainer's Guide to Cycling.** Richmond Hills, Ont., Firefly Books, 2013. 160p. illus. $24.95pa. ISBN 13: 978-1-77085-171-9.

Students of athletic training have no shortage of books and other media to help them achieve peak physical fitness. The field of training manuals for cyclists is not as crowded as for runners, but it has solid offerings, such as *The Cyclist's Training Bible* by Joe Friel, now in its 4th edition. Jennifer Laurita, a national-level cycling instructor and coach, has added to the athletic training bookshelf with *Anatomy of Cycling: A Trainer's Guide to Cycling.*

Anatomy of Cycling is well illustrated, has clear and concise instructions, and is logically organized into four units: flexibility, leg-strengthening, core-strengthening, and balance and posture. It also includes text boxes directing the user what to "aim for" and "avoid," and what the exercise is best for. Practitioners will also appreciate sidebars which point out what the specific exercise "targets" and "benefits," and when performing it is not advisable.

Although aimed at cyclists, the book does not live up to its title; it does not tie illustrations or descriptions of exercises to cycling per se. There are only 10 pages of narrative, and these are aimed at beginners. One expects a book with this title to be more geared to cycling. A recent book with nearly the same title, *Cycling Anatomy* (see ARBA 2011, entry 729), opens with a chapter entitled "The Cyclist in Motion," and it includes the cycling-specific information that one might expect. Readers might also prefer the male model dressed in spandex, rather than gym shorts, for a clearer picture of technique and anatomy. *Anatomy of Cycling* is a useful general exercise manual and will benefit all athletes. Libraries looking for a cycling-specific reference source are advised to look elsewhere.—**John P. Stierman**

Extreme Sports

709.   Beal, Becky. **Skateboarding: The Ultimate Guide.** Santa Barbara, Calif., Greenwood Press/ABC-CLIO, 2013.]150p. illus. index. (Greenwood Guides to Extreme Sports). $37.00. ISBN 13: 978-0-313-38112-6; 978-0-313-38113-3 (e-book).

710.   Robinson, Victoria. **Rock Climbing: The Ultimate Guide.** Santa Barbara, Calif., Greenwood Press/ABC-CLIO, 2013. 165p. illus. index. (Greenwood Guides to Extreme Sports). $37.00. ISBN 13: 978-0-313-37861-4; 978-0-313-37862-1 (e-book).

This series from Greenwood Press takes an in-depth look at our fascination with extreme sports. Two new titles have been added to the series--*Rock Climbing* and *Skateboarding*--joining previous titles in the series on base jumping, snowboarding, and surfing. While very different in skill level and acceptance, each sport has similarities, including very few rules, little to no coach involvement, and they tend to be more dangerous and involve more risk than typical sports. They also typically appeal to the young, many involve new technologies, and they reflect the culture of the time and have cult followings of their own. The volumes look at the history, equipment and techniques, and important individuals associated with the sport. They also discuss links to culture, history, social issues, and trends and are written in an informal conversational manner. These are reference books that students will enjoy using for research and browsing and may make them think more critically about the extreme sports they enjoy and what makes them relevant in sports culture. These titles are recommended as select purchases for middle and high school libraries.—**ARBA Staff Reviewer**

Fitness

711.   Liebman, Hollis Lance. **Anatomy of Core Stability: A Trainer's Guide to Core Stability.** Richmond Hills, Ont., Books, 2013. 160p. illus. $24.95pa. ISBN 13: 978-1-77085-170-2.

The "core" of the human body has been a popular area of focus for a number of years now, and there is no shortage of books on the topic. *Anatomy of Core Stability* is an excellent addition to the materials currently existing on the topic. The content includes warm-up exercises, static and dynamic exercises for the core, and workouts for beginners through more advanced users. A glossary that includes the Latin terms for the body's musculature is provided at the end.

The most impressive aspect of the title, other than the content itself which is very valuable, is the high quality of the photographs. Each exercise is demonstrated using photographs of a real person performing the exercise, as well as images of a human with the muscular anatomy utilized during the exercise highlighted with each specific muscle identified. Tips to "do it right" and things to avoid while performing the exercise are also included.

Anatomy of Core Stability is an extremely informative and high-quality publication that will be of use to anyone interested in improving their core strength and stability. It is suitable for all levels, from beginner to advanced, and would be a worthwhile addition to any public, high school, or undergraduate library.—**Alicia Brillon**

Football

712.   Grasso, John. **Historical Dictionary of Football.** Lanham, Md., Scarecrow, 2013. 559p. (Historical Dictionaries of Sports). $125.00; $119.95 (e-book). ISBN 13: 978-0-8108-7856-3; 978-0-8108-7857-0 (e-book).

From the Alabama Crimson Tide to legendary coach Bob Zuppke, football remains America's favorite sport. This historical dictionary includes in excess of 600 alphabetic entries, players, coaches, and teams that have contributed to professional and college football. Examples are a one-page entry on Virginia Tech and its rich football tradition, a similar entry on the Washington Redskins, the Sugar Bowl, and terms such as flea flicker and pylon—word count for terms are briefer and teams and players are longer. The entries are both factual and interesting, and cross-references are in bold print. Some may argue with omitted teams such as Maryland and Oklahoma State or included terms and concepts like Massillon (Ohio) High School or the simplicity of an incomplete pass, but the dictionary aims at a general audience and successfully so. There are 16 appendixes covering Championship teams and games, Heisman Trophy winners, and football films. There is a 20-page chronology and a 24-page bibliography, but no index. In all, this 14th volume in Scarecrow's Historical Dictionary of Sports series adds to the literature of football and sports.—**Boyd Childress**

Golf

713.   Williams, Robert, and Michael Trostel. **Great Moments of the U.S. Open.** Richmond Hills, Ont., Firefly Books, 2013. 216p. illus. index. $35.00. ISBN 13: 978-1-77085-188-7.

The authors of this work are the director and the curator of the U.S. Golf Association's Museum. This fully illustrated volume provides a history of the U.S. Open, an internationally recognized golf tournament that since 1895 identifies the best golfer of the year. The work has contributed essays by both the authors of this volume as well as from other experts in the field. One of the more interesting essays explains how the course itself is a "competitor" in the golfing competition due to its level of difficulty and the challenge it presents to players. There are photographs interspersed throughout the text, both of live shots and of collectibles found within the museum. Lovers of the game will find this work an interesting and fun read and will enjoy the historical element that the authors bring to this volume due to their work at the museum.—**Shannon Graff Hysell**

Ice Hockey

714.   **Hockey Hall of Fame Book of Players.** Steve Cameron, ed. Richmond Hills, Ont., Firefly Books, 2013. 335p. index. $29.95. ISBN 13: 978-1-77085-224-2.

Ballet on skates or mayhem on ice, hockey is an exciting and graceful game often marred by physical play but most true fans want to see the speed and violence that is professional hockey. The Hockey Hall of Fame in Toronto is home to the game's greats—men and a handful of women—who are recognized as hockey's best, over 250, brothers (the Richards), fathers and sons (Bobby and Brett Hull), names from the past and more recent hockey history. Divided into six major sections representing positions (rover is the position no longer recognized), the entries feature player career highlights, notes, records, and some great photographs. In some instances a brief textual note is added for noteworthy players (Bobby Clarke and Doug Harvey for example) with four pages on Wayne Gretzky. An additional 50-page section lists career statistics of each player. Black-and-white and color photography provide remarkable visuals. Not expensive, the *Hockey Hall of Fame Book of Players* is a worthwhile addition to public and academic libraries as well as collection with a sports emphasis.—**Boyd Childress**

715.   Malolepszy, Thomasz. **European Ice Hockey Championship Results since 1910.** Lanham, Md., Scarecrow, 2013. 169p. $85.00. ISBN 13: 978-0-8108-8781-7.

This book charts the growth and history of ice hockey in Europe. It is largely a statistical recap of men's and women's competitions dating from the first competition of the sport in Europe in 1910 through 2012. Since then a total of 66 championships have been competed, most of which were world championships or the Olympics. The work also chronicles the history of women's European championships, which, unfortunately, only included five championship games from 1989-1996 before being discontinued. The work begins with a two-page introduction to the history of the sport. As expected, two pages does not give much space to give a thorough overview of over 100 years of sports history. The bulk of the volume consists of statistics on game results, team rosters, medalists, and standings for European championship games. The work also includes a list of unique records, some of which have never been published. A book like this will appeal to a very small audience in the United States and should be reserved for purchase by libraries that have comprehensive sports collections or have clientele with a keen interest in international sports.—**Shannon Graff Hysell**

716.   Zeisler, Laurel. **Historical Dictionary of Ice Hockey.** Lanham, Md., Scarecrow, 2013. 419p. (Historical Dictionary of Sports). $115.00; $109.95 (e-book). ISBN 13: 978-0-8108-7862-4; 978-0-8108-7863-1 (e-book).

Zeisler, an independent researcher and member of the Society for International Hockey Research and International Society of Olympic Historians, has written this historical dictionary on the evolution of hockey as well as the sport's highlights. This dictionary also provides statistical data and lists information about international organizations and governing bodies. An introductory timeline-arranged chronology spanning from the seventeenth century to May 2012 includes the most pivotal points in the history of ice hockey. The 600-plus entries comprising the body of this dictionary offer well-written, cross-referenced paragraphs that address both the historical aspects of the sport along with the key figures of the sport. A nice balance of historical and biographical entries is achieved and the items chosen for inclusion make for interesting reading. Finally, nine informative appendixes and a thorough bibliography round out the work. *Historical Dictionary of ice Hockey* is available in either print or e-book format and is recommended for public libraries, for academic libraries supporting sports curricula, and for ice hockey aficionados. [R: LJ, 15 June 13, p. 115]—**Philip G. Swan**

Soccer

717.   Malolepszy, Tomasz. **European Soccer Championship Results Since 1958.** Lanham, Md., Scarecrow, 2013. 127p. $60.00; $59.95 (e-book). ISBN 13: 978-0-8108-8779-4; 978-0-8108-8780-0 (e-book).

This book charts the growth and history of soccer in Europe, a sport that has experienced enormous growth in the past 50 years. In fact, the 2012 European Soccer Championship was attended by nearly 1.5 million people and was the third most watched sporting event in the world. This work is largely a statistical recap of men's and women's competitions dating from the first competition of the sport in Europe in 1958 through 2012. The work begins with a two-page introduction to the history of the sport. As expected, two pages does not give much space to give a thorough overview of over nearly 50 years of sports history. The bulk of the volume consists of statistics on game results, team rosters, medalists, and standings for European championship games. The work also includes a list of unique records, some of which have never been published. While soccer is a popular sport in Europe and has experienced grow over the years, it may have less appeal to an American audience. This work should be reserved for purchase by libraries that have comprehensive sports collections or have clientele with a keen interest in international sports.—**Shannon Graff Hysell**

718.   **Soccer Source Series.** New York, Crabtree, 2013. multivolume. illus. index. $26.60/vol.; $8.95pa./vol.

This multivolume series from Crabtree Publishing, a company known for their multivolume, nonfiction series designed specifically for children, provides a series designed specifically for this age group on one of their favorite sports—soccer. The series currently includes four titles: *Play Life a Pro: Soccer Skills and Drills*, *Score! The Story of Soccer*, *Soccer's Superstars: The Best of the Best*, and *Winning Big: World and Euro Cup Soccer*. With the use of color photographs and easy-to-understand text, each volume covers its topic in child-friendly style. Each volume concludes a glossary, a list of further references, and a very short index, all of which can be used to teach young students basic researching skills. This series is recommended as an additional purchase for elementary school libraries and juvenile collections in public libraries where there is an interest in soccer.—**Shannon Graff Hysell**

Stock Car Racing

719.   Freedman, Lew. **Encyclopedia of Stock Car Racing.** Santa Barbara, Calif., Greenwood Press/ ABC-CLIO, 2013. 2v. illus. index. $189.00/set. ISBN 13: 978-0-313-38709-8; 978-0-313-38710-4 (e-book).

Joining the ranks of such classics as *The Stock Car Racing Encyclopedia* (Macmillan, 2009) and *The Encyclopedia of Stock Car Racing* (MetroBooks, 1998), this updated title on this popular American sport provides 250 entries on subjects that have defined the sport since its inception in 1948. Today, stock car racing is a multibillion dollar industry that is entrenched in American pop culture and commands top dollar for advertising within the United States. This work, organized alphabetically, covers all of the main races (e.g., Daytona 500, Indianapolis 500), famed tracks across the country (e.g., Talladega

Superspeedway, Bristol Motor Speedway), and key historical figures and top drivers today (e.g., Richard Petty, Jimmie Johnson, Dale Earnhardt Jr.). The work begins with a thorough history of the sport as well as its impact on pop culture and its financial influences. This is followed by a chronology that begins with the first race held in Daytona Beach in 1936 and concludes with the 2012 win of team owner Rick Hendrick who won his 200th career NASCAR Cup race. Each entry runs several pages in length, many include a black-and-white photograph, and each concludes with *see also* references and a list of references for further information. Volume 2 concludes with an appendix of Cup and Race Champions, a six-page bibliography, and an index.

There are very few up-to-date reference titles available on this popular topic. Much of the information in the work can likely be found through Internet searches; however, this is a fun resource to browse and users will come across many names, races, and interesting facts that they are likely to overlook with a basic Internet search. This work would be a useful addition in the recreation collections of public libraries.—**Shannon Graff Hysell**

Volleyball

720.   Malolepszy, Thomasz. **European Volleyball Championship Results Since 1948.** Lanham, Md., Scarecrow, 2013. 177p. $85.00. ISBN 13: 978-0-8108-8785-5.

This book charts the growth and history of volleyball in Europe. It is largely a statistical recap of men's and women's competitions dating from the first competition of the sport in Europe in 1948 through 2012. The sport has grown in popularity across Europe over those years and today the European Championship has 55 participating nations; 16 of whom can qualify to play for the gold in the championships. The work begins with a two-page introduction to the history of the sport. As expected, two pages does not give much space to give a thorough overview of over nearly 70 years of sports history. The bulk of the volume consists of statistics on game results, team rosters, medalists, and standings for European championship games. The work also includes a list of unique records, some of which have never been published. While volleyball is a popular sport in Europe and has experienced grow over the years, it is unlikely that this work will have much appeal to an American audience. This work should be reserved for purchase by libraries that have comprehensive sports collections or have clientele with a keen interest in international sports.—**Shannon Graff Hysell**

16 Sociology

General Works

Catalogs and Collections

721. **Gender Studies Database. http://www.ebscohost.com/academic/gender-studies-database.** [Website]. Ipswich, Mass., EBSCO. Price negotiated by site. Date reviewed: 2013.

This site offers over 920,000 records through *Women's Studies International* and *Men's Studies* databases. It includes scholarly, popular, official, and alternative sources since 1972. Several thousand links to freely available and indexed full-text articles and documents on the Internet are available. Source documents include professional journals, conference papers, theses & dissertations and other sources.—**Noriko Asato**

722. **Sociological Abstracts. http://md1.csa.com/factsheets/supplements/saguide.php.** [Website]. Ann Arbor, Mich., ProQuest. Price negotiated by site. Date reviewed: 2013.

This site is a respected source for abstracts to over 2,700 journals in disciplines related to sociology with coverage from 1963 to the present. The CSA Sociological Abstracts database offers access to the international literature in sociology and related disciplines in the social and behavioral sciences. Many records from key journals in sociology, added to the database since 2002, also include the references cited in the bibliography of the source article. Each individual reference may also have links to an abstract and/or to other papers that cite that reference; these links increase the possibility of finding more potentially relevant articles. Key topics covered include culture and social structure, economic development, religion and science, and women's studies.—**Noriko Asato**

Dictionaries and Encyclopedias

723. Harris, John, and Vicky White. **Dictionary of Social Work and Social Care.** New York, Oxford University Press, 2013. 560p. $22.95pa. ISBN 13: 978-0-19-954305-2.

For anyone looking for an international perspective on the field of social work and social welfare, this volume will provide a good overview. Written from a UK perspective, a *Dictionary of Social Work and Social Care* has entries covering theories, terms, methods, policies, legislation, and organizations. Users will find up-to-date definitions on things like confidentiality, addiction counseling, and working with older populations. The work is multidisciplinary in scope. Many entries provide further reading resources (both print and online). This work belongs in the social work collections of large public and academic libraries. While it will not replace such standards as the National association of Social Work's

The Social Work Dictionary, it will provide a nice supplement for those interested in an international perspective. [R: LJ, 1 June 13, p. 140]—**Shannon Graff Hysell**

Handbooks and Yearbooks

724.   Gay, Kathlyn. **Bigotry and Intolerance: The Ultimate Teen Guide.** Lanham, Md., Scarecrow, 2013. 174p. illus. index. (It Happened to Me). $50.00; $49.99 (e-book). ISBN 13: 978-0-8108-8360-4; 978-0-8108-8361-1 (e-book).

Bigotry and Intolerance: The Ultimate Teen Guide is designed with the high school age student in mind who wants a broad overview of the emotional and societal issues behind bigotry and intolerance of people with different cultural, social, political, and religious backgrounds. While the teenage years are a time of great emotional and psychological change, there are many issues that may arise for the teen dealing with intolerance. The work focuses on what it means to be discriminated against, the various types of bigotry (e.g., religious, cultural), the difference between bigotry and racism, and how to cope with discrimination. Information in this work is presented through the personal stories of teens and young adults who have lived through these experiences; most of the stories focus on teenagers who have experienced discrimination and the various emotions and steps they took to resolve them. Specific chapters address bullying, the language of bigotry and racism, censorship, and the role of hate groups. The volume includes discussion questions at the end of each chapter to help teens verbalize their questions, up-to-date statistics, and first-hand advice from professionals. Teens who are experiencing strong emotions surrounding intolerance and racism and who have questions about how to cope with intolerance in their lives will find this guide useful. The personal experiences shared in this book will appeal to this target audience and could be useful for students this age researching this topic.—**Shannon Graff Hysell**

725.   **The State of the World's Children 2013: Children with Disabilities.** By the United Nations Children's Fund. Lanham, Md., Bernan Press, 2013. 152p. $25.00pa. ISBN 13: 978-9-28064-656-8.

The 2013 edition of this annual report focuses on ways in which world government should be ensuring that children with disabilities are not marginalized or made to be vulnerable. The chapters discuss the barriers that disabled children face, which oftentimes include discrimination, lack of health care, and lack of material goods. Best practices are discussed that will be of interest to those in politics, social work, health care, and education. Solutions focus around access to health care and education, proper nutrition, prevention of abuse and illness, protection from violence, elimination of abuse and exploitation, emergency response procedures, and how technology can be utilized to help in communication during these efforts.—**Shannon Graff Hysell**

Disabled

726.   **Arts and Humanities.** Gary L. Albrecht, ed. Thousand Oaks, Calif., Sage, 2013. 304p. index. (The Sage Reference Series on Disability). $80.00/vol.; $650.00/set. ISBN 13: 978-1-4129-8818-6; 978-1-4129-8015-9 (set).

727.   **Assistive Technology and Science.** Gary L. Albrecht, ed. Thousand Oaks, Calif., Sage, 2013. 304p. index. (The Sage Reference Series on Disability). $80.00/vol.; $650.00/set. ISBN 13: 978-1-4129-8798-1; 978-1-4129-8015-9 (set).

728.   **Disability Through the Life Course.** Gary L. Albrecht, ed. Thousand Oaks, Calif., Sage, 2013. 230p. index. (The Sage Reference Series on Disability). $80.00/vol.; $650.00/set. ISBN 13: 978-1-4129-8767-7; 978-1-4129-8015-9(set).

729.   **Education.** Gary L. Albrecht, ed. Thousand Oaks, Calif., Sage, 2011. 360p. index. (The Sage Reference Series on Disability). $80.00/vol.; $650.00/set. ISBN 13: 9781412986908; 978-1-4129-8015-9 (set).

730.   **Employment and Work.** Gary L. Albrecht, ed. Thousand Oaks, Calif., Sage, 2013. 448p. index. (The Sage Reference Series on Disability). $80.00/vol.; $650.00/set. ISBN 13: 978-1-4129-9292-3; 978-1-4129-8015-9 (set).

731.   **Ethics, Law, and Policy.** Gary L. Albrecht, ed. Thousand Oaks, Calif., Sage, 2013. 360p. index. (The Sage Reference Series on Disability). $80.00/vol.; $630.00/set. ISBN 13: 978-1-4129-8747-9; 978-1-4129-8015-9 (set).

732.   **Rehabilitation Interventions.** Gary L. Albrecht, ed. Thousand Oaks, Calif., Sage, 2013. 352p. index. (The Sage Reference Series on Disability). $80.00/vol.; $650.00/set. ISBN 13: 978-1-4129-9491-0; 978-1-4129-8015-9 (set).

This timely and important series is edited by the same authority who compiled the *Handbook of Disability Studies* (2003) and the *Encyclopedia of Disability* (see ARBA 2006, entry 805). The eight volumes in this set provide a cross-disciplinary look into the varied fields of study that make up disability studies. Incorporated throughout the volume are research from history, theory, and clinical application that will help researchers and practitioners learn more about the many ways in which those living with disabilities are affected on a day-to-day basis and how to best help them live better. The volumes are written in an engaging style that is not too technical in nature. Along with the text users will have access to statistical data, recommendations for further reading, a guide to organizations and associations, and ample cross-references between related topics. The series titles focus on: Ethics, Law, and Policy; Arts and Humanities; Employment and Work; Education; Disability Through the Life Course; Health and Medicine; Assistive Technology and Science; and Rehabilitation Interventions. The books are designed to be used together, but can easily be used individually. The tone of the series is positive in nature and focuses on new directions and trends in which the field of disability studies is moving. This series will be a worthwhile addition to large public libraries. All academic libraries offering courses in health care and social work should consider it a must-purchase.—**Shannon Graff Hysell**

733.   **The Complete Directory for People with Disabilities, 2014.** 22d ed. Millerton, N.Y., Grey House Publishing, 2013. 988p. index. $165.00pa.; $300.00 (online database; single user); $400.00 (print and online editions). ISBN 13: 978-1-61925-132-8.

Intended for individuals with disabilities, service providers, and family members and friends, this directory is a massive guide to a wide variety of resources and services. Some 9,009 directory entries are arranged under 27 chapters and more than 100 subchapters. Section 1 contains 24 chapters arranged by topic, including assistive devices, camps, computers, travel and transportation, veteran services, foundations and funding resources, independent living, and rehabilitation facilities. Many of these chapters include subcategories, appropriate to the topic, that aid in locating resources. For example, the chapter for assistive devices includes automobiles, hearing aids, chairs, kitchen and eating aids, ramps, scooters, wheelchairs, beds, and much more. Section 2 includes nine chapters for various disabilities, including aging, blind and deaf, cognitive, dexterity, hearing, mobility, specific disorders, speech and language, and visual. These, too, include subcategories for associations, camps, print and nonprint resources, and support groups, among others. The entries themselves are brief, usually including an address, telephone and fax numbers, e-mail and Website addresses, names of a few top personnel, and a very brief description of the resource or service. There are also three extensive indexes, including an alphabetic entry and publisher index, a geographic index arranged by state, and a disability and subject index that is quite detailed. This work can also be accessed as an online database through the publisher (http://gold.greyhouse.com). By using the database users can conduct subject-specific searches and find direct links to listee's Websites and e-mail addresses. Overall, this directory would be a valuable resource for public and academic libraries as well as for social service professionals in related fields. It will be a useful guide to caregivers as well as teachers, therapists, and health care providers.—**Stephen H. Aby**

Family, Marriage, and Divorce

Dictionaries and Encyclopedias

734.   **Encyclopedia of Domestic Violence and Abuse.** Laura L. Finley, ed. Santa Barbara, Calif., ABC-CLIO, 2013. 2v. illus. index. $189.00/set. ISBN 13: 978-1-61-69-001-0; 978-1-61069-002-7 (e-book).

This work looks at, as it title says, domestic violence and abuse. There are 173 articles written by 60 different contributors that look at this worldwide problem. There is an alphabetic list of topics as well as a topical list. Topics covered include articles on the historical information on abuse and forms of abuse such as acid throwing, dowry killings, honor killings, human trafficking, workplace violence, and domestic abuse. Other topics discuss the victims and offenders as well as the middle and upper classes and domestic abuse. There are articles on understanding and explaining abuse, the effects of abuse, and the correlates of abuse. Key people are listed as well as laws, court decision, and policies. Articles on interventions, prevention, and organizations and resources to combat abuse are included. The articles are often extremely grim and thought provoking. Most of the articles come with sources for further reading as well as suggestions for other articles to read in the encyclopedia.

There is a timeline of abuse that demonstrates that this is not a new social occurrence. It helps put this topic into perspective. There are two appendixes. The first consists of 4 documents that take up over 25 percent of the book, all of which are available online and could easily have been referenced in several of the entries. It appears as though they were used just to enlarge the book. The second lists organizations at the state, national, and international level that deal with domestic violence. A glossary is included as well as a section that recommends other books, journals, articles, and videos. There is also a section mentioning the contributors, who range from people with advanced degrees in a variety of academic departments to those with no degrees, but who were asked to contribute for a variety of reasons. A very good index is included. This will be a useful place to start discussing domestic violence.—**Robert L. Turner Jr.**

735.   Monger, George P. **Marriage Customs of the World: An Encyclopedia of Dating Customs and Wedding Traditions.** Santa Barbara, Calif., ABC-CLIO, 2013. 2v. illus. index. $189.00/set. ISBN 13: 978-1-59884-663-8; 978-1-59884-664-5 (e-book).

The author, a freelance heritage conservation consultant, folklorist, and writer, provides a timely and fascinating update to the 1st edition of this title published in 2004. He provides a thorough update to the original entries of this volume, while also including many new topics of interest on the subject of marriage and marriage customs around the globe. All of the articles are thoroughly documented, which adds greatly to the reference value of this title.

The book is set up like an encyclopedia with articles under the entries that are listed in the table of contents. Citations to other works follow each article. The articles are from two to three pages in length and the text is liberally sprinkled with black-and-white photographs. Within the articles there are cross-references to other topics that are related to the current one.

The content is fascinating. It covers most of the world, including places like the Middle East, South East Asia, Russia, Tibet, and Niger. Topics are different kinds of ceremonies, special objects related to marriage (e.g., ribbons, rice, favors, henna), people important to the marriage, and particular styles of wedding dress. It also covers the special topics related only to marriage, such as wife-selling, dowries, common-law marriage, same-sex marriage, or marriage by capture. The work includes the reasons behind customs and identifies their origins; provides comparative material across cultures; and discusses contemporary marriage customs and controversial subjects. His style is reminiscent of an academic text, but the language is very clear and uncomplicated.

Access to the content is especially good, which makes this a good book for reference collections. There is access through the table of contents (which is a listing of the article headings), but everyone should use the index because it is especially good. It was obviously done by a professional because it brings out all of the richness of the text. The table of contents alone does not do the book justice. There is a very good *see* and *see also* structure and there are no long strings of locators to chase down. The indexer did a good job of using subheadings to keep the searching easy.

The readability of the book makes it appropriate for all ages above middle school. As a reference book it would be very good in academic and public libraries. It could also be used as a text for comparative marriage customs.—**Lillian R. Mesner**

Handbooks and Yearbooks

736.   Apelqvist, Eva. **LGBTQ Families: The Ultimate Teen Guide.** Lanham, Md., Scarecrow, 2013. 197p. illus. index. (It Happened to Me). $50.00; $49.99 (e-book). ISBN 13: 978-0-8108-8536-3; 978-0-8108-8537-0 (e-book).

LGBTQ Families: The Ultimate Teen Guide is designed with the high school age student in mind who wants a broad overview of the issues and questions that teens from LGBTQ families may experience. While the teenage years are a time of great emotional and psychological change, there are many issues that may arise for the teen growing up in a LGBTQ family, including not being accepted by their peers, being perceived as different, or bullying. Information in this work is presented through the personal stories of teens and young adults who have lived through these experiences; most of the stories focus on teenagers growing up in an untraditional family and how their family deals with legal issues, the images pop culture gives of LGBTQ families, and activism. The book features sidebars with interesting facts related to the topic, up-to-date statistics, personal stories, and resources for further information. This book will be useful to teens with parents who of LGBTQ, teens who are LGBTQ, and anyone interested in modern-day families and the teen experience.—**Shannon Graff Hysell**

737.   **Child Abuse Sourcebook.** 3d ed. Valarie R. Juntunen, ed. Detroit, Omnigraphics, 2013. 629p. index. (Health Reference Series). $85.00. ISBN 13: 978-0-7808-1277-2.

The 3d edition of this sourcebook in the Omnigraphics Health Reference Series is needed even more today than the 1st edition was in 2004 (see ARBA 2005, entry 801). More than three million reports of child abuse are reported each year according to the U.S. Department of Health and Human Services. Sadly, this abuse often leads to long-lasting issues, including difficulty in social interaction and physical disabilities. This updated compilation of information from private sources and government documents is useful for parents, caregivers, social workers, and libraries when used in conjunction with updated Websites and addresses. Timeliness of information is difficult when budgets are cut in agencies and policies, personnel, and procedures change rapidly.

Divided into seven parts, this reference volume covers things such as child malnutrition, physical and sexual abuse, child neglect and emotional abuse, adult survivors of child abuse, preventions and interventions, and other sources for more information. It covers a wide range of topics, including some controversial ones, such as child exploitation, abuse by other children, Munchausen by Proxy

Syndrome, medical neglect, and Safe Haven laws. This book has something for every issue dealing with the mistreatment of children. A listing of telephone numbers, addresses, and Websites help those who need to contact the right organizations to help a child out of a bad situation or help a parent get aid to be a better parent. A bibliography of sources at the end of each chapter or at the end of the book would greatly enhance this work. The *Child Abuse Sourcebook* is recommended for social welfare agencies and school, public, and academic libraries.—**Robert L. Turner Jr.**

738.   **Domestic Violence Sourcebook.** 4th ed. Sandra J. Judd, ed. Detroit, Omnigraphics, 2013. 642p. index. (Health Reference Series). $85.00. ISBN 13: 978-0-7808-1261-1.

Judd, a regular editor in Omnigraphics' Health Reference Series, presents a starter reference on domestic violence for teachers, students, writers, and social service professionals. The book begins with a careful definition of the types of behavior commonly described as "domestic violence," most often but not exclusively effectuated by men against women. There is a succinct historical rundown on the topic, including myths and truths about domestic violence, the statistics surrounding this type of abuse, the cycle of abuse within families, and the progression of abuse in relationships. The first chapter presents a lot of current data and statistics on domestic violence in the United States, explaining the characteristics of abusers and victims, risk factors for domestic violence, detecting abuse, stalking, and sexual harassment. The following sections address the types of relationships in which abuse can be found (e.g., intimate) and abuse in specific populations (e.g., children, teen dating, abuse of men, elder abuse, abuse in the LGBT community). The final sections address remedies to the problem and how to spot and assist those being abused. Useful chapters in these sections include those on intervening in child abuse; men's role in domestic violence prevention; and methods of intervention by the workplace, religious communities, and legal system. There are even some chapters that address issues many may not have given previous thought to, such as protecting your pets in a violent situation, and the psychological and emotional reasons people stay with abusers. The work concludes with a glossary of terms, a directory of domestic violence resources and hotlines, and state child abuse reporting numbers. Because this problem is so wide spread and because this book includes a lot of issues within one volume, this work is recommended for all public libraries.—**Adrienne Antink**

739.   Slade, Suzanne Buckingham. **Adopted: The Ultimate Teen Guide.** rev. ed. Lanham, Md., Scarecrow, 2013. 211p. illus. index. (It Happened to Me). $50.00. ISBN 13: 978-0-8108-8568-4; 978-0-8108-8569-1 (e-book).

This revised edition of *Adopted: The Ultimate Teen Guide* is designed with the high school age student in mind who wants a broad overview of the emotional issues that the adopted teen may feel. While the teenage years are a time of great emotional and psychological change, there are many issues that may arise for the adopted teen, including questions about where they came from, why their birth parents chose adoption, the idea of meeting their birth parents, and questions about what defines "family." Information in this work is presented through the personal stories of teens and young adults who have lived through these experiences; most of the stories focus on adopted teenagers and the various emotions and steps they took to resolve them. Within there are stories of meetings with birth parents, fitting in to peer and family situations, finding out one's been adopted, and the realities behind international and transracial adoptions. This revised edition has added discussion questions at the end of each chapter to help teens verbalize their questions, up-to-date statistics, and first-hand advice from adoption professionals. Teens who are experiencing strong emotions surrounding their adoption and who have questions about how others have handled the questions behind locating birth parents will find this guide useful. The personal experiences shared in this book will appeal to this target audience and could be useful for students this age researching this topic.—**Shannon Graff Hysell**

Gay and Lesbian Studies

740.   **Feminist and Queer Information Studies Reader.** Patrick Keilty and Rebecca Dean, eds. Duluth, Minn., Litwin/Library Juice Press, 2013. 700p. illus. index. $60.00pa. ISBN 13: 978-1-936117-16-1.

Edited by an Assistant Professor in Information and member of the Bonham Centre for Sexual Diversity Studies in conjunction with a gender and technology researcher with a background in Information Studies and Women's studies, this volume presents an interdisciplinary approach to the fields of feminist and queer information studies from a technology and digital perspective for the library and information science practitioner. Organized into 7 parts, these 27 chapters authored by 30 international students, scholars, and practitioners in their fields offer a diverse range of informative chapters, both new and reprinted, to appeal to those in the intersecting fields of gender, sexuality, race, and technology through a library and information science lens. Nineteen of these chapters are based on or are directly from previously published materials, properly cited and acknowledged both in the introductory materials and on the entries themselves. These scholarly and academic chapters address information as gendered labor, cyborgs and cyberfeminism, the online environment, information organization, information extraction, and information flow, archives, and performance. The writing style is highly research-based, and the work offers inspiration and ideas for current and future practitioners, although the novice might be lost at the technical and subject-specific language used. Each chapter includes a bibliography, and there is an index that can be used in conjunction with the informative chapter titles to locate chapters of interest. This is a recommended book for any upper-level or graduate library where there is a growing interest on queer and feminist theory as a field that intersects technology, information science, and digital humanities.—**Sara Marcus**

741.   Myers, JoAnne. **Historical Dictionary of the Lesbian and Gay Liberation Movements.** Lanham, Md., Scarecrow, 2013. 453p. (Historical Dictionaries of Religions, Philosophies, and Movements). $120.00; $119.99 (e-book). ISBN 13: 978-0-8108-7226-4; 978-0-8108-7468-8 (e-book).

This remarkable collection of material on lesbian and gay liberation movements both foreign and domestic was compiled by a college academic whose previous publications include the *Historical Dictionary of the Lesbian Liberation Movement* (see ARBA 2004, entry 825). This new dictionary is divided into four parts. The first is a chronology of over 30 pages that traces developments related to same sex love from Ancient Greece to 2013 (many of these entries are related to countries outside the United States). The second is a 44-page introduction that deals in narrative form with key issues, movements, and general concerns related to lesbian and gay liberation. These include topics related to politics, sociology, and health. The third, and largest part, is a dictionary of about 600 entries, each averaging about 10 lines in length, which deal with important people, legislation, terms, concepts, movements, organizations, events, and key publications. The longest entries (a page or two in length) are those dealing with individual countries. The cross-referencing in this section is outstanding (necessary because there no general index). Bold type is used within entries to indicate related material and generous *see also* references are found at the end of each entry. Coverage in the dictionary emphasizes lesbian-related topics. For example, there are entries for authors June Jordan, Patricia Highsmith, and Lorraine Hansbury, but none for such influential gay writers as Edmund White, Andrew Holleran, or James Baldwin. The fourth section is an outstanding bibliography of about 1,200 unannotated books and articles arranged by subjects that cover all aspects of lesbian and gay life, including reference books, material on historical developments, and coverage on such contemporary social issues as employment, human rights, and coming out. Because of the wealth and breadth of the information found in this volume (plus its up-to-date coverage), this work is highly recommended for academic and public libraries where source material on the subject is in demand.—**John T. Gillespie**

Philanthropy

742.   Miner, Jeremy T., and Lynn E. Miner. **Proposal Planning & Writing.** 5th ed. Santa Barbara, Calif., Greenwood Press/ABC-CLIO, 2013. 268p. index. $41.95. ISBN 13: 978-1-4408-2967-3; 978-0-313-05027-5 (e-book).

As in earlier editions, this book discusses funding from government, foundation, and corporate sponsors. The title includes practical advice and examples on developing proposal ideas, identifying funding sources, creating systems and procedures to support grantseeking activities, developing procedural components, budget forecasting, submission procedures, and follow-up techniques. This latest edition includes a new chapter on "sustainability," or how to provide evidence that the project will sustain growth after the granting period. It also provides expanded chapters on assessment and evaluation, advanced writing tips to make your grant proposal stand out, and more examples. This standard resource helps grantseekers navigate the funding process and helps grantseekers pinpoint why grants proposals fail or succeed. The volume also includes checklists and a bibliography.—**ARBA Staff Reviewer**

Sex Studies

743.   Ratsch, Christian, and Claudia Muller-Ebeling. **The Encyclopedia of Aphrodisiacs: Psychoactive Substances for Use in Sexual Practices.** Rochester, Vt., Park Street Press, 2013. 734p. illus. index. $125.00. ISBN 13: 978-1-59477-169-9.

One only has to turn on a computer to discover advertisements for substances guaranteed to enhance sexual performance. The search for aphrodisiacs is as old as civilization. This encyclopedia by two anthropologists who have studied the subject in diverse cultures provides a detailed overview of the subject. Introductory chapters explain what aphrodisiacs are, how they are used, their effects on the senses, and their use in art. An alphabetic encyclopedia follows. Entries for each substance include the name, the type of substance (e.g., plant, mineral), history, ethnopharmacological use, and references. Color illustrations augment the text and shaded boxes offer bits of folklore about the various substances. Some entries have commentary about experiences with the various drugs. This is a comprehensive resource, covering both ancient (datura) and modern (ecstasy) aphrodisiacs. Health sciences and large public libraries will want to add it to their collections.—**Barbara M. Bibel**

Substance Abuse

Dictionaries and Encyclopedias

744.   **Alcohol and Alcohol Problems Science Database. http://etoh.niaaa.nih.gov/.** [Website]. Free. Date reviewed: 2013.

The National Institute on Alcohol Abuse and Alcoholism (NIAAA) has created this portal to support researchers and practitioners searching for information related to alcohol research. This page includes links to a number of databases, journals, and Websites focused on alcohol research and related topics. This database also includes a link to the archived ETOH database, which is the premier Alcohol and Alcohol Problems Science Database. It was produced by NIAAA from 1972 through December 2003. Although it is a fairly academic site, there are parts of it that can be of value to high school teachers and students as they discuss and research the topics of alcohol abuse and alcoholism in their classes.—**William O. Scheeren**

745. **Alcohol and Drugs in North America: A Historical Encyclopedia.** David M. Fahey and Jon S. Miller, eds. Santa Barbara, Calif., ABC-CLIO, 2013. 2v. illus. index. $189.00/set. ISBN 13: 978-1-59884-478-8; 978-1-59884-479-5 (e-book)

First published as *Alcohol and Temperance in Modern History: An International Encyclopedia* in 2003 (see ARBA 2005, entry 820), this encyclopedia has been revised and updated to reflect the latest research on alcohol and drugs. The 250 alphabetic entries cover issues related to alcohol and drug use and abuse in the United States and Canada, but it also includes information on Mexico, Central America, and the Caribbean. Approximately 100 contributors, scholars in the field, have written articles ranging in length from 500 to 7,000 words. Some 85 entries are completely new. The others have been revised or rewritten. Some of the older articles have been shortened and some have been dropped from this edition.

The *Encyclopedia* is interdisciplinary, looking at alcohol and drugs from many different perspectives. There are articles on the arts and religion, businesses, government and national groups, health, history and research, individuals and families, laws and enforcement, prohibition, geographic regions, setting for consumption, special populations, specific substances, temperance and pressure groups, and treatment and rehabilitation. They cover topics such as the representation of alcohol and drugs in film and television, microbreweries, organizations, people (e.g., Henry Anslinger, Timothy Leary), pro- and anti-alcohol groups, and alcohol as medicine. All articles have bibliographies. The book also has a chronology beginning with the founding of Bakers Chocolate Company in 1765 and continuing to the present An appendix contains documents, including the Harrison Narcotics Tax Act of 1914 and the Volstead Act of 1919. There is a bibliography of recommended bibliographies and reference works and an annotated list of online resources. This is a useful resource for school and public libraries.—**Barbara M. Bibel**

746. **Salem Health: Addictions & Substance Abuse.** Robin Kamienny Montvilo, ed. Hackensack, N.J., Salem Press, 2013. 2v. illus. index. $275.00/set. ISBN 13: 978-1-58765-959-1.

Drug abuse and misuse is a major public health problem in the United States. There is a need for information about substance abuse and other addictive behaviors. This new encyclopedia from Salem, part of its Salem Health series, offers current information on the subject for lay readers. Edited by a nurse and written by health care professionals and medical writers, the set contains more than 325 alphabetic entries covering all aspects of the field. They include information about psychological issues and behaviors (e.g., bulimia, hoarding), social issues (e.g., advertising for alcohol, celebrities and substance abuse), substances (e.g., aerosols, mushrooms/psilocybin), treatment (e.g., behavioral therapies for addictions, support groups), diagnosis and prevention (e.g., blood alcohol content, prevention methods and research), and health issues and physiology (e.g., cross-addiction, emphysema). The entries range in length from one to five pages and all are signed by the authors. They include references for further reading, relevant Websites, and cross-references. Black-and-white photographs augment the text. A series of appendixes offer a glossary, a bibliography, a directory of Websites, a list of substances of abuse with cross-references, pharmaceutical treatments, a directory of treatment centers and programs, a directory of addiction support groups and organizations, and a timeline of major developments in addictions and substances abuse. Categorical and subject indexes make it easy for users to locate information. This is an excellent overview of the substance abuse and addiction field for general readers and students. Purchase of the print set includes access to the online encyclopedia with remote access, a very useful benefit for public and school libraries.—**Barbara M. Bibel**

Handbooks and Yearbooks

747. **Alcohol Information for Teens.** 3d ed. Karen Bellenir, ed. Detroit, Omnigraphics, 2013. 371p. index. (Teen Health Series). $62.00. ISBN 13: 978-0-7808-1313-7.

Although teen alcohol abuse fluctuates over time, the overall pattern of abuse is alarming. The physical, mental, emotional, and behavioral effects of alcohol can be substantial. This handbook, written for a teenage audience, provides information on the causes, effects, and preventive measures related to alcohol abuse among teens. Overall, there are 45 chapters grouped into 7 sections or parts: basic information about alcohol and alcohol abuse, underage drinking, alcohol's physical effects, mental health and behavioral risks associated with alcoholism, alcoholism treatment and recovery, alcoholism in the family, and resources for more information.

The chapters in parts 1 and 2 explain the pressure for teens to drink, the scope of the problem, and the adverse consequences of drinking. Sections 3 through 4 address alcohol's effect on the body, brain, and the process of becoming addicted. Addressed within these sections are the effects of binge drinking, the association of drinking with reckless behavior, drinking and driving, diagnosing alcoholism, and withdrawal symptoms. All chapters are excerpted or adapted from other sources, which are cited. Chapters also include definitions of technical terms, things to remember, quick tips, and important facts. A final section of the book provides directory information on state and national organizations that provide additional information or assistance. There are also suggestions for further reading, as well as a combined subject/name/title index.

The chapters are quick to make a connection to their teenage reading audience. The prose is straightforward and the book lends itself to spot reading. It should be useful both for practical information and for research, and it is suitable for public and school libraries.—**Stephen H. Aby**

748.   Bestor, Sheri Mabry. **Substance Abuse: The Ultimate Teen Guide.** Lanham, Md., Scarecrow, 2013. 181. illus. index. (It Happened to Me). $50.00; $49.99 (e-book). ISBN 13: 978-0-8108-8558-5; 978-0-8108-8559-2 (e-book).

Substance Abuse: The Ultimate Teen Guide is designed with the high school age student in mind who wants a broad overview of the physical and emotional issues associated with substance abuse and teen use of drugs and alcohol. While the teenage years are a time of great emotional and psychological change, there are many issues that may arise for the teen dealing with substance abuse. The work focuses on the exposure that teens today have to substances, the reasons that teens experiment with drugs and alcohol, the physical and emotional aspects of addiction, and relapse and recovery. Information in this work is presented through the personal stories of teens and young adults who have lived through the experience of drug and alcohol abuse; most of the stories focus on teenagers who have experienced substance abuse first-hand. Specific chapters address the experimentation stage, prevention of addiction, holistic methods of recovery, and recovery and relapse. The volume includes discussion questions at the end of each chapter to help teens verbalize their questions, up-to-date statistics, and first-hand advice from professionals. Teens who are experiencing issues with substance abuse first-hand, either themselves or with a parent or friend, will find this guide useful. The personal experiences shared in this book will appeal to this target audience and could be useful for students this age researching this topic.—**Shannon Graff Hysell**

749.   **Drug Abuse Sourcebook.** 4th ed. Laura Larsen, ed. Detroit, Omnigraphics, 2014. 636p. index. (Health Reference Series). $85.00. ISBN 13: 978-0-7808-1307-6.

The human, social, and economic costs of drug abuse in this country are staggering. The medical and social costs of drug abuse are near $200 billion a year according to the U.S. Department of Justice. Yet, even figures like these fail to fully capture the breadth and depth of the effects of drug abuse. This volume, compiled from government and copyrighted sources, is an effort to map the causes and consequences of this social problem. The book is divided into seven parts: facts and statistics about drug abuse in the United States; drug abuse and specific populations; drugs of abuse; the causes and consequences of drug abuse and addiction; drug abuse treatment and recovery; drug abuse testing and prevention; and additional help and information. Each of these parts, in turn, is subdivided into numerous chapters that focus on more specific topics. For example, part 1 includes the prevalence of drug abuse, economic costs, and related deaths as well as discussions of the legal use of controlled substances, such as medical marijuana and prescriptions for controlled substances. Part 2 is new to this addition and includes articles on drug abuse and children, college students, women, and veterans. While part 3 provides an overview of many specific drugs, part 4 talks about the causes and consequences of abusing illicit and over-the-counter drugs. Equally important, this sourcebook includes other major sections dealing with treatment, recovery, and prevention. The last section includes glossaries of terms, a directory of state agencies for substance abuse, and a directory of organizations providing information about drug abuse. There is also a detailed name/title/subject index. While many of the sources consulted for this work are publicly available, the compilation and synthesis of that information for users of this volume is invaluable. This work is highly recommended for most academic and public libraries.—**Stephen H. Aby**

17 Statistics, Demography, and Urban Studies

Demography

Catalogs and Collections

750. **American Time Use Survey. http://www.bls.gov/tus.** [Website]. Free. Date reviewed: 2013.

The American Time Use Survey (ATUS) tracks the amount of time individuals spend doing various activities, such as work, child care, volunteering, and socializing. Like the Consumer Expenditure Survey, its original impetus is economic, and the study was created to measure the value of unpaid work (including housework) and labor productivity. In addition, it has been used by other federal researchers and social scientists to make international comparisons about American life, and to study sleep deprivation, eating habits, geriatric well-being, and work-life balance.

The ATUS is important to target market researchers because it provides nationally comparable estimates for American lifestyles and product usage. The tables contain itemized data of "time spent in detailed primary activities" for weekdays and weekends, with percentages and by gender. There is a section of colorful bar graphs and charts on such special topics as students, leisure and sports, household activities, and older Americans. In the data files section of the Website, there is an eating and health module with multiyear comparisons. Other items of special interest may be found in the "News Release" section (e.g., there is a table on "married parents' use of time").

The Website is well supported by tools and documentation. In addition, in the Overview section there are links to published academic studies and journal articles.— **Wendy Diamond**

751. **SimplyMap. http://geographicresearch.com/simplymap.** [Website]. Geographic Research. $7,197 (small school and public library discounts available). Date reviewed: 2013.

SimplyMap is an important Web-based mapping and reporting application with a rich collection of local-level data sets. Its key value derives from the combination of an innovative interface and its data partnerships with high-level providers such as MediaMark, D&B, Nielsen, and Experian Simmons. *SimplyMap* offers extensive demographic variables from government sources such as the Census and Bureau of Labor Statistics, plus additional material on business locations and media market profiles not typically found in other sources. Data can be retrieved for Tract and Block Groups, as well as for ZIP codes, counties, and states. The database provides an exceptional depth of information at the neighborhood level.

SimplyMap enables the novice or nonprofessional user to create complex and sophisticated maps and reports. The GIS-based interface is easy to learn, and maps can readily be exported to Word, PowerPoint, and Websites. The software has tools for customizing reports, creating bar charts, and rankings.—**Wendy Diamond**

752.   **U.S. Census Bureau. http://www.census.gov/.** [Website]. Free. Date reviewed: 2013.

This Web page is the best place to start searching for the multitude of data produced by Census programs, publications, and statistics. The home page groups the data under People, Business, Geography, Newsroom, At the Bureau, and Special Topics. Under Business, you can click on the Economic Census, NAICS, Survey of Business Owners, E-Stats, and Foreign Trade. Under People, business owners will be interested in income statistics, housing data, and more. Analyzing the Demographic trends in the United States allows businesses to forecast future demands for their products or services. The "New to Using Census Bureau Data" page is very helpful in helping users locate what they need quickly. The Catalog, a Search feature, and links to related sites are also accessible on the left side of the home page. Users can check this site frequently to learn more about local demographics and even help start and grow a business.—**Susan C. Awe**

Dictionaries and Encyclopedias

753.   **Immigrants in American History: Arrival, Adaptation, and Integration.** Elliott Robert Barkan, ed. Santa Barbara, Calif., ABC-CLIO, 2013. 4v. illus. index. $415.00/set. ISBN 13: 978-1-59884-209-7; 978-1-59884-220-3 (e-book).

This encyclopedia is arranged chronologically for its first three parts. The editor believes a chronological arrangement increases interest, appeal, accessibility, and relevance in the issues of immigration. These include the context of a common time, intermixing of cultures, and politics. Within each period ethnic groups are arranged alphabetically. These periods are 1600-1870, 1870-1940, and 1940-Present. Part 4, "Issues in U.S. Immigration," covers trends, themes, and the commonalities and differences between the various periods and people in parts 1-3. The 4 volumes contain 163 extensive essays. Of these, part 4 has 30 essays about the issues. Each essay concludes with a bibliography.

In addition, for access, each volume includes a comprehensive index to the entire set. And there are multiple approaches via this index. Several newspapers are listed. Also listed are broad concepts, like Nativism, Anti-Semitism, Religion and American Ethnicity, Politics, and Education. There are broad generic religious groups listed, such as Protestants, Jews, and Islam; also indexed are specific groups, Mennonites, Methodists, Baptists, and Dutch Reformed Church. Several geographic areas, from South Carolina to California present regional coverage. Issues include laws and court decisions, religious practices, demographic shifts from rural to urban, and language preservation, particularly of Native Americans.

Within the essays, contributors attempt to identify the origin of each group, and present the demographics of migration for each group. This was particularly difficult in reference to African Americans due to their involuntary immigration. Some essays contain several tables and statistics (e.g., "Canadians and Canadian Americans to 1870"). Others relate the ethnic group to their status during the Revolutionary and Civil Wars, later conflicts, and languages spoken. Contributors address how various ethnic groups' labor was utilized, industries which they influenced, their working conditions, and reaction by residents already in the United States, including racism towards several ethnic groups. Certain groups constructed ethnic communities, while others assimilated into the society at large. Other contributors, like the writer of "Immigrant Ports of Entry," display useful graphs that depict trends at various times. One can determine how peak immigration times differed between Boston and New Orleans. *Immigrants in American History* provides a useful overview and lists basic resources of ethnic immigration and the issues that surround this. [R: SLJ, June 13, p. 68]—**Ralph Hartsock**

Handbooks and Yearbooks

754.   Aiken, Charles Curry, and Joseph Nathan Kane. **The American Counties: Origins of County Names, Dates of Creation, Area, and Population Data, 1950-2010.** 6th ed. Lanham, Md., Scarecrow, 2013. 491p. $135.00; $129.95 (e-book). ISBN 13: 978-0-8108-8761-9; 978-0-8108-8762-6 (e-book).

The 1st edition of *The American Counties* by Joseph Nathan Kane came out in 1953 and was welcomed widely because it was among the first reference books to deal exclusively with American counties and provide information on the names of counties and because its author was one of the most respected producers of reference books at that time. Kane died in 2003 and the task of the first revision of the book in 22 years fell on Charles Curry Aiken. This 6th edition uses much of the same information in the earlier editions with updated population figures from 1950 to 2010.

There a number of titles on the market that address many of the same topics and statistics as this title, including Bernan's *County and City Extra* (21st ed.; see entry 778). The 6th edition of *American Counties* provides updated population figures, information on counties created since the last edition, and information on persons who have more than one county named after them. Also new to this edition is an appendix ranking all counties nationally by population and area as well as an appendix listing counties that have been eliminated. In the age of Google, it is not enough for reference books to provide information readily available on the Internet or in books, like population figures. Information should be intensive as well as extensive and should provide historical as well as current data. This title is not an essential purchase since most of the information it provides can be found through free online sites.—**George Thomas Kurian**

755.   **This Is Who We Were: In the 1950s.** Millerton, N.Y., Grey House Publishing, 2013. 443p. illus. index. $150.00. ISBN 13: 978-1-61925-179-3; 978-1-61925-180-9 (e-book).

Works such as this offer a wealth of readily accessible factual information about a particular period and are usually targeted for a general audience. Hence, they are extremely useful to high school and college students as well as to teachers in preparing reports, term papers, and lectures. Included in Grey House Publishing's Working American Series, this outstanding volume is no exception. As shown here, popular stereotypes of the 1950s as something of a sterile, conservative, anti-intellectual wasteland are overly simplistic. Complex better describes the era, as evidenced by its contrasts and contradictions. If optimism and confidence characterized the 1950s, so too did fear and paranoia, seen by a morbid obsession with Communism near and far. Down South many white southerners were convinced the Communist Party's pernicious influence was being exercised through the NAACP. If conformity was the reigning principle, those youngsters who rocked with Elvis, Fats Domino, and Little Richard were oblivious, to the dismay of their elders. And if domesticity was the prevailing sentiment, many women nonetheless ventured beyond the fireside hearth. The percentage of wives working outside the home increased from 25 percent in 1950 to 40 percent by 1959.

The work is divided into five parts. Section 1 consists of profiles of 34 ordinary folks, their homes, jobs, and neighborhoods, from a former slave in South Carolina, Ann O'Connor's crusade against violent comic books, and a casino operator in Las Vegas to a science teacher in Oklahoma City, a rock 'n' roll musician in Tennessee State Prison, and an Italian immigrant in New Jersey. This is good social history, for collectively the profiles give a sense of what it was like to live in the 1950s. Section 2 provides historical snapshots of the decade in the early 1950s, the mid-1950s, and the late 1950s, covering politics, movies, technology, books, and much more. Economic matters are the subject of section 3, including: advertisements for products; the cost of food, clothing, and housing; annual income; and a useful index of the dollar's value from 1860 to 2010. Making up Section 4 are 33 reprints of magazine and newspaper articles and excerpts from speeches and books, such as "Desegregation's Hot Spots" from *Time*, October 1954, and "Lyndon Pledges Satellite Probe" from *The Paris News* (Texas), October 1957. And section 5 is a treasure trove of census data from 1950 to 2010. Enhanced by an abundance of photographs, charts, graphs, and maps, an extensive bibliography, and an adequate index, this work will be a worthy addition to the reference collections of high school and colleges.—**John W. Storey**

756.   **Transforming America: Perspectives on U.S. Immigration.** Michael C. LeMay, ed. Santa Barbara, Calif., Praeger/ABC-CLIO, 2013. 3v. illus. maps. index. $163.00/set. ISBN 13: 978-0-313-39644-1.

This three-volume set addresses immigration throughout U.S. history in chronological order. The volume is edited by emeritus professor of California State University, San Bernardino, who is assisted by a team of well-established academics and doctoral students as well as practicing immigration lawyers and policy makers. Volume 1 coves immigration to the end of the Civil War. Volume 2 covers Reconstruction through World War II. And, volume 3 discusses immigration from the Cold War to the present day. The chapters provide interesting details of immigration during the intended time period and present the issues that were at the forefront at that time. The book is supplemented with photographs, illustrations, charts, and graphs, and each chapter has its own bibliography. Unfortunately, there is no cumulative index. This book could be useful in the reference collection or in the circulating collection of academic libraries. [R: Choice, June 2013, pp. 1814-1815]—**Philip G. Swan**

757.   **Yearbook of Immigration Statistics 2011.** By the U.S. Department of Justice. New York, United Nations, 2013. 212p. $26.00pa. ISBN 13: 978-0-16091-717-2.

The *Yearbook of Immigration Statistics 2011* is a compendium of data in tabular form that provide data on foreign nations who have been granted lawful permanent residence into the United States for the year 2011. It also provides statistics on those that were admitted into the United States on a temporary basis, those who applied for asylum or refugee status, and those that were naturalized. Information on law enforcement action taken against illegal immigrants is also noted within the tables. This work will be useful for those research immigration statistics of the United States; however, the dated nature of the statistical figures may limit its usefulness.—**ARBA Staff Reviewer**

Statistics

United States

758.   **Bureau of Economic Analysis (BEA) http://www.bea.gov.** [Website]. Free. Date reviewed: 2013.

This government Website from the Department of Commerce produces a wealth of statistical information on the U.S. economy. Its mission is to produce and circulate accurate, timely, relevant, and cost-effective statistics and to provide a comprehensive, up-to-date description of U.S. economic activity. The ups and downs of the U.S. economy and regional economic development affect every business (both large and small) in some way. Use the BEA to keep a close eye on what is happening in the economy. The BEA's "US Economy at a Glance" section will help you do just that. The BEA also produces the *Survey of Current Business*, a monthly publication that provides data on personal income, state and regional economic statistics, and more.—**Susan C. Awe**

759.   **County Business Patterns. http://www.census.gov/econ/cbp/index.html.** [Website]. U.S. Census Bureau. Free. Date reviewed: 2013.

County Business Patterns (CBP) is an annual statistical series about economic activity in small areas. Arranged according to the NAICS, it provides data on the number of establishments, number of employees, and total payroll dollars. Business planners use CBP to evaluate market potential, assess competition, manage sales territories, and plan advertising campaigns. Despite its title, data are not limited to counties. For local planning, statistics at the ZIP code and metropolitan area levels are useful. The information is presented in tabular form at the Website and can be accessed from American FactFinder (http://factfinder.census.gov/home/). In addition, downloadable files are available for time series analysis and other statistical operations.—**Wendy Diamond**

760.   **Data.gov. http://www.data.gov/.** [Website]. Free. Date reviewed: 2013.

FedStats, the official Website of the Federal Interagency Council on Statistical Policy, is a gateway to statistics from over 100 U.S. Federal agencies and is well organized and easy to use. Users can find under Links to Statistics, "Topic Links A-Z," "MapStats," and "Statistics By Geography from U.S. Agencies." MapStats provides statistical profiles of states, counties, cities, Congressional Districts, and federal judicial districts. The "Statistical Reference Shelf," a bit further down on the homepage, is a large collection of online reference sources like the *Statistical Abstract of the United States* (131st ed.; see entry 866). You will find a variety of other sources such as the *State and Metropolitan Area Data Book* and *Digest of Education Statistics*, which will provide statistics on many topics of interest to entrepreneurs. On the other half of the page, Links to Statistical Agencies, under "Agencies by Subject," click Economic on the drop down arrow to lead you to a list of Periodic Economic Censuses. Below this area, you'll find "Data Access Tools," which link users to agency online databases.

Data.gov is a portal to statistics and data sets produced by federal government agencies and offices. Eventually it will replace the FedStats site (http://fedstats.gov; see ARBA 2012, entry 863), which has been available since 1997 and allows users to access statistical data produced by the federal government without having to know which agency produces what particular statistics. It is best consult both Websites for now, however, since FedStats often times provides some data that Data.gov does not.—**Susan C. Awe**

761.   Dulberger, Michael D. **America's Ranking Among Nations: A Global Perspective of the United States in Graphic Detail.** Lanham, Md., Bernan Press, 2013. 201p. maps. index. $65.00pa. ISBN 13: 978-1-59888-603-0.

America's Ranking Among Nations by Michael D. Dulberger provides a graphical portrayal of the status of the United States and its position relative to other nations over a wide spectrum of topics including demographics, education, the economy, international trade, employment, energy, health, innovation, and defense. Bar charts are utilized to present cross-sectional data and include the values of data points. Line charts show time series data, many of which offer a vista of 50 or more years. The value of data used to create line charts are given only for the most recent year, since incorporating all values would result in clutter. Pie charts depict relative share with share values shown. A few maps indicate country membership in key blocs, (e.g., European Union). Charts are quite current, utilizing, in most case, information through 2010. Comparisons are provided in many instances for the top 10 countries as well as pertinent bloc, such as OECD. All data were drawn from reliable national and international sources. The author has restricted his presentation to "facts" and has made no attempt to analyze or interpret. A table of contents and an index facilitate finding specific subjects of interest. Much useful data have been gathered in this single volume and it is presented in a manner offering accessibility to a wide range of readers.—**William C. Struning**

762.   **Easy Stats. http://www.census.gov/easystats/.** [Website]. Free. Date reviewed: 2014.

Designed to make statistics "quicker and easier to access," this Website from the U.S. Census Bureau is an interactive tool for those looking for statistics on everything from finance and jobs, to housing, people, and education in the United States. The data on this site are from the American Community Survey and the 2010 Census. Users can choose from a limited number of predefined data sets to find the need statistics. The data are presented in tables, which can be exported to Microsoft Excel. The site is easy to navigate with its pull-down menus and easy-to-find navigation buttons. The data set provided here will be better for undergraduates and general audiences. Those needing more robust and sophisticated statistics will want to search *American FactFinder* (see ARBA 2012, entry 833) or *State and County Quick Facts* (http://quickfacts.census.gov/).—**ARBA Staff Reviewer**

763.   **Economy at a Glance. http://www.bls.gov/eag/eag.us.htm.** [Website]. Washington, D.C., U.S. Bureau of Labor Statistics. Free. Date reviewed: 2013.

The Bureau of Labor Statistics compiles and publishes a number of prominent economic indicators, available from its Economy at a Glance Website. Data on unemployment and consumer prices (usually called inflation) highlight BLS's data. Another popular indicator available from Economy at a Glance is productivity, a measure of the productive output of the nation's workers. Unlike many economic indicators, many of those available from the BLS, including unemployment and prices, include data at the state and metro level (also available from economy at a Glance).—**Eric Forte**

764.   **Housing Statistics of the United States, 2012.** 5th ed. Shana Hertz Hattis, ed. Lanham, Md., Bernan Press, 2013. 401p. index. $160.00. ISBN 13: 978-1-59888-575-0. ISSN 1521-5601.

This reference contains some 250 tables on housing stock, demand, production, investment, market data, financing, and utilization of federal housing programs. Examples of the information provided are the number of owned housing units versus those rented, broken out by state. Other variables are included, such as how many rooms the house has and the ethnic and age composition of the households. The reader will find median rents and sale prices reported by state. Even the nature of the neighborhood (e.g., vandalism, trash, bars on the windows) and the condition of the units (e.g., broken windows, sagging roofs, exposed wiring) are noted.

The statistics reflect a range of dates, but the majority are multiyear indicators with 2010 and 2011 being the most recent years available. The table of contents and detailed index give easy access to the broad array of information available. The introductory preface gives an overview of the past decade in the real estate industry, describing the housing bubble, housing characteristics, and housing financials. The two appendixes identify the reporting source for each table, definitions for the headings used in each figure, and descriptions of the surveys and censuses used to collect the data. Everything one will ever want to know about housing can be found in this useful resource. It will be useful for those in the industry as well as general users needing insight into current living conditions across the country.—**Adrienne Antink**

765.   **Ranking America's Fifty States: A Comparison in Graphic Detail.** Lanham, Md., Bernan Press, 2013. 222p. $39.00; $38.99 (e-book). ISBN 13: 978-1-59888-669-6; 978-1-59888-670-2 (e-book).

Ranking America's Fifty States presents graphic comparisons of socioeconomic characteristics of U.S. states. A wide range of attributes are portrayed by means of 173 graphs grouped into 10 chapters: demographics, health, lifestyle, education, crime, environment, resources, personal finance, state economy, and federal influence. Bar charts are utilized to portray the analyses. In single characteristic charts (solid bars), the four most heavily populated states (California, Texas, New York, and Florida) are shown in individual colors positioned among the ordered array of bars. In multiple characteristic charts (segmented bars), colors identify individual characteristics, again in an ordered array of bars. A national average is given for each chart. An overview, as well as a summary table, precedes each chapter. The summary tables are displayed alphabetically by state with the highest five ranking states highlighted in green and the lowest five in red. Included in an appendix are a map of the United States and a listing of all 50 states showing top honors for highest and lowest characteristics earned by each state. Data sources are provided for each chapter and an appendix summarizes database resources and Website portals for further investigation. An introduction to the charts, a table of contents, and an index aid in orienting the reader and in locating specific items of interest. The book is formatted not only to enable easily absorbed graphic comparisons among states, but to provide useful insights into the national life style as well.—**William C. Struning**

766.   **State and Metropolitan Area Data Book 2013.** Deirdre A. Gaquin and Gwenavere W. Dunn, eds. Lanham, Md., Bernan Press, 2013. 450p. index. $89.00; $88.99 (e-book). ISBN 13: 978-1-59888-627-6; 978-1-59888-630-6 (e-book).

This databook provides a summary of statistics on the social, political, and economic organization of the states and metropolitan areas in the United States, and it serves as a supplement to the *Statistical Abstract of the United States* (2014 ed.; see entry 767). Source citations allow it to act as a statistical reference and guide to other statistical publications and sources form the U.S. Bureau of the Census. Emphasis is, of course, one the states and metropolitan areas, but tables are also included that provide data for the counties that comprise the metropolitan area as well as its central city. This edition includes the 2010 census counts and even more recent population counts. There is expanded information on vital statistics, communication, and criminal justice data, as well as data on health insurance and housing and financials. Demographic and statistical data are provided for population, birth and death rates, school enrollment, crime rates, income and housing, employment, government, and transportation. Source notes now appear at the bottom of each page of tables and also in the source notes and explanations appendix. Also included is directory information for federal agencies with major statistical programs. Each agency's mailing address, telephone number, and Internet address is given. This inexpensive volume belongs in every library.   **William C. Struning**

767.   **Statistical Abstract of the United States 2014: The National Data Book.** Lanham, Md., Bernan Press, 2014. 1025p. index. $179.00. ISBN 13: 978-1-59888-639-9.

The latest edition of this venerable reference work has added 55 new tables on topics as varied as firearm-related violence and deaths, homeless population, prevalence of allergies among children, sexual assault in the military, student loans of bachelor's degree recipients, and online course enrollment. This annual report provides detailed statistics on a variety of subject in U.S. life, including health, education, elections, income, communications, transportation, construction and housing, and geography and environment. As the most comprehensive and authoritative source for statistics on the United States since 1878, every library, whether public, research, special, or academic, must own at least one copy of the current *Statistical Abstract of the United States.*—**Gregory A. Crawford**

International

768.   **Balance of Payments Statistics Yearbook.** By International Monetary Fund. Lanham, Md., Bernan Press, 2013. 1075p. $153.00. ISBN 13: 978-1-61635-403-9.

The *Balance of Payments Statistics Yearbook 1998* is an in-depth reference organized into 3 parts. Part 1 is the detailed tables on balance of payments and statistics for participating countries, and the international investment position data for nearly 50 countries. Part 2 aggregates the country data by major balance of payments components. For each component, data for countries, country groups, and the world are provided. Data for international organizations are also included in part 2. Part 3 is the formulas, practices, and data sources for deriving each country's balance of payments statistics. This part outlines the government agency that provided the statistical information, the currency used, and supporting documentation for calculation of statistics. This publication is recommended for special government libraries, business libraries, and large academic libraries that have a need for economics statistics information.—**Kay Stebbins Slattery**

769.   **Government Finance Statistics Yearbook 2012. Volume 36.** By International Monetary Fund. Lanham, Md., Bernan Press, 2013. 633p. $102.00pa. ISBN 13: 978-1-61635-405-3.

This volume provides in-depth financial data for central, state, and local governments of countries across the world. The data tables are presented in world, country, and international categories. The tables can best be used to do international comparisons between countries by allowing users to discover major components as percentages of total expenditure and lending minus repayment. It all allows users to discover the types of revenue as percentages of total revenue as well as find expenditures by function as percentages of total expenditure. Overall, users will be able to use these figures to examine the structure and magnitude of each government's operation. Data are presented on government revenue, grants, expenditures, financing, and debt.—**William C. Struning**

770.   **International Yearbook of Industrial Statistics 2013.** By the United Nations Industrial Development Organization. Northhampton, Mass., Edward Elgar, 2013. 848p. $310.00. ISBN 13: 978-1-78195-564-2; 978-1-78195-565-9 (e-book).

The *International Yearbook of Industrial Statistics 2013*, published by United Nations Industrial Development Organization, provides comprehensive statistical data on world manufacturing. The 2013 publication is the 19th annual edition in the series. The purpose of the series is to place manufacturing in global perspective as well as to enable comparisons. The first part of the book treats world manufacturing as a whole and offers comparisons among nations and subgroups. The second part, by far the largest, shows the role of manufacturing in individual countries, thus enabling comparisons of categories of manufacturing within nations. Some countries, mostly small, were not included in the current edition since the present book is already quite large and since the omitted countries were already included in recent editions. The concept of value added by manufacturing (MVA) is widely utilized. Documentation is provided to clarify nuances in meaning, specification, and scope. The yearbook represents a massive effort in data collection, data harmonization, and tabular presentation—well beyond the constraints of time and resources available to the average researcher or investigator. Therefore, the yearbook presents a vast amount of information in a convenient form. Sources and methods are discussed in an introduction, along with explanatory notes on the tables.—**William C. Struning**

771.   **National Accounts Statistics: Analysis of Main Aggregates.** New York, United Nations, 2012. 250p. $80.00. ISBN 13: 978-92-11615-56-2.

772.   **National Accounts Statistics: Main Aggregates and Detailed Tables 2010.** New York, United Nations, 2010. 5v. $350.00/set. ISBN 13: 978-92-11615-55-5.

National Accounts Statistics: Analysis of Main Aggregates and *National Accounts Statistics: Main Aggregates and Detailed Tables* provide national accounts estimates for more than 200 countries and areas, covering years 1970 through 2010. This series is issued in accordance with the recommendation of the Statistics Commission that the statistics division of the United Nations should publish regularly the most recent available data on national accounts for as many countries and areas as possible. Information concerns gross domestic product by expenditures in current and constant prices and on the relations among product, income, savings and net lending aggregates. For each country covered, sources of the data (other than from the survey data) are described and statistics are presented in the currency of each country. Each country contains the following statistical tables: gross domestic product by expenditures at current prices; gross domestic product by expenditures at constant prices; relations among product, income, savings, and net lending aggregate; value added by industries (at current prices); value added by industries (at constant prices); output, gross value added, and fixed assets by industries (total economy); output, gross value added, and fixed assets by industries (tables are presented for specific industries); government final consumption expenditure by function at current prices; and individual consumption expenditure of households, NPSHs, and general government in current prices. *National Accounts Statistics* should be a part of larger research and academic library collections.—**Lucy Heckman**

773.   **OECD Factbook 2013: Economic, Environmental, and Social Statistics.** Lanham, Md., Bernan Press, 2013. 292p. index. $70.00pa. ISBN 13: 978-9-26-417706-2.

For individuals seeking statistical information on the countries that belong to the Organisation for Economic Co-Operation and Development (OECD), this is the best source available. The OECD is composed of some 30 major democracies from around the world, including countries such as Australia, Belgium, Canada, Mexico, Norway, Poland, Turkey, the United Kingdom, and the United States. Thus, the statistics included in this volume span the world and most of the largest industrial nations. This year the *OECD Factbook* features a focus chapter on gender.

The work is divided into sections: population and migration, macroeconomic trends, prices, energy, labor market, science and technology, environment, education, public policies, quality of life, and a special section focusing on economic globalization. Within each section, the charts are prefaced by a textual introduction that discusses trends and provides a definition of what is being measured, in addition to providing the sources for the information. The charts generally give data for each country of the OECD over a specific time period, most often up until 2011. Thus, time trend data are easy to generate from the tables. The index, while short, does provide adequate access to the tables. A Web link is provided for each table that directs the user to a Web page where the corresponding data are available in Excel format, a useful feature for researchers.

While not a mandatory purchase for most libraries, especially since the data are available freely online, many academic and special libraries will want to purchase this volume for their reference collections. The data are provided in an easy-to-use format that researchers and students will find valuable.—**Gregory A. Crawford**

774. **OFFSTATS: Official Statistics on the Web. http://www.offstats.auckland.ac.nz/.** [Website]. Free. Date reviewed: 2013.

There are plenty of statistics sites, but not many are as comprehensive and well maintained as the University of Auckland Library's OFFSTATS, a centralized collection of links to free, official sources. The site is arranged into three sections: country, region, and subject. The sections are accessible through pull-down menus. Each set of sources provides information on the publisher name or acronym when relevant. There are very few outdated links and it appears that the sites are double-checked at least on an annual basis. While the site does link to larger sources of statistics, the site's true value is in its links to smaller, more difficult-to-find sources, such as those put out by individual countries and smaller organizations. Many times these sources provide deeper information than do the larger databases. While the site was developed for residents and students of Australia and New Zealand and those areas a well represented, its coverage of global statistical sites is very complete and makes it worth noting. Another bonus: no registration is required to access the site and all information is available for free.—**ARBA Staff Reviewer**

775. **Statistical Yearbook 2010: Fifty-Fifth Issue.** New York, United Nations, 2012. 650p. $155.00. ISBN 13: 978-92-10613-15-6.

Prepared by the Statistics Division, Department of Economic and Social Affairs of the United States Secretariat, *Statistical Yearbook* provides international statistics on various social and economic issues. It is complemented by the *Monthly Bulletin of Statistics* published by the same Division.

This edition presents 60 tables on nearly 20 topics, primarily for 2000-2010, and consists of 4 parts. Part 1 provides key world and regional statistics, and parts 2 through 4 present data concerning individual countries or areas. Part 2, "Population and Social Statistics," includes Population and Human Settlement; Literacy; Health, Childbearing and Nutrition; and Culture and Communication. Part 3, "Economic Activity," includes National Accounts and Industrial Production; Financial Statistics; Labour Force; Wages and Prices; Agriculture, Forestry and Fishing; Manufacturing; Transport; Energy; Environment; and Science and Technology and Intellectual Property. Part 4, "International Economic Relations," includes International Merchandise Trade, International Tourism, Balance of Payments, International Finance, and Development Assistance. The emphasis seems to be on economic data. Each chapter includes a section titled "Technical Notes," which describes the data. The data sources are presented in the "Statistical Sources and References" at the end of the publication.

Although the noncomparability of data due to currency conversion rate fluctuations, differences in sources, and variations in the institutional patterns of countries should not be ignored, this publication continues to be a core reference title for international statistics and is recommended for any serious reference collection.—**Mihoko Hosoi**

776. **UNCTAD Handbook of Statistics 2012.** By the World Trade Organization. New York, United Nations, 2012. 190p. $65.00. ISBN 13: 978-92-87038-46-3.

The *UNCTAD Handbook of Statistics* provides a comprehensive collection of statistical data relating to international trade, investment, and development. The tables are designed primarily for government officials, planners, and researchers involved in transnational trade and development, especially in assessing the growth patterns and imbalances. The tables are organized in eight parts: international merchandise trade; international merchandise trade by region; international merchandise trade by product; international merchandise trade indicators; international trade in services; commodities; international finance; and development indicators. A number of these tables and indicators are available in other World Bank and UN statistical publications, but a number of others are unique to this *UNCTAD Handbook*. These include workers' remittances; import and export concentrations and structural change indexes; import MFN tariff rates; and diversification indexes. For specialized trade and development data *UNCTAD Handbook of Statistics* is an indispensable resource. The only drawback is that there is no analytical introduction or interpretive commentary, and the data can be used only by trained professionals.—**George Thomas Kurian**

777. **World Statistics Pocketbook 2011.** New York, United Nations, 2012. 256p. $20.00pa. ISBN 13: 978-92-11615-58-6.

World Statistics Pocketbook is a small handbook that brings together statistical information for the countries and regions of the world. The data provided are for the most part uniform except in cases where certain statistics do not apply. The most recently compiled information for each country is provided and generally covers the years 2000-2011. For each country the following information is provided: general information (e.g., region, currency, surface area, United Nations membership date), economic indicators (e.g., exchange rate, unemployment, number of people owning automobiles and with access to the Internet), social indicators (e.g., population growth rate, life expectancy, infant mortality, number of educated citizens), and environment (e.g., threatened species, energy consumption per capita). The "Technical Notes" section at the back of the volume illustrates how data were gathered and the "Data Dictionary" defines the statistical terms used. Because this volume is small and meant to be used only for ready-reference use, the publisher has provided additional United Nations resources that researchers can consult to find more information. This is not a necessary purchase but at such a low price it may be useful for its ready-reference value.—**Shannon Graff Hysell**

Urban Studies

778. **County and City Extra, 2013: Annual Metro, City, and County Data Book.** 21st ed. Lanham, Md., Bernan Press, 2013. 2v. maps. $150.00/set; $149.99 (e-book). ISBN 13: 978-1-59888-633-7; 978-1-59888-634-4 (e-book).

Because the *County and City Data Book* from the U. S. Bureau of the Census is on a five- to six-year publication cycle, Bernan Associates continues to fill in the gaps with this very useful series. Now in its 21st edition, this volume follows the format established by the Census Bureau. A series of large color maps highlight major population shifts in the United States—migration, ethnic populations, age distribution, population density, educational attainment, unemployment, and land use. This reference compiles information from many sources to provide all the key demographic and economic data for every state, county, metropolitan area, congressional district, and for all cities in the United States with a 2010 population of 25,000 or more. As with most Census Bureau compilations (most notably the *Statistical Abstract of the United States* [see entry 767]), the currency of information varies from table to table.

Depending on budgets and need, this is a title that might not have to be purchased every year. However, all editions are highly recommended for large public and academic libraries where it will be used heavily as a ready-reference resource.—**Thomas A. Karel**

18 Women's Studies

Bibliography

779. **GenderWatch.** http://www.proquest.com/en-US/catalogs/databases/detail/genderwatch. shtml. [Website]. Ann Arbor, Mich., ProQuest. Price negotiated by site. Date reviewed: 2013.

GenderWatch, updated quarterly, contains more than 125,000 full-text items from academic and scholarly journals, magazines, newspapers, newsletters, regional publication, books, booklets and pamphlets, conference proceedings, government publications, and nongovernmental organization (NGO) and special reports. It also includes archival material, in some cases as far back as the 1970s, with new archival material added as it becomes available. The database supports programs in gender and women's studies, public policy, political science, sociology and contemporary culture, education, literature and the arts, health sciences, history, business, and more. Like *Contemporary Women's Issues* from Gale (see ARBA 2005, entry 856), *GenderWatch* is interdisciplinary and international in scope, with a focus on English-language materials, and provides only abstracts for articles in scholarly journals. Unlike *Contemporary Women's Issues*, *GenderWatch* provides cover-to-cover contents. The database was originally produced by Softline Information and called *Women "R"*.—**Linda Friend**

780. **Studies on Women and Gender Abstracts.** http://www.routledge.com/genderstudies/. [Website]. New York, Routledge/Taylor & Francis Group. Price negotiated by site. Date reviewed: 2013.

This database covers from 1995 to the present, although print copies of *Studies on Women* Abstracts began in 1983. It provides access to citations on research related to women's studies and gender. On these pages users will find information on titles that cover sexuality, feminist theory, feminism, gender, gay and lesbian studies, queer theory, women's studies, and much more. Users will also find information on research books, series, reference titles, and books for courses.—**Noriko Asato**

Biography

781. **Distinguished Women of the Past and Present.** http://www.distinguished women.com. [Website]. Free. Date reviewed: 2013.

This Website offers biographies of women who contributed to their fields in different ways, including writers, educators, scientists, heads of state, politicians, artists, entertainers, and more. The site's creator, Danuta Bois, developed this site to provide a more in-depth analysis of women's achievements than can be found in the typical history book. Users can search by name or by subject. There are special sections of the site that provide information on women's contribution is black history, movies and books that are about women, and music by women. To date, the site features over 5,500 links to sites on nearly 2,000 featured women and continues to grow.—**ARBA Staff Reviewer**

Catalogs and Collections

782. **Contemporary Women's Issues. http://www.cengage.com/.** [Website]. Stamford, Conn., Gale/ Cengage Learning. Price negotiated by site. Date reviewed: 2013.

Contemporary Women's Issues (CWI) contains more than 65,000 full-text items covering a broad range of topics pertaining to women, such as human rights, health and reproductive issues, violence, work, development, feminism, and legal information. It contains articles from more than 600 sources worldwide, including periodicals, newsletters, reports, fact sheets, and pamphlets. Coverage is international, with a focus on English-language materials, and the database is updated weekly. For several major women's studies journals, CWI provides only abstracts of articles (but full-text book reviews) and does not always include cover-to-cover contents. It is, however, an excellent source for ephemera not always readily available in libraries and for background and factual information.—**Linda Friend**

Handbooks and Yearbooks

783. Nadeau, Kathleen, and Sangita Rayamajhi. **Women's Roles in Asia.** Santa Barbara, Calif., Greenwood Press/ABC-CLIO, 2013. 208p. illus. index. (Women's Roles Through History). $58.00. ISBN 13: 978-0-313-39748-6; 978-0-313-39749-3 (e-book).

Contrary to the conventional notion that Asian women are submissive and mysterious, women in Asia have played a substantial and active role through history as evidenced by several prominent women political leaders. Nadeau and Rayamajhi provide a broad understanding of women's lives in historic and contemporary Asia and seek to challenge stereotypical images of Asian women as portrayed by Western media in this well-researched book. The volume begins with a chronology that expands from 3100 B.C.E. to 2011 that encompasses 18 countries from East, South, to Southeast Asia. In the introduction the authors highlight the varied and important roles women throughout Asia have played while recognizing their diverse historical, social, and cultural similarities and differences. The main body of the text is organized under six thematic topics with the first four chapters exploring the roles of Asian women in religion, work, family, and politics. Chapter 5 examines women's contributions to literature and the last chapter focuses on the changing roles women have undertaken, from both historical and contemporary perspectives, to achieve at today's status in society. The volume also contains black-and-white illustrations, a glossary, nearly 100 selected bibliographies, and a dictionary Index. This well thought-out survey on women in Asia is suitable for high school students to the general public. Readers are encouraged to consult other sources if requiring more in-depth research into one particular country or individual.—**Karen T. Wei**

784. Shouse, Aimee D. **Women's Rights.** Santa Barbara, Calif., ABC-CLIO, 2014. 195p. index. (Documents Decoded). $79l00. ISBN 13: 978-1-61069-199-4; 978-1-61069-200-7 (e-book).

Taking a broad view of the ongoing efforts to attain rights for women, this work provides unique insight into the context of the issues and reveals the range of factors that can influence a particular policy decision. This book presents an overview of women's rights that also addresses specific policy decisions. Within each policy entry, the author explains the factors that can influence a particular policy decision, such as the current American political culture, prevailing views of women as mothers and caretakers, perceptions of female/male relationships, systemic governmental influences, and conflicting opinions over the role of government in decisions related specifically to women's lives. A dominant theme that prevails throughout the volume is the idea that rights that have historically been assumed by men oftentimes must be granted to women—a concept that may be new to students using this volume. Primary source documents that have had a role in the history of women's rights are listed chronologically.

The are organized into subjects, including "Women and Work," "Women and Education," "Women and Politics," "Women's Health and Reproduction," "Women and Violence," and "Women's Rights in the Twenty-First Century." Each primary source document is introduced with several paragraphs from the author describing the circumstances around the event and why it was important. The document is then presented, allowing students to experience firsthand what citizens at the time may have been experiencing. Side notes are provided to explain difficult concepts or to provide context to what is being discussed.

This work will provide students with a deeper understanding of the evolution of women's rights in this country and what work still needs to be done to ensure equity among for all people. This will be a particularly useful book in high school libraries and undergraduate libraries.—**ARBA Staff Reviewer**

Part III
HUMANITIES

19 Humanities in General

General Works

Biography

785. **Who's Who in Research: Cultural Studies.** Bristol, United Kingdom, Intellect; distr., Chicago, University of Chicago Press, 2013. 1v. (various paging). $115.00. ISBN 13: 978-1-84150-498-8.

The intention of this volume is to provide an easily accessible guide of the names and research interests of the leading academics who have been published with Intellect, Ltd. This is a two-volume A-Z compendium with volume one featuring comprehensive profiles of scholars in the area of cultural studies, including their name, institution, a short biography, current research interests, and a list of their articles published with Intellect. To make the volume user friendly, an index based on key words is included. This volume will be a valuable resource for scholars and librarians, or for any person seeking more detailed information about one of Intellect's authors.—**Joseph P. Hester**

Indexes

786. **British Humanities Index. http://www.proquest.com/en-US/catalogs/databases/detail/bhi-set-c.shtml.** [Website]. Bethesda, Md., ProQuest. Price negotiated by site. Date reviewed: 2013.

The *British Humanities Index* provides an index and abstracts of periodical literature from humanities journals, magazines, and newspapers published in the United Kingdom. The BHI broadly covers the humanities and arts including art and architecture, archaeology, antiques, cinema, gender studies, history, language and linguistics, literature, music, philosophy, religion, and theater. The index also includes current and foreign affairs, political science, economics, environment, and law; thus being a very good source for interdisciplinary humanities and social sciences topics. Links to full-text sources are offered for some entries.—**ARBA Staff Reviewer**

787. **Humanities & Social Sciences Index Retrospective, 1907-1984. http://ebscohost.com/academic/humanities-social-sciences-index-retrospective.** [Website]. Bronx, N.Y., H. W. Wilson. Price negotiated by site. Date reviewed: 2013.

788. **Humanities Full Text Index. http://ebscohost.com/academic/humanities-full-text.** [Website]. Bronx, N.Y., H. W. Wilson. Price negotiated by site. Date reviewed: 2013.

789.   **Humanities Index Retrospective, 1907-1984. http://ebscohost.com/academic/humanities-index-retrospective-1907-1984-h.w.-wilson.** [Website]. Bronx, N.Y., H. W. Wilson. Price negotiated by site. Date reviewed: 2013.

Dating from 1974 when the H. W. Wilson *Social Sciences and Humanities Index* (1965-1974) was separated into two publications. The Humanities Index is one of the leading cumulative indexes to English-language periodicals in the humanities. The contents of some 600 periodicals from all areas of the humanities and, in some cases, the social sciences, are indexed in the Humanities Index. The same can be said of the Social Sciences Index, treating interdisciplinary subjects such as anthropology. These indexes are an ideal place to begin a search. The Humanities Full Text Index includes bibliographic indexing and abstracts for full-text articles from over 600 scholarly journals in the humanities. Updating is monthly.

Humanities Index Retrospective is a separate database that contains the contents of nearly 800,000 articles from the period 1907-1984. Humanities & Social Sciences Index Retrospective contains citations to more than 1,300,000 articles, including over 240,000 book reviews from 1,200 periodicals as far back as 1907.—**Anna H. Perrault**

20 Communication and Mass Media

General Works

Biography

790. **Who's Who in Research: Media Studies.** Bristol, United Kingdom, Intellect; distr., Chicago, University of Chicago Press, 2013. 1v. (various paging). $115.00. ISBN 13: 978-1-84150-497-1.

Who's Who in Research: Media Studies, a publication of Intellect and distributed by the University of Chicago Press, is an interesting concept but ultimately not worth the price tag ($115), in the opinion of this reviewer. The series purports to gather the names of leading academics who have published in journals sponsored by Intellect; five volumes in the series cover cultural studies, film studies, performing arts, visual arts, and media studies. Included in each volume is a number of academics' names, institutional information, a brief biography, research interests, and one to two citations of articles published in Intellect journals (a very small number of authors included have more than two citations included). An index offers keywords with authors' names connected; for example, the keyword "identification" is linked to Richard Wilkins and Karen Wolf, while "media theory" is linked to David W. Park and Johanna Dorer. Given the frequency with which academics move to new institutions and embrace new research areas, such a volume—despite its intentions to provide up-to-date information on distinguished names in certain fields—is sure to rapidly fall out of date. While the volumes will be updated annually, it would make more sense to create an online database that could be searchable for a fee, a far more green solution, rather than continually print hard copies of such a publication.—**Stephanie Vie**

Dictionaries and Encyclopedias

791. **Encyclopedia of Media and Communication.** Marcel Danesi, ed. Toronto, University of Toronto Press, 2013. 738p. $48.00pa. ISBN 13: 978-1-4426-1169-6.

Marcel Danesi (professor of Linguistic Anthropology at the University of Toronto) edited this compendium of media and communication-related terms that aims for both breadth and depth. As he states in the introduction, the thrust of this volume is to offer "the bulk of the ideas that the media student or the interested general reader will need to know in order to understand what is going on in the field" (p. x). Its foundational emphasis on semiotics ensures that the overall treatment of the field is grounded in meaning.

At 738 pages, including timelines of print media, radio and recordings, film and video, television, the Internet and World Wide Web, and advertising, the *Encyclopedia of Media and Communication* offers a substantial number of entries overall. Entries range from brief biographic profiles of famed media studies scholars and critics (such as Theodor Adorno, Donna Haraway, and Marshall McLuhan) to lengthier, research-heavy discussions of major theoretical perspectives. For instance, the entry for "text theory" compiled by Thomas F. Broden is twenty-six pages long, is divided into multiple sections for ease of reading, and includes approximately 300 references for further consultation. Unfortunately, the encyclopedia lacks an index, which makes searching through such a lengthy volume a bit more difficult. Similarly, few images are included; their inclusion might have added more imagistic emphasis and thus appealed to those whose learning style is primarily visual. Overall, this encyclopedia can meet the needs of both undergraduate students and graduate students as well as researchers in the field; the entries are written with clarity and precision but offer enough depth and suggest further research in their bibliographies for more advanced readers.

The *Encyclopedia of Media and Communication* is a recommended volume for media studies scholars and teachers. While Danesi notes that the *Encyclopedia* is "the first comprehensive encyclopedia for the growing fields of media and communication studies," others published in 2009 and 2010 by M. E. Sharpe, Sage, and The University of Chicago Press may have already filled that niche. However, Danesi's work offers one of the most up-to-date and current encyclopedias of media and communication currently available.—**Stephanie Vie**

792. **Encyclopedia of Media Violence.** Matthew S. Eastin, ed. Thousand Oaks, Calif., Sage, 2013. 456p. index. $295.00; $369.00 (e-book). ISBN 13: 978-1-4129-3685-9; 978-1-4522-9965-5 (e-book).

The *Encyclopedia of Media Violence* brings together the work of experts from a range of fields. The volumes contain a table of contents, an alphabetic list of entries, and a reader's guide of topical entries. The volume contains a list of contributors with names and affiliations. There are 134 signed entries covering topics ranging from general aggression, media effects, media policy, and society and the media, to media content and theories of media influence. The entries range in length from 400 to 5,000 words. All entries are followed by citations for further readings and references. Because of the broad coverage, the reader's guide is essential. The category names in the reader's guide are accessible to the general public. The contributors have strived to cover the latest information in this area of study to make the work as up to date as possible. Overall, this is a very good resource for the general public and undergraduate students. This work is recommended for public and academic libraries.—**ARBA Staff Reviewer**

793. **Encyclopedia of Public Relations.** 2d ed. Robert L. Heath, ed. Thousand Oaks, Calif., Sage, 2013. 1152p. index. $325.00; $406.00 (e-book). ISBN 13: 978-1-4522-4079-4; 978-1-4522-7623-6 (e-book).

The 2d edition of this work is an authoritative compilation of essays on topics related to public relations. Edited by well-known public relations scholar Robert Heath and an impressive group of public relations educators, the encyclopedia focuses on the history and evolution of the profession, the key figures and concepts, and the myriad challenges and opportunities facing the profession. Entries include contributions from practitioners, scholars and representatives of public relations organizations, resulting in a valuable cross section of viewpoints from both the academy and the "real world" of the public relations professional. This new edition has been updated to reflect the ever-increasing role that the Internet and social media now play in the field of public relations.

Defining public relations is a difficult task and the profession continues to struggle with the negative perceptions often associated with it. The acknowledgement of these issues and the inclusion of entries detailing challenges in the areas of ethical concerns and social responsibility result in a generally well-balanced coverage of the profession. Due to the reality that the overwhelming majority of the growth of the public relations profession has historically been based in the United States there is an understandably U.S.-centric emphasis. Despite this, there has been a clear attempt to acknowledge the growing emphasis on the "internationalization" of the profession and there are a number of entries dedicated to global public relations.

This work includes over 500 alphabetic entries and nine appendixes, which include women pioneers in public relations, milestones in the history of public relations, and public relations online resources. A "Readers Guide" groups the entries into subject areas ranging from "crisis communication and management" to "theories and models," a tool that should be helpful for readers unfamiliar with the topic. The entries are all extensively indexed at the back of both volumes. There is also a listing of illustrations and tables; however, while many of the tables are useful, most of the illustrations add minimal value to the entries.

The uniqueness of this encyclopedia makes it a resource with value to a broad cross-section of libraries. It should be a core resource in the reference collections of academic libraries supporting mass communications programs, but should also be considered for broader use in any academic library that supports undergraduates or for inclusion in public library collections.—**ARBA Staff Reviewer**

794. **International Encyclopedia of Communication Online. http://www.communicationencyclopedia. com/public/.** [Website]. Hoboken, N.J., Wiley-Blackwell. Price negotiated by site. Date reviewed: 2013.

This site covers communication studies (from mass media to communication theory), interpersonal communications, journalism, and public relations. Since 2009, there have been over 300 updates adding a total of 30 new entries to the collection and updating a further 274. The editors are continually revising and adding new entries to keep this site up to date. Students, lecturers, and researchers will find the *International Encyclopedia of Communication Online* an invaluable learning, teaching, and research resource—**Noriko Asato**

Directories

795. **Plunkett's Entertainment & Media Industry Almanac.** 2014 ed. Jack W. Plunkett, ed. Houston, Tex., Plunkett Research, 2014. 580p. $349.99pa. ISBN 13: 978-1-60879-725-7.

The *Almanac* is divided into four parts. "Major Trends Affecting the Entertainment & Media Industry," the first part of the book, has several short essays on recent topics and trends in the industry. Here users will find essays on historical entertainment and media industry trends, a discussion of trend sin e-commerce and internet-based entertainment, and an essay on the trends in electronic games and online gambling. "Entertainment & Media Industry Contacts" supplies the addresses, telephone numbers, Websites, and a one-sentence description of the most relevant contacts in the field. The list is broken down into more than 25 subjects, making searching an individual company difficult unless you know in which category it was placed. Finally, the heart of the book is titled "Entertainment & Media 400," which provides individual data profiles for over 400 firms that are primarily located in the United States. Industries include: entertainment chain stores, cable television and satellite companies, top publishing companies, leading music publishers and recording firms, and leading broadcasters. Each profile includes company name, ranks, business activities, type of business, brands/divisions/affiliations, contacts, address, financials, apparent salaries/benefits, competitive advantage, "other thoughts," growth plans/special features, and locations. The profiles give an excellent overview of each company. This section is the strongest feature of the *Almanac*. Also included are an "Entertainment & Media Industry Glossary" and an index of firms noted as "Hot Spots for Advancement for Women & Minorities"; both are particularly attractive to students and job-seekers.

Overall, *Plunkett's Entertainment & Media Industry Almanac* is an important tool any special libraries serving the media, entertainment, public relations, and advertising industries as well as employment centers, academic libraries with programs in these fields, and any public research library.—**Rob Laurich**

Handbooks and Yearbooks

796.   Licona, Adela C. **Zines in Third Space: Radical Cooperation and Borderlands Rhetoric.** Albany, N.Y., State University of New York Press, 2012. 191p. illus. index. $75.00; $24.95pa; $24.95 (e-book). ISBN 13: 978-1-1384-4372-0; 978-1-4384-4373-7 (e-book).

Authored by an Associate Professor of English at the University of Arizona and co-editor of *Feminist Pedagogy: Looking Back to Move Forward* (Hopkins Fulfillment Service, 2009), this work presents five chapters on the third-space theory that engages in the subcultural space of zines as alternate media. Looking specifically at the zines of feminist and queer of-color groups that challenge the dominant knowledge and presentation of knowledge and history, this work opens readers' eyes to other views of current, past, and future knowledge and history. Beginning with a chapter on borderlands rhetoric and third-space sites, the work continues to explore the role of imagination in challenging everyday dominations through the articulation at work in producing antiracist and egalitarian social agendas. The third chapter addresses embodied intersections through a reconsideration of subject formation beyond binary borders, followed by a chapter offering queer inquiries and third-space subversions as related to queer consumption and production. The final chapter offers an epilogue on third-space theory and borderlands rhetoric applied theory and the everyday. Including numerous illustrations, this well-researched and well-documented work will open all readers' eyes to alternate ways of looking at the world, and new materials that can be used to explore the histories of both majority and hidden communities, materials that present ideas and memories that are not often represented in the mainstream materials often used for scholarship. This is a valuable book for any student of public history, culture, or any underrepresented group.—**Sara Marcus**

Authorship

797.   Hopper, Vincent F., and Cedric Gale. Benjamin W. Griffith. **Essentials of English.** 6th ed. Hauppauge, N.Y., Barron's Educational Series, 2010. 240p. index. $11.99pa. ISBN 13: 978-0-7641-4316-8.

This updated and expanded edition of *Essentials of English* provides a review of English grammar, sentence structure, correct word usage, and punctuation for students and writers. There is advice and samples of how to alter writing for difference environments, such as classroom assignments, writing for the business environment, and electronic communication. The best advice comes in the form of providing readers with detailed instructions on how to begin a classroom essay, including the importance of outlining the subject, writing a first draft, editing, and final proofreading. A sample research paper is provided that explains how to cite sources, create a reference list, and format papers. MLA style is used throughout the volume so it is important that students are aware of this so they can alter their style if other styles, such as APA or Chicago Manual of Style, are required.—**Lori D. Kranz**

798.   **A Manual for Writers of Research Papers, Theses, and Dissertations.** 8th ed. By Kate L. Turabian. Revised by Wayne C. Booth, Gregory G. Colomb, and Joseph M. Williams. Chicago, University of Chicago Press, 2013. 448p. index. $18.00p. ISBN 13: 978-0-226-81638-8.

This latest interpretation and implementation of the *Chicago Style* has been enhanced by a section on research and writing adapted from Booth, Colomb, and Williams' *Craft of Research*. This section focuses on the gathering, organizing, and presenting of information and ideas and serves as a separate supplement to the mechanics of the style guidelines. It includes an examination of the ethics of scholarly research, as well as the technical aspects. The style guidelines are based on the 16th edition of *The Chicago Manual of Style* (2010). The guidelines are meant to be standard practice, but may be altered by the requirements of specific disciplines or departments, if needed. The text is further enhanced by the use of blue typeface to highlight headings and examples. A section of citation formats is followed by another on style. An appendix displaying paper formats and submission guidelines with sample pages is followed by a bibliography of additional sources; a short biography of Booth, Colomb, and Williams; and an index. The newest edition in over 7 years accounts for changes in technological applications and revised guidelines for formatting research papers, theses, and dissertations.—**Martha Lawler**

Journalism

799.   **Hudson's Washington News Media Contacts Directory 2013.** 46th ed. Amenia, NY., Grey House Publishing, 2013. 350p. index. $289.00pa. ISBN 13: 978-1-61925-111-3.

Now in its 46th edition, this directory has retained the same general format as found in preceding editions. Founded by respected public relations professional Howard Penn Hudson in 1968, the directory is the single most comprehensive source available for Washington, D.C. area press contact information.

The Washington Press Corps consists of "the largest concentration of journalists in the world," thus the more than 4,000 news organizations and media contacts. Directory entries are arranged into 7 major media categories with 20 subdivisions. Included within is contact information for newspapers, news services and wire, radio/television, magazines and periodicals, foreign news, and special services. There are additional sections specific to media headquartered in Washington, D.C., along with an entry name index, geographic/foreign media index, personnel index, magazine subject index, and assignment locator index. Cross-listing of entries provides several options for locating relevant listings. While the majority of the content is comprised of standard directory contact information, the added value lies in the detailed personnel listings accompanying each entry, which include contact information for individuals within the organizations.

The directory, while comprehensive, obviously has a very narrow focus and therefore a limited use for anyone outside of the mass media professions. It is suggested primarily for special libraries, but may also have some value to academic libraries supporting journalism/mass communication programs. It will be valuable to government press offices, public relations and marketing professionals, journalists, and association officials around the Washington D.C. area.—**Patrick J. Reakes**

800.   **News Media Yellow Book: Who's Who Among Reporters, Writers, Editors and Producers in the Leading National News Media. Winter 2013 ed.** New York, Leadership Directories, 2013. 1135p. index. $595.00pa. (annual subscription); $566.00pa. (automatic renewal). ISSN 1071-8931.

News Media Yellow Book is one of 14 Leadership Directories covering government, non-profit organizations, businesses, and professional institutions. Published quarterly since 1990, the 2012 editions cover approximately 33,000 positions at over 1,900 national media organizations. Entries include major news wires, newspaper chains and syndicates, major daily and ethnic newspapers, major networks, television and radio stations and programs in the top 30 markets, leading consumer, government and trade magazines, and independent journalists and columnists. Headquarters and U.S. bureaus of over 178 foreign-owned media are also included.

Five general sections covered in the entries include: General Information (e.g., contact information, editorial content, circulation information, ownership), Chief Editorial Officer (e.g., photograph, educational/career background), News Executives (hierarchical listing with direct contact information), Administrative Services (e.g., managers of supporting departments such as libraries, information technology, public relations, circulation), and Headings (news staff reporting to the News Executives section). Indexes include: assignment, Washington-based regional assignment, online media, program, periodical, geographical, name, and media. One notable feature of the listings is the detailed contact information for specific people within each organization, including e-mail addresses for many of the individuals listed. There is also an electronic edition available that includes daily updates and additional content, including beat information, additional journalist entries, "pitching notes," and a Leadership

Mobile feature that provides access to content from a handheld device.

This is one of the most comprehensive of the media directories available and the relatively narrow focus makes it especially useful for special libraries and media professionals. It is also recommended as a core resource for academic libraries supporting journalism and mass communication programs and for general reference collections in larger academic libraries.—**Patrick J. Reakes**

Newspapers

801.   **NewsBank. http://www.newsbankschools.com.** [Website]. Naples, Fla., NewsBank. Price negotiated by site. Date reviewed: 2013.

This useful provider of newspaper information has several products for school libraries. KidsPage offers materials from documents, magazines, newspapers, Websites, and reference sources on all curriculum topics carefully selected for elementary audiences. Access World News is a daily updated news source from 200 countries and is appropriate for both middle level and high school students. NewsBank Retrospective is based on newspapers from the United States and shows broad perspectives of recent historical issues such as the Vietnam War, the end of the Soviet Union, and the administrations of Nixon, Ford, Carter, Reagan, and Bush. A particularly strong set is America's Historical Newspapers (1690-1992), which offers content from newspapers, both national and regional, and supports American history, government, and literature classes. Other collections are also available, including some in Spanish.—**Barbara Ripp Safford**

802.   **World News Digest. http:/www.infobase.com/.** [Website]. New York, Facts on File. Price negotiated by site. Date reviewed: 2013.

This is an excellent factbook resource for school libraries. It covers political, social, cultural, and athletic events. Published by Infobase Publishing and updated twice weekly, this resource contains an archive of seven decades of news along with current events. It includes 200 biographies, more than 100 key events, overviews of 50 controversial issues, and thousands of hyperlinks. The resource is appropriate for middle school and high school students and is an excellent source for introducing young adults to people and events that have shaped and are shaping our world. The cost is reasonable for school libraries, and the cope of content is very broad.—**ARBA Staff Reviewer**

Radio, Television, Audio, and Video

803.   Martland, Peter. **Recording History: The British Record Industry 1888-1931.** Lanham, Md., Scarecrow, 2013. 361p. illus. index. $80.00; $79.99 (e-book). ISBN 13: 978-0-8108-8252-2; 978-0-8108-8253-9 (e-book).

Recording History presents the history of Great Britain's musical recording industry from 1888 to 1931. Its 11 essays are presented in chronological order and illustrate the founders of the industry, the successes and failures experienced, the major recording companies (e.g., Atlantic, The Gramophone Company, EMI), key marketing strategies to get the industry off the ground, and its role in World War I and after. Also discussed are the changes the performers had to make in order to reach a new audience through records and how the recording industry led to a new appreciation of music to an entirely new audience. Written from a historian's point of view the author uses a multitude of archival sources in his research and each chapter ends with a notes section. The work concludes with a currency converter, glossary, bibliography, and an index. There is an inset in the middle of the book with black-and-white photographs of live performances, promotional materials, and recording equipment of the day.—**Shannon Graff Hysell**

804. **Radio Rides the Range: A Reference Guide to Western Drama on the Air, 1929-1967.** Jack French and David S. Siegel, eds. Jefferson, N.C., McFarland, 2014. 232p. illus. index. $49.95pa. ISBN 13: 978-0-7864-7146-1; 978-1-4766-1254-6 (e-book).

The American cowboy appeared briefly on the historical stage from the period of about 1860 until 1890. Their legends and stories have lasted longer through stories told in movies, television programs, and radio shows. *Radio Rides the Range* is a handy guide to over 100 cowboy radio shows that were aired during the period from the early 1920s to the advent of mass market television programs around 1967 (*The Lone Ranger*, for example, ended live on air production on September 3, 1954). Recordings of these shows live on in the hearts of die-hard fans who eagerly listen to past programs via a number of audio copies, some available on the Internet. The entries in this encyclopedia are written by a variety of authors, all of whom have ties or interest in old-time radio. Interestingly, of the 20 article authors only 2 are women. Some program entries are very short (such as *Buffalo Billy Bates*), while major shows, such as *Bobby Benson*, extend for nine pages. There is a list in appendix 1 of shows that the editor knows existed, but insufficient information is available to write even a brief description of the show.

Typical show entries include name, network, format, duration of run, sponsor, number of audio copies known to exist, and location of know transcript copies. Next follows the actual show narrative, which as noted above can extend to several pages and include a number of photographs of the cast often inside the studio where the show was produced. The entries end with a list of sources used to obtain information about the show. Appendixes for the book include: a list of known shows for which limited data are available; a timeline of important show introductions; a list of shows included on mainstream radio programs; audio sources on the Internet; and a list repositories that have copies of show transcripts. The encyclopedia concludes with a very useful bibliography (including Web sources), brief biographies of the contributors, and an index. Overall, the book is a fascinating glimpse into the world of the American cowboy and its portrayal on old-time radio.—**Ralph Lee Scott**

21 Decorative Arts

Collecting

General Works

805. Contemporary Collecting: Objects, Practices, and the Fate of Things. Kevin M. Moist and David Banash, eds. Lanham, Md., Scarecrow, 2013. 273p. illus. index. $80.00; $79.99 (e-book). ISBN 13: 978-0-8108-9113-5; 978-0-8108-9114-2 (e-book).

The idea of collecting as a reflection of historical and cultural development is examined in a series of scholarly essays written by various authors, differing from the usual price guides and how-to sources on collecting. An introduction gives an overview of the types and techniques of collections and collecting, as well as the arrangement of the essays. The 12 new essays and one reprinted essay are grouped into four basic themes: collecting in a virtual world, relationships between collector and their collections, collecting as a reflection of identity (both personal and political), and how collecting practices relate to cultural development. The essay topics range from whimsical to sobering (i.e., from toys to Nazi propaganda), from the curiosity cabinets of the seventeenth and eighteenth centuries to the more modern MP3 files. Each essay is followed by a bibliography and some are enhanced with illustrations. There is an index and information about the essay contributors at the end. This is an interesting examination of collections and collecting that would serve as a beginning place for scholarly research.—**Martha Lawler**

Art

806. Price It! Antiques and Collectibles. http://www.gale.cengage.com/PriceIt/. [Website]. Stamford, Conn., Gale/Cengage Learning. Price negotiated by site. Date reviewed: 2013.

This database is an identification, research, and pricing tool for collectors, dealers, appraisers, and anyone interested in the trade. Price and sales data are provided from eBay, TIAS.com, land-based auction houses, and antique businesses. The database has 127 searchable categories with 41 million records and more than 60 million images. It is a useful resource for public libraries with clientele interested in art collecting.—**ARBA Staff Reviewer**

Coins and Currency

807.   Friedberg, Arthur L., and Ira S. Friedberg. **Paper Money of the United States: A Complete Illustrated Guide with Valuations.** Clifton, N.J., Coin & Currency Institute, 2013. 305p. illus. index. $67.50; $42.50pa.; $29.50 (e-book version). ISBN 13: 978-0-87184-720-1; 978-0-87184-202-2 (e-book).

This venerable resource is in its 20th edition representing a span of more than 50 years. The authors have compiled a reference source embracing nearly every form of paper recognized and used as money from colonial to current times.

The resource is arranged chronologically from the date U.S. currency was first issued in 1861, and then subdivided by variety and denomination. Each note is shown in obverse and reverse half-tone images. Detailed information is given in series order, including the issuing bank, the number printed, and the valuation of two to three different conditions. Then follows several sections devoted to an assortment of paper monies used prior to 1861, such as those issued by the colonies or the treasury notes of the War of 1812, as well as special circumstances post 1861, such as the use of encased postage stamps when coins were nearly nonexistent during the Civil War. There is also a section on Confederate currency. This new edition provides all color photographs, most of which illustrate the collections of the American Numismatic Association in Colorado Springs, Colorado, and the Federal Reserve Bank of San Francisco. Also included for the first time is a section on U.S. paper money errors and a complete listing of large size star notes. Supplementary sections include an introduction and guide to using the resource, a list of national banks, signatures on U.S. currency, and a discussion of uncut sheets.

For the collector of United States currency, this reference is the "bible" of the hobby. The Friedbergs, recognized authorities in the numismatic world, continue the high standards of quality established by their father, Robert Friedberg. With the many recent modifications in U.S. currency, this latest edition is highly recommended for public libraries and special collections where identification and dating of historical notes is needed.—**Margaret F. Dominy**

808.   Shafer, Neil, and Tom Sheehan. **Panic Scrip of 1893, 1907 and 1914: An Illustrated Catalog of Emergency Monetary Issues.** Jefferson, N.C., McFarland, 2013. 406p. illus. index. $75.00pa. ISBN 13: 978-0-7864-7577-3; 978-1-4766-0570-8 (e-book).

During times of economic crisis real currency was difficult to come by for many reasons. To maintain business and commerce, the U.S. government would allow banks and businesses to print scrip money, essentially promissory notes, for payroll and trade. This was the situation during the panics of 1893, 1907, and 1914 in the United States. This book is an illustrated catalog of the emergency monetary issues for each of these years. Background information of the economic crisis leads each section of the book giving a context of the period. For each crisis, issues are listed alphabetically by state. Issues are illustrated (sometimes both front and back) as a high resolution half tone images. Details such as condition and rarity are also provided. Occasionally additional notes are included. Several appendixes offer additional insights, 1907 Pseudo or Parody Scrip, Miscellaneous Scrip, the Clearing House Certificate, and G.B. DeBernardi Labor Exchange Scrip of 1895-1905 round out this important resource. Enthusiasts, historians, and collectors of this numismatic niche will find this work indispensable.—**Margaret F. Dominy**

Crafts

809.   **Hobbies and Crafts Reference Center. http://www.ebscohost.com/public/hobbies-crafts-reference-center.** [Website]. Ipswich, Mass., EBSCO. Price negotiated by site. Date reviewed: 2013.

It would be difficult to find any hobby or craft that is not included in this comprehensive database. The full text of more than 760 magazines and books, 720 instructional videos, and more than 140 full-text hobby reports are included on more than 140 specific topics. The topics range from the broad, as in antiques and genealogy, to the daring, as in bungee-jumping or hang gliding, to the secondary, such as embroidery and quilting. Every public library could use this fun database that will appeal to a wide range of patrons.—**Anna H. Perrault**

810.   **Native Village Arts and Crafts Library. http://www.nativevillage.org/.** [Website]. Free. Date reviewed: 2013.

Although the links focus on North American native peoples, there are links to Japanese, Caribbean, and Aboriginal artisans located in this site. Many of the links feature videos of artists at work as well as instructions for making pieces, such as dream catchers and cornhusk dolls. The links are not categorized in any discernible fashion, which makes it more difficult for users to find appropriate information. However, a patient researcher will find links that would be valuable for teaching and scholarly pursuits alike.—**ARBA Staff Reviewer**

811.   **Textile Technology Complete (TTI). http://www.ebscohost.com/academic/textile-technology-complete.** [Website]. Ipswich, Mass., EBSCO. Price negotiated by site. Date reviewed: 2013.

Formerly the Institute of Textile Technology's *Textile Technology Digest*, this database traces the body of knowledge in textile science and technology as far back as the early years of the twentieth century. The database contains indexing and abstracting for more than 470 periodical titles and for thousands of titles drawn from sources such as books, conferences, theses, technical reports, and trade literature. Subject coverage includes manufacturing techniques, textile end products, chemicals and dyes, the properties of natural and synthetic fibers and yarns, environmental issues, and the related areas of chemistry, biology, and physics. Coverage spans the domestic and international arenas and includes publications covering the major resources from the scientific community, as well as the apparel, home furnishings, flooring, and polymer industries. The database also includes full text for nearly 50 journals, as well as over 50 books and monographs.—**Anna H. Perrault**

Fashion and Costume

812.   Chico, Beverly. **Hats and Headwear Around the World: A Cultural Encyclopedia.** Santa Barbara, Calif., ABC-CLIO, 2013. 531p. illus. index. $100.00. ISBN 13: 978-1-61069-062-1; 978-1-61069-063-8 (e-book).

With the publication of this title, researchers in fashion and costume history now have a well-researched reference work in which to find the history, significance, and meaning behind hats and headwear worn throughout the world. The book spans from ancient history up to the modern era. The alphabetic entries reveal the significance of religion, geography, ethnicity, culture, and of course fashion in the selection of headwear. The book includes black-and-white photographs, sidebars with historical events and terms defined, and literary references to hats (e.g., *The Cat in the Hat*). The volume concludes with a bibliography and an index. The author is a history/humanities professor at Regis University in Denver and has been a consultant for museums on hats and headwear from around the globe. While not a necessary acquisition for most university or public libraries, this work does add to the research in this area of fashion and culture.—**ARBA Staff Reviewer**

813.   **Encyclopedia of National Dress: Traditional Clothing Around the World.** Jill Condra, ed. Santa Barbara, Calif., ABC-CLIO, 2013. 2v. illus. index. $189.00/set. ISBN 13: 978-0-313-37636-8; 978-0-313-37637-5 (e-book).

The two-volume set is continuously paginated, split between Afghanistan-Japan and Kenya-Yemen. The two-page alphabetic Entry Guide at the beginning of each volume lists the full set of countries discussed, including some cross-references, such as "Jordan, see The Palestine Region and Jordan" and "Latvia, see Estonia, Latvia, and Lithuania." A few countries or areas are lacking, such as Borneo-New Guinea. This organization is problematic. Defining by country is a simple way to organize entries; however, cultural relationships are lost, since many cultural groups cross nineteenth- and twentieth-century defined borders. In the context of the essays the term "traditional," is used to describe a cluster of historical/pre-industrial, rural, or festival clothing, representing a specific cultural identity.

The content is good, containing articles by 45 authors. Most articles are from 9-14 pages each. The essays contain a historical background, then focus on what people wear. It appears that contributors had leeway to include other sections they deemed useful, such as geography, adornment, textiles, special-occasion dress, or a specific cultural group within a country. Most photographs are credited with a source and date (with the exception being a few examples of woodcuts or drawings), thus offering contextual information. It would have been helpful to have included a small map at the beginning of each entry marking a country within a continent.

The Further Reading and Resources at the end of each entry are up-to-date, with references as recent as 2011 and in-text statistical information from 2012. Information at the end of volume 2 includes "Museums with National Dress and Textile Collections," a selected bibliography, information on the editors and contributors, and a comprehensive 21-page index.

The main editorial drawback is the encyclopedic arrangement. A regional focus would have been much more useful. A consistent set of sections such as "Central African" or "South American" throughout the books would have been useful. Yet an advantage of the alphabetic arrangement makes it fun to open a volume at random and learn a little bit about the history, culture, and clothing of very different regions. For example, sequential entries are: Native North American Dress (United States and Canada), The Netherlands and Belgium, New Zealand (concentrating on Maori), Niger and Burkina Faso, Nigeria, and Norway. Overall, the *Encyclopedia of National Dress* offers a good introduction to an important visual marker of any cultural group's clothing.—**Lizbeth Langston**

814. **Fashion, Costume, and Culture: Clothing, Headwear, Body Decorations, and Footwear Through the Ages.** 2d ed. Sara Pendergast, Tom Pendergast, and Drew D. Johnson, eds. Stamford, Conn., Gale/Cengage Learning, 2013. 6v. illus. index. $450.00/set. ISBN 13: 978-1-4144-9841-6; 978-1-4144-9848-5 (e-book).

This six-volume set from U*X*L provides a broad overview of how clothing and fashion represent our cultural, religious, and societal beliefs, both now and in centuries past. The set is arranged chronologically chapters that focus on either a specific time period or a specific cultural tradition. Each chapter is arranged in the same format. They begin with an overview that discusses the historical time period and major cultural and economic factors of the time. Following this are four sections on clothing, headwear, body decoration, and footwear. For example, in volume 1, "The Ancient World," users learn about the significance of the clothing in Ancient Egyptian life, including the use of wigs, headdresses, fragrant oils, and sandals. In the fourth volume, " Modern World Part I: 1900-1945," users learn how economic and social hardships have affected clothing and style—how short hair and short flapper dresses represented wealth and freedom for women in the 1920s and how the Depression and World War II sent hem lines down and made simple clothing fashionable. The work is supplemented by more than 390 color photographs, which will aid the reader substantially. Other supplementary material include a timeline, a glossary, "For More Information" sections at the end of each entry, and a "Where to Learn More" section that offers lists of books and Websites students can consult for more information.

This set does an excellent job of describing the changes and significance of clothing and fashion in relation to society's cultural and societal beliefs. The photographs add significantly to the text and create a work that is fun to use for both research and for browsing. *Fashion, Costume, and Culture* is highly recommended for school libraries and the children's reference collections of large public libraries.—**Shannon Graff Hysell**

815.   Snodgrass, Mary Ellen. **World Clothing and Fashion: An Encyclopedia of History, Culture, and Social Influence.** Armonk, N.Y., M. E. Sharpe, 2014. 2v. illus. index. $249.00/set. ISBN 13: 978-0-7656-8300-7.

The subtitle for this set, *An Encyclopedia of History, Culture, and Social Influences*, succinctly indicates what this encyclopedia covers. It explores the colorful and diverse history of clothing from prehistoric times to the twenty-first century, commenting on its utility, style, production, commerce, and cultural influences. Unlike most multivolume encyclopedias, all of the entries for this volume were written by one author.

The basic structure of the encyclopedia is exemplary. The black-and-white images are clear and attractive. The volume has a table of contents that lists all of the alphabetic entries as well as a topic finder that will assist those needing more specialized help. The topics include the various types of clothing for men, women, and children; dress for different climates; occupational clothing; recreational clothing; religious clothing; dress for rites of passage; and information on textiles used in the making of clothing. Some social issues are addressed here as well, including dress as a reflection of social status, fashion that resulted from economic conditions, influential figures in fashion, and the role of media and marketing in fashion. Most entries include a list of further resources, *see also* references, and black-and-white images of maps or photographs. The work concludes with a chronology, a glossary, a bibliography, and an inclusive index.

In terms of content, this encyclopedia is excellent. The entries are balanced and informative. It joins several other titles on this subject that have been released within the last year, including *Fashion, Costume, and Culture: Clothing, Headwear, Body Decorations, and Footwear Through the Ages* (2d ed.; see entry 814) and *Encyclopedia of National Dress: Traditional Clothing Around the World* (see entry 813). This set is recommended for high school and undergraduate collections.—**Anita Zutis**

816.   Taylor, Kerry. **Vintage Fashion and Couture: From Poiret to McQueen.** Richmond Hills, Ont., Firefly Books, 2013. 223p. illus. index. $39.95. ISBN 13: 978-1-77085-262-4.

Kerry Taylor specializes in providing collectors with historic fashion pieces and has gathered an informative collection of information on the history and technique of fashion design, construction, and utility. A foreword by Herbert de Givenchy and a prologue by Christopher Kane seem a bit superfluous, but are followed by an introduction outlining the definition and importance of vintage designs and the art of collecting them. Each decade from the early twentieth to the twenty-first century is treated separately with an introduction to the time period and how it affected fashion aesthetics. Although not all major fashion designers are included, a cross-section of individual designers are highlighted (e.g., Chanel, Dior, Quant, McQueen), as well as fashion icons of each period (e.g., Wallis Simpson, Grace Kelly, Princess Diana, Kate Moss). Some designers are highlighted in more than one decade. The text is enhanced with both black-and-white and color illustrations, including details such as designer labels and accessories. A section on where and how to collect vintage fashions, including how to take care of a collection and how to spot forgeries, is followed by a bibliography and an index. There is a note in the introduction about price estimates, which refers the reader to further information that seems to be missing from the publication. This source would serve more as an overview of the topic and as a starting point for potential collectors.—**Martha Lawler**

22 Fine Arts

General Works

Bibliography

817. ARTBIbllographies Modern. http://www.proquest.com/en-US/catalogs/databases/detail/artbm-set-c.shtml. [Website]. Bethesda, Md., ProQuest. Price negotiated by site. Date reviewed: 2013.

As the title implies, the database does not furnish full text, but indexes journal articles, books, essays, exhibition catalogs, dissertations, and exhibit reviews of English and foreign-language materials beginning with the late 1960s. The bibliography is comprehensive for modern art, with more than 13,000 new entries being added each year. Coverage includes famous and lesser-known artists, movements, and trends from the late nineteenth century onwards. The bibliography thoroughly covers all art fields including illustration, painting, printmaking, photography, sculpture, and drawing. In the design fields, crafts, ceramic and glass art, calligraphy, computer and electronic art, graphic and museum design, fashion, video art, and theater arts are included. In addition to the traditional art forms, ethnic arts and modern forms such as performance art and installation works, body art, graffiti, artists' books, and more are included.—**ARBA Staff Reviewer**

818. Bibliography of the History of Art (BHA). http://www.getty.edu/research/tools/bha/index.html. [Website]. Los Angeles, Calif., J. Paul Getty Trust. Free. Date reviewed: 2013.

Although the Getty Research Institute ceased maintaining the BHA in 2009, it still provides access to the Bibliography and to the Répertoire de la literature de l'art (RILA) for no charge on its Website. The databases, searchable together, cover material published between 1975 and 2009. RILA covers the years 1975-1989. It was produced at the Sterling and Francine Clark Art Institute, and Michael Rinehart was the editor in chief. In 1982, Getty began to support RILA and in 1990 the Getty began to collaborate with INIST-CNRS to produce the BHA, which was a merger of RILA and the Répertoire d'art et d'archéologie. For material published after 2007, see the International Bibliography of Art (http://www.csa.com). The Getty Website offers both basic and advanced search modules for BHA and RILA, and they can be searched easily by subject, artist, author, articles or journal titles, and other elements. The Getty Search Gateway allows users to search across several of the Getty repositories, including collections databases, library catalogs, collection inventories, and archival finding aids.—**Anna H. Perrault**

Biography

819.   **Who's Who in Research: Visual Arts.** Bristol, United Kingdom, Intellect; distr., Chicago, University of Chicago Press, 2013. 1v. (various paging). $115.00. ISBN 13: 978-1-84150-495-7.

Part of the Who's Who in Research five-volume series by the University of Chicago Press, the current volume on visual arts presents researchers working on various topics in art, aesthetics, culture, and cross-disciplinary areas. Other volumes in the series cover performing arts, film studies, cultural studies, and media studies. The researchers listed in the volume are located internationally showing the growth of international cooperation in research areas. With the increase in international scholarship comes the need for understanding and collaboration transcending national boundaries, and the need to connect with other researchers in a thorough review and dialog on the research topic. Arranged alphabetically by scholar, each listing includes the scholar's name, institutional affiliation, short biography, current research interests, and a short list of articles published. Also included in each entry are keywords relating to the research interests of the scholar. These keywords are used as an index at the end of the volume to create a simple-to-use topical organization to research areas and interests. A second index by nationality of the researcher might be useful in a 2d edition for the user if they need to see the list of researchers in a particular region of the world.

With the increasing interconnectedness and internationality of the research community, knowing who is researching in a particular area or topic is vital to today's creation of knowledge and moving discussions forward on all fronts and in all regions. The current volume, and the series, is a valuable resource in that endeavor. The usefulness of the resource will be enhanced by continuing revisions and additions of scholars with new editions to the series. The current volume, and the series, is well worth including in collections for researchers interested in the arts, aesthetics, cultural, intellectual, visual and performing arts, media studies, film, and cross-disciplinary studies.—**Gregory Curtis**

Catalogs and Collections

820.   **Art & Architecture Complete. http://www.ebsco.com.** [Website]. Ipswich, Mass., EBSCO. Price negotiated by site. Date reviewed: 2013.

The "Complete" in the title of this database refers to the wide number of disciplines and fields indexed as well as the range of resources covered. More than 800 periodicals and over 230 books are fully indexed in *Art & Architecture Complete* with selective coverage for another 70 publications. Major subject areas covered include art, antiques, archaeology, architecture and architectural history, art history, decorative arts, painting, sculpture, photography, printmaking, costume design, interior and landscape design, and graphic arts. The database is appropriate for both academic and public library users.—**ARBA Staff Reviewer**

821.   **Art Full Text. http://www.ebscohost.com/academic/art-full-text.** [Website]. Bronx, N.Y., H. W. Wilson. Price negotiated by site. Date reviewed: 2013.

822.   **Art Index Retrospective. http://www.ebscohost.com/academic/art-index-retrospective.** [Website]. Bronx, N.Y., H. W. Wilson. Price negotiated by site. Date reviewed: 2013.

The long-running Wilson print *Art Index* was replaced by Art Full Text. This bibliographic database indexes and abstracts articles published worldwide from periodicals in Dutch, English, French, German, Italian, Japanese, Spanish, and Swedish. Coverage includes art reproductions that appear in indexed periodicals, museum bulletins, yearbooks, and more. This is the database most likely to be found in public libraries. The Art Index Retrospective database includes the contents of the *Art Index* from 1984 back to the beginning.—**ARBA Staff Reviewer**

823. **Art Museum Image Gallery. http://www.ebscohost.com/academic/art-museum-image-gallery.** [Website]. Ipswich, Mass., EBSCO Publishing, Inc.. Price negotiated by site. Date reviewed: 2014.

Art Museum Image Gallery boasts 165,000 attractive, high-quality images of artwork. The sheer number of images in this database has nearly doubled in seven years. Two outstanding features are apparent: the high-quality, high-resolution reproductions and the opportunities for users to analyze the artwork. Images are available in three sizes: the thumbnail version appears in a search results list, a mid-sized version with full bibliographic data about the image, and a high-resolution image. The site continues to provide opportunities for users to explore the content of over 1,800 worldwide museums of fine and decorative art form 3000 B.C. E. through the 20th Century. The full bibliographic information includes most of the following for each image: the object type, title of work, date the work was created, artists(s), nationality, description of work, museum Website, copyright information link, accession number, subjects, key terms, and a persistent URL link to the image. The description of work varies, with some images having no more than the title, while others include a paragraph description content note. The content note may include background information about he painting, the style, additional information about when it was created, and what experts view as significant about the work. Users can do a browse search by such field as birthplace, date of birth, date of death, location of work, object type, nationality publication year, and subject. Unfortunately, no clickable list of any of these options is available; however, entering simply the letter "a" constitutes a search, which then allows the user to begin to browse and scroll through the possibilities.

A final outstanding feature of this database is the Content Discovery Keys sidebar that relates to a search results list form any type of search (basic, advanced, or browse). The Content Discovery Keys are hyperlinked subject terms related to the current results list. These links perform a subject search on the related term and activate a new results list. The *Art Museum Image Gallery* provides a number of learning and teaching opportunities.—**ARBA Staff Reviewer**

824. **Art Source. http://www.ebscohost.com/academic/art-source.** [Website]. Birmingham, Ala., EBSCO. Price negotiated by site. Date reviewed: 2013.

Art Source was formed in the merger of EBSCO Publishing and H. W. Wilson in 2011. The Wilson databases *Art Abstracts*, *Art Full Text*, and *Art Index Retrospective* were merged with the EBSCO *Art & Architecture Complete* database to form Art Source. All of the databases are also available separately as well as within the Art Source database.—**ARBA Staff Reviewer**

825. **ARTstor. http://www.artstor.org.** [Website]. New York, ARTstor. Price negotiated by site. Date reviewed: 2013.

The Andrew W. Mellon Foundation, founders of the JSTOR database, started ARTstor as a nonprofit entity in 2000 to enhance scholarship and teaching in the arts. Part of its mission is "to create an organized, central, and reliable digital resource that supports noncommercial use of images for research, teaching, and learning." The project was begun to address technical problems with digitization, issues with standardization and copyright, and the challenge of bringing together a collection from artifacts and objects scattered around the world. ARTstor is a repository of one million images in the arts, architecture, humanities, and social sciences. Collections comprise contributions from outstanding museums, photographers, libraries, scholars, photo archives, and artists and artists' estates. ARTstor contains dozens of collections from a wide variety of cultures across all major time periods including a collection of 190,000 old master drawings originally photographed at over 100 different repositories, 20 years of contemporary New York City gallery shows, archives of Islamic textiles, the restored Ghiberti "Gates of Paradise," African masks, medieval manuscripts, images of all exhibitions shown at MOMA, and many others. For a fee, nonprofit organizations can become members of ARTstor, securing access to over one million images, with more constantly being added. Additionally, ARTstor provides the technology for users to create presentations, zoom in on the artwork, and save personal collections. This excellent resource is vital for all study and research in the arts fields.—**Anna H. Perrault**

826. **Cultural Objects Authority File (CONA). http://www.getty.edu/research/tools/vocabularies/cona/.** [Website]. Los Angeles, Calif., The Getty Research Institute. Free. Date reviewed: 2013.

CONA, a new vocabulary being developed, is a thesaurus in structure and includes titles, attributions, and other information for works of art and architecture. CONA comprises authority records for cultural works, including architecture and moveable works such as paintings and sculpture. The minimum fields in a CONA record are the types of information typically captured in a visual resources catalog, repository catalog records, or included on a museum wall label.

The Getty Research Institute has published a number of guides on cataloging, metadata, controlled vocabularies records, standards, and tools that promote best practices for managing information in libraries, archives, and museums. Many are issued in both print and e-book formats. Other similar titles from the Getty Research Institute are *Introduction to Metadata* (2008); *Introduction to Imaging* (2003); and *A Guide to the Description of Architectural Drawings* (2000). All are available online.—**Anna H. Perrault**

827. **Symbols in Christian Art and Architecture. http://www.planetgast.net/symbols/symbolsc/symbolsc.html.** [Website]. Free. Date reviewed: 2013.

This free Website contains a gallery of images you are likely to find in many Christian churches along with explanations to help you understand their meaning and significance. Church features and architectural symbols are also explained. An alphabetical search leads to images with explanations, while it is even easier to find items by browsing. It is also possible to search on basics like color, numbers, and patterns. Referrals to Amazon's offerings on symbols and symbolism help support the costs of maintaining the Website; however, they do not interfere with the interface or ease of use of the site.—**ARBA Staff Reviewer**

Dictionaries and Encyclopedias

828. **Axis: The Online Resource for Contemporary Art. http://www.axisweb.org/.** [Website]. Free. Date reviewed: 2013.

Axis is the best online resource for information about contemporary art. The Website features profiles of professional artists and curators, interviews, discussion, art news, and debates, and showcases the artists to watch. Students can use the constantly expanding directory of more than 2,500 profiles of artists and curators. This Website offers audio, video, biographies, and even an events listing. Those artworks selected for this directory reflect both the high quality and diversity in the art being produced today. A few disclaimers: first, the scope is limited to the United Kingdom, and second, it deals exclusively with contemporary art.—**William O. Scheeren**

Handbooks and Yearbooks

829. Andrews, Julia F., and Kuiyi Shen. **The Art of Modern China.** Berkeley, Calif., University of California Press, 2012. 364p. illus. index. $39.95. ISBN 13: 978-0-520-27106-7.

The peaceful rise of China on the world stage since the 1980s has attracted academia to conduct research on site that has also brought Chinese crucial contact with the West. Taking advantage of the circumstances, co-author Andrews became the first American art historian to travel to China to consult primary resources for her dissertation research on the emerging field of modern Chinese art. This was made possible with the normalization of U.S.-China relations in 1979 and offered previously unavailable resources to outsiders. This comprehensive and award-winning book that follows the authors successful collaboration on an exhibition catalog titled "A Century in Crisis: Modernity and Tradition in the Art of 20th Century China" has received assistance from over 60 museums, academic institutions, and art publishers in China, Hong Kong, Taiwan, Japan, and Europe. The volume is chronologically organized in 13 chapters beginning with the Opium War between Britain and China in 1839 to the first decade of the twenty-first century. Special attention focuses on the fundamental changes in Chinese visual art, and representative works, with extensive discussion and debates of contemporary and traditional arts for each period. More chapters are devoted to the PRC period from 1949 to the present. The introduction section outlines the content of each chapter. A glossary and a list of characters are helpful. Major Events in Modern Chinese Arts section details significant events that occurred between 1839 to 2012. Nearly 270 selected bibliographies are extremely useful for further research. A dictionary index completes the volume. This well-researched, well-written, and beautifully illustrated book is a significant contribution to the modern Chinese art. This work is highly recommended to scholars and students in the field as well as art collectors and anyone interested in Asian arts.—**Karen T. Wei**

830.   **The Books That Shaped Art History: From Gombrich and Greenberg to Alphers and Krauss.** Richard Shone and John Paul Stonard, eds. New York, Thames and Hudson, 2013. 264p. illus. index. $34.95. ISBN 13: 978-0-500-23895-0.

This book provides 16 articles on the books and their authors that shaped art history during the twentieth century. All but one of the articles is a reprint from the *Burlington Magazine*, of which Shone is the editor. Some of the key titles covered include: Rosalind Krauss's *The Originality of the Avant-Garde and Other Modernist Myths* and Clement Greenberg's *Art and Culture*. Arranged chronologically, the essays discuss the author's contribution to art history, how the book influenced art at the time, and provide a thorough overview of what the world of art looked like during the movement or era covered. The essays are supplemented with photographs and the work includes a bibliography of all of the art historians mentioned in the book. Although written with scholars and students in mind, this book will also appeal to general readers with an interest in art history. It is a worthwhile addition to university and large public library collections. [R: LJ, 15 June 13, p. 88]—**R. K. Dickson**

831.   Daniels, Lawrence J. **The Graphic Designer's Business Survival Guide.** New York, AMACOM/ American Management Association, 2013. 207p. index. $24.95pa. ISBN 13: 978-0-8144-3241-9.

This easy-to-use work offers practical advice on starting and running a successful commercial graphic design firm. The author stresses that most design school training lacks a business component so he applies his many years of professional experience to educate readers. The focus is exclusively on the business aspect of graphic design, not the artistic elements. There is information on managing a design firm that fills a niche in the industry, how to successfully communicate with clients and build relationships, how to promote your business, establishing fees and billing processes, time management, developing professional partnerships, and presenting to potential clients. He stresses the importance of communicating with customers and understanding that their main interest is on their return on investment and the building of their brand. This will be a useful guide for academic libraries with graphic design programs as well as public libraries.—**Shannon Graff Hysell**

832.   Dickerson, Madelynn. **The Handy Art History Answer Book.** Canton, Mich., Visible Ink Press, 2013. 294p. illus. index. $21.95pa. ISBN 13: 978-1-57859-417-7.

Numerous well-known art survey books have lined library shelves for decades, but most are heavy, expensive, and dense or overly academic in their coverage. In her new book, Dickerson (art teacher and writer) offers plain-language answers for curious readers' commonly asked questions. She manages to keep her comprehensive coverage of world art and architecture from ancient to modern times under 300 pages, while addressing a variety of primarily "what, who, and why" questions.

This book, published under an apparently new subject heading ("Art—History—Miscellanea"), is arranged in eight chapters. Dickerson begins her book with questions and answers first surrounding basic art principles and history, including the most basic question of all: "What is art?" This introductory chapter is followed by ones covering the periods of ancient, medieval, baroque, early modern, industrial, modern, and contemporary art. Coverage is not limited to the Western world but includes also art of tribal and prehistoric regions and periods. Chapters are conveniently tabbed by color code. They are followed by a glossary of nearly 200 terms, defining both the expected (e.g., camera obscura, De Stijl) and the lesser-known (e.g., sfumato, Fluxus). The book closes with a two-page bibliography and a comprehensive index. Part of a growing series of Handy Answer books, this low-priced paperback is surprisingly sturdy, featuring sewn pages. Although modestly illustrated, the book does contain high-quality color images on semi-gloss paper.

Devoting one to three paragraphs to each answer, Dickerson asks over 600 questions, from "What is megalithic art?" to "Who was Henry Moore?" Entries range from approximately 100 to as many as 500 words. Most are brief but the language is engaging and lively. Occasional sidebars offset the main text to expand on topics relating to several entries. For example, she further describes the "Classical Pantheon" or points out a handful of little-known female artists of the fifteenth and sixteenth centuries. Some sidebars do address topics as basic as the difference between Manet and Monet, making this book truly accessible to the art novice. Also included is a handy two-page timeline of major art historical periods.

The only immediate flaw this reviewer noticed was a number of typographical errors, perhaps due to hasty production. Otherwise this book is recommended for most any library shelf. Nearest comparable titles might be the likes of *Art History for Dummies* (2007), *Art: The Whole Story* (2010), or *Art: A Beginner's Guide* (2012).—**Lucy Duhon**

833.　　**An Eye for Art: Focusing on Great Artists and Their Work.** Judy Metro, ed. Chicago, Chicago Review Press, 2013. 177p. illus. $19.95. ISBN 13: 978-1-61374-897-8.

An Eye for Art: Focusing on Great Artists and their Work is a collection of National Gallery news pieces from their quarterly letters that feature artists and works from their museum; the book is more than just a collection of these pieces that have been updated, revised, and expanded. Rather, the book is a fantastic reference work for children and young adults interested in learning about art. This volume features not only painters but sculptors, and crosses the time span and Western world from Giotto and Fra Angelico to Roy Lichtenstein and Andy Goldsworthy; from Italy to America, the thirteenth century to today. It is hoped that volumes on other countries and artists are forthcoming—such as on Eastern Europe and Africa. A timeline is presented at the back of the book, color-coded for easy indexing to find an artist of a particular nationality, and all the artists are arranged by time period. The books is carefully laid out with an artist's work gracing a full page then into a set of three or four important expanded facts about the artwork and the artist—whether on what was influential to him or her at the time; the details and symbolism in the particular work shown in the book; the artist's evolution or perhaps the revolution they sparked with their new theories or images. Ending the chapter on the artist is a segment that encourages the reader to consider criticism on the painting, attempt journaling to spur his own creativity, or encouragement to paint, draw, or sculpt something similar to the artist's work. This is a must-have for public and school libraries. From children to young adults, this book will be a valuable introduction and exploration of art and will encourage young artists to experiment outside their own comfort zones or improve what they already are learning.—**Michelle Martinez**

Indexes

834.　　**Arts and Humanities Citation Index. http://thomsonreuters.com/products_services/science/ science_products/a-z/arts_humanities_citation_index/.** [Website]. New York, N.Y., Thomson Reuters. Price negotiated by site. Date reviewed: 2013.

This multidisciplinary database is a module within the *Web of Knowledge* subscription database from Thomson Reuters. International in scope, *Arts and Humanities Citation Index* covers 1,300 of the leading arts and humanities journals. Implicit citations are added for material such as paintings, musical compositions, literary works, films and records, along with dance, music, and theatrical performances. Dates covered are from 1980 to the present and the database is updated weekly. The database is most suitable for academic research.—**Anna H. Perrault**

Architecture

835. **archINFORM: International Architecture Database. http://eng.archinform.net/index.htm.** [Website]. Free. Date reviewed: 2013.

This database has become the largest online database about worldwide architects and buildings from past to present. The contents are concentrated on architecture of the twentieth century and include records of interesting building projects from architecture students, and on "more than 29,000 built and unrealized projects from various architects and planners." With the indexes or by using a query form, it is possible to look for a special project using an architect's name, town, or keyword. Most entries give name, address, keywords, and information about further literature. Some entries include images, comments, and links to other Websites or internal links. The site has several mobile phone apps to become connected to the same information, automatically reading the user's location and giving a list of architecturally significant buildings nearby.—**Anna H. Perrault**

836. **Avery Index to Architectural Periodicals. http://library.columbia.edu/indiv/avery/avery_index.html.** [Website]. New York, Columbia University. Free. Date reviewed: 2013.

The Avery Index to Architectural Periodicals is a comprehensive listing of journal articles published internationally germane to architecture and design. The online index contains over 638,000 records dating back to 1934 and is one of the largest listings of journal articles, including over 440,000 entries surveying over 700 American and international journals. Some major areas of coverage included are architectural design, history of architecture, interior design, and city and urban planning.—**ARBA Staff Reviewer**

837. **National Register of Historic Places Database (NRHP). http://nrhp.focus.nps.gov.** [Website]. Free. Date reviewed: 2013.

The National Register is well known to local preservationists and tourists alike. The NRHP Database allows access to documentation associated with properties listed in the National Register that have been digitized, including registration forms, photographs, and maps. The database is also searchable by location (city, county, or state), resource name, and National Park Service park name if searching for an NPS park.—**ARBA Staff Reviewer**

838. **SAH Architecture Resources Archive (SAHARA). http://www.sah.org/publications-and-research/sahara.** [Website]. Price negotiated by site. Date reviewed: 2013.

The SAHARA is an archive of architectural and landscape images from throughout the world. Funded by a grant from The Andrew W. Mellon Foundation, and built in partnership with ARTstor (www.ARTstor.org), SAHARA includes not only high-quality images but also rich, searchable metadata for each of those images. The SAHARA collection has been developed for all who study, interpret, photograph, design, and preserve the built environment worldwide. SAH members can use the archive to store their own digital photographs or download images from the archive for teaching and research.—**Anna H. Perrault**

Photography

839.   **Photography Collections Online. http://geh.org/.** [Website]. Rochester, N.Y., George Eastman House. Free. Date reviewed: 2013.

This Website provides access to a digital storehouse of the George Eastman photography holdings. Photography collections are organized as follows: Indexed by Photographer, Stereo Views, Lantern Slides, Subject, and Books and Albums. Other resources on the site include: A Collection Guide: Photography from 1839 to Today; a sampler of The Gabriel Chrome Collection; the Pre-Cinema Project; and the Technology Collection, which contains images of photography and related equipment. The project is supported by grants from Irv Schankman, National Endowment for the Humanities, Pew Charitable Trusts, and the Getty Grant Program.—**Anna H. Perrault**

23 Language and Linguistics

General Works

840.   Crystal, David. **Spell It Out: The Curious, Enthralling and Extraordinary Story of English Spelling.** New York, St. Martin's Press, 2013. 336p. illus. index. $22.99pa. ISBN 13: 978-1-25000-347-8; 978-1-25002-886-0 (e-book).

This work, written by a linguistics scholar from the University of Wales, provides a history of the etymological background of words. The author discusses how words have changed over the centuries due to influences from other regions as well as the shift in cultural attitudes. Crystal writes in a conversational tone that will appeal to many readers, but he stays close to his linguistics roots by using some technical terms that may throw readers new to the subject off course. The work can serve as a reference or a primer to those studying the history of language and the evolution of spelling in the English language. It will be useful to those with an interest in language and linguistics. [R: LJ, 15 June 13, p. 89]—**John B. Romeiser**

841.   **CSA Linguistics & Language Behavior Abstracts (LLBA). http://www.proquest.com/en-US/catalogs/databases/detail/llba-set-c.shtml.** [Website]. Bethesda, Md., ProQuest. Price negotiated by site. Date reviewed: 2013.

Published by Cambridge Scientific Abstracts, LLBA provides access to abstracts of journal articles and books, book chapters, and dissertations as well as citations to book reviews selected from over 1,500 periodical publications. The chronological scope of coverage extends from 1973 to the present with monthly updates. As of April 2012, LLBA contained over 480,000 records. LLBA covers all subfields of linguistics as well as related disciplines such as psychology, speech and hearing sciences, cognitive psychology, and educational psychology.—**Anna H. Perrault**

842.   **Ethnologue: Languages of the World. http://www.ethnologue.com/.** [Website]. Free. Date reviewed: 2013.

This site is an online version of M. Paul Lewis's *Ethnologue: Languages of the World* (16th ed.; SIL International, 2009). This encyclopedic work includes useful information on 6,909 known living languages. *Ethnologue: Languages of the World* is a comprehensive reference work cataloging all of the world's known living languages. Since 1951, the Ethnologue has been an active research project involving hundreds of linguists and other researchers around the world. It is widely regarded to be the most comprehensive source of information of its kind. The information in the Ethnologue will be valuable to anyone with an interest in cross-cultural communication, bilingualism, literacy rates, language planning and language policy, language development, language relationships, endangered languages, writing systems and to all with a general curiosity about languages.—**Noriko Asato**

843. **Lexicons of Early Modern English (LEME). http://leme.library.utoronto.ca/.** [Website]. Toronto, University of Toronto Press. $75.00-$1,260.00 (based on institution size). Date reviewed: 2014.

The *Lexicons of Early Modern English*, from the University of Toronto Press, is designed to give scholars access to books and manuscripts that document the English language from the first printings to 1702. To date there are over 150 dictionaries and glossaries here, including monolingual, bilingual, and polyglot. Linguistic works can be found here as well, giving linguists access to one-half million entries that have been created by modern-day speakers of early modern English. Many of the entries also have their equivalents in different languages, including French, Italian, Spanish, Latin, and Greek. Some 800 bibliographies of primary lexical texts and critical literature are included as well as biographies of prominent lexicographers.

The site can be searched by simple or advanced search as well as can be browsed by date, author, title, or subject. For scholars of the English languages as well as historians this site provides a wealth of information in one convenient format that would be hard to track down otherwise.—**Shannon Graff Hysell**

844. **Routledge Encyclopedia of Language and Teaching and Learning.** 2d ed. Michael Byram and Adelheid Hu, eds. New York, Routledge/Taylor & Francis Group, 2012. 817p. index. $360.00. ISBN 13: 978-0-4155-9376-2.

Designed for an audience of those actively engaged in the teaching of language and of language learning, this comprehensive encyclopedia includes more than 35 updated overview articles on topics such as early language learning, applied linguistics, teaching methods, literary theory, and research methods. Another 160 updated articles treat a variety of related issues, such as bilingualism, gender and language learning, study abroad, reading, and classroom research. More than 50 articles on conceptual frameworks are presented.

While alphabetically arranged, the work is prefaced by a thematic list of entries that groups articles into nine broad categories: learners and learning; teachers and teaching (including assessment); methods and materials; curriculum and syllabus; systems and organization of foreign language teaching and learning; languages; history and influential figures; evaluation and research; and contexts and concepts. Entries range from very brief to 3,000 words. Entries are signed and include lists of references and further reading. All entries are cross-referenced as appropriate, and the volume includes a full analytic index that provides quick access to related topics and subtopics. More than 200 international specialists have contributed to the volume.

This work is recommended primarily for academic, large public, and school libraries. Broad in scope and current in content, this encyclopedia will likely become a mainstay for professionals and researchers alike. Entries on language teaching in individual countries will be of value to the multicultural and diversity initiatives that currently prevail in the academic sector.—**ARBA Staff Reviewer**

English-Language Dictionaries

General Usage

845. **Webster's American English Dictionary.** expanded ed. Darien, Conn., Federal Street Press, 2013. 504p. $4.99pa. ISBN 13: 978-1-59695-154-9.

An expanded version of that reliable stand-by, the *Webster's American English Dictionary* is a simplified dictionary of American English. It includes more than 40,000 succinct definitions and features pronunciation guidance and spelling variations. The expanded edition includes special sections featuring items like biographical names, geographical names, English word roots, and basic English grammar. It is a remarkably concise dictionary, perfect for desktops of students and professional writers alike. It includes lists of self-explanatory words associated with certain prefixes (like co- and in-) rather than including separate definitions for each.

A highly concise and accessible title, the *Webster's American English Dictionary* is good for every day dictionary-related needs. It gets the job done. This work is recommended for public libraries, K-12 school libraries, and for individuals with basic dictionary-related needs.—**Megan W. Lowe**

846.   Yates, Jean. **Master the Basics: English.** 3d ed. Hauppauge, N.Y., Barron's Educational Series, 2013. 349p. index. (Barron's Language Guides). $14.99pa. ISBN 13: 978-1-4380-0164-7.

Designed with the English as a Second Language (ELS) student in mind, this volume presents the user with the fundamentals of English grammar. This series from Barron's provides similar titles for students of German, Italian, Japanese, Russian, and Spanish. Inside users will find English grammar broken down with descriptions of nouns, pronouns, adjectives, verbs, prepositions, adverbs, and conjunctions. Rules for sentence formation and for capitalization and punctuation are also provided. There is a special section on numbers, dates, time, and weather that will help the student new to English. New to this edition are helpful hints that will help them avoid mistakes with pronunciation. Quizzes are presented throughout the volume so students can test themselves on what they just learned. This inexpensive volume would be useful as a supplement to a textbook in high school or college courses or for international travelers wanting to brush up on their language skills.—**Shannon Graff Hysell**

Sign Language

847.   **A Basic Dictionary of ASL (American Sign Language) Terms. http://www.masterstech-home.com/ASLDict.htm..** [Website]. Free. Date reviewed: 2013.

Designed to help people communicate more easily with people who can see but cannot hear, this dictionary provides signing definitions to more than 1,270 terms, the basic alphabet, and numbers 1-10. This dictionary has both animated and text definitions. The text definitions also have letter or number sign images to aid in visualizing the sign. This will allow you to quickly locate a word, read how to sign the word, and choose to view the animated sign if you wish. The sign images are displayed from the perspective of the viewer, not the signer. In Sign Language, facial expression including the raising or lowering of the eyebrows while signing, and body language are integral parts of communicating. These actions help give meaning to what is being signed, much like vocal tones and inflections give meaning to spoken words.—**ARBA Staff Reviewer**

Slang

848.   Axelrod, Alan. **Whiskey Tango Foxtrot: The Real Language of the Modern American Military.** New York, W. W. Norton, 2013. 224p. $12.95pa. ISBN 13: 978-1-62087-467-3.

This is one of those fun slang dictionaries that will take the reader through both the fun and the functional side of military language—with a focus on the fun side of things. While some of the entries do come from official sources, such as the *Department of Defense Dictionary of Military Terms*, the bulk of the terms represent the more colorful side of military life and many of the terms will be new to readers. The work is arranged into six chapters, each with a descriptive title. There is no index, which would have helped readers navigate through the work a little easier. Luckily, this is a fun reference to browse. This is an inexpensive reference that will serve as a supplement to language and linguistic collections. It will be useful for those studying military history as it provides a different point of view from the average dictionary. It will also be useful for aspiring novelists writing from a military point of view. [R: LJ, 15 June 13, p. 115]—**Shannon Graff Hysell**

849.   Mohr, Melissa. **Holy Sh*t: A Brief History of Swearing.** New York, Oxford University Press, 2013. 368p. $24.95pa. ISBN 13: 978-0-19-974267-7.

As the author of this book notes, swearing has a direct response on people's emotions and physical responses to their surroundings. Swearing causes the speakers heart rate to rise and their pain tolerance to go up, and it can cause the listener either a sympathetic response or can turn them off entirely. In this volume Renaissance scholar Melissa Mohr takes a look at the history of swearing from early Western civilization to the present day. The chapters highlight those words that were considered the most offensive at the time and provides a historical overview of the era. The author pulls out interesting examples from the Bible as well as from Ancient Rome. She also discusses how censorship came into play in the eighteenth century as well as how racial slurs came into being. The author presents her findings in a scholarly manner but is also humorous in her approach, which makes this book an interesting read. [R: LJ, 15 June 13, p. 90]—**Shannon Graff Hysell**

850.   **Ware's Victorian Dictionary of Slang and Phrase.** By J. Redding Ware. Oxford, United Kingdom, Bodleian Library; distr., Chicago, University of Chicago Press, 2013. 271p. $45.00. ISBN 13: 978-1-85124-262-7.

A facsimile reproduction of J. Redding Ware's Victorian-era dictionary *Passing English*, this title contains an introduction that covers Ware's biography and the development of the dictionary. Initially released as a supplement to Farmer and Henley's one-volume *Dictionary of Slang and Colloquial English*, Ware's dictionary and its tone, style, and voice made it stand out. Intending to "amuse as well as inform" (p. viii) and using evidence from "newspaper and other ephemeral sources" (p. viii), including quotations and extrapolation, Ware highlighted slang and colloquialisms in Victorian/nineteenth-century England, mostly British English, although he did include some American terms and phrases. Most entries emerge from the 1880s and 1890s, though the latest definition is dated 1902. He sought to represent the "vocabulary of his day" (p. x).

The "amuse" element of the "amuse as well as inform" part of Ware's approach includes a peculiar labeling system to identify the context of usages and origins of entries. Furthermore, his definitions are as much commentary and critique as they are descriptions of meaning and usage. Additionally, as John Simpson notes in the Introduction, there are also problems with the etymology of words, despite Ware's extensive citations and reading. Ware seemed to have guessed at the etymology of words when he could not satisfy himself on their actual etymology. Of course, this can be amusing at times, and – again – seems to serve as commentary or critique, but it does thwart scholars of language.

A sometimes vaguely offensive but nonetheless charming and amusing compilation, *Ware's Victorian Dictionary of Slang and Phrase* provides more than just definitions: it provides a look at Victorian England via the language heard in its streets, and a view of its people via the language they used. This work is highly recommended, especially for colleges/universities.—**Megan W. Lowe**

Terms and Phrases

851.   Sommer, Elyse. **Similes Dictionary: 16,000 Figures of Speech on More than One Thousand Topics.** 2d ed. Canton, Mich., Visible Ink Press, 2013. 625p. index. $29.95. ISBN 13: 978-1-57859-433-7; 978-1-57859-469-6 (e-book).

Amended and updated from the 1st edition this listing has similes taken from various literature and media sources and arranged by basic categories. A section on how to use the book and an introduction are followed by a table of thematic categories, arranged alphabetically with any appropriate *see* and *see also* references. The actual listings of similes are arranged by these basic categories (with the *see* and *see also* references repeated) and listed alphabetically by the first letter of the first word. Each simile is quoted with the original spelling, along with the name or title of the original source and any historical background information. Quotes by specific individuals can be found with the help of an author index at the end. The choice of similes offers a broad range of sources and would be an excellent resource for writers or for those interested in cultural or philological development.—**Martha Lawler**

Non-English-Language Dictionaries

Yiddish

852.   **Comprehensive Yiddish-English Dictionary.** Solon Beinfeld and Harry Bochner, eds. Bloomington, Ind., Indiana University Press, 2013. 704p. $45.00. ISBN 13: 978-0-253-00983-8.

The *Comprehensive Yiddish-English Dictionary* provides over 37,000 word definitions and idioms compiled by a team of expert Yiddish linguists. The work includes a comprehensive User's Guide that will help readers new to this language find the terms they are looking for. Words included come from Hebrew-Aramaic, Slavic, and Romance as well as Germanic origin. A wide range of colloquial usage and dialect forms are represented here. It is a true reference dictionary that will be of great value to those needing an English-language tool to translate all of the riches that can be found in Yiddish literature. [R: Choice, June 2013, p. 1798]—**Simon J. Bronner**

24 Literature

General Works

Bibliography

853.   **The Annual Bibliography of English Language & Literature (ABELL). http://www.mhra. org/uk/Publications/Journals/abell.html.** [Website]. Alexandria, Va., Chadwyck-Healey. Price negotiated by site. Date reviewed: 2013.

   ABELL has been the standard bibliography for literature written in English in Great Britain and the Commonwealth countries since 1920. All aspects and periods of English literature are covered, from Anglo-Saxon times to present. The bibliography contains more than 880,000 records for monographs, periodical articles, critical editions of literary works, book reviews, collections of essays, and doctoral dissertations published anywhere in the world, including scholarly material in languages other than English, and also records for unpublished doctoral dissertations for the period 1920-1999.—**Anna H. Perrault**

854.   **A Bibliography of Literary Theory, Criticism and Philology. http://www.unizar.es/ departamentos/filologia_inglesa/garciala/bibliography.html.** [Website]. Free. Date reviewed: 2013.

   This is a bibliography of literary studies, criticism, and philology, listing well over 150,000 items, including books, book chapters, articles, films, Websites, and so forth. The main focus is on English-speaking authors and criticism or literary theory written in English. There are, however, many listings on linguistics, cultural studies, discourse analysis, and other philological subjects as well. The site can be searched by a subject directory, authors/schools directory, or by keyword.—**ARBA Staff Reviewer**

855.   Frolund, Tina. **Read On ... History: Reading Lists for Every Taste.** Santa Barbara, Calif., Libraries Unlimited/ABC-CLIO, 2013. 197p. index. (Read on Series). $30.00pa. ISBN 13: 978-1-61069-034-8; 978-1-61069-432-2 (e-book).

   Both fiction and nonfiction books on history are filled with inspiring stories that can engage readers of all ages. Included in this collection are titles that were either well reviewed, considered bestsellers, won awards, or have enduring appeal. The titles are arranged into five basic categories that focus on particular aspects of the stories that are especially significant. These categories include stories that focus on an engaging story, interesting characters, fascinating settings, language, or mood/tone of the story or storyteller. At the beginning of each chapter is a discussion of a basic aspect followed by a listing of the titles used as examples. Each title is represented by a full citation and a brief synopsis. An introduction at the beginning of the book gives a discussion of the concept of life stories, an overview of the arrangement of the listing, and a small bibliography. An index is available at the end of the book. The titles included are representative of a broad range of historic events and personalities covering several time periods.—**Martha Lawler**

856.   **Literature Online Reference. http://collections.chadwyck.co.uk/.** [Website]. Alexandria, Va., Chadwyck-Healey. Price negotiated by site. Date reviewed: 2013.

Literature Online Reference is a reference database, rich in content, containing a large number of separate databases, digital collection, and reference works. The database combines and indexes the texts of over 357,250 words of poetry, drama, and prose fiction in the English language written from the 7th century to the present. In addition to classic and standard works, *Literature Online Reference* includes all of an author's works that can be found to make as complete a corpus as possible. *Literature Online Reference* also contains the complete text of a number of reference works including *The Concise Oxford Dictionary of Literary Terms* and the *New Princeton Encyclopedia of Poetry and Poetics*. Also within the database are the full texts of 312 current literature journals that are indexed in *The Annual Bibliography of English Language and Literature* (ABELL). The *Literature Online Reference* database also includes multimedia with a collection of nearly 1,000 videos of poetry readings.

The *Literature Online Reference* database is an all-encompassing resource for the historical study of English literature, but as it continues to grow, increasing numbers of works by the major authors of the twentieth century are being added as well as new reference works and digital collections.—**Anna H. Perrault**

857.   **Pulitzer Prizes. http://www.pulitzer.org/.** [Website]. Free. Date reviewed: 2013.

The Pulitzer Prizes site contains the complete list of Pulitzer Prize winners from 1917 (the first year the Prizes were awarded) to the present. The site also lists nominated finalists from 1980 (the first year finalists were announced) through the present. Furthermore, this site offers the full text of journalism winner categories after 1995 as well as selected material from winners in the Letters, Drama and Music, and Special Awards and citations categories. From this data, you can also find biographies of winners and information on board members and nominating jurors. If your students aspire to be a Pulitzer winner, they can find entry forms for the upcoming prizes, photographs, press releases, and contact information for the Pulitzer Prizes office. Another use of this Website might be the crossword puzzle fanatic who needs an answer to a clue.— **William O. Scheeren**

Bio-bibliography

858.   **Knowledge Rush. http://www.knowledgerush.com.** [Website]. Free. Date reviewed: 2013.

This open access Website includes a directory of authors from a variety of genres. The site includes reading lists, keyword searches, and books by category. Topics included are banned books, romance, horror, mystery, and science fiction, among other popular games of literature. Additionally, the Website links specific works to public domain Websites. It also contains an encyclopedia of many topics including literature.—**Anna H. Perrault**

859.   **The Literature of Autobiographical Narrative.** Thomas Riggs, ed. Farmington Hills, Mich., St. James Press/Gale Group, 2013. 2v. illus. index. $418.00/set. ISBN 13: 978-105862-870-0; 978-1-55862-873-6 (e-book).

The Literature of Autobiographic Narrative seeks to explore the rich history of autobiography as a genre and literary form of its very own. Rather than a simple encyclopedic list of autobiographies and related writings throughout history, this three-volume set more fully explores these writings and provides some basic literary analysis.

The three volumes of this set are divided into Autobiography and Memoir, Diaries and Letters, and Oral Histories. Each volume is then further subdivided into sections such as adversity and resistance, coming of age, theories, war experiences, and more. Each entry consistently includes sections discussing historical and literary context, themes and style, critical discussion, and a detailed bibliography.

Occasional graphics and sidebars also dot the volumes with other pertinent information. Entries range from "The Autobiography of Charles Darwin" to "Brokenburn" to "Daring Hearts."

The writing style throughout these volumes is easy to understand and the content is wonderful in not only discussing a particular work, but conveying its literary and historical importance. The entries are detailed enough to provide an excellent introduction to each work, while providing a bibliography to use as a stepping stone for additional information. *The Literature of Autobiographic Narrative* does an admirable job of conveying the importance of autobiography as its very own literary genre. Considering autobiographies from virtually all walks of life are included, this publication would be an excellent addition to most collections.—**Tyler Manolovitz**

860.　**The Literature of Propaganda.** Thomas Riggs, ed. Farmington Hills, Mich., St. James Press/ Gale Group, 2013. 3v. illus. index. $418.00/set. ISBN 13: 978-1-55862-858-8; 978-1-55862-878-6 (e-book).

When is writing literature and when is it propaganda? According to this reference, it is a thin line. Propaganda is a charged word usually associated with manipulation but the editors of this series take a broader view. They define propaganda as information that is intended to influence our beliefs, attitudes, and actions, which raises the question—isn't all literature meant to persuade? The 300 authors featured in this survey are drawn from the Ancient Greeks to the present day and across the globe. As a taste of the selections, we find: the Federalist Papers; *Uncle Tom's Cabin*; the writings of Fidel Castro, Simon Bolivar, and Mao Zedong; *J'Accuse*; *Animal Farm*; and more recent works such as a speech by Harvey Milk, Persepolis, writings from the Nigerian civil war, *The Hunger Games*, and the WikiLeaks Manifesto. For each selection the contributor provides the historical context for the work, an explanation of the author's themes and style, a summary of the critical reception at the time of the piece's publication, and sources for further reading. As George Orwell said, "Propaganda in some form or other lurks in every book." This series explores the complexities of persuasive literature and invites debate on its use and impact.—**Adrienne Antink**

861.　**The Manifesto in Literature.** Thomas Riggs, ed. Farmington Hills, Mich., St. James Press/Gale Group, 2013. 3v. illus. index. $418.00/set. ISBN 13: 978-1-55862-866-3; 978-1-55862-880-9 (e-book).

Manifestos, as defined in the Editor's Note, "challenge a traditional order, whether in politics, religion, social issues, art, literature or technology, and propose a new vision of the future." This set is a reference guide to manifestos, rather than an anthology—only a few very short manifestos are included in their entirety. Each of the three volumes in the set covers a certain time period (pre-1900; 1900-World War II; Late 19th century to 21st century). Each volume is divided into sections (e.g., Artists and Writers, Church and State), and each volume contains the author, title, and subject indexes to the set and the same introduction, Editor's Note, and list of contributors and reviewers. Over 300 manifestos are provided, including the *Ars Poetica* of Horace, the *Magna Carta*, and Luther's *Ninety-Five Theses* as well as current manifestos (up to 2012) such as the *Declaration of the Occupation of New York City* by Occupy Wall Street, the *Contract with America* issued by the Republican Party, and the *WikiLeaks Manifesto*. Each manifesto gets a three- to four-page treatment in four parts: Overview, Historical and Literary Context, Themes and Style, and Critical Discussion, with short bibliographies of the sources and critical works and a half-page illustration, usually in color. Contributors are usually academics.

While the treatment of the manifestos are generally readable and informative, the obscurity of many of the manifestos, the lack of texts, and the price of the set will probably militate against its purchase by all but the largest libraries. Academic libraries will find some use in reference sections for students writing term papers on a fairly wide range of subjects.—**Jonathan F. Husband**

Dictionaries and Encyclopedias

862. **Bloom's Literary Reference Online.** http://online.infobaselearning.com/Login. aspx?app=Infobase&returnUrl=/Default.aspx. [Website]. New York, Facts on File. Price negotiated by site. Date reviewed: 2013.

Bloom's Literary Reference Online contains the published works from Facts on File's print literature monographs and series. A major portion of the contents are from the Bloom's monograph series of critical articles by noted scholars and also hundreds of Harold Bloom's essays on the lives and works of great writers throughout the world. In the database there is information on more than 46,000 characters; extensive entries on literary topics, themes, movements, genres, and authors; almost 170 video segments; and more. It has a "Did You Mean …?" search feature. MARC records can be downloaded to a library's catalog. The database is suitable for schools and public libraries for which it would be a major resource. Along with Harold Bloom's many works, this resource contains such resources as the *A to Z of African-American writers*, *A to Z of Latino American Writers and Journalists*, and *A to Z of Women Writers*, as well as many of Facts on Files encyclopedias of American literature, British literature, world writers, and literary movements.—**Anna H. Perrault**

863. **Johns Hopkins Guide to Literary Theory and Criticism.** http://litguide.press.jhu.edu. [Website]. Baltimore, Md., Johns Hopkins University Press. $100.00 (individual annual subscription); $325.00 (institution annual subscription). Date reviewed: 2013.

Compiled by 275 specialists from around the world and including more than 240 entries, this online subscription database provides a comprehensive historical survey of the field's most important figures, schools, and movements. Some specific subjects include African American feminist literary criticism, British New Left criticism, Classical literary criticism, literary criticism on fantasy fiction, historical novel criticism, modernist literature criticism, and gay literary criticism, among many others. This resource is updated annually to reflect the rapidly changing scholarship.—**ARBA Staff Reviewer**

Handbooks and Yearbooks

864. **Critical Insights: American Road Literature.** Ronald Primeau, ed. Hackensack, N.J., Salem Press, 2013. 347p. index. $85.00. ISBN 13: 978-1-4298-3819-1.

865. **Critical Insights: American Sports Fiction.** Michael Cocchiarale and Scott D. Emmert, eds. Hackensack, N.J., Salem Press, 2013. 271p. index. $85.00. ISBN 13: 978-1-4298-3824-5.

866. **Critical Insights: Contemporary Speculative Fiction.** M. Keith Booker, ed. Hackensack, N.J., Salem Press, 2013. 263p. index. $85.00. ISBN 13: 978-1-4298-3820-7.

867. **Critical Insights: Crime and Detective Fiction.** Rebecca Martin, ed. Hackensack, N.J., Salem Press, 2013. 265p. index. $85.00. ISBN 13: 978-1-4298-3822-1.

868. **Critical Insights: Crisis of Faith.** Robert C. Evans, ed. Hackensack, N.J., Salem Press, 2013. 262p. index. $85.00. ISBN 13: 978-1-4298-3825-2.

869. **Critical Insights: Literature of Protest.** Kimberly drake, ed. Hackensack, N.J., Salem Press, 2013. 279p. index. $85.00. ISBN 13: 978-1-4298-3826-9.

870.   **Critical Insights: Pulp Fiction of the '20s and '30s.** Gary Hoppenstand, ed. Hackensack, N.J., Salem Press, 2013. 230p. index. $85.00. ISBN 13: 978-1-4298-3827-6.

871.   **Critical Insights: Southern Gothic Literature.** Jay Ellis, ed. Hackensack, N.J., Salem Press, 2013. 280p. index. $85.00. ISBN 13: 978-1-4298-3823-8.

872.   **Critical Insights: The American Dream.** Keith Newlin, ed. Hackensack, N.J., Salem Press, 2013. 266p. index. $85.00. ISBN 13: 978-1-4298-3821-4.

Salem Press's Critical Insights series highlights critical discussions of important authors, literary works, and literary themes. Eight new volumes in the series have recently been published, covering broad topics such as crime and detective fiction to much narrower topics, such as southern gothic literature and contemporary speculative fiction.

Each volume begins with an introductory essay on the topic, explaining its rise in popularity as a literary theme in the twentieth and twenty-first centuries. The volumes then provide essays discussing key topics surrounding the theme. For example, in *Crisis of Faith* there are articles on the crises of faith and renewal through poetic tides, the crisis of faith theme as experienced through the Harlem Renaissance writers, and the theme of faith in Elie Wiesel's *Night*. The Critical Readings sections provide 10-11 essays on novels that highlight the aspect of literature being discussed. For example, in the *Crisis of Faith* volume *All the King's Men* is discussed as well as the short fiction of Flannery O'Connor. In *Literature of Protest* the themes surrounding George Orwell's *Nineteen Eighty-Four* are covered as well as the themes of paranoia and pacifism in e. e. cumming's *The Enormous Room*.

The text is written at a level appropriate for high school and undergraduate-level students, precisely the age that would be reading these titles and authors' works and needing resources to write critical papers for class. These resources will be useful for high school and undergraduate library collections. Online access is available with purchase of the print volume, which will be a huge benefit for classroom use since many students will be able to access the same information at one time. Once activated by the student's library the database can be accessed at the library or from their home or dorm room. This aspect of the product more than justifies the cost for high school or university libraries needing this type of critical literature information.—**Shannon Graff Hysell**

873.   **Magill's Literary Annual 2013.** Eve-Marie Miller, Liza Oldham, and Christi Showman Farrar, eds. Hackensack, N.J., Salem Press; distr., Millerton, N.Y., Grey House Publishing, 2013. 2v. illus. index. $195.00/set. ISBN 13: 978-1-4298-3809-2; 978-1-4298-3812-2 (e-book).

Magill's Literary Annual 2013 highlights 200 of titles published in the United States in English from 2012. Covering a wide gamut of genres, the *Literary Annual* is essentially a collection of essay-reviews, describing and analyzing the works' strengths and weaknesses, incorporating reviews and material from a variety of sources to present balanced accounts of the works. Included with a purchase of the two-volume print set is access to its electronic version. Types of works included in the *Literary Annual*, which also serve as parameters in searching in the electronic version of the title, are autobiography, biography, fiction, general non-fiction, literary non-fiction, poetry/drama, and short fiction.

Entries are arranged alphabetically by title of the work and contain: the author; a picture of the book cover; publication details; type of work; time period in which the work is set; locales/geography in which the work is set; a brief overview of the work; a listing of principal characters (fiction) or principal personages (nonfiction) appearing in the work; the critical examination of the title; and a bibliography of "Review Sources." In addition to the entries, the *Literary Annual* contains a brief annotated bibliography of all the titles, which translates to either to brief plot summaries or brief descriptions of content, depending on the genre, as well as three indexes: category (subject), title, and author.

The online component contains the same kind of entry content (although the book covers are in color in the online version). It offers citations for entries (including exporting into biographical managers) and printing, e-mailing, and saving of entries. The title provides several types of searches, including full text (preferred by this reviewer over the "top matter/keywords" search which is clunky); abstract; title; and the aforementioned top matter/keywords. In addition to the genre search mentioned earlier, other search parameters include geographical, identity (biographies only), and gender (biographies only). The online version also provides a listing of titles in the set, arranged alphabetically, which is simply too long to be user-friendly; this reviewer would have recommended at least dividing the list into alphabetic groupings. The indexes are not available in the online version.

The mechanism of selection for inclusion for the *Literary Annual* is not transparent to the reader, which bothers this reviewer. The introduction describes the selection process intending "to cover works that are likely to be of interest to general readers, that reflect publishing trends, that add to the careers of authors being taught and researcher in literary programs, and that will stand the test of time" (p. vii). This reviewer would have liked to see more detail or criteria than that. Other than these complaints, this title is very good, and considering that it comes with free access to an electronic version, a library will get a lot of bang for its buck, especially with such a relatively low cost. This title is highly recommended for both public and academic libraries, especially at institutions with strong literature programs for both the undergraduate and graduate levels.—**Megan W. Lowe**

874.   **Social Issues in Literature Series.** Farmington Hills, Mich., Greenhaven Press/Gale/Cengage Learning, 2012. multivolume. illus. index. $28.45/vol.

Greenhaven Press has several series available to young adults that deal with social issues, including the Opposing Viewpoints series and the At Issues series. This is yet another look at social issues; however, this series focuses on how social issues have been presented in classic literature. Each volume presents major social issues and explores how the author's work explores the historical and social context of that issue. Each volume presents selected excerpts from the text that represent a variety of perspectives on the social themes of the time. There are currently more than 40 titles in this series, with some of the new titles including *Class Conflict in Charles Dickens' Tale of Two Cities* , *Race in the Poetry of Langston Hughes*, *Coming of Age in Sue Monk Kidd's The Secret Life of Bees* , and *Sexuality in William Shakespeare's A Midsummer Night's Dream* . These books provide a unique perspective to the social issues both past and present and are likely to spur new interest from young readers in these classic titles. The titles provide biographical information and a timeline of the author's life, excerpts that offer historical and contemporary viewpoints on the social issue examined, a "For Further Reading" section, and a subject index. They combine the sociology and literature in a complementary format that supports cross-curricular studies.—**Shannon Graff Hysell**

Indexes

875.   **Essay and General Literature Index. http://ebscohost.com/wilson.** [Website]. Bronx, N.Y., H. W. Wilson. Price negotiated by site. Date reviewed: 2013.

876.   **Essay and General Literature Index Retrospective, 1900-1984. http://www.ebscohost.com/ academic/essay-and-general-literature-retrospective.** [Website]. Bronx, N.Y., H. W. Wilson. Price negotiated by site. Date reviewed: 2013.

As a long-running printed tool, the *Essay and General Literature Index* (EGLI) provided indexing for articles in collections and anthologies that were not indexed in other periodical indexes. Although other areas of the humanities are covered in this standard work, literature receives the greatest emphasis. Originally, the work succeeded the *ALA Index . . . to General Literature* (2d ed., American Library Association, 1901-1914), that indexed books of essays, travel, sociological matters, and so forth up to 1900. A supplement covered the publications of the first decade of the twentieth century. EGLI indexes essays in books published since 1900, the initial volume covering the first 33 years. Two comprehensive printed editions have been issued covering the periods 19001-1989 and 1990-1994. The EGLI is now an online database with citations to over 86,000 essays from some 7,000 collections published in the United States, Canada, and Great Britain. Hundreds of collections and anthologies (about 300 added annually) serve as sources of the indexed essays on authors, forms, movements, genres, and individual titles of creative works. Essay and General Literature Index Retrospective is a separate online collection that contains the publication from the years 1900-1984.—**Anna H. Perrault**

Children's and Young Adult Literature

Bibliography

877.   Barr, Catherine. **Best Books for High School Readers: Grades 9-12.** 3d ed. Santa Barbara, Calif., Libraries Unlimited/ABC-CLIO, 2013. 1102p. index. (Children's and Young Adult Literature Reference Series). $85.00. ISBN 13: 978-1-59884-784-0.

Best Books is a comprehensive list of 12,699 young adult titles. The contents divides the books into 11 major subject areas. In each subject area, books are divided into alphabetized subcategories. For example, the Fiction section begins with "Adventures and Survival Stories" and ends with "Short Stories and General Anthologies." Entries are numbered and listed in alphabetic order by author's last name. Each entry includes hardbound publication information and price, suitable grade levels, and a brief annotation. Illustrations, Dewey Decimal classification number, paperback information, and audio version information are provided when applicable. *Best Books* also provides an alphabetic list of major subjects along with entry numbers facilitating the readers' ability to locate a book's annotation. Readers can also use the title index or author index to locate a book.

The authors consulted a wide array of current sources in compiling the bibliography. Among those consulted were *Booklist*, *Library Media Connection* (formerly *Book Report*), *School Library Journal*, and *VOYA* (*Voice of Youth Advocates*). Each annotation references the review source and date of the review.

The authors realize that reading levels are elastic, meaning readers cannot be labeled by grade levels. Rather the bibliography provides books from a wide range of topics that accommodate the reading interests of readers from grades 9-12. One of the book's tasks is to help librarians and media specialists provide reading guidance to young adults. The other three tasks are: evaluating the adequacy of existing collections, building new collections or strengthening existing holdings, and preparing bibliographies and reading lists. The information provided in *Best Books for High School Readers* would greatly assist a young adult librarian or media specialist build or refine their collection as well as help them provide reading suggestions to their users.—**Susan E. Montgomery**

878.   Barr, Catherine. **Best Books for Middle School and Junior High Readers: Grades 6-9.** 3d ed. Santa Barbara, Calif., Libraries Unlimited/ABC-CLIO, 2013. 1188p. index. (Children's and Young Adult Literature Reference Series). $85.00. ISBN 13: 978-1-59884-782-6.

As part of the Children's and Young Adult Literature Reference series, which also includes *Best Books for Children* (9th ed.; see ARBA 2011, entry 909) and *Best Books for High School Readers* (3d ed.; see entry 877), the purpose of this 3d and updated edition of *Best Books for Middle School and Junior High Readers: Grades 6-9* is to provide librarians with the tools they need to evaluate existing collections, establish new collections, and build reading lists and bibliographies. It is also designed to be a helpful tool for young adult readers, guiding them to make informed decisions about their choice of reading material.

This work clearly achieves its purpose. Its scope is comprehensive, including 14,028 annotations for books published up to July 2012. In most cases these books have received two or more positive reviews. Each entry contains succinct information about the book's content: suggested grade range, a short summary, and references to other books by the same author. An evaluation of the content is not included. Each entry also gives helpful purchasing information: availability of an audio version, ISBN, publisher and price, and citations of the book's reviews. Books from all genres and subject areas have been annotated, from classics such to recent publications.

Not only is the scope of this work comprehensive, but its information is also easily accessible. Comprehensive indexes allow readers to locate books by subject, title, and subject/grade level. The subject/grade level index is an especially helpful feature, allowing both librarians and young adult readers to find books on a particular subject and grade level at one glance. Because of these strengths, *Best Books for Middle School and Junior High Readers* is an invaluable resource for all those who make purchasing decisions or compile reading lists in the area of young adult books.—**Helen Margaret Bernard**

879.   Cart, Michael. **Cart's Top 200 Adult Books for Young Adults: Two Decades in Review.** Chicago, American Library Association, 2013. 126p. index. $50.00pa.; $45.00pa. (ALA members). ISBN 13: 978-0-8389-1158-7.

Cart's reading advice for "adultescents" supplies the compiler's personal suggestions for teen tastes and reading ventures. The range of works—Satrapi's *Persepolis*, Sebold's *The Lovely Bones*, McCarthy's *The Road*, Watson's *Montana 1948*, Alvarez's *In the Time of the Butterflies*—stresses the diversity of recent publications in terms of genre, theme, and style. Cart omits drama, depriving his list of such treasures as August Wilson's *Gem of the Ocean* and Margaret Edson's *Wit*. The list presses beyond average comprehension, particularly the choices of O'Brien's *The Things They Carried* and Kingsolver's *The Poisonwood Bible*, while pandering to the pop appeal of Brown's *The Da Vinci Code* and Martel's *The Life of Pi*. The list slights historical romance, which combines passion with plans for a full adult life, the focus of Robin Oliveira's *My Name Is Mary Sutter*, E. L. Doctorow's *The March*, and Virginia Ellis's *The Wedding Dress*. Cart also overlooks two classics of multicultural adventure lore, Isabel Allende's *Zorro* and Peter Carey's *The True History of the Kelly Gang*, which revisit Latino and Australian frontier legends that appeal to both genders. Cart also omits a substantial contribution to Native American nonfiction, Leslie Marmon Silko's desert musings in *The Turquoise Ledge*, which outlines the Indian's reverence for nature as obligation and legacy. This pricey reference guide leaves too many holes to be forgiven, and can therefore not be recommended.—**Mary Ellen Snodgrass**

880.   **Children's Literature Web Guide. http://people.ucalgary.ca/~dkbrown/.** [Website]. Free. Date reviewed: 2013.

The Children's Literature Web Guide is an attempt to gather together and categorize the growing number of Internet resources related to books for children and young adults. While created and maintained by David K. Brown, a librarian and director of Director, Doucette Library of Teaching Resources, much of the information that users can find on these pages is provided by others: fans, schools, libraries, and commercial enterprises involved in the book world. This Website includes Features, Discussion Boards, Quick Reference, and many more links to Children's and Young Adult authors and their books.—**ARBA Staff Reviewer**

881.   Crosetto, Alice, and Rajinder Garcha. **Death, Loss, and Grief in Literature for Youth: A Selective Annotated Bibliography for K-12.** Lanham, Md., Scarecrow, 2013. 245p. index. (Literature for Youth, no.13). $75.00; $74.99 (e-book). ISBN 13: 978-0-8108-8560-8; 978-0-8108-8561-5 (e-book).

Authored by experienced, professional librarians whose backgrounds include working the University of Toledo Libraries, this impressive bibliography begins an introduction introducing the reader to working with children and teens dealing with the loss of a loved one. This book contains almost 1,000 entries for print and nonprint resources and is divided into 12 chapters. The works are arranged according to the relationship to the loved one lost: death of a family member, death of a teacher or schoolmate, death of a friend or neighbor, or death of a pet. The remaining chapters address various aspects of death and the afterlife, including folktales, nonfiction resources, animal and nature stories, resources for parents and professionals, and media and Internet resources. For each entry, there is extensive bibliographic information that includes ISBNs and grade level suitability (but no prices), and a lengthy critical annotation of about 10 lines that describes the contents and often supplies quotes from reviews. Choices for this section were made by consulting reviewing journals like Booklist and standard retrospective sources, including the Best Books series from Libraries Unlimited. The titles are in print and almost entirely published since 2000 (some as late as 2011). The result is that many recommended imprint titles from before 2000 are not included. The chapters on adult resources are also current and well annotated. There are two brief appendixes: one of book and media awards in these fields and the other provides information on children's Grief awareness Day. The extensive indexes include ones for authors, titles, series, subject, and grade levels.

This is a valuable, useful resource not only for librarians but also for other professionals working with young people who are experiencing the loss of a loved one or who have questions about death. It is recommended for professional collections in both school district and college libraries as well as large public libraries.—**John T. Gillespie**

882.   Crosetto, Alice, and Rajinder Garcha. **Native North Americans in Literature for Youth: A Selective Annotated Bibliography for K-12.** Lanham, Md., Scarecrow, 2013. 267p. index. (Literature for Youth, no.14). $90.00; $89.99 (e-book). ISBN 13: 978-0-8108-9189-0; 978-0-8108-9190-6 (e-book).

Approximately 800 annotated titles of books on various aspects of Native American history form the body of this work, which is compiled by two specialists in children's literature who are also library school faculty members. The books range in difficulty from picture books for pre-school children to adult titles suitable for senior high students. Unfortunately, there is no mention of selection criteria, sources consulted, selection limitations, cut-off dates, or in-print status of books chosen. However, the choices appear to be judicious and prudent. The books are listed in 12 chapters that cover geographic regions, history, religion, social life and customs, nations, oral literature, biographies, fiction, general reference, media resources, books for educators, and Internet resources. The descriptive annotation for each book is four or five lines in length. At the pre-school through sixth grade level many of the books listed can also be found in general bibliographies; coverage is about the same and as up-to-date as in *Best Books for Children* (8th ed.; see ARBA 2007, entry 886). However, the wide range of age and grade levels covered makes this book unique. The appendixes include lists of book awards, and information on Native American Heritage Month. The book can easily be search with its multitude of indexes, including author/editor, title, illustrator/photographer, nations, series, subject, grade/level, and book award index. This specialized tool will be valuable in school and public libraries where there is a great demand for material and other resources on Native American history.—**John T. Gillespie**

883.   **Database of Award-Winning Children's Literature. http://www.dawcl.com.** [Website] Free. Date reviewed: 2013.

Under various names, this excellent resource has been in existence for several years. It was founded and is maintained by Lisa R. Bartle, now a librarian at California State University at San Bernadino. It covers over 100 awards. Background information, including selection criteria, and a link to each award's home page are given under "Explanation of Awards." The "Instructions" section explains each of the search choices—age of reader, genre, and setting, for example. In the "Search the Database" mode, one can search by a number of access points including those mentioned above, plus format, setting/period, gender of protagonist, and more. Individual title entries contain bibliographic information and a two-line annotation. There are now more than 10,000 records from 6 English-speaking countries contained in this amazing site.—**John T. Gillespie**

884.   Griffith, Susan C. **The Jane Addams Children's Book Award: Honoring Children's Literature for Peace and Social Justice Since 1953.** Lanham, Md., Scarecrow, 2013. 161p. index. $65.00; $64.99 (e-book). ISBN 13: 978-0-8108-9202-6; 978-0-8108-9203-3 (e-book).

Griffith's book is far more than an annotated bibliography of the Jane Addams Children's Book Award winners and honor books; she provides discussions of the complex Addams and her representation in biographies; the controversial granting of the award to Theodore Taylor for The Cay and the issues this title raised in evaluating books as promoters of racial harmony and understanding; and reviews of some noteworthy biographies of Addams. Part 2 begins with a history of the work of the Book Award committee, and then lists the Award winner and honor books in reverse chronological order. Each entry includes a bibliographic citation and a one-paragraph synopsis. Appendixes include a list of winners by three broad themes and 26 subjects; the 1957 and 1994 guidelines; and a timeline of events in the life of Jane Addams and her publications. General, author/illustrator, and title indexes complete the volume. Given the wealth of information provided, the insightful discussion of issues, and the importance of this award, it is highly recommended for all school, public, and academic libraries that support children's literature collections.—**Rosanne M. Cordell**

885.   Jones, Cherri, and J. B. Petty. **Multiethnic Books for the Middle-School Curriculum.** Chicago, American Library Association, 2013. 284p. index. $55.00pa.; $49.50pa. (ALA members). ISBN 13: 978-0-8389-1163-1.

Jones and Petty have produced an up-to-date list of multiethnic books arranged in seven broad categories (Health; Language Arts; Performing Arts: Dance, Music, and Theater; Physical Education; Science and Mathematics; and Social Studies) to coordinate with middle school curricula. Each broad area is subdivided and includes fiction and information books. Entries include the title, series title, author, whether it is fiction or nonfiction, the grade level, curricular area, the standards the book might fulfill, and the ethnic groups covered. The annotation gives a brief summary and a review statement. The authors have read every book listed and have drawn on their own vast experience in middle school literature and curricula to make excellent choices from recently published titles. Appendixes cover the National Curriculum Standards to which the entries refer, the cultures included in the list, and Sources for Further Information on Multiethnic Literature. A comprehensive title-author-subject index completes the volume. Although this work was written specifically for middle school use, public libraries may also find it a welcome addition to their professional literature. This work is highly recommended.—**Rosanne M. Cordell**

Handbooks and Yearbooks

886.   Stover, Lois Thomas, and Connie S. Zitlow. **Portraits of the Artist as a Young Adult: The Arts in Young Adult Literature.** Lanham, Md., Scarecrow, 2014. 275p. index. (Scarecrow Studies in Young Adult Literature, no.46). $65.00; $64.99 (e-book). ISBN 13: 978-0-8108-9277-4; 978-0-8108-9278-1 (e-book).

Stover, author of *Teaching the Selected Works of Katherine Paterson and Jacqueline Woodson: The Real Thing*, and Zitlow, author of *Teaching the Young Adult Novels of Walter Dean Myers* and *Lost Masterworks of Young Adult Literature*, bring their considerable knowledge and experience to this work, defining "artist" broadly and exploring the characteristics of the literature as well as the possibilities for the study of it. This is not a reference work; rather it provides insightful essays on the development of an identity as an artist in young adults in various works, common themes in these works, and the role of adults in young adult artists' lives. The essays use works to explain the authors' ideas about young adult literature, going into considerable depth about the titles discussed. The appendixes include an annotated bibliography of young adult books about the arts and a chapter on the use of the arts in pedagogy. This work is highly recommended for professional collections in school libraries and in academic libraries that support teacher preparation programs.—**Rosanne M. Cordell**

Fiction

General Works

887.　**American Short Fiction.** Hackensack, N.J., Salem Press, 2013. 278p. illus. index. (Introduction to Literary Context). $165.00. ISBN 13: 978-161925212-7.

The second in the series of Introduction to Literary Context, *American Short Fiction* consists of 40 essays on works by major American writers beginning with 9 on Poe short stories and 2 by Hawthorne to works by twentieth-century Canadian Alice Munro and Antiguan Jamaica Kinkaid. The stories themselves are not included, but a Content Synopsis gives an intensive account of plot, setting, and characters. A few of the six- to eight-page essays are introduced by a portrait of the writer and all have a biographical account. Sections entitled Historical, Societal, Religious, and Scientific and Technological (which in modern times includes Environmental) contexts show how much fiction and attitudes have changed since the nineteenth century. Both Updike and Hawthorne use the same general geographical setting, but with very different results.

Presented alphabetically by title, each essay ends with a list of books cited, questions for discussion, and topics for student essays. The collection ends with an intensive bibliography of critical works both of the individual writers and the genre in general. The index lists topics such as phrenology, symbols, and technology as well as the names of titles and authors.

A desirable library reference book, the concentration on specific short stories might limit it as a classroom text. Both teachers and students, however, would profit from the careful analysis of important American writers and the way they reveal the beliefs and behavior of the society of their times.—**Charlotte Lindgren**

888.　**Genreflecting: A Guide to Popular Reading Interests.** 7th ed. Cynthia Orr and Diana Tixier Herald, eds. Santa Barbara, Calif., Libraries Unlimited/ABC-CLIO, 2013. 622p. index. $75.00; $65.00pa. ISBN 13: 978-1-59884-840-3; 978-1-59884-841-0pa.

This is the 7th edition of the standard guide to genre fiction. This edition is a completely rewritten version of the 6th edition (see ARBA 2007, entry 917), with new editors and mostly new contributors. This edition is divided into three parts: Parts 1 and 2 consist of six chapters all by co-editor Cynthia Orr, on the basics of readers' advisory services for libraries and readers. Part 3, which is the predominant section, consists of chapters on the types of genre fiction—historical, mystery, thriller, western, romance, women, fantasy, horror, and science fiction—plus chapters on mainstream fiction, nonfiction, and other popular reading interests, which include Christian fiction, urban fiction, and graphic novels. Each chapter has several subdivisions with annotated lists of book authors and titles. Name, subject, and title indexes, a general introduction, and a section on the editors and contributors complete the volume. Recent titles (last 20 years) predominate among the titles listed and annotated—the mainstream fiction section contains only titles published from 2008 through 2011. Many young adult titles are included, and there is a distinct tilt toward younger readers. Useful Web sources are listed. *Genreflecting* remains a useful reference source for libraries, especially for public and school libraries. Libraries owning earlier editions should keep them.—**Jonathan F. Husband**

889.　**NoveList. http://www.ebsco.com.** [Website]. Ipswich, Mass., EBSCO, 2013. Price negotiated by site. Date reviewed: 2013.

NoveList is a database designed to be an aid to librarians for readers' advisory services to adults, teens, and younger readers. According to the publisher's description, the database provides access to information on 155,000 fiction titles, over 60,000 being juvenile fiction records. The database goes beyond just records for fiction titles and has several built-in features which make it suitable for teachers and readers including curriculum-driven material designed to help integrate NoveList into the classroom. The Readers' Advisory section includes RA training, novelist newsletters, Genre Outlines, hundreds of reading lists, book talks, and feature articles by notable librarians and subject matter experts. Lists of award titles and recommended reading lists by genres and topics are included. The database has an easy-to-use interface with a single search bar. Results can be sorted by popularity and/or Lexile scores. Records can be linked to a library catalog, making it easy to find a desired title in the local library. Several different customized versions of Novelist can be subscribed to include NoveList Plus and NoveList K-8 and K-8 Plus.—**Anna H. Perrault**

890. **Street Lit: Representing the Urban Landscape.** Norris, Keenan, ed. Lanham, Md., Scarecrow, 2014. 214p. index. $38.000; $37.99 (e-book). ISBN 13: 978-0-8108-9262-0; 978-0-8108-9263-7 (e-book).

Norris provides an introductory survey of the new, fast growing genre of street lit—also referred to as urban fiction, hip-hop lit, and gangsta lit. It is made up of edgy stories focusing on personal relationships and survival of the fittest. In this volume Norris provides readers with articles, essays, interviews, and poems that capture the spirit of this edgy literature. Making its appearance in the 1950, the genre draws readers who tend to be young, African American, and female. Urban fiction is characterized by stories of life on the streets and in the projects using brutal descriptions of drugs, violence, sex, abuse, and prison. The work begins with an introduction that explores the roots of this literature and provides insight into how it captures today's culture in much the same way that hip-hop music does for the music industry. The author provides critical discussions of works by Goines, Japer, and Whitehead, and gives interviews with such literary icons as David Bradley, Gerald Early, and Lynel Gardner. Norris helps scholars, avid readers, and librarians understand the significance of this sometimes controversial but up-and-coming form of literature.—**Adrienne Antink**

891. Vnuk, Rebecca, and Nanette Donohue. **Women's Fiction: A Guide to Popular Reading Interests.** Santa Barbara, Calif., Libraries Unlimited/ABC-CLIO, 2013. 233p. index. (Genreflecting Advisory Series). $55.00. ISBN 13: 978-1-59884-920-2.

A glance at the title of this work might lead one to believe that it is a straightforward bibliography of women's fiction. It is instead a scholarly discussion and review of the literature, aimed principally at librarians who buy this literature and who must satisfy eager readers. The work begins with an introductory chapter on the history of women's fiction and its distinctive characteristics. The authors provides some general hints to librarians on how to approach collection development in this area, recommending that collection development librarians talk to colleagues and to regular readers of the genre, read reviews, and monitor circulation statistics. For those responsible for personnel allocation, the authors recommend designating a librarian to be responsible for collection building in this area.

The main body of the book is devoted to sections on subgenres of the field: grand dames of women's fiction, contemporary women's fiction, gentle reads, issue-driven women's fiction, chick lit and beyond, romantic women's fiction, and genreblends (e.g., Christian fiction, romantic suspense). Each of these sections begins with a lengthy definition of the subgenre, followed by a discussion of its appeal. Hints on advising the reader follow, including such topics as what other subgenres a reader might find appealing and specific series that might be of interest. An annotated bibliography of selected authors rounds out each section. Other material includes a list of 30 contemporary women's fiction authors to know, read-alike lists, a further reading list, and a list of selected online resources. This work is for the collection development librarian with a commitment to building a women's literature collection and the budget to support that commitment as well as for the scholar or student with an interest in the genre.—**Terry Ann Mood**

Crime and Mystery

892. Gunn, Drewey Wayne. **The Gay Male Sleuth in Print and Film: A History and Annotated Bibliography.** new ed. Lanham, Md., Scarecrow, 2013. 426p. index. $85.00. ISBN 13: 978-0-8108-8588-2; 978-0-8108-8589-9 (e-book).

This updated edition of Gunn's original volume provides all new gay male sleuth detectives stories in print and on film that have been published since 2005, as well as includes any titles that were overlooked in the original edition. With a discussion of more than 800 works of literature and 100 films and nearly 20 television or video series, *The Gay Male Sleuth in Print and Film* is the definitive reference work on this topic, and it belongs in any library whose patrons might be researching this subgenre. This outstanding book is divided into three highly readable and well-organized sections. In part 1, Gunn explores how this doubly marginalized subgenre (mysteries receiving relatively little respect to begin with, gay mysteries even less) has evolved from its beginnings in 1953 with Rodney Garland's *The Heart of Exile* to the present. Developing an extended analogy between gay sleuthing and all gay men's journey to self awareness, Gunn provides a chronological narrative from 1953-1969 (when early gay sleuth novels intimated to readers the possibility for gay men to lead happy and productive lives, a relatively unusual idea for the time) to the 1970s (a period of great productivity for the gay mystery) to 1981-1994 and 1995-2004 (when images of pathfinders in the dark time of AIDS and builders in years of loss and gain are the prevailing metaphors for gay male sleuths) to more recent releases of *Kiss Kiss Bang Bang* (2005) and *The Walker* (2007). Part 2 is mostly an extensive annotated bibliography listing novels, short stories, plays, and comics with gay male sleuths (1953-2011). It is organized alphabetically by author's name, as are two briefer annotated bibliographies, for other fictional investigators of interest and for non-sleuthing police officers. Part 3 presents four annotated bibliographies focused on the electronic media: films and television (organized alphabetically by film director's or show creator's name); erotic videos; other on-screen investigators of interest; and non-sleuthing police officers. Along with a superb index, this highly recommended work concludes with two very useful appendixes, the first on critical and bibliographic resources and the second on the Lambda Literary Awards for Best Gay Men's Mystery (1988-2011).—**G. Douglas Meyers**

893. **The Mystery Reader. http://ww.themysteryreader.com.** Dede Anderson. [Website]. Free. Date reviewed: 2013

The Mystery Reader offers hundreds of book reviews for mystery novels. One who indulges in this Website can also meet new authors and learn about forthcoming mystery novels. It reviews books in six categories: Latest Police/Detective, Latest Romantic Suspense, Latest Thrillers, Latest Cozy, Latest Suspense, and Latest Historical. Each book is priced, reviewed, and given from 5 stars (outstanding) to 1 star (don't bother). Its other features include New Faces (introducing new authors), Eagerly Awaited (upcoming releases), Author Directory, Small Press, Mail Bag, News, Crime Scene (news from authors), and Author Freebies.—**Anna H. Perrault**

Science Fiction and Fantasy

894. Gunn, James. **Paratexts: Introductions to Science Fiction and Fantasy.** Lanham, Md., Scarecrow, 2013. 229p. index. $75.00; $74.99 (e-book). ISBN 13: 978-0-8108-9122-7; 978-0-8108-9123-4 (e-book).

This book contains introductions and prefaces written by the author for a series of leather-bound collector editions by Easton Press in the mid-1980s called *Masterpieces of Science Fiction* and *Masterpieces of Fantasy*, along with a series called *Signed First Editions of Science Fiction*. They are compiled into this volume, along with reprinted prefaces for 13 of the author's own books. These prefaces and introductions are of value in their own right, as compilations of historical and genre-specific timepieces related to the growth and popularity of science fiction and fantasy from the 1980s onward; putting them all into one volume, as a timeline for these genres as well as a glimpse into the author's own writing and scholarship on the topics, is a gem for science fiction and fantasy readers, especially since many of these books have since become classics in the literature.—**Bradford Lee Eden**

895.   Joshi, S. T., and Darrell Schweitzer. **Lord Dunsany: A Comprehensive Bibliography.** 2d ed. Lanham, Md., Scarecrow, 2014. 296p. index. $100.00; $99.99 (e-book). ISBN 13: 978-0-8108-9313-9; 978-0-8108-9314-6 (e-book).

Known primarily for his literary contributions in the area of fantasy literature in the early 1900s, there has been a renewed interest in Lord Dunsany's work in recent years, which is reflected in recent volumes published on this influential author, including *Critical Essays on Lord Dunsany* (Scarecrow Press, 2013) and *Lord Dunsany, H.P. Lovecraft, and Ray Bradbury: Spectral Journeys* (Scarecrow Press, 2013). This volume is a revision a 1993 bibliography that provided a much-needed compilation of all of Lord Dunsany's works. This volume has been updated to reflect dozens of new editions of Dunsany's work and new titles that have been identified in the past 20 years. The new material includes short stories, newspaper articles, poems, books, essays, and critical reviews of Dunsany's published works. The volume is arranged into three sections: Works by Dunsany in English; Works by Dunsany in Translation; and Dunsany Criticism. The work has been indexed by name, title, and periodical titles to make navigating the work easier for the user. This will be a useful volume for the literature collections of college and university libraries.—**Shannon Graff Hysell**

896.   **The Twilight Saga: Exploring the Global Phenomenon.** Claudia Bucciferro, ed. Lanham, Md., Scarecrow, 2014. 253p. index. $60.00; $59.99 (e-book). ISBN 13: 978-0-8108-9285-9; 978-0-8108-9286-6 (e-book).

Stephenie Meyer's Twilight series, a dark romantic fantasy saga between mortals, vampires, and werewolves, had an astounding reception when it hit the shelves in 2005. Since that time the books have gone on to be international bestsellers and the movies adaptations have been just as well received. The fact that this series has been an international success makes it worthwhile to examine what it is about the characters, the storyline, and the genre that make it appeal to such a wide audience. In this volume the editor has compiled 15 essays, written by contributors from the United States, France, Spain, Chile, and Australia, that examine the intercultural relevance of the Twilight series.

The book is arranged into five parts: Contextualizing Twilight's Appeal; Twilight Audiences; Characters and Their Cultural Referents; Issues of Gender, Sex, Class, and Race in Twilight; and Beyond the Twilight Universe. Many of the essays look at how the series fits within larger contexts including historical, philosophical, and sociological studies. Designed for scholars and students of media, this work will be a valuable addition to larger university collections.—**Shannon Graff Hysell**

National Literature

American Literature

General Works

Bibliography

897.   **Bibliography of American Literature (BAL). http://collections.chadwyck.com/marketing/ home_bal.jsp.** [Website]. Alexandria, Va., Chadwyck-Healey. Price negotiated by site. Date reviewed: 2013.

Between 1955and 1991, Yale University Press published the nine volumes of BAL for the Bibliographical Society of America. A selective index to the set was published in 1995. A new printing was issued by the Oak Knoll Press in 2003. BAL's accuracy is widely recognized. Jacob Blanck led a team of bibliographers over the years of the project and the bibliography became known by his name. Originally projected for eight volumes, this monumental but highly selective series was finally concluded with publication of the ninth volume some 36 years following volume 1.The Bibliography complements the work of the early American bibliographers Charles Evans and Joseph Sabin. Some 300 American writers, dating from the Federal period to moderns who died before 1930, are covered. BAL contains close to 40,000 records of nearly 300 American writers' literary works. The works of about 30 writers are covered in each volume in systematic fashion, including first editions, reprints containing textual or other changes, and a selected listing of biographical, bibliographical, and critical works. Only authors of literary interest (popular in their time but not necessarily recognized today as major writers) are included. The online BAL allows researchers to search all volumes together. Each author is searchable with lists of works divided into sections, including principal works, reprints, and references. Each primary book listed has a title page transcription along with information about the collation, pagination, binding, and publication history. The location of at least one copy is given, as well as a selected list of bibliographic and biographical works. The database also provides a list of general references, principal periodicals consulted, and initials and pseudonyms. The printed BAL is usually found in academic libraries and is now available in electronic form through the *Literature Online Reference* (see entry 856).—**Anna H. Perrault**

Biography

898.   **Critical Insights: James Joyce.** Albert Wachtel, ed. Hackensack, N.J., Salem Press, 2013. 259p. index. $85.00. ISBN 13: 978-1-4298-3834-4.

899.   **Critical Insights: Kurt Vonnegut.** Robert T. Tally Jr., ed. Hackensack, N.J., Salem Press, 2013. 314p. index. $85.00. ISBN 13: 978-1-4298-3832-0.

900.   **Critical Insights: Philip Roth.** Aimee Pozorski, ed. Hackensack, N.J., Salem Press, 2013. 254p. index. $85.00. ISBN 13: 978-1-4298-3829-0.

901.   **Critical Insights: Raymond Carver.** James Plath, ed. Hackensack, N.J., Salem Press, 2013. 271p. index. $85.00. ISBN 13: 978-1-4298-3830-6.

902.   **Critical Insights: Sylvia Plath.** William K. Buckley, ed. Hackensack, N.J., Salem Press, 2013. 325p. index. $85.00. ISBN 13: 978-1-4298-3833-7.

903.   **Critical Insights: William Faulkner.** Kathryn Stelmach Artuso, ed. Hackensack, N.J., Salem Press, 2013. 298p. index. $85.00. ISBN 13: 978-1-4298-3828-3.

904.   **Critical Insights: Zora Neale Hurston.** Sharon L. Jones, ed. Hackensack, N.J., Salem Press, 2013. 351p. index. $85.00. ISBN 13: 978-1-4298-3831-3.

Salem Press's Critical Insights series highlights critical discussions of important author's and literary works. Several new volumes in the series have recently been published—new authors covered here are on critically acclaimed American authors Philip Roth, Kurt Vonnegut, Sylvia Plath, Zora Neale Hurston, William Faulkner, and Raymond Carver. Because each volume covers one author they are much more detailed than your average reference source. Each volume is about 250 pages in length and includes information on the author's career, life, and influences; critical contexts; critical readings (the bulk of each volume), and further resources (a chronology of the author's life, works by the author, a bibliography, and index). The text is written at a level appropriate for high school and undergraduate-level students, precisely the age that would be reading these titles and authors' works and needing resources to write critical papers for class.

An added bonus with purchase of the Critical Insights series is free online access to Salem's Literature database (http://www.literature.salempress.com). This will be a huge benefit for classroom use since many students will be able to access the same information at one time. Once activated by the student's library the database can be accessed at the library or from their home or dorm room. This aspect of the product more than justifies the cost for high school or university libraries needing this type of critical literature information.—**Shannon Graff Hysell**

Catalogs and Collections

905.   **Early American Fiction, 1789-1875. http://www.proquest.com/en-US/catalogs/databases/ detail/early_am_fiction.shtml.** [Website]. Ann Arbor, Mich., ProQuest. Price negotiated by site. Date reviewed: 2013.

The contents of *Early American Fiction, 1789-1875* are based upon two standard bibliographies: *The Bibliography of American Literature* and *Lyle H. Wright's American Fiction 1774-1850*. The collection began with a microform collection published by Research Publications and later digitized by Chadwyck-Healey. This collection incorporates the contents of the Chadwyck-Healey collection based upon the Wright bibliography and extends the coverage up to 1875, adding more than 300 additional titles and over 50 new authors. The collection was sponsored by the Andrew W. Mellon Foundation and the University of Virginia Library and published in collaboration with the University of Virginia. *Early American Fiction 1789-1875* contains the full text of more than 730 first editions of American novels and short stories by such authors as Louisa May Alcott, Herman Melville, Harriet Beecher Stowe, and Mark Twain, as well as minor writers of the period. Not typical of many digital collections, the pages of the texts are available in full color, enabling the viewer to see details of the originals such as their illustrations, typography, bindings, design, and construction. The collection will most likely be useful in research libraries serving graduate programs in American literature.—**Anna H. Perrault**

906. **PAL: Perspectives in American Literature—A Research and Reference Guide. http://www. csustan.edu/English/reuben/home.htm.** [Website]. By Paul P. Reuben. Free. Date reviewed: 2013.

The *Perspectives in American Literature* (PAL) guide is maintained by California State University professor Paul P. Reuben. The project began as a book, but is now available online. The guide is divided into chapters and appendixes. It is free, quite easy to use, and is updated regularly. The resource covers American literature from 1700 to the late twentieth century. The appendixes include selected bibliographies on poetry, fiction, folklore, and drama, as well as literary history. The resource also provides an alphabetic listing of 452 American authors. Each of these pages includes a brief biography, a list of primary works, and a selected bibliography.—**ARBA Staff Reviewer**

Dictionaries and Encyclopedias

907. **Encyclopedia of the Environment in American Literature.** Geoff Hamilton and Brian Jones, eds. Jefferson, N.C., McFarland, 2013. 350p. index. $75.00pa. ISBN 13: 978-0-7864-6541-5.

This easy-to-use encyclopedia consists of well-written and well-researched essays on American writers and ideologies with different viewpoints concerning environment, from exploiting or subduing nature to recognizing the need for preservation. Topical essays include such subjects as the Bible, American Pastoralism and Naturalism, Utopian, Transcendentalism, and Conservation. Biographical and critical discussions range in time from Indian myths and European explorers such as Christopher Columbus and Bartolome Las Caras to modern day conservationists Rachel Carson and Al Gore.

Each author's name and date is followed by an extensive biographical account and bibliography. Usually there is also a separate critical discussion of the major work that made him or her pertinent to environment with its own separate bibliography. In addition to poetry and fiction there are also articles on those who closely studied nature: Lewis and Clark, Muir, Thoreau, and E. O. White. The editors have made sure that women's voices have been included as well as different ethnic groups. Some of the nostalgic regionalist writers have been omitted though, including Sarah Orne Jewett and John Greenleaf Whittier who were only briefly cited under Celia Thaxter. A useful index aids researchers by referencing works by regions, birds, climate change, and such industries as oil, logging, fishing, and railroads. It would have helped to also have a timeline of authors to make it easier to connect ideas to eras.

Environment has become increasingly important as it becomes more endangered. In this volume the term has been broadly defined. This means that scholars of American literature, history, ecologists, or just general readers will find useful information as well as pleasurable reading. [R: LJ, 1 June 13, p. 132]—**Charlotte Lindgren**

Handbooks and Yearbooks

908. **American Post-Modernist Novels.** Hackensack, N.J., Salem Press, 2013. 328p. illus. index. (Introduction to Literary Context). $165. ISBN 13: 978-161925210-3.

American Post-Modernist Novels is the first of a series entitled Introduction to Literary Context. Designed primarily as a reference source for undergraduates, this volume contains essays on 37 novels published between 1960 and 2000 by a diverse selection of African American, Latin American, and Native American male and female writers. They differ from the more traditional Modernists in that their stories end unhappily or may have no real ending at all.

Each essay is organized into six sections: Symbols and Motifs, Historical, Societal, Religious, Scientific and Technological, and Biographical. Unfortunately, the latter topic especially has not been updated; for example, J.D. Salinger who died in 2010 is described as a recluse who "still lives" in Cornish, New Hampshire. Critical studies later than 2008 have also not been included in the final bibliography.

Especially useful for students and teachers are 10 questions for discussion and 4 or 5 essay ideas at the end of each of the novels analyzed. The Index too is especially useful since it not only includes names and titles, but also subdivides major subjects such as Religion, which has 29 sub-texts ranging from Catholicism to Voodoo. The volume includes material rarely gathered in one book and clearly reveals how life and literature have changed since the 1960s.—**Charlotte Lindgren**

909.   **Toward a Literary Ecology: Places and Spaces in American Literature.** Karen E. Waldron and Rob Friedman, eds. Lanham, Md., Scarecrow, 2013. 207p. index. $85.00; $84.99 (e-book). ISBN 13: 978-0-8108-9197-5; 978-0-8108-9198-2 (e-book).

Editors Karen E. Waldron (College of the Atlantic) and Rob Friedman (New Jersey Institute of Technology) have brought together several authors in this collection of essays on ecocriticism, a rapidly growing field of literary studies. The book is divided into three parts. In part 1, "Ecological Identities," three chapters examine American authors and works of the nineteenth and twentieth centuries, including Gary Snyder, Sherman Alexie, Simon Ortiz, and Kimberly Blaeser. Part 2, "Ecological Cityscapes," examines urban semiotics and geography of two works: Walter Mosley's *Always Outnumbered, Always Outgunned* and Tei Yamashita's *The Tropic of Orange*. In Part 3, "Ecological Rhetoric," examines texts such as Rachel Carson's *Silent Spring* and Virgil's *Georgics*, as the authors explore the language and linguistic strategies used to discuss the environment and the cultural history in which it exists. There is an extensive works cited list at the back as well as information about the contributors to this volume. The chapters are well written and include a notes section at the end. This reviewer recommends this title for students interested in ecocriticism in literary studies, particularly for upper-level undergraduates and graduate students who are already well versed in the authors and texts discussed.—**Michelle Martinez**

Individual Authors

F. Scott Fitzgerald

910.   Batchelor, Bob. **Gatsby: The Cultural History of the Great American Novel.** Lanham, Md., Scarecrow, 2014. 299p. illus. (Contemporary American Literature). $45.00; $44.99 (e-book). ISBN 13: 978-0-8108-9195-1; 978-0-8108-9196-8 (e-book).

In what seems to be the first in the Contemporary American Literature series, Bob Batchelor, James Pedas Professor of Communication and executive director of the James Pedas Communication Center at Thiel College, author or editor of more than 20 books, founding editor of the *Popular Culture Studies Journal*, and editor of the Contemporary American Literature series, gives a narrative history of the critical and cultural fortunes of F. Scott Fitzgerald and the novel *The Great Gatsby* from its publication in 1925 until 2013, when a new movie version starring Leonardo DiCaprio was released. The author includes extensive notes, a bibliography, and an index, but no illustrations are included.

Batchelor covers the ground well, pointing up the similarities between the 1920s and the 2010s in America—the culture of fame, the gap between rich and poor, and the conspicuous consumption of the rich. There are some annoying stylistic tics in the narrative—everyone Batchelor quotes has to be identified with designations such as "famous writer" or "eminent critic," sometimes several times for the same person and, perhaps with the potential high school or undergraduate in mind, he hammers the same points again and again. There have been numerous book-length studies about the novel, including those by Fitzgerald experts such as Matthew J. Bruccoli, but this is the most up-to-date source on its reputation and relevance for our times. This work is not a reference book, but it could be assigned to the reserve rooms or reserve shelves in high school or college libraries where *The Great Gatsby* is taught.— **Jonathan F. Husband**

Ernest Hemingway

911. Hays, Peter L. **Fifty Years of Hemingway Criticism.** Lanham, Md., Scarecrow, 2014. 257p. index. $70.00; $69.99 (e-book). ISBN 13: 978-0-8108-9283-5; 978-0-8108-9284-2 (e-book).

Hays, a professor emeritus at the University of California, Davis, has collected his writings about Hemingway published over 50 years in such sources as *The Hemingway Review*, *South Atlantic Quarterly*, and *Studies in Humanities*. The 32 essays cover such topics as Hemingway's style, themes, and reading, autobiographical elements in his fiction, his debts to such writers as Herman Melville, Henry James, and William Faulkner, and teaching Hemingway. There are essays about the cinematic quality of his style, his clinical depression, and similarities between "The Killers" and Harold Pinter's *The Birthday Party*. One of the most interesting essays explains parallels between F. Scott Fitzgerald's *The Great Gatsby* and *The Sun Also Rises*. Hays has updated the endnotes for older essays and provides an extensive bibliography. There is a name and title index, as well as seven photographs. The collection serves as a good introduction to Hemingway studies and also demonstrates the variety of approaches to interpreting his novels and stories.—**Michael Adams**

Zora Neale Hurston

912. **Zora Neale Hurston: An Annotated Bibliography of Works and Criticism.** Cynthia Davis and Verner D. Mitchell, eds. Lanham, Md., Scarecrow, 2013. 279p. index. $90.00; $89.99 (e-book). ISBN 13: 978-0-8108-9152-4; 978-0-8108-9153-1 (e-book).

In addition to its extensive annotated bibliography, the volume contains three excellent original essays indicating new directions in the assessment of Hurston's works. Although she had received a number of awards, her work fell into oblivion during the 1950s when her use of folklore and depictions of rural blacks living rich, fulfilling lives in segregated communities in the South became antithetical to the urban Northern Harlem Renaissance movement. Now in the twenty-first century, thanks partly to the feminist movement and new African studies programs, the complexities, sophistication, and artistry of her writings are once more being appreciated.

The bibliography section is divided into two parts, further subdivided into Books and Articles and Chapters, for many works listed include other writers. All books are identified by consecutive numbers with the first number showing the genre and the second number the alphabetically by author listed work. Part 1 separates by genre: biographies, general criticism, 40 pages devoted to her most popular novel *Their Eyes Were Watching God*, and her other novels and short stories. Part 2 reveals the breadth of her interests, influence, and writings under the headings Plays, Films, Dance, Folktales, Anthropology, Comparative Literature, Letters, Journalism, and Essays.

The volume concludes with three appendices. Appendix A lists doctoral dissertations written between 1975 and 2012 in which Hurston is often part of a larger topic or group. Appendix B names her books written for children and young adults, and appendix C divides all her primary works by genre including sound recordings and unpublished writings. The index identifies only the authors of works cited by their individual numbers. Beyond its practical use to discover as much as possible about Zora Neale Thurston, the book is also valuable to any reader interested in understanding how cultural attitudes have expanded in the past few decades.—**Charlotte Lindgren**

Margaret Mitchell

913. Davis, Anita Price. **The Margaret Mitchell Encyclopedia.** Jefferson, N.C., McFarland, 2013. 233p. illus. index. $75.00pa. ISBN 13: 978-0-7864-6855-3.

Fans of *Gone with the Wind* and all the people and places with whom it is associated will find this encyclopedia informative and pleasurable. Believing that biographies of Margaret Mitchell have distorted certain details such as her possible racism, the editor presents facts to allow readers to determine for themselves. It includes also much new material since the publication in 1992 of her last biography.

The volume begins with an extensive Chronology covering the period between 1892, when Margaret Mitchell's parents married, to the year 2000 when the author's name was finally added to the Georgia Writers Hall of Fame. The carefully documented entries of the encyclopedia range from "abuse," detailing the harsh treatment by her first husband "Red" Upshaw, to "Zanuck, Darryl," the director who tried and failed to get the movie rights to her novel. Sometimes there is an overabundance of information about tangential figures. Many illustrations enliven and elucidate the text. An extensive bibliography fully references books, articles, blogs, and Websites about Mitchell and her world, followed by an additional 6 related Websites and over 30 theses and dissertations written between 1954 and 2010. The oversimplified index is sometimes difficult to follow for the uninformed. For example, one must look under *Gone with the Wind* postage stamps, not under U.S. Postal Service or postage stamps, to get a complete listing of the stamps issued to commemorate the movie. The similarity of typeface also makes it difficult to separate the major titles from subtitles, of which there are many.

Gone with the Wind aficionados will enjoy learning the facts of Margaret Mitchell's life and her great Civil War classic. More general scholars will gain considerable knowledge about the attitudes and life style of southern society, Hollywood, and events of the first half of the twentieth century.—**Charlotte Lindgren**

British Literature

General Works

914.   **Early English Prose Fiction. http://www.proquest.com/en-US/catalogs/databases/detail/ early_eng_prose_fict.shtml.** [Website]. Ann Arbor, Mich.,, ProQuest. Price negotiated by site. Date reviewed: 2013.

915.   **Eighteenth   Century   Fiction.   http://www.proquest.com/en-US/catalogs/databases/ detail/18th_century_fiction.shtml.** [Website]. Ann Arbor, Mich., ProQuest. Price negotiated by site. Date reviewed: 2013.

The Early English period in the case of this database is defined as those writings before the inauguration of the fiction novel in the eighteenth century. This digital collection has more than 200 works from the period 1500-1700, a larger number than one might expect for a time period in which religion and politics occupied much of the printed output. Included in the collection are the full text of works by key writers such as John Bunyan, Sir Philip Sidney, Thomas Nashe, and Aphra Behn. The collection has been produced in association with the Salzburg Centre for Research on the Early English Novel (SCREEN).

The Eighteenth Century Fiction Collection, also a subscription database from ProQuest, continues with 96 works by writers from the British Isles from 1700 to 1780. Both of these collections will most likely be found in research libraries serving graduate programs in literature.—**Anna H. Perrault**

916.   **Romantic Era Redefined. http://Alexanderstreet.com/.** [Website]. Alexandria, Va., Alexander Street Press. Price negotiated by site. Date reviewed: 2013.

In partnership with Pickering & Chatto Publishers, Alexander Street Press is publishing *The Romantic Era Redefined*, with over 170,000 pages of text by writers from Britain, the British Empire, and North America. Included are poetry, prose, drama, letters, and diaries, along with political, philosophical, scientific, and sociological works. In addition to Pickering & Chatto's critical editions, *The Romantic*

Era Redefined includes the only complete digital version of *The Wordsworth Circle*, the international academic journal devoted to the study of English literature, culture, and society during the Romantic era.—**ARBA Staff Reviewer**

Individual Authors

917.   **Online Chaucer Bibliographies. http://englishcomplit.unc.edu/chaucer/chbib.htm.** [Website]. Free. Date reviewed: 2013.

This site provides an organized navigation aid for Chaucer resources on the Web, including Chaucer pages, Chaucer works, life and times, and more. For each bibliographic entry there are several sentences noted on the sites content and on its arrangement. The site has not been thoroughly updated in several years so there may be broken links on the site; however, none were noted at the time of this review.— **Shannon Graff Hysell**

African Literature

918.   **African Writer Series. http://collections.chadwyck.com/marketing/home_aws.jps.** [Website]. Alexandria, Va., Chadwyck-Healey. Price negotiated by site. Date reviewed: 2013.

This collection is based on the Heinemann African Writers Series and covers works published from 1973. Although some were written decades earlier to the end of the twentieth century, the series includes works from author of all regions of Africa. Many authors' works appear in English translation for the first time in this series. Each volume contains introductory materials and glossaries to aid in the understanding of the work. The collection is indexed by author name, gender, nationality, and dates of birth and death.—**Anna H. Perrault**

European Literature

919.   **WESSWeb: Online Text Collections in Western European Literature. http://wessweb. info/index.php/Online_Text_Collections_in_Western_European_Literature.** [Website]. Free. Date reviewed: 2013.

Western European literature is defined broadly by the Western European Studies Section of the ALA Association of College and Research Libraries to include the majority of the countries in Europe. The WESSWeb site provides links to online collections of literary texts from Europe. The organization is by language. Within the language areas, headings describe electronic texts (primary materials), literary criticism (secondary materials), as well as resources on language and linguistics and online library or museum exhibits. The links to the literary texts themselves includes both original language versions and English translations.—**Anna H. Perrault**

French Literature

920.   Flower, John. **Historical Dictionary of French Literature.** Lanham, Md., Scarecrow, 2013. 587p. (Historical Dictionaries of Literature and the Arts). $130.00. ISBN 13: 978-0-8108-6778-9; 978-0-8108-7945-4 (e-book).

The latest contribution to Scarecrow's Historical Dictionaries of Literature and the Arts series covers the major authors, works, literary movements and philosophical and social developments of French literature in one alphabetic list. By far the greatest number of entries is dedicated to individual authors and includes all the writers one is likely to encounter in the standard repertoire, and then some, keeping in mind though that the coverage is France only—no representation from Canada, the Caribbean, or Francophone Africa. Alas, the contribution of playwrights is given short shrift; the perfunctory entries (barely 200 words each) for Ionesco, Molière, and Racine, for example, are exceedingly short. The reason for this shortcoming is that drama is covered as a whole in a separate volume, the *Historical Dictionary of French Theater* (see ARBA 2011, entry 1089); unfortunately, users probably will not know this as there is no indication anywhere in this volume that such is the case. Within author entries, the titles of published English translations, usually the most recent one, are given in italics; if no published English translation exists, a version is given in roman. The handful of individual works that have separate entries of their own are in French with no cross references from an English-language title. Thus users will need to know ahead of time, for example, to find *The Hunchback of Notre Dame* under Notre Dame de Paris, though the write-up on Victor Hugo will direct them correctly.

As for the supplementary material, the opening chronology, which spans 1,200 years from the death of Charlemagne in 814 to 2012, is more factual than the more interpretive introductory survey which follows. An extensive, fairly current bibliography, broken down into general studies for each literary epoch and then titles for specific authors and texts, aimed heavily at an academic clientele, concludes the work.

Cross-references are a little more problematic, however. An end-of-entry system of *see* and *see also* references effectively pulls together related terms, but within individual entries, terms with their own entries are in boldface type. However, it is not always easy to locate them in the text proper owing to the fact that this book violates one of the cardinal rules of indexing by usually alphabetizing the articles la, le, and les in regular word order instead of the noun they modify. Thus *Les Misérables* will be found in the L's, not M's; Camus' *L'Etranger* is sandwiched between "Lesbian Writing" and Lettres Persanes. But the literary review *Le Mercure de France* is listed as "Mercure de France, Le."

The author, John Flower, is emeritus professor of French at the University of Kent (UK) and a recognized scholar of French literature. Among single volumes, this dictionary's closest competitor is the *New Oxford Companion to Literature in French* (Oxford University Press, 1995), which has a broader geographic and thematic coverage but is now almost 20 years old. Even older is Sandra Dolbow's *Dictionary of Modern French Literature: From the Age of Reason Through Realism* (Greenwood Press, 1986), which, though very limited chronologically, still provides a lucent supplement to the works and authors of its 200-year coverage.

In sum, this work's currency and coverage of prose and poetry provide a useful introduction to French literature; the bibliography serves as a steppingstone to more advanced research. The dictionary is appropriate for academic and public libraries despite the annoying but minor access problems.— **Lawrence Olszewski**

Latin American Literature

921.　**Caribbean Literature. http://alexanderstreet.com/products/cali.htm.** [Website]. Alexandria, Va., Alexander Street Press. Price negotiated by site. Date reviewed: 2013.

The focus of this collection is the literary production of the entire Caribbean region from 1900 to the present. The collection includes more than 10,000 pages of works written in languages such as Papiamento, French Creole, Jamaican Creole, Belizean Kriol, Singlish, and Sranam Tongo. Translations of major works, dictionaries, and reference materials are included. All genres are represented in the works selected for inclusion. In addition, there are manuscript and archival materials, photographs, and interviews. Multiple versions of a work are often including; for example, the original language as well as translations to English or other European languages.—**Anna H. Perrault**

922.   **Latin American Women Writers. http://alexanderstree.com/products/laww.htm.** [Website]. Alexandria, Va., Alexander Street Press. Price negotiated by site. Date reviewed: 2013.

This collection offers a broad overview of literary works by women from 20 different countries, extending from colonial times to the present. Although most of the works in the collection are in the original language, this database is included here because it interfaces with other Alexander Street collections. The works selected for inclusion represent all literary genres as well as memoirs and essays. The sophisticated indexing of the collection offers not only the traditional points of access: nation, dates of birth/death, and literary movements, but also key words that deal with issues of gender, politics, slavery, and the struggle for independence.—**ARBA Staff Reviewer**

923.   Snodgrass, Mary Ellen. **Isabel Allende: A Literary Companion.** Jefferson, N.C., McFarland, 2013. 360p. index. $39.95. ISBN 13: 978-0-7864-7127-0.

An interesting examination of the Chilean author who enfolded her own experiences and observations into a variety of woks is a very good starting place for further research of both this author and Latin American literature. A preface and introduction are followed by an exhaustive, highly detailed chronology of her life (with a significant bibliography) and a genealogical diagram of the Allende family. The main text is an alphabetic listing of aspects or topics incorporated, examined or used to enhance her work (such as "evil," which is followed more in-depth by "military evil" and "civil struggles"). There are also sections on individual works and the genealogies of characters' families. Each section concludes with a brief bibliography. Tables and diagrams help to enhance the text and make the discussion clearer. A glossary offers not only definitions of terms, but also abbreviations and page number citations for the works in which each term can be found. Appendix A offers a timeline of historical events as seen in Allende's works. Appendix B offers an extensive listing of suggested writing and research topics. At the end is a general bibliography (divided into primary and secondary resources and then again by general titles, biographies, and sources that examine individual works) and an index. The exhaustively researched and arranged information focuses mainly on the more profound aspects of Allende's life and work.—**Martha Lawler**

Poetry

924.   **Irish Women Poets of the Romantic Period. http://alexanderstreet.com.** [Website]. Alexandria, Va., Chadwyck-Healey. Price negotiated by site. Date reviewed: 2013.

The description of this collection stresses that this group of women poets has been neglected in studies of the Romantic period in England and Ireland. This thought is born out in that the names of the 50 poets, such as Henrietta Battier, I. S. Anna Liddiard, Adelaide O'Keeffe, and Elizabeth Ryves, are not generally recognized by even those with an advanced graduate degree in literature. The collection contains 80 rare words owned by only a small number of libraries in the world. In addition to the original texts, there are critical essays written by prominent scholars on the subject, especially commissioned by Alexander Street Press. Other elements of the collection include a critical introduction providing context for the poetry; a bibliographic introduction and a general bibliography; and criticism, reviews, and links to related Web resources. The collection was carefully compiled and edited by Stephen Behrendt, the George Holmes Distinguished Professor of English at the University of Nebraska, along with a board of distinguished scholars. Irish Women Poets of the Romantic Period is available on the Web, either through subscription or one-time purchase of perpetual rights.—**Anna H. Perrault**

925.   **20th Century American Poetry. http://collections.chadwyck.co.uk/.** [Website]. Alexandria, Va., Chadwyck-Healey. Price negotiated by site. Date reviewed: 2013.

Two existing Chadwyck-Healey literature collections have been combined to comprise this database: Twentieth-Century American Poetry and Twentieth-Century African American Poetry. The collection brings together the most important and influential poems representing the full range of movements and traditions in American poetry from 1900 to the present day. The database covers African American writers from both the North and South. The database is also available as an add-on to the Literature Online database (see ARBA 2013, entry 863).—**Anna H. Perrault**

25 Music

General Works

Bibliography

926.   Carman, Judith E., William K. Gaeddert, and Rita M. Resch. **Art Song in the United States, 1759-2011: An Annotated Bibliography.** 4th ed. Lanham, Md., Scarecrow, 2013. 613p. index. $120.00. ISBN 13: 978-0-8108-8307-9.

Art Song in the United States, 1759-2011 is the latest iteration of a bibliography of art songs for solo voice and piano by American composers that was first published in 1976. Staying true to the intent of the original edition, the 4th edition is an extensively annotated reference tool aimed primarily at singers and studio voice teachers. This edition adds 11 years worth of new works and collections since the 3d edition was published in 2002, adding a total of 450 new entries. Each annotation contains information about the composer of the art song, the poet, publication data, key structure, vocal range, vocal tessitura, meter, tempo indications, and length of the song. Remarks about the subject or mood of the song, and an appraisal of the difficulties of both the vocal line and the piano part, are also included in the annotations. In addition to song title entries, this bibliography also contains a key to song anthologies and collections, a discography, a composer index, and a poet index.

The annotations do suffer from an element of redundancy. The last category in each entry is marked "uses" and is intended to provide information about the quality and suitability of the song for performance use. However, the information given in this category is often so perfunctory as to be meaningless. The authors, all experienced professional vocal music educators, have done an admirable job of collating and analyzing a large number of American art songs and this book remains an important resource for musicians interested in researching and performing the art song literature of the United States.—**ARBA Staff Reviewer**

Catalogs and Collections

927.   **Archival Sound Recordings. http://sounds.bl.uk/.** [Website]. Free. Date reviewed: 2013.

The online resource provides access to more than 45,000 recordings of music, speech, and human and natural environments. The database resulted from a project to increase access to the British Library's enormous archive of sound recordings, totaling some 3.5 million items originating in countries all over the world. The online archive includes examples of accents and dialects; poetry, theater, and other spoken word recordings; classical music; jazz and popular music; sounds of nature and the environment; oral history; and world and traditional music. Anyone with an Internet connection can search the database and listen to approximately 24,000 recordings. UK library members may listen to all the recordings and also add information to the metadata via user tags.—**ARBA Staff Reviewer**

928.   **Catalogue of Printed Music in the British Library. http://www.bl.uk/reshelp/findhelprestype/ music/muiccollprinted/musiccollprinted.html.** [Website]. Free. Date reviewed: 2013.

For many years, the *Catalogue of Printed Music in the British Library* was available as a print publication. Print publication ceased as of 2010, and all of the records in the printed catalogue have been incorporated into the online catalogue. The printed music collection is vast and contains music published in every European country from the late fifteenth century to the present day. Fascinating examples of the earliest printed music have been digitized and can be viewed online. The collection is strongest in music published in the United Kingdom. Like the Library of Congress, the British Library is a national copyright depository, and receives one copy of every piece of music published in the United Kingdom and the Republic of Ireland.—**Anna H. Perrault**

Dictionaries and Encyclopedias

929.   Collins, Irma H. **Dictionary of Music Education.** Lanham, Md., Scarecrow, 2014. 339p. $75.00; $74.99 (e-book). ISBN 13: 978-0-8108-8651-3; 978-0-8108-8652-0 (e-book).

The top-quality *Dictionary of Music Education* is an alphabetic dictionary of words utilized in the learning of music including important associations, people, words, and occurrences. Author Irma H. Collins has a Temple University music education DMA. The dictionary contains a contents, foreword, preface, acknowledgments, list of acronyms and abbreviations, organizations and abbreviations, chronology, introduction, the A-Z dictionary, and four appendixes (a list of organizations, a list of publications, and instructions for examining institutions for music. The work concludes with a bibliography.

The 11-page chronology is from 6th c. Greece B.C.E. to 2011 with divisions B.C.E., A.D., Medieval/ Middle Ages (5th-15th c.), and Beginning of the Discipline of Music Education. The 17-page List of Organizations has sections for Australia and New Zealand, Canada, International, United Kingdom and Republic of Ireland, and United States divulges for example Early Music America (EMA) in Pittsburgh, Pennsylvania. The 20 page List of Publications is divided into sections Australia and New Zealand, Canada, International, United Kingdom and Republic of Ireland, and United States.

The Bibliography is separated into categories: "Dictionaries and Encyclopedias" and "Books and Journal Articles." Examining Institutions for Music includes two parts: Australia and United Kingdom. The *Dictionary of Music Education* will be very useful for music learners, public and academic libraries, and music libraries.—**Melinda F. Matthews**

930.   Cooper, John Michael, with Randy Kinnett. **Historical Dictionary of Romantic Music.** Lanham, Md., Scarecrow, 2014. 740p. (Historical Dictionaries of Literature and the Arts). $150.00; $149.99 (e-book). ISBN 13: 978-0-8108-7230-1; 978-0-8108-7484-8 (e-book).

Beginning in the late eighteenth century and lasting well into the 1850s, Romanticism as a philosophical and artistic movement embraced the awakening of modernism while at the same time reinterpreting the classical tradition that came before it. Many of the composers and musicians we associate with the nineteenth century find their roots in romanticism. This work, by a professor of music noted for his work in the artistic period, has a lengthy introduction discussing the roots, changes, and influences on the future that Romanticism brought to the world. The major portion of the work is an alphabetically arranged listing of composers and musicians, instrument makers, patrons and publishers, specific works and significant events associated with Romanticism. Each entry is from a half-page to one and one-half pages in length. In the case of individuals birth and death dates are given where known. Each entry discusses the importance to the Romantic idea with bold typeface referencing other topics in the dictionary. An extensive bibliography for further reading and research completes the volume. No index appears at the end of the volume, but with the alphabetic arrangement and the cross-referencing of topics little value is lost by it being left out.

This volume will find ready use in music and music history collections. Well bound in hardcover format and with its easy to use alphabetic format, the work should stand up to years of use in the library setting. Any library with collecting interests in the music, arts, philosophy, or the history of the eighteenth and nineteenth centuries will find this a useful addition.—**Gregory Curtis**

931. **The Garland Encyclopedia of World Music Online. http://alexanderstreet.com/products/ garland-encyclopedia-world-music-online.** [Website]. Alexandria, Va., Alexander Street Press, 2013. Price negotiated by site. Date reviewed: 2013.

The Garland Encyclopedia of World Music Online offers an overview of the many regions of the world; a survey of each region's musical heritage, traditions, and themes; and a description of specific musical genres, practices, and performances. It contains photographs, images, and maps, and is ideal for ethnomusicology research. The online version offers the entire 10-volume print set with additional features.—**Noriko Asato**

932. **Music in American Life: An Encyclopedia of the Songs, Styles, Stars, and Stories That Shaped Our Culture.** Jacqueline Edmondson, ed. Santa Barbara, Calif., Greenwood Press/ABC-CLIO, 2013. 4v. illus. index. $415.00/set. ISBN 13: 978-0-313-39347-1; 978-0-313-39348-8 (e-book).

This encyclopedia, in four volumes, paged continuously, illustrates the degree to which music pervades life in the United States. More than 280 contributors wrote over 500 articles on several aspects of music in America. Each volume contains a complete alphabetic list of entries, a guide to related topics, and the index. The chronology, located in volume 1, while not indexed, includes many persons, places, and songs that are presented in the index.

Several forms and genres are described with simple and clear explanations. Sidebars show the influences of Ray Charles, or a list of the most famous musicals in America. Articles are on styles, genres, and the people that symbolize these. This includes Classical (with other articles on composers and performers, like Aaron Copland, Charles Ives, George Gershwin, and John Philip Sousa); Folk (Stephen Collins Foster, Pete Seeger); Pop (John Denver, Neil Diamond, Irving Berlin), Rock (Bo Diddley, Beach Boys), Jazz (Big Band Music; Miles Davis, Buddy Holly); Country (Reba McEntire); Blues (B.B. King); and Instruments (Banjo, Ukulele). The encyclopedia goes as far as including humorous musicians, including poet Shel Silverstein.

Several articles address social or political aspects of music, like the Recording Industry, Vinyl Records, Antiwar songs, and Environmental Activism in Music. Religious influences, including not only Gospel, but also Judaic, Shaker, Slave, and Native American music, are presented. This gives the encyclopedia a wide base for readership. To illustrate the usage, the article on "Blues" uses staff notation to illustrate key or mode, and utilizes parallel text and numbers with lyrics to indicate rhythmic patterns. The contributor presents clear explanations of the form, melody, harmony, venues, history, reference sources and magazines, and a brief listing of great blues musicians. Like each article, it concludes with a set of *see also* references and a bibliography. Several photographs are also scattered throughout the volumes.

This set serves as a fine introduction to various influences, venues, forms, genres, and styles of music that affected American life, and the musicians with whom these forms are associated.—**Ralph Hartsock**

Directories

933. **Musical America. http://www.musicalamerica.com.** [Website]. Heights Town, N.J., Musical America. $135.00 (annual subscription). Date reviewed: 2013.

This directory requires a subscription for complete access. It provides contact information for performing arts organizations, as well as artist managers, competitions, music schools and departments, and services and products. The database is updated frequently, and the coverage is international in scope. One very useful function is the ability to search for jobs. Listings include performance jobs as well as administrative and teaching jobs. The Website also offers travel booking services for helping to manage the logistics of going on tour. Numerous other features are offered including information about grants, a career advice blog, feature articles about up-and-coming artists, and a searchable archive of back issues of the directory. The print version of *Musical America* is published annually for $99.—**Anna H. Perrault**

Handbooks and Yearbooks

934.   **Black Recording Artists, 1877-1926: An Annotated Discography.** Craig Martin Gibbs, comp. Jefferson, N.C., McFarland, 2013. 490p. index. $95.00pa. ISBN 13: 978-0-7864-7238-3.

From the end of the nineteenth century through the early twentieth century, home entertainment often consisted of listening to disk recordings made in the acoustic era of recording technology. This discography covers all of the studio recordings of black artists from the period of 1877-1926. Listing year, month, and date in which the recording was made, the title is arranged in chronological order and includes information on the name of the artist(s), location of recording, matrix number(s), title of recording, label name, and a source where the entry can be heard. The work includes cross-references to related bibliographies and recording sessions. It also provides information on piano rolls performed by black artists, a filmography detailing the visual record of black performing artists from this time period, and Caribbean and Latin American recordings. A bibliography and indexes by artist's name, recording titles, and commercial labels and field recordings conclude the volume.

Some of these artists are known to collectors and fans of music yet are not generally recognizable to modern scholars. The earlier artists created much of their own material, which if it was good, was often repeated and revised by later musicians. So alive is the author's handling of the material that even if the reader has never actually heard any of these recordings, the sense of the original material is there, and some social insight is gained into otherwise dated performances. This work should be in the collection of major libraries and in the home libraries of many record collectors.—**Shannon Graff Hysell**

935.   Howe, Sondra Wieland. **Women Music Educators in The United States: A History.** Lanham, Md., Scarecrow, 2014. 335p. illus. index. $75.00; $74.99 (e-book). ISBN 13: 978-0-8108-8847-0; 978-0-8108-8848-7 (e-book).

During the colonial period women sang in church choirs and taught children in homes. In the nineteenth century, many women published hymns, taught in schoolhouses, and held positions as performers in church. More recently, women have earned college degrees, taught in public school and colleges, and have become involved in national organizations. Howe narrates the story of music teaching in the United States, focusing on women as the educators, chronologically from colonial times until the conclusion of the twentieth century. The author broadly defines "music education" to include informal settings, such as home, and formalized education, be it public or private. She hopes to rectify the lack of historical records of these women's educational careers. Howe approaches this in an interdisciplinary fashion, building her research upon several fields of study—the history of American education, musicological studies of women and music, and feminist writings. The review of literature explores several aspects, including the general history of education, musicology, and feminist issues. Each chapter has numerous endnotes, some of which are annotated. The extensive index serves navigation well, and includes persons (male and female), institutions, ensembles, and titles of works or journals relevant to music education. Howe's volume adds to Kristin Burns's *Women and Music in America Since 1900* (see ARBA 2004, entry 1080) and Judith Zaimont's *The Musical Woman* (Greenwood, 1983-1991).—**Ralph Hartsock**

936.   **The Music Library Series.** Farmington Hills, Mich., Lucent Books/Gale/Cengage Learning, 2013. multivolume. illus. index. $34.10/vol.

Throughout this series Stuart A. Kallen traces the evolution of specific musical genres from their earliest compositions influenced by African and European immigrants to contemporary artists. Included are brief biographical sketches of artists or groups who made significant contributions and gave birth to various subcategories within each genre. Numerous photographs documenting influential musicians and their most successful hits are featured throughout each chapter. Appendixes include a source for listening music and additional resources. The series would be especially useful in a school with a sophisticated music program. Each volume includes a bibliography, a glossary, and an index.—**ARBA Staff Reviewer**

Indexes

937.   **Index to Printed Music (IPM). http://www.ipmusic.org/index.php.** [Website]. Ipswich, Mass., EBSCO. Price negotiated by site. Date reviewed: 2013.

This online subscription database makes it possible to search for particular works published in scholarly editions, anthologies, and collections. The database continues and expands on Hill's *Collected Editions, Historical Series & Sets & Monuments of Music: A Bibliography*. It is regularly updated, and currently contains approximately 412,000 index records. It is possible to search the Index by title, composer, librettist, poet, and edition or anthology title. The Names Index allows searches by alternate spellings of a name, and thus makes it possible to retrieve all titles associated with all known spellings of the name. A user can also search by a frequently used title, such as *Missa l'hammearme*, and find the names of all the composers who wrote a Mass with this title, where each Mass is published, and in what library the manuscript of the work is held. At this point, the index includes very few twentieth-century composers, and for these composers, it is better to consult the works listed in Grove Music Online (http://www.oxfordmusiconline.com/public/book/omo_gmo).—**ARBA Staff Reviewer**

938.   **International Index to Music Periodicals (IIMP). http://iimp.chadwyck.com/marketing.do.** [Website]. Alexandria, Va., Chadwyck-Healey. Price negotiated by site. Date reviewed: 2013.

This site provides indexing and abstracts for music journals from 1874 to the present—scholarly to the popular. It has over 900,000 indexed articles, including an extensive backfile, encompassing music education, performance studies, composition, theory, and ethnomusicology to all forms of popular music. The full-text version, *IIMP Full Text*, is available for those needed more in-depth access to this information.—**Noriko Asato**

939.   **RILM Abstracts of Music Literature. http://www.ebscohost.com/academic/rilm-abstracts-of-music-literature.** [Website]. Ipswich, Mass., EBSCO. Price negotiated by site. Date reviewed: 2013.

This is a comprehensive music bibliography featuring citations, abstracts, and subject indexing. It provides broad yet detailed coverage including music-related works, articles, books, bibliographies, dissertations, film video, concert reviews, and recording notes. It deals with classical and popular music, ethnomusicology, music education, and theory. The site's coverage spans 1967 to the present.—**Noriko Asato**

940.   **ThemeFinder. http://www.themefinder.org.** [Website]. Free. Date reviewed: 2013.

This online thematic catalog is freely available through collaboration between the Center for Computer Assisted Research in the Humanities at Stanford University and the Cognitive and Systematic Musicology Laboratory at the Ohio State University. At present, there are three searchable databases: Classical and Instrumental Music, European Folksongs, and Latin Motets from the sixteenth century. Together, these total more than 35,000 themes. Searching the database requires some basic knowledge of musical notation. It is possible to search for the title of a work by entering the intervals or notes of a melody, either by note name or scale degree. It is possible to search by the contour of a melody. Browsable composer work lists display the *incipits* of the themes of each work included in the database.—**Anna H. Perrault**

Individual Composers

941.   Schroeder, David. **Experiencing Mozart: A Listener's Companion.** Lanham, Md., Scarecrow, 2013. 215p. index. $45.00; $44.99 (e-book). ISBN 13: 978-0-8108-8428-1; 978-0-8108-8429-8 (e-book).

Until the 1984 movie *Amadeus*, not many Americans knew much more than the name Mozart. It's a pity, too, as the movie proved a chockablock of errors and innuendo, yet great fun. Older readers will recalled the Dick Van Dyke episode in which Robert Petrie made the colossal mistake of being a talent judge in his New Rochelle neighborhood. They saw the bratty enfant terrible mimic his mother's pronunciation of the musician's name as "Moat-ZART!" But if either or both got the general public turning a kind ear to Mozart, and really listening to him, then so be it.

The current volume is more determined to turn our ears to Mozart by turning first our eyes. As Horace says somewhere, our minds are more easily tuned by the eye than by the ear. The *Listener's Companion* is meant to be just that: an unpedantic account in words that it is hoped will give life to the ears. If any life was a fury slinging flame, as Tennyson had it, it was Mozart's, and this volume helps give a sense of both the man and his music.

Schroeder, professor emeritus from Dalhousie, has written widely on music and film. He has provided many pre-concert talks at the Lincoln Center in New York and has appeared on many radio and television shows to talk about music. His style is straightforward, easygoing but delightful and full of panache. He gives readers explanations of both technical and scholarly aspects but also important points of what we should be listening for. He traces Mozart from his early struggles to his mature music. Along the way he provides readers chapters with important historical and musical insights into *Cosi fan tutte*, *Don Giovanni, The Abduction from the Seraglio, Figaro, The Magic Flute*, and of course the magisterial *Requiem*. An index makes it easy to find specific topics, persons, places, or musical pieces.

As good as this book is—and it is wonderful—it cannot bear scrutiny as a reference tool. Rather, it is a monograph on the life and music of perhaps the finest of eighteenth-century composers.—**Mark Y. Herring**

Musical Forms

Classical

942.   Swain, Joseph P. **Historical Dictionary of Baroque Music.** Lanham, Md., Scarecrow, 2013. 363p. (Historical Dictionaries of Literature and the Arts). $105.00; $99.99 (e-book). ISBN 13: 978-0-8108-7824-2; 978-0-8108-7825-9 (e-book).

Joseph Swain, an organist and teacher of music history at Colgate University, authored his second historical dictionary. This dictionary provides basic information about traditions, persons, compositions, places, terminology, and institutions of Baroque music—music that dominated Western Europe from about 1600 to 1750. Nearly half of the entries are biographical, mostly composers, but the author also describes theorists, critics, and poets. However, Swain excluded the modern performers of early music.

Another one-fifth of the entries are Baroque era genres—concerto, cantata, opera seria, and more. Other areas covered are techniques (e.g., figured bass, double dotting), theoretical terms (e.g., inversion, counterpoint, continuo, Baroque pitch), instruments (e.g., harpsichord, bassoon, theorbo), and places (e.g., Venice, Vienna, London, Paris). Swain gives titles of compositions in modern English form; for example, *Art of Fugue* and *Christmas Oratorio*. He presents detail lists of J. S. Bach's *Brandenburg Concertos*; some works are known by their work numbers, such as *Opus 3*, a set of 12 concertos by Antonio Vivaldi, and *Opus 6*, 12 concerti grossi by Arcangelo Corelli. Swain lists dramatic works by several composers, including George Frideric Handel, Francesco Cavalli, Claudio Monteverdi, and Jean Baptiste Lully. Treatises, such as *Gradus ad Parnassum* (Johann Joseph Fux) and *Traite de l'Harmonie* (Jean Philippe Ramaeu) are given in their original languages.

Swain also presents examples in musical notation. Most entries provide a sufficient, yet succinct, first source for users. *See* references are numerous and given in bold font. The chronology is of events outside of births (pp. xv-xxix). The bibliography is extensive and well organized, and is presented in great detail. The *Historical Dictionary of Baroque Music* serves as a quality ready-reference source, with resources cited for those seeking more detailed information.—**Ralph Hartsock**

Folk Music

943.   Beviglia, Jim. **Counting Down Bob Dylan: His 100 Finest Songs.** Lanham, Md., Scarecrow, 2013. 201p. index. $35.00; $34.99 (e-book). ISBN 13: 978-0-8108-8823-4; 978-0-8108-7847-1 (e-book).

Counting Down Bob Dylan: His 100 Finest Songs is the first publication in a new series titled Counting Down that ranks and discusses the best songs by famous musicians. This foundational volume tackles the iconic Bob Dylan and his nearly 60-year career. Beviglia has scoured Dylan's catalog and has come up with not just a list, but an actual ranking of his best songs from 100 to 1.

Unlike other "best of" lists that can be found online by the hundreds, this publication provides its value in the analysis of each song. *Counting Down Bob Dylan* does not simply count down one person's opinion of Dylan's best songs, but provides a mini-essay for each song that includes interesting facts, historical information, and more. These mini-essays provide insight into the songs themselves as well as into Dylan as a figure. Beviglia obviously spent quite a bit of time researching these songs, although this reviewer was a bit surprised to find the bibliography is only six items long. Regardless, *Counting Down Bob Dylan* is an entertaining and informational read. The text is very easy to follow and also includes an index and a short list of an additional 100 songs. This book could serve as a great introduction to those interested in Dylan or a great source of previously unknown trivia for Dylan fans.—**Tyler Manolovitz**

Jazz

944.   **The Jazz Discography. http://www.lordisco.com.** [Website]. $280.00-$930.00 (institution price). Date reviewed: 2013.

This online subscription database, also available in CD-ROM format, was first published as a 26-volume reference book from 1992-2001. It covers more than 400,000 jazz recordings released from 1895 to the present. *The Jazz Discography* lists not only albums and sessions that were released, but also those that were broadcast on radio and television, and albums that were recorded but not released. The database can be searched by musician name, bandleader, session date or number, record label, and tune title. Each listing includes personnel; recording date and place; album title, record label and number (when applicable); and complete track listings. The multi-search function makes it possible to search for two or three musicians simultaneously and discover what recordings they made together. The ability to search by tune title is also interesting since it makes it possible to see the recordings of all musicians who recorded a particular tune.—**Anna H. Perrault**

945.   Stephans, Michael. **Experiencing Jazz: A Listener's Companion.** Lanham, Md., Scarecrow, 2014. 488p. illus. index. (Listener's Companion Series). $45.00; $44.99 (e-book). ISBN 13: 978-0-8108-8289-8; 978-0-8108-8290-4 (e-book).

Stephans, a prominent jazz musician, has written widely on jazz music and has written promotional material for many fine musicians. His style is straightforward and easygoing, and will help long-time listeners of jazz and those new to the genre cultivate an understanding and appreciation of jazz music. He gives readers explanations of both technical and scholarly aspects but also important points of what we should be listening for. He provides a survey in the art of listening to jazz and provides an insider's perspective to its ever-changing culture. Along the way he provides readers chapters with important historical and musical insights into the history and styles of jazz during the 1940s and 1950s, discusses the functions and forms of jazz on and off the bandstand, gives details on small groups and big bands, and discusses the key instrument and their significant roles in music (e.g., trombone, saxophone, piano, clarinet). An index makes it easy to find specific topics, persons, places, or musical pieces.

As good as this book is—and it is wonderful—it cannot bear scrutiny as a reference tool. Rather, it is a monograph on the history, styles, and movements of jazz music.—**ARBA Staff Reviewer**

946.   Yanow, Scott. **Great Jazz Guitarists: The Ultimate Guide.** San Francisco, Calif., Backbeat Books, 2013. 238p. $24.99pa. ISBN 13: 978-1-61713-023-6.

This highly readable book offers profiles of over 500 representative jazz guitarists that have made (or are making) their mark on the music world today. Each entry includes biographical data, a stylistic analysis, and a discussion of the guitarist's contributions to the development of the guitar in jazz. A Website for each guitarist is provided at the end of each entry. Guitarists are listed in alphabetic order, which proves useful since no index is provided. One feature that makes this work unique are the profiles that feature musician's recollections of other artists featured in the book. All of these features have been collected by the author and are therefore unique to this book. The author has written other titles on this subject, including *Classic Jazz: The Musicians & Recordings That Shaped Jazz, 1895-1933* (see ARBA 2003, entry 1139), which was well received. [R: LJ, 15 June 13, p. 115]—**Shannon Graff Hysell**

Opera

947.   Balthazar, Scott L. **Historical Dictionary of Opera.** Lanham, Md., Scarecrow, 2013. 537p. (Historical Dictionaries of Literature and the Arts). $125.00; $119.99 (e-book). ISBN 13: 978-0-8108-6768-0; 978-0-8108-7943-0 (e-book).

The latest entry in Scarecrow's Historical Dictionaries of Language and the Arts series covers the entire gamut of opera, from the earliest productions through such contemporaries as Glass and Adams. The dictionary section contains about 350 entries, ranging from a short paragraph to three pages, and mostly focuses on composers. Fewer entries cover significant performers, impresarios, venues, works, and terminology. Every entry includes bolded cross-references, and many feature additional *see also* references that lead to other entries within the volume. Entries are well written but necessarily limited in detail, and all are objective rather than subjective. Coverage is heaviest in the golden age of opera, the nineteenth and early twentieth centuries, and no attempt is made for comprehensiveness. As with other dictionaries in the series, the current volume includes a brief timeline, a short introductory essay, and a good secondary bibliography (although the author excludes Operabase.com, an essential source for living opera). Although some might question the need for still another opera reference book, Balthazar does a better job with uniting information on composers, terms, and works than other excellent but more focused single-volume works, including Hamilton's *The Metropolitan Opera Encyclopedia* (Simon & Schuster, 1987), Mesa's *Opera: An Encyclopedia of World Premieres and Significant Performances, Singers, Composers, Librettists, Arias and Conductors, 1597-2000* (see ARBA 2008, entry 979), and

Batta's *Opera: Composers, Works, Performers* (rev. ed.; see ARBA 2011, entry 1014). For libraries without Stanley Sadie's four-volume *New Grove Dictionary of Opera* (Macmillan, 1992), Balthazar will suffice for the basics. This work is recommended for all music collections.—**Anthony J. Adam**

948.　　Griffel, Margaret Ross. **Operas in English: A Dictionary.** rev. ed. Lanham, Md., Scarecrow, 2013. 2v. index. $160.00/set; $159.99 (e-book). ISBN 13: 978-0-8108-8272-0; 978-0-8108-8325-3 (e-book).

This scholarly and interesting volume is now the standard reference work in its field. Its succinct preface gives informative surveys of opera in the United States, the British Isles, Canada, South Africa, Australia, and New Zealand. It traces the history of opera from its beginnings in the seventeenth century masque to its transition into musical comedy and musical drama. In opera, as in most art forms now, the lines between genres have crumbled. The format of this revised edition remains the same as the 1st edition (1999). Many of the original 3,500 entries have been updated with new information and 900 more works have been added.

The slant of the work is markedly American. Entries for American operas or musicals at times supply details of repeat performances, cast, and even evaluations. English operas do not receive the same attention. What most arouses the editor's warm appreciation is American musical comedy; her entries on the musical comedies to which she accords status comparable to that of operas are excellent for the 1970s, but she loses interest when they decline in the 1980s.

The work is thoroughly cross-indexed. By far the largest section is devoted to an alphabetic list of the operas in English, often giving brief story outlines and, in contemporary American operas, details of cast. There are other important indexes for composers and librettists (both usually with dates), authors and sources of the story, and a chronology of opera performances from 1634 through 2011. This useful and detailed work will be useful to scholars, performers, and opera lover and deserves a place in most academic library music collections as well a larger public libraries.—**John B. Beston**

949.　　Marek, Dan H. **Giovanni Battista Rubini and the Bel Canto Tenors: History & Technique.** Lanham, Md., Scarecrow, 2013. 420p. index. $55.00pa.; $54.99 (e-book). ISBN 13: 978-0-8108-8667-4; 978-0-8108-8668-1 (e-book).

Drawing on a distinguished career as an educator, writer, and most notably, a principal tenor at numerous major opera houses, Malek has authored the definitive biography of Giovanni Battista Rubini, the legendary nineteenth-century tenor who gained international fame as the first non-castrati romantic lead in Italian operas. In addition, Malek provides an exceptional historical overview of the singing style known as bel canto as well as an examination of the vocal techniques employed by Rubini and his contemporary bel canto tenors.

Twenty-six chapters are sub-divided into three parts: Historical Antecedents of the Bel Canto Tenor; Giovanni Battista Rubini; and Vocal Technique of Rubini and the Bel Canto Tenors. Complementing the text are the copious black-and-white illustrations that include portraits of notable musicians, including Rubini himself, and musical examples. Most noteworthy are the three appendixes that document Rubini's prolific career. Appendix 1, titled "Twelve Lessons in Modern Singing—For Tenor or Soprano," contains exercises that Rubini himself composed prior to 1840. Appendix 2 contains a list of Rubini's "Operatic Repertoire by Year of First Performance" noting work, composer, role, theater, and year. A "Chronology of Rubini's Concert Performances" that includes date of performance, place and theatre, and performers and works, is provided in appendix 3. A bibliography, name index, and subject index conclude the text.

Giovanni Battista Rubini and the Bel Canto Tenors: History & Technique stands as a testament to Malek's personal and professional devotion to the world of music. While vocal coaches, students, and opera historians will find Malek's opus indispensable, the casual reader will also enjoy the wealth of information that documents the fascinating evolution of the fine high voice, which has been admired throughout history. This wonderful publication, the only English-language text on high tessitura for tenor and soprano singing, is a must for all libraries.—**Alice Crosetto**

950.   Martin, Nicholas Ivor. **The Opera Manual.** Lanham, Md., Scarecrow, 2014. 442p. index. $85.00; $84.99 (e-book). ISBN 13: 978-0-8108-8868-5.

The original edition of this work was published in 1998 as *The Da Capo Opera Manual.* The author of both editions is the director of operations at the Lyric Opera in Chicago, and he refers to the work as an opera "cookbook" because it lists all the ingredients needed to produce each of the 550 operas contained within.

The operas included fall into several categories: standard repertory works, all works by major composers, works by major non-opera composers, works that were once very popular, and small-scale works frequently staged by schools. The entries themselves, listed by title, are rich in details, relaying for each opera: composer, librettist, language, story source, premier date, revision notes, setting, running time, number of sets and scenes, difficult stagings, rights and publisher info, arias, major and minor roles, bit parts, chorus parts, dance parts and instrumentation breakdown for the orchestra. A very brief summary is provided for each scene.

Generally, standard one-volume opera reference books, such as Henry W. Simon's *100 Great Operas and Their Stories* (Bantam, 2001) or Amanda Holden's *The New Penguin Opera Guide* (Penguin, 2001), offer much more in-depth plot summaries and musical analysis, but the focus here is on production. This book aims to help a producer stage an opera by gathering all the "ingredients" needed. It answers such questions as: where to get the rights, how many clarinetists or dancers or choral members are required, and what type of challenging sets and actions have to be planned. Not intended for a general audience, it is a godsend for those working in the opera world.

The book also lists the operas by title and composer as well as including a separate register of one-act operas. The overall title list is redundant, though, since the entries themselves are in title order. In addition, operas are indexed by librettist, and arias are indexed by voice type. This no-nonsense work packs a lot of basic details into one volume and would be useful for any library that supports either opera students or an opera production team.—**John Maymuk**

951.   **MetOperaDatabase.**   **http://archives.metoperafamily.org/archives/frame.htm.**   [Website]. Free. Date reviewed: 2013.

This database provides complete information about every opera staged at the Metropolitan Opera from its opening night on October 22, 1883 to the present day. The database is updated five days a week during the opera season. Searching the database by singer produces a list of all performances at the Met by that singer. It is then possible to click on one performance and see a complete listing of cast and production members, as well as a review of the production. Links to other Metropolitan Opera features include free audio streaming of selected performances and paid subscription and audio and video services.—**Anna H. Perrault**

952.   Sanders, Donald. **Experiencing Verdi: A Listener's Companion.** Lanham, Md., Scarecrow, 2014. 255p. index. (The Listener's Companion). $45.00pa.; $44.99 (e-book). ISBN 13: 978-0-8108-8467-0; 978-0-8108-8468-7 (e-book).

Sanders, a professor of music at Samford University in Birmingham, Alabama, has written widely on opera music. His style is straightforward and easygoing, and will help long-time listeners of opera and those new to Verdi cultivate an understanding and appreciation of this great composer's music. He gives readers explanations of both technical and scholarly aspects but also important points of what the listener should be listening for. He provides a biography of Verdi alongside an easy-to-understand musical analysis. He summarizes the evolution of Italian opera and analyzes in depth 11 of Verdi's key operas. He examines Verdi's influence on later composers, including Giacomo Puccini, as well as takes a look at his role in modern opera. The author includes a timeline, a glossary of musical terms, and selected reading and recording recommendations. An index makes it easy to find specific topics, persons, places, or musical pieces.—**ARBA Staff Reviewer**

Orchestral

953.   Green, Jonathan D. **A Conductor's Guide to Selected Baroque Choral-Orchestral Works.** Lanham, Md., Scarecrow, 2014. 267p. $85.00; $84.99 (e-book). ISBN 13: 978-0-8108-8649-0; 978-0-8108-8650-6 (e-book).

This work, a companion to the author's *A Conductor's Guide to the Choral-Orchestral Works of J. S. Bach*, covers the music of the Baroque era from Monteverdi through many of Bach's contemporaries. The arrangement is alphabetic by composer, subarranged by date of composition. The basic information on the compositions is also the same, listing title; date of composition; duration; source of text; detailed list of performing forces required; date, place, and principal performers of the premiere; editions currently available; location of the autograph score; historical notes; an extensive analysis of performance issues; a discography; and a selective bibliography of reviews and criticism. Performance difficulty is rated separately for choir and orchestra. Short composer biographies (including brief bibliographies) are provided. This is a useful guide for choral conductors and advanced music students.—**Paul B. Cors**

954.   Manning, Lucy. **Orchestral "Pops" Music: A Handbook.** 2d ed. Lanham, Md., Scarecrow, 2013. 460p. index. $85.00; $84.99 (e-book). ISBN 13: 978-0-8108-8422-9; 978-0-8108-8423-6 (e-book).

Many bibliographies of orchestral music contain lists of pops music, but few provide as complete a list (over 2,000) as is found in this handbook. This updated volume provides up-to-date information due to changes in publishers and agents, presses that have gone out of business, and discontinuation of publications of certain original material, music directors, orchestra conductors, and instrumentalists. Lucy Manning points out that this handbook is an attempt to alleviate some of the time consuming work of locating pops music by creating a comprehensive and informative repertoire list for "pops" concerts." She provides an interesting definition of "pops" music from which the list is based. Numerous orchestras and composers were contacted to develop the theory of "pops" used for selecting the titles included. The list is arranged alphabetically by composer, and each entry contains the title of the work, instrumentation, duration, themes (e.g., animals, Broadway musicals, circus, dance), publisher, and availability for purchase or rental. In addition to the alphabetic list, the work contains listings by publishers and sources, instrumentation, duration, and theme. In addition, a list of abbreviations is provided. No attempt to annotate any of the entries has been made.

This work is extremely valuable for its listing of pops music by theme. Pops orchestra conductors and music programmers should find it useful to be able to find listings by such themes as space, seasons, and travel. Few bibliographies provide such listings. This updated work is highly recommended for all orchestra libraries, larger public and academic libraries, and the libraries of professionals concerned with orchestral programming.—**ARBA Staff Reviewer**

Popular

955.   **Encyclopedia of Latin American Popular Music.** George Torres, ed. Santa Barbara, Calif., Greenwood Press/ABC-CLIO, 2013. 484p. index. $100.00. ISBN 13: 978-0-313-34031-4; 978-0-313-08794-3 (e-book).

The author seeks to create an encyclopedia that defines major concepts and milestones related to Latin American music, covering only the popular music. There exists a large body of work on Latin American folk music and art music. This encyclopedia is alphabetical, with 200 entries, a chronology, and 37 biographical sidebars. Entries are countries, genres and ensembles (e.g., boleros, conjunto, Hip-Hop, reggae, salsa, samba), concepts (e.g., Afro-Cuban, Protest Song), and instruments (e.g., claves, maracas, marimba, vihuela).

Each entry includes text about the genre or instrument. If the commonly used word is English, it will be found there (i.e., guitar, not *guitarra*). When feasible, each entry is alphabetical in its original language (i.e., Claves). Entry size depends on content. There is at least one bibliographic entry for further reading with each entry, most being English-language sources. The chronology, while not comprehensive, is intended to place significant events within a wider context. Biographical sidebars must be accessed via the index as they are positioned next to their relevant genre: Machito adjacent to "Latin Jazz;" Rita Montaner precedes "Afro-Cuban." The boundaries are not simply geographic, but also political, cultural, and linguistic, including influence from inside the United States. For this encyclopedia, Latin America comprises the Spanish-, Portuguese-, and French-speaking countries of the western hemisphere that lie south of the United States.

In previous years, Don Michael Randel's *New Harvard Dictionary of Music* (Belknap Press, 1986, 2003) provided concise and informative articles on Latin American musical genres. The *Encyclopedia of Latin American Popular Music*, by and large, presents more detail on popular music in entries for countries, and more extensive information on genres (i.e., tango). Articles on forms and genres name composers and performers most often associated with these, and also note geographic coverage. Articles on instruments note genres and forms performed by instrumentalists and where these are prevalent geographically. The text includes numerous cross-references in bold font. The author provides a few selective photographs, illustrations, and musical examples. This encyclopedia serves as a preliminary reference on the most common topics in Latin American popular music. [R: LJ, 1 June 13, p. 132-134]—**Ralph Hartsock**

956.   Leszczak, Bob. **Who Did it First? Great Rhythm and Blues Cover Songs and Their Original Artists.** Lanham, Md., Scarecrow, 2013. 293p. index. $35.00. ISBN 13: 978-0-8108-8866-1.

This book provides information on 380 R&B songs that where made famous by someone other than, or in addition to, the original artists. The majority of songs were first recorded in the 1950s and 1960s with a few songs from the 1970s and a couple of songs from the 1940s and the 1980s. Songs are arranged alphabetically by title and each entry provides the composer of the song, the original artists, year of release, the record label and number, and how it ranked on the charts. This is followed by the cover artist, year of release, record label and number, and how it ranked on the charts. Following each entry is a brief history of both the original release and the release that made the song famous. References to other "honorable mention" versions are included (with appropriate record label and number). Historical descriptions are usually 2-3 brief paragraphs of 200 words on average. Over 40 pictures of original 45 rpm records with half a dozen photos of artists are included. The 32-page index proves quite valuable for identify the various people and artists mentioned in the historical narratives.

Depending on the age of the reader, one may believe the original recording of a song was the more popular version. "Ain't That a Shame" by Fats Domino is still being played on the radio today even though the Pat Boone version charted #1. All in all, music fans of the popular R&B genre of this time period will enjoy this work. The book will also be sought out by fans of popular culture trivia.—**Mike Burgmeier**

957.   **Rock's Backpages. http://www.rocksbackpages.com.** [Website]. $200.00 (annual subscription). Date reviewed: 2013.

Rock's Backpages is a subscription database of rock journalism from the 1950s to the present. The database includes more than 17,000 articles and reviews from rock magazines, including >*Creem*, *Rolling Stone*, *New Musical Express*, and *Melody Maker*. The database can be searched by artist, genre, writer, or keyword. Also included are more than 100 audio interviews with rock artists.—**ARBA Staff Reviewer**

958.   Sullivan, Steve. **Encyclopedia of Great Popular Song Recordings.** Lanham, Md., Scarecrow, 2013. 2v. illus. index. $200.00/set. ISBN 13: 978-0-8108-8295-9.

Lists of popular song recordings and hit books abound, covering various genres and time periods. Rarer are sources that bring these recordings together into one "great list," and which also treat readers to a musical journey with an in-depth examination of each song—from little-known root influences to interesting claims to fame, alternate recordings, and other trivia.

Sullivan's new two-volume set covers all popular genres, from blues and jazz to country and hip-hop—even world music—and spans all recorded time periods, from 1889 to the present. Interestingly, it presents songs based not only on their established greatness in various compiled lists, but also on the quality of the recordings themselves.

Sullivan opens volume 1 by establishing the criteria for his selections. Acknowledging the difficulty of drawing on so many sources and covering so much ground, he explains the importance of weighting his selections based on recognition by standard award agencies and media outlets. These include the Grammy Hall of Fame, the National Recording Registry, NPR, the Rock and Roll Hall of Fame, *Rolling Stone*, and to a lesser extent other hit lists, such as *Billboard*. Sullivan also acknowledges consulting earlier compilations similar to his.

Chapters are presented as 10 themed but somewhat enigmatic "playlists," each of which chronologically lists and describes 100 loosely related song recordings representing a variety of genres and eras. The idea is not to include every great song ever recorded, but to present threads of musical evolution, from roots to branches. Thus the reader realizes that elements of The Who's "Baba O'Riley" can be found in the 1897 recording of the African-American folk song, "Poor Mourner." The over 1,000 richly descriptive entries range from one paragraph in length to two or three pages. Sullivan paints aural images even of songs we have never heard. Both lyric-based songs and instrumentals are included in this encyclopedia. Most are placed in the context of the historical, societal, and political backdrops of their time. One minor irritation is that Sullivan occasionally injects his own political viewpoints.

Sparsely illustrated but heavily footnoted, Sullivan's enjoyable, worthwhile reference work includes an extensive bibliography including biographical sources and discographies. Separate title and subject/name indexes are included. Nearest comparable titles include *1,000 Recordings to Hear Before You Die; 1001 Songs: The Great Songs of All Time and the Artists, Stories and Secrets Behind Them*; or *Time Out: 1000 Songs to Change Your Life.*—**Lucy Duhon**

26 Mythology, Folklore, and Popular Culture

Folklore

959. Bane, Theresa. **Encyclopedia of Fairies in World Folklore and Mythology.** Jefferson, N.C., McFarland, 2013. 419p. index. $75.00pa. ISBN 13: 978-0-7864-7111-9; 978-1-4766-1242-3 (e-book).

Theresa Bane's *Encyclopedia of Fairies in World Folklore and Mythology* is a concise compilation of fairies, fairy-like beings, ancestral spirits, nature spirits, fairy animals, and other fay-related entities as derived from world folktales and mythologies. Bane includes both named fairies (singular, unique beings) and types of fairies (subspecies of the larger fay species). These "concise description[s]" (p. 2) were culled from a variety of sources, some dating back to the 1700s. Bane further indicates that "If the specifics [of a fairy] were not consistent in my sources, the fairy did not make it into this book" (p. 3). This constitutes the clearest parameter for exclusion from the work; as for inclusion, entities such as Tuatha de Danann, banshees, sirens, nymphs, dryads, brownies, leprechauns, minor gods and goddesses, and the offspring of gods and goddesses are detailed. The scope of the work is global, representing the Americas, Mexico, the Middle East, China, Japan, Vietnam, Guam, the United Kingdom, the European continent (west and east), Russia, Africa, Greece, Native American cultures (including the Inuit), Australia, the Maori, India, Burma, Iceland, and cultural stories such as Shinto and Islam.

Each entry contains the name of the entity, including variations of the name and variations of the spelling, translations of the name (where appropriate, often literal), a short description of the fairy, and a brief list of source material. The average entry is about two paragraphs long, although some are as short as one. Entries for concepts, like fairy, can run three or more paragraphs, if not pages.

This reviewer has a few criticisms regarding the title. There are no pronunciations, either as a guide or an appendix, or within the entries themselves, which is bothersome, especially as regards difficult languages like Gaelic or Welsh. The book is also all text—no pictures are included to depict these colorful creatures. Folk depictions from the source materials or at least illustrations would have been appreciated. Furthermore, for a paperback book without images and the most to-the-point information possible, the $75 price tag is a bit much to swallow.

Apart from these critiques, the title is very user-friendly and contains succinct but descriptive descriptions of fairies. Its global approach is deeply appreciated. This work is definitely recommended for public and academic libraries, particularly at undergraduate institutions with folklore or mythology studies.—**Megan W. Lowe**

960. **Critical Survey of Mythology and Folklore: Heroes & Heroines.** Hackensack, N.J., Salem Press, 2013. 403p. illus. index. $195.00. ISBN 13: 978-1-61925-181-6.

961. **Critical Survey of Mythology and Folklore: Love, Sexuality, and Desire.** Thomas J. Sienkewicz, ed. Hackensack, N.J., Salem Press, 2013. 2v. index. $295.00/set. ISBN 13: 978-1-4298-3765-1.

Both in print and electronic versions, these masterful collection of essays on world love stories and heroes and heroines surpasses other collections for their succinct, readable surveys of literature on passion and heroism. Remarkably consistent in tone and style for a multi-author text, the works summarize and analyzes conflict and theme from artistic, humanistic, existential, feminist, and cosmic perspectives. In *Love, Sexuality, and Desire*, bibliographies mesh classic criticism—Edith Hamilton, James Frazer, Karl Jung, Joseph Campbell—with re-settings of ageless stories by James Baldwin and Oscar Wilde as well as by artists and librettists. The timeline and chronological list of world love stories orient young readers, researchers, and teachers to landmarks of global literature. Notable omissions from coverage include Polynesian folklore compiled by David Kalakaua, Mesoamerican myth from the Popol Vuh, and Aboriginal dreamtime stories. These volumes are superb additions to the public, high school, college, or university library. They offer a grounding for an up-to-date reference shelf on world mythology.—**Mary Ellen Snodgrass**

962. **World Oral Literature Project. http://oralliterature.org/.** [Website]. Free. Date reviewed: 2013.

This project is primarily the work of researchers at Cambridge University, although Yale University has been a co-site collaborator since 2011. Oral literature in the scope of this project includes epic poems, folk tales, creation talks, myths, legends, proverbs, word games, and autobiographical and historical narratives, as well as ritual texts and curative chants. The texts themselves are in the form of sound files. Access is facilitated by an interactive world map that shows the location of the field and archival recordings.—**ARBA Staff Reviewer**

Mythology

963. **GreekMythology.com.** [Website]. Free. Date reviewed: 2013.

Greek Mythology.com provides links to many aspects of Greek mythology including sites on gods, goddesses, heroes, places, creatures, and full-text of important myths. A handy family tree of the gods is on the home page for reference. This online resource is logically organized but lacks visual appeal. However, it does provide some links to the basics of mythology in the Greek tradition and the site is free. Links to *Bulfinch's Mythology* and other classic sources are valuable for students and those with curiosity about Greek mythology. The Website sponsors a discussion forum whose threads are categorized under the topical areas that organize the resources on the Website; Olympian gods, Titans, The Myths, Creatures, and more.—**Anna H. Perrault**

964. **Mythology and Culture Worldwide Series.** Farmington Hills, Mich., Lucent Books/Gale/ Cengage Learning, 2013. multivolume. illus. index. $34.45/vol.

This multivolume series covering the origins, cultural importance, and impact of world mythologies is aimed at upper middle and high school students. This new series discusses one cultural or national mythology and discusses such topics as major myths, characters, gods, and typical themes represented. The authors continually show how the myth related to the cultures geography, history, social organization, religions, and values, giving students an overall feel for the specific culture being covered. Recently published volumes are on the mythologies of the British, the Celts, Egypt, and Babylonia. All of the volumes feature informative sidebars, full-color illustrations, lists for recommended listening, a glossary, bibliography, and an index. These additional features add to the value of the series by providing young readers with information for further research and discussion topics.

The authors are writers of books for young people. Because mythology may be a new topic to the students this series is aimed at, the authors write in a straightforward style that covers the topic as thoroughly as possible. They could easily be used as a jumping off point for research projects. At $34.45 for the hardcover copies, this set could be expensive to collect as a whole, but school librarians have the freedom to select the titles that will best suit their collection. Many of the versions are also available in e-book versions.—**Shannon Graff Hysell**

965.   **Theoi Greek Mythology. http://www.theoi.com.** [Website]. By Aaron J. Atsma. Free. Date reviewed: 2013.

This free Website explores Greek mythology and the gods in classical literature and art. The developer states the aim of the project is to provide a comprehensive, free reference guide to the gods (*theoi*), spirits (*daimones*), fabulous creatures (*theres*), and heroes of ancient Greek mythology and religion. This site is visually attractive and well organized, and serves as a guide to Web resources and an encyclopedia, with well-documented entries. The organizational scheme is simple: Greek Mythology Introduction has definitions and links on A-Z Gods, Cults, Bestiary, and similar topics; Greek Mythology and Biographies links to more information on gods, goddesses, heroes, and other persons important to mythology (e.g., giants); and a Gallery provides access to photographs of art, such as vases, that depict mythological events, person, and stories. An impressive Library provides links to important works by major authors, such as Aeschylus, Homer, and other less popular ones as well. A gods and heroes family tree and a list of most popular links are included. While there are many mythology Websites, a large proportion of them have not been recently updated. This Website appears to be well maintained.—**Anna H. Perrault**

Popular Culture

Biography

966.   **100 Entertainers Who Changed America: An Encyclopedia of Pop Culture Luminaries.** Robert C. Sickels, ed. Santa Barbara, Calif., Greenwood Press/ABC-CLIO, 2013. 2v. illus. index. $189.00/set. ISBN 13: 978-1-59884-830-4; 978-1-59884-831-1 (e-book).

This two-volume set, arranged alphabetically, provides information on a wide range of entertainers, from Walt Whitman and Walter Winchell to Chuck D and Quentin Tarantino. Articles include portraits of the subjects, and briefly provide biographical information along with the subject's accomplishments and broader context. For example, the entry on Martha Stewart describes her life prior to her publishing and television career, her achievements in those fields, her legal woes, and her subsequent return to the spotlight. Each article concludes with a list of references and additional resources.

The credentials of the authors of the articles varies, as does the quality of the articles and the sources listed as references. For example, one contributor is "pursuing a graduate degree" (with no discipline specified) and another is "an independent scholar" (again, with neither discipline nor relevant degrees specified). The entry for Jim Henson lists only DVDs of Jim Henson's productions as references; no biographical sources are cited. The article on Andrew Lloyd Webber has a list of references that is drawn almost entirely from Websites—aside from one book, there are no resources listed beyond what can be found on the open Web—but that may not be an issue depending on the community your library serves. Many of the other articles do include an appropriate mix of sources given the content. That said, the conversational tone of the encyclopedia does make for an easy-to-understand introduction.

The simple and clear writing style and the accessibility of many of the references makes this most suitable for middle school, high school, and public libraries, but for those wishing to present good models of writing and referencing, there may be better sources.—**Amanda Izenstark**

967.   **Superstars! Series.** New York, Crabtree, 2013. multivolume. illus. index. $26.60/vol.; $8.95pa./vol.

This multivolume series from Crabtree Publishing, a company known for their multivolume, nonfiction series designed specifically for children, provides biographical volumes on pop culture's most famous teen and young adult stars. New celebrities added to the series include: Sidney Crosby, Carrie Underwood, Lindsey Vonn. With the use of color photographs and easy-to-understand text, each volume covers the celebrity's childhood, their school life, their start into fame, and what's next on the horizon. Each volume concludes a timeline, a glossary, a further reading list, and a very short index, all of which can be used to teach young students basic researching skills. This series is recommended for elementary school libraries and juvenile collections in public and school libraries if this type of information is needed.—**Shannon Graff Hysell**

968.   Tracy, Kathleen. **Superstars of the 21st Century: Pop Favorites of America's Teens.** Santa Barbara, Calif., Greenwood Press/ABC-CLIO, 2013. 227p. illus. index. $89.00. ISBN 13: 978-0-313-37736-5; 978-0-313-37737-2 (e-book).

Superstars of the 21st Century: Pop Favorites of America's Teens is a 227-page volume of biographical essays about some of the most popular figures in today's pop culture landscape. Kathleen Turner has selected 20 athletes, singers, and actors that represent the most popular role models for today's teenage population.

The 18 essays in this book (some individuals were combined into a single chapter) are geared toward a high school audience and provide a mini-biography of each performer, including such information as his/her childhood, career beginnings, and professional accomplishments. Each essay also includes additional notes while some essays include citations for further reading. The volume also includes an index and selected bibliography.

Superstars of the 21st Century is very easy to comprehend and organized in a way that is very easy to pick up and enjoy immediately. Unfortunately, the fleeting nature of fame, stardom, and popularity make this work a risky investment. Although the basic historical details of each person will remain the same, the information is only current up to the point in which the book was written. Each essay reads similarly to a Wikipedia article, but without the ability to be updated with current information. With only 20 included individuals, this book is also limited in its scope. To be clear, the information included in this resource is accurate, interesting, and certainly worthwhile to a certain audience, but the limitations and $89 cost must also be taken into account. Many public libraries, in particular, could be well served to provide this resource to its patrons.—**Tyler Manolovitz**

Catalogs and Collections

969.   **Comicsresearch. http://www.comicsresearch.org.** [Website]. By Gene Kannenberg. Free. Date reviewed: 2013.

Maintained by Gene Kannenberg, author of *500 Essential Graphic Novels*(Harper Design, 2008), this site is a comprehensive bibliography with listings and reviews of works about comics, organizations, library resource guides, and more. Included on the site is *Comic Art in Scholarly Writing: A Citation Guide* by Allen Allis (http://www.comicsresearch.org/CAC/cite.html), a guide to citing comic art as suggested by the Popular Culture Association.—**ARBA Staff Reviewer**

970.   **Grand Comics Database (GCD). http://docs.comics.org.** [Website]. Free. Date reviewed: 2013.

The slogan for GCD is "indexing every comic book ever made from all over the world." The GCD is a nonprofit, noncommercial, fan-based volunteer effort with the goal of documenting and indexing all comics for the free use of scholars, historians, researchers, and fans. The GCS is an ongoing project to build a detailed comic-book database that is international, accurate, and complete from the beginning of the art form to the present. It is truly international with comic series in almost 50 languages, quite a few of them minor. The database includes information on creator credits story details, and other information useful to comic-book readers, fans, collectors, and scholars. Over 7,000 publishers, 4,000 brands, 300,000 covers, and 900,000 stories are represented in the database. Searchers for covers show the cover images that are copyrighted by their respective current copyright holders. The GCD is a fully searchable wiki that is easy to use and understand, and also easy for contributors to add information to it. A disclaimer warns about content that may be objectionable. The GDC is only one of many comic databases. The various comic publishers each have their own database (e.g., DC Comics Database, Marvel Comics Database) as well as characters (e.g., Spiderman, Batman).—**Anna H. Perrault**

971.   **Snopes. http://www.snopes.com.** [Website]. Free. Date reviewed: 2013.

This interesting site includes the topics of urban legends, music, luck, business, horrors humor, and holidays, just to name a few. What they began in 1995 as an expression of the originator's shared interest in researching urban legends has since grown into what is widely regarded by folklorists, journalists, and laypersons as one of the World Wide Web's essential resources. Snopes.com is routinely included in annual "Best of the Web" lists and has been the recipient of two Webby awards.—**ARBA Staff Reviewer**

972.   **Underground and Independent Comics, Comix, and Graphic Novels. http://comx. alexanderstreet.com/.** [Website]. Alexandria, Va., Alexander Street Press. Price negotiated by site. Date reviewed: 2013.

This digital comics collection claims to be the first ever scholarly, primary source database focusing on adult comic books and graphic novels. According to the publisher's description, the collection documents the entire spectrum of underground and independent North American and European comics and graphic novels, with 75,000 pages of original material from the 1950s to today along with more than 25,000 pages of interviews, commentary, theory, and criticism from journals, books, and magazines, including *The Comics Journal*. Among the notable contents is *The Seduction of the Innocent* by Dr. Frederick Wertham, the book that led to one of the largest censorship programs in U.S. history, and the complete transcripts of the senate subcommittee hearings that resulted in the Comics Code Authority and, inadvertently, the underground commix movement. These publications were not generally collected by academic or even public libraries. The database provides a complete collection in the genre all in one place. Because of the adult content it is most suitable for academic libraries and research.—**Anna H. Perrault**

Dictionaries and Encyclopedias

973.   **The Christmas Encyclopedia.** 3d ed. Crump, William D. Jefferson, N.C., McFarland, 2013. 527p. illus. index. $75.00pa. ISBN 13: 978-0-7864-6827-0; 978-1-4766-0573-9 (e-book).

This single subject encyclopedia offers a treasure trove of information on a huge array of Christmas-related subjects through more than 760 well-constructed and clearly arranged entries. This represents an increase of 300 entries since the last edition published in 2006. Readers can find information on almost every popular Christmas song and traditional carol, including composition history, arrangement, and ranking among the 25 most popular Christmas songs. Fans of the Rankin/Bass Christmas cartoons can find summaries of each television show as well as a listing of who provided the voice talents. Many other television specials, episodes, and movies are also summarized with notable events highlighted. Much attention is paid to the meaning of every Christmas related date, such as Candlemas, St. Nicholas Day, or Boxing Day, as well as to the different Christmas traditions around the world (arranged by national entries). All the principal figures of the Christmas story, season, and history are also included, be they religious or secular. In addition, a lot of general information is covered; for example, how each President celebrated the season and decorated the official White House Christmas tree and the images used on Christmas stamps from 1962-today. This provides a nice "thumb through" element to the resource that makes it as useful for browsing as it does for answering a specific question. New entries added to this edition include specific countries and their traditions (e.g., China, India, Iran, South Africa) as well a more secular holiday traditions such as football bowl games, animated cartoons, and literature. A massive index provides access to even more of the content than can be found following the alphabetic arrangement, which makes this reference especially user friendly. With its expanded interest in how other countries celebrate Christmas, while containing all the other expected and unexpected entries, this resource is a delight for the casual browser and will support almost all Christmas-related research in both academic and public libraries.—**ARBA Staff Reviewer**

974.   **Icons of the American Comic Book: From Captain America to Wonder Woman.** Randy Duncan and Matthew J. Smith, eds. Santa Barbara, Calif., Greenwood Press/ABC-CLIO, 2013. 2v. illus. index. (Greenwood Icons). $189.0/set. ISBN 13: 978-0-313-39923-7; 978-0-313-39924-4 (e-book).

One hundred of comic book's most influential creators, characters, publishers and titles are treated in this set, as well as comic-related terms such as *Fanboy*. The choice of entries is based on those that are most significant to American culture. Regarding characters or comic book titles, the list of entries is exclusive to those that originated in comic books. Most of the entries in this set provide more in-depth information than the standard reference article. A historical overview for each subject is provided as well as an examination of the topic as an icon, providing an analysis of the subject's impact on comic books as well as American culture. Breakout boxes offer expanded information and reading suggestions are available. The set is more than just a list of what's popular as some of the titles are not necessarily popular in the mainstream, but have had a broad impact on the industry. Readers looking to bridge the gap between a reference book and book-length sketches will find this meaty and desirable.—**Brian J. Sherman**

975.   **St. James Encyclopedia of Popular Culture.** 2d ed. Thomas Riggs, ed. Farmington Hills, Mich., St. James Press/Gale Group, 2013. 5v. illus. index. $767.00/set. ISBN 13: 978-1-55862-852-6; 978-1-55862-853-3 (e-book).

Since the inaugural publication of the *St. James Encyclopedia of Popular Culture* in 2000 (see ARBA 2001, entry 1199), the world has become enamored by the love affairs of teenage vampires and New York advertising executives. With a paucity of reference literature on the subject, the 2d edition of this comprehensive popular culture encyclopedia is well received. Providing a broad historical overview to this five-volume set is Jim Cullen's introductory essay, underscoring the special case of American popular culture. With an additional decade included in the 2d edition, ranging from 1900-2010, the topics expand to 3,034 items. Entries not only cover celebrities and television but also businesses (AT&T) and belief structures (Astrology). Entries are alphabetically arranged, cross-referenced, and complete with a brief bibliography for further reading. Volume 5 provides two indexes to facilitate discoverability: the time-frame index and subject index. Whereas the subject index is alphabetically arranged and useful in locating specific entries by volume and page number, the time-frame index is demarcated by decade and confusingly constructed. Without an explanation of the time-frame index organization, the reader is left to wonder why electric trains is indexed in the 2010s. Much like the 1st edition, the encyclopedia includes a general reading list on popular culture and a brief biographies on the advisers and contributors to the 2d edition. Overall, there is much to applaud in the expanded 2d edition, namely the update from black-and-white to color images. An invaluable resource to public and academic libraries, this encyclopedia will continue to be a foundational reference resource on the subject of popular culture.—**Josh Eugene Finnell**

Handbooks and Yearbooks

976.   **Celebrations in My World Series.** New York, Crabtree, 2013. multivolume. illus. index. $19.95/vol.; $8.95pa./vol.

This multivolume series from Crabtree Publishing, a company known for their multivolume, nonfiction series designed specifically for children, provides historical and social information on about

45 holidays celebrated throughout the world. Some students will be familiar with, such as Presidents' Day, Independence Day, Valentine's Day, and St. Patrick's Day, while others may be new to them, such as Eid al-Adha, Juneteenth, Purim, Victoria Day, and 100th Day of School. Each key topic covered is presented in a two-page spread and covers history behind the holiday, rituals associated with it, and the people and parts of the world that celebrate it. Each volume ends with a two-page quiz that emphasizes the key points in the book and reinforces the concepts being taught. Each volume concludes with a glossary and a very short index, both of which can be used to teach young students basic researching skills. This series is recommended for elementary school libraries and juvenile collections in public libraries. They provide a good introduction to holiday and rituals celebrated around the world, particularly those that are students are unfamiliar with.—**Shannon Graff Hysell**

977.   Hillstrom, Kevin, and Laurie Collier Hillstrom. **Woodstock.** Detroit, Omnigraphics, 2013. 226p. illus. index. (Defining Moments). $49.00. ISBN 13: 978-0-7808-1284-0.

This slim volume on the Woodstock Festival of 1969 is the latest installment in the Defining Moments series, designed for students grades 8-12, on pivotal events in U.S. history from the twentieth century forward. This volume, like others in the series, is divided into three primary sections: narrative overview, biographies, and primary sources. The narrative overview section provides a factual account of the topic, outlining origin, key players, major events, and impact. In *Woodstock*, the authors explore the role that the civil rights movement and the anti-Vietnam War movement played in the popular music of the time and the hippie counterculture lifestyle. The author examines the generational tension at the time and how rock music contributed to that tension, as well as how that compares to the generational gaps we see today. The biographies section provides sketches of 10 leading figures of the event, most of which are performers (e.g., Joan Baez, Bob Dylan, Jimi Hendrix) as well as Woodstock promoters. It may have been useful to provide a few biographies of opponents of this counterculture revolution to give students a more balanced look at both sides. Sources for further study accompany each sketch. Primary sources include essays, first-hand accounts, and articles on the role of Woodstock on the mood of the country, what it was like to be there (both good and bad experiences), and an article from Ayn Rand denouncing the "phony" values of Woodstock. Additional useful materials include photographs, a chronology, a glossary, a bibliography that also includes Websites and videotapes, and a subject index.

Woodstock is a well-organized, balanced, and approachable reference source for its intended audience, undoubtedly reflective of the composition of the series advisory board (public and school librarians and educators) and hopefully indicative of the quality of other titles in the series. Although its title reflects this one event in the 1960s counterculture movement, much of the information and material it provides reflects the deeper meaning behind the movement and the feeling behind it.—**John T. Gillespie**

978.   Martin, Judith, and Nicholas Ivor Martin. **Miss Manners Minds Your Business.** New York, W. W. Norton, 2013. 302p. $26.95. ISBN 13: 978-0-393-08136-7.

Miss Manners has addressed at least 16 topics of etiquette in her previous books. Her newest guide is the first on workplace etiquette. This edition of Miss Manners tries to cool the fires of office staff with concise useful solutions and comments. Each of the 15 chapters begins with a synopsis of the chapter topic. This is followed by several "Gentle Readers" questions and her response. A detailed index completes this compendium. Miss Manners had thought that business manners existed to maintain personal dignity and show respect for others, instead she was told that manners existed so as to dominate one's coworkers. Miss Manners does not think this works well. While everyone agrees that family is of paramount importance, business is allowed to trump any personal obligation or occasion.

Miss Manners emphatically does not advocate a return to old-style office behavior. She prefers orderly change that preserves what is needed from the past while rectifying what is bad. To do this you must cede final authority to Miss Manners. Being the master of manners for the modern age, her job is to equip the "Gentle Readers" with the practical, pertinent, and correct advice necessary to win, keep, and leave the job with sanity and dignity intact. She has successfully solved many business etiquette problems. This reviewer highly recommends *Miss Manners Minds your Business* for anyone who wants to learn business etiquette and its roles of business and family situations. [R: LJ, 15 June 13, p. 115]—**Nadine Salmons**

979.   **Mystery Files Series.** New York, Crabtree, 2013. multivolume. illus. index. $20.70/vol.; $9.95pa./vol.

This four-volume set from Crabtree Publishing, a company known for their multivolume, nonfiction series designed specifically for children, attempts to unlock some of the secrets behind some of the most outrageous stories in history. The volumes in the series discuss: Astonishing Bodies, Conspiracy, Forgotten Cities, Ghost Ships, Hidden Worlds, Impossible Science, Secret Signs, and Weird Nature. The volumes explore how these mysterious stories originated, how they have been explained in different cultures, and what the common belief is today surrounding the mystery. The books are organized by these topics and within each chapter specific mysteries are explored in depth to show children how the mystery was used to explain the circumstances in the lives of people at that time. Within each volume are plenty of color photographs and illustrations as well as sidebars full of additional information. The book provides sidebars called "Mystery File," which define key aspects of the mystery. Each volume ends with a glossary, a list of resources for further research that includes both books and Internet sites, and a very short index, all of which can be used to teach young students basic researching skills. This series is recommended for upper-elementary and middle school libraries and juvenile collections in public libraries.—**Shannon Graff Hysell**

27 Performing Arts

General Works

Biography

980. Lentz III, Harris M. **Obituaries in the Performing Arts, 2012.** Jefferson, N.C., McFarland, 2013. 315p. illus. $49.95pa. ISBN 13: 978-0-7864-7063-1.

Dick Clark, Whitney Houston, and Phyllis Diller are just a few of the notable performers that passed away last year. This one-volume, A-Z encyclopedia includes over 1,000 obituaries of performers that died in 2012. Compiled by Harris M. Lentz III, this is the latest volume in a serial publication issued annually since 1994. The volumes include the obituaries of reality television show contestants and celebrity animals. Entries are arranged alphabetically, and include a photograph, cause of death, and brief biography. Lent's brief introduction serves as a year-in-review, highlighting notable celebrity deaths while pointing out less-remembered celebrities whose impact on their field warrant pause and reflection. It is here that Lentz sets the tone for this seemingly macabre work as a labor of reverence for individual performers that dedicated their lives to entertaining the masses. A brief reference bibliography consisting of books and Internet sources gives the curious reader an opportunity to explore celebrity culture more in depth. The inclusion of an index, a common critique by past reviewers of this series, would be a welcome addition to future volumes in the series. However, the compilation is a solid reference work that deserves inclusion in all public libraries.—**Josh Eugene Finnell**

981. **Who's Who in Research: Performing Arts.** Bristol, United Kingdom, Intellect; distr., Chicago, University of Chicago Press, 2013. 1v. (various paging). $115.00. ISBN 13: 978-1-84150-494-0.

This book was designed to increase self-knowledge and facilitate communication and collaboration with those who are involved in the performing arts, mainly in the United Kingdom. It is basically a published contact sheet, and would probably be more visible and able to be updated on a regular basis if it were designed as an Internet Web page or database. Given that, each entry lists the person's name, affiliation, and some keywords on the left hand side, while the center area contains a short biography of the person, their interests and research, and some publications. It is interesting that only mailing addresses are listed and not e-mail addresses. All of the keywords are combined at the end of the book as an index, so one can see individuals who are working in the same subject area. While I can understand the need for this information, it is outdated as soon as it is published, and the expenditure of money to obtain it would probably not be worth it. The publisher should examine providing this service through a Website.—**Bradford Lee Eden**

Catalogs and Collections

982. **Creating Digital Performance Resources: A Guide to Good Practice. http://www.ahds.ac.uk/ creating/guides/.** [Website]. Oxford, England, Oxbow Books. Free. Date reviewed: 2013.

This work is part of the Arts and Humanities Data Service series of guides to good practice. The guides are meant to educate those in the humanities and arts who create, preserve, and use digital resources. Guides in the series address a number of humanities disciplines and the arts; this one relates to performing arts resources. According to the publisher's Website, this resource "covers various issues related to digital resources in the performance arts. It examines the construction of Web-based databases, digital archives, e-journals and teaching applications, all in the context of performing arts datasets." Three sections with individual chapters by expert editors give practical advice. Finally, a section on the use of electronic resources in the practice of the performing arts is included. A glossary and bibliography, including Web resources, complete this small volume.—**Anna H. Perrault**

Dictionaries and Encyclopedias

983. **Performing Arts Encyclopedia. http://www.loc.gov/performingarts/.** [Website]. Washington, D.C., Library of Congress. Free. Date reviewed: 2013.

The Performing Arts Encyclopedia Website of the Library of Congress is a rich resource for information across the performing arts. The following divisions at the Library are represented in this rich Web resource: The Music Division; the Motion Picture, Broadcasting and Recorded Sound Division; the American Folklife Center; the Manuscript Division; the Rare Books and Special Division; and the Prints and Photographs Division. The Library's description of the site states that the encyclopedia provides information about the Library's "collections of scores, sheet music, audio recordings, films, photographs, and other materials." Users can find digitized items from the collections; special Web presentations on topics and collections; articles and biographical essays; finding aids to collections; databases for performing arts resources; information on concerts at the Library; and a special Performing Arts Resource Guide which contains entries for hundreds of Library collections, Websites, databases, and exhibits. This free resource will open the door to the wealth of performing arts information, including programs and Web presentations, of the Library of Congress.—**Anna H. Perrault**

Directories

984. **The Grey House Performing Arts Directory 2013/14.** 8th ed. Millerton, N.Y., Grey House Publishing, 2013. 1191p. index. $250.00pa.; $357.00 (online access; single user); $475.00 (print and online editions). ISBN 13: 978-1-59237-879-1.

A no-frills, straightforward fund of information, the 8th edition of *The Grey House Performing Arts Directory* is an updated continuation of the methodically detailed resource. The scope of this directory (like those in the past) focuses on dance, instrumental music, vocal music, theater, and series and festivals. It also provides information regarding facilities and venues, as well as other sources of information regarding the performing arts. The *Directory* is divided into seven chapters focusing on the aforementioned performing art categories, six on facilities, and seven on information resources. Prior to the start of the chapters, there is a brief section on promotion and planning for promotions. Within the chapters concerning the performing arts categories, entries are arranged by state, and then alphabetically. The entries themselves, ranging from dance troupes to choirs to theater troupes, contain (when available) the title of the entity (e.g., association, troupe), mailing address, telephone number, fax number, Web address, officers, and management. Entries in the facilities chapter, which is arranged by state, then alphabetically, also contain this information and include 307 new entries. The information resources chapter contains data drawn from Grey House's *Directory of Business Information Resources* (20th ed., 2013) and includes 732 individual resources, ranging from newsletters, listservs, databases, periodicals, trade shows, directories, and Websites. Prices are included for resources that can be purchased.

Six indexes offer users a variety of ways to look up information: entry name (e.g., association, venue, performing group); executive name (this edition provides names for 2,651 key individuals); facilities; specialized field (which is divided into general categories with 257 specific subdivisions); geographical index; and information resources. This last index seems a little superfluous, since that particular chapter is arranged by type of resource and is self-explanatory.

Clear-cut, easy-to-use, uncomplicated but comprehensive, the *Directory* is a great resource for public and academic libraries alike, as well as any performing arts-related entity. For those looking for electronic access, the work is available online via the publisher's G.O.L.D. platform (Grey House Online Database).—**Megan W. Lowe**

Indexes

985.   **International Index to the Performing Arts (IIPA). http://iipa.chadwyck.com/marketing.do.** [Website]. Alexandria, Va., Chadwyck-Healey. Price negotiated by site. Date reviewed: 2013.

IIPA full text covers a broad spectrum of the arts and entertainment industry including dance, film, television, drama, theater, stagecraft, musical theater, broadcast arts, circus performance, comedy, storytelling, opera, pantomime, puppetry, magic, and more. Prior to the IIPA full-text edition with abstracts, the product was issued in CD-ROM. The database, begun in 1999, indexes 200 scholarly and popular periodicals in the performing arts and other content, such as biographical profiles, conference papers, obituaries, interviews, discographies, reviews, and events.—**Anna H. Perrault**

Dance

986.   **International Encyclopedia of Dance. http://www.oxford-dance.com/.** [Website]. New York, Oxford University Press, 2013. Price negotiated by site.

This is a digital version of a six-volume work containing around 2,000 signed scholarly articles on the full spectrum of dance—theatrical, ritual, dance-drama, folk, traditional, ethnic, and social dance. It includes many national overviews, such as the Asian national overview, as well a specific entries on dance forms, music, costumes, performances, as well as entries on leading dancers and choreographers.— **Noriko Asato**

987.   **Voice of Dance. http://voice of dance.com.** [Website]. Free. Date reviewed: 2013.

Voice of Dance is a resource for dance fans, dance professionals, and dance students. The history of the site states that it began as a forum at a time when message boards and discussions were the way to communicate within a community. The site now covers multiple areas of interest, from finding tickets to criticism to finding classes and more. The developers state that "the database technology at the core of the site cross references this information in a fully integrated way that is not possible in the off-line work." This site is a true mix of directory, newsletter, resource guide, and encyclopedia.—**ARBA Staff Reviewer**

Film, Television, and Video

Biography

988.   **Who's Who in Research: Film Studies.** Bristol, United Kingdom, Intellect; distr., Chicago, University of Chicago Press, 2013. 1v. (various paging). $115.00. ISBN 13: 978-1-84150-496-4.

This intriguing but oddly incomplete resource offers potentially helpful and interesting information about 1,354 international film scholars. The entries provide short biographies of the subjects, including their current research interests as of 2011, and a list of their articles published in any of the 23 film journals, such as *Film International, Journal of Screenwriting, Studies in Documentary Film*, and *The Soundtrack*, published by Intellect, Ltd. The scholars range from such well-known authorities as Ian Christie, Gina Marchetti, Patrick McGilligan, and Ginette Vincendeau to graduate students. The subject index is based on keywords these scholars have used in their articles, but too many are vague, as with American cinema and suspense. Alfred Hitchcock and Martin Scorsese receive one mention each, the same as for Adolf Hitler, Hillary Clinton, and the Rolling Stones. The entry for Greil Marcus gives no indication that he is perhaps the leading rock-and-roll historian. Despite such limitations, the volume may be useful for locating film scholars and finding out what kinds of articles are in vogue in current scholarship.—**Michael Adams**

Catalogs and Collections

989.   **Cinema Image Gallery. http://ebscohost.com/academic/cinema-image-gallery.** [Website]. Bronx, N.Y., H. W. Wilson. Price negotiated by site. Date reviewed: 2013.

The Cinema Image Gallery is one of the most comprehensive collections of still images from movies, television, and the entertainment industry, providing over 150,000 superior-quality images, along with 4,000 post-art and lobby cards used to promote movies. It presents the history of movie-making; still images of films in production; directors working on-set; set, costume, and production design; hair and make-up shots; and rare behind-the-scenes material. The gallery also offers an extensive television stills archive, covering comedies, dramas, series, television movies, game shows, and thousands of pictures of stars.—**Anna H. Perrault**

Dictionaries and Encyclopedias

990.   Burton, Alan, and Steve Chibnall. **Historical Dictionary of British Cinema.** Lanham, Md., Scarecrow, 2013. 542p. (Historical Dictionary of Literature and the Arts). $120.00; $199.99 (e-book). ISBN 13: 978-0-8108-6794-9; 978-0-8108-8026-9 (e-book).

Until now, students and scholars interested in the broad scope of British cinemas had few collected sources to begin their research, most notably Brian McFarlane's *Encyclopedia of British Film* (4th rev. ed.; Manchester University Press, 2013) and Geoff Mayer's *Guide to British Cinema* (see ARBA 2004, entry 1155). Together Alan Burton and Steve Chibnall have created a work of broad historical synthesis. Coupled with a chronology, a detailed and thorough introduction contextualizes Britain's film industry within the historical confines of both national and global issues. Entries are arranged alphabetically and mostly consist of four categories: film studio, actor, film, and genre. However, broader entries such as "women" and "gay and lesbian issues" fill out the sociocultural development of identity within British cinema. Although varying in length, each entry averages three paragraphs. Moreover, to facilitate searching, phrases with individual entries are highlighted in bold and cross-referenced. Two appendixes are included in the dictionary: British Academy of Film and Television Arts Annual Awards, and the Evening Standard British Film Awards. However, perhaps outshining the rest of the dictionary is the sizeable bibliography, requiring its own table of contents and seven-page introduction. Ranging from silent cinema to individual journals, this robust bibliography reflects the deep subject knowledge both editors bring to the compilation. Overall, this dictionary is constructed for both the novice and expert. Students will inevitably thumb to the entry on Harry Potter, while scholars will devour the bibliography on Derek Jarman.—**Josh Eugene Finnell**

991.   Mayo, Mike. **The Horror Show Guide: The Ultimate Frightfest of Movies.** Canton, Mich., Visible Ink Press, 2013. 477p. illus. index. $19.95pa. ISBN 13: 978-1-57859-420-7.

This guide to horror movies covers this popular genre of filmmaking very well. It provides reviews of over 1,000 of the scariest (and wackiest) movies from the beginning of horror movies. The work highlights each era's top films, noting what that particular decade's top fear was; for example, there were the silent killers of the 1920s, Frankenstein in the 1930s, teenage horror movies of the 1980s, and serial murders in the 1990s. Along with reviews users will find top 10 lists, photographs, and film credit information. The book is organized alphabetically for ease of use. This work is sure to be a popular choice in most public library film collections.   **ARBA Staff Reviewer**

992.   Terrace, Vincent. **Encyclopedia of Television Pilots 1937-2012.** Jefferson, N.C., McFarland, 2013. 372p. index. $145.00pa. ISBN 13: 978-0-7864-7445-5.

The author, a specialist in radio and television history, has written over 30 books on this and related subjects including *Encyclopedia of Television Shows, 1925 through 2010* (2d ed.; see ARBA 2012, entry 1018). The present volume supplies information on over 5,000 pilot films (a pilot film is defined as "a sample episode of what such a series could provide"), aired and unaired that were produced from 1937 through 2012 but failed to become regular television series. This includes information on rejected pilots of shows that later were accepted with changes, such as *I Love Lucy* in 1951 and *Star Trek* in 1964-1965. Entries range in length from 5 to 25 lines depending on the data available. Each entry is numbered and, after the title, a typical entry consists of materials on the show's classification (e.g., comedy, crime drama), company for which it was produced (e.g., Fox, ABC), dates of production, and, when applicable, air date, material on antecedents (spin-offs from other shows), a description of show's contents, producer's name, and cast list of actors and the parts they played. There is an extensive name index of all the people involved with these shows including both actors and producers. This is a remarkable fascinating book but one wishes that the author had supplied material on the sources of his material. Because of the highly specialized nature of the subject, this book will be useful in libraries with extensive materials on media studies.—**John T. Gillespie**

993.   Welsh, James M., and Donald M. Whaley. **The Oliver Stone Encyclopedia.** Lanham, Md., Scarecrow, 2013. 345p. illus. index. $80.00; $79.99 (e-book). ISBN 13: 978-0-8108-8352-9; 978-0-8108-8353-6 (e-book).

Welsh, author of *The Francis Ford Coppola Encyclopedia* (see ARBA 2011, entry 1071), and Whaley take a "kaleidoscopic" approach to examining the life and career of Oliver Stone, combining facts with opinion that make each entry more "personalized" than is found in other similar reference works. Their self-stated goal is for each thematic entry to read like a personal essay and each biographical entry "like an interconnected but self-contained short story," although many of the biographies are too short to merit more than factual consideration. Each of Stone's 20-plus films receive three to four pages of treatment, with at least one black-and-white photograph, a few secondary bibliographic references, and further cross-references. All entries include secondary bibliographies, with additional references in the end material. Most of the nonbiographical and film entries help elucidate Stone's personal philosophy towards filmmaking and writing, and these entries are often enlightening for the casual filmgoer who is not as familiar with the director complete oeuvre. Although opinionated, the entries are well written and thoughtful, but readers should also be aware that many of the biographical entries on individuals who only appeared in a single Stone film (e.g., Val Kilmer) will only skim over that person's complete career. This work is recommended for comprehensive public and academic library film collections.—**Anthony J. Adam**

Filmography

994.   Boggs, Johnny D. **Billy the Kid on Film, 1911-2012.** Jefferson, N.C., McFarland, 2013. 281p. illus. index. $39.95pa. ISBN 13: 978-0-7864-6555-2; 978-1-4766-0335-3 (e-book).

In 2011, the author, an award-winning writer of fiction and nonfiction about the American West, published *Jesse James and the Movies* (McFarland, 2011). Using roughly the same format, Boggs extends his coverage to movies related to the name of the notorious American outlaw known as Billy the Kid, a.k.a. William H. Bonney (real name Henry McCarty) who lived from 1859 to 1881, and at age 22 was shot by Sheriff Pat Garrett.

The first chapter is a biography of Billy, which explodes many myths related to his name. For example, he was not left-handed as portrayed by Paul Newman in the 1958 western *The Left Handed Gun*. The second chapter traces the career of Billy the Kid from history to popular culture figure, and the next nine deal, in chronological order, with his portrayal in films, beginning with the silent film *Billy the Kid* (1911) and ending with *Young Guns II* (1990). (Coverage in other formats ends in 2012.) Movies are included in which Billy appears in only cameo roles, like *Strange Lady in Town* (1955), which starred Greer Garson, and 1971s *The Last Movie*. Also included are movies in which a character named Billy the Kid appears without any connection to the real Billy. For example, a whole chapter is devoted to the B-movie series from IFP studio of 17 movies that featured a conventional western hero, usually played by Buster Crabbe, whose nickname happened to be Billy the Kid. A total of about 80 movies are covered. For the more important films, entries are usually six to eight pages in length and consist of five parts: a listing of the actors and technical personnel, a synopsis of the plot, a historical fact check, background material on the stars and the production, and a brief critical analysis. The last four chapters cover Billy as featured in foreign films, in television movies (plus movies released directly to television), and in television series such as *Death Valley Days*. The book concludes with a section of chapter notes, which cite sources chapter by chapter; an extensive bibliography; and a thorough index.

The author writes with clarity, authority, and an obvious zest for his subject. Although the topics covered in this book are of interest primarily to film buffs, this is an enjoyable browsing item for the general reader and is recommended.—**Anthony J. Adam**

995.   Curti, Roberto. **Italian Crime Filmography 1968-1980.** Jefferson, N.C., McFarland, 2014. 323p. illus. index. $55.00pa. ISBN 13: 978-0-7864-6976-5; 978-1-4766-1208-9 (e-book).

After the decline in popularity of the Spaghetti Western in the early 1960s, Italian filmmakers turned to a different genre, one that also originated in Hollywood—the crime drama. This book, which was written by a noted Italian film critic, analyzes over 220 Italian crime films released from 1968 through 1980. The films are arranged first by year of release and then alphabetically by their title in English (the Italian title follows in parenthesis). Most of these titles had very limited release (if any) in the United States. Each annotation is divided into three parts. First is a detailed list of credits that begins with an extensive list of production personnel followed by a complete cast list (with the names of characters portrayed) arranged by their importance in the film (starts first). The film's availability in other media like DVDs is also indicated. A second section gives brief plot summary and the third consists of a critical analysis of the film, which emphasizes production values, quality of the script, acting and direction, use of settings, the development of themes and subjects, innovative aspects of the film, and critical responses. These critiques are both insightful and probing. Appendixes include a brief overview of Italian crime films from 1982 to the present (2013), profiles of nine of the most significant directors of crime films during the late

1960s and 1970s, and biographical sketches of nine of the most important stars of this genre. Scattered throughout the test are many black-and-white illustrations mostly of film posters. The book concludes with a bibliography of both Italian and English-language books and articles on the subject, followed by a brief index of film titles and the most important personal names involved. This is a fine addition to the growing number of quality books of film criticism; however, the specialized nature of its subject matter will probably restrict its purchase to libraries specializing in media studies.—**John T. Gillespie**

996.   **Directory of World Cinema: Turkey.** Eylem Atakav, ed. Bristol, United Kingdom, Intellect; distr., Chicago, University of Chicago Press, 2013. 215p. illus. index. $25.00pa. ISBN 13: 978-1-8415-0620-3.

This is the 1st edition of *Turkey*, a volume in the *Directory of World Cinema* series from Intellect. It was created to help give Turkish cinema some of the attention it has been lacking in recent years. The goal of the editor is to highlight the extraordinary history of Turkey's film industry, noting its ties to transnational identity and its political, economic, and social conditions. The entries focus mainly on major genres (e.g., science fiction and fantasy, drama, transnational cinema, blockbusters), movements, and prominent figures in the industry. After introductory chapters on the film of the year (*Once Upon a Time in Anatolia*), festivals, film locations, directors, and celebrities. Black-and-white illustrations add interest and information. Individual entries include film title, credits, synopsis, critique, cast, and year of release. The work concludes with a recommended reading list, Websites to go to for more information, notes on the contributors, and a brief filmography. This title and others in the series will be useful for students of film and will be useful in academic libraries.—**Ralph Hartsock**

997.   Levine, Sanford. **Best Movie Scenes: 549 Memorable Bank Robberies, Car Chases, Duels, Haircuts, Job Interviews, Swearing Scenes, Window Scenes and Others, by Topic.** Jefferson, N.C., McFarland, 2013. 198p. index. $29.95pa. ISBN 13: 978-0-7864-7091-4.

The 1st edition of this title listed the author's picks for the best 247 movies scenes (McFarland, 2011). This 2d edition, published 12 years later, provides more than 300 additional movie scenes that cinema fans have found memorable and "spurred their adoration" for the film at hand. The work is organized alphabetically by theme, with each theme providing anywhere from 5 to 10 scenes on that topic. Themes in this volume include the expected (e.g., bank robbery, cemetery, car chase, marriage proposal, swearing) to the unexpected (e.g., false teeth, funny walk, library, Viagra). For each movie selected it provides a detailed one-paragraph description of the imagery of the scene, the actors involved, and the critical reception of the movie and the scene in particular. As expected, a book like this is highly subjective and many scenes that have been influential in movie making have been left out. The author also does not include detailed information on each film mentioned (e.g., cast, production notes, date of release) so it is not as complete as it could have been from a reference point of view. It is, however, an interesting book to browse through for inspiration and is a fun read overall.—**Anita Zutis**

998.   McCall, Douglas. **Monty Python: A Chronology, 1969-2012.** 2d ed. Jefferson, N.C., McFarland, 2013. 392p. index. $45.00pa. ISBN 13: 978-0-7864-7811-8.

Although the BBC weekly television program of zany satirical sketches and songs known collectively as *Monty Python's Flying Circus* aired only from 1969 through 1974, the number of histories, critical studies, and biographies on the subject plus spin-offs and reruns continues to the present. This volume (an edited and expanded version of the 1st edition of 1991) covers, in diary format (i.e., day to day), topics related to *Monty Python* and its members from January 1969 through December 2012. In addition to his own research and a thorough examination of primary sources (i.e., the programs themselves), the author, an American writer and avid Python fan, has consulted a number of secondary sources listed in an appended bibliography. The body of the work consists of 4,208 numbered entries averaging 8 to 10 lines, each arranged chronologically. The most important information is found in the articles that cover the years during which the show was in progress. Most valuable are the entries for each of the shows. They include contents notes, the names of skits and songs used (plus credits), and listings of specific authors and participants. Other entries cover spin-offs like books and movies inspired by the show (e.g., *Monty Python and the Holy Grail* of 1975, and 1979's *Monty Python's Life of Brian*). There are also entries on awards received, books and articles of importance, and personal information about individual cast members (e.g., birthdays, marriages). The entries for years after the show ended concentrate on subsequent activities of cast members like personal appearances, important interviews, and awards received. Most important is material on subsequent professional activities of the members like John Cleese's role in *Fawlty Towers* and Michael Palin's film career, which includes *A Fish Called Wanda* (1988). The book's indexes are outstanding. There is one on sketches and songs from the various episodes, another on material written by the show's mainstay, Eric Idle, plus an exhaustive general index using references to the number of a specific article. Presumably, because of the large number of entries involved, there are no entries in this index for the six creators/principal performers. There are also no illustrations. Nevertheless, this is an excellent one-volume reference work on one of the most influential entertainment phenomena of the late twentieth century—**John T. Gillespie**

999.   Neibaur, James L., and Terri Niemi. **Buster Keaton's Silent Shorts 1920-1923.** Lanham, Md., Scarecrow, 2013. 253p. illus. index. $60.00; $59.99 (e-book). ISBN 13: 978-0-8108-8740-4; 978-0-8108-8741-1 (e-book).

As well as books about the silent films of Charlie Chaplin and Harry Langdon, the film historian, James L. Neibaur, has written an earlier book about Buster Keaton (1895-1966), *The Fall on Buster Keaton* (Scarecrow, 2010), which deals with Keaton's career in talking pictures. Even before he carved out an important place in silent film history with such full-length classics as *The General* (1926) and *Steamboat Bill, Jr.* (1928), Keaton starred in 19 two-reelers released between 1920 and 1923. Beginning with *The High Sign* (1920) and continuing with such titles as *One Week* (1920), *The Haunted House* (1921), *The Playhouse* (1921), and *The Frozen North* (1922), the series ends with *The Love Nest* (1923). This volume describes thoroughly each of these films with a detailed (practically frame-by-frame) plot summary plus an evaluative analysis of the film, material on film techniques utilized, and reasons for the film's importance. Background information on production details, audience reception, and a present-day evaluation of the film are also included. The material on each film is preceded by a brief table of basic information like releasing company, film credits (e.g., producers, cinematographers), and a cast list. Coverage for each film averages 10 pages. Throughout the text there are many black-and-white stills from the films and reproductions of movie posters. The book's introduction and epilogue briefly cover Keaton's career before and after the making of these short films. There is also a brief bibliography (although where the author found the wealth of material for this book is not divulged) and a four-page index (mostly names of cast members). This is a fascinating book that covers a little-known segment of film industry. One wishes that a DVD of these films could have been included with the book. This work is recommended for large media collections.—**John T. Gillespie**

1000.   Parrill, Sue, and William B. Robison. **The Tudors on Film and Television.** Jefferson, N.C., McFarland, 2013. 344p. illus. index. $75.00pa. ISBN 13: 978-0-7864-5891-2.

Given the prevalence of dramas about the Tudors from the silent film era to the present, it is odd that this topic has never been given the detailed study offered by Parrill, emeritus professor of English at Southeastern Louisiana University, and Robison, history and political science at the same institution. This guide also fills a void since so many of the silent films have been lost and the numerous television productions, especially from the 1950s and 1960s, impossible to see. The filmography's format includes credits, including running times, synopsis of the titles the authors were able to see, critical reception and awards, and critical analysis, including commentary on historical accuracy. Note is made of actors appearing in one dramatization who have appeared in others. For miniseries there is summary and analysis of each episode. *Elizabeth R* (1971) is described over 14 pages, and *The Tudors* (2007-2010) is examined in 43 pages. As with any such work, there is occasional sloppiness, as when the credits for *The*

Young Elizabeth, a 1964 BBC production, fails to list who plays the title character, but errors are rare. There is an introduction by Robison, a name-and-title index, a bibliography, and a helpful chronology. There are few photographs.—**Michael Adams**

1001.   Pitts, Michael R. **Western Movies: A Guide to 5,105 Feature Films.** Jefferson, N.C., McFarland, 2013. 483p. illus. index. $49.95pa. ISBN 13: 978-0-7864-6372-5.

The author of this title has written over 30 books on entertainment, including another title on Westerns from McFarland, *Western Film Series of the Sound Era* (see ARBA 2009, entry 1068). This title covers 5,105 western films from the silent era to the present, nearly 900 more than the 1st edition (1986). Pitts includes both Hollywood feature productions as well as Westerns made in other countries, frontier epics, north woods adventures, and nature productions. He also includes films that cross genres, such as horror western films and science fiction western films. The book is arranged in alphabetic order by film name and each includes: release company, year, whether it is in color or black-and-white, running time, list of cast members, a plot synopsis, and a brief critical review. More than 100 black-and-white photographs of movie stills and film posters accompany the text. The volume provides with two appendixes: a list of cowboys and cowgirls and their horses, and a list of screen names. A selected bibliography and a name/title index conclude the volume making the title easy to use for reference purposes. This updated 2d edition will be a useful addition in public libraries and in academic libraries offering film studies collections. It continues to be a highly recommended selection.—**Shannon Graff Hysell**

Handbooks and Yearbooks

1002.   **Contemporary Westerns: Film and Television since 1990.** Andrew Patrick Nelson, ed. Lanham, Md., Scarecrow, 2013. 178. index. 75.00. ISBN 13: 9780810892569.

Instead of a conventional chronological approach to tracing the history of American TV and movie westerns produced from 1990 on, this volume consists of 11 monographic essays by media-study academics, nine of which deal with individual titles, one with western themes utilized in science fiction films, and one on the career of country music singer George Straight who is supposedly the prototype of the modem non-traditional cowboy hero. The films analyzed begin (chronologically) with *Dances with Wolves* (1990) and end with the 2010 remake of *True Grit* (later releases like Quentin Tarantino's 2012 popular *Django Unchained* are not covered). Some of the other films analyzed include Clint Eastwood's 1992 *Unforgiven*, *No Country for Old Men* (2007), *There Will Be Blood* (2007) and *The Assassination of Jesse James by the Cowardly Robert Ford* (2007). There are separate chapters for the TV series *Deadwood* and *Justified*. Amazingly, there is a chapter on Ang Lee's 1999 *Rider with the Devil* but none for his ground-breaking *Brokeback Mountain* (2007). Other notable omissions include such titles as *Last of the Mohicans* (1992), *3:10 to Yuma* (2007) and *The Pledge* (2010). Accepting these limitations, the individual essays and an overview introduction by the editor supply much insightful information on the films discussed and are scholarly in nature and well documented. Some stress plot construction or character development others film techniques, script writing, and themes explored, both obvious and subtle. The main thrust, however, is twofold: how each differs from the classic western of earlier times and what are the distinct qualities and importance of each that makes it significant in film history. Each essay ends with copious footnotes and a list of works cited. The book ends with a brief name index mainly of film titles. This work will be of more value in library circulation departments rather than reference. As such, it is recommended for collections that emphasize media studies.—**John T. Gillespie**

1003.   **Directory of World Cinema: American Independent 2.** John Berra, ed. Intellect Books, Bristol, United Kingdom; distr., Chicago, University of Chicago Press, 2013. 397p. illus. $25.00. ISBN 13: 978-1-84150-612-8.

This is the 2d edition of American Independent, a series-within-the-series of *Directory of World Cinema*. It was made possible by dedicated contributors from the fields of film journalism and academic, whose different approaches enable an informed analysis of American independent cinema. Its rich history and cultural diversity are discussed. This entry covers key genres and thematic concepts and focuses on specific timely and socially relevant films and directors. Black-and-white illustrations add interest and information. Individual entries include film title, credits, synopsis, critique, cast, and year of release information. Some of the key topics covered in this 2d edition include: "Stardom," "The American Nightmare," "Brutal Youth," "Exploitation USA," and "Queer Cinema."

Sections on recommended reading, American independent cinema online, and notes on contributors complete the volume. If American independent cinema can be considered similar to the open road, then the editor hopes that this work will provide an appropriate route map to an, as yet, unspecified destination.—**Anita Zutis**

1004.   **Directory of World Cinema: Brazil.** Natalia Pinazza and Louis Bayman, eds. Bristol, United Kingdom, Intellect; distr., Chicago, University of Chicago Press, 2013. 320p. illus. index. $35.00pa. ISBN 13: 978-1-78320-009-2.

Motion pictures from Brazil have been getting noticed on the international stage in recent years, with prominent placing at global film festivals and high acclaim from critics. This volume can serve as both an introduction to the newcomer to Brazilian film as well as provide new information for scholars of Brazil's rich history in filmmaking. Much of the focus of the volume is on the genres featured in Brazil's film, including musicals and avant-garde styles. The work also addresses the many themes from this region, such as gender, indigenous and diasporic communities, Afro-Brazilian identity, class division, liberation struggles, and dictatorship. The editor never loses sight of the countries rich artistic and cultural history, making this work a worthwhile study of this country's film history.—**Shannon Graff Hysell**

1005.   **Directory of World Cinema: Russia 2.** Birgit Beumers, ed. Bristol, United Kingdom, Intellect; distr., Chicago, University of Chicago Press, 2013. 320p. illus. index. $35.00pa. ISBN 13: 978-1-7832-010-8.

This handbook on Russian film is a 2d edition of a previously published work. The focus of this work is on the key genre's found in Russian cinema, which differ somewhat from genres found in other parts of the world. For example, the main identifiable genres in Russian film are Cold War spy movies, science fiction, blockbusters, horror films, adventure films, and *chernukha* films and serials. This work builds off of the 1st edition, which focused primarily on the time of the tsars to the Putin era. The work provides introductory essays that provide director biographies, key players in Russian filmmaking, and the role of genres in filmmaking. Russia has a complex and fascinating history and this is reflected in the films that originate from this country.—**Richard W. Grefrath**

1006.   **Directory of World Cinema: Argentina.** Beatriz Urraca and Gary M. Kramer, eds. Bristol, United Kingdom, Intellect; distr., Chicago, University of Chicago Press, 2013. 320p. illus. index. $35.00pa. ISBN 13: 978-1-78320-007-8.

This is the 1st edition of *Argentina*, a volume with the *Directory of World Cinema* series from Intellect. It was created to help give Argentinean cinema some of the attention it has been lacking in recent years. The goal of the editor is to represent this country's vast array of cinematography efforts, which showcase its geographical area, rich history, and varied political concerns. Chapters highlight the Buenos Aires film festival, influential directors (e.g., Maria Luisa Bemberg, Pablo Trapero), and human rights dramas and groundbreaking documentaries. Film reviews from scholars, critics, and filmmakers are included, providing commentary on both blockbusters and small independent films. Other features include full-color stills, interviews, and trivia. Individual entries include film title, credits, synopsis, critique, cast, and year of release information. The work concludes with a list of recommended reading, Websites to go for more information, notes on the contributors, a glossary, and a brief filmography. This title and others in the series will be useful for students of film and will be useful in academic libraries.—**Shannon Graff Hysell**

1007.   **Directory of World Cinema: Latin America.** Isabel Maurer Queipo, ed. Bristol, United Kingdom, Intellect; distr., Chicago, University of Chicago Press, 2013. 251p. illus. index. $25.00pa. ISBN 13: 978-1-84150-618-0.

This is the 1st edition of *Latin America*, a volume with the *Directory of World Cinema* series from Intellect. It was created to help give Latin American cinema some of the attention it has been lacking in recent years. The goal of the editor is to represent Latin America's vast array of cinematography efforts, which showcase its vast geographical area, rich history, and varied political concerns. Its rich history and cultural diversity are discussed. The entries cover key genres and thematic concepts, and the work focuses on specific timely and socially relevant films and directors. The book is arranged into chapter according to genre. Color illustrations add interest and information. Individual entries include film title, credits, synopsis, critique, cast, and year of release information. The work concludes with a list of recommended reading, Websites to go for more information, notes on the contributors, a glossary, and a brief filmography. This title and others in the series will be useful for students of film and will be useful in academic libraries.—**Shannon Graff Hysell**

1008.   **Dracula's Daughters: The Female Vampire on Film.** Douglas Brode and Leah Deyneka, eds. Lanham, Md., Scarecrow, 2014. 310p. illus. index. $65.00; $64.99 (e-book). ISBN 13: 978-0-8108-9295-8; 978-0-8108-9296-5 (e-book).

Vampires have long been a popular cultural icon in Western films and have more recently come back into the spotlight with the public fascination with the Twilight fiction series of books and movies. While men were the original stars, women vampires have been popular in movies and television as well since their debut in *Dracula's Daughters* in 1936. In this volume the editors have compiled 16 essays that discuss women vampires in popular movies, television, book, and pop culture roles. A number of interesting topics are addressed within the essays, including the role of violence toward and by women, the reaction of these characters by feminists and antifeminists, and the role of race in the characterization of female vampires. The work includes more than 30 black-and-white photographs (mostly movie stills or movie posters) and a thorough introduction to the topic by editor Douglas Brode. This work can be recommended as a supplemental selection for academic film collections.—**Joseph L. Carlson**

1009.   Gitlin, Martin. **The Greatest Sitcoms of All Time.** Lanham, Md., Scarecrow, 2014. 419p. illus. index. $65.00; $64.99 (e-book). ISBN 13: 978-0-8108-8724-4; 978-0-8108-8725-1 (e-book).

The top 70 situation comedies (sitcoms) are ranked and described in Martin Gitlin's *The Greatest Sitcoms of All Time*. Shows such as *I Love Lucy*, *Arrested Development*, *Leave It to Beaver*, *30 Rock*, and *M*A*S*H* are included. Rankings are based on ratings, awards, impact, humor, legacy, and longevity, and each entry includes such information as cast members and character list, a black-and-white cast photograph, network and airing dates, ratings, an overview of the series and outstanding episodes, awards, sample dialogue, and fun facts. Appendixes list Emmy award-winners, top 10 sitcoms from each decade (1950s-2000s), the top male and female funniest sitcom characters of all time, and the 10 best sitcom spin-offs. An alphabetic index is also included. Students, scholars, and television fans will find this title of interest.—**Denise A. Garofalo**

1010.   **International Westerns: Re-Locating the Frontier.** Cynthia J. Miller and A. Bowdoin Van Riper, eds. Lanham, Md., Scarecrow, 2014. 447p. illus. index. $85.00; $84.99 (e-book). ISBN 13: 978-0-8108-9287-3; 978-0-8108-9288-0 (e-book).

While most American probably think that the western movie genre is unique to the United States, in fact there are many countries that celebrate this genre, including Asia, Central and Eastern Europe, and Latin America. This book presents 20 chapters organized into 5 subject-specific parts that look at the contributions other countries have made to the western film, how those films were received in their native country, and insight into how they challenge or support the image of the American western. Written by an international team of contributors this book looks at westerns that have come from France (*The*

Adventures of Lucky Joe), Brazil (*O Cangaceiro*), Eastern Europe (*Lemonade Joe*), and Asia (*Sukiyaki Western Django*), among others. The chapters include black-and-white photographs and all end with notes and a bibliography. This book will mainly be of interest to film scholars.—**Shannon Graff Hysell**

1011.   MacDonald, Laurence E. **The Invisible Art of Film Music: A Comprehensive History.** 2d ed. Lanham, Md., Scarecrow, 2013. 605p. index. $115.00pa.; $114.99 (e-book). ISBN 13: 978-0-8108-8297-0; 978-0-8108-8397-0 (e-book).

When the 1st edition of this history of Hollywood film music appeared in 1998, one reviewer called it "the best (history) available in the market." In this 2d edition, the author, a retired college professor, has expanded coverage to 2012. As in the 1st edition, a chronological arrangement is used to cover composers and their scores written as background music for films (Hollywood musicals like *Singin' in the Rain* are excluded). After a chapter on music that was used to accompany the silent films, each of the chapters that follows cover a decade of film history. These chapters begin with an overview of the decade, followed by year-by-year coverage. For each year, the author highlights a few outstanding scores and their composers, followed by a section, "Short Cuts," that mentions briefly a few other important film scores. For example, in the section "1939," Max Steiner's score for *Gone with the Wind* and Aaron Copeland's *Of Mice and Men*, get extensive coverage and brief mention is made of other film scores of the year by such composers as Erich Korngold and Dimitri Tiompkin. Each entry discusses both the music and the film (e.g., brief plot outlines). Coverage is nontechnical and anecdotal, often bordering on entertainment gossip. Scattered throughout the text are page-long profiles (each with a photograph) of 102 important composers beginning with Max Steiner and ending with Michael Giacchino, who composed the score for the 2009 animated feature *Ratatouille*. Each chapter also contains a list of sources used in the text. The book ends with an extensive six-page bibliography of books and articles on the subject of film music, followed by three indexes: the first on general topics, the second of film titles, and the third of names (because of the book's chronological arrangement the use of this index is essential to trace a composer's output). The book is both informative and entertaining. For a more scholarly approach to the subject Marvyn Cooke's *A History of Film Music* (Cambridge University Press, 2008) is recommended, but the present volume is also an excellent source of information on this subject.—**John T. Gillespie**

1012.   Niemi, Robert. **Inspired by True Events: An Illustrated Guide to More Than 500 History-Based Films.** Santa Barbara, Calif., ABC-CLIO, 2013. 606p. illus. index. $100.00. ISBN 13: 978-1-61069-197-0; 978-1-61069-198-7 (e-book).

Films inspired by true events have long been a stable of the motion picture world, and here Niemi, author of a number of books on cultural studies, surveys the field to judge the factualness of some of those works. The 500-plus films here include big screen fictionalizations, documentaries, and television films. Thus for every *The Benny Goodman Story* there is a *Say Amen, Somebody* or *Ken Burn's Jazz*. Perhaps space was a consideration, but some well-known films are missing, including *Till the Clouds Roll By* and *Five Pennies*. Some categories are left out altogether— literary biographies and true disasters (e.g., *Alive!*, any of the Titanic films). The volume divides into 10 broad topics—four on military history and one each on sports, music, art, labor/business, race relations, and crime. Films are arranged chronologically within each section, arranged first by specific event (e.g., basketball) and further chronologically by the film's release date. Most entries are two paragraphs long, although some are only a single paragraph. For each film Niemi gives a brief summation of the plot and cast and compares the film version to the actual events. Comparisons are brief, although whenever possible Niemi cites other books on which the film is based. Black-and-white stills are scattered throughout, and a secondary bibliography and index complete the work. Although handy as a single-volume guide to this genre, Niemi must be supplemented by a range of titles, including Mike Mayo's *Videohound's War Movies* (see ARBA 2000, entry 1198) and Ian Aitken's *Encyclopedia of the Documentary Film* (Routledge). This work is recommended for comprehensive film collections.—**Anthony J. Adam**

1013.   San Juan, Eric, and Jim McDevitt. **Hitchcock's Villains: Murders, Maniacs, and Mother Issues.** Lanham, Md., Scarecrow, 2013. 185p. illus. index. $38.00. ISBN 13: 978-0-8108-8775-6.

In 2011, San Juan and McDevitt wrote the well-received *A Year of Hitchcock* (Scarecrow Press), which analyzed the over 50 silent and sound films that Alfred Hitchcock directed. In this follow-up volume the same authors examine the various forms of villainy that have been portrayed in his films. Each of the nine forms of evil identified by the authors is dealt with in two chapters. The first surveys this topic as covered in all of Hitchcock's films and the second singles out one of these films for an in-depth analysis. For example, the chapter that deals with authority figures as villains, is followed by one that analyzes the actions and character of Alexander Sebastian (Claude Rains) in *Notorious* (1946), and the chapter featuring villainous mothers follows with a discussion of Bruno Anthony (Robert Walker) in *Strangers on a Train* (1951). Other chapters explore intellectual villains (*Rope*, 1948), innocent villains (*Vertigo*, 1958), and psychotic villains (*Psycho*, 1960). The films (and topics) are organized chronologically beginning with *Sabotage* (1936) and ending with Hitchcock's penultimate thriller, *Frenzy* (1972). Other important miscreants given a detailed, probing analyses are those in *Shadow of a Doubt* (1943) and *North by Northwest* (1959). The coverage is thorough and probing and the authors' insight into this material is impressive. The writing style is informal and often chatty. Scattered throughout the text are black-and-white stills from the highlighted films. The book closes with a three-page bibliography and a name index. Although the contents of this volume are perhaps too esoteric for general collections, it will be a fine addition to libraries specializing in film studies.—**John T. Gillespie**

1014.   Senn, Bryan. **The Most Dangerous Cinema: People Hunting People on Film.** Jefferson, N.C., McFarland, 2014. 286p. illus. index. $45.00pa. ISBN 13: 978-0-7864-3562-3; 978-1-4766-1357-4 (e-book).

In 1932, while filming the original *King Kong*, the producers at its studio, RKO, decided to use some of its sets and personnel to film another adventure story, *The Most Dangerous Game*. This is based on a 1924 short story of that title by Richard Connell and tells of a shipwrecked hunter who finds himself on a South Seas island deserted except for a huge mansion inhabited by a deranged count whose favorite sport is also hunting, but, in his case, the prey are those unfortunate humans who happen into his island lair. In the movie a love interest is added in the form of another captive played by Fay Wray, the screamer from *King Kong*. This book, by a frequent writer on films, explores the theme of humans hunting humans for sport and its variations as depicted in films and related media. Each of the first 14 chapters in this book is devoted to an analysis of a single film beginning with *The Most Dangerous Game* and ending with the unfunny comedy of 1997, *The Pest*, starring John Leguizamo. With the exception of a remake of *The Most Dangerous Game*, the 1945 *A Game of Death*, the movies dealt with are mostly trashy B films intended for the lower half of double bills. Titles like *Confessions of a Psycho Cat* (1968) and *Slave Girls Beyond Infinity* (1987) are typical, but, regardless of quality, the author lavishes each with perceptive scrutiny and telling analysis. Each chapter is divided into four parts: a detailed synopsis; behind-the-scenes information; a lengthy, perceptive critique (usually several pages); and production details. The last five chapters, which represent almost half of the book, are perhaps the most valuable. The first covers in less detail films with this theme that were either released directly to television or made specifically for television. The next covers 24 films where the human hunting human theme is present but as a secondary theme; for example, *The Hunting Party* of 1971 and *The Naked Prey* of 1966, which starred and was directed by Cornel Wild. Another chapter deals with movies in which humans hunt humans for the entertainment of others. Included here are the first of the *Hunger Games* movies (2012) and Schwarzenegger's 1987 film *The Running Man*. There follows a chapter devoted to science fiction films where aliens hunt humans, and lastly, a chapter on television games that also contain the hunting theme. The book ends with a section of chapter footnotes, a bibliography, and a name index. Scattered throughout the text are black-and-white illustrations, many of which are lobby cards for the films discussed. This is a fascinating, hugely entertaining book that will be particularly welcome in collections specializing in media studies.—**John T. Gillespie**

1015.   Terrace, Vincent. **Television Introductions: Narrated TV Program Openings Since 1949.** Lanham, Md., Scarecrow, 2014. 391p. index. $85.00; $84.99 (e-book). ISBN 13: 978-0-8108-9249-1; 978-0-8108-9250-7 (e-book).

Television programs past and present often have opening narrations; for example, for the 1950s show *Superman* it was "And who, disguised as Clark Kent, mild-mannered reporter for a great metropolitan newspaper, fights a never ending battle for truth, justice, and the American Way," and for the long-running Soap Opera *Days of Our Lives* it is "Like sands through the hour glass, so are the Days of Our Lives." Terrace's reference source is a directory of over 900 television series and their introductory vocal narratives. Terrace is also the author of 36 books on television, including the *Encyclopedia of Television Subjects, Themes and Settings* and *The Television Specials*. The programs are divided into alphabetically arranged chapters by specific genres: Comedy Programs, Drama and Adventure Programs, Westerns, Science Fiction Programs, Anthology Programs, Children's Programs, Soap Operas, Talk and Variety Programs, Game and Quiz Shows, and Court Programs. Each entry includes the name of the show; network where show aired; original broadcast years; brief description of plot, cast, theme (song), and opening narrative; and original ad pitches for products, including Sanka Coffee, Maybelline, Chrysler, and General Motors. If the narrative varies season by season this is reflected; for example, all *Twilight Zone* narrative changes are provided. The appendixes include an alphabetic listing of theme song credits and a list of televisions series available on DVD or VHS. Indexes are provided for actors, vocalists, and composers. Researchers can find entries for classic programs like *I Love Lucy*, *The Fugitive*, and *Jeopardy* as well as for the more obscure ones such as *The Adventures of Hiram Holliday*, *Mr. Terrific*, and *It's Always Jan.*

This reference guide should be of value to students of commercial broadcasting, communications and media studies, and to anybody interested in television history. It is recommended to public libraries and academic libraries supporting media and communications programs.—**Lucy Heckman**

1016.   Terrace, Vincent. **Television Specials: 5,336 Entertainment Programs, 1936-2012.** Jefferson, N.C., McFarland, 2013. 479p. index. $95.00pa. ISBN 13: 978-0-7864-7444-8; 978-1-4766-1240-9 (e-book).

This 2d edition updates the 1993 version with over 2,000 additional entries. The alphabetic listings include variety shows, holiday specials, award shows, dramas, musicals, and much more. Each record includes an entry number as well as a brief summary and additional information such as the host (if applicable), guest stars, director, producer, writer, music, cast, date aired, and the network. The index includes the entry number rather than the page number, which facilitates access to the information. Researchers, students, and television devotees will find this title of use.—**Denise A. Garofalo**

1017.   **Undead in the West II: They Just Keep Coming.** Cynthia J. Miller and A. Bowdoin Van Riper, eds. Lanham, Md., Scarecrow, 2013. 358p. illus. index. $75.00; $74.99 (e-book). ISBN 13: 978-0-8108-9264-4.

Focusing on portrayals of the western frontier and the undead in cinema and television, the first *Undead in the West* (2012) book confined its analysis to a specific medium. Here, Miller and Van Riper widen their editorial scope to essays examining a myriad of Western genre bending formats: pulp fiction, comics, board games, video games, and blogs. The volume is thematically partitioned into four segments, each reflecting an iconic element of traditional Western narratives: pioneers, lawmen and gunmen, men of god, and communities. The first collection of essays examines the pioneering work of Robert E. Howard, Joe R. Landsdale, and many other writers, in broadening the boundaries of the Weird Western. Complicating the simplistic binary of "good guy versus bad guy" in the Western narrative, the second collection of essays critically assess the genre hybridity of Stephen King's *The Gunslinger*, the development of steampunk horror, and the ideology of *Red Dead Redemption*. Encounters with the undead by men of faith shapes the third part of the volume, exploring Clint Eastwood's *Pale Rider* and the graphic novel *Priest*. Analyzing the concept of community in AMC's *The Walking Dead*, the role-playing game Deadlands, and fan Websites, the authors in the final section of the book parse concepts of gender, race, and national memory in portrayals and fans of the undead. Coupled with the first volume, Miller and Van Ripper have created a work of broad historical and critical synthesis. Ranging from pulp to video games, this robust collection of essays provides a much-needed foundational text in this ever-evolving genre. This work is recommended for both public and academic libraries, given the breadth and depth of the topic.—**Josh Eugene Finnell**

Indexes

1018. **Film and Television Literature Index: With Full Text. http://www.ebscohost.com/public/ film-television-literature-index-with-full-text.** [Website]. Ipswich, Mass., EBSCO. Price negotiated by site. Date reviewed: 2013.

Film and Television Literature Index covers material from some 300 periodicals, which are scanned for pertinent articles. Recently, it has included television periodicals as well. Since it was first issued in 1973, in print as *Film Literature Index*, it has developed an excellent reputation not only for its coverage of some 160 journals from 30 countries but also for its organization and ease of use. Developed originally as a pilot offering at SUNY-Albany with a grant from the New York State Council on the Arts, this work has continued without interruption and occupies a prominent position among such tools. The full text online offering includes *Variety* movie reviews from 1914 to the present.—**ARBA Staff Reviewer**

1019. **Film Indexes Online ProQuest Information and Learning. http://film.chadwyck.com/ home.** [Website]. Ann Arbor, Mich., ProQuest. Price negotiated by site. Date reviewed: 2013.

This resource is comprised of three valuable resources that have been brought together online under a single portal. The databases are Film Index International, the American Film Institute Catalog, and FIAF International Index to Film Periodicals. Subscribers to Chadwyck-Healey Film Indexes Online can search across these three resources or search the individual databases separately.

Film Index International offers records on international films that were released over the past 90 years and indexed by the British Film Institute. The database is updated twice each year and now consists of over 128,000 film records and more than 880,000 records on persons working in the film industry. This is a rapidly growing tool; for example, in 2009, 700 film and 21,000 person records were added. The record on each film includes information on director, cast, crews, year of release, production information, and awards. A synopsis of each film is included. Person records give biographical information, awards, and films in which the individual appeared. There are references from film journals within the records, and also links among the records so that the user can navigate between the records in the database.

American Film Institute Catalog has long been a standard for American film information. Its scope is the history of American film from 1893 to 1974, with records for selected major films from 1975-2008. The print catalog is updated annually. This database is also updated twice per year.

The International Index to Film Periodicals indexes scholarly film periodicals. This database is provided by the International Federation of Film Archives. The index begins in 1972 and extends to present day. It is searchable by topic, not just by film title, and thus adds a type of accessibility unavailable through the Film Index International above.—**Anna H. Perrault**

Theater

Biography

1020.   **International Women Stage Directors.** Anne Fliotsos and Wendy Vierow, eds. Champaign, Ill., University of Illinois Press, 2013. 327p. index. $60.00. ISBN 13: 978-0-252-03781-8.

Anne Fliotsos and Wendy Vierow follow their *American Women Stage Directors of the Twentieth Century* (see ARBA 2009, entry 1073) with this detailed overview of women working in 24 countries. Each essay is by someone who has lived or worked in the country in question. The entries offer accounts of early women directors, examinations of the working climates in the twenty-first century, and profiles of three to five representative contemporary directors, including such well-known figures as Ariane Mnouchkine of France and Garry Hynes of Ireland. The profiles are full of interesting details. The productions of Lída Engelová of the Czech Republic have been informed by her experience as an intern to Great Britain's legendary Peter Brook. India's Zuleikha Chaudhari, whose mother is director Amal Allana, presented Henrik Ibsen's *John Gabriel Borkman* as if it were a series of paintings. The staging of William Shakespeare's *Macbeth* by Maja Kleczewska of Poland emphasized sex and violence and was compared to Quentin Tarantino's *Pulp Fiction*. Mumbi Kaigwa of Kenya staged Eve Ensler's *The Vagina Monologues* even though using the word vagina in public was forbidden. There are many other accounts of how these directors have dealt with societal pressures. This valuable study includes photographs of some directors and their productions; a forward by Roberta Levitow, founder of Theatre Without Borders; an introduction by Fliotsos; profiles of the contributors; and a name, title, and subject index.—**Michael Adams**

Catalogs and Collections

1021.   **American Drama. http://www.proquest.com/en-US/catalogs/databases/detail/american_ drama.shtml.** [Website]. Bethesda, Md., ProQuest. Price negotiated by site. Date reviewed: 2013.

This ProQuest database offers online access by play, title, keywords, character, place, date of first performance, and genre to more than 1,500 plays by 500 playwrights from 1714 to 1915, although plans seem to be afoot to expand the scope. ProQuest also lists several other theater databases: *Source Materials in the Field of Theater*, *Twentieth-Century Drama* (2,500 plays in English from around the world), and *English Drama*, which contains more than 3,900 plays from 1280 to 1915.—**Anna H. Perrault**

1022.   **Lortel Archives: The Internet Off-Broadway Database. http://www.lortel.org/LLA_ archive/index.cfm.** [Website]. Free. Date reviewed: 2013.

Echoing the Internet Broadway Database (IBDB), the Lortel Archives attempts to provide users the same kind of searchable resource for off-Broadway productions. The scope of the database includes play titles, casts, and crews from productions that appeared in houses with between 100 and 499 seats, the range of seating that defines off-Broadway in labor contracts. The site states that its staff members have entered complete off-Broadway seasons going back to 1958 (more than 5,000 shows as of January 2009). Through an advanced search, the database is accessible by actor name, company name, play title, playwright, crew members, or awards. Like the IBDB, search results produce first a clickable name; once clicked, a list of productions from the individual appears (in reverse chronological order). A further click on the show title brings up the listings from the programs. A click on individual names or company names will yield a list of credits. Clicking on a venue will produce a list of plays produced there. If used in conjunction with the IBDB, the Lortel site will give researchers a fuller picture of the careers of actors, playwrights, production companies, and other theatrical practitioners on the New York City scene.—**ARBA Staff Reviewer**

1023.   **North American Theatre Online. http://asp6new.alexanderstreet.com/antho/index.shtml.** [Website]. Alexandria, Va., Alexander Street. Price negotiated by site. Date reviewed: 2013.

This is an essential tool for ferreting out plays, performers, theater artists, and other information on theater in the United States and Canada. The site provides online access to dozens of theater reference works going back into the nineteenth century (categorized either as primary or secondary material), including a 1919 history of the American theater, *The Oxford Companion to the American Theatre* by Gerald Boardman, *A Record of the Boston Stage* (published in 1853), *Notable Women in the American Theatre: A Biographical Dictionary* (Greenwood Press, 1989), and *American Theatre: A Chronicle of Comedy and Drama 1969-2000* by Thomas Hischack. Information can be found on most theatrical professionals from the twentieth century and many from the nineteenth century, through either a simple search or in an alphabetic listing. Calling up names gives the user access to their mentions in the indexed reference material; for playwrights, users also may find complete play texts, because the database accesses the other drama full-text databases published by Alexander Street. The interface is basic and easily usable; a table of contents gives access to a list of works indexed as well as indexes of people, plays, productions, companies, years, characters, and subjects. The site also features photographs and playbills from image databases, including the Theatre Scrapbook Collection at Virginia Tech. This resource is a great place to start when researching an American theater, performer or artist, and it is a fair substitute for a basic collection of theater reference. The database is as good as the material fed into it, and the works used are among the foundations of theater research.—**Anna H. Perrault**

1024.   **Theatre Communications Group Tools & Research. http://www.tcg.org/tools/index.cfm.** [Website]. $550.00 (institution); $35.00 (individual). Date reviewed: 2013.

Founded in 1961 with a grant from the Ford Foundation, the Theatre Communications Group serves as a national organization and advocacy group for regional theaters in the United States. The group has more than 700 member theaters and 12,000 individual memberships. In additional to its extensive publications division, the group features a Website with numerous resources for researching trends in employment and theatrical production. The advantage to the researcher lies in the picture the site gives of American theaters outside of New York City. The Theatre Profiles section features a searchable database of profiles of member theaters; some of the profiles go back to 1995. Information provided includes an annual budget figure, seating capacity, and an artistic statement. The Theatre Facts series provides a yearly overview of the financial state of American nonprofit theaters. In addition, the site has an index to American Theatre. Some materials are open only to members. A recent addition, New Plays in Production, features production information and press on world premier plays presented at member theaters.—**Anna H. Perrault**

Chronology

1025.   Wearing, J. P. **The London Stage 1890-1899: A Calendar of Productions, Performers, and Personnel.** 2d ed. Lanham, Md., Scarecrow, 2014. 609p. index. $125.00; $119.99 (e-book). ISBN 13: 978-0-8108-9281-1; 978-0-8108-9282-8 (e-book).

1026.   Wearing, J. P. **The London Stage 1900-1909: A Calendar of Productions, Performers, and Personnel.** Lanham, Md., Scarecrow, 2014. 709p. index. $150.00; $149.99 (e-book). ISBN 13: 978-0-8108-9293-4; 978-0-8108-9294-1 (e-book).

1027.   Wearing, J. P. **The London Stage 1910-1919: A Calendar of Productions, Performers, and Personnel.** 2d ed. Lanham, Md., Scarecrow, 2014. 773p. index. $150.00; $149.99 (e-book). ISBN 13: 978-0-8108-9299-6; 978-0-8108-9300-9 (e-book).

The 1st editions of these volumes were published in 1976, nearly 40 years ago. Since that time several new research aids have become available in the form of digitization of newspapers and periodicals, making this update a worthwhile purchase. The 2d editions provide a chronological calendar of London productions from January 1890 through December 1899; from January 1900 through December 1909; and from January 1910 through December 1919. More than 20 percent of the material is new to these editions, particularly information on adaptations and translations, plot sources, and comments. *The London Stage 1890-1899* chronicles more than 3,000 productions at over 30 London theaters. *The London Stage 1900-1909* presents more than 3,000 productions at 35 major central London theaters. *The London Stage 1910-1919* chronicles some 3,000 productions at 35 major central London theaters during this 10-year span. For each users will find the following information: title, author, theater, actors, assisting personnel, opening and closing dates, and the number of performances. There is also information on the type of genre, the number of acts, and reviews. Comments have been expanded in this edition and include details on the plot, audience reception, and noteworthy performances. The works are thoroughly indexed by play title, genre, and theater. A longer general index provides users access. These volumes will be useful in academic and public libraries where theater students, writers, and theater historians will have access to their many treasures.—**Shannon Graff Hysell**

Dictionaries and Encyclopedias

1028.	Grantley, Darryll. **Historical Dictionary of British Theatre Early Period.** Lanham, Md., Scarecrow, 2013. 519p. (Historical Dictionaries of Literature and the Arts). $125.00; $119.99 (e-book). ISBN 13: 978-08108-6762-8; 978-0-8108-8028-3 (e-book).

This volume is part of the Historical Dictionaries of Literature and the Arts series from Scarecrow Press. It deals with British theater from its earliest stage presentations (1311 C.E.) to 1899. The dictionary's entries cover authors, trends, genres, literary and historical concepts, plays, actors, and great eras.

A year-by-year chronology that highlights important theatrical events leads off the volume. That is followed by a condensed historical essay. The author divides his essay into historical eras. The alphabetically organized entries include some of the greatest playwrights of all time—William Shakespeare, Christopher Marlowe, and George Bernard Shaw.

A very extensive bibliography organized by eras closes this handy volume. There are no indexes, but there is extensive cross-referencing in the dictionary entries. The dictionary entry portion of the book is nearly 450 large type pages. This book can be of great value as an introduction to the early British theater, which can make for pleasant reading and lead to further research. It will be of interest to both the general reader interested in the theater as well as theater scholars. It covers periods that not well known or well documented making it useful to a broad range of readers.—**Charles Neuringer**

1029.	**Musicals 101: The Cyber Encyclopedia of Musical Theatre, TV and Film. http://www. musicals101.com/.** [Website]. Free. Date reviewed: 2013.

This is an entertaining Website offering a great deal of information about musicals, with pages on musical theater history, on staging musicals, and on the elements that go into creating musicals. There are numerous reviews of shows, recordings, books, and DVDs, as well as features on famous composers, lyricists, and performers. It will be a great site for researchers of the history of musicals as well as musical theater buffs.—**ARBA Staff Reviewer**

1030.	Sampson, Henry T. **Blacks in Blackface: A Sourcebook on Early Black Musical Shows.** Lanham, Md., Scarecrow, 2014. 2v. illus. index. $250.00/set; $249.99 (e-book). ISBN 13: 978-0-8108-8350-5; 978-0-8108-8351-2 (e-book).

As a follow-up to his earlier book *The Ghost Walks*, which covered the period 1865 to 1910, Sampson in *Blacks in Blackface* focuses on African American musical entertainment between 1900 and 1940. The range of genres is fascinating, including vaudeville and nightclub acts but also minstrel shows, medicine shows, circus sideshows, carnivals, and other forms of variety. Rather than critically analyzing the era, Sampson lets the contemporary commentators speak for themselves through hundreds of brief reviews almost exclusively from the African American press from across the United States. As an introduction to forgotten performers or a reminder of the greats of this period, the reviews are eminently browsable and often illuminate the difficulties black performers had getting and keeping jobs at that time. Each chapter gathers reviews on a specialized topic, such as black theatres or cabarets, and a series of appendixes list shows, theatres, and routings for the TOBA and Dudley Circuits, the main avenues for black performers before World War II. Black-and-white photographs are scattered throughout the volumes. As interesting as these volumes are, the chronological rather than by performer organization of the chapters weakens the ease of use, and spot checking the index against the text revealed problems in citing individuals. Despite that difficulty, Sampson is an excellent primary sourcebook for African American musical entertainment that will be a fine addition for all large academic and public libraries.—**Anthony J. Adam**

Handbooks and Yearbooks

1031.   **Theories of the Avant-Garde Theatre: A Casebook from Kleist to Camus.** Bert Cardullo, ed. Lanham, Md., Scarecrow, 2013. 185p. index. $75.00; $74.99 (e-book). ISBN 13: 978-0-8108-8704-6; 978-0-8108-8705-3 (e-book).

This work is a collection of essays and articles written by many of the key leaders in the avant-garde theater movement of the late nineteenth and twentieth centuries. Writers include directors, playwrights, performers, and designers and the writing varies from discussions of specific plays or theater performances to national movements to theories of the avant-garde movement. The authors include such seminal artists as Antonin Artaud, Alfred Jarry, Luigi Pirandello, and August Strindberg. The articles demonstrate the dramatic shift in the aesthetics of theater during this time frame and the desire to create a new, distinctive type of theater apart from the traditional. Chapters vary in length from a few pages to over 10 pages and the writing style is equally as diverse, with some essays being easy to comprehend and others more scholarly in their approach. As such, this volume will be most useful in the hands of theater scholars interested in theater history in general or the avant-garde movement in particular.—**Charles Neuringer**

28 Philosophy and Religion

Philosophy

Bibliography

1032. PhilPapers: Online Papers in Philosophy. http://philpapers.org/. [Website]. Free. Date reviewed: 2013.

PhilPapers is a comprehensive directory with links to online articles and books by academic philosophers designed to facilitate the exchange and development of philosophical research through the Internet. It gathers and organizes philosophical research from journals, archives, and personal papers, and provides tools for philosophers to access, organize, and discuss this research. Manuscripts can be submitted for discussion, too. PhilPapers started in 2006 as part of MindPapers, and now includes much of the material from Online Papers in Philosophy. The developers of this resource understand that philosophy is about "the argument" and so they make available opportunities for discussion, categorization, and editing of papers. The coverage is good, too: a search on "animal ethics" yielded 402 items and they were categorized into a handy group of five subtopics ranging from "animal cruelty" to "vegetarianism." Some features require that users sign in, but creating an account is easy and free.

Included with PhilPapers is *Contemporary Philosophy of the Mind: An Annotated Bibliography* (http://consc.net/mindpapers). This is a collection of the texts of over 28,000 papers in *Philosophy of the Mind* and the *Science of Consciousness*. The library is organized by eight major themes, and then further subdivided by topic. Both online and print items are included with links to those that are freely available online.—**Anna H. Perrault**

Catalogs and Collections

1033. The Philosophy Documentation Center (PDC). http://www.pdcnet.org/. [Website]. Charlottesville, Va., Philosophy Documentation Center. Free with additional subscription services. Date reviewed: 2013.

The PDC provides access to information resources in philosophy, applied ethics, religious studies, classics, and fields related to the discipline of philosophy. The nonprofit Center, which began its work in 1966, has grown over the years to offer membership management for professional organizations, secure hosting of full-text, service as a fulfillment house for print and electronic journals, rights and permissions management, conference registration management, and otherwise ranging services to the philosophy researcher, associations, and libraries.

New products of the PDC include the Philosophy Research Index. This is advertised on the Center's Website as the new standard for bibliographic research in philosophy, and it will compete with the older Philosopher's Index. Another new product offered by the PC is the e-collection, which contains complete electronic coverage of 90 journals and other series publication, with each article accompanied by permission and copyright information. Libraries are also offered a Collection Development Bundle consisting of access to some 20 journals in the field. Most of those that are offered are recent (1990 forward) but a few date back to the 1920s. Finally, the newly available (since 2010) online *International Directory of Philosophy* (http://secure.pdcnet.org/idphil) consolidates the long-running print tools *Directory of American Philosophers*, and the *International Directory of Philosophy and Philosophers*. The print directories continue to be published by PDC as well. The PDC is still growing in its offerings, and so the librarian will do well to make contact about the host of products and services available to the discipline and those interested in it.—**Anna H. Perrault**

Dictionaries and Encyclopedias

1034.   Diethe, Carol. **Historical Dictionary of Nietzcheanism.** 3d ed. Lanham, Md., Scarecrow, 2014. 433p. (Historical Dictionaries of Religions, Philosophies, and Movements). $120.00; $119.99 (e-book). ISBN 13: 978-0-8108-8031-3; 978-0-8108-8032-0 (e-book).

Diethe's expanded 3d edition of her *Historical Dictionary of Nietzscheanism* fulfills its goals admirably. A lengthy introductory essay details the reception of Nietzsche's works and its effects on scholarship throughout Europe and in Japan, China, Russia, and the United States. The bulk of the volume is composed of short entries on Nietzsche's works and ideas, and on the persons, concepts, and phrases significant to his life. The book includes several photographs of Nietzsche and people and places related to him.

Most historical dictionaries on philosophical topics or thinkers should not include photographs or extensive biographical information; in the case of Nietzsche, such materials and information is crucial. Nietzsche's writings are both deeply personal and cryptic. This work seeks to illuminate not by ignoring the difficulties of Nietzsche scholarship, but by making information available to scholars and novices alike. Indeed, this volume would be an excellent introduction to Nietzscheanism, and it should help answer questions posed by those more familiar with his work. This volume will be useful to students and researchers needing information on Nietzsche's life, works, and teachings.—**Delilah R. Caldwell**

1035.   **Encyclopedia of Philosophy and the Social Sciences.** Byron Kaldis, ed. Thousand Oaks, Calif., Sage, 2013. 2v. index. $350.00/set. ISBN 13: 978-1-4129-8689-2.

The studies of philosophy and the social sciences have long been interconnected but rarely has their interdisciplinary nature been examined so thoroughly as it is in this multivolume set. This comprehensive two-volume encyclopedia covers the major theories, research, and issues in the interdisciplinary and multidisciplinary study of the links between philosophy and the social sciences. Many of the topics discussed are at the cutting edge of this topic and some are controversial in nature. Editor Byron Kaldis from the Hellenic Open University in Greece, assembled international experts in the field to write more than 150 entries.

The work contributes to the renewal of the philosophy of the social sciences and will help to promote new modes of thinking about classic problems of society. The entries are diverse in nature, touching on economics, sociology, ethics, genealogy, and more. Entries range from about 600 to 2,000 words, with related entries, further readings, and Websites noted. Entries are listed alphabetically and by theme, and an index completes both volumes. Several longer framing essays provide an overview of contemporary research. Addressing complex philosophical topics, the *Encyclopedia of Philosophy and the Social Sciences* is a cohesive, usable reference source for both public and academic libraries and is well worth its high price.—**Margot Note**

1036.   **Meta-Encyclopedia of Philosophy. http://www.ditext.com/encyc/frame.html.** [Website]. Free. Date reviewed: 2013.

This is a dynamic resource that enables the user to compare topics in key online philosophy reference tools. The user can compare entries in Runes, IEP, SEP, *Dictionary of the Philosophy of the Mind*, *The Ism Book*, the 1913 *Catholic Encyclopedia*, and *Dictionary of Philosophical Terms and Names*. Arranged alphabetically, the Meta-Encyclopedia retrieves entries and associated sources in a simple data format that can be clicked for full information. While this resource lacks visual appeal and extensive documentation, the feature allowing for comparisons across seven electronic tools is worthwhile.—**ARBA Staff Reviewer**

1037.   **Stanford Encyclopedia of Philosophy. http://plato.stanford.edu/.** [Website]. Metaphysics Research Lab, CSLI, Stanford University. Date reviewed: 2013.

This open-access database offers scholarship refereed by members of a distinguished editorial board. This dynamic reference work maintains academic standards while evolving and adapting in response to new research. Users can cite fixed editions that are created on a quarterly basis and stored in the site's Archives (every entry contains a link to its complete archival history, identifying the fixed edition the reader should cite). The table of contents lists entries that are published or assigned. The site also provides a projected table of contents that lists entries which are currently unassigned but projected.—**Noriko Asato**

Indexes

1038.   **Philosopher's Index. http://philindex.org/.** [Website]. Ipswich, Mass., EBSCO. Price negotiated by site. Date reviewed: 2013.

Available in print and online editions, this index is the leading bibliography of scholarly articles from 1,500 journals coming from 139 countries in 37 languages. The literature coverage dates back to 1940 and includes print and electronic journals, books, anthologies, contributions to anthologies, and book reviews. Covering scholarly research in all major areas of philosophy, The Index features informative, author-written abstracts. The extensive indexing, which includes proper names along with subject terms, enhances the search capability.—**Noriko Asato**

Religion

General Works

Catalogs and Collections

1039.   **Association of Religious Data Archives (ARDA). http://www.thearda.com/.** [Website]. Free. Date reviewed: 2013.

ARDA strives to democratize access to the best data on religion. Founded as the American Religion Data Archive in 1997 and going online in 1998, the initial archive was targeted at researchers interested in American religion. Since 1998, the database has been expanded in both audience and data collection now including American and international collections and developing features for educators, journalists, religious congregations, and researchers. Contributors to the data included in the ARDA include the foremost religion scholars and research centers in the world. It is currently housed in the Social Science Research Institute, the College of Liberal Arts, and the Department of Sociology at the Pennsylvania State University.—**William O. Scheeren**

1040.   **Religion & Philosophy Collection. http://www.ebscohost.com.** [Website]. Ipswich, Mass., EBSCO. Price negotiated by site. Date reviewed: 2013.

This is a comprehensive database of full-text articles and reviews on topics such as world religions, major religious denominations, biblical studies, religious history, epistemology, political philosophy, moral philosophy, and the history of philosophy. The collection provides access to more than 300 full-text journals and its coverage of the subject areas listed is extensive. *Religion & Philosophy Collection* is an essential tool for scholars searching for journal articles, librarians seeking book reviews, or the general user wanting magazine articles or photographs and other graphic materials. Searching through the EBSCO system is familiar to librarians and scholars and allows for differentiation between scholarly journals that are peer reviewed or not, magazines, and book reviews; limiting by document type, date of publication, and type of image; and the choice of EBSCO's "visual search" or other search options (e.g., Boolean or Smart Text Searching).—**Anna H. Perrault**

1041.   **Religion Data Archive. http://www.thearda.com.** [Website]. Free. Date reviewed: 2013.

The ARDA, which was founded as the American Religion Data Archive in 1997, provides statistical information on all manner of religious topics, both U.S. and international in scope. Housed at the Pennsylvania State University, the ARDA Data Archive is a collection of surveys, polls, and other statistical data on denominational memberships, data from surveys of the public and denominational members, and geographical information. Especially useful are the denominational family trees and profiles. This collection of data archives is available on the organization's free Website. It is funded by the Lilly Endowment, the John Templeton Foundation, and the Pennsylvania State University. The best approach to locating needed data is to browse files by category, alphabetically, view the newest additions, most popular files, or search for a file. After a file has been selected, the user can preview the results, learn about how the data were identified and collected, save survey questions, and download the data file. The ARDA website also includes materials and ideas for teachers (the learning center), information for the press (the press room), and resources for congregations.—**Anna H. Perrault**

1042.   **Wabash Center Internet Resources in Theology and Religion. http://www.wabashcenter. wabash.edu/resources/guide_headings.aspx.** [Website]. Charles K. Bellinger, ed. Free. Date reviewed: 2013.

The Wabash Center provides broad support for teachers of religion and theology in institutions of higher education. Along with grants, workshops, consulting, and the publication of a peer-reviewed scholarly journal, the Center has a selective annotated guide to Internet resources. Subject headings for the guide include best of the Web; aspects of religion; religious thought, archaeology, Bible, and classics; religions (organized by faith tradition); geographical or demographic groups; Christianity; and pedagogy. An especially useful feature from the latter is the "syllabi collection," a collaborative project between the American academy of Religion and the Wabash Center that provides access to and sharing of syllabi on a variety of topics from teachers at numerous universities and seminaries.—**Anna H. Perrault**

Dictionaries and Encyclopedias

1043.   **The Encyclopedia of Caribbean Religions.** Patrick Taylor and Frederick I. Case, eds. Champaign, Ill., University of Illinois Press, 2013. 2v. index. $250.00/set. ISBN 13: 978-0-252-03723-8.

This reference source lies at the juncture of religion and regional geography. It employs varied approaches to provide data about the various religions in the Caribbean. This area includes the islands of the West Indies, the greater and lesser Antilles, and select portions of the northern coast of South America (Guyana, Guyane, and Suriname).

The editors and contributors approach the subject through ethnic groups (Maya, Nago), geography of nations (Cuba, Guyana, Bahamas, Jamaica), religions (Christianity, Islam, Judaism, Hinduism, Krishna, and Kumina), denominations (Lutheran Church, Methodist Church), and ceremonies and culture (African Caribbean Funerary Rites, Carnival, Nation Dance, Quimbois, Vodou). Many topical articles are subdivided geographically, sometimes with separate contributors. These include detailed descriptions of rituals and sacred practices by Maya, and tables illustrating the varied Orisha rites of the Santeria.

Articles devoted to geographic territories present an overview of the religions, indigenous and currently used languages, culture, and societies of the country or island, followed by some specific religious rites or traditions practiced there. In the entry on Cuba, for instance, in 26 pages 5 contributors discuss government relations to churches, various popular religions and rituals, and how art, film, and music manifest themselves in the country.

Many of the articles explain their historical background, such as the entry on Mennonites, and clarifies its differences with other religions. Entries are followed by substantial bibliographies, with some sources written in Spanish. Linkage is achieved through several cross-references (indicated by bold font) and a quality index. Volume 1 concludes with 16 color plates, mostly art works, with high image quality. The only downside is the presence of but one map, prior to the title page of each volume. This encyclopedia serves as an in-depth resource for those interested in Caribbean geography, religions, or languages.—**Ralph Hartsock**

1044.   **Encyclopedia of Religious Controversies in the United States.** 2d ed. Bill J. Leonard and Jill Y. Crainshaw, eds. Santa Barbara, Calif., ABC-CLIO, 2013. 2v. illus. index. $189.00/set. ISBN 13: 978-1-59884-867-0; 978-1-59884-868-7 (e-book).

The United States is a religiously pluralistic society that has experienced many religious controversies from its colonial origins in the seventeenth century through the present. Shriver and Leonard have conceived and edited a useful reference work that admirably surveys the main topics of U.S. religious controversies. It consists of more than 400 entries by some 50 qualified contributors and covers people (Wallie Amos Criswell, Joseph Smith, Jr.), concepts (anti-Semitism, feminism), groups (Branch Davidians, Jehovah's Witnesses), and events (Antinomian Crisis, Scopes Trial). This updated edition gives particular attention to new religious trends and the controversies surrounding sexuality, gender, race, and politics. There is also a strong focus on the inner struggles going on within many Christian denominations and the differing viewpoints over doctrine and practice within the church. Many of the entries from the 1st edition have been updated with new commentary and more recent bibliographies. Individual entries range from about 250 to 1,500 words and include a bibliography for further reading. Cross-references are provided to related entries and are provided in bold text. A master bibliography of about 350 books on religious controversies and a general index conclude the volume. This fine encyclopedia belongs in any library with an interest in U.S. religion.—**ARBA Staff Reviewer**

Handbooks and Yearbooks

1045.   Omer, Atalia, and Jason A. Springs. **Religious Nationalism: A Reference Handbook.** Santa Barbara, Calif., ABC-CLIO, 2013. 328p. index. (Contemporary World Issues). $58.00. ISBN 13: 978-1-59884-439-9; 978-1-59884-440-5 (e-book).

In this investigation of religious nationalism the authors provide an account of how different forms of religious nationalism emerge and examine the debates about whether nationalism is a recent development or predates the modern era. Two objectives dominate its writing: to challenge the common understanding that religious nationalism is a uniquely volatile and anti-modern form of nationalism; and to challenge the idea that secular nationalism is more stable than religious nationalism. The debates that encircle these two questions are taken up in chapters 1-3, and are organized around four questions: Is religion uniquely prone to cause violence? What are the links between organized religion, the potentially harmful and potentially beneficial ways that religiously motivated actors and ideas might be present in public and political life, and the links between manifestations and assertions of national identity? How does the inter-relation of religion and nationalism challenge the idea that the religious and the secular are distinct and easily separable? Why is nationalism itself a form of religion? In answering these questions the authors explore possibilities for thinking differently about the ways that national and religious forms of identification have and do intersect, reinforce, or conflict with one another. These debates comprise the heart of this book and make it a valuable supplement to college courses in the humanities and social sciences examining the concept of religious nationalism. The authors open up future paths for exploration and debate for a contemporary issue that is puzzling to many because of its historical depth and emotional nature. The authors complete this book by providing valuable resources (chapters 4-8) for the reader or potential researcher including chronologies of religious nationalism and conflict zones, biographical sketches, dates and documents, a directory of organizations, and print resources. A thorough glossary is provided for those who require more information about people, concepts, events, and documents.—**Joseph P. Hester**

1046.   **The Religions of Canadians.** Jamie S. Scott, ed. Toronto, University of Toronto Press, 2012. 468p. illus. index. $46.95. ISBN 13: 978-1-4426-0516-9.

Stressing religion as a cultural phenomenon and as having community importance, this volume pays homage to the cultural significance of religion in Canada illustrating Canadian society's multicultural development and social diversity. Drawing on the expertise of scholars from various academic fields, the chapters in this book introduce the beliefs and practices of nine major religious Canadian religions that have shaped and continue to shape Canadian culture, social, and legal practices. Important to teachers and students especially, each of these nine chapters provides the following information: definitions of key terms, key dates relating to this particular religion, key readings, key Websites, and key questions for dialogue and discussion. The book has two major appendixes providing 2001 census data of selected religions and by immigrant status within selected time periods. For the scholar or student of North American religion, this volume is highly recommended.—**Joseph P. Hester**

Bible Studies

Atlases

1047.   Lawrence, Paul. Johnson, Richardson, ed. **The IVP Concise Atlas of Bible History.** Downers Grove, Ill., InterVarsity Press, 2013. 191p. illus. maps. index. $20.00. ISBN 13: 978-0-8308-2928-6.

This book is a shortened version of the 2006 classic *IVP Atlas of Bible History* (see ARBA 2007, entry 1094), which has been updated with a newer four-color design and made easier to carry. There are over 100 maps, a number of panoramic reconstructions, numerous site plans, chronological charts, and an index and gazetteer. Bible history from Creation to the 4th century C.E. is covered. One of the more interesting sections covers the great archives and libraries of the ancient world, featuring Mesopotamia, Egypt, Palestine, the Persian Empire, the Greek world, the Roman world, and a short discussion of what manuscripts survive to the present day. The maps, reconstructions, and photographs provide a wonderful reference work for the present-day student of the Bible, as well as an excellent resource for any library.—**Bradford Lee Eden**

Dictionaries and Encyclopedias

1048.   Taliaferro, Bradford B. **Encyclopedia of English Language Bible Versions.** Jefferson, N.C., McFarland, 2013. 543p. index. $75.00pa. ISBN 13: 978-0-7864-7121-8.

For those scholars and enthusiasts of biblical studies this will be an interesting reference tool. It covers 1,400 versions of the Bible that are in English. The user of this tool will need to read the preface to learn how to use this encyclopedia. It is not an easy reference source to use for the non-scholar of the Bible. There is a list of abbreviations, a glossary with short definitions, and a list of tables. This is followed by the versions of the Bible arranged alphabetically. There are many cross-references in the entries that refer to other works on the Bible in English. Five passages from the Bible are given to show examples of the version. The *Encyclopedia* has a list of translators, revisers, and editors with some having short biographies, but most have notes referring to another biographical source. There are 10 appendixes that cover variants, confusing names, list of unfinished or abandoned Bibles, and other topics. There is bibliography and an index. The *Encyclopedia* has a Website at EELBV.biblereadsmuseum.com. This encyclopedia is recommended to Bible colleges, seminaries, and to scholars of the Bible.—**Benet Steven Exton**

Handbooks and Yearbooks

1049.   **Handbook for Biblical Interpretation: An Essential Guide to Methods, Terms, and Concepts.** 2d ed. W. Randolph Tate, ed. Grand Rapids, Mich., Baker Academic, 2012. 528p. index. $39.99. ISBN 13: 978-0-8010-4862-3.

W. Randolph Tate professor at Evangel University and the author of *Biblical Interpretation: An Integrated Approach* (2008) in the preface of his 1st edition says this about the handbook: "It is essentially an extended glossary of the terminology currently used in interpreting the Bible." In his 2d edition he has deleted some "terms that lacked clear relevance to literary concerns," removed appendixes A and B since they were similar to a biblical commentary, naturally added more terms, updated the indexes, and changed the name of the handbook to avoid confusion with his other book. There is an abbreviation list at the front of the book. Many of the entries have one bibliographic reference at the end. The length of the entries varies. There is cross-referencing. There are no maps or illustrations. The bibliography is divided into: critical theory: general; critical theory: biblical; hermeneutics; Bible as literature; general biblical studies: Hebrew Bible; and general biblical studies: New Testament. There are an authors' index and a scripture index. This book is recommended to academic and theological libraries. [R: Choice, June 13, p. 1802]—**Benet Steven Exton**

1050.   **Old Testament Pseudepigrapha: More Noncanonical Scriptures. Volume 1.** Richard Bauckham, James R. Davila, and Alexander Panayotov, eds. Grand Rapids, Mich., William B. Eerdmans, 2013. 808p. index. $90.00. ISBN 13: 978-0-8028-2739-5.

This work, which will ultimately be part of a two-volume set, sets out to assemble Old Testament pseudepigrapha that have not been included in other, recent collections, such as James H. Charlesworth's *The Old Testament Pseudepigrapha*. In addition, with a few exceptions, works that are included in other collections, such as the Dead Sea Scrolls, are not included, as Bauckham, Davila, and Panyotov strive to introduce readers to potentially unfamiliar writings. The editors provide a collection of writings spanning a vast range of genres and origins. Unlike previous collections, writings are not excluded based on the author's religion; even the works by authors of polytheistic faiths are included. As a collection of pseudepigrapha written throughout time would be far too vast, the editors have limited the included works to those written prior to the 7th century C.E.

The majority of the writings are organized chronologically by biblical event, while items spanning multiple time periods and events are arranged by theme. This first volume covers biblical chronology from Adam Octipartite/Septipartite through the Latin Vision of Ezra, while the thematic section covers The Cave of Treasures, Palaea Historica, Quotations from the Lost Books in the Hebrew Bible, and Hebrew Visions of Hell and Paradise. Each entry, written by experts, includes helpful text that offers an explanation of the writing and its contents. In addition, many entries include sections on the manuscripts and versions, genre and structure, date and provenance, and literary context, as well as a bibliography. This is followed by exceptional English translations of the text. This volume is intended for both the specialist and the novice and it would be a valuable addition for anyone studying Judaism or the evolution of early Christendom.—**Julia Frankosky**

Buddhism

1051. **BuddhaNet: Buddhist Studies. Http://www.buddhanet.net/.** [Website]. Buddha Dharma Education Association. Free. Date reviewed: 2013.

This free web resource is packed with timely information for the user interested in all things Buddhist. This comprehensive guide to Buddhism answers many basic questions, while the Buddhism e-Library provides a multilingual online resource suitable for the librarian or researcher. News from the Buddhist world is updated daily. A directory of Buddhism worldwide; annotated video, audio, and e-book lists; and resources for meditation are included. Buddhist Weblinks to blogs, meditations, and other Internet resources, and a daily readings link to the word of the Buddha complete this comprehensive Web resource.—**Anna H. Perrault**

1052. **Digital Dictionary of Buddhism. http://buddhism-dict.net/ddb/index.html.** By Charles Muller. [Website]. Free. Date reviewed: 2013.

University of Tokyo professor A. Charles Muller compiled this online dictionary with over 55,000 entries on Buddhist concepts, famous temples, individuals and schools. The work was initiated by Muller in 1986, moving into online format in the late 1990s, and has grown over the years to include not only Chinese Buddhist canon but also Indian, Central Asian, Tibetan, and other cultural manifestations of Buddhism.—**Noriko Asato**

1053. **East Asian Buddhist Studies: A Reference Guide. http://alc.ucla.edu/refguide/refguide.htm.** [Website]. Free. Date reviewed: 2013.

This work contains scriptural collections, bibliographies and translations of scriptures, history of Buddhist studies, and dictionaries. First compiled by Robert Buswell, and subsequently revised and updated by several other scholars, this site links to the UCLA library catalog but has not been fully updated since 2005. It will provide the researcher with a lot of information on the multitude of Buddhist literature available.—**Noriko Asato**

1054. **The Princeton Dictionary of Buddhism.** By Robert E. Buswell Jr. and Donald S. Lopez Jr. Princeton, N.J., Princeton University Press, 2014. 1265p. $65.00. ISBN 13: 978-0-69115-786-3; 978-1-40084-805-8 (e-book).

The creation of a relatively comprehensive dictionary on Buddhism would be a challenging goal, due to the religions long history, wide geographic range, and the variety of cultures and languages involved. According to its preface, this impressive volume is the largest dictionary of Buddhism ever produced in English. Including some 5,000 main entries, it is the result of a 12-year project by the authors and their teams of graduate students. The dictionary is based on terms from the six major Buddhist languages: Sanskrit, Pali, Tibetan, Chinese, Japanese, and Korean, and includes a smaller number of entries in regional languages such as Burmese, Mongolian, and Thai. The entries concentrate on three major areas: the terminology of doctrines and practices in Buddhism, texts and scriptures, and biographical entries on major figures (historical or mythical). Also, notable geographical locations are covered, as are the various schools and sects of Buddhism.

Rather than providing a brief definition, this works aims to be an encyclopedic dictionary, and the entries are in short essay format, typically four to five per page, although some are much longer. The main entry terms are usually listed in their original language. For key concepts that are important in more than one language, main entry cross-references lead users to the term in the original language. Also for terms that are significant in more than one language, translations of the term (or a closely related concept if that term does not exist in one of the languages) are also provided in the entry. Cross-references in the body of the entries appear in all upper case letters. The entries are not included. The front matter includes explanations of the conventions used for creating the entries and the transcriptions systems chosen (e.g., pinyin versus Wade-Giles for transcribing Chinese); tables of the historical periods of India, China, Korea and Japan; a chronology of Buddhist history arranged in five columns (four for geographic regions and one for general world history); and selected maps of ancient India, China, and the mythical region of Mount Sumeru. Appendixes include a "List of Lists." Buddhism makes frequent use of numerical lists to elucidate key doctrinal points, such as the Four Noble Truths and the Noble Eightfold Path. This section lists these lists in order of the number of key points and includes each of the individual doctrinal points. The wide scope, detailed entries, and intercultural cross-references offered by this dictionary make it a highly recommended purchase for all academic and larger public libraries.—**Kenneth M. Frankel**

Christianity

Biography

1055.   Price, Joann F. **Pope Benedict XVI: A Biography.** Santa Barbara, Calif., Greenwood Press/ABC-CLIO, 2013. 154p. illus. index. (Greenwood Biographies). $37.00. ISBN 13: 978-0-313-35123-5; 978-0-313-35123-5 (e-book).

Joann F. Price's biography of the Pope Benedict XVI is part of the Greenwood Biographies Series, which is written for the high school or college freshman writing a research paper. It includes a series foreword, an introduction, a timeline of events in the life of Pope Benedict XVI, 8 well-referenced chapters, a glossary, a selected bibliography with both print and electronic sites, and an index. Black-and-white photographs appear throughout the volume.

This authoritative biography uses four main sources of information: books, magazine and newspaper articles, governmental documents, and correspondence. Additionally, it is well referenced with most of the main sources being taken from the Internet. These notes are listed at the end of each chapter. The chapters cover his early life, his early career in the church, and his theological convictions. Unfortunately, there is no discussion of his decision to step down from his role as Pope in February of 2013, probably due to the fact that the work went to press before this controversial announcement. This work is recommended not only to students, but also to the general reader interested in a concise life of the Fourteenth Dalai Lama.—**Nadine Salmons**

Dictionaries and Encyclopedias

1056.   **Dictionary of Jesus and the Gospels.** 2d ed. Joel B. Green, Jeannine K. Brown, and Nicholas Perrin, eds. Downers Grove, Ill., InterVarsity Press, 2013. 1087p. index. $60.00. ISBN 13: 978-0-8308-2456-4.

For the scholar, pastor, or layperson interested in the history and theology of Jesus and the Gospels, this clearly written and excellently researched dictionary provides an A-Z topical guide to each Gospel, major themes in the Gospels, key episodes in the life of Jesus, and issues and methods of interpretation. Bibliographies are full and up to date, providing users with the latest scholarship in the field. In the more than 20 years since this dictionary was first published (1992) there has been significant research and scholarship in the area of Jesus' life. Therefore, more than 90 percent of the articles have been replaced or completely rewritten (many by new contributors), with the remainder being revised and updated. The work also has two new editors at its helm, both of whom are specialists in Jesus and the Gospels.

The work begins with a brief introduction, a guide to abbreviations and transliterations used in the text, and information on how to use the dictionary. The A-Z entries are scholarly in tone and provide ample cross-references between entries to guide readers to other subjects of interest. The work concludes with a substantial and useful index. The scope and breadth of this dictionary makes it a volume for every religious library, regardless of one's theological commitments.—**Benet Steven Exton**

1057.   Kapic, Kelly M., and Wesley Vander Lugt. **Pocket Dictionary of the Reformed Tradition.** Downers Grove, Ill., InterVarsity Press, 2013. 140p. $8.00; $6.40 (e-book). ISBN 13: 978-0-8308-2708-4.

This is an inexpensive quick reference tool of the Reformed tradition created by Kelly M. Kapic (Ph.D., King's College, University of London) and Wesley Vander Lugt (Ph.D., University of St. Andrews). The dictionary covers over 300 terms that has entries for persons, historical events, and theological terms of the Reformed tradition. Most of the entries are short and to the point with more important terms a bit longer. Cross-referencing is indicated by asterisks. There are no maps or illustrations. The bibliography is divided into: select reference works, introductory literature, and a sampling of classic works from the Reformed tradition. This book is recommended to academic and public libraries and to scholars, students, and general readers interested in the Reformed tradition.—**Benet Steven Exton**

1058.   **New Catholic Encyclopedia. Supplement 2012-2013: Ethics and Philosophy.** Stamford, Conn., Gale/Cengage Learning, 2013. 4v. index. $654.00/set. ISBN 13: 978-1-4144-8085-5; 978-1-4144-8225-5 (e-book).

Philosophy (love and pursuit of wisdom by intellectual investigation) and ethics (fundamental moral norms) are standard in Roman Catholic tradition and teaching. They are based on natural reason coupled with divine guidance and are presented as guidelines to universal moral norms and acceptable just behavior between persons and nations of diverse background, belief, and worldview. The intent of the 2012-2013 supplement to the *New Catholic Encyclopedia* (NCE; 2d ed., see ARBA 2003, entry 1245) is to update and revise entries on philosophy and ethics that appeared in previously published volumes of the *Encyclopedia*. Articles of various length, written by professors and several by Ph.D. graduate students of four Catholic universities, embrace a gamut of philosophical ideas and ethical issues. Entries engage concepts (theory and practice), technical terms, thinkers, movements, and history of philosophy. Essays on the philosophy of Africa, Islam, and Judaism are responsibly authored by co-ethnic and co-religionists. Noteworthy is the co-mingling of sacred tradition and secular thought from antiquity to the present assuring the Catholic commitment to faith and reason. Helpful features include in-text cross-references, references to previous NCE articles, and a select bibliography. In sum, this resource is highly recommended.—**Zev Garber**

1059. Yrigoyen, Charles, Jr., and Susan E. Warrick. **Historical Dictionary of Methodism.** 3d ed. Lanham, Md., Scarecrow, 2013. 487p. (Historical Dictionaries of Religions, Philosophies, and Movements). $110.00; $109.99 (e-book). ISBN 13: 978-0-8108-7893-8; 978-0-8108-7894-5 (e-book).

Editors Charles Yrigoyen Jr., general secretary of the General Commission on Archives and History of The United Methodist Church, and Susan E. Warrick, former assistant general secretary, once again serve as co-authors of this well-received reference title.

The text, an alphabetically arranged dictionary of church leaders, events, and doctrines, is preceded and augmented by a list of acronyms used in the work, a chronology of important dates, and a brief history of Methodism. Entries about the history of Methodism in specific geographic regions are understandably longer than those that provide information about doctrine and people. Entries about doctrine are longer than entries about people. Coverage of the subject of Methodism is very broad. Entries range from a short paragraph to several pages in length and some provide black-and-white photographs (mainly of influential church leaders). Additional information on topics in this work can be found in sources that comprise the extensive bibliography. This work will be useful for students, researchers, and the general layperson interested in the Methodist church and its history.—**Lois Gilmer**

Handbooks and Yearbooks

1060. Farrell, Michael. **Modern Just War Theory: A Guide to Research.** Lanham, Md., Scarecrow, 2013. 413p. index. (Illuminations: Guides to Research in Religion). $100.00; $99.95 (e-book). ISBN 13: 978-0-8108-8344-4; 978-0-8108-8345-1 (e-book).

While theological concepts may be theoretical and abstract to most people, they occasionally deal with issues that touch upon the average person. One such topic is the Just War Theory as in *Modern Just War Theory: A Guide to Research*, written by scholar and librarian Michael Farrell as part of the Illuminations: Guides to Research in Religion series. This work will appeal to "students and scholars of theology, military history, international law, and Christian ethics." The book is solid and well done. Examples are provided and terms are clearly defined. Chapters include research on topics ranging from History to International Law to Realism to Pacifism to Non-Christian Religious traditions.

From the early days of the Romans to the early days of Christianity, where this topic was systematically explored and developed by great scholars like Saint Augustine of Hippo in the City of God and Saint Thomas Aquinas, many scholars of have addressed "the challenges from competing ideologies as well as these presented by the changing nature of warfare." Most of the more influential literature was written by twentieth and twenty-first century authors and scholars. Farrell not only gives a brief overview of the theorists, but discusses the key terminology and surveys and evaluates key primary and secondary sources for researchers. This title will be a valuable addition to larger academic libraries.—**Scott R. DiMarco**

1061. **Voices of Early Christianity: Documents from the Origins of Christianity.** Kevin W. Kaatz, ed. Santa Barbara, Calif., Greenwood Press/ABC-CLIO, 2013. 277p. illus. index. $100.00. ISBN 13: 978-1-59884-952-3; 978-1-59884-952-3 (e-book).

This is a wonderful introduction into the writings of early Christianity edited by Kevin W. Katz. Six major areas are covered: early Christian life, the Church, early Christian women, conflicts of the early Christians, persecution, and the church and politics. Within these major areas are subsections with the excerpts which are the primary part of the book. The writings include excerpts from the Bible and writings from the early Christian era. The subsection begins with an introduction that provides basic background information about the work the excerpt is from. This is followed by information that helps the reader to understand the context of the text. The excerpt then follows and each varies in length. The source for the excerpt is given at the end. The excerpt is followed by an "Aftermath" which discusses the effects of the writing on the early Christian community. This is followed by questions for personal or group reflection. A short bibliography of mainly English-language sources is given. There are a few black-and-white photographs. There are two appendixes; the first is short biographies and the second is a glossary. There is a bibliography of written material, a bibliography of Websites, and an index. This book is highly recommended to those studying the writings of early Christianity and is recommended to public, academic, and theological libraries.—**Benet Steven Exton**

Islam

1062.   **The Bloomsbury Companion to Islamic Studies.** Clinton Bennett, ed. New York, Bloomsbury, 2013. 419p. index. $190.00. ISBN 13: 978-1-4411-2788-4.

Often in scholarly work, one spends more time searching for sources than extracting data from them. Indeed, knowledge of where to search is just as valuable as the knowledge one is seeking. Furthermore, an awareness of the trajectory of how we have constructed our body of knowledge adds another dimension of understanding which helps one appreciate the current state of scholarship, regardless of one's point of view. As a starting reference, this work is well suited for those in the field of Islamic Studies.

The introductory chapter summarizes the subsequent chapters in the book and outlines the evolution of Islamic Studies from medieval to contemporary times. The following chapter discusses the current state of scholarship. The next series of chapters addresses specific areas of research within Islamic studies. These include Koranic and Hadith studies, Jurisprudence, Sufism, Shiite Islam, Contemporary Salafi Islam, Islamic Art and Architecture, and the relationship between Islam and the West. Gender is not separately discussed, but is incorporated within the individual chapters. The last chapter speculates on possible novel areas of study within Islamic Studies. The chronology starts with the birth of Muhammad and outlines major academic events and turning points until 2011. Next is an extensive resource guide subdivided by topic, followed by a glossary of key term

It is difficult for one reference—especially a single-volume work—to cover all facets of a field as vast, nuanced and rich as Islamic Studies. Given the enormity of the book's scope and limitations of a single volume, this is an excellent reference for scholars starting their research in Islamic Studies. [R: LJ, 1 June 13, p. 134]—**Muhammed Hassanali**

1063.   **The Princeton Encyclopedia of Islamic Political Thought.** Gerhard Bowering, ed. Princeton, N.J., Princeton University Press, 2013. 656p. index. $75.00. ISBN 13: 978-0-691-13484-0; 978-1-4008-3855-4 (e-book).

Islamic political thought is an enormous topic that derives principles for governance from both religious and philosophical developments as well as local pre-Islamic customs. This work explores Islamic political thought from five lenses. The first is major themes, which includes topics from authority and religion, although philosophy is missing. The second is historical developments with a special interest in dynasties, geographic regions, and schools of thought. Third is a focus on modern development, which can be viewed as an extension of historical developments into modern times. The next lens is Islamic law and traditional Islamic societies, which looks at primarily Islamic jurisprudence (essentially theology and governance). The last theme is thinkers, personalities, and statesmen. The primary focus here is more on implementers rather than on those who originally envisioned novel ideas.

Most entries end by cross-referencing other relevant entries in the encyclopedia and with a reference list of additional sources for the interested reader. The longest entries are those 15 that comprise the major themes. The work seems to concentrate on the contemporary Sunni thought, but there are entries on Shi'a and pre-modern thought as well. Space limitations of a single volume prohibit greater coverage of West Africa, Southeast Asia, and areas where Muslims are a significant minority—concentrating instead on Islam's traditional heartlands.

Overall, it is a good reference to introduce a topic related to Islamic political thought, but it should be supplemented by other works for those who are looking for more than just cursory exposure to the subject matter. [R: Choice, June 13, p. 1813]—**Muhammed Hassanali**

Judaism

1064.   **Text Messages: A Torah Commentary for Teens.** Rabbi Jeffrey K. Salkin, ed. Woodstock, Vt., Jewish Lights Publishing, 2012. 284p. $24.99. ISBN 13: 978-1-58023-507-5.

This volume offers two commentaries for each weekly Torah portion, or reading selection in the Jewish tradition of the Pentateuch, geared for Jewish teenagers. These commentaries focus on conduct of life, bringing out aspects of each weekly reading as related to today's contemporary teen. Written for teens by over 100 North American Jewish congregational rabbis of all denominations, cantors, musicians, educators, youth workers, Hillel rabbis, camp directors, professors, writers, social activists, community leaders and philanthropists the lessons are appropriate for any teen, not just Jewish teens. Any professional or parent looking for biblical insights that are relatable for today's teens will appreciate these insights, although limited to the first five books of the Old Testament. The brief commentaries offered teachings on their own, but can also be used as a starting point for lessons or one's own expanded speech or writing. The lens through which the Bible is looked at is unique and valuable to teens and those working with teens, although the lack of a specific Jewish-focus leads this book to be appropriate for all collections and might not be appropriate for the more observant or traditional Jewish collections.—**Sara Marcus**

Part IV

SCIENCE
AND
TECHNOLOGY

29 Science and Technology in General

Biography

1065. **Great Lives from History: Scientists & Science.** Joseph L. Spradley, ed. Hackensack, N.J., Salem Press, 2013. 3v. illus. index. $395.00/set. ISBN 13: 978-1-58765-968-3.

Intended for high school students, undergraduates, and general readers, *Great Lives from History: Scientists & Science* provides 350 biographical essays of 2,000-2,500 words highlighting the lives of scientists and the stories behind their discoveries and contributions to science. The signed essays from the more than 100 contributors are arranged alphabetically by inventor. Scientists were selected for inclusion based upon the significance of their contribution to their field, whether their scientific theory or development contributed to furthering the knowledge base within their field, and their appeal to the intended audience. Women are well represented in the list of entries. Essays are divided into three parts: Early Life, Life's Work, and Impact. Each essay contains a sidebar highlighting one of the scientist's most important contribution. Two-thirds of the essays contain black-and-white photographs depicting the scientist. Every entry contains a brief annotated bibliography for further reading. While the brevity of the articles limit the details that could be provided, the articles are well written and maintain a consistency throughout the set. Sample articles can be viewed at the publisher's Website.

The publisher should be commended for providing many avenues into the text. Each volume contains a complete table of contents and a list of inventions along with the scientist's name. The last volume contains a chronological list of scientists, a timeline of scientific discoveries, and a category index listing scientists by their field of study. There is a geographical index of scientists by country with over 30 countries represented. The majority of scientists come from the United States. The set concludes with a modest subject index. Part of the Great Lives from History series, Salem Press offers free online access to the electronic version when a print copy is purchased.—**Mike Burgmeier**

Catalogs and Collections

1066. **AccessScience. http://www.accessscience.com/.** [Website]. Price negotiated by site. Date reviewed: 2013.

This is the McGraw-Hill Encyclopedia of Science and Technology on the Web. It provides full access to articles, dictionary terms, and hundreds of research updates in all areas of science and technology. Applied Science and Technology Abstracts (ASTA)—1983 to the present; abstracts 1994 to the present. Applied Science and Technology Abstracts covers core English-language scientific and technical publications. Topics include engineering, acoustics, chemistry, computers, metallurgy, physics, plastics, telecommunications, transportations, and waste management. Periodical coverage includes trade and industrial publication, journals issued by professional and technical societies, and specialized subject

periodicals, as well as special issues such as buyers' guides, directories, and conference proceedings.—
James E. Bobick

1067.   **Applied Science and Technology Abstracts (ASTA). http://www.hwwilson.com/ast/applieds. cfm.** [Website]. Bronx, N.Y., H. W. Wilson. Price negotiated by site. Date reviewed: 2013.

Applied Science and Technology abstracts covers core English-language scientific and technical publications. Topics include engineering, acoustics, chemistry, computers, metallurgy, physics, plastics, telecommunications, transportation, and waste management. Periodical coverage includes trade and industrial publications, journals issued by professional and technical societies, and specialized subject periodicals, as well as special issues such as buyers' guides, directories, and conference proceedings. The site provides access to more than 220 periodicals as far back as 1997. Also, nearly 800 periodicals have been fully indexed and abstracted, including 400 peer-reviewed journals, going back as far as 1984. The abstracts range in length from 50 to 300 words. Other features of the database include podcasts from well-respected museums, links to full-text articles, .pdf and page images, and the ability to link to your library's OPAC so patrons can easily find the cited materials on your shelves.—**James E. Bobick**

1068.   **Digital Science Online. http://www.visuallearningco.com/.** [Website]. Brandon, Vt., Visual Learning Systems. Price negotiated by site. Date reviewed: 2013.

Digital Science Online provides an interactive science experience for students. The curriculum is divided into three levels: primary (K-12); elementary (3-5); and middle school (5-8). All levels include Physical, Earth, and Life Science collections, and middle school also offers Integrated Science and Health. Each collection features several broad subtopics, which comprise multiple videos. Supplementing each video lesson is a quiz, an assortment of downloadable worksheets, and a teacher's guide. The worksheets are concise, well written, and relate strongly to the lessons. However, most of the videos seem dated, and the onscreen quizzes do not provide enough time for answering. This site would make a worthwhile additional selection to supplement other electronic science curriculum sources.—**Shanna Shadoan**

1069.   **HSTM: History of Science, Technology, and Medicine. http://www.hstm.umn.edu/index1. html.** [Website]. Dublin, Ohio, OCLC. Price negotiated by site. Date reviewed: 2013.

This resource contains references to journal articles, chapters, and reviews within the fields of general science, technology, and medicine. It covers the influence of these fields on society and culture from prehistory to the present. Citations reflect the contents of nearly 9,500 journals. Covering a vast array of topics, from agricultural sciences to anthropology, medical sciences to military technology, the site can be searched by key word or browsed by subject. The site links to a number of other scholarly databases, including ABI/INFORM, Electronic Collections Online, and Wilson Select Plus. It will be useful to a wide range of science historians.—**James E. Bobick**

1070.   **ISI Web of Science. http://scientific.thomson.com/isi/.** [Website]. Price negotiated by site. Date reviewed: 2013.

The Institute for Scientific Information (ISI) is a multidisciplinary database with searchable author abstracts, covering the literature of the sciences, social sciences, and the arts and humanities. Users may choose to search across all entire database, or select just one specific area. This unique database indexes and links cited references for each article. All formats provide complete bibliographic data and additional features, such as cited reference searching, links to related articles, and author and publisher addresses.—**James E. Bobick**

1071.   **Knovel: Answers for Science and Engineering. http://why.knovel.com.** [Website]. Knovel, New York. Price negotiated by site. Date reviewed:2013.

Knovel contains online interactive reference books and databases. It has a database of some of the leading science and engineering reference handbooks, databases, and conference proceedings from publishers such as McGraw-Hill, Elsevier, John Wiley & Sons, ASME, SPE, and ASM International. Knovel's collection includes over 3,000 leading reference works and databases from over 90 leading technical publishers and professional societies. Users can search by keyword or phrase, or by unlimited Boolean searching.—**James E. Bobick**

Handbooks and Yearbooks

1072.   **Agricultural Inventions.** New York, Crabtree, 2014. 46p. illus. index. (Inventions that Shaped the Modern World). $23.95/vol.; $10.95pa./vol. ISBN 13: 978-0-7787-0213-9.

1073.   **Communication Inventions.** New York, Crabtree, 2014. 46p. illus. index. (Inventions that Shaped the Modern World). $23.95/vol.; $10.95pa./vol. ISBN 13: 978-0-7787-0222-1.

1074.   **Medical Inventions.** New York, Crabtree, 2014. 46p. illus. index. (Inventions that Shaped the Modern World). $23.95/vol., $10.95pa./vol. ISBN 13: 978-0-7787-0212-2.

1075.   **Transportation Inventions.** New York, Crabtree, 2014. 46p. illus. index. (Inventions that Shaped the Modern World). $23.95/vol.; $10.95pa./vol. ISBN 13: 978-0-7787-0223-8.

This four-volume series from Crabtree Publishing, a company known for their multivolume, nonfiction series designed specifically for children and middle school students, demonstrates how the creation of new technologies can lead to and inspire future inventions. The volumes in the series discuss innovations in transportation, agriculture, communications, and medicine. Significant inventions throughout history are profiled featuring information about the person or people behind the idea, the development process, the impact of the invention, and the future inventions it inspired. Also included is a list of other resources (e.g., books, Websites), a timeline, a glossary, and a very short index, all of which can be used to teach young students basic researching skills. This series is recommended for middle school libraries and young adult collections in public libraries.—**Shannon Graff Hysell**

1076.   Berger, Lee R., and Marc Aronson. **The Skull in the Rock: How a Scientists, a Boy, and Google Earth Opened a New Window on Human Origins.** Washington, D.C., National Geographic Society, 2012. 64p. illus. $18.95. ISBN 13: 978-1-4263-1010-2.

Engaging text invites readers to take part in the excitement and challenge of looking for early humans through a close-up look at the discovery of an almost two million year-old fossil by Lee Berger and his son. Berger uses Google Earth for a different perspective of familiar terrain and uncovers much of the skeleton named Karabo along with other hominins he names sediba. Photographs demonstrate key aspects of the discovery with artistic interpretations of what Karabo might have looked like and how he died. Young readers are brought into the ongoing research with the inclusive use of "we" and a promise by the authors to update readers with an explanation of any new research through a dedicated Website. Readers will be entranced with this story. A bibliography, glossary, list of Websites, and index enhance the usefulness of this work.—**Sue C. Kimmel**

1077.   **Building Blocks of Science.** Chicago, World Book, 2013. 10v. illus. index. $269.00/set. ISBN 13: 978-0-7166-1420-3.

Information in this set is presented in a graphic novel format with a few real images interspersed. The few small photographs are supportive to the text and are clear and crisp. Each cartoon character presents their concept in a basic and easy-to-understand manner. The information is direct and moves smoothly from questions to facts or statements. The graphic novel format in this series is geared toward younger students who are comic book fans. Each volume presents a good informational resource to basic science concepts. The work is supplemented with a glossary, additional Websites, and an index.—**Eileen Wright**

1078. **Conquering the Sky.** New York, Rosen Publishing, 2013. 32p. illus. index. (Discovery Educational Discoveries and Inventions Series). $25.25/vol.; $10.00pa./vol. ISBN 13: 978-1-4777-1504-8.

1079. **Creating and Cracking Codes.** New York, Rosen Publishing, 2013. 32p. illus. index. (Discovery Education: Discoveries and Inventions Series). $25.25/vol.; $10.00pa./vol. ISBN 13: 978-1-4777-1500-0.

1080. **The Industrial Revolution: Age of Invention.** New York, Rosen Publishing, 2013. 32p. illus. index. (Discovery Education: Discoveries and Inventions Series). $25.25/vol.; $10.00pa./vol. ISBN 13: 978-1-4777-1332-7.

1081. **Leonardo da Vinci: The Greatest Inventor.** New York, Rosen Publishing, 2013. 32p. illus. index. (Discovery Education: Discoveries and Inventions Series). $25.25/vol.; $10.00pa./vol. ISBN 13: 978-1-4777-1330-3.
    Students in the upper elementary grades with a passion for inventions and inventing will find these books to be inspiring and engaging. The books provide information on the inventions of the day that changed the way that citizens of the time lived and also shaped the inventions that change our lives today. Timelines run along the bottom of the pages to give students an idea of what else was going on during the time of the invention. The text is a little more complex than most reference books geared to this age group; however, the many illustrations help explain the text and will provide young students with the visual cues they need for learning. The *Leonardo da Vinci* title is more biographical in nature, focusing on the life of the man as well as his many inventions. These titles fill a niche for this age group and will be welcome additions to most school and public library collections.—**Shannon Graff Hysell**

Indexes

1082. **Scitopia. http://scitopia.org/.** [Website]. Free. Date reviewed: 2013.
    Scitopia searches more than three and a half million documents, including peer-reviewed journal content and technical conference papers from leading voices in major science and technology disciplines. Through simple and advanced searches users can find bibliographic records in each partner's electronic library; patents from the U.S. Patent and Trademark Office, European Patent Office, and Japan Patent Office; and U.S. government documents on the Department of Energy Information Bridge site.—**James E. Bobick**

30 Agricultural Sciences

General Works

1083. **Agricultural Statistics 2012.** Lanham, Md., Bernan Press, 2013. 549p. index. $49.00pa. ISBN 13: 978-0-1609-1518-5.

Agriculture Statistics is a yearly publication of reliable reference material on agricultural production, supplies, consumption, facilities, costs, and returns. Foreign agricultural trade statistics include government as well as nongovernment shipment of merchandise from the United States and its territories to foreign countries. The world summaries are taken from statistics supplied by foreign governments and foreign source material. The book of tables is particularly valuable to individuals who want a current overview of agricultural production in the United States as well as worldwide, including world trade. This reviewer knows of no other source where this information is so current, readily available, and accurate. This paperback publication is on average paper, with average binding and print large enough to be useful when looking only at specific information. An adequate index is provided to assist in locating specific information desired.—**ARBA Staff Reviewer**

Food Sciences and Technology

Bibliography

1084. Stoeger, Melissa Brackney. **Food Lit: A Reader's Guide to Epicurean Nonfiction.** Santa Barbara, Calif., Libraries Unlimited/ABC-CLIO, 2013. 350p. index. (Real Stories). $60.00. ISBN 13: 978-1-59884-706-2; 978-1-61069-376-9 (e-book).

Stoeger, a readers' services librarian at Deerfield Public Library in Deerfield, Illinois, has written *Food Lit: A Reader's Guide to Epicurean Nonfiction* and it is a welcome guide. There are plenty of nonfiction books for the "foodies" of the world, but the issue is finding them. Food is a hot topic today and people are hungry for titles addressing the histories of food, extreme cuisines, and life stories of those who have dedicated their lives to cooking and serving delicious foods. The nine chapters representing specific genres—Life Stories; Food Biographies; Food Travel; Food Adventure; History of Food; Food Science; Investigative Food Writing; Narrative Cookbooks, and Food Essays—follow a straightforward format that offer definitions, the appeal of the work (or why there is interest), and how the specific chapter is organized before it launches into individual titles. After each title, the subjects of the book are listed as well as suggestions for interested readers on what to try next. One of the best things about this book is that there is a "Consider Starting With . . ." section for each chapter that allows a reader to become familiar with the topic. While the title focuses on titles published in the past decade, several significant landmark titles are presented as well. The appendix includes great resources such as cooks and their books, food in fiction, and food writing awards. There is a title/author index as well as subject index. This book would find a welcome place in public libraries as well as universities.—**Nadine Salmons**

Catalogs and Collections

1085.   **Nutrition and Food Sciences Database. http://www.cabi.org/nutrition/.** [Website]. Center for Agriculture and Biosciences International. Price negotiated by site. Date reviewed: 2013.

This is a specialist database covering human nutrition, food science, and food technology. No other database can provide such a comprehensive view of the food chain or of the interactions between diet and health. This database contains more than 880,000 records dating back to 1973, with over 50,000 added annually. It annually selects records from over 5,000 serials, as well as 400-500 nonserial publications, covering literature from 125 countries. It also covers books, conference proceedings, bulletins, reports, and published theses.—**James E. Bobick**

Dictionaries and Encyclopedias

1086.   Difford, Simon. **Cocktails: The Bartender's Bible.** 11th ed. New York, Firefly Books, 2013. 504p. illus. index. $49.95pa. ISBN 13: 978-1-77085-222-8.

One of the most popular areas in most public libraries is the cooking and food section. *Cocktails: The Bartender's Bible* will be a great addition to most public libraries needing some new life in their collection. The title begins with an introductory section to bartending that includes "the basics," essential tools, glassware, garnishes, and key ingredients. From here the book is arranged alphabetically by drink name. For each drink the author recommends the glass, garnish, recipe, variants (if any), author comments, and the origin of the drink. Tips from the bartender are provided throughout the volume that will ensure that users have all the facts before making a drink and will be sure to create high-quality beverages. Those cocktails that were featured in the previous volume and have updated recipe direction are provided with a "New/Updated" designation so that users of the 1st edition will know that the recipe has been tweaked or variations have been added.—**Shannon Graff Hysell**

1087.   Smith, Andrew F. **Food and Drink in American History: A "Full Course" Encyclopedia.** Santa Barbara, Calif., ABC-CLIO, 2013. 3v. illus. index. $310.00/set. ISBN 13: 978-1-61069-232-8; 978-1-61069-233-5 (e-book).

Food plays a major role in the culture and history of the United States. Andrew F. Smith, who teaches the history of American food and drink at the New School University in New York, has created an encyclopedia covering this interesting subject. The first two volumes contain 664 alphabetic entries covering a wide range of subjects. They include agriculture (factory farms, organic food), beverages (bourbon, tea), Business and commercial products including companies (A&P, Spam), cooking instruction including the media (celebrity chefs, home economics), culinary icons (Aunt Jemima, Ronald McDonald), equipment (cups, microwave ovens), ethnic, religions, and special interest foods (baby food, gluten-free diets), specific foods (abalone, rhubarb), food and beverage distribution (automats, food courts), public policy (farm bills, menu labeling), historical periods (colonial food, slave food), biographies (Gail Borden, Fannie Farmer Merritt), and more.

The book begins with a chronology covering 3000 B.C.E. to 2012. The entries range in length from one paragraph to several pages. Black-and white illustrations, shaded text boxes with interesting supplementary facts, and recipes from historic cookbooks provide additional insight. All articles have references for further research. Volume 3 contains primary source documents from various historical periods such as an account of bread made from maize written in 1539 by a member of Hernando De Soto's expedition and an excerpt from Moby Dick describing chowder. This volume also has a glossary, six appendixes listing food history organizations, listservs, Websites, periodicals, libraries with major culinary collections, food-related museums, and universities with food studies programs, and a bibliography. This is an entertaining and useful resource for school, public, and academic libraries.—**Barbara M. Bibel**

1088. **Street Food Around the World: An Encyclopedia of Food and Culture.** Bruce Kraig and Colleen Taylor Sen, eds. Santa Barbara, Calif., ABC-CLIO, 2013. 504p. illus. index. $100.00/set. ISBN 13: 978-1-59884-954-7; 978-1-59884-955-4 (e-book).

This book covers 395 countries, illustrates 72 recipes, and is indexed with recipes per country. It is estimated that 2.6 million people eat street food in some form every day and this is an overview of the world's street food by country or region. The contributors include oral readings of food historians, academics, and journalists. The introduction of the book asks the question: what is street food and where can it be found? It also discusses how it is prepared. The book offers advice of how street food can be safe food. It then has an alphabetic listing according to countries and often where these products can be found in specific areas. Most countries are followed by sections on the photographs of establishments. This is a major volume since the book requires 471 pages. Following these entries, there is a section about the editors and contributors to the book indicating their qualifications. This is followed by an extensive index requiring 53 pages. The book is well written and the authors are well qualified for such an undertaking. The font size is adequate, paper quality is average, and the book binding is acceptable. This book should be of interest to anyone traveling internationally or wanting to experience how the natives obtain a great portion of their food.—**Herbert W. Ockerman**

Directories

1089. **Plunkett's Food Industry Almanac.** 2014 ed. Jack W. Plunkett, ed. Houston, Tex., Plunkett Research, 2014. 600p. $349.99pa. ISBN 13: 978-1-60879-730-1.

The food industry is one of the most globally linked and competitive of all industries. Large chains, such as Starbucks and McDonalds are well known throughout the world and have to compete with other American brands as well as regional favorites. It also features an ever-changing food market industry that is extremely cost competitive while trying to break into the Internet/home delivery markets. This almanac starts with a glossary of terms, followed by an introduction and how to use each section. Chapter 2 covers the statistics of these industries. Chapter 3 covers important food and beverage industry contacts. Chapter 4, which is a major portion of the book, is in a table format listing company names; industry and location; and a complete table of sales, profits, and ranks including individual profiles of each of the "Food 400." Indexes follow including "hot spots" for advancement for women and minorities. An index of subsidiaries, brand names, and selected affiliations is also included. This would be valuable to anyone in the food industry that needs specific information on companies, products, contacts, and more. It would be a useful addition to most general purpose libraries and particularly those that are located in food production areas. The paperback binding, paper, font size, and organization are acceptable for the purpose.—**Herbert W. Ockerman**

Handbooks and Yearbooks

1090. **FAO Statistical Yearbook 2013: World Food and Agriculture.** By Food and Agriculture Organization. Lanham, Md., Bernan Press, 2013. 356p. $125.00pa. ISBN 13: 978-92-51073-96-4.

Accepted as one of the leading collections of statistical data on food and agriculture worldwide, this latest edition provides data on agricultural economics, environmental factors, and social trends and issues. Gathered from around the world, the statistics are broken down into four major sections: the state of the agricultural resource base; hunger dimensions; feeding the world; and sustainability. This work provides hard-to-find statistics and presents them in a way that is meaningful to the users. It will be useful to researchers and statisticians in need of current agricultural statistics. Large academic and research libraries will benefit the most from this publication.—**Shannon Graff Hysell**

1091.   Fenster, Michael S. **Eating Well, Living Better.** Lanham, Md., Rowman & Littlefield, 2012. 319p. index. $18.95. ISBN 13: 978-1-4422-1340-1.

Americans are in love with food. Many are overweight, making them vulnerable to serious health problems. The author, a board-certified cardiologist who struggles to control his weight, offers practical advice to help people eat well, maintain a healthy lifestyle, and lose weight. In addition to his medial training, Fenster is a trained chef with restaurant experience. He takes a common-sense approach, telling people to set realistic goals. He offers basic information about nutrition and exercise; an introduction to basic cooking techniques; and information about foods, kitchen equipment, spices, and wine. He provides recipes for stocks and sauces as well as an assortment of tasty dishes such as wood plank chicken, zucchini stuffed with herbed chevre, and tea-smoked salmon. He uses fresh, quality ingredients and encourages moderation and portion control. He shows readers how advertising encourages consumption of junk food and teaches them how to choose healthy alternatives. This is a useful addition to circulating collections in public and consumer-health libraries.—**Barbara M. Bibel**

1092.   Herbst, Sharon Tyler, and Ron Herbst. **The New Food Lover's Companion.** 5th ed. Hauppauge, N.Y., Barron's Educational Series, 2013. 916p. $16.99pa. ISBN 13: 978-1-4380-0163-0.

This 5th edition has exploded with 500 new and expanded terms not only from Great Britain and America but also from Persia, South America, and other international food markets. There are now 7,200 entries describing foods, cooking techniques, herbs, spices, desserts, wines, and ingredients. The original author (Ms. Herbst) is deceased and he has attempted to update this tome as he would think Ms. Herbst would have wanted it updated. There an extensive breakdown of food labels and nutritional facts, but eliminating the Food Guide Pyramid, and some of the popular entries such as Garlic. There are several additions added: MyPlate (USDA), apple varieties, and suggested uses and Blood Alcohol Concentration charts. He has individualized each section of Meat. It now lists beef, lamb pork, and veal. Multiple appendixes that include many charts and topics are followed by a bibliography and then About the Authors and books they have published. Four pages of new acknowledgements have also been added. This reviewer highly recommends this edition for all levels of cooks, be it professional or neophyte, and their respective libraries.—**Nadine Salmons**

1093.   **Nutrition & Health Series.** Farmington Hills, Mich., Lucent Books/Gale/Cengage Learning, 2012. multivolume. illus. index. $30.95/vol.

This multivolume series on nutrition and food science is aimed at middle and high school age students. The series aims to provide young people with up-to-date information on nutrition and healthy living, especially since there is much published in this area and much of it is contradictory. All of these volumes achieve that aim through clear writing, comprehensive, age- and grade-level information, and attractive and colorful illustrations that bring each topic to life. Recently published volumes are on eating disorders and sports nutrition, which complement previous volumes on childhood obesity, food allergies, and food regulation.

The authors are writers of books for young people. Each volume provides information on new trends in the topic, the science behind the facts, and any controversies surrounding the subject. All volumes provide personal anecdotes, sidebars with highlighted information, and fact boxes. Full-color photographs, charts, and graphs provide visual interest that is important for this age group and further enhance the text. The works conclude with a glossary, bibliography, and subject index. This set is highly recommended for school and public libraries.—**Shannon Graff Hysell**

1094.   Smith, Merril D. **History of American Cooking.** Santa Barbara, Calif., ABC-CLIO, 2013. 188p. illus. index. $37.00. ISBN 13: 978-0-313-38711-1; 978-0-313-38712-8 (e-book).

This is a fascinating book that not only covers the different forms and types of cooking but is also a good history book. The book describes different ingredients and their history within food categories in the United States. It also provides recipes to try for the different categories. The book is full of information, has a bibliography, an extensive index, and is a fun read. At this price it is a good buy for any public library or as a gift for a cook who likes history.—**Betsy J. Kraus**

1095.   **State of Food and Agriculture 2012: Investing in Agriculture for a Better Future.** By the Food and Agriculture Organization. Lanham, Md., Bernan Press, 2013. 180p. $75.00pa. ISBN 13: 978-92-51073-17-9.

1096.   **State of Food Insecurity in the World 2012: Economic Growth is Necessary But Not Sufficient to Accelerate Reduction of Hunger and Malnutrition.** By the Food and Agriculture Organization. Lanham, Md., Bernan Press, 2012. 62p. $30.00pa. ISBN 13: 978-92-51073-16-2.

This volume in the FAO Agriculture Series is an assessment of the world's food supply, especially as it relates to the economic and social welfare of rural nonfarm people in the developing countries. *State of Food and Agriculture 2012* provides essays and reports on the future of agriculture in regions where there is not enough agriculture to support the nutritional needs of the people. It discusses the prospective demands in growth over the coming years and how this will place increasing pressure on the natural resource base. The work stresses the need for a significant increase in agricultural investments—and in their effectiveness—in order to ensure that these countries can support the nutritional needs of the people.

State of Food Insecurity in the World 2012 provides users with new estimates of how many people in the world are undernourished. It shows that there has been marked improvement to decrease malnourishment in the poorest of countries in the past 20 years. It focuses on the need for sustainable agricultural growth in reducing undernourishment in rural areas. Policies for the reduction of hunger are also discussed, including supporting increased dietary diversity, providing access to safe drinking water, improving sanitation services, and educating consumers in nutrition and child nutritional needs.

For a thorough assessment of the availability of food and the economic status of the rural nonfarm population in the developing countries, this is the definitive source. The writing is excellent and the tables and charts use colors, which provide exceptional clarity and ease of interpretation.—**John Laurence Kelland**

Horticulture

Dictionaries and Encyclopedias

1097.   Biggs, Matthew, and Jekka McVicar. **Vegetables, Herbs, & Fruit: An Illustrated Encyclopedia.** paperback ed. New York, Firefly Books, 2013. 640p. illus. index. $29.95pa. ISBN 13: 978-1-77085-200-6.

Now issued as a more affordable paperback edition, this work is ideal for gardeners looking to grow their own vegetables, herbs, and fruits. Solid gardening tips and tempting recipes mix, quite naturally.

That applies to vegetables, herbs, and fruits. Take rosemary. Across four pages, the reader sees how lovely rosemary looks growing in a diverse bed of perennials, learns about the herb's history and symbolism (for fidelity), and finds a recipe for vegetarian goulash. Some 70 vegetables, 100 herbs, and 100 fruits are introduced at a level deep enough to teach even experienced gardeners new tricks. Vegetable and herb sections are each arranged alphabetically by name of genus. Throughout, there are recipes for everything from onion and walnut muffins to gooseberry fool. Culinary uses stand alongside details of the medicinal properties, companion plants, cultivation, and varieties of each species covered. The fruit section is subdivided by four types of growth, with a fifth category for nuts. The fastest route to a particular species is often through the excellent index. A full 80 pages of the book provide good advice on everything from garden design to soil preparation to the ways of common insect pests. Visually, the book is a match for the mind's eye of any gardener.—**Diane M. Calabrese**

1098.   Lord, Tony, and Andrew Lawson. **The Encyclopedia of Planting Combinations.** repr. ed. New York, Firefly Books, 2013. 464p. illus. index. $45.00. ISBN 13: 978-1-55407-997-1.

Now back as a reprinted edition, this book continues to be a visual delight. The color photography alone makes it a worthwhile purchase. The author describes his work as "a menu of suggestions from which readers can choose or reject, revise or augment combinations to suit their own tastes and conditions" as they combine plants to achieve personal works of art in the garden. There are over 4,000 color photographs of plants in lovely color, and more than 1,000 plant descriptions, offering cultural and descriptive notes. The first section of the book is called "The Art of Combining Plants." It looks at assessing the garden site, choosing plants, harmonious form and texture, pleasing color combinations, and the overall affect of a planted border. The largest section of the book provides individual plant descriptions divided by plant types such as shrubs, climbers, bulbs, perennials, annuals, and so on. The section on roses is especially detailed with descriptions of types and individual varieties. The author asserts that roses are the most versatile of all garden plants. What makes this book quite different from numerous plant books with descriptions of plants and their culture is that the author comments on what other plants go well with the plant to achieve pleasing combinations, based on color, texture, and growing conditions. He succeeds, as the results pictured are quite beautiful. There is a brief glossary of common plant names with their scientific counterparts, and a full index, with each plant and variety fully listed.

While the author, Lord, is well qualified, special recognition also should be given to the photographer, Andrew Lawson, who has been named "Garden Photographer of the Year" and certainly deserves any and all accolades. As with many garden books on the market today, this is a British publication, subsequently published in Canada, and then in this U.S. edition. It has hardiness zones listed for Europe, North America, and Australia. This reviewer recognizes many of the plant varieties as available in the United States, and certainly the combination advice transcends continental borders. The only criticism is that the cultivators described are those that grow in a temperate climate with moisture, either rain or irrigation. The desert southwest of the United States is not addressed here, nor is the now very popular and often necessary xeriscaping garden plan.

This book is recommended for libraries, although not necessarily for the reference collection. It is beautiful to look at, informative to read, and offers first-rate suggestions for making one's garden truly a work of art.—**Janet Mongan**

1099.   Rice, Graham. **Powerhouse Plants: 510 Top Performers for Multi-Season Beauty.** Portland, Oreg., Timber Press, 2013. 282p. illus. index. $24.95pa. ISBN 13: 978-1-60469-210-5.

Splendid is the word for this book. The author has a way of speaking to gardeners. In this volume he has compiles more than 500 diverse plants that he considers to be "hardworking" in that they survive and bloom through several seasons, provides multiple looks over their life span, are easy to grow, and are hardy in nature. The author has included a multitude of perennials, annuals, groundcovers, vines, shrubs, and trees as examples. Many provide summer flowers, fall foliage, and even color in the winter. The book begins with a 20-page introduction describing what to look for when selecting plants for a year-long garden and what color changes to expect throughout the year. It then presents the 510 plants in alphabetic order from *Abelia* to *Weigela* describing the plant's strongest season, how to nurture it in your garden, how much sun or shade it requires, what it is best matched with, and what to expect from it in terms of color variation. Full-color photographs enhance the text and give the reader an idea of what to expect from the plant throughout the seasons. The work concludes with a list of nursery sources and an index.—**Diane M. Calabrese**

Handbooks and Yearbooks

1100.   Adams, Denise Wiles, and Laura L. S. Burchfield. **American Home Landscapes: A Design Guide to Creating Period Garden Styles.** Portland, Oreg., Timber Press, 2013. 303p. illus. index. $39.95. ISBN 13: 978-1-60469-040-8.

This work examines the best practices in restoring the landscape of historical homes. While the restoration of historical properties is well covered in the literature, the topic of restoring the landscaping to its original design but with modern efficiencies has largely been ignored. This book rectifies that beginning with a chapter on researching design elements for a particular time period or property. It is then arranged into chapters that address specific time periods—from the Colonial period to the last decades of the twentieth century. Prominent features from each period are featured with detailed descriptions and full-color photographs. These include: paths, driveways, fences, seating, hedges, and landscaping accessories. Plants are also recommended to ensure the landscaping stays true to the home's historical roots.

Special libraries of landscape architecture or architecture in general should most certainly have this title in their reference sections. Public libraries will also want to have it available to their patrons. This work is highly recommended.—**Mary Ellen Snodgrass**

1101.   Adams, George. **Gardening for the Birds: How to Create a Bird-Friendly Backyard.** Portland, Oreg., Timber Press, 2013. 443p. illus. index. $24.95pa. ISBN 13: 978-1-60469-409-3.

Information on how to create a "sustainable ecosystem" (p. 9) in your backyard is the focus of this book. Adams recommends using native plants to feed and shelter birds and other wildlife. He includes calendars outlining when hummingbird plants and wildflowers bloom and when trees and shrubs have fruit, all of which sustain birds and butterflies. His broad focus is North America, giving regional information for native plant species and birds. As it is difficult to provide specific regional information on bird species and native plants, Adams suggests connecting to local resources to learn more about the plants and birds of a particular location, and how to obtain native plants.

Gardening for the Birds is lavishly illustrated, with excellent photographs, many featuring birds using the plants under discussion. It is organized into four large sections, with the first two focusing on gardening and the last two serving as directories of native plant and bird species. Each bird in the Bird Directory is depicted in pen-and-ink drawings by the author and accompanied by color photographs. All photographs have accurate and descriptive captions, including the common and botanical names for plants.

With so much information to impart, more thought might have been given to organization. Some charts go across, others down. Some charts are organized by region, others by perennial/annual status. Some calendars have photographs interspersed, others simply list the plants. There is no map of USDA plant hardiness zones, although readers are directed to the Internet to find plant hardiness information for regions in the United States and Canada. There is no documentation of sources, so some facts may not be verified.

Despite those shortcomings, this is an excellent reference for those wishing to provide bird habitat at their house. Small areas of bird habitat are becoming increasingly important as bird-sustaining habitat is destroyed. Excellent information combined with engaging photographs of the plants and birds provide for a pleasant experience while learning about gardening for the birds.—**Sally Bickley**

1102.   Bennett, Jennifer. **Dryland Gardening: Plants that Survive and Thrive in Tough Conditions.** repr. ed. New York, Firefly Books, 2013. 192p. illus. index. $24.95pa. ISBN 13: 978-1-55407-031-2.

This well-received title is now available again as a reprinted edition. Bennett's attractive, reasonably priced text is a useful handbook to landscaping in unpromising terrain. Her advice extends to which plants to grow, how to water and enrich the soil, and how to protect the land with windbreaks. Generous listings cover herbs and grasses, bulbs, annuals and perennials, climbers, and shrubs. Attractive photographs display individual plants as well as groupings, such as colorful annuals and perennials for borders, rock gardens, strawberry jars, and a wildflower meadow. Entries specify individual plants by name and height, such as the six best asters and the seven most promising cacti. Additional tips include how to guard trees from drought stress, how to curb pesty invaders, and how to protect gardeners from sunstroke. Back matter provides a zone map of the 50 states and Canada and a 4-page listing of 73 specialist nurseries and equipment and information sources along with postal and e-mail addresses, telephone numbers, and Websites. Indexing by common and proper names increases the appeal to librarians, horticulturists, and home gardeners.—**Mary Ellen Snodgrass**

1103.   Chace, Teri Dunn. **How to Eradicate Invasive Plants.** Portland, Oreg., Timber Press, 2013. 336p. illus. index. $24.95pa. ISBN 13: 978-1-60469-306-5.

The many books dealing with invasive plants range from comprehensive, scholarly volumes to briefer studies pertinent to specific geographic regions or individual states. Given existing books and newer Websites such as invasive.org, this book's niche is as an inexpensive, compact, color-illustrated guide for homeowners and gardeners. Chace, a garden writer and editor, is a long-time gardener who presents enough information to enable readers easily to identify 200 unwelcome plants commonly encountered in yards and gardens across the United States, to choose from various types of strategies for control or eradication of those plants, and to alert neighbors or the community. She defines invasive as weeds, "plants that are problems in human-made environments," but also are "understood to be a threat to biodiversity and natural systems as a whole" (p. 12).

Chapter 1, "Know Thy Enemy," outlines nine ways to prevent weeds before they become established and lists the characteristics of potential weeds. Chapter 2, "Combat Thy Enemy," suggests a four-step approach: intervene early, time the intervention appropriately, concentrate removal efforts, and persist. Chace favors less toxic controls beginning with hand-pulling and smothering under plant to applying boiling water or using a propane torch. She offers a homemade weed killer recipe and describes chemical remedies from simple household supplies to name brands. Also included are weed disposal options. Chapters 3-8 feature descriptions and color photographs of various categories of invasives, including water and bog plants, annuals, biennials and tropical perennials, herbaceous perennials, grasses and bamboos, vines, shrubs, and trees. Within chapters, the one-page individual plant profiles are arranged alphabetically by scientific name with common name, descriptions, problem origin, reproduction, notes, noninvasive alternatives, and types of controls. Also included are a short "Problem Areas for Problem Plants" section, suggested reading, four recommended Websites, and an index with invasive plant names in boldface type. This is a very useful book for all public libraries and for smaller academic libraries.— **Julienne L. Wood**

1104.   Cox, Tom, and John M. Ruter. **Landscaping with Conifers and Ginkgo for the Southeast.** Gainesville, Fla., University Press of Florida, 2013. 290p. illus. index. $29.95pa. ISBN 13: 978-0-8130-4248-0.

A handsome text packed with useful data, Cox and Ruter's guide to lawn greenery offers a wealth of suggestions for boosting year-round color and texture. Photographs feature the angles, shades, and structure of bark, leaves, needles, and cones. Names of species pinpoint the plantings promising the most benefit and longest service to the grower. An appendix identifies trees and shrubs by height and width, essential details for the home builder proportioning the landscape for future growth. Additional hardiness and heat zone charts and nursery sources take the work out of researching the best choices in the southeastern United States. A long-lived reference for the public library, community college, and professional nursery shelf, this reasonably priced work is both engaging and practical.—**Mary Ellen Snodgrass**

1105.   Crandell, Gina. **Tree Gardens: Architecture and the Forest.** New York, Princeton Architectural Press, 2013. 165p. illus. index. $40.00. ISBN 13: 978-1-61689-121-3.

The author of this title, a landscape architect and author of books on related topics, provides clear and descriptive studies on 15 parks worldwide that demonstrate the use of trees in landscaping. While the majority of the examples modern there are a few ancient examples (e.g., André Le Notre's Versailles). Most of the examples are located in Europe; however, there are several examples from the United States as well, such as Brooklyn's Bridge Park's Pier 1 and the 9/11 Memorial Forest. For each tree garden the author discusses the artistic design behind the landscaping, and demonstrates how the landscape architect uses tree selection, spacing, and pruning to create the desired effect. She also discusses the maintenance involved in maintaining the beauty of the parks. The author uses color photographs and landscaping plans to provide visual aid to the reader. This book will appeal to landscape architects, gardeners looking for inspiration, and armchair travelers. [R: LJ, 15 June 13, p. 88]—**Shannon Graff Hysell**

1106.   Dakin, Karla, Lisa Lee Benjamin, and Mindy Pantiel. **The Professional Design Guide to Green Roofs.** Portland, Oreg., Timber Press, 2013. 300p. illus. index. $39.95. ISBN 13: 978-1-60469-312-6.

Aiming to survey and inspire, the authors tap a variety of intellectual spheres to encourage those who would add plants to their roofs. Even the artist Arthur Dove gets a mention. The two biggest constraints in adding flora to a roof are structural load and time. The plants, the biomass that accumulates and the soil all have mass and weight. One cannot simply throw soil on a roof and start growing things. To prevent biomass accumulation or structurally unsupportable succession, a wholly green roof requires regular attention and an investment of time. For the idea seeker, there are plenty of schemes to ponder, ranging from planters to roofs entirely planted with sedum to the middle course of a sky trapezium. Examples, which are documented with dazzling photographs, come from around the world. Interest in green roofs is not new. For thousands of years, green roofs have provided aesthetic and relaxing views from above; and rooftop gardens have expanded contemplative and recreational space. But the contribution green roofs make to slowing rain so that it nourishes and permeates locally increasingly garners attention. Structures can be fortified with supplemental framing to accommodate a green roof, but the best opportunity for a sustainable green roof begins in the architectural design phase. Expect to see green roofs more in the future and expect them to be part of more fully sustainable buildings with necessities such as water treatment and thermal regulation incorporated.—**Diane M. Calabrese**

1107.   Deardorff, David, and Kathryn Wadsworth. **What's Wrong with My Fruit Garden? 100% Organic Solutions for Berries, Trees, Nuts, Vines, and Tropicals.** Portland, Oreg., Timber Press, 2014. 312p. illus. index. $24.95pa. ISBN 13: 978-1-60469-358-4.

Anyone who has tried to grow berries, applies, melons, and exotic fruits without the aid of synthetic pesticides knows how challenging it can be to ward off pests and diseases. This book provides help for those who are intent on foregoing the chemicals and growing their own healthy organic vegetables. After an introduction on preparing for success, the work is arranged into chapter based on fruit or nut type. The chapters range from the expected (apples, blueberries, melons, and plums) to more exotic offerings (gooseberries, figs, kiwi, loquat, and persimmon). The author offers advice on providing each an optimal growing environment, including temperature, soil, light, and water requirements. The author then provides solutions to some of the most persistent problems one might encounter, providing a detailed account of symptoms, a diagnosis, a color illustration of the culprit, and a detailed organic The work concludes with a list of resources, conversion charts, the USDA hardiness zones, and an index. For the gardener aiming to produce a healthy organic fruit garden, this is an excellent resource.—**Lori D. Kranz**

1108.   Diacono, Mark, and Lia Leendertz. **The Speedy Vegetable Garden.** Portland, Oreg., Timber Press, 2013. 207p. illus. index. $18.95pa. ISBN 13: 978-1-60469-326-3.

As the title suggests *The Speedy Vegetable Gardener*'s focus is on getting vegetable crops from planting to the table in the least amount of time. The authors' focus is on introducing the reader to those crops that require the least amount of time to mature. For example, users will discover that dwarf French beans can be harvested a mere 60 days after planting, cherry tomatoes after only 65 days, and cilantro, arugula, and fennel in only 10-14 days. Some 50 crops are highlighted with complete information on how to sow and harvest each plant. This is a fun book that will give both novice and experienced gardeners plenty of new crops to try.

This book is an ideal read for gardener's looking to grow the healthiest vegetables in an environmentally friendly and quick manner. It will be useful in most public library gardening collections.—**Diane M. Calabrese**

1109.   Fox, Jim. **How to Buy the Right Plants, Tools & Garden Supplies.** Portland, Oreg., Timber Press, 2013. 222p. index. $14.95pa. ISBN 13: 978-1-60469-214-3.

Readers familiar with other Timber Press titles filled with lavish color photographs and treating specialized garden or landscape topics many not recognize this slim volume with two-color print and amusing black-and-white illustrations as a Timber Press book. Author Jim Fox, a nursery owner and horticultural consultant, offers his best advice in this book based on years of questions he has received from customers. He explains in layperson's terms how to stretch your landscaping dollars and get the best products, at the best time, and for the right price. He begins by providing the user with advice from a nursery insider even before you get to the nursery, including how to navigate the nursery, as well as how to successfully garden once you get your haul of horticultural materials home. You'll get insider advice on how to determine the health of a plant, how to read the plant tags, and how to select the best tools for your gardening needs. This encouraging book will be of value to public library patrons who wish to learn gardening basics.—**ARBA Staff Reviewer**

1110.   Lowenfels, Jeff. **Teaming with Nutrients: The Organic Gardener's Guide to Optimizing Plant Nutrition.** Portland, Oreg., Timber Press, 2013. 250p. illus. index. $24.95. ISBN 13: 978-1-60469-314-0.

Poor soil turns many garden dreams to dust. Organic matter and essential plant nutrients are inextricably tied together in good soil. The last quarter of this book provides valuable, basic information about how to improve soil by adding organic fertilizers, instead of just dumping on nitrogen, phosphorous, or potassium because a soil test shows one or more as deficient. The same section also includes easily replicated homemade fertilizer mixes that work well and suggestions for how to augment the organic material in soil—grass clippings will do in a pinch. Addition of organic material encourages microorganisms that build a subterranean community and support the growth of plants, sometimes directly as in the case of symbiotic mycorrhizal fungi. Most of the book is filled by three general biology textbook-level reviews: organelles in plant cells; structure and function of tissues that transport water and nutrients; and structure of organic compounds. Von Liebig's law of the minimum is a recurring theme, as in it takes only one missing or deficient essential element to impede plant growth. Some readers will be jarred by the repeated references to plants eating; only an organism that ingests food via a mouth eats. Plants are autotrophic, as the author points out, which means they are self-feeding. Plants depend on physical chemistry—absorption, osmosis, gas exchange—to take in nutrients and water and carbon dioxide; then, they use the energy from sunlight to convert that precious mix to the carbohydrates that support life on earth.—**Diane M. Calabrese**

1111.   Nagel, Vanessa Gardner. **The Professional Designers Guide to Garden Furnishings.** Portland, Oreg., Timber Press, 2013. 308p. illus. index. $34.95. ISBN 13: 978-1-60469-293-8.

For this ardent gardener who recently began experimenting with painted concrete structures amongst flora of all kinds, this volume is as timely as it is gorgeous and informative. Garden objects, which the author calls furnishings, are first put in context historically. Who does not love the Lutyens bench, also known as Thakeham seat? Then readers will find a survey of some of the most familiar architectural styles and environs, such as Craftsman and Victorian and woodland and tropical, sets the tone for thinking about complementary structures, plants, and objects. With imagination ignited, the reader turns next to discussion of some of the most familiar materials used in garden objects, beginning with wood. Each material discussed, including metal, glass, stone, and fabric, is treated in enough depth to give confidence to the gardener who would enhance a garden space with objects. The reader might be pleasantly surprised, for instance, to find lucid illustrations of sawn lumber patterns and joinery. Resources for garden furnishings include an icon-driven guide to vendor company Websites. There is also a robust index and a list of design centers that includes real- and virtual-world addresses. Each photograph is credited. Although this gardener will never be persuaded a sculpture made from aluminum cans or anything made from fabric belongs in a green space, there is so much to embrace in this volume that it must be recommended most highly. The book is delectable. A future volume might put some focus on flower boxes and bricks, which want for attention here.—**Diane M. Calabrese**

1112.   Oudolf, Piet, and Noel Kingsbury. **Planting: A New Perspective.** Portland, Oreg., Timber Press, 2013. 280p. illus. index. $39.95. ISBN 13: 978-1-60469-370-6.

Beauty, an invitation to wildlife, sustainability, and even greater resilience in the context of climatic instability, are just some of the good outcomes that derive from combining long-lived perennials with woody plants. Beginning with that premise, the authors move to exemplars of planted spaces that are less obviously structured gardens than complementary enhancements to a place. The authors both have roots in nursery work and they know plants. They showcase abundant strong landscape designs and reveal many equally strong opinions. Be prepared to read about the connection between imperialism and aggressive humanity in the loss of legacy gardens, the garish nature of annuals, the cliché that is a sedum roof or the notion of a mixed planting, and a dislike of snakes. Perhaps to meet the authors and rebut points is the answer. Until then, readers will find the focus the authors put on form in the context of an annual cycle very useful. Consider the section on combining plants. It encourages visualization of what a given perennial will add in terms of breadth, depth and height. There's also attention to color. Charts provide a realistic look at the interval of the year that flowers can be expected for a particular plant. The authors put the emphasis on seasonal interest instead of blooms and rightly so. Foliage and complexity of plant morphs add dimensions that are just as visually captivating as flowers. The plant directory that rounds out the book is concise and accurate. As a guide to planting perspective or perspective in planting, this volume is excellent.—**Diane M. Calabrese**

1113.   Rubin, Greg, and Lucy Warren. **The California Native Landscape: The Homeowner's Design Guide to Restoring Its Beauty and Balance.** Portland, Oreg., Timber Press, 2013. 372p. illus. index. $34.95. ISBN 13: 978-1-60469-232-7.

This classic Timber Press book, beautifully designed, brimming with 270 color photographs, and written by two passionate gardening professionals, is an essential purchase for California academic and public libraries, but also belongs in larger library gardening collections in other states with similar physical environments. Authors Greg Rubin, the respected owner of a well-known native landscape design firm, and Lucy Warren, former editor of *California Garden* magazine and gardening columnist for a San Diego newspaper, maintain that gardeners should "think and buy local" (p. 10) because native plants are both attractive and easy to maintain. Chapters 1-3 introduce readers to California's environment and survey the human effects on soil and plants. Chapters 4 and 5 introduce the concepts of garden design and style. The heart of the book, chapter 6, offers more than 100 pages of detailed plant selection advice featuring native trees, shrubs, ground covers, perennials, vines, and monocots. Chapters 7 and 8 explain specialized native plant installation, care, and maintenance techniques. The next two chapters detail pest, disease, and weed-related problems. The authors devote their final chapter to debunking the myth that native plants fuel wildfires and contend that properly sited or managed native plants can actual or slow fires.

The Resources section includes books, articles, and online sources, notably contact information for regional chapters of the California Native Plant Society and for California native plant nurseries. In conclusion, the authors write, "we envision a new approach to landscape in California; one that is much more purposeful, healthier, and sustainable" (p. 349). Readers who share the view that "a shift to a wiser, more natural protocol where native plants are predominant, rather than the exception" (p. 30) and find that gardening motto desirable will find ample inspiration and guidance in this book.—**Julienne L. Wood**

1114.   Stibolt, Ginny, and Melissa Contreras. **Organic Methods for Vegetable Gardening in Florida.** Gainesville, Fla., University Press of Florida, 2013. 326p. illus. index. $24.95. ISBN 13: 978-0-8130-4401-9.

It is good to see garden hygiene, including proper hand washing and vegetable waste disposal, get the attention it deserves. Any gardener, even a veteran, can find some new bit of information here. Garden wagons to easily move plants and change their exposure to sun, and the collection of rabbit feces for fertilizer are among the interesting possibilities. Guidance with soil preparation, design and build of raised beds, drip irrigation and rain barrels, plant selection and seed collection are part of the book. There are even a few recipes. Novice gardeners living anywhere will benefit from the discussion of the basics of gardening and organic gardening. Florida gardeners, especially recent arrivals, get a great start on what they need to know about growing vegetables in the Sunshine State. In an appendix, North, Central, and South Florida each receive a separate month-by-month set of recommendations for what a gardener should be doing. The glossary is adequate, but a few of the entries are not well defined. The distinction between ecology and environment is made clear, however, and that is a beautiful thing. We are wholly in favor of gardens here, there, and everywhere. Somehow, though, it seems that two books—a how-to on organic gardening in Florida and a philosophical-political tome on trends in edible gardening—would be far better. The mention of politically tied, quasi-organic gardens could then be omitted from the how-to. Gardening is transcendent; organic gardening is a specific sort. And inspiration, wishful thinking, and politics do not mix.—**Diane M. Calabrese**

1115.   **The Timber Press Guide to Vegetable Gardening in the Mountain States.** By Mary Ann Newcomer. Portland, Oreg., Timber Press, 2014. 223p. illus. index. $19.95pa. ISBN 13: 978-1-60469-427-7.

1116.   **The Timber Press Guide to Vegetable Gardening in the Northeast.** By Marie Iannotti. Portland, Oreg., Timber Press, 2014. 231p. illus. index. $19.95pa. ISBN 13: 978-1-60469-421-5.

1117.   **The Timber Press Guide to Vegetable Gardening in the Pacific Northwest.** By Lorene Edwards Forkner. Portland, Oreg., Timber Press, 2013. 231p. illus. index. $19.95pa. ISBN 13: 978-1-60469-361-5.

1118.   **The Timber Press Guide to Vegetable Gardening in the Southeast.** By Ira Wallace. Portland, Oreg., Timber Press, 2014. 215p. illus. index. $19.95pa. ISBN 13: 978-1-60469-371-3.

These four volumes, which have been written to address the growing requirements in the various regions of the United States, have been written by four well-qualified and experienced authors. The guides are written in an easy-to-read style that can be used for a quick look-up or read all the way through. Each work begins with a section titled "Get Started" in which the author addresses the unique climate of the region, gardening basics, and how to plan a garden that will be fruitful all year long. Section two, "Get Planting," provides monthly planning guide to depict what you can do in your garden from January through December. Each month the authors provide information on what you can be doing to ensure that you have a bountiful garden, including starting the garden in March, reaping the rewards in August, putting the garden to bed in October, and gift ideas from the garden in December. The final section is an A to Z guide to vegetables that are sure to grow in the specific environment being addressed, whether it is the damp environment of the Northwest, the dry and colder environment of the mountain states, or the warm humid environment of the Southeast. The final section includes a list of resources and services, a list of further reading, metric conversions, and an index. These books are an ideal read for gardener's looking to grow the healthiest, most problem-free plants and vegetables in the various regions in the United Sates. They will be useful in most public library gardening collections in their respective regions.—**Diane M. Calabrese**

1119. Tychonievich, Joseph. **Plant Breeding for the Home Gardener: How to Create Unique Vegetables & Flowers.** Portland, Oreg., Timber Press, 2013. 215p. illus. index. $19.95pa. ISBN 13: 978-1-60469-364-5.

Author Joseph Tychonievich, nursery manager for Arrowhead Alpines and gardening blogger, boldly declares that "if you garden, you can breed plants" (p. 11). This clearly written, basic guide, built on Tychonievich's knowledge of horticulture, plant breeding and genetics, and personal experience dating from his childhood experiments with violas in northeastern Ohio, could stimulate even the most skeptical or inexperienced readers to launch their own plant breeding experiments.

In chapter 1 the author provides a brief history of plant breeding featuring corn and tomatoes and compares the goals of gardeners and commercial growers. Chapter 2 urges gardeners to develop breeding goals based both on the plant they hope to create and the already available plants, then engage in slow and steady experiments such as his own work with zucchini and peppers. Chapter 3, "How to Make a Cross," delivers technical information about plant pollination in easy-to-understand language and yields useful details about equipment, labels, and notebook entries. Chapter 4 gently introduces the principles of genetics, including genes, chromosomes, inheritance patterns, outcrosses, and cloning. In chapter 5 the author indicates how to select, name, and share favorites. In chapter 6 he outlines advanced techniques used by commercial breeders.

Chapter 7 reveals more specifics about breeding popular flowers and vegetables such as coleus, daffodils, roses, zinnias, beans, cabbage, corn, lettuce, squash, and tomatoes. The book closes with a short list of Recommended Readings, a page of Useful Websites, 12 Plant Sources (including several foreign seed suppliers), and an index. Inspirational for current and potential gardeners, this encouraging book could also guide teachers and students exploring the basics of botany. This work is appropriate for middle and high school libraries, all public libraries, and college or university undergraduate collections.—**Julienne L. Wood**

1120. Wilson, Andrew. **Small Garden Handbook: Making the Most of Your Outdoor Space.** New York, Firefly Books, 2013. 224p. illus. index. $24.95pa. ISBN 13: 978-1-77085-192-4.

Gardeners seeking privacy, contemplative space, added living space, or just a gorgeous assemblage of flora take note: This book if stuffed with useful nuggets and gorgeous ideas and essential advice. Especially welcome is the attention given to the basics, such as being realistic about the size of a prospective garden space, capitalizing on existing features, and ridding the soil of nuisance plants first. It is good to see geometric shapes, textures, and hardscapes get the attention they deserve. The basic how-to for raised beds, preparing soil, stratifying plantings, incorporating water, and making certain a roof garden does not outmatch the loading bearing of a structure are all here. And, although this reviewer is not excited about plastic furniture or artificial turf in the garden, I can say the author thoroughly covers the possibilities, including screens and woven hangings. Recommendations for annuals and shrubs are geared to the latitude and longitude of England, but even novice gardeners can extrapolate. My two concerns with the handbook are minor and stem from intense interest. I would like to know more about the wind turbines around an industrial recycling center that are partly obscured by a yew hedge (page 71) ; and so, it would be wonderful to have more information on places photographs were taken. The photograph credits relegated to one-page acknowledgement section do not serve the reader or the photographer well. Overall, however, the book is nothing less than a robust packet of informative delight.—**Diane M. Calabrese**

Indexes

1121.   Garden, Landscape & Horticulture Index. http://www.ebscohost.com/academic/garden-landscape-horticulture-index. [Website]. Ipswich, Mass., EBSCO. Price negotiated by site. Date reviewed: 2013.

One of the Gale InfoTrac collections, the *Gardening, Landscape and Horticulture Collection*, much like EBSCO's *Garden, Landscape & Horticulture Index*, is heavily concentrated in horticulture, but there are also resources dealing with landscape planning, design, and conservation. The EBSCO database focuses on horticulture; however, the indexing and abstracting of content does cover areas of architectural overlap and intersection, such as landscape design. The majority of the more than 500 titles that are covered by this database are in English and are from publications dating back only to the early 2000s. Both of these sources are reliable and rich in content.—**Anna H. Perrault**

31 Biological Sciences

Biology

Catalogs and Collections

1122. **Bacteriology Abstracts. http://www.csa.com/factsheets/bacteriology-set-c.php.** [Website]. Ann Arbor, Mich., ProQuest. Price negotiated by site. Date reviewed: 2013.

Covering topics ranging from bacterial immunology and vaccinations to disease of humans and animals, the journal provides access to far-reaching clinical finding as well as all aspects of pure bacteriology, biochemistry, and genetics. Main coverage includes bacteriology and microbiology, bacterial immunology, vaccinations, antibiotics, and immunology. General microbiologists and bacteriologists aren't the only specialists who will find value in this database for important perspectives in the field. The journal is also valuable to environmentalists, medical and veterinary laboratory staff, agricultural researchers, cell biologists, geneticists, toxicologists, and many others.—**James E. Bobick**

1123. **Biosis Previews. http://thomsonreuters.com/biosis-previews/.** [Website]. New York, Thomson Reuters. Price negotiated by site. Date reviewed: 2013.

Biosis Previews is a key database for literature searching in biological and life sciences. It covers medical topics with focus on basic research and its coverage of clinical medicine. The site combines journal content from Biological Abstracts with supplemental, non-journal coverage from Biological Abstracts/RRM (Reports, Reviews, Meetings). Specialized indexing helps users discover more accurate, context-sensitive results.—**James E. Bobick**

1124. **CSA Biological Sciences. http://www.csa.com/factsheets/biolclust-set-c.php.** [Website]. Ann Arbor, Mich., ProQuest. Price negotiated by site. Date reviewed: 2013.

This site covers resources in life sciences disciplines, including cell and molecular biology, neuroscience, biochemistry, entomology, ecology, immunology, microbiology, genetics, immunology, and agriculture. Supporting over two dozen areas of expertise, this CSA database provides access to literature from over 8,000 serials, as well as conference proceedings, technical reports, monographs and selected books and patents. Biological Sciences supplements the Biological Sciences Database and select related files with access to deep indexing for tables, figures, graphs, charts and other illustrations from the scholarly research and technical literature for selected records. Records from the database appear with searches of the Biological Sciences Database and related databases to provide an additional path for discovery.—**James E. Bobick**

1125.   Genetics Home Reference. http://ghr.nlm.nih.gov/. [Website]. United States National Library of Medicine. Free. Date reviewed: 2014.

This site is a guide to understanding genetic conditions—more than 900 of them. The site can be searched by genetic conditions, genes, or chromosomes, with the explanation for each topic clearly explained and with hyperlinks to other relevant topics inserted. Also included are resources for understanding how genes work, including information on mutations, genetic testing, inheritance, and genetic research; a glossary; and a Resources page that links to relevant organizations.—**Shannon Graff Hysell**

Dictionaries and Encyclopedias

1126.   Grzimek's Animal Life Encyclopedia: Extinction. Norman MacLeod, ed. Stamford, Conn., Gale/Cengage Learning, 2013. 2v. illus. maps. index. $282.00/set. ISBN 13: 978-1-4144-9067-0; 978-1-4144-9070-0 (e-book).

Intended as a complement to *Grzimek's Animal Life Encyclopedia: Evolution* published in 2011 (see ARBA 2012, entry 1176), *Grzimek's Animal Life Encyclopedia: Extinction* is a two-volume set addressing the diverse field of evolutionary research. Instead of focusing on either ancient extinctions or modern biodiversity issues as previous publications, *Evolution* attempts to unite these disparate disciplines into a single work. Unfortunately, this is not done through an intuitive organizational structure. The entries on the table of contents appear random, making it hard to know where to look for specific information. For example, if you want to learn about the passenger pigeon do you look under Birds (modern), Historical Extinctions (1850 – present), Modern Biodiversity Crisis, or somewhere else? Actually, the most complete entry is under Endangered Species, with no coverage under Birds (modern) or Historical Extinctions (1850 – present). For topical access most users will need to rely on the 30-page index at the back of the book. Aside from this shortcoming, the entries themselves are thorough (approximately 10 pages in length), well written, and include occasional illustrations, photographs, figures, or tables. At the end of the book there is a bibliography for further reading of approximately 200 sources. This is in addition to the references included at the end of each entry. Written by approximately 200 contributing scholars, this source does provide a good scientific introduction to the concepts and processes of extinction. Yet, at the same time, it is a hard book to recommend. Because the topics are so disparate, with no unifying themes or categories, there isn't a good context to frame the information. As a result, both public library users, and lower level undergraduates, will likely turn to other sources.—**Kevin McDonough**

1127.   Kelly, Evelyn B. Encyclopedia of Human Genetics and Disease. Santa Barbara, Calif., Greenwood Press/ABC-CLIO, 2013. 2v. illus. index. $189.00/set. ISBN 13: 978-0-313-38713-5; 978-0-313-38714-2 (e-book).

The *Encyclopedia of Human Genetics and Disease* is a two-volume encyclopedia that brings together short essays on a variety of genetic diseases and general topics related to genetics. It includes 376 entries—varying in length from 550-1,700 word entries on specific disorders to 1,000-3,000 word "Special Topics." Most of the entries are about specific disorders, from "Aarskog-Scott Syndrome" to "Zellweger Syndrome," while the 18 "Special Topics" are on general topics related to genetics, such as "Eugenics." The entries are arranged alphabetically. Each disease/disorder entry follows a standard format that includes information such as prevalence of the disease, additional names, general information, genetic cause, treatment, and further reading. In addition to the main entries there are three overview essays on "Genetic Disorders 101," "Proteomics 101," and "The Genome and the Foundations of Genetics, with Timelines," as well as an index and a list of some helpful additional resources for further study. According to the introduction, this work is aimed primarily at high school students, undergraduates, and lay people rather than professionals or practitioners.

This resource is a quick guide that will be of particular use for high school students beginning a research paper, but may also be useful to early undergraduates looking for basic information on a particular genetic disease. The entries are short, providing relevant information, especially regarding the genes involved with the disorder. The entries will not overwhelm a student new to the topic, but they also provide additional resources as a gateway to more in depth information if a student wishes to go further. While the content will be useful to young students, there are some issues with the encyclopedia's formatting and the quality of the index. For example, the contents does not provide page numbers for entries except the three main overview essays; the Further Reading sections contain mostly URLs, better suited to the e-book version of this encyclopedia where they could be hyperlinked; and the index does not include gene names. Even with the formatting and index issues, this encyclopedia will be useful to students looking for an introduction to human genetics and genetic diseases.—**Megan Toups**

1128. **NatureServe Explorer: An Online Encyclopedia of Life.** http://www.natureserve.org/explorer/. [Website]. Free. Date reviewed: 2013.

   NatureServe Explorer provides conservation status, taxonomy, distribution, and life history information for more than 70,000 plants, animals, and ecological communities and systems in the United States and Canada. The data available through *NatureServe Explorer* represent a snapshot of the U.S. and Canadian data managed in the NatureServe Central Databases. Hundreds of natural heritage program scientists and other collaborators offer input to these databases. The database is "periodically updated from these central databases to reflect information from new field surveys, the latest taxonomic treatments and other scientific publications, and new conservation status assessments." These updates are somewhat too infrequent. In order to have more value, the updates should be done more frequently.—**William O. Scheeren**

Handbooks and Yearbooks

1129. **Building Blocks of Science—Life Science.** Chicago, World Book, 2014. 8v. illus. index. $239.00/set. ISBN 13: 978-0-7166-1840-9.

   Information in this set is presented in a graphic novel format with a few real images interspersed. The few small photographs are supportive to the text and are clear and crisp. Each cartoon character presents their concept in a basic and easy-to-understand manner. The information is direct and moves smoothly from questions to facts or statements. The whimsical characters guide the reader through the human body systems. Throughout there are illustrations of the different systems within the body. The graphic novel format in this series is geared toward younger students who are comic book fans. Information is included about how scientists use their knowledge of the topic and the importance of that knowledge. Each volume presents a good informational resource to basic science concepts. The work is supplemented with a glossary, additional Websites, and an index.—**ARBA Staff Reviewer**

Botany

General Works

Dictionaries and Encyclopedias

1130. **Encyclopedia of Cultivated Plants: From Acacia to Zinnia.** Christopher Cumo, ed. Santa Barbara, Calif., ABC-CLIO, 2013. 3v. illus. index. $294.00/set. ISBN 13: 978-1-59884-774-1; 978-1-59884-775-8 (e-book).

This three-volume set covers information for specific plants and food crops. Each entry has background information with additional material such as details on the origin, diffusion, description, production, history of the plant; the attributes, nutrients, cultivation; mythology, folklore, and religion. The work also covers breeding and cultivars; habitat and ecological impact; disease and pests; threats to the plant; varieties and/or species; the useful of the plant, horticultural uses, culinary uses, medicinal uses, and cosmetic uses; effects on agriculture; and further readings. The content is predominantly text, although there is the occasional black-and-white photograph. The title also includes a guide to related topics so the reader is directed from the more general term to the specific plants, such as from fiber plants to flax, or from herbs to dill. A selected bibliography and index as well as a listing of organizations providing information on cultivated plants are also included. Researchers, students, and gardeners will find this title of use.—**Denise A. Garofalo**

1131.   Hodge, Geoff. **Practical Botany for Gardeners: Over 3,000 Botanical Terms Explained and Explored.** Chicago, University of Chicago Press, 2013. 2013. illus. index. $25.00. ISBN 13: 978-0-226-09393-2.

This work will shed light on the world of botanical science for the novice and experienced gardener alike. The work provides the user with scientific definitions and explanations right alongside gardening tips. The authors easy prose will help reveal the secrets of the botanical universe. Chapters are arranged by theme, including plant types, plant parts, inner workings, and external factors. Alongside the clear definitions are sidebars on "Great Botanists" and "Botany in Action," which provide interesting facts and tips for gardeners. A major highlight in this book is the 200 botanical illustrations and diagrams that demonstrate the concepts of botanical science. This work is an introductory survey of the field of botany presented in layperson's terms. This work is recommended for anyone wanting to know the how and why of the most commonly used garden plants.—**Shannon Graff Hysell**

Handbooks and Yearbooks

1132.   Musselman, Lytton John, and Harold J. Wiggins. **The Quick Guide to Wild Edible Plants: Easy to Pick, Easy to Prepare.** Baltimore, Md., Johns Hopkins University Press, 2013. 133p. illus. $24.95pa. ISBN 13: 978-1-4214-0871-2.

This small, practical, and fun book adds value to the growing literature on wild plants in North America. The eminently qualified botanist authors, who have both published other books and scientific articles on plants, describe their latest book as "quirky." Quirky because the plants are generally "easy to pick and prepare" (as the subtitle indicates) in the Middle Atlantic States and Northeast, and the authors say they taste good too. They are also "underutilized" plants, meaning you will not find them frequently in other books on the subject.

One striking feature of the slightly large pocket-sized book is the over 100 excellent color photographs which make identification of the 50 wild edibles straightforward. Plus, importantly, these 50 plants do not have toxic look-alikes. Indeed, the first chapter after the introduction, is "Deadly Harvest: Plants you Should Avoid." The other edible plant chapters are uniquely divided into: Condiments, Aperitifs, Greens, Starches, Grains, Flowers, Sweets, Cordials, and Mushrooms. Each plant has a recipe where the wild plant is the main ingredient, not just a minor addition. Quirky examples are: Cattail Corndogs, Nettle Omelets, Crunchy Kudzu Leaf Chips, Fungus Chicken Fingers, Oyster Mushroom Soup, Pawpaw Bread, Red Sorrel Pilaf, and Wild Blueberry Cordial.

The book cover has an endorsement from Garrison Keillor, which will send many *Prairie Home Companion* aficionados into the outdoors searching for a unique menu item to prepare. Public libraries and any library supporting biological sciences will benefit from this charming book.—**Georgia Briscoe**

1133.   Walker, Timothy. **Plant Conservation: Why it Matters and How It Works.** Portland, Oreg., Timber Press, 2013. 303p. index. $29.95. ISBN 13: 978-1-60469-260-0.

This unique work, author by the Director of the University of Oxford Botanic Garden and a member of the group of conservation biologists helping to develop the Global Strategy for Plant Conservation, explores the implications associated with the possible extinction of plants currently under environmental threat. The author argues that many of the plants that could become extinct have the potential to be used for tomorrow's foods, fuel, or medical cures. The book explains in plain language the most crucial areas of plant conservation and how the general public can contribute toward ensuring further plant extinctions. He demonstrates how gardeners can contribute by growing their own food to decrease the reliance on large farms as well as how critical it is to make smart choices for the garden to ensure that invasive plants do not threaten plant life native to the region. The book is divided into four parts: The Global Garden List; Oath of a Plant Steward: To Conserve and Protect; And Justice for All: Diversity Without Adversity; and What Can You Do? Partnership and Practice in Plant Conservation. The work concludes with a further reading list, a list of organizations, conversion tables, and an index.—**Diane M. Calabrese**

Flowering Plants

1134.   Taylor, Walter Kingsley. **Florida Wildflowers: A Comprehensive Guide.** Gainesville, Fla., University Press of Florida, 2013. 567p. illus. index. $29.95pa. ISBN 13: 978-0-8130-4425-5.

Author Walter Kingsley Taylor, professor emeritus of biology at the University of Central Florida, has lived in Florida 42 years, has visited all of its counties at least once, and clearly loves his adopted state. He defines wildflowers as "any flowering plants growing in a natural state" (p. xiii). Librarians who purchased his popular earlier book, *Florida Wildflowers in Their Natural Communities* (1998), may ask why this new title. As Taylor accurately asserts, this title reflects "numerous major changes in plant taxonomy and nomenclature" and "a major update and reassessment of Florida's natural communities by Florida Natural Areas Inventory," provides rewritten natural community and species descriptions, adds more than 350 photographs with all other images improved, includes a substantial new section on some 400 species in major wetland communities, and offers notation of native/non-native and threatened/endangered status for all species (p. xi). What both books share is an unorthodox organization presenting plants by well-defined habitat areas and Taylor's two aims—making it easy and fun for hikers and flower seekers to find and identify flowers and encouraging his readers to become active to protect those flowers.

A useful section on Florida's geography, geology, and soil precedes an introduction designed to assist readers as they learn to identify wildflowers, understand the basics of flower structure and flowering times, and visualize the distribution of wildflowers. Parts 1-4 detail wildflowers found in Florida's Hardwood Forested Uplands and wetlands. Numbered, individual species descriptions appear under their specific environment, then by common name, scientific name and its source, description, flowering time, habitat, range (counties), comment, native or not, threatened or endangered, and synonym. Detailed color photographs clearly picture both the various habitats and 752 wildflowers.

Taylor's friendly writing style and authoritative content make this guide an essential purchase for all Florida libraries and for other academic and public libraries with large biology collections. Comprehensive but perhaps a bit too heavy to carry into the field, it will delight both active and armchair wildflower enthusiasts as well as biology students and professionals.—**Julienne L. Wood**

Trees and Shrubs

1135.   Jones, Ronald L., and B. Eugene Wofford. **Woody Plants of Kentucky and Tennessee: The Complete Winter Guide to Their Identification and Use.** Lexington, Ky., University Press of Kentucky, 2013. 143p. illus. index. $45.00. ISBN 13: 978-0-8131-4250-0; 978-0-8131-4309-5 (e-book).

Almost all plant identification guides deal with plants during the growing season when they have leaves. This guide fills in by helping users identify woody plants during the winter, by focusing on leaf scars, buds, fruits, and seeds. Users should use the detailed keys to identify plants to species, and then confirm their identification with species accounts and photographs. The species accounts include common names, habitat and range, frequency, and notes. Each generic account also provides a description of bark, twig, leaf scar, bud, and other descriptive notes, as well as information on the use of members of the genus for food, medicine, fiber, and weapons both historically and currently. Appendixes list plants useful for food, medicine, cordage, and for constructing bows and arrows. There is also a glossary, bibliography, and genus and species index as well as extensive introductory information.

While the guide focuses on the woody plants of Kentucky and Tennessee, it will be useful in the surrounding states as well since many of the plants have wider distribution. It is a good purchase for special and academic libraries that focus on botany, forestry, or plant use, and for public libraries in and near the core states.—**Diane Schmidt**

1136.   More, David, and John White. **The Illustrated Encyclopedia of Trees.** 2d ed. Princeton, N.J., Princeton University Press, 2013. 832p. illus. index. $49.95. ISBN 13: 978-0-691-15823-5.

The Illustrated Encyclopedia of Trees covers more than 1,900 trees consisting of natural species and cultivars, which are trees bred for desirable characteristics such as ornamental flowers. The brief descriptions include physical attributes, what the wood is used for, and native region. A specific tree can be found by checking the Index of Scientific Names or Index of English Names sections.

Colorful illustrations show unique characteristics that help identify a tree more easily. For instance, depictions of Rauli Beech show the "spiky green" fruit, elliptical leaf shape, and bark pattern. The "Trees for Problem Sites or Special Needs" listings show types that should or should not be considered under certain conditions. For instance, the Sweet Gum provides especially good fall leaf colors and the Ash is better suited for clay soils. The names of natural species are in boldface; cultivars have the scientific name italicized followed by the word "cultivar" but have English names in the written text. For example, the Lawson Cypress is followed by the cultivars "Somerset" and "Pottenni." Separate categories further distinguish features such as height in 10 and 20 years and full grown.

The foreword has only the two authors' initials but the full names should come first to clarify what these letters refer to. The foreword and introduction state trees in Western Europe and or North America are featured in the book, but many from other places. For example, the Engler Beech grows in China. The introduction should clarify the geographic areas. The "Unusual Garden Trees" list includes Antarctic Southern Beech, but there is no separate entry. A new entry could include history on why this tree received the name "Antarctic" even though it actually grows in rainforests and native to Chile. This publication has exceptional illustrations and is a good starting point to find general information on a wide variety of trees.—**Mike Parchinski**

Natural History

Catalogs and Collections

1137.   **Biological Inventories of the World's Protected Areas. http://www.ice.ucdavis.edu/ bioinventory/bioinventory.html.** [Website]. Free. Date reviewed: 2013.

This database was developed by The Information Center for the Environment (ICE), a part of the Department of Environmental Science & Policy at the University of California, Davis. Numerous collaborators helped in developing databases containing documented, taxonomically harmonized species inventories of plants and animals reported from the world's protected areas." This allows students and teachers access to information that is otherwise largely unavailable via the Internet and provide a mechanism for protected areas and protected area systems to publish their species inventories when they would otherwise be unable to do so. With the focus of many groups on saving endangered plants and animals, this site would help them choose a species of interest.—**William O. Scheeren**

1138. **CSA Illustrata: Natural Sciences. http://www.csa.com/factsheets/objectsclust-nats-set-c. php.** [Website]. Ann Arbor, Mich., ProQuest. Price negotiated by site. Date reviewed: 2013.

This Cambridge Scientific Abstracts database indexes tables, figures, graphs, charts, and other illustrations from scholarly literature in agriculture, biology, conservation, earth sciences, environmental studies, fish and fisheries, food and food industries, forests and forestry, geography, medical sciences, meteorology, veterinary sciences, and water resources since 1997.—**James E. Bobick**

Handbooks and Yearbooks

1139. **Essential Readings in Wildlife Management & Conservation.** Paul R. Krausman and Bruce D. Leoppold, eds. Baltimore, Md., Johns Hopkins University Press, 2013. 682p. illus. index. $50.00. ISBN 13: 978-1-4214-0818-7.

Intended as an essential resource to influential leaders in the field of wildlife management, *Essential Readings in Wildlife Management & Conservation* provides practical and conceptual topics on nearly every aspect of this field. Each of the 42 essays is written by one or more experts from academia, those practicing in the field, or government. The editors introduce each article with commentary explaining the article's relevance to the field and the inspiration behind it. The work is divided into four sections: "Our Philosophical Roots," "Animals, Ecology, & Populations"; ""Habitat"; and "Human Dimensions." Each article runs 10-20 pages in length and many have charts, references, and lists of related readings. The articles reflect the history of wildlife management, with many dating back to the early and mid-twentieth century. This manual would be useful for large public libraries and for academic libraries supporting zoology or wildlife management.—**ARBA Staff Reviewer**

1140. Latham, Donna. **Backyard Biology: Investigate Habitats Outside Your Door with 25 Projects.** White River Junction, Vt., Nomad Press, 2013. 128p. Illus. index. $15.95. 978-1-6193015-1-1.

Although basic, the activities and background information in this slim volume will keep young explorers busy as they learn about the natural environment in their community. Designed with the urban and suburban lifestyle in mind, these projects and experiments can be completed using items easily found. The author does a nice job of explaining each step clearly. Each chapter begins with an introduction to the area of biology, starting with the most basic unit cells, and progressing into animal life cycles and conservation; simple cartoon-style illustrations and diagrams enhance content and engage young readers. The introductions include a plethora of scientific vocabulary, definitions of which can be found in the "words to know" box on the same page. The activities require a fair amount of outside exploration and digging in the dirt, but for the adventurous explorer this volume is sure to provide hours of fun. The work is supplemented with a bibliography, glossary, additional Websites, and an index.—**Diane S. Hance**

1141. Newton, David E. **The Animal Experimentation Debate: A Reference Handbook.** Santa Barbara, Calif., ABC-CLIO, 2013. 322p. index. (Contemporary World Issues). $58.00. ISBN 13: 978-1-61069-317-2; 978-1-61069-318-9 (e-book).

The Animal Experimentation Debate is part of the publisher's Contemporary World Issues series, which collects statistics, primary sources, and wide-ranging opinion essays on various controversial topics, similar to Gale's Opposing Viewpoints series. An ideal source for high school and undergraduate projects, the book begins with a short history of dissection and vivisection, as well as the movement opposing these practices which first arose in the nineteenth century. Subsequent chapters summarize key facets of the debate and collect essays by leading voices from all sides, as well as profiles of well-known organizations and individual activists. The final chapters are more like appendixes: statistics, primary sources (such as key legislation), an extensive annotated bibliography of print and online sources, and a glossary. Concise, clearly written, and balanced, *The Animal Experimentation Debate* is a good choice for high school and academic libraries.—**Maren Williams**

Zoology

General Works

1142.   Campbell, Iain, and Sam Woods. **Wildlife of Australia.** Princeton, N.J., Princeton University Press, 2013. 286p. illus. maps. index. (Princeton Pocket Guides). $19.95pa. ISBN 13: 978-0-691-15353-7.

This book is an identification guide to those mammals (70 species), birds (350 species), reptiles (30 species), and frogs (16 species) most likely to be encountered in Australia's most popular tourist destinations. After a section with descriptions and photographs of major habitats, species are described (2-6 per page) with color photographs on facing pages. Descriptions include identification features plus brief range, habitat, and natural history information. The descriptions are well written and pack in much interesting information. The coverage is very selective; comprehensive guides are listed in the bibliography. The book is compact and easy to use. Aimed especially at travelers, this guide is an excellent purchase for any library.—**Frederic F. Burchsted**

1143.   **The Habitats of Baby Animals Series.** New York, Crabtree, 2013. multivolume. illus. index. $19.95/vol.; $8.95pa./vol.

All authored by one person, Bobbie Kalman, this multivolume set at informs and educate as they entertain. Written in simple language with many colorful photographs and brief paragraphs and sentences the volumes teach about ecology, animals, geography, and biomes such as rivers, northern forests, islands, and cities. The books do not have consistent tables of content, although each teaches about parents, babies, eating habits, and the food chain in that particular environmental area. Words to know are combined with the index, although there is no glossary. This is good for reading aloud and for independent research in the lower to middle elementary grades.—**Sara Marcus**

1144.   **Zoological Record Plus. http://thomsonreuters.com/products_services/science/.** [Website]. New York, N.Y., Thomson Reuters. Price negotiated by site. Date reviewed: 2013.

This database, currently produced by Thomson Scientific and formerly by BIOSIS and the Zoological Society of London, provides extensive coverage of the world's zoological and animal science literature, covering all research from biochemistry to veterinary medicine. The database provides an easily searched collection of references from over 5,000 international serial publications, plus books, meetings, reviews, and other nonserial literature from over 100 countries.—**James E. Bobick**

Birds

1145.   Hirschfeld, Erik, Andy Swash, and Robert Still. **The World's Rarest Birds.** Princeton, N.J., Princeton University Press, 2013. 360p. illus. maps. index. $45.00. ISBN 13: 978-0-691-15596-8.

    This is a compendium of up-to-date information about rare birds worldwide from *Birdlife International*. Some 590 species of endangered or critically endangered birds, or birds who exist only in captivity, are described. There are 515 species accounts accompanied by color photographs. Colored illustrations by Tomasz Cofta are included for the 75 species for which color photographs are not available. Included are narrative chapters giving a general picture of birdlife and rare birds, as well as chapters on the threats that birds face, threats without borders, and the need for conservation. Descriptions of each species are included within one of six regional sections or a section on "data-deficient species" for which there is little up-to-date information. Each entry includes a color photograph or illustration of the bird, a range map, estimated population of the species, a list of primary threats to the species, a paragraph of about 100 words describing where the bird can be found, an explanation of threats to the species, and conservation efforts to preserve it. A chart listing extinct species of birds and a list of globally threatened bird families are included in appendixes. There is an index that includes the English and scientific names of all bird species mentioned in the book. There is no bibliography, but each species description includes a QR code linked directly to the relevant species factsheet on *Birdlife International*'s Website. The editors are variously described as consultants in ornithology, wildlife photographers, naturalists, or graphic artists.

    This is a sumptuous book that is well worth its price, and it belongs in every library. It has considerable potential reference use, especially in libraries that service a population engaged in natural history courses or birders. The only remotely similar book is *Atlas of Rare Birds* by Dominic Couzens (MIT, 2010).—**Jonathan F. Husband**

1146.   **The New Stokes Field Guide to Birds: Eastern Region.** By Donald Stokes, and Lillian Stokes. New York, Little, Brown, 2013. 592p. illus. maps. index. $19.99pa. ISBN 13: 978-0-316-213929.

1147.   **The New Stokes Field Guide to Birds: Western Region.** By Donald Stokes and Lillian Stokes. New York, Little, Brown, 2013. 512p. illus. maps. index. $19.99pa. ISBN 13: 978-0-316-21393-6.

    Fans of birdwatching will be thrilled to find these updated Stokes field guides on the shelves of their public library. While much of the information from the 1996 edition remains intact, the photographs have been updated along with any new information found by the authors during the 20 years since the last publication. The images appear much larger than in the past edition and there are far more of them, which will appeal to birders who rely on visual guides. Range maps are included, which will provide users with information on summer, winter, and migration ranges. Although some birds fit nicely into either the Western or the Eastern region, many of the bird flocks mentioned appear in both editions since they pass through both regions. The photographs are the most impressive addition to these new volumes. They include vivid shots of bids in flight, juvenile and adult plumage, seasonal and gender variations, and color variations. These volumes will make great additions to a public libraries birding collection and will serve to supplement other popular birding guides. [R: LJ, 15 June 13, p. 113]—**Charles Leck**

1148.   Swanson, Sarah, and Max Smith. **Must-See Birds of the Pacific Northwest.** Portland, Oreg., Timber Press, 2013. 243p. illus. maps. index. $19.95pa. ISBN 13: 978-1-60469-337-9.

    This is a guide to 85 birds likely to be seen in the western parts of the states of Washington and Oregon and how to find them. One or two pages, illustrated by one or two color photographs of the bird, describe basic information about each bird—food and foraging, pairing and parenting, migrations and movements, where to find them, and other birds to see. The bird descriptions are arranged under rubrics such as Beach Birds, Big Birds, Singing Birds, and more. There is a short introduction to the basics of birding, a section describing places to go and weekend trips to take in search of these birds, an eclectic bibliography of two dozen (mostly) journal articles, and an index of popular bird names and places to go birding. Swanson is an environmental educator and Smith is a wildlife biologist with the U.S. Forest Service.

Because of its selectivity, reference vale of this book is minimal, even within the area covered. However, *Must-See Birds of the Pacific Northwest* is an attractive, readable, affordable volume that could be used as an introduction to birds and birding in public and school library collections within the states of Oregon and Washington.—**Jonathan F. Husband**

Fishes

1149.   Murdy, Edward O., and John A. Musick. **Field Guide to Fishes of the Chesapeake Bay.** Baltimore, Md., Johns Hopkins University Press, 2013. 345p. illus. index. $24.95pa. ISBN 13: 978-1-4214-0768-5.

The text of this field guide gives a brief biological overview of each fish. The introduction explains the history, watershed, and hydrology of the Chesapeake bay; seasonal fish faunal changes; and conservation and environmental management of the area. The illustrations, created by Val Kells, an experienced marine science illustrator, provide detailed accounts of each species. This field guide features full-color illustrations of more than 200 species found in the Chesapeake Bay. Each has a detailed description with mention of their physical characteristics, range, occurrence in the bay, reproduction, diet, and statistics from fishery research. The illustrations are presented adjacent from the text for easy reference. Fish that appear differently throughout the life span have multiple illustrations. Four appendixes round out the text: a key to the orders and families of Chesapeake Bay Fishes; a key to the families of Perciformes Fishes in the Chesapeake bay; keys to species within families; and fish species rarely record from the Chesapeake Bay. A glossary and index conclude the volume.

This book should be of interest to anyone with an interest in fish, oceanography, or conservation. It is an attractive purchase for any academic or public library.—**Elaine Ezell**

1150.   **The State of the World's Fisheries and Aquaculture, 2012.** New York, United Nations, 2012. 209p. $65.00. ISBN 13: 978-9-25-10722-57.

Divided into four sections, this biennial reference source will be useful to fishery biologists, students, conservationists, and anyone employed by the fishing industry. Part 1 provides statistics of the status of and trends in the fishery industry. The next two parts are concerned with recreational fisheries, fuel-efficient fishing, marine protected areas, ecosystem management, and certification. Part 4 focuses on the future of fisheries. The well-written chapters call attention to the issues, trends, and future of fisheries throughout the world. The work provides copious notes and references throughout but no bibliography for the whole volume. This volume will be useful in academic libraries offering courses in ecological and biological conservation and fisheries.—**Elaine Ezell**

Insects

1151.   Lebuhn, Gretchen. Illustrated by Noel B. Pugh. **Field Guide to the Common Bees of California: Including Bees of the Western United States.** Berkeley, Calif., University of California Press, 2013. 175p. illus. index. $55.00; $21.95pa. ISBN 13: 978-0-520-27283-5; 978-0-520-27284-2pa.

This field guide explores the lives of honey bees in California and offers tools for identifying the most common bees of the region. Readers will be introduced to 30 genera of native bees, and provided with an explanation of their importance in our own food supply and in our habitat. The author also suggests ways to support bee life within your own backyard. The author, a professor of biology at San Francisco State University and the Director of the Great Sunflower Project (a program designed to share information about bees and their importance), shares her expertise and observations from years of tracking California's bee species. The book is arranged into topical chapters that provide an introduction to bees and provide bee family and genus accounts. The volume is filled with photographs and illustrations that serve as example; the illustrations have been contributed Noel B. Pugh. The book concludes with two appendixes (bee families and genera found in California, and a key to females of genera included in this book) as well as a glossary, list of resources, and an index. This guide book is highly recommended for all libraries with natural history collections. Those on the Pacific Coast will want to order multiple copies.—**Shannon Graff Hysell**

Mammals

1152.　Petter, Jean-Jacques, and Francois Desbordes. **Primates of the World.** Princeton, N.J., Princeton University Press, 2013. 186p. illus. maps. index. $29.95. ISBN 13: 978-0-691-15695-8.

This attractive book features color paintings of all the living primate species. An introductory section on primate evolution, paleontology, and general biology is followed by a family tree and outline classification showing all the species. The bulk of the book is divided into geographical sections: Madagascar, South America, Asia, and Africa. There are paragraph-length descriptions of each family, subfamily, and genus, accompanied by superb color paintings of each species. The species list with each plate is keyed to a range map. There is also a short bibliography and species index.

The book is most comparable to Noel Rowe's 1996 *The Pictorial Guide to the Living Primates* (see ARBA 98, entry 1472; updated version available online to member of Primate Conservation Inc.). *The Pictorial Guide* is illustrated by color photographs and has a brief description of each species and thus offers more detailed information. *Primates of the World* has the advantage of a uniform format for the illustrations. The generic level descriptions in *Primates of the World* often give a more accessible perspective than the family and species level descriptions in *The Pictorial Guide*. It is also less than half the price of *The Pictorial Guide*. The text author died in 2002, and the roughly 20 species discovered since 2002 are not included, so it is not markedly more up-to-date. This work is an excellent purchase for academic and public libraries.—**Frederic F. Burchsted**

Marine Animals

1153.　Cole, Brandon, and Scott Michael. **Reef Life: A Guide to Tropical Marine Life.** Richmond Hills, Ont., Firefly Books, 2013. 616p. illus. maps. index. $35.00. ISBN 13: 978-1-77085-190-0.

This colorful, eye-catching title provides the reader with in-depth text on tropical marine ecosystems accompanied by brilliant photography. The work is essentially a field guide to hundreds of species, including ray-finned fish, marine mammals and reptiles, and invertebrates that reside in the reef ecosystem. The book centers around the "coral belt." There are maps of coral areas in the Maldives, the Eastern Caribbean Sea, and French Polynesia, to name a few. Along with information on the marine life in these areas the authors provide users with what they are likely to see while diving in these areas. For each wildlife creature described there is information on its size, location, common names, Latin classification, and any other interesting facts. The authors write from a stance that encourages conservation of these areas and provide users with information on how to be considerate to these environments. This title will be a welcome addition to both lower-level academic libraries and public libraries. It is useful as an identification guide as well as for those who want to browse the incredible photographs. [R: LJ, 15 June 13, pp. 112-113]—**Mark A. Wilson**

1154.   Johnson, William S., and Dennis M. Allen. **Zooplankton of the Atlantic and Gulf Coasts.** 2d ed. Illustrated by Marni Fylling. Baltimore, Md., Johns Hopkins University Press, 2012. 453p. illus. maps. index. $50.00. ISBN 13: 978-1-4214-0618-3.

Now in its 2d edition, this reference catalogs "hundreds of the most commonly encountered species" among the smaller residents off our southern and eastern shores. While not comprehensive, *Zooplankton* includes detailed descriptions and clear black-and-white line drawings of several species from each class or subclass presented. Descriptions incorporate geographic and seasonal distribution, mating and feeding habits, and references to further research on the species.

An introductory section covers basics like key terms, geographic features, and plankton collection methods. "Quick Picks," which prefaces the identification chapters, groups together a few drawings from each class so that users may visually approximate which one is likely to contain the species under study. Appendixes include a glossary and further information on collecting, preserving, and observing specimens. This work is recommended for university libraries supporting programs in marine science.— **Maren Williams**

1155.   **Starfish: Biology and Ecology of the Asteroidea.** John M. Lawrence, ed. Baltimore, Md., Johns Hopkins University Press, 2013. 266p. illus. $100.00. ISBN 13: 978-1-4214-0787-6.

This is a lovely book discussing one of the more fascinating animals in the world's oceans—starfish, or asteroids, as they are known by the scientists that study them. The text, by a professor of integrative biology at the University of South Florida, gives a brief biological overview of each starfish species. *Starfish* explores the biology and ecology of this animal. Chapters explore reproduction, biology, and the ecological role of starfish within their habitat. The work examines the functions of these invertebrates on the marine environment and how they influence the ocean food chain. Because the starfish is rare in its ability to regenerate its own body parts it is of particular interest to many other types of scientists well beyond marine biologists. A 10-page color plate of photographs in the middle of the book illustrates the many types of starfish. This book should be of interest to anyone with an interest in fish, oceanography, or conservation. It is an attractive purchase for any academic or public library.—**Shannon Graff Hysell**

Reptiles and Amphibians

1156.   Dixon, James R. **Amphibians & Reptiles of Texas: With Keys, Taxonomic Synopses, Bibliography, and Distribution Maps.** 3d ed. College Station, Tex., Texas A&M University Press, 2013. 447p. illus. maps. index. $39.95pa. ISBN 13: 978-1-60344-734-8.

This is a 3d edition of a book that now covers the 230 native and exotic species (284 taxa) of Texas herpetozoans. Texas A&M professor emeritus Dixon, a much-published herpetologist, has done a superb job of updating a volume that covers the state's salamanders, frogs, turtles, lizards, snakes, and alligator. The text and references are updated and the book now has a more attractive and useful format. Superb color photographs by professional photographer Toby J. Hibbits replace the monochrome photographs of the earlier editions and significantly improve the appearances and add immeasurably to the book's usefulness for species identifications.

Acknowledgments and the introduction begin the narrative. The introduction provides historical perspectives, comments on species conservation, notes on Texas herpetological literature, explanations of maps and keys, and recent nomenclatural changes affecting Texas herpetozans. The author has chosen to utilize generic names from the 2d edition but includes new generic names in parentheses in the keys, checklist, and species accounts.

Dichotomous keys to the amphibians and reptiles of Texas succeed the introduction. Black-and-white lined drawings illustrate a few of the key choices. The keys are followed by lists of common and scientific names of Texas species. Detailed species accounts are next. Each account includes scientific and common names, a brief synonymy, comments, and a list of numbers representing literature citations in the bibliography. Texas county spot maps and one or more color photographs are included with each account. Some accounts have additional shaded Texas distribution maps and shaded sections titled special comments. A glossary, numbered and alphabetized bibliography, and indexes of common and scientific names complete the book.

This is an easily readable and information-packed book on Texas amphibians and reptiles. The nearly complete listing of Texas herpetological literature will be invaluable to readers and researchers needing more detailed information on southwestern reptiles and amphibians. Highly recommended for municipal and college libraries in the southwestern and southern United States.—**Edmund D. Keiser Jr.**

1157.   Dodd, C. Kenneth, Jr. **Frogs of the United States and Canada.** Baltimore, Md., Johns Hopkins University Press, 2013. 2v. illus. maps. index. $180.00/set. ISBN 13: 978-1-4214-0633-6.

Frogs of the United States and Canada is a beautiful, two-volume encyclopedia that includes thoroughly researched entries on all 100 native species and 6 established non-native species of frogs in this region. Entries are organized alphabetically by family name, followed by genus and species. Entries vary in length and include color photographs and distribution maps. Each species entry is subdivided into subtopics on nomenclature; etymology; identification; distribution; fossil record; systematics and geographic variation; adult habitat; terrestrial and aquatic ecology; calling activity and mate selection; breeding sites; reproduction; larval ecology; diet; predation and defense; population biology; diseases, parasites, and malformations; susceptibility to potential stressors; and status and conservation. If information on a particular subtopic is not known for that species it is indicated in the text. Each entry is heavily cited and the encyclopedia includes a bibliography of over 4,500 references published between the 1700s to mid-2011. In addition to the individual entries there is a short introduction that discusses frog evolution, life history, and conservation. The introduction ends with a short section on resources for finding additional information and includes books, websites, herpetological atlases, sound recordings, and professional herpetological societies.

This resource is a comprehensive guide to the frogs of the United States and Canada. According to the author, this encyclopedia is not designed as a field guide, but rather the objective of the work is to "synthesize the literature on all frogs of North America north of the Mexican border through May 2011" (p. xx). This resource will be incredibly useful to anyone interested in learning more about a particular species of frog in this region, from undergraduates to field biologists. It is written in accessible language, but goes into depth on what is known about each species. The references included throughout the text will provide additional published resources to explore. While other books may be more useful in frog identification in the field, such as *The Frogs and Toads of North America: A Comprehensive Guide to Their Identification, Behavior, and Calls* by Lang Elliott, Carl Gerhardt, and Carlos Davidson that provides a CD of frog calls, this work provides an immense amount of in-depth information about each species. This is a fantastic, easily accessible, but thoroughly referenced and beautifully illustrated encyclopedia that is highly recommended to anyone with an interest in different frog species of the United States and Canada.—**Megan Toups**

32 Engineering

General Works

Catalogs and Collections

1158.   **EI Compendex. http://www.ei.org/compendex.** [Website]. San Diego, Calif., Elsevier Science. Price negotiated by site. Date reviewed: 2013.

Compendex, also knows as the Engineering Index, is the most comprehensive bibliographic database of scientific and technical engineering research available, covering all engineering disciplines, including chemical, civil, mining, mechanical, and electrical. It includes millions of bibliographic citations and abstracts from thousands of engineering journals and conference proceedings. When combined with the engineering index Backfile (1884-1969), Compendex covers well over 120 years of core engineering literature. It currently holds 12 million records across 190 engineering disciplines and provides users access to 1,031 journals. It is a standard resource in most academic science and engineering library.—**James E. Bobick**

1159.   **INSPEC. http://www.theiet.org/publishing/inspec/.** [Website]. Price negotiated by site. Date reviewed: 2013.

This site contains literature in electrical engineering, electronics, physics, control engineering, information technology, communications, computers, computing, and manufacturing and production engineering. The database contains nearly 12 million bibliographic records taken from 3,850 scientific and technical journals and 2,200 conference proceedings. Approximately 330,000 new records are added to the database annually. Users can subscribe by purchasing individual journals or magazines, purchasing individual articles, or subscribing to have access to the entire database.—**James E. Bobick**

1160.   **NTIS. http://www.ntis.gov/.** [Website]. Springfield, Va., U.S. Department of Commerce, National Technical Information Service. Free. Date reviewed: 2013.

The National Technical Information Service maintains and disseminates a large collection of scientific, technical, engineering, and business-related information produced for and by U.S. government agencies. The freely accessible NTIS database contains the records of millions of publications from 1990 forward, along with audiovisual materials, computer data files, and software. All records include an abstract; some of the publications are freely available on the Internet. Other documents and materials may be purchased from NTIS or found in depository libraries. To find earlier references consult Government Reports Announcements & Index or one of its predecessors; or search a pay per search version that covers 1964 forward, available from Dialog, DataStar, Ovid, EINS, and STN. Subscription versions are available from Dialog, Questel-Orbit, STN, Ovid, Cambridge Scientific Abstracts, and EBSCO. CD-ROM and DVD versions are available from Dialog and Ovid. NTIS and Ovid offer it on magnetic tape.—**Michael Knee**

Directories

1161. **Plunkett's Engineering & Research Industry Almanac.** 2014 ed. Jack W. Plunkett, ed. Houston, Tex., Plunkett Research, 2014. 720p. $349.99pa. ISBN 13: 978-1-60879-735-6.

This 720-page, 2014 edition of Plunkett's engineering and research reference almanac offers an in-depth look at the top engineering and research companies. This is a group of companies chosen specifically for their prominence and leadership in engineering- and research-related segments: design and development, technology-based research and development, and manufacturing. Only publicly traded companies are featured because of the editorial requirement that each firm have "sufficient objective data" (i.e., financial data and vital statistics to facilitate broad-based comparisons).

The almanac is written in lay terms to help the general reader compare financial records, company growth statistics, employment opportunities, and investment possibilities. The six industries represented are energy, entertainment and hospitality, health care, information technology, manufacturing, and services.

Although these industry and company profiles will provide an excellent overview for students, researchers, and executives, a caveat must be stated: this volume, as are all print volumes that include corporate data, is a snapshot in time. Changes occur rapidly in the corporate arena—financials change daily, and mergers and acquisitions, downsizing, and division elimination occur every year. It may behoove the reader to delve more deeply into a given industry by contacting specific companies, industry associations, key individuals, and some government agencies to garner the most current information. Perhaps more valuable for planning purposes are the chapters devoted to major trends and industry outlooks. The glossary of engineering and research industry terms should help clarify the concepts presented in those chapters. The index provides about 160 firms noted as "Hot Spots for Advancement for Women and Minorities." Also included is an index of subsidiaries, brand names, and affiliations.

The content of this reference resource will provide many answers for researchers, students, and general information seekers. It is recommended for reference collections in public and academic libraries.—**Laura J. Bender**

1162. **Plunkett's Nanotechnology & MEMS Industry Almanac.** 2014 ed. Jack W. Plunkett, ed. Houston, Tex., Plunkett Research, 2014. 440p. $349.99pa. ISBN 13: 978-1-60879-738-7.

Plunkett's Nanotechnology & MEMS Industry Almanac provides industry trends, a glossary of industry terms, categorized lists of important industry contacts, and detailed profiles of the 250 "most important" firms. It is targeted at sales and marketing researchers and job-seekers.

Nanotechnology and MEMS are hot industries right now with billions of dollars of funding from world governments and private investors; therefore, an almanac on this subject is timely and could be very useful. In the list of industry trends, it correctly lists health, safety, and environmental implications of nanotechnology; however, for sources of more information it lists only top-level government agency Websites (e.g., www.epa.gov) from which one would be hard pressed to locate any information on this subject. Users will find up-to-date information on the history of nanoscience, biotechnology and pharmaceuticals based on nanoscience, and optics based on nanotechnology. To the book's credit, it has a helpful glossary. The company profiles are well indexed and easy to read. The information can also be accessed through the publisher's online version, which is free with purchase of the print volume. The industry list with NAIC numbers will help researchers access the literature in other more general resources. Overall, this book is on the right subject at the right time but the industry contacts section needs revisions. This volume is recommended for engineering and nanotechnology business collection.—**Christina K. Pikas**

Handbooks and Yearbooks

1163.   **Audio Engineering and the Science of Sound Waves.** New York, Crabtree, 2014. 32p. illus. index. (Engineering in Action). $20.70/vol.; $9.95pa./vol.. ISBN 13: 978-0-7787-1196-4.

1164.   **Chemical Engineering and Chain Reactions.** New York, Crabtree, 2014. 32p. illus. index. (Engineering in Action). $20.70/vol.; $9.95pa.vol. ISBN 13: 978-0-7787-1197-1.

1165.   **Environmental Engineering and the Science of Sustainability.** New York, Crabtree, 2014. 32p. illus. index. (Engineering in Action). $20.70/vol.; $9.95pa./vol. ISBN 13: 978-0-7787-1213-8.

1166.   **Optical Engineering and the Science of Light.** New York, Crabtree, 2014. 32p. illus. index. (Engineering in Action). $20.70/vol.; $9.95pa./vol. ISBN 13: 978-0-7787-1228-2.

The four new volumes in this series from Crabtree Publishing, a company known for their multivolume, nonfiction series designed specifically for children and middle school students, discuss the various ways that technology is connected to our everyday lives and how engineers work to address problems and identify solutions. The latest volumes in the series discuss audio engineering, optical engineering, environmental engineering, and chemical engineering. In a very elementary style the volumes discuss what is involved in the various branches of engineering, pioneers in the field, how an idea is brought into being, the importance of testing, future trends, and the path to becoming an engineer. Also included is a list of other resources (e.g., hotlines, Websites), a glossary, and a very short index, all of which can be used to teach young students basic researching skills. This series is recommended for middle school libraries and young adult collections in public libraries.—**Shannon Graff Hysell**

Biomedical Engineering

1167.   **Plunkett's Biotech & Genetics Industry Almanac.** 2014 ed. Jack W. Plunkett, ed. Houston, Tex., Plunkett Research, 2013. 600p. $349.99pa. ISBN 13: 978-1-60879-714-1.

This volume of *Plunkett's Biotech & Genetics Industry Almanac* is the 2014 edition. The editors continue to provide the first step for researchers in the biotech and genetics industry. Not written for in-depth analysis of the industry, the monograph instead provides students and researchers with self-contained segments readers can access without going through the entire book. Structured into four chapters dealing mainly with the industry in America, the sections give snapshots of different components of the industry. The first chapter contains several sections of varying length dealing with current trends. These trends include the interest in ethanol as a fuel alternative and hot topics such as stem cell research and rising drug prices. The almanac also provides key statistical information on funding and company rankings. One of the most useful parts of the text was the company profiles for the biotech 400. The companies listed, predominately based in the United States, have significant presence in the industry and openly accessible financial information. The typical entry includes company name, Web address, NAIC code, company ranking, types of business, brands, basic financial data, and contact information. Other useful aspects of the book include a short glossary; an index of subsidiaries, brand names, and affiliations; and an index of companies noted for promoting women and minorities.

The language is relatively jargon-free. The paper binding will not stand up to heavy use but the pages are thick with large clear type. With the purchase of the print edition users will also be given access to the online edition. Overall, this directory will complement the collections of large public and academic libraries.—**Melissa M. Johnson**

Civil Engineering

1168. **BuildingGreen Suite. http://www.buildinggreen.com/.** [Website]. $199.00 (individual subscription); $499.00 (10-member team subscription). Date reviewed: 2013.

The BuildingGreen Web resources include access to green product listings, articles related to green building, and hundreds of green building case studies, searchable by name, owner, or location of the project, or by energy type and building details. This is a substantial resource for those working in the field as well as students of green building.—**Anna H. Perrault**

1169. **Multitasking Architectural Database for Computer Aided Design (MADCAD). http://www. madcad.com/index.php.** [Website]. Price negotiated by site. Date reviewed: 2013.

MADCAD is a state-of-the-art subscription-based reference online database, containing building codes, knowledge-based design solutions, and guidelines to meet the codes. MADCAD contains building, electrical, mechanical, plumbing, fire, and maintenance codes and published standards, including but not limited to ASCE, ASME, ASTM, BHMA, BOCA, ICBO, ICC, IEEE, EFPA, SBCCI, and others. Electronic subscriptions for each of the standards are required for access through MADCAD, but the advantage to MADCAD is that all of the standards and codes can be searched through one site in a combined search result. MADCAD also gives access to comprehensive state and local codes, a very valuable asset to the database.—**ARBA Staff Reviewer**

Electrical Engineering

1170. **IEEE Xplore. http://ieeexplore.ieee.org/Xplore/guesthome.jsp?reload=true.** [Website]. Price negotiated by site. Date reviewed: 2013.

This site provides full-text access to IEEE transactions, journals, and conference proceedings and IEE journals from 1988 to the present, as well as all current IEEE standards. This database provides users with a single source leading to almost one-third of the world's current electrical engineering and computer science literature, with unparalleled access to IEEE and IEE publications.—**ARBA Staff Reviewer**

Energy Engineering

1171. Thumann, Albert, and D. Paul Mehta. **Handbook of Energy Engineering.** 7th ed. Boca Raton, Fla., CRC Press, 2013. 442p. index. $129.95. ISBN 13: 978-1-4665-6161-8.

A great deal of progress has been made since 1989 when the 1st edition of this energy engineering handbook was published. Codes, standards, and local and national regulations have been modified to reflect the adoption of "green" technologies and science. This handbook has been a go-to reference for engineering students for years, and the latest edition will continue in that role as the country adapts to climate change.

The book consists of 14 chapters dealing with all the updated codes and standards, energy economic analysis, electrical system optimization (new to the 7th edition), waste heat recovery, HVAC equipment, control systems, financing energy projects, and energy auditing and accounting. The appendix beginning on page 395 contains several important tables: A-1 through A-8 list 10 percent through 50 percent impact factors. Tables A-9 through A-12 list five-year to 20-year escalation tables. Table A-13 features figures for Saturated Steam measures. Table A-14 features figures for Superheated Steam. References begin on page 433, and a comprehensive index begins on page 435. Students and engineering practitioners should find the graphs, diagrams, and sample problems of particular value to their studies and projects.

This resource is highly recommended for academic science and engineering libraries, practicing engineers, and community college and public libraries with large science collections.—**Laura J. Bender**

Materials Science

1172. **Materials Research Database with Metadex. http://www.csa.com/factsheets/materials-set-c.php.** [Website]. Ann Arbor, Mich., ProQuest. Price negotiated by site. Date reviewed: 2013.

This database includes leading materials science databases with specialist content on materials science, metallurgy, ceramics, polymers, and composites used in engineering applications. The collection provides coverage on applied and theoretical materials processes including welding and joining, heat treatment, and thermal spray. Everything from raw materials and refining through processing, welding, and fabrication to end-use, corrosion, performance, and recycling is covered in depth. There are over 3,000 periodicals, conference proceedings, technical reports, trade journals, patents, books, and even press releases and newsletter items indexed here. The deep indexing includes that of tables, graphs, charts, and illustrations from each resource as well.—**James E. Bobick**

Mechanical Engineering

1173. **Applied Mechanics Reviews. http://journaltool.asme.org/Content/JournalDescriptions. cfm?journalId=20&Journal=AMR.** [Website]. Free. Date reviewed: 2013.

This site reviews books and journal articles related to mechanical engineering. It includes complete review articles. It serves as an archival repository for state-of-the-art and retrospective survey articles and reviews of research areas and curricular developments across all sub-disciplines of applied mechanics. The journal invites commentary on research and education policy in different countries and regions in the area of applied mechanics, including material that provides an international comparison of different regional frameworks for collaboration and networking. The journal also invites original tutorial and educational material in applied mechanics targeting non-specialist audiences, including undergraduate and K-12 students.—**James E. Bobick**

1174. **SAE Publications and Standards Database. http://www.libraries.uc.edu/libraries/ceas/ selfhelp/sae.html.** [Website]. Free. Date reviewed: 2013.

This database contains bibliographic data for more than 69,000 documents published by the Society of Automotive Engineers, including technical papers since 1906, magazine articles, books, all ground vehicle and aerospace standards, specifications, and research reports.—**James E. Bobick**

33 Health Sciences

General Works

Catalogs and Collections

1175. **Consumer Health Complete. http://www.ebscohost.com/public/consumer-health-complete.** [Website]. Ipswich, Mass., EBSCO. Price negotiated by site. Date reviewed: 2014.

This site is a comprehensive resource for consumer-oriented health content. *Consumer Health Complete* provides content covering all areas of health and wellness from mainstream medicine to the many perspectives of complementary, holistic, and integrated medicine. This full-text database covers topics such as aging, cancer, diabetes, drugs and alcohol, fitness, nutrition and dietetics, men's and women's health, and children's health. It provides a unique search interface and intuitive means for searching specific information.—**W. Bernard Lukenbill**

1176. **Health Source: Consumer Edition. http://www.ebscohost.com/public/health-source-consumer-edition.** [Website]. Ipswich, Mass., EBSCO. Price negotiated by site. Date reviewed: 2014.

This commercial source is a rich collection of consumer health information providing access to nearly 80 full-text, consumer health magazines, including *American Fitness*, *Better Nutrition*, *Fit Pregnancy*, *Harvard Health Letter*, *Health Facts*, *Men's Health*, *Muscle & Fitness*, *Prevention*, *Vegetarian Times*, and many others. This database also includes searchable full text for current, health-related pamphlets and more than 130 health reference books.—**W. Bernard Lukenbill**

1177. **My Family Health Portrait. http://www.hhs.gov/familyhistory.** [Website]. U.S. Surgeon General's Office. Free. Date reviewed: 2014.

This site from the U.S. Surgeon General's Office will help library patrons and students map a family health history. Many common diseases such as heart disease, cancer, and diabetes, and rare diseases, like hemophilia, cystic fibrosis, and sickle cell anemia, are hereditary. By tracing the illnesses suffered by parents, grandparents, and other blood relatives, users can learn how to take action to keep themselves healthy. The printable chart or online chart is good for participation of multiple family members located in different geographic areas. These resources are also available in Spanish.—**Marty Magee**

Dictionaries and Encyclopedias

1178.   **Atlas of Health and Climate.** By the World Health Organization. Lanham, Md., Bernan Press, 2013. 68p. $36.00pa. ISBN 13: 978-9-24156-452-6.

This new study is the product of the collaboration between the public health and meteorology communities. Based on evidence-based research the work provides concrete examples of how weather and climate affect the health of citizens. This includes such examples as diseases that arise due to poverty, to health concerns that arise during extreme weather events, to the notable increase in noncommunicable diseases. The work stresses the importance of being aware of the link between how climate conditions can make the public vulnerable to physical and mental health problems as well as how being aware of climate can help professionals lower the risk to the public during weather events.—**Laura J. Bender**

1179.   Danner, Horace Gerald. **A Thesaurus of Medical Word Roots.** Lanham, Md., Scarecrow, 2013. 630p. $120.00; $199.99 (e-book). ISBN 13: 978-0-8108-9154-8; 978-0-8108-9155-5 (e-book).

New medical students, medical practitioners, and students of language will benefit from using this resource for their work. It can also be a source of fun for curious word lovers who will no doubt discover many surprises in the meanings of the roots, prefixes, and suffixes listed in the book.

With the help of 17 medical dictionaries, encyclopedias, and several Internet resources, Danner compiled this reference of medical word roots. The presentation is clear and concise. As the author states, "this thesaurus is designed for a user to refer to when an unknown medical word of mainly Greek or Latin origin is encountered. By seeing other words in the same family, users can better associate, and therefore better remember the meaning of the root."

The thesaurus itself is an alphabetic listing of terms in four columns: element (the root), from (the origin), meaning, and examples. Within the examples column there are leading root compounds (root under consideration comes at the beginning of the word comprised of at least two roots) and trailing root compounds (the root under consideration comes after another root). There are cross-references and root notes when the meaning of the root is different from the original meaning or there is an important aspect to the root's background. Appendix A consists of a very useful English to root index (e.g., alimentary canal: esophag); appendix B lists prefixes and appendix C lists suffixes.

This thesaurus would be a valuable addition to large public, community college, science, and medical library reference collections. In addition, medical practitioners would benefit by having a copy in their private offices.—**Laura J. Bender**

1180.   **The Gale Encyclopedia of Diets: A Guide to Health and Nutrition.** 2d ed. Kristin Key, ed. Stamford, Conn., Gale/Cengage Learning, 2013. 2v. illus. index. $549.00set. ISBN 13: 978-1-4144-9884-3; 978-1-4144-9887-4 (e-book).

The choices made regarding what we eat have a major impact on our health. A great deal of money is spent in the United States on various "diets" that help people lose or gain weight or control a medical problem. This encyclopedia is a one-stop comprehensive resource regarding these diets. Three general topics are included in the more than 275 entries: basics of nutrition; medical problems that are related to nutrition (e.g., gout); and diets. Over 115 different diets are included, from well-known commercial diets like Weight Watchers to lesser-known diets, like the "Caveman." All entries are organized in a standard format, averaging three to four pages in length. Each submission includes a discussion on benefits, risks, precautions, research evidence, and acceptance. Entries conclude with a bibliography of reputable journals, books, organizations, and Websites. Entries are written by professionals in the field. The book is aimed at consumers, but would be helpful to healthcare professionals who are less than knowledgeable about specifics of each of the various commercial or popular diets. The Gale series has a reputation for presenting reliable health information in a succinct, usable format. This new edition supports that reputation. The greatest value of this book is that it is a single, reliable reference for all the various commercial, medical, or popular ("fad") diets that are available to the public.—**Mary Ann Thompson**

1181.   **The Gale Encyclopedia of Environmental Health.** Jacqueline L. Longe, ed. Stamford, Conn., Gale/Cengage Learning, 2013. 2v. index. $549.00/set. ISBN 13: 978-1-4144-9880-5; 978-1-4144-9883-6 (e-book).

Hurricanes, chemical spills, antibiotic resistance, and contaminated foods are among the issues considered when discussing environmental health. This new encyclopedia from Gale contains more than 250 articles covering this important topic. The alphabetic entries provide information on historic, natural, and manmade environmental health events. They include environmentally related health conditions and diseases and public health practices affecting the world. The articles are written by health professional, academics, and science writers. They include color photographs, text boxes with definitions of key terms, interesting historical information, and questions to ask physicians, as well as resource lists of online and print information and organizations. Topics covered include environmental health crises (e.g., acid rain, drought), organizations and legislation (e.g., UNICEF, Occupational Health and Safety Act), and diseases and conditions (e.g., ammonia exposure, emergent diseases). The entries are comprehensive, ranging in length from 1-12 pages. The articles on environmental crises and diseases include a definition, description, demographics, causes and symptoms, common diseases and disorders, treatment, public health role and response, prognosis, and prevention. Those on organizations and legislation include a definition, purpose, demographics, description, results, research and general acceptance, interactions, complications, aftercare, and parental concerns. The book begins with a chronology of major environmental health events up to 165 to 2013. It ends with a list of organizations, a glossary, and a comprehensive index.

With articles on contemporary issues such as climate change, food safety, and traveler's health as well as fracking and Gulf War Syndrome, this will be a useful resource for students with assignments as well as anyone interested in the environment or public health.—**Barbara M. Bibel**

1182.   **The Gale Encyclopedia of Public Health.** Laurie J. Fundukian, ed. Stamford, Conn., Gale/Cengage Learning, 2013. 2v. illus. index. $549.00/set. ISBN 13: 978-1-4144-9876-8; 978-1-4144-9879-9 (e-book).

The 2013 two-volume edition of *The Gale Encyclopedia of Public Health* contains a wealth of information on over 200 public health topics. This set is for the nonmedical researcher, it is not heavily worded with medical terminology. The articles include references to the scientific articles and the statistical data used to write the entry. Also included are timelines of historic events that were important during specific entries origins. Some sidebars that include historical facts and some include people that were involved with health and medicine such as well-known scientist Louis Pasteur and not so well known scientists Gladys Dick and her husband George Dick who isolated the bacteria which caused scarlet fever in 1923.

Included are cross-references for related topics and primary entries. There are data and statistics included in many of the entries and the sources for these data are handily available in the resources at the end of the entry. The resources section includes books, periodicals, Websites, and popular organizations for deeper information digging. The diseases and conditions included in this set include articles on historical conditions such as scarlet fever and polio and current issues such as second hand smoking and West Nile Virus.

The end of volume 2 includes a comprehensive glossary and an index with bolded page numbers indicating main topical essays. A practical aspect of this encyclopedia is that there are text boxes included in the topics such as "Questions To Ask Your Doctor"; therefore, this set would be beneficial to have in a public library setting in a reference collection. This set would also be beneficial in an academic setting for undergraduate students in the nursing and health sciences looking for scholarly articles to launch their public health research.—**Amy B. Parsons**

Directories

1183.   **The Complete Directory for Pediatric Disorders, 2014.** 7th ed. Millerton, N.Y., Grey House Publishing, 2013. 1066p. index. $165.00pa.; $300.00 (online database; single user); $400.00 (print and online editions). ISBN 13: 978-1-61925-116-8.

The 7th edition of *The Complete Directory for Pediatric Disorders* is a comprehensive and current listing of helpful information about hundreds of pediatric and adolescent conditions. The directory is organized into six sections. The first, which comprises the majority of the book, presents clear and understandable descriptions for 212 disorders. A listing of disorder-specific resources is provided after each description. These resources include state and national associations, research centers, Websites, hotlines and support groups, and print materials. The second section contains information about general resources for finding information about pediatric disorders, including government agencies, libraries, camps, and Wish Foundations (including contact information as well as Website and e-mail addresses where available). Basic background information on major bodily systems, such as the endocrine or nervous system, is found in the third section. The fourth section contains glossary, while the fifth section provides guidelines for obtaining additional information and resources. The final section provides three indexes—an entry index, a geographic index, and a disorder & related term index. Several new topics have been added to this edition including social anxiety disorder, the eating disorders of restrictive eating and orthorexia (the obsession of pure foods), and noise induced hearing loss, which can be caused from loud music and mechanical equipment. The new edition is also available as an online subscription with continuous updates. The online edition gives the user access to more than 5,500 disorder-specific and general resources. This carefully written directory will be useful to families, caregivers, counselors, nurses, teachers, and anyone else coping with children's illnesses.—**Denise A. Garofalo**

1184.   **The Complete Directory for People with Chronic Illness 2013/2014.** 11th ed. Millerton, N.Y., Grey House Publishing, 2013. 864p. index. $165.00pa.; $300.00 (online edition); $400.00 (print and online edition). ISBN 13: 978-1-61925-114-4.

The 11th edition of *The Complete Directory for People with Chronic Illness* provides information on 89 chronic illnesses, including support services and additional resources. This is a revised and updated edition (10th ed.; see ARBA 2012, entry 1243).

The directory begins with a table of contents and introduction, then presents a cross-referenced chart of Chronic Illness to Body System. Next, several narrative pages are dedicated to suggested steps to take after a diagnosis. The 89 chronic illness chapters are then presented, and include a brief description of the condition, cause, symptoms, and common treatment options. Also presented are a wide range of condition-specific associations, state agencies, resources centers, support groups, and print and electronic resources. These are broken down into categories, including national agencies & associations, state agencies and associations, support groups and hotlines, books, magazines, newsletters, pamphlets, audio and video, and Websites. Extensive contact information (e.g., mailing address, telephone numbers, e-mail and URLS, contact persons) are also included, as available to the editors. The directory concludes with an entry name index (alphabetic listing of all entries) and a geographic index (listing agencies and organizations by state).

Buyers of the 2013/2014 edition will receive a one-year free subscription to the online version of this directory. Users can search the information by entry name, major category (e.g., AIDS, Asthma), minor category (e.g., books, foundations, libraries and research centers), keyword, executive last name, or state. The directory allows users to save their searches and search results, download contact sheets, and click through to e-mail and Website links.

The strength of this source is not so much in the description of the illness itself, but in the information referral portion for each entry: the wide range of resources and organizations presented that can assist with additional information and support. Like other medical reference books, it is not meant to be a substitute for professional medical care. This resource is most appropriate for public libraries and academic libraries that field medical questions.—**Caroline L. Gilson**

1185. **HMO/PPO Directory, 2014: Detailed Profiles of U.S. Managed Healthcare Organizations & Key Decision Makers.** 26th ed. Millerton, N.Y., Grey House Publishing, 2014. 603p. index. $325.00pa.; $650.00 (online subscription; single user); $800.00 (print and online edition). ISBN 13: 978-1-61925-134-2.

This resource is designed primarily for all types of businesses seeking to make decisions about plans to offer employee health care coverage. However, it could also be valuable for individuals seeking information about different states as they enter into job searches, or want more facts about current medical insurance offerings in their respective states. The sections for each state are broken down as follows: Type of Plan, Type of Coverage, Type of Payment Plan, Subscriber Information, Financial History (loss and expense ratios), Average Compensation Information, Employee References and Member Enrollment, Hospital Affiliations, Number of Primary Care and Specialty Physicians, Federal Qualification Status, For-Profit Status, Specialty Managed Care Partners, Regional Business Coalitions, Employer References, Peer Review Information, and Accreditation Information. All organizations are listed alphabetically within state chapters, and feature the names, telephone numbers, and e-mail addresses of key executives. This edition has updated listings that include information on 1,215 HMOs, PPOs, POS plans, and dental and vision plants, many of which are new to this edition.

The *HMO/PPO Directory* is available online in addition to the print version. The online version can be searched by health plan name, city or state name, plan type (e.g., HMO, PPO), number of affiliate hospitals, number of primary physicians, number of specialty physicians, number of members enrolled, plan specialties (e.g., behavioral, dental), and types of coverage. The print edition has five indexes: Plan Index, Personnel Index, Primary Care Physician Index, Referral/Specialty Physician Index, and the Membership Enrollment Index (a list of organizations by member enrollment in descending order). This reference resource is recommended for corporate, large public and academic, medical and law libraries.—**Laura J. Bender**

1186. **Leadership Health Focus.** http://www.leadershipdirectories.com/Products/Leadership OnlineDirectories/Business/LeadershipHealthFocus. [Website]. New York, Leadership Directories. $2,800.00 (annual subscription). Date reviewed: 2014.

Leadership Directories has long been providing a library of 14 directories that cover such topics as congress, state and municipal governments, associations, law firms, and nonprofits. They now offer an online directory designed to help users identify and contact leaders in the health and health care field. Much like the print volumes on government and law, this online resource on health and health care offers contact for leaders in the business sector of health care, the government sector of health care, and in the nonprofit sector of health care. It currently provides name, title, addresses, telephone and fax numbers, and biographical and organization information. Organization information includes annual revenue, endowments, budget number of employees, annual emergency room visits, and inpatient and outpatient visits annually. For those in sales or even job-seeking, the site can be searched by specialty.

This unique directory provides useful contact information on people within the health care industry that library patrons frequently request. The steep price, however, may limit the purchase to larger public and academic libraries or those specializing in health care.—**Shannon Graff Hysell**

1187. **Medical Device Register, 2013: The Official Directory of Medical Manufacturers.** 33d ed. Millerton, N.Y., Grey House Publishing, 2013. 2v. index. $350.00pa./set; $699.00 (database). ISBN 13: 978-1-59237-880-7.

The 33d edition of the *Medical Device Register* is a two-volume resource divided into five main sections. Volume 1 contains the keyword index and product directory, and volume 2 contains the manufacturer profiles, geographical index, a trade name index, and a subsidiary index. The keyword index provides an access point for locating the name of a specific product, and the product directory provides a list of suppliers by product. The subsidiary index provides an alphabetic list of manufacturers and their subsidiaries. Volume 2 begins with the manufacturer profiles, which in most cases provides the name of the company followed by basic corporate information similar to that provided in business directories, like Standard & Poor's, followed by a list of products the company produces or supplies. The geographical index provides medical manufacturers by state and city, and the trade name index displays product names linked to the manufacturing company.

On the verso of the title page is a disclaimer that the publisher does not guarantee that the information is 100 percent accurate. Mistakes in the information supplied are present but not easily apparent. Overall, however, this work has been thoroughly researched and contains listings for more than 13,000 North American manufacturing companies, several hundred more than the last edition (32d ed.; see ARBA 2013, entry 1243). Data presented in the manufacture profiles are also inconsistent with some entries providing Web addresses, e-mails, and company information, while other entries only include a street address and telephone number. Some of the missing information, such as e-mail addresses, can be easily obtained from a Web search on the company's name. An online version is also available (http://www. mdrweb.com) and appears to offer more information than the print edition. The online version also offers additional features not provided in the print resource, such as the ability to place an information request with multiple suppliers and create mailing lists.—**Susan E. Thomas**

1188.   **Plunkett's Health Care Industry Almanac.** 2014 ed. Jack W. Plunkett, ed. Houston, Tex., Plunkett Research, 2012. 720p. $349.99pa. ISBN 13: 978-1-60879-718-9.

This almanac is a thorough compendium on the business of healthcare, focusing mainly on the United States but also including some international data. The *Almanac* includes chapters describing trends in health care and the outlook for technology. Another section includes statistics from U.S. government and United Nations sources on health care expenditures, Medicare and Medicaid, insurance coverage, and vital statistics. The bulk of the *Almanac* is a directory of the so-called "Health Care 500"<197>the top for-profit health care firms located mainly in the United States, based on size, growth, and for which the editors could confirm the statistics and financial data from outside sources. Each entry includes a description of the company, executive staff, financials, salaries and benefits, and types of business. This directory is also available online and is free with the book. There are a number of indexes in the print almanac (e.g., corporate headquarters by state, a list of subsidiaries, NAICs and SIC codes) that facilitate competitive intelligence, job searching, sales contact lists, and so forth. This resource is highly recommended for adult collections in all libraries.—**ARBA Staff Reviewer**

Handbooks and Yearbooks

1189.   Brunton, Deborah. **Health and Wellness in the 19th Century.** Santa Barbara, Calif., Greenwood Press/ABC-CLIO, 2014. 240p. illus. index. (Health and Wellness in Daily Life). $58.00. ISBN 13: 978-0-313-38511-7; 978-0-313-38512-4 (e-book).

This new series from Greenwood Press explores the history of health and medicine during different times in history, explaining the reasoning behind various medical practices and the way that medicine has progressed throughout the ages. The series also focuses on how medicine is tied to politics, ethics, economics, and social conditions. This projected seven-volume series will follow the same format for each book so that students will be able to see how things changed and progressed over time. The first two volumes focused on Antiquity through the Middle Ages and Colonial America; the latest volumes progress chronologically into heath and wellness in the Renaissance and Enlightenment eras and into the nineteenth century. Each volume has 13 chapters covering such topics as education and training of those working in medicine, religion and medicine, women's health, health throughout the lifespan, infectious disease, surgery, mental health, war and health, apothecary and early pharmaceuticals, and health institutions. The volume discussing nineteenth-century medicine examines the dramatic changes and development in the field of surgical medicine during this century. It also has chapters on folk medicine and herbal medicine that was popular at this time. It discusses the challenges brought about by urbanization and industrialization during this era. The volume concludes with a glossary, suggestions for further reading, and an index. This work would be useful in high school and undergraduate libraries.—**Adrienne Antink**

1190.   Byrne, Joseph P. **Health and Wellness in the Renaissance and Enlightenment.** Santa Barbara, Calif., Greenwood Press/ABC-CLIO, 2013. 268p. illus. index. (Health and Wellness in Daily Life). $58.00. ISBN 13: 978-0-313-38136-2; 978-0-313-38137-9 (e-book).

This title is part of a projected seven-part series on health and wellness across the ages, beginning with a volume on Antiquity through the Middle Ages. The first few titles provide a panoramic sampling of world cultures. Forthcoming titles will address Colonial America and America in the 19th and 20th centuries. In the series foreword to this volume, author Joseph P. Byrne explains the series' structure, beginning with selection of authors who are, first and foremost, medical historians and teachers. Each author will strive to provide equivalent chapter titles to allow easy comparison of particular issues.

This title covers the Renaissance and the Age of Enlightenment, which equates to roughly 300 years. A chapter on "Surgeons and Surgery" includes sections addressing issues of the Chinese, the Aztecs, the Islamic World, and the Europeans. Other chapters cover similar worldwide representation. Chapter titles include: infants and children, infectious diseases, mental and emotional health and disorders, apothecaries and their pharmacopeias, women's health and medicine, and healing and the arts. Each chapter ends with references for further study. Coverage is broad and includes perspectives from across the globe, each topic necessarily informed by the history, medicine, politics, and religion/spirituality of the particular time/place. Topics within the book are brief enough to allow glimpses of many cultures; for example, the mental and emotional health issues of Caribbean slaves being brought to the "New World."

This series is at once accessible and yet interesting enough to satisfy curious readers of the history of health and wellness. Black-and-white art prints and line drawings are sprinkled throughout the text. A glossary, a bibliography, and an index round out the work. This work is recommended for public and academic libraries as a valuable layperson's introduction to health and wellness across time and spanning the globe.—**Linda D. Tietjen**

1191.   **Fitness Information for Teens: Health Tips About Exercise and Active Lifestyles.** 3d ed. Elizabeth Bellenir, ed. Detroit, Omnigraphics, 2013. 387p. index. (Teen Health Series). $62.00. ISBN 13: 978-0-7808-1267-3.

This is another excellent offering from Omnigraphics in their Teen Health Series. As usual, the information is reprinted from its original sources and reorganized into the Omnigraphics format. The original sources are without question the most reliable available; for example, the federal government's Centers for Disease Control and National Institutes of Health, and professional organizations like the American Academy of Family Physicians and American Academy of Orthopedic Surgeons. The material is as up to date as possible. Although there are no photographs or glossy insets, the work is kept visually appealing for this age group with plenty of bullet lists and sidebars with quick facts. The reading level is appropriate to the target audience. The work addresses many key aspects of fitness, including how it affects each part of the body, maintaining a fitness plan, activities to choose from, sports safety, and addressing the obstacles to fitness (e.g., obesity, asthma, physical disabilities). The last part, "If You Need More Information," provides useful contact information to sports organizations and a bibliography of books and articles. This book will be a great addition to any public, junior high, senior high, or secondary school library.—**ARBA Staff Reviewer**

1192.   **Healthy Living.** 2d ed. By Barbara Wexler. Elizabeth Manar, ed. Farmington Hills, Mich., U*X*L/Gale, 2013. 3v. illus. index. $247.00/set. ISBN 13: 978-1-4144-9865-2; 978-1-4144-9869-0 (e-book).

This three volume set is aimed at middle and early high school students. It provides 14 chapters on ways students can incorporate healthy habits into their lifestyle and manage personal health issues. Material from the 1st edition (2000) has been updated and the work now contains more full-color images.

A cumulated table of contents and a glossary are repeated at the beginning of each volume. Each chapter begins with a summary, a table of contents, and a glossary of terms specific to that chapter's main subject. There are inset boxes throughout the chapters that offer interesting facts and health and safety tips relevant to the discussion. The further readings and pertinent Websites listed at the end of each chapter provide additional information, but are limited. Each volume ends with a repeated cumulated bibliography and index. The very useful index is cross-referenced and denotes illustrations associated with a subject. The text is liberally sprinkled with photographs and illustrations to visually demonstrate the main points of the text. The text itself is organized more like a textbook than an encyclopedia.

Overall, *Healthy Living* presents a balanced discussion of most topics and is suitable for high school libraries, especially if a thorough discussion of alternative health care and medicine is desired.—**Shannon Graff Hysell**

1193.   **Vital Statistics of the United States 2012: Births, Life Expectancy, Deaths, and Selected Health Data.** 5th ed. Lanham, Md., Bernan Press, 2012. 464p. index. $110.00; $109.99 (e-book). ISBN 13: 978-1-59888-538-5; 978-1-59888-539-2 (e-book).

This 2012 edition of *Vital Statistics of the United States* provides data on births, mortality, health, marriage, and divorce in the United States. It includes detailed data on multiple births; tables on abortion rates and contraception; information on caloric intake; and subchapters with detailed statistics on health personnel, health expenditures, and health insurance. Each statistical table is complemented by explanatory text, and some include figures. Many of the tables end at the years 2010 or 2009 due to data availability lags.

The same contents are freely available on the Websites of the National Center for Health Statistics (http://www.cdc.gov/nchs/) and the U.S. Census Bureau (http://www.census/gov/). Additionally, a summary of these data can also be found in the *Statistical Abstract of the United States*, compiled by the U.S. Department of Commerce and published by Bernan Press (see entry 767). Still, this title is nicely packaged in one volume, including a list of sources, a glossary of terms, and a topical index. It is recommended for large academic and public libraries.—**Mihoko Hosoi**

Medicine

General Works

Catalogs and Collections

1194.   **FamilyDoctor.org: Health Information for the Whole Family. http://familydoctor.org/ online/famdocen/home.html.** [Website]. Free. Date reviewed: 2013.

This Website is operated by the American Academy of Family Physicians (AAFP), a national medical organization representing more than 93,700 family physicians, family practice residents, and medical students. The information on this site was written and has been reviewed by physicians and patient education professionals at the AAFP. Visiting the AAFP Website will allow users to learn more about this organization. Links on the left of the home page provide additional information about this Website. The AAFP also welcomes feedback if you wish to click on the Contact Us link for both the e-mail and the mailing address. This is a more accessible medical database for the average user. However, users should not use this site (or any site for that matter) for self-diagnostic purposes.—**William O. Scheeren**

1195.   **MedlinePlus. http://www.nlm.nih.gov/medlineplus/.** [Website]. Date reviewed: 2013.

MedlinePlus offers a wide variety of health information for consumers, including current health news, a medical dictionary, a medical encyclopedia, information about diseases and conditions, drug information, and directories of health professionals and institutions. There are also tutorials and real-time videos of diagnostic and surgical procedures, information in many languages, and easy-to-read articles. It is an excellent starting point for almost all medical questions. *Medline* (also a product of the National Library of Medicine) is very much a professional tool. Medical librarians can go through weeks of training learning all of its functions and what they mean. For general consumer health queries, however, *MedlinePlus* is a much better option and will fill most reference librarian's need.—**ARBA Staff Reviewer**

1196.   **PubMed. http://www.ncbi.nlm.nih.gov/pubmed/.** [Website]. Free. Date reviewed: 2013.

PubMed is much more than a super-sized database of medical citations, however. It is a portal to databases from the National Center for Biotechnology Information (NCBI)—of gene sequences, molecular structures, and more—and to "Services" such as citation matchers and a special interface for clinical queries, as well as "Related Resources" such as Clinical Trials and Consumer Health information. Its huge, first-class, professional information, and it is freely available on the Web.

Many of the same features found in *MEDLINE* are found here. Under the Limits tab is the opportunity to limit to a particular Author or Journal title, as well as the Full Text or abstracts options, Dates, Humans or Animals, Gender, Languages, Subsets, Type of Article, and Ages. The Preview□Index tab provides the ability to search in a particular field, and the History tab provides a list of previous searches. In the drop-down list of "Search" options, and linked on the sidebar under *PubMed* Services, is access to the MeSH Database, giving users access to the thesaurus to explore terms and their relationships.

Other features are unique to the *PubMed* interface, and are quite handy, such as a spell checking feature that suggests alternative spellings for *PubMed* search terms that may include misspellings. In the results lists, there are additional links to Related Articles and Links. The Related Articles feature in *PubMed* makes use of a word-analysis algorithm, and is very effective: the results are almost always quite useful.—**Suzanne Bell**

Handbooks and Yearbooks

1197.   **Antibiotics.** By Kristi Lew. Tarrytown, N.Y., Marshall Cavendish, 2014. 64p. illus. index. (Advances in Medicine). $23.95/vol.; $119.75/set. ISBN 13: 978-1-60870-465-1.

1198.   **Cancer Treatments.** By George Capaccio. Tarrytown, N.Y., Marshall Cavendish, 2014. 62p. illus. index. (Advances in Medicine). $23.95/vol.; $119.75/set. ISBN 13: 978-1-60870-466-8.

1199.   **Organ Transplants.** By Henry Wouk. Tarrytown, N.Y., Marshall Cavendish, 2014. 62p. illus. index. (Advances in Medicine). $23.95/vol.; $119.75/set. ISBN 13: 978-1-60870-467-5.

1200.   **Pain Treatments.** By L. H. Colligan. Tarrytown, N.Y., Marshall Cavendish, 2014. 62p. illus. index. (Advances in Medicine). $23.95/vol.; $119.75/set. ISBN 13: 978-1-60870-468-2.

1201.   **Vaccines.** By Carol Ellis. Tarrytown, N.Y., Marshall Cavendish, 2014. 62p. illus. index. (Advances in Medicine). $23.95/vol.; $119.75/set. ISBN 13: 978-1-60870-470-5.

These first five volumes in the Advances in Medicine series provide young readers in the middle and high school grades up-to-date information on new ways that people are being treated to prevent disease. The book is filled with photographs and infographics that explain difficult concepts in a way that students will comprehend. Many of the illustrations and photographs are in 3D and the photographs are indexed. The text of the series have many Common Core connections, including definitions of scientific terms and phrases, and procedures for scientific observation. Each title provides an introduction to the subject, a history of its use in medicine, the controversies surrounding it, and its future in medical treatments. For middle and high school age students interested in the medical sciences and biology, this series will provide a good starting off point for research into several key topics.—**Shannon Graff Hysell**

1202.   **Congenital Disorders Sourcebook.** 3d ed. Sandra J. Judd, ed. Detroit, Omnigraphics, 2013. 642p. index. (Health Reference Series). $85.00. ISBN 13: 978-0-7808-1295-6.

Congenital Disorders Sourcebook is part of the Omnigraphics' Health Reference Series. As the title implies, the focus of this edition is to provide information on the most noted congenital birth defects. Congenital disorders are nongenetic or non-inherited birth defects resulting from complications during pregnancy or birth. As noted in the preface, the 3d edition is intended to provide an update on current medical research, advances, and practice with regard to pregnancy and congenital birth defects. The preface also notes that this sourcebook provides an easy-to-comprehend overview on medical conditions, but specifically explains that it is not intended to serve as a replacement for care from an appropriate health care practitioner.

The sourcebook is divided into four parts. The first two parts provide an excellent introduction and overview of the health and medical aspects of pregnancy. Part 1 provides information to answer many of the questions that may arise during pregnancy, such as chapter 9 on "Infectious Diseases with Adverse Fetal Effects" or the section in chapter 2 on "Vaccinations for a Healthy Pregnancy." Part 2 covers delivery complications, including the complications of having a premature baby, concerns with multiple births, and screening tests for newborns. Part 3 is the longest section covering congenital abnormalities and impairments. Each chapter examines a different group of disorders. For example, there is a chapter covering craniofacial defects, another chapter covers heart defects, and some chapters cover specific disorders such as cerebral palsy. With each disorder a definition and/or description is provided, and as applicable, causes, signs and symptoms, diagnosis, risk factors, prevention (if appropriate), and treatment are covered. Part 4 contains a glossary and a listing of additional information and support resources. Overall, the *Congenital Disorders Sourcebook* provides an excellent, nontechnical overview of many aspects of pregnancy with the focus, as indicated, on congenital disorders.—**Susan E. Thomas**

1203.   **Diseases & Disorders Series.** Farmington Hills, Mich., Lucent Books/Gale/Cengage Learning, 2013. multivolume. illus. index. $34.95/vol.

Written for the high school student, but also appropriate for the undergraduate student, the volumes of the Diseases & Disorders series contain well-researched text and numerous full-color illustrations to assist in bringing to life topics that can be hard to understand if one is not currently facing them. Each volume begins with a foreword and introduction, and ends with a list of notes by chapter, a glossary, an annotated list of organizations to contact, and a set of three annotated lists under the collective heading "For Further Reading" of fiction, nonfiction, and Websites. The volumes end with lengthy indexes to assist in locating specific information needed, while the writing style encourages reading further and the descriptive table of contents assists readers wanting broader overviews. New titles recently added to the series include the topics of cholera, cystic fibrosis, radiation sickness, sleep disorders, and teen depression. These scholarly yet accessible volumes are a valuable addition of new research on topics that change frequently for any young adult collection or community college collection.—**Sara Marcus**

1204. **Men's Health Concerns Sourcebook.** 4th ed. Sandra J. Judd, ed. Detroit, Omnigraphics, 2013. 655p. index. (Health Reference Series). $85,00. ISBN 13: 978-0-7808-1263-5.

This is a comprehensive resource on men's health. It is likely to be useful for individuals who are interested in learning more about the general health of men. Students and professionals may find this to be a valuable resource. The cover provides insight to the book's contents through the use of effectively key word text that is displayed in an easy to read format. Examples include Self-Examinations Recommended for Men, Guidelines for Nutrition, Gender-Specific Health Differences, Alcohol and Drug Abuse, and Sexual Concerns.

This work contains more than 600 pages. It includes a preface, five parts, and an index. The body of the text is comprehensive. It is separated into five parts with subsequent chapters followed by sections. The following are the headings for each part: Men's Health Basics; Leading Causes of Death in Men; Sexual and Reproductive Concerns; Other medical Issues of Concern to Men; and Additional Help and Information.

Chapter topics are contemporary. Content is presented in an easy-to-read format. Examples include: Gender-Specific Health Differences, Aim for a Healthy Weight, Lung Cancer, Vasectomy and Vasectomy Reversal, Male Menopause, Chronic Liver Disease, and Male Pattern Baldness. The text does not include figures, tables, charts, or pictures.

The editor has successfully produced a timely and relevant text. Chapter 50 includes several pages that provide a useful directory of resources. Readers are likely to find this to be a useful text that is easy to navigate and understand. This text would complement personal, professional, and medical libraries.— **Paul M. Murphy III**

1205. **Pain Sourcebook.** 4th ed. Karen Bellenir, ed. Detroit, Omnigraphics, 2013. 653p. index. (Health Reference Series). $85.00. ISBN 13: 978-0-7808-1299-4.

Whether it is headaches or backaches or managing arthritis, pain is something that all of us are challenged with at times. The 4th edition of the *Pain Sourcebook*, edited by Karen Bellenir, is a consumer healthcare and wellness handbook that describes many types of pain, causes, symptoms, diagnosis and treatments, and where to go for more in-depth information outside of this book. This book covers a large number of types of pain, descriptions, symptoms, and treatments as well as the effects of chronic pain on mental health and the effects of substance use when in pain. The *Pain Sourcebook* has had a different organization with each edition. This latest edition has chapters dedicated to specific types of pain. There are specific chapters on musculoskeletal pain, pain-related injuries, and the medical management of pain. A glossary of pain-related terminology and bibliographic information with Website addresses is included.

Although information in this book is taken from scholarly journals and professional Websites in the health and medical fields, this is a book that is excellent for ready-reference uses and can be used for beginning students in the health fields. The *Pain Sourcebook* would be appropriate for consumer health library collections in both public and academic libraries.—**Amy B. Parsons**

1206. **Perspectives on Diseases & Disorders Series.** Farmington Hills, Mich., Greenhaven Press/ Gale/Cengage Learning, 2012. multivolume. $38.95/vol.

Greenhaven's Perspectives on Diseases & Disorders series discusses the more controversial aspects of each disease covered, including discussion on understanding the disease, controversies surrounding the disease, and personal stories from those coping with the disease. The series first explores each disease in detail, covering symptoms, causes, treatments, and medical advances. It then goes on to provide pro/con essays on controversies surrounding the disease, and finally provides first-person accounts from those living with the disease. Full-color photographs will catch the attention of young readers and the sidebars highlight interesting facts and stories. Supplementary materials include a glossary, further reading lists, a chronology, and organizations to contact for further information. New topics covered in this series include: food allergies, sports injuries, dissociative disorders, traumatic brain injuries, and

Tourette Syndrome. The content in each book is thorough and covers many angles. This series is more appropriate for high school age students with the critical thinking skills to understand the more complex language in the pro/con essays.

In general, these books are excellent sources for high school readers to enhance their critical thinking skills. They could easily be used as jumping off points for research projects and debate topics. At $40.45 for the hardcover copies, these set as a whole is expensive. School librarians will most likely need to be selective if they choose to purchase books within this series.—**Shannon Graff Hysell**

1207.   **Skin Health Information for Teens.** 3d ed. Lisa Esposito, ed. Detroit, Omnigraphics, 2013. 387p. index. (Health Reference Series). $62.00. ISBN 13: 978-0-7808-1317-5.

The Teen Health Series from Omnigraphics provides health and hygiene information specifically designed to help adolescents make the right decisions concerning their health. This volume focuses specifically on skin conditions and skin care. Hormonal changes within the teenage body as well as external factors such as the use of cosmetics, body piercing, and tattoos, make this work extremely relevant to teenagers. New to this generation is an increased interest in the prevention of skin cancer, which has a key place in this title.

As with all of the volumes in this series, the articles and excerpts are taken from publications issued by government agencies, with full bibliographic citations accompanying each article. This volumes features articles from the Centers for Disease Control and Prevention, the Food and Drug Administration, and the National Cancer Institute, just to name a few. Part 1 provides information on skin basics, such as skin types, brown spots and freckles, blushing, and the effects of smoking. Part 2 discusses acne, a topic of particular interest to this population. Included is information on treating acne, how boys and girls experience acne differently, and psychological effects of acne. Part 3 discusses infectious conditions of the skin, while part 4 discusses the other disorders affecting the skin (e.g., eczema, melanoma, rosacea). Parts 5 and 6 cover skin injuries (e.g., scars, burns, frostbite) and caring for your skin (e.g., indoor tanning, tattoos, piercings). Finally, part 7 provides directory information for further resources to consult and suggested reading. The material in this work will be easily understood by teenagers and young adults. The publisher has liberally used bulleted lists and sidebars to keep the reader's attention. This volume, as with others in the series, will be a useful addition to school and public library collections.—**Shannon Graff Hysell**

1208.   **Surgery Sourcebook.** 3d ed. Amy L. Sutton, ed. Detroit, Omnigraphics, 2013. 655p. index. (Health Reference Series). $85.00. ISBN 13: 978-0-7808-1291-8.

The *Surgery Sourcebook* is part of Omnigraphics' Health Reference Series. The Agency for Healthcare Research and quality found that more than 15 million people undergo surgery each year at hospitals or same-day surgery centers in the United States. This work includes information for inpatient and outpatient procedures. The book is divided into six major sections as follows: "Introduction to Surgery"; "Preparing for Surgery"; "Common types of Surgery and Surgical Procedures"; "Managing Pain and Surgical Complications"; "Recovering from Surgery"; and "Additional Help and Information." The publication has a comprehensive index and surgery statistics. It also contains Website information for further information. Large public libraries and medical libraries would benefit from this material in their reference collections.—**Theresa Maggio**

1209.   **Women's Health Concerns Sourcebook.** 4th ed. Laura Larsen, ed. Detroit, Omnigraphics, 2013. 697p. index. (Health Reference Series). $85.00. ISBN 13: 978-0-7808-1303-8.

This useful resource provides information about a wide range of topics that will help women understand their bodies, prevent or treat disease, and maintain health. The book begins with a general overview of women's health in the United States, highlighting major health problems, statistics of women's health, and the health of special populations (e.g., disabled, lesbians and bisexuals). Chapters about maintaining health and wellness are included, such as health aging, managing stress, obesity and weight loss, and alternative medicine techniques. Gynecological concerns, breast health, sexuality, reproductive issues, menopause, and women's cancers as well as other diseases affecting women (heart disease, diabetes, thyroid disease, lupus, and migraines) receive good basic coverage. Other chronic health conditions and special concerns for women, such as arthritis, irritable bowel syndrome, and osteoporosis, are highlighted as well. Missing from this new edition is a section on mental and emotional health issues, which would have been a valuable addition. The information about all of these subjects comes from government and nonprofit health organizations. A glossary and directories of organizations and government agencies providing information and health assistance to women complete the work. A detailed index helps readers locate information. This is a useful addition to public and consumer health library collections.—**Barbara M. Bibel**

Indexes

1210.   **List of Serials Indexed for Online Users 2012.** National Library of Medicine; distr., Lanham, Md., Bernan Press, 2013. 358p. $59.00pa. ISBN 13: 978-1-60175-876-7.

The 2012 edition of the *List of Serials Indexed for Online Users* provides 14,417 serial titles. The work provides bibliographic information for journals whose articles have historically have been indexed with the MeSH vocabulary and cited in MEDLINE. (These serve as the backbone of the NLM PubMed database.) The list includes titles that are no longer in publication, those that have changed titles, and those that are no longer indexed.—**ARBA Staff Reviewer**

Alternative Medicine

1211.   **Alt HealthWatch. http://www.ebscohost.com/academic/alt-healthwatch.** [Website]. Ipswich, Mass., EBSCO. Price negotiated by site. Date reviewed: 2014.

This site focuses on the many perspectives of complementary, holistic, and integrated approaches to health care and wellness, and it provides full-text articles from more than 200 international and often peer-reviewed journals, reports, proceedings, and association and consumer newsletters. In addition, there are hundreds of pamphlets, booklets, special reports, original research, and book excerpts.—**W. Bernard Lukenbill**

1212.   Buhner, Stephen Harrod. **Herbal Antibiotics.** 2d ed. North Adams, Mass., Storey, 2012. 467p. index. $24.95pa. ISBN 13: 978-1-60342-987-0.

Herbal medicine offers an alternative to pharmaceuticals that are increasingly ineffective. Expert Stephen Harrod Buhner offers compelling scientific evidence that medicinal herbs should be our first line of defense against disease. He explains the roots of drug resistance and why medicinal herbs can work better than pharmaceutical drugs. Plants have long been and still are humanities primary medicines. Additionally, the plants are free or nearly so, and are quite safe if used properly cause minimal side effects. Buhners contention that basically there are too many useless generic antibiotics, which is at the root of diseases evolving into resistant strains.

Besides a foreword (one for each edition) there is a chapter on How to use this Book. Also included are a herbal formulary, a large index, and extensive footnotes and documentation all based on scientific evidence with a detailed list of books and journals. Herbal antibiotics are separated into three categories. Comments are made by Buehner. He explains how to use herbs and learn to grow, harvest, store, and use these herbs. It is obvious that Buhner is against pharmaceuticals except in rare instances. This reviewer recommends this title to everyone, either for simple cold or flu or for more serious conditions that doctors cannot treat anymore.—**Nadine Salmons**

1213.   **Complementary and Alternative Medicine Information For Teens.** 2d ed. Lisa Bakewell, ed. Detroit, Omnigraphics, 2013. 389p. index. (Teen Health Series). $62.00. ISBN 13: 978-0-7808-1311-3.

This title is intended to provide an overview of complementary and alternative medicine (CAM) for teenage readers. The initial chapters define CAM and discuss issues that should be considered when choosing these healthcare options, such as how to select a practitioner, and telling healthcare providers about CAM use. Guidelines for evaluating Web-based health resources are provided. The next six sections look at various aspects of CAM, including whole medical systems (e.g., Traditional Chinese Medicine and Naturopathy); manipulative practices and manual therapies (such as Chiropractic Medicine and massage therapy); mind-body medicine (e.g., biofeedback, meditation); biologically based practices (e.g., nutritional supplements, dietary regimes); energy medicine; and creative arts therapies. Most chapters are five to ten pages in length, and describe the treatment, how it may work, the status of current research, side effects and risks, and training, licensing, and certification needed by practitioners. The formatting of the chapters varies: some use an outline format, others take a question-and-answer approach to the topic. These sections on treatment modalities are followed by a section that describe CAM treatments for several diseases, including cancer, asthma, diabetes, irritable bowel syndrome, and attention deficit hyperactivity disorder. These chapters take a similar format: the ailment is described, CAM treatment approaches are listed, and sections on what the scientific research says about these approaches, as well as safety precautions that users should take are included. This work is not illustrated. There are some shaded text boxes that highlight key points. The final section, "If You Need More Information," includes resources on clinical trials, recommendations for further reading on CAM, and a list of government and private organizations that can provide additional information. An index lists main entries in bold.

Much of the content of this book is excerpted from various Websites, including many from the NIH National Center for Complementary and Alternative Medicine, as well as other agencies and professional associations. Although most of this information could be accessed through searching the Web, this book provides a degree of resource evaluation and quality control that teen researchers may lack, and is therefore recommended for middle school, high school, and public libraries.—**Kenneth M. Frankel**

Specific Diseases and Conditions

Allergies

1214.   **Allergy Information for Teens.** 2d ed. Karen Bellenir, ed. Detroit, Omnigraphics, 2013. 388p. index. (Teen Health Series). $88.00. ISBN 13: 978-0-7808-1288-8.

Allergies are a common health problem about which library patrons often need information. This title consists of reprinted information from U.S. government publications, supplemented with materials from medical associations and online resources, like Omnigraphics earlier work entitled *Allergies Sourcebook* (2d ed.; see ARBA 2003, entry 1461). As such, the information it contains is generally available elsewhere, often for free; however, one could argue that this is a convenient compilation of material from scattered sources. An introductory section explains the mechanisms and types of allergic reactions. Other parts explain allergy symptoms and complications, food allergies, other common allergies, and managing allergies in daily life. An important limitation of the book is that it does not cover asthma, the topic of another title in this series. The subject matter is as relevant to adults as teens. There is a list of medical organizations and Websites to consult for further information, and a bibliography. Given the varied sources of the information, the language and style of different sections vary; however, the information is more popular than technical. Other books on the subject may be more consistent in style and coverage, and include information on asthma. Nonetheless, this book does provide some useful information and would be of use particularly to larger public libraries.—**Marit S. Taylor**

Cancer

1215.   **Cancer Information for Teens.** 3d ed. Lisa Esposito, ed. Detroit, Omnigraphics, 2014. 410p. index. (Teen Health Series). $62.00. ISBN 13: 978-0-7808-1319-9.

Cancer is often thought of as a disease of aging, but in reality it is a killer in all age groups, and is, in fact, a leading cause of death in teenagers. Many more teens have to deal with cancer in family members and friends. And perhaps most important, all teenagers are at a point in their lives when they are making lifestyle decisions that will affect their chances of developing many cancers later down the road. During the teenage years, choices on tobacco use, sexual activity, eating habits, and sun exposure are presented on a daily basis. Teens who view these choices from a position of knowledge have a better chance at making wise decisions. Arming teenagers with all the facts they need to understand cancer and its causes, effects, and treatments should be a major part of any school health curriculum.

Like most Omnigraphics publications, this volume is a collection of materials previously published elsewhere—government documents, pamphlets by nonprofit organizations, and magazine and journal articles. The editors have grouped these materials in an easy-to-use arrangement, in six sections. An introduction defines cancer, its types, its symptoms, and risk factors. A very useful second section outlines the types of cancer that most affect children and young adults. Further sections detail the medical aspects of detection, diagnosis and treatment, surviving cancer, and coping strategies for patients, friends, and family. The last section is a listing of sources of further information.

Although all of these articles are (or were at one time) available elsewhere, finding them all would be difficult. The collection of all of this material here, and the addition of user-friendly information boxes, charts, and a comprehensive index, make this a valuable educational tool.—**Carol L. Noll**

Diabetes

1216.   **The Medical Library Association Guide to Finding Out About Diabetes.** By Dana L. Ladd and Alyssa Altshuler. Chicago, American Library Association, 2013. 322p. index. $80.00pa.; $72.00pa. (ALA members). ISBN 13: 978-1-55570-890-0.

With the incidence of diabetes increasing rapidly, the need for information about this disease is also rising. This volume by two medical librarians and an advisory board of health care practitioners specializing in diabetes provides current information from reliable sources. The materials included have been vetted for authorship, authority, reliability, currency, and reading level. They are suitable for lay readers.

The book has four sections. The first contains basic resources that provide an overview of the different types of diabetes: type 1, type 2, and gestational. This explains diagnosis, treatment, and basic essential information. Part 2 covers disease management: lifestyle changes, managing a chronic condition, drug therapy, and complementary and alternative treatments. Part 3 discusses life with diabetes and includes useful information about financial and legal issues, travel, and work. The last section covers complications and care resources, explaining what they are and how to prevent them as well as how to treat them when they occur. Skin conditions, foot problems, cardiovascular disease, renal disease, and eye problems are among the conditions covered. Each section begins with an overview of the topic followed by annotated lists of print, Web, and audiovisual resources. Easy-to-read materials, materials for children and teens, and materials in other languages are included.

This is a very useful resource for consumer health and public libraries, although it is rather expensive. It will also need periodic updating to remain current.—**Barbara M. Bibel**

Eating Disorders

1217. **Eating Disorders Information for Teens.** 3d ed. Elizabeth Bellenir, ed. Detroit, Omnigraphics, 2013. 380p. index. (Heath Reference Series). $85.00. ISBN 13: 978-0-7808-1269-7.

Omnigraphics' Teen Health Series has been running for several years now and has covered a wide range of issues, including alcohol abuse, asthma, skin problems, and suicide. This volume discusses the important and at times deadly topic of eating disorders, which affect more than eight million Americans, many of which are teenagers. This 3d edition is arranged into six parts, each of which covers a different aspect of eating disorders, including risk factors, understanding body image disorders, medical consequences, diagnosis and treatment, and maintaining health eating and fitness habits. Each of the main eating disorders is discussed: anorexia nervosa, bulimia, binge eating disorders, laxative abuse, compulsive exercise, and night eating disorder. New to this edition is a special section on healthy weight management and exercise plans. More in-depth articles cover such topics as medications and therapies for eating disorders, improving body image and self esteem, and eating disorders relapse and relapse. The work concludes with directory-type information on additional reading and organizations that help those with eating disorders.

This work is written in a straightforward style that will appeal to its teenage audience. The author does not play down the danger of living with an eating disorder and urges those struggling with this problem to seek professional help. This work, as well as others in this series, will be a welcome addition to high school and undergraduate libraries.—**Shannon Graff Hysell**

1218. **Eating Disorders: An Encyclopedia of Causes, Treatment, and Prevention.** Justine J. Reel, ed. Santa Barbara, Calif., Greenwood Press/ABC-CLIO, 2013. 498p. illus. index. $100.00. ISBN 13: 978-1-4408-0058-0; 978-1-4408-0059-7 (e-book).

Eating Disorders: An Encyclopedia of Causes, Treatment, and Prevention is a one-volume reference source that explores subjects related to body image and eating disorders. Topics covered include anorexia, bulimia, and binge eating, as well as media and cultural influences, treatment options, and prevention programs. The target audience for this source would include students and general readers interested in introductory material on eating disorder-related topics.

Entries are arranged alphabetically; most articles are one to three pages in length and include narrative text along with occasional black-and-white photographs. Entries are signed and have been written by experts in health and psychology-related fields. *See also* references to other entries are given at the end of some entries. Most entries have an accompanying bibliography. The book also includes a timeline of eating disorder history, brief case studies, and a topic index.

Eating Disorders offers a solid overview of information related to eating disorders. This reviewer appreciates having a working bibliography within the entries and would also suggest libraries place this title in the circulating collection for higher use. Issues and topics relating to eating disorders continues to be a popular research area for high school and college students, so this title would be a useful addition to high school libraries, public libraries, and university libraries.—**Caroline L. Gilson**

Fibromyalgia

1219. McCrindle, Louise S., and Alison C. Bested. **The Complete Fibromyalgia Health, Diet Guide & Cookbook.** Toronto, Robert Rose, 2013. 288p. index. $24.95. ISBN 13: 978-0-7788-0453-6.

Fibromyalgia is a condition that is becoming more common, possibly due to increased awareness. It is a syndrome, rather than a disease, with a wide range of symptoms: pain all over the body, fatigue, sleep disorders, and cognitive problems. Until recently it was dismissed as a psychosomatic condition. The majority of those affected are women.

Diagnosis and treatment are based on medical history. There are no standard tests. Holistic treatment, which is personalized and patient-centered, seems to be the most effective. This book written by a naturopath and a physician offers a plan based on diet, exercise, pain relief, and complementary and alternative therapies. The authors suggest that patients set realistic goals for improving their health. They offer treatment options including prescription and non-prescription pain relievers, meditation, exercise, body work, and diet and nutrition. The book has a number of questionnaires and planners for readers to fill in. It also provides detailed advice about dietary supplements, vitamins, and foods to use and avoid. There are meal plans and recipes with vegetarian and fish options. Red meat is one of the foods that fibromyalgia patients should avoid. This is a useful book for circulating collections in public and consumer health libraries with a caveat about the forms to fill in.—**Barbara M. Bibel**

Genetic Disorders

1220.   **Genetic Disorders Sourcebook.** 5th ed. Sandra J. Judd, ed. Detroit, Omnigraphics, 2014. 716p. index. (Health Reference Series). $85.00. ISBN 13: 978-0-7808-1301-4.

The arrangement of the 5th edition of this title is very similar to the last edition (2010); however, all of the content is new to this edition and reflects the latest research in the area of genetic disorders. The first, "Introduction to Genetics," provides a basic explanation of how genes work, genetic mutations, how genetics are inherited, and genetic testing. The major focus of the book, divided into parts 2 through 4, covers individual disorders associated with specific genes (e.g., cystic fibrosis, growth disorders), chromosome disorders (e.g., blood disorders, growth disorders), and complex disorders having genetic and environmental components (e.g., cancer, diabetes, obesity). Part 5 looks at genetic research, including the Human Genome Project, behavioral genetics, and gene therapy. Information for parents of children with genetic disorders is covered in part 6 and includes information on babies born with birth defects, education opportunities for children with special needs, and government benefits available. The final part offers further help to the user via a glossary and lists of additional resources. The intended audience, parents, and other concerned laypeople, makes this a good acquisition for public libraries.—**Barbara MacAlpine**

Graves' Disease

1221.   Moore, Elaine A., and Lisa Marie Moore. **Advances in Graves' Disease and Other Hyperthyroid Disorders.** Jefferson, N.C., McFarland, 2013. 278p. index. (McFarland Health Topics). $35.00pa. ISBN 13: 978-0-7864-7189-8; 978-1-4766-0622-4 (e-book).

This well-written guide is a timely and valuable resource. It is likely to be useful to individuals, including healthcare providers, who are involved or interested in learning more about topics related to hyperthyroid disease in general or Graves' Disease in particular. The contents of the guide are comprehensive. It begins with a table of contents that lists the book's 11 chapters. Topics discussed in depth include an overview of what hyperthyroidism is, its signs and symptoms, causes of hyperthyroidism, genetic and environmental factors, coexisting conditions, conventional and alternative treatments, and hyperthyroidism in special populations (e.g., children, pregnant women). This text also includes a selected bibliography, a list of references and resources, and an index. The text is easy to read and understand and provides plenty of first-person accounts to help users determine how common their symptoms are and the extent of their health problems.

This text is likely to be useful to individuals diagnosed with Graves' Disease or hyperthyroidism or their relatives. It is also a resource that a variety of healthcare providers may find helpful, especially if they are involved in providing care to patients who suffer from these conditions.—**Shannon Graff Hysell**

Heart Disease

1222.   DeSilva, Regis A. **Heart Disease.** Santa Barbara, Calif., Greenwood Press/ABC-CLIO, 2013. 276p. index. (Biographies of Disease). $45.00. ISBN 13: 978-0-313-37606-1; 978-0-313-37607-8 (e-book).

This small book is packed with information on heart disease. It opens with a history of the disease and the advancement of medical procedures to cure it. The following chapters cover what it is, the structure and function of the heart, disorders of coronary circulation, diseases of the heart valves, disorders of the heart muscle, disorders of cardiac rhythm, congenital heart disease, tests for heart disease, surgical treatments and implantable cardiac devices, and cardiac arrest and resuscitation. The final chapter provides some of the most thought-provoking information on future trends in heart disease, including advances in genomics and genetics, the role of stem cell research, and longevity research. The book includes a glossary, bibliography, and extensive index. The book is very readable and recommended for public and health care libraries. It is a good purchase for the cost.—**Betsy J. Kraus**

1223.   **Stroke Sourcebook.** 3d ed. Amy L. Sutton, ed. Detroit, Omnigraphics, 2013. 606p. index. (Health Reference Series). $85.00. ISBN 13: 978-0-7808-1297-0.

This volume is truly a reference volume. It is an encyclopedic handbook on stroke that is written in a language the layperson will understand. It is divided into seven sections: introduction to stroke, types of stroke, stroke risk factors and prevention, diagnosis and treatment of stroke, post-stroke complications and rehabilitation, life after stroke, and additional help and information. These different sections explain in detail their topic, giving examples for further clarity. No illustrations are included.

Each chapter lists additional sources of information. The chapter on "Life after Stroke" gives information that would be hard for the average family to find. Adapting your home after stroke, sleep and sex after stroke, health insurance and disabilities concerns, and choosing long-term care for those disabled by stroke. A glossary and a directory of stroke resources, which lists telephone numbers and toll-free numbers (if available) and e-mail and Website addresses is included. An index with cross-references completes the volume. This is one of the most helpful, readable books on stroke. This volume is highly recommended and should be in every medical, hospital, and public library; in addition, every family practitioner should have a copy in his or her office.—**Betsy J. Kraus**

Respiratory Disorders

1224.   **Respiratory Disorders Sourcebook.** 3d ed. Amy L. Sutton, ed. Detroit, Omnigraphics, 2014. 651p. index. (Health Reference Series). $85.00. ISBN 13: 978-0-7808-1305-2.

This title is a great addition for public and school libraries because it provides concise health information on the respiratory conditions. Readers can start with this reference source and get satisfactory answers before proceeding to other medical reference tools for more in-depth information.

There are eight parts to this reference tool: an introduction to respiratory disorders; "Understanding and Preventing Respiratory Problems"; "Infectious Respiratory Disorders"; "Inflammatory Respiratory Disorders"; "Other Conditions That Affect Respiration"; "Pediatric Respiratory Disorders"; "Diagnosing and Treating Respiratory Disorders"; "Living with Chronic Respiratory Problems"; and "Additional Help and Information." The introduction presents the lung disease statistics, the affects of air pollution, and smoking and respiratory disease. At the end of each chapter there is information for where readers can get more information from support groups. "Understanding and Preventing Respiratory Problems" explains how physical activity can improve lung function, the factors that affect lung function, and the impact from indoor and outdoor pollution. The section on "Infectious Respiratory Disorders" provides explanations on cols and influenza, pneumonia, and viral and fungal infections. "Pediatric Respiratory Disorders" discusses asthma in children, croup, respiratory distress syndrome of the newborn, and sudden infant death syndrome (SIDS). "Additional Help and Information" provides a glossary as well as contact information for national organizations for lung cancers, asthma resources, and sleep disorder clinics. Most of the general research documentations are from Centers for Disease Control and Prevention (CDC) and Department of Health and Human Services (DHHS) as well as many other governmental entities— generally authoritative sources. However, readers should not treat this book as a replacement for medical professional care but use it as a good guide for health education on lung disorders.—**Polin P. Lei**

Sexually Transmitted Diseases

1225. **Sexually Transmitted Disease: An Encyclopedia of Diseases, Prevention, Treatment, and Issues.** Jill Grimes, Kristyn Fagerberg, and Lori Smith, eds. Santa Barbara, Calif., Greenwood Press/ ABC-CLIO, 2014. 2v. illus. index. $189.00/set. ISBN 13: 978-1-4408-0134-1; 978-1-4408-0135-8 (e-book).

This is a well-written encyclopedia set that is focused on sexually transmitted diseases, commonly referred to as STDs. The editors have also included a variety of topics that are related to STDs, which makes the set even more informative, timely, and appropriate. This two-volume encyclopedia set is likely to be of interest to individuals who want to learn more about STDs, including educators, clinicians, counselors, and public health officials. This encyclopedia is timely and provides a thorough review of a topic that has the potential to impact any individual.

The encyclopedia includes a contents page, a list of entries, a Guide to Related Topics, preface, introduction, timelines, A-Z entries, selected resources, information on the editors and contributors, and an index. The list of entries pages are comprehensive. Topics range from Acquired Immune Deficiency Syndrome to Malaria to Zoster. The broad topics include: Anatomy, Contraception, Diagnostic and Surgical Interventions, Diseases, History, Individuals, Legal Issues, Medical Consequences, Microbiology, Pregnancy and Childbirth, Sexual Behavior, Societal Issues, Teens and STDs, Testing, Treatment, and Vaccinations and Prevention. Each broad topic includes a list of subtopics that is comprehensive. The Index is extensive with corresponding page references.

Throughout both encyclopedias there are text boxes that include such things as case studies. The text boxes are easy to read and are effective in providing highlights on the respective topic. Black-and-white illustrations are included and are easy to read. The pictures are clear and include detailed descriptions. This two-volume set encyclopedia set is well written and timely. Readers will likely find the text's organization and layout to be user-friendly. This encyclopedia set will likely complement libraries in settings such as healthcare facilities, schools, public health systems, or other locations where the topic of sexually transmitted diseases may be discussed or reviewed.—**Paul M. Murphy III**

1226. **Sexually Transmitted Diseases Sourcebook.** 5th ed. Amy L. Sutton, ed. Detroit, Omnigraphics, 2013. 580p. index. (Health Reference Series). $85.00. ISBN 13: 978-0-7808-1281-9.

The 5th edition of the *Sexually Transmitted Diseases Soucebook*, part of Omnigraphics' Health Reference Series, is a welcome update. The organization is the same as in previous editions with 6 major sections (focusing on broad areas of interest) subdivided into 51 total chapters (focusing on single topics within each section). Highlights include part 3, which discusses the complications that may occur with an STD infection, and part 5, which covers STD risks and prevention, which includes advice on talking to your partner as well as the teenage population about STDS and an updated section on vaccines and microbicides that can help prevent the spread of STDs.

This edition includes updated information about the transmission, diagnosis, and treatment of STDs; reports on current research and clinical trials; updated statistical information; and information on STD testing and treatment concerns. A comprehensive index, glossary of terms, Website and hotline directories, and contact information for organizations complete this resource.

The majority of the information comes from U.S. government agency publications, and is thus in the public domain (and free), but this does not detract from the source's value. The *Sexually Transmitted Diseases Sourcebook* provides a wealth of information for the layperson in one compact volume, including bulleted fact sheets, easy-to-read guides, and extensive endnote references. This resource is highly recommended for academic and public libraries.—**Shannon Graff Hysell**

Sports Medicine

1227. **Pediatric Sports Medicine: Essentials for Office Evaluation.** Chris Koutures and Valarie Wong, eds. Thorofare, N.J., Slack, 2014. 322p. illus. index. $82.95pa. ISBN 13: 978-1-61711-052-8.

This work is a ready-reference designed to be in the hands of pediatric doctors and sports medicine specialists working with children. The work is designed in a question-and-answer format that is organized into three main sections—General Information, Medical Issues, and Musculoskeletal Issues. Each section has several chapters, with the chapter on musculoskeletal issues having over 20 chapters. The questions make it easy for the researcher to look up an answer quickly, but also provides the practitioner with questions to ask their patient that they may not have considered. There are several practical elements involved in this work, including a section on medical terms and phrases, information on how to take a sports history, guidelines on how to decide which imaging studies to order, and how long to recommend a child be sidelined when musculoskeletal concerns occur. The work has contributions from over 60 experts in the field, all with credentials listed in the front matter of the volume. While this book is designed to be in the hands of medical practitioners for quick and easy reference, it will also be a useful addition to medical libraries and university libraries offering programs in pediatrics and sports medicine.—**Mila C. Su**

Nursing

1228. **CINAHL: The Cumulative Index to Nursing and Allied Health Literature. http://www.ebscohost.com/cinahl/.** [Website]. Ipswich, Mass., EBSCO. Price negotiated by site. Date reviewed: 2013.

This database is the most comprehensive resource for nursing and allied health literature. CINAHL subject headings follow the structure of the Medical Subject Headings, or MeSH, used by the National Library of Medicine. There are currently over 12,000 subject heading used in this database, which efficiently and effectively retrieves information for literature citations and text. It covers the literature in the fields of nursing, allied health, and related fields from 1981 to the present.—**James E. Bobick**

1229. **The Gale Encyclopedia of Nursing & Allied Health.** 3d ed. Brigham Narins, ed. Stamford, Conn., Gale/Cengage Learning, 2013. 6v. illus. index. $1,407.00/set. ISBN 13: 978-1-4144-9888-1; 978-1-4144-9895-9 (e-book).

This new edition continues to be a valuable quick reference for the target audience of students in the health sciences. Approximately 1,100 entries are included over 6 volumes. General topics include diseases and disorders, lab tests and procedures, equipment, human biology, the professions, and current health issues. The entries, written by health professionals, average two to three pages in length. The information provided is evidenced-based and accurate. Each entry is followed by a succinct bibliography of relevant books, journal articles, organizations, or Internet sites. Helpful color photographs or illustrations, as well as tables, are included throughout. Each of the volumes has an alphabetized list of all 1,100 entries in the table of contents and in the index. The reference is written in a style that is easily accessible to students in a number of health fields, including those studying to become a registered and licensed practical nurse, nurse practitioner, nurse midwife, medical technologist, pharmacy technician, or physical therapist.—**Mary Ann Thompson**

34 Technology

General Works

1230. Enhancing Instruction with Visual Media: Utilizing Video and Lecture Capabilities. Ellen G. Smyth and John X. Volker, eds. Hershey, Pa., Information Science Reference, 2013. 315p. index. $175.00; $265.00 (e-book); $350.00 (print and online editions). ISBN 13: 978-1-46663-962-1; 978-1-46663-963-8 (e-book).

Two professors bring together 18 chapters by scholars and practitioners that focus on new and improved technologies being integrated into student instruction to enhance student engagement and performance. The work is designed to provide researchers and educators with insights into new visual media being used in the instructional environment, placing them into their correct social and cultural contexts and evaluating challenges and benefits that arise with their implementation. The book illustrates how to use these new technologies to enhance teaching and learning to every student regardless of their learning style or disabilities. This work includes both a basic table of contents, and a detailed table of contents that includes abstracts for each chapter. Each chapter includes examples and references as well as a discussion of what has been done in the situation. The work might benefit from cross-references between chapters, and a glossary either within each chapter or for the work as a whole. It will be useful for professors, researchers, and instructional designers looking to use innovative video technologies in teaching a wide range of learners, including learning disabled, non-English speakers, and those with nontraditional learning behaviors.—**Sara Marcus**

1231. Exploring Technology for Writing and Writing Instruction. Kristine E. Pytash and Richard Ferdig, eds. Hershey, Pa., Information Science Reference, 2013. 418p. index. $175.00; $265.00 (e-book); $350.00 (print and online editions). ISBN 13: 978-1-46664-341-3; 978-1-466664-342-0 (e-book).

Edited by an Assistant Professor in Teaching, Learning, and Curriculum Studies and co-director of the secondary Integrated Language Arts teacher preparation program in collaboration with the Summit Professor of Learning Technologies and Professor of Instructional Technology at Kent State University, this volume is part of the Advances in Educational Technologies and Instructional Design series. With the growth of technology has come a writing revolution, from forming the letters, to thinking, collaborating, sharing, and the language itself. The growth of digital writing and associated technologies has led to a social change that needs to be explored, an exploration initiated and guided by the 20 chapters authored by 42 scholars and practitioners mainly from the United States. These entries examine and provide evidence of the use of technology for writing and writing instruction at all levels of instruction. Organized into five sections, the work examines new tools and theories, new tools for revision and feedback, online spaces for writing, writing instruction, and writing and identity. This volume is appropriate for educators at all levels who integrate writing into their subject or class.—**Sara Marcus**

1232.   **Project Management Approaches for Online Learning Design.** Gulson Eby and T. Volkan Yuzer, eds. Hershey, Pa., Information Science Reference, 2013. 344p. index. $175.00; $265.00 (e-book); $350.00 (print and e-book editions). ISBN 13: 978-1-46662-830-4; 978-1-46662-831-1 (e-book).

Two Turkey-based scholars and educators bring together 17 chapters by international scholars and practitioners that focus on the best practices planning, organizing, and managing the necessary resources to successfully complete online goals and objectives. Although the focus is on project development and management, the six sections are appropriate for an educator in any discipline seeking knowledge of online learning tools. The seven sections address: an introduction to the topic, communication management, implementation management, human resources management, quality insurance management, and risk management. The contributors present theoretical points of view as well as empirical evidence of how to effectively design online learning modules that will enhance learning environments and student experiences. This work includes both a basic table of contents, and a detailed table of contents that includes abstracts for each chapter. Each chapter includes examples and references as well as a discussion of what has been done in the situation. Many chapters also include a glossary of key terms. The editors provide a compiled list of references from all chapters, and an index to the work as a whole.—**Sara Marcus**

1233.   **Technological Tools for the Literacy Classroom.** Jeff Whittingham, Stephanie Huffman, Wendy Rickman, and Cheryl Wiedmaier, eds. Hershey, Pa., Information Science Reference, 2013. 354p. index. $175.00; $265.00 (e-book); $350.00 (print and e-book editions). ISBN 13: 978-1-46663-974-4; 978-1-46663-975-1 (e-book).

Edited by three faculty at the University of Central Arkansas, and Cheryl Wiedmasier who is affiliated with the University of Central Arkansas but not identified in the biography area, this work brings together 17 chapters authored by 27 scholars and practitioners in the United States. Organized into five sections, the work begins with a historical overview of literacy and technology, followed by four chapters on Web-based and online tools for use in the literacy classroom. The third section presents seven chapters focusing on hardware and software applications in the literacy classroom. The fourth section presents four chapters on teacher training, while the fifth section addresses the future use of technology in literacy.

A detailed table of contents enables the user to preview each of the chapters through abstracts in order to locate the most relevant information, while a brief index enables seekers of specific information to find individual pages of interest. This book will help educators of all subjects to integrate both literacy and technology into the curriculum and classroom, at any level, particularly K-12, although higher education practitioners will also find chapters of benefit. Combining theoretical and practical chapters, this work will offer research-based evidence to support implementations of the practical ideas offered. Each chapter concludes with references and a list of key terms and definitions. What would add value to this volume is a compiled list of key terms and definitions, offering a unified usage of terminology throughout the chapters and serving as a glossary for those new to the field. A compilation of references enables one to see a comprehensive bibliography on the topic of technology and literacy in the K-12 classroom, in addition to the lists at the end of each chapter.—**Sara Marcus**

Computers

1234.   **Computer Sciences.** K. Lee Lerner, ed. New York, Macmillan Reference USA/Gale Group, 2013. 4v. illus. index. (The Macmillan Science Library). $657.00/set. ISBN 13: 978-0-02-866220-6; 978-0-02-866225-1 (e-book).

The original edition of this four-volume set appeared in 2002, so a revised edition is appropriate a decade later. The roughly 300 unsigned articles, some new and some updated, in this encyclopedia are arranged thematically in four, nearly independent volumes, making the index even more important than normal for this work.

The overlapping themes of the four volumes are: Foundations: Ideas and People; Software and Hardware; Social Applications; and Electronic Universe. Each of the four volumes has the same front pages that include the set's preface, How to Use This Book, a reference section of measurements and conversions, a timeline of computing history, and a timeline of programming languages. Each volume also shares the same back pages that include a glossary, the cumulative index, and a directory of computer science organizations.

The clearly written set is aimed at "younger students and general readers" and features a very attractive layout with broad margins to display sidebars, definitions, captions, photographs, and figures. Photographs and figures are also incorporated into the main text. Each article has *see also* references and a brief bibliography or resources.

Giants in the history of computing like Charles Babbage, Bill Gates, and Steve Jobs have their own entries. Several other notable innovators, such as Tim Berners-Lee, Jeff Bezos, and Larry Page, are grouped in the Entrepreneurs article. Entries fall in a number of categories. There are obvious ones like Abacus, E-Mail, and Hypertext; general ones like Animation and Games; applied ones like Medical Systems and Library Applications; and conceptual ones like Privacy and Ethics.

The main difficulty with this set is that the organizational scheme is so arbitrary at times. Music, Computer is in volume 2, while Music Composition is in 3. Entries on Astronomy, Biology and Physics are in volume 3, while those on Art and Chemistry are in 4. The Library Applications piece is in volume 3, but Political Applications is in 4. The aforementioned entry on Entrepreneurs is in volume 4 rather than 1, and the Social Impact article is in 4 instead of 3. As noted above, the index is essential in locating a topic. For example, the index will direct the user to the Security entry for information on the Stuxnet malware; it will also confirm that there is no mention of Wikileaks – indeed, there is no mention there of Wikipedia even, which is very surprising. Despite the organizational challenges, there is much to recommend here, and the set is best suited to high school and public libraries.—**John Maxymuk**

1235.   **Computer Technology Innovators.** Millerton, N.Y., Grey House Publishing, 2013. 414p. index. $95.00. ISBN 13: 978-1-4298-3805-4; 978-1-4298-3806-1 (e-book).

This is an informative resource that is focused on the innovators of computer technology. This text is likely to be appealing to individuals such as students, professors, and professionals that are interested in learning more about the men and women who shaped computer technology as it is known today. This is timely as we continue to experience the rapid expansion of computer technology and computing on a global basis. The cover provides clear insight to the book's contents through the use of an effectively placed color picture of Steve Wozniak, Apple's cofounder.

This book spans more than 300 pages. The first few pages include content, publisher's note, and a list of the contributors. The Content page is a nice feature as it lists the individuals that are included in the text alphabetically by last name.

A majority of this book is a biography of more than 100 individuals who influenced computer technology. Each biography is presented in an easy-to-read format. The beginning of each biography includes a summary of information including Name, Born, Died, Professional Field, Specialty, and Primary Company/Organization. This is followed by an Introduction, Early Life, Life's Work, Personal Life, and Affiliation. The end of each biography includes a Further Reading section. The text does not include any tables or graphs. Each bibliography includes a gray portrait sketch of the individual. Color pictures are not included. The text's index is useful as it includes information by topic as well as the innovator's last name. Topics range from ABC, to programming language, to Konrad Zuse.

The editors of this text have produced a timely, relevant, and informative resource. Readers that are interested in computers, technology, and the men and women who influenced the industry will likely find this text to be of interest. [R: LJ, 1 June 13, p. 138]—**Paul M. Murphy III**

1236.   Holt, Thomas J., and Bernadette H. Schell. **Hackers and Hacking: A Reference Handbook.** Santa Barbara, Calif., ABC-CLIO, 2013. 354p. index. (Contemporary World Issues). $58.00. ISBN 13: 978-1-61069-276-2; 978-1-61069-277-9 (e-book).

This is an informative resource that is focused on technology, the world of hackers, and the act of hacking. The text is likely to be of interest to individuals who want to learn more (or are intrigued) about hackers, hacking, and technology in general. This is a timely and well-written resource. Technology and technology-related crime continues to experience rapid growth.

The text's cover provides great insight to the content. This is accomplished through the use of an effectively placed color photograph of an individual who appears to be typing on a computer. Interestingly, the book's title partially covers the individual's face. This can be correlated with the hacker's desire not to be recognized, identified, or caught.

This book spans more than 300 pages. The first few pages include a contents section, list of figures and tables, and a preface. The contents section is easy to reference and includes corresponding page numbers. The actual content of the book includes seven main sections: Background and History; Problems, Controversies, and Solutions; Perspectives; Profiles; Data and Documents; Resources; and a Chronology. The end of the text includes a glossary, an About the Authors section, and an index.

A variety of tables and figures are included in the book. They are easy to read and understand. Black-and-white pictures are also included throughout. The pictures range from hardware to hackers using computers to ex-hackers who are presenting at speaking engagements. Each picture is accompanied with a brief explanation. This is a nice feature. References include traditional printed materials as well as online resources.

This text is well written and timely. Individuals will find the book's organization and layout to be user-friendly. This text will complement a variety of libraries, including personal and professional libraries.—**Paul M. Murphy III**

Games

1237.   **Cases on Digital Game-Based Learning: Methods, Models, and Strategies.** Youngkyun Baek and Nicola Whitton, eds. Hershey, Pa., Information Science Reference, 2013. 592p. index. $175.00; $265.00 (e-book); $350.00 (print and e-book editions). ISBN 13: 978-1-4662-848-9; 978-1-4662-849-6 (e-book).

Presenting 26 chapters authored by 59 international educators, scholars, and practitioners, this book is organized into 7 sections. Beginning with a chapter on teaching with commercial games, there next are four chapters on teaching with educational games, followed by three chapters designing games for learning. Section four addresses learning through game design, followed by sections on games for teacher education, game-based learning in practice, and ending with four chapters on researching games and learning. The volume includes a compilation of references as well as an index, making this valuable not only for finding a chapter of one's interest through the detailed table of contents, but also for research and future research. This book is appropriate for educators at all levels who want to learn more through reading case studies of those who explore the methods, models, and strategies of digital game-based learning for various purposes and levels. Not all chapters have lists of key terms and definitions, although it is not necessarily needed in each chapter. The international scope of the cases presented enable a range of concepts and implementations to be explored, although the technologies and games used might not be familiar to those in other cultures. Regardless, these case studies are valuable resources for seeing what has been done, and also for guidance in how to try these techniques in one's own settings through the detailed guidance and plans presented in each chapter for reproducing the case.—**Sara Marcus**

1238.   Fox, Matt. **The Video Games Guide: 1,000+ Arcade, Console and Computer Games, 1962-2012.** Jefferson, N.C., McFarland, 2013. 376p. index. $55.00pa. ISBN 13: 978-0-7864-7257-4.

This resource is a guide for anyone researching the arcade, console, and computer video games of 1962-2012, including today's latest PlayStation 3, Xbox 360, and Wii games. The work is arranged alphabetically by game name and each entry provides an in-depth review of the video game being discussed. Each review includes the year of release, developer, the reviewer's number of stars (from 1 to 5), and a description of the game and its features. Titles of games within a review that are reviewed themselves elsewhere in the book are bolded, while those that are listed only in the appendixes are italicized. The author writes his reviews in a candid, sometimes humorous manner that most game fans will appreciate. In addition to reviews, the author provides full-color gallery of games throughout the decades, and seven appendixes (e.g., a games chronology, list of video game awards, video game resources). In reading the descriptions video game players of this generation will remember many of the popular games. Although not a necessary purchase for most libraries it may be useful in college libraries that offer courses in video game development as well as large academic and public libraries.—**Shannon Graff Hysell**

1239.   **Plunkett's Games, Apps, & Social Media Industry Almanac.** 2014 ed. Jack W. Plunkett, ed. Houston, Tex., Plunkett Research, 2013. 322p. $349.99pa. ISBN 13: 978-1-60879-707-3.

Plunkett Research is a well-known publisher of industry directories and almanacs. This particular title covers fast-growing industry of games, apps, and social media. This new edition focuses on the role the internet and mobile devices play in business collaboration and online retailing. Games, both online and offline, continue to be very popular and a high-dollar industry as well. This work is designed for the general reader and business owner to compare the top 300 American game, app, and social media companies. An overview of the industry trends is provided and graphs and tables are provided for easy interpretation of the information.

The top gaming and social media companies included here are the largest and most successful companies from all areas of the industry. The alphabetic listing of these top companies provides the industry group, types of business, brands, divisions, subsidiaries, plans for growth, current news, contact information for the officers, annual financials, salaries and benefits, and provides an assessment of the company's hiring and advancement of minorities and women. Within the volume users will find industry analysis and market research. Topics include: social media privacy concerns, 3-D games and new opportunities, the latest trends in mobile table entertainment devices, and virtual worlds opening up new revenue sources. Indexes to the industry, sales, brand names, and the subsidiaries are provided. The information in this book is also available online through the publisher. This work is a fine addition of Plunkett Research's growing list of industry guides and will be useful in academic and large public library's business collections.—**Kay Stebbins Slattery**

1240.   **Serious Games and Virtual Worlds in Education, Professional Development, and Healthcare.** Klaus Bredl and Wolfgang Bosche, eds. Hershey, Pa., Information Science Reference, 2013. 361p. index. $175.00. ISBN 13: 978-1-4666-3673-6.

Edited by a Professor for Digital Media at the Institute for Media and Educational Technologies at Ausburg University (Germany) and an Interim Professor at the Institute of Psychology at the University of Education Karlsruhe (Germany), this volume brings together research projects, case studies, examples, and literature reviews about games and virtual environments specifically in health education, counseling, and therapy. The 18 chapters authored by 33 predominantly German scholars and practitioners look at a variety of technologies, such as multi-user virtual environments (MUVEs), massive multiplayer online role-playing games (MMORPGs), and virtual worlds, as well as single-player games. This volume explores their use in several areas, including individually, in health education, and in counseling and therapy practice. Organized into four sections, these chapters address factors and key components of serious games and multi-user virtual environments, including authoring, control, and evaluation in serious games for education; games and virtual worlds in education; and games and virtual worlds in healthcare. While the focus is specifically on healthcare, therapy,. and counseling, the concepts and techniques discussed can be applied to education and other situations as well, offering a view of these technologies that is often not seen. A detailed table of contents, in conjunction with an index, enables the reader to find the section or chapter of most interest and value, while the compiled list of references enables further research on the topic in general. This book is of exceptional value to practicing counselors and therapists seeking ways to reach today's generation as well as to reach previously noncommunicative or noncompliant patients.—**Sara Marcus**

Internet

1241.   **Complete Planet: A Deep Web Directory. http://www.completeplanet.com/.** [Website]. Free. Date reviewed: 2013.

According to the creators of this database, "there are hundreds of thousands of databases that contain Deep Web Content. CompletePlanet is the front door to these Deep Web databases on the Web and to the thousands of regular search engines." They consider it a first step in trying to find highly topical information. By tracing through CompletePlanet's subject structure or searching Deep Websites, you can go to various topic areas, such as energy or agriculture or food or medicine, and find rich content sites not accessible using conventional search engines." CompletePlanet is one of the Websites that the literature describes as a good starting point for entrance into the Invisible Web (Websites that cannot be accessed by search engines such as Google or Yahoo).—**William O. Scheeren**

1242.   **InfoMine. http://infomine.ucr.edu/.** [Website]. Free. Date reviewed: 2013.

InfoMine is a virtual library of Internet resources relevant to faculty, students, and research staff at the university level. It contains useful Internet resources such as databases, electronic journals, electronic books, bulletin boards, mailing lists, online library card catalogs, articles, directories of researchers, and many other types of information. *InfoMine* was created by librarians from the University of California, Wake Forest University, California State University, the University of Detroit—Mercy as well as other universities and colleges. Because it is a very scholarly site, it is most appropriate for academic and public librarians.—**William O. Scheeren**

1243.   **Internet Innovators.** Ipswich, Mass., Salem Press; distr., Millerton, N.Y., Grey House Publishing, 2013. 464p. index. $95.00. ISBN 13: 978-1-58765-993-5; 978-1-4298-3762-0 (e-book).

Internet Innovators, the first volume in the new Salem Press Innovators series, contains 120-plus clearly written, to-the-point biographies of significant and influential individuals in the arena of Internet innovation, with an advertized emphasis on dot-com initiators and leaders. Entries include highlights of the entrant's activities, an introduction, early life, life's work, personal life, further reading recommendations, and sketches of the entrant. Also included in entries are insightful insets regarding site or product affiliation (for example, Netscape co-founder Marc Andreessen's entry contains an inset on Netscape) which provide a snapshot of the site or product and its development.

The appendixes of this accessible biographical dictionary also contain an excellent timeline regarding the development of the Internet and its constituencies (e.g., browsers, social media); a useful (although only briefly) annotated bibliography; a seemingly redundant biographical directory, which "briefly summarizes the achievements" of the entrants (p. 425); a company index; and a traditional index.

This reviewer's main complaint regarding the print version (which also applies to the electronic version as well) is the lack of cross-referencing of entries. This title also includes complementary access to an online version of the book that contains all the features and content described above. It offers citations for entries (including exporting into biographical managers) and printing, e-mailing, and saving of entries. The title provides several types of searches including full text (preferred by this reviewer over the "top matter/keywords" search), abstract, title, and the aforementioned clunky top matter/keywords.

The electronic version has a few negatives, including the aforementioned lack of cross-referencing. The listing of names/entries is just that—a long alphabetic listing of the entries. This reviewer would have recommended at least dividing the list into alphabetic groupings. Furthermore, the timeline, which is easy to read in the print version, did not translate well in the online version and is difficult to decipher. Furthermore, the indexes do not link directly to content within the title. This would be very useful and user-friendly, especially with regard to the biographical, company, and regular indexes.

Other than these complaints, this title is very good, and considering that it comes with free access to an electronic version, a library will get a lot of bang for its buck, especially with such a relatively low cost. This title is highly recommended for both public and academic libraries, especially at institutions with strong computer science, history of computer science, media studies, and business programs (particularly those that emphasize entrepreneurship).—**Megan W. Lowe**

1244.   **RefDesk. http://www.refdesk.com.** [Website]. Free. Date reviewed: 2013.

Refdesk.com is the brainchild of Bob Drudge, and represents his personal attempt, underway since 1995, "to bring some semblance of order to the chaos of the Internet." In contrast to the cluttered and somewhat overwhelming main page of *Refdesk.com*, the "Reference Desk" page (at the URL given above) offers a clean listing of sources neatly organized into 32 categories. There are also links to "Essential Reference Tools," "Fast Facts," and more. Users will have access to such resources as a diction, a thesaurus, news stories, "Today in History," current events topics, and much more.—**Charlotte Ford**

35 Physical Sciences and Mathematics

Physical Sciences

General Works

1245. **Careers in Chemistry.** Donald R. Franceschetti, ed. Hackensack, N.J., Salem Press; distr., Millerton, N.Y., Grey House Publishing, 2013. 482p. index. $95.00. ISBN 13: 978-1-58765-993-5.

1246. **Careers in Physics.** Donald R. Franceschetti, ed. Hackensack, N.J., Salem Press, 2013. 475p. index. $95.00. ISBN 13: 978-1-58765-992-8.

This new series from Salem Press, and distributed by Grey House Publishing, provides overviews of career options in some of science and technologies most rewarding and challenging fields. What makes the titles in this series unique is that there is a connection between the area of science covered and how it relates to other STEM-related (Science, Technology, Engineering, and Mathematics) careers or occupations. The works are arranged into 20 specific occupations, each highlighting a particular career within that branch of science. For example, in *Careers in Physics* highlighted careers include: Aeronautics and Aviation, Astrophysics, Cryogenics, Geophysics, Nuclear Physics, and Systems Engineering. Each chapter begins with an overview of the field of study, including a study of its history, technological advances, and future prospects. Also discussed is how this area of science has impacted U.S. industry in the areas of private industry, government, military, and academic research. Each occupational profile provides data on median annual income, employment outlook, education and coursework, daily tasks and technology used, future applications, and transferable skills. The appendixes provide useful resources for students looking into these fields. They include: a bibliography, detailed STEM undergraduate majors, colleges to consider, career guidance portals, occupational resources, and Nobel Prize winners in the area of study.

Designed to align with high school curriculum standards, these titles are ideal for students at both the high school and undergraduate level.—**Shannon Graff Hysell**

Chemistry

Biography

1247.   **Contemporary Biographies in Chemistry.** Ipswich, Mass., Salem Press; distr., Millerton, N.Y., Grey House Publishing, 2013. 301p. index. $95.00. ISBN 13: 978-1-58765-997-3; 978-1-58765-998-0 (e-book).

Contemporary Biographies in Chemistry compiles 31 short biographies of current leaders in the field of chemistry along with 10 short historical biographies of chemists who have had a significant impact on the field. Each article is between 1,000 and 4,000 words and includes information on the scientist's early life, education, and life's work; a short bibliography is included at the end of each article. In addition there is a larger bibliography at the end of the book, a list of selected works, and two indexes (one by name and one by geographical location).

The strength of this resource is that the biographies for current practicing chemists go in greater depth than most resources easily accessible on the Web, such as Wikipedia, making it a useful source for students looking for current biographical information on practicing chemists.

There are a number of weaknesses to this resource, however. First of all, at least 8 of the 31 entries are not biographies of chemists, but instead include a number of geneticists, plant biologists, and one oncologist. Second, there are a number of editorial errors. For example, in the Publisher's Note it is stated, "Contemporary Biographies in Chemistry is a collection of thirty-one biographical sketches of 'living leaders' in the fields of physics" (p. vii). Another example of an error can be found in the article on Olufunmilayo Olopade, an oncologist, where the author writes that she and her family "...live in the Kenwood community, outside Chicago" (p. 137) when Kenwood is actually a neighborhood within Chicago. Third, the binding of the book is of poor quality; the pages have begun to separate from the spine with only minimal use. While this resource provides useful biographical information on contemporary chemists, this should be weighed against the noted issues with this resource.—**Megan Toups**

Catalogs and Collections

1248.   **Household Products Database. http://hpd.nlm.nih.gov.** [Website]. National Library of Medicine. Free. Date reviewed: 2014.

This is a great Website to discover if any given household product can be hazardous to your health. This database includes product information for auto products, pesticides landscape/yard, pet care, and more with manufacturer, health effects, handling/disposal, and ingredients. A lot of useful and enlightening information can be found here by browsing either by category or by and A-Z listing of products. This site is supported by the National Library of Medicine.—**Marty Magee**

1249.   **Periodic Table. http://periodictable.rosendigital.com/.** [Website]. New York, Rosen Publishing. Price negotiated by site. Date reviewed: 2014.

This Web resource makes chemistry and complex scientific concepts interesting and easier to understand for elementary and middle school students. Supportive of STEM learning, this site provides students with an interactive interface in which they can explore the 118 chemical elements. They will learn about the building blocks of each element as well as how it was discovered, its uses throughout history, and more. Individual articles are broken into screen-sized segments that can be read aloud for the user. Users can access information by a keyword search or following the hierarchical menu. Each segment includes brief text, an enlargeable photograph, plus occasional audio or video files. Teacher resources include lesson plans and instructional materials that provide step-by-step instructions for further exploration. There is a text-to-speech feature that supports ESL students. It is also compatible for iPad and iPod Touch for schools that have these tools available. Purchase this for elementary and middle school libraries if teachers are enthusiastic about using it.—**Shannon Graff Hysell**

1250.   **SciFinder. http://www.cas.org/products/scifinder.** [Website] Columbus, Ohio: Chemical Abstracts Service. Starting at $2,700.00. Date reviewed: 2013.

SciFinder Scholar is an interface to the *Chemical Abstracts Service* (CAS). It allows users to search millions of chemical references and substances by research topic, author name, structure and substructure, chemical name or CAS Registry Number, company/name organization, as well as browse the table of contents in journals, and enable a reaction query.—**James E. Bobick**

Handbooks and Yearbooks

1251.   Coelho, Alexa, and Simon Quellen Field. **Why Is Milk White? And 200 Other Curious Chemistry Questions.** Chicago Review Press, 2013. 288p. Illus. $14.95pa. ISBN 13: 978-1-6137-4452-9.

This question and answer chemistry book came about because of an eleven-year-old's curiosity and interest in science. She came up with 200 questions about chemistry and enlisted the help of her chemist neighbor. He agreed to answer all of her questions and they co-authored this book. Questions and answers are divided into broad chapters, including sections on Food, Health and Safety, Things that Stink, Household Chemistry, and People and Animals. The beginning of the book explains how to read structural formulas, and several of these diagrams are included in the text. There are also projects for readers to try on their own. Overall, the writing is a bit lofty, and students will benefit from having a basic chemistry background in order to fully understand the answers. However, students will be eager to learn the answers to their questions. This book is perfect for browsing and for the first steps into research.— **Anne Bozievich**

1252.   Stewart, Ian C., and Justin P. Lomont. **The Handy Chemistry Answer Book.** Canton, Mich., Visible Ink Press, 2013. 388p. illus. index. $21.95pa. ISBN 13: 978-1-57859-374-3.

The Handy Chemistry Answer Book is an ideal supplemental resource for high school and college students in introductory and intermediate chemistry courses. Using a question-and-answer format with an engagingly informal tone, the authors effectively make the often-feared topic accessible but also do not skimp on details in their explanations of everything from polymers to CO_2 pollution to the many types of reactions. In addition to the basics required for understanding the subject and conducting lab work, the book also includes numerous questions that emphasize the application of chemistry in everyday life, such as "Why do farts stink?" and "What makes string cheese stringy?" Many questions are illustrated with structural formulas or black-and-white photographs.

Questions are arranged in 19 chapters on broad subtopics. The final chapter contains a selection of simple experiments that can be done at home, such as making "slime," rock candy crystals, and, the old standby, baking-soda-and-vinegar volcano. A detailed index makes topics easy to locate, and appendixes include charts of physical constants and conversion factors, a glossary, a historical timeline, and short descriptions of every Nobel Prize in Chemistry since 1901. The book would be a valuable addition to libraries at the high school and college levels.—**Maren Williams**

Earth and Planetary Sciences

General Works

1253.   **Earth Science: Earth Materials & Resources.** Stephen I. Dutch, ed. Hackensack, N.J., Salem Press, 2013. 2v. illus. index. $295.00/set. ISBN 13: 978-1-58765-981-2.

Earth Science: Earth Materials & Resources is a 2-volume encyclopedia with accompanying online access that includes over 100, 3-6 page entries on a range of introductory earth science topics. It is part of a larger 8-volume series that is being released in 4, 2-volume sets on different earth science subtopics. The Earth Science series is a revision of an earlier work published by Salem Press in 2001, *Earth Science* (see ARBA 2002, entry 1542), which was released as 5 volumes with "Earth Materials & Resources" being one of those volumes. The work has been updated from the previous edition to include information on new technologies and historical events such as hydraulic fracturing; the 2011 nuclear disaster at Fukushima, Japan; and the Deepwater Horizon explosion in 2010. In addition, there is now online access available to the encyclopedia.

The broad scope of topics covered in *Earth Science: Earth Materials & Resources* ranges from entries on earth materials, such as "Diamonds," to issues related to earth science, such as "Nuclear Waste Disposal." As noted in the publisher's note, this work is largely directed toward high school students and college students being introduced to earth science topics. Each entry is comprised of five parts—a short summary; a list of a few key definitions; an essay on the topic, sometimes including black-and-white photographs or diagrams; an annotated bibliography of books related to the topic; and a *see also* section with cross-references to other entries pertinent to the topic. In addition, the work contains a number of appendixes with useful reference information including a periodic table of the elements; a Mohs scale of mineral hardness; a glossary; a bibliography; and a subject index.

This resource will be very useful to high school students or undergraduate students being introduced for the first time to earth science topics. It gives them a good introduction to these topics and the annotated bibliographies at the end of each entry are an excellent way to provide students with additional resources to deepen their knowledge. While the written content of the entries is very useful, the accompanying black-and-white photographs are not. When looking at photographs of different rock types it is essential to be able to see colors to aid in identification. Overall, however, this resource should be useful to students being introduced for the first time to information on earth materials.—**Megan Toups**

1254.   **GeoBase. http://www.geobase.ca/geobase/en/index.html.** [Website]. Canadian Council on Geomatics. Free. Date reviewed: 2013.

GeoBase is a multidisciplinary database covering human and physical geography, geology, oceanography, geomechanics, alternative energy sources, pollution, waste management, and nature conservation. The product's goal is to provide geospatial reference for a broad variety of thematic data for government, business, and personal applications. It is considered throughout the industry to be a primary tool in planning and execution due to its high-quality geospatial information.—**James E. Bobick**

1255.   **GeoRef. http://www.agiweb.org/georef/index.html.** [Website]. Price negotiated by site. Date reviewed: 2013.

Established by the American Geological Institute in 1966, this database provides access to the geoscience literature of the world. GeoRef is the most comprehensive database in the geosciences. The database contains over 3.4 million references to geoscience journal articles, books, maps, conference papers, reports, and theses. Users can gain access to this vast amount of information through searching on the worldwide web, online, or on GeoRef CDs. To maintain the database, GeoRef editor/indexers regularly scan more than 3,500 journals in 40 languages as well as new books, maps, and reports. They record the bibliographic data for each document and assign index terms to describe it. Each month between 6,000 and 9,000 new references are added to the database.—**James E. Bobick**

1256.   Spellman, Frank R., and Melissa L. Stoudt. **The Handbook of Geoscience.** Lanham, Md., Scarecrow, 2013. 547p. index. $125.00. ISBN 13: 978-0-8108-8614-8; 978-0-8108-8615-5 (e-book)

This hefty handbook is designed by the authors as a "user-friendly overview" of geoscience. They have defined the geosciences broadly, including in their coverage the atmosphere, biosphere, hydrosphere, lithosphere, pedosphere (soils), environmental science, geographic systems, geodesy, surveying, and cartography. The authors stress the "readability" of the text, and it is indeed written in an attractive style, although sometimes the whimsy is a bit irritating. (For example, the "What is Life?" section contains an "after-thought" about living as a "state of mind".)

The variety of topics in this single volume is extraordinary. It begins with the basics like measurements, units, and the scientific method, and then proceeds through the major disciplines of the geosciences, covering a little bit of almost every major topic. There are a good number of black-and-white photographs and several good to mediocre line drawings. Each section has an extended (although not particularly up-to-date) bibliography.

A common problem with all-inclusive volumes like this is that there are errors of detail in topics beyond the collective expertise of the authors. For example, a "recumbant" (misspelled) fold is defined as an overturned fold with an "axial plant that is nearly horizontal." The geologic time scale (table 22.1) is considerably outdated, lacking the Ediacaran, Carboniferous, Paleogene, and Neogene Periods. Evolution is only briefly mentioned twice in this book, despite a large section on the biosphere. In short, the coverage is broad but it would not be a good idea to rely on this book for detailed information.

Which leads to the most important question: how useful is this book? In an age where we can call up accurate information from nearly every computer or smart phone, why would we reach for a book on a shelf for basic information about the geosciences, especially if the information may be inaccurate or out of date? Libraries may want to consider whether purchasing such volumes is worth the cost and shelf space.—**Mark A. Wilson**

Astronomy

1257.   Aguilar, David A. **Space Encyclopedia: A Tour of Our Solar System and Beyond.** Washington, D.C., National Geographic Society, 2013. 192p. illus. index. $24.95. ISBN 13: 978-1-4263-0948-9.

This is one of those wonderful reference books that is so engaging and visually fascinating that it is hard to put down. Even if a student were to reach to it for a quick reference question, it is likely they would spend much more time flipping through the pages and discovering more about our solar system and galaxy. The work features full-color NASA photography along with original art and computer images. The language is designed with middle to high school students in mind; however, the images make the work engaging enough that younger students and older general readers will find it interesting as well. Terms are fully defined and analogies are oftentimes used to provide students with a better understanding of difficult concepts. A glossary and an index make the book user-friendly for the reference collection and for student research. At just $24.95, this book is sure to be a hit in school and public libraries.— **Shannon Graff Hysell**

1258.   **Astronomical Almanac for the Year 2014.** Lanham, Md., Bernan Press, 2013. 618p. $40.00. ISBN 13: 978-0-70774-142-0.

The Astronomical Almanac has been a joint annual production of the governments of the United Kingdom and the United States for many years and a separate publication of each government for a century. Its former title, before 1981, was *The American Ephemeris and Nautical Almanac*, which better describes what it is about. The *Almanac* provides current astronomical data for use in making observations. The work contains data for astronomy, space sciences, geodesy, surveying, and navigation, among others. The 2014 edition gives highly accurate positions of the Sun, Moon, planets, satellites, and a few asteroids and comets for the year. Positions for the brighter stars are also provided, as are the latitudes and longitudes of the major observatories and much more. This annual publication is essential for navigating, surveying, and observing for skilled, amateur, and professional astronomers. As the information provided becomes out of date at the end of 2014, libraries will need to replace it with next year's edition.—**Robert A. Seal**

1259.   Liu, Charles. **The Handy Astronomy Answer Book.** 3d ed. Canton, Mich., Visible Ink Press, 2013. 359p. illus. index. $21.95pa. ISBN 13: 978-1-58759-419-1.

The Handy Astronomy Answer Book offers clear, detailed explanations of the many fascinating and diverse aspects of astronomy with over 120 illustrations and photographs. Topics include the fundamentals of astronomy, the universe, galaxies, stars, the solar system, the Earth and moon, space programs, exploring the solar system, life in the universe, space programs, and astronomy today (e.g., use of telescopes, photometry, spectroscopy). The book is written in understandable language, but the answers are not over-simplified and provide sufficient detail for understanding the concept or feature described, making this book appropriate for readers from high school to college. Unfamiliar terms are briefly explained within the text and a comprehensive subject index is provided as well. This book covers many aspects of astronomy and the space sciences that will be of interest to students and general readers, including facts about planets and stars, information on space mission programs, and the latest science behind the new discoveries in space. This title will be useful for high school and public library reference collections.—**Polly D. Boruff-Jones**

1260.   Trefil, James. **Space Atlas: Mapping the Universe and Beyond.** Washington, D.C., National Geographic Society, 2013. 2012. illus. index. $50.00. ISBN 13: 978-1-4262-0971-0.

This visually appealing atlas to the planets, stars, and beyond provides full-color photography and computer graphics of our galaxy. Along with the stunning photographs are biographies of leading scientists in astronomy, facts about the planets, and information on stars, galaxies, moons, and nebulae found in our solar system. The index guides readers through the use of bold type to illustrations, scientists' biographies, and facts. A place-name index is also included. This is one of those rare reference titles that can be used to identify fast facts as well as provide users will hours of pleasure as they browse its eye-catching pages. It will be a hit with both students and adults and can therefore be recommended for both school and public libraries. [R: SLJ, June 13, p. 70]—**Shannon Graff Hysell**

Climatology and Meteorology

Catalogs and Collections

1261.   **AMS Journal Online. http://journals.ametsoc.org/.** [Website]. Boston, Mass., American Meteorological Society. Price negotiated by site. Date reviewed: 2013.

This database is a freely searchable site that contains the full text of all AMS journals (fee-based access to the full text via subscription). The entire journal database, including accepted manuscripts not yet formally published, is searchable by all, with access restricted to subscribers for the full-text Early Online Release manuscripts and articles from the most recent two years.—**James E. Bobick**

Dictionaries and Encyclopedias

1262.   **Climate Change: An Encyclopedia of Science and History.** Brian C. Black, ed. Santa Barbara, Calif., ABC-CLIO, 2013. 4v. illus. maps. index. $399.00/set. ISBN 13: 978-1-59884-761-1; 978-1-59884-762-8 (e-book).

The growing impact of climate change is on a global scale and includes extreme weather patterns. Human activity is a main factor and increasingly so because of the growing population and developing countries' increasing energy needs. *Climate Change: An Encyclopedia of Science and History* covers scientific, political, and economic aspects associated with this real threat to human health as well as permanent alteration to the Earth.

Each volume begins with complete list of entries in alphabetic order and includes specific entries covered in each of the four volumes. An entry discussion includes subtopics to highlight interrelationship between activities, conditions, and more, and how these relate to climate change. For example, "China's National Climate Policy" covers five-year plans on economic and social development. Subtopics associated with this goal to reduce greenhouse gas emissions include a program for companies to reduce energy use, 10 projects to increase energy efficiency, a broad national plan (but lacking resources to fully implement), and regulations supporting transition to a more developed country. Many individuals and organizations that made an impact on better understanding the cause and effects of climate change are covered. For example, Charles David Keeling (1928-2005) was an American scientist and determined, in the early 1960s, a direct relationship between increasing levels of carbon dioxide in the atmosphere caused by additional fossil fuel burning. Additional entry sections include speeches by individuals involved with an activity and historical timelines.

The "Leadership in Environmental Energy and Environmental Design" (LEED) entry describes this voluntary program on "environmental sustainability" of buildings and includes safeguarding human health. Subtopics include the role of U.S. Green Building Council organization, a rating system to certify a building meets specific requirements, and LEED credentials for professionals. The subject "Green Technology" is a growing field that covers aspects such as energy efficient buildings and using renewable energies to decrease greenhouse gas emissions. Adding a separate section on this technology in the LEED entry, or a new separate entry, is useful. The "Waxman-Markey Climate Bill: American Clean Energy and Security Act of 2009" deals with a cap-and-trade approach on emissions effecting climate change. An excerpt from Congressman Henry Waxman's speech (2011) highlights the real difficulty of having Democrat and Republican politicians both agree on the same policies.

The 16 appendixes cover a wide range of topics including individual speeches, federal court cases, climate reports, and international countries' agreement on reducing greenhouse gas emissions. A list containing specific title of each appendix should be added to the first page of the appendixes section so a topic found more easily.

A figure showing many potential environmental catastrophes (such as, melting Antarctic glaciers) caused by human activities is difficult to read because the words are very small. Larger words and global map diagram would improve how information is shown. In the "Tipping Point" entry, the word "perturbation" is associated with a nonlinear system going from one fixed point to another but this scientific meaning is not clearly stated. A better word might be "change" in the context of passing threshold of a "global climate system" and causing a different condition(s) to begin. This volume set is a good resource for high school students and college undergraduates to find general information on a wide variety of topics associated with climate change. A nice feature is the Further Reading section at the end of each entry that lists publications and Websites providing additional material. [R: LJ, 15 June 13, p. 112]—**Mike Parchinski**

Handbooks and Yearbooks

1263. Climate Change in the Midwest: Impacts, Risks, Vulnerability, and Adaptation. S. C. Pryor, ed. Bloomington, Ind., Indiana University Press, 2013. 266p. illus. maps. index. $65.00; $59.95 (e-book). ISBN 13: 978-0-253-00682-0; 978-0-253-00774-2 (e-book).

Pryor explores the historical, current, and future issues of climate change in the Midwest. Written from a graduate level perspective, the work explores climate change in the context of agriculture issues, Midwest water resources, area energy use, infrastructure impact, and the impact of change on human health in the region. The series of 17 topical chapters in the book are written by 41 contributors, all of whom are well qualified to write on the topic of climate change. A typical chapter is one written by J. A. Winkler and others on the impact of climate change on Michigan's Tart Cherry industry. The author describes three decision tools, including the Historical Tart Cherry Yield Tool, Historical Weather Tool, and Future Scenarios Tool, which were developed as part of the Pileus Project that has been helping farmers since the early 1940s to "better understand the impact of weather and climate on tart cherry yield." This tool helped farmers understand the almost total loss of their crops in 2002 due to an early freeze. The research shows that an enhanced global warming greenhouse effect on the Great Lakes cannot be assumed to provide a better growing climate for Tart Cherry producers in Michigan. Other chapters explore topics such as extreme heat stress in Midwestern urban areas, the vulnerability of the area electric and water supply to climate change, drought risk management in the Midwest, and Midwest floods and Great Lakes water levels in a time of climate change. The work is very well written and includes a number of color charts and diagrams, keyed to each chapter, which illustrate concepts discussed in that chapter. Some of the illustrations are rather small when reproduced in the book, but they are backed up for the most part by online files and can be viewed by the reader in a larger screen format. The book is modestly priced especially when one considers the wealth of information contained inside and an e-book version is available for $10 less than the price of the hardback. The cover of the book features a neat graphic showing a gathering storm descending upon an open stretch of Midwest highway. Overall, the book is very inviting to the reader.—**Ralph Lee Scott**

1264. Earth Science: Earth's Weather, Water, & Atmosphere. Margaret Boorstein and Richard Renneboog, eds. Hackensack, N.J., Salem Press, 2013. 2v. illus. index. $295.00/set. ISBN 13: 978-1-58765-985-0.

This two-volume set is essentially a textbook-type reference work for high school and college-level Earth Science students. The work consists of 118 topical essays that range from three to seven pages in length. Each essay, written by a different contributor, contains an introduction of principal terms used, a basic essay introduction to the topic, followed by several pages of topical text, and ends with a bibliography. Contributors come from places as varied as MIT and Maharishi International University. A number are "independent scholars." Typical topics covered include: air pollution, auroras, climate change theory, Great Lakes, hurricanes, nitrogen cycle, radon gas, tornadoes, water table, and weather forecasting. Appendixes at the end of the set consist of a glossary, a general bibliography, a table of atmospheric pressure above and below sea level, a map of major oil spills, a table of the earth's bodies of water and a table of major severe weather events in history (e.g., hurricanes, tornadoes), and an index. The work is illustrated with a small number of the drawings, tables, and photographs. Most of the work consists of long blocks of textual materials. An online subscription to the printed text of the set is available. This reviewer tried to access this online component but was unable to log in using the instructions provided by the publisher. Overall, this set is a good introduction to basic concepts in Earth Science.—**Ralph Lee Scott**

1265. Schimel, David. Climate and Ecosystems. Princeton, N.J., Princeton University Press, 2013. 222p. illus. index. (Princeton Primers in Climate). $80.00; $27.95pa. ISBN 13: 978-0-691-15196-0.

The Princeton Primers in Climate series is intended to introduce readers to the current state of climate science research. Previous titles in the series include David Archer's *The Global Carbon Cycle*, Geoffrey K. Vallis' *Climate and the Oceans*, and Shawn J. Marshall's *The Cryosphere*. Written by David Schimel, Senior Research Scientist at the Jet Propulsion Laboratory in Pasadena, California, this latest volume focuses on the manner that climate impacts all levels of life, including individual organisms, different ecosystems, and the biosphere. It also explores how ecosystems in turn influence the climate. Special attention is paid to modeling the manner that rapid climate change is presently altering respective ecosystems and what that means for the future.

Although this work is an authoritative introduction to the topic, it has limited utility as a reference work because it is designed to be read in its entirety. The author also assumes that the readers have a fundamental grasp of advanced mathematical concepts and writes accordingly, which limits its audience. The work's greatest utility may be as a textbook for upper-level undergraduate and graduate students. All academic libraries should strongly consider buying this volume for its circulating collection.—**John R. Burch Jr.**

1266.   Spellman, Frank R. **The Handbook of Meteorology.** Lanham, Md., Scarecrow, 2013. 223p. index. $85.00; $84.99 (e-book). ISBN 13: 978-0-8108-8612-4; 978-0-8108-8613-1 (e-book).

Designed for undergraduate students and interested lay readers, *The Handbook of Meteorology* serves as an introduction to the science of meteorology and the study of weather. In clear terms it describes how our weather functions and will serve to answer questions in easy-to-understand terms that nonspecialists will understand. After a general introduction the book has three parts addressing meteorological basics (e.g., weather elements, the atmosphere, precipitation, seasons, the Greenhouse Effect), weather and climate (e.g., El Nino, microclimates, air masses), and atmospheric dynamics (e.g., global air movement, predicting weather, meteorological tools). The author provides illustrations and simple equations that illustrate how to read weather patterns and translate technical information. Each chapter concludes with a select bibliography. The volume concludes with a 62-page glossary and an index.—**Shannon Graff Hysell**

1267.   **Weather Close-Up Series.** New York, Crabtree, 2013. multivolume. illus. index. $22.60/vol.

This series includes informational texts with large, colorful photographs that contain captions that supply interesting facts. Each book ends with a data collection idea including journaling, charting, and creating calendars. Each title introduces measurement and graphing and could be used in an integrated math lesson. Thinking questions end each book sending the reader off more knowledgeable and excited to investigate weather. Additional resources provided include other titles and Websites that are age-appropriate and connected to the information covered. Each volume also includes a glossary and index.—**Barbara Johnson**

Ecology

1268.   **Biomes & Ecosystems.** Robert Warren Howarth, ed. Hackensack, N.J., Salem Press, 2013. 4v. illus. index. $395.00/set. ISBN 13: 978-1-4928-3813-9; 978-1-4928-3818-4 (e-book).

Biomes & Ecosystems is a four-volume multi-authored set that introduces general concepts and location-specific information related to world biomes and ecosystems. Narrative text introduces readers to general concepts and specific geographic environments.

Part 1 (volume 1) introduces five major categories of biomes (Marine and Oceanic, Inland Aquatic, Desert, Forest, and Grassland/Tundra/Human), with detailed extended essays describing specific systems within each category. The Topic Finder at the beginning of volume 1 groups the entries by ecosystem. This will be useful for students who want to locate all the Forest Ecosystem articles or all the Tundra

Grassland entries, for example. Part 2 (volumes 2, 3, and 4) contain over 500 entries covering place-based ecosystems. Entries are one to three pages in length (written by various contributors) and describe a specific location (e.g., river, lake, forest, desert) and its animal and plant diversity. Environmental threats, conservation, historical perspective, and human impact are topics addressed in some entries. There are occasional black-and-white photographs to illustrate the text. A further reading list is provided at the end of each entry. Volume 4 ends with several appendixes, including a timeline of important events, a glossary, a resource guide (e.g., books, journals, Websites), and a subject index. Each of the four volumes contains a table of contents for the entire set.

This reviewer was disappointed with the poor quality of illustrations and photograph images. The wonderful illustrations at the beginning of volume 1 depicting eight ecosystems are dull and blurry, as are all the black-and-white photographs in the entries in volumes 2-4. Clearer, color illustrations and photographs would have added much more to the text.

Overall, *Biomes & Ecosystems* provides a basic introduction to the concepts and characteristics of the world's major types of biomes and ecosystems. Content presented is introductory and will need to be supplemented with other sources. This work is best suited for high school or public libraries.—**Caroline L. Gilson**

1269.   **Habitats and Ecological Communities of Indiana: Presettlement to Present.** Whitaker, John O., Jr. and Charles J. Amlancer, Jr., eds. Bloomington, Ind., Indiana University Press, 2012. 493p. illus. maps. index. $35.00; $24.99 (e-book). ISBN 13: 978-0-253-35602-4; 978-0-253-00520-5 (e-book)

Edited by John O. Whitaker, Professor of Biology at Indiana State University, and Charles J. Amlaner, Jr, Vice President for Research and Dean of the Graduate College at Kennesaw State University, are joined by 14 additional scholars in producing a reference that examines approximately two centuries of ecological transformation in Indiana. It also documents the present condition of the state's habitats and how they impact the plant and wildlife found therein.

The work includes 14 chapters that are divided into 4 parts: "A Statewide Overview: Land Use, Soils, Flora, and Wildlife"; "Natural Habitats: Changes over Two Centuries"; "Man-Made Habitats: Changes over Two Centuries"; and "Species Concerns: Declining Natives and Invading Exotics." The text is supplemented by numerous maps and photographs, many of which are in color. Following the respective chapters is an overview that charts directions for future research. Extremely detailed information is provided in the nine appendixes that make up more than 220 pages of the book: "General Information"; "Soils"; "Plants"; "Fishes"; "Amphibians and Reptiles"; "Birds"; "Mammals"; "Invertebrates"; and "ASTER Mapping." The work concludes with an extensive bibliography. Although this book is written in a manner that makes it useful for researchers, it is also accessible by educated lay readers. It is an essential purchase for all public and academic libraries in Indiana. This reference is highly recommended for academic libraries outside Indiana supporting programs in agriculture, biology, or ecology.—**John R. Burch Jr.**

Geology

1270.   **AAPG Datapages. http://www.datapages.com/.** [Website]. Free. Date reviewed: 2013.

A subsidiary of the American Association of Petroleum Geologists, this site contains digital databases and utilities for the petroleum geologist. Datapages digitally captures geological publications and archives them to electronic media, thereby ensuring their future viability by making them indispensable to the geological professionals who need them most. By doing this, publications are easily accessible, searchable, and affordable. A combined publications database of over 20 geoscience societies, this full-text database covers petroleum geology and related fields.—**James E. Bobick**

1271. **Dictionary of Metals.** Harold M. Cobb, ed. Materials Park, Ohio, ASM International, 2012. 357p. illus. $149.00. ISBN 13: 978-1-61503-978-4.

This highly specialized reference work provides a wealth of well-organized information pertinent to engineering, metallurgy, chemistry, and even history from antiquity through the Industrial Revolution and the present day. It defines not only the various alloys and 73 naturally occurring metals, but also the tools, processes, and test methods that are employed in metalworking. Some concepts are illustrated with black-and-white line drawings.

Appendixes include a Metals History Timeline of discoveries and significant structures, a bibliography, and 19 property and conversion tables showing things like density, conductivity, thermal expansion, and melting range of metals and alloys. Academic libraries serving engineering or construction departments will certainly want to obtain this title, especially as it appears to be the only comprehensive English-language reference book published on the topic in the past several decades.—**Maren Williams**

Oceanography

1272. **Oceanic Abstracts. http://www.csa.com/factsheets/oceanic-set-c.php.** [Website]. Ann Arbor, Mich., ProQuest. Price negotiated by site. Date reviewed: 2013.

The database focuses on marine biology and physical oceanography, fisheries, and aquaculture. It is comprehensive in its coverage of living and nonliving resources; meteorology and geology; and environmental, technological, and legislative topics. The database has long been recognized as a leading source of information on topics relating to oceans.—**James E. Bobick**

Paleontology

1273. **If These Fossils Could Talk Series.** New York, Crabtree, 2013. multivolume. illus. index. $27.60/vol.; $9.95pa./vol.

This new multivolume series from Crabtree Publishing, a company known for their multivolume, nonfiction series designed specifically for children, provides an insider's look into the history behind and the creation of fossils. The volumes thus far in the series discuss: human fossils, plant fossils, animal fossils, and dinosaur fossils. These books are written with children in mind so they begin at the most basic level and answer questions that children will be interested in. Within each volume are plenty of color photographs and illustrations as well as sidebars full of additional information. Each volume ends with a glossary, resources to consult for further information, an activity that can be done at home or school, and a very short index, all of which can be used to teach young students basic researching skills. This series is recommended for elementary and middle school libraries and juvenile collections in public libraries. They provide a good introduction to the basic concepts of fossils and the science behind their study.—**Shannon Graff Hysell**

1274. Kielan-Jaworowska, Zofia. **In Pursuit of Early Mammals.** Bloomington, Ind., Indiana University Press, 2013. 254p. illus. index. $60.00; $49.99 (e-book). ISBN 13: 978-0-253-00817-6; 978-0-253-00824-4 (e-book).

This well-authored book does an excellent job at both introducing the early mammals of the Mesozoic era and covering the latest evolutionary and paleoecological ideas in professional detail. Each chapter is well organized with clear headings, clean diagrams and photographs, and summary comments. Mammals of this era lived amongst the dinosaurs. This book goes into detail about their origins, anatomy, systematics, paleobiology, and distribution. The book also has a strong focus on the paleontologists who have studied these species, with much of the focus being on the career of the author, Zofia Kielan-Jaworowska. As one of the first women to lead a large-scale paleontological expedition, she shares her pleasures and difficulties of her work. She also discusses the changing views on early mammals that were discovered due to her work in the field. This is an attractive book at the cutting edge of paleontology. It also has a reasonable price. This resource is highly recommended for professionals in the field and libraries with strong paleontology and evolution collections.—**ARBA Staff Reviewer**

1275.   **Tyrannosaurid Paleobiology.** Parrish, J. Michael, Ralph E. Molnar, Philip J. Currie, and Eva B. Koppelhus, eds. Bloomington, Ind., Indiana University Press, 2013. 297p. illus. maps. index. $60.00; $49.99 (e-book). ISBN 13: 978-0-253-00930-2; 978-0-253-00947-0 (e-book).

Although there were only seven known specimens of Tyrannosaurus rex in 1980, it was already one of the best known and beloved dinosaurs. The number of specimens had grown to at least 45 by 2008, but there was great diversity between them. Did they represent the same species or were some examples of different types of Tyrannosauridae, such as Nanotyrannus? The questions led to two different symposia on the tyrannosaurids being held in 2005. Some of the papers presented at the symposium at the Black Hills Natural History Museum in Hill City, South Dakota were published in 2008 in *Tyrannosaurus Rex, The Tyrant King*, edited by Peter Larson and Kenneth Carpenter. Selected papers from "The Origin, Systematics, and Paleobiology of Tyrannosauridae" symposium held at Rockford, Illinois, sponsored by the Burpee Museum of Natural History and Northern Illinois University, are published in the volume under review. Together, the books provide a comprehensive overview of the research being conducted on the Tyrannosauridae at the present time and also pose new questions for researchers to explore in the future.

Edited by J. Michael Parrish (San Jose State University), Ralph E. Molnar (University of California, Berkeley), Philip J. Currie (University of Alberta), and Eva B. Koppelhus (University of Alberta), *Tyrannosaurid Paleobiology* includes 15 articles divided into three parts: "Systematics and Descriptions"; "Functional Morphology and Reconstruction"; and "Paleopathology, Paleoecology, and Taphonomy." The articles include a large number of illustrations and photographs, along with an extensive number of bibliographic citations. Written for specialists, this work is highly recommended for libraries supporting programs in paleontology. Libraries should also consider Donald F. Glut's excellent *Dinosaurs: The Encyclopedia* and all its supplements as a complementary scholarly reference (McFarland).—**John R. Burch Jr.**

Physics

1276.   **arXiv.org. http://arxiv.org/.** [Website]. Free. Date reviewed: 2013.

Originally developed by Paul Ginsparg in 1991, the site provides open access to over 890,000 e-prints in physics, mathematics, computer science, quantitative biology, and statistics. The site, which is Open Archives Initiative (OAI) compliant, is owned, operated, and funded by Cornell University, and is partially funded by the National Science Organization.—**James E. Bobick**

1277.   **Contemporary Biographies in Physics.** Millerton, N.Y., Grey House Publishing, 2013. 315p. index. $95.00. ISBN 13: 978-1-58765-996-6; 978-1-58765-998-0 (e-book).

Contemporary Biographies in Physics is a collection of biographical articles that originally appeared in Current Biography magazine. The main text covers 31 living scientists, while 11 more historical pioneers appear in an appendix. While a list of 61 contributors is included at the front of the volume, no author information is included with the individual articles, which is unfortunate considering that they vary widely in readability and concision. Some of the articles chosen for inclusion also have scant connection to physics, like the one on Fabien Cousteau, grandson of Jacques and an oceanographer himself.

Articles are organized alphabetically by the subject's surname. Most include sections on the scientist's early life and education, major contributions to the field, and personal life. Each article also has its own bibliography of further resources for consultation. Despite a claim in the Publisher's Note that "selections span the Eastern and Western Hemispheres," all but four of the living scientists hail from North America or Europe. Purchasers also receive access for all users to the full text of the volume in Salem Press' online database. Considering the somewhat scattered editing and the fact that the same information is relatively easy to find through other sources, however, most libraries can probably do without the book.—**Maren Williams**

1278.   **Encyclopedia of Medical Physics.** Slavik Tabakov, ed. Boca Raton, Fla., CRC Press, 2013. 2v. illus. index. $595.00/set. ISBN 13: 978-1-4398-4652-0.

Co-published by the European Medical Imaging Technology e-Encyclopedia for Lifelong Learning Consortium and the International Organization for Medical Physics, this two-volume set provides short entries (50-500 words each) on the subject of medical physics that have been contributed by an international team of specialists in the field. The work is arranged into seven sections: General Terms, Diagnostic Radiology, Nuclear Medicine, Radiotherapy, Magnetic Resonance Imaging, Ultrasound Imaging, and Radiation Protection. In all there are more than 2,800 entries, many of which have accompanying black-and-white images, graphs, or diagrams, along with a section of colored-plates in each volume. While this print version is sturdily built and will be useful in the reference setting, all of the contents in this publication are readily available for free online at. http://www.emitel2.eu in a searchable site that is updated regularly. The content of this set will be useful to graduate students and researchers; however, libraries should check out the Website before making a purchasing decision. [R: Choice, June 13, p. 1804]—**ARBA Staff Reviewer**

1279.   *The New York Times* **Book of Physics and Astronomy: More Than 100 Years of Covering the Expanding Universe.** Cornelia Dean and Neil DeGrasse Tyson, eds. New York, Sterling Publishing, 2013. 576p. index. $24.95. ISBN 13: 978-1-40279-320-2.

Compiled from articles within *The New York Times*, this work provides readers with articles in the areas of physics and astrophysics. The focus is on important discoveries within the twentieth century. The work is arranged into three topical categories—"The Nature of Matter," "The Practical Atom," and "The Fate of the Universe." Within each category the articles are presented in chronological order allowing the user to see how science progressed throughout the century. This work is designed with the student or the lay reader in mind. It is not going to be of much value to the serious researcher on the higher academic level. It would make a nice addition to the science collection of most public libraries and lower-division college libraries.—**ARBA Staff Reviewer**

Mathematics

Catalogs and Collections

1280.   **The Math Forum Internet Mathematics Library. http://mathforum.org/library/.** [Website]. Free. Date reviewed: 2013.

Nicely organized, this popular online forum and library is recommended as a first stop for math librarians and mathematicians. It has over 8,500 links to selected online resources in mathematics and mathematics education. They are arranged by topics, resource types, and education level and can be searched by any of these variables. Each record is annotated. The library is part of the larger *Math Forum@Drexel* site, which also offers a variety of links such as "Ask Dr. Math" and its archive, problems of the week, and "Teacher2Teacher." Originally funded by the National Science Foundation, *Math Forum* is now administered by Drexel University.—**Martha A. Tucker**

1281. **MathSciNet. http://www.ams.org/mathscinet/.** [Website]. Free. Date reviewed: 2013.

This is an electronic publication offering access to a carefully maintained and easily searchable database of reviews, abstracts, and bibliographic information for much of the mathematical sciences literature. More than 80,000 new items are added each year, most of them classified according to the Mathematics Subject Classification, and contains over 2 million items and over 700,000 direct links to original articles. It continues in the tradition of the paper publication *Mathematical Reviews*, which was first published in 1940. MathSciNet bibliographic data from retro-digitized articles dates back to 1864.—**James E. Bobick**

1282. **MathWorld. http://mathworld.wolfram.com/.** [Website]. Champaign, Ill., Wolfram Research. Free. Date reviewed: 2011. Date reviewed: 2013.

MathWorld continues to be the most popular and most visited mathematics site on the Internet and its mathematical content continues to steadily grow and expand. MathWorld is the Web's most extensive mathematical resource, provided as a free service to the world's mathematics and Internet communities as part of a commitment to education and education outreach by Wolfram Research, the makers of *Mathematica* (http://www.wolfram.com/mathematica/). The site includes several special features, including: pop-up summaries for more than 300 mathematical terms; extensive citations to books and journal articles (with hyperlinks); and many interactive entries to help users train in mathematical concepts.—**James E. Bobick**

1283. **Zentralblatt MATH. http://www.emis.de/.** [Website]. Free. Date reviewed: 2013.

This is the world's most complete and longest-running abstracting and reviewing service in pure and applied mathematics. The Zentralblatt MATH database contains more than 2 million entries drawn from more than 2,300 serials and journals and covers the period from 1868 to the present by the recent integration of the Jahrbuch database (JFM). The entries are classified according to the Mathematics Subject Classification Scheme (MSC 2000).—**James E. Bobick**

Directories

1284. **AMS Digital Mathematics Registry. http://www.ams.org/dmr/.** [Website]. Ann Arbor, Mich., AMS Digital Mathematics Registry. Free. Date reviewed: 2013.

The aim of the AMS-DMR is to provide centralized access to certain collections of digitized publications in the mathematical sciences. The registry is primarily focused on older material from journals and journal-like book series that originally appeared in print but are now available in digital form. The registry is organized both by the collections and by the individual journals (or series) themselves, providing links to each that will be regularly verified and updated. All versions of the Digital Mathematics Registry (DMR) are in the public domain; they may be downloaded, modified, and posted on other sites. Each version is dated, and the AMS requests that modifications of any version retain this date.—**James E. Bobick**

Handbooks and Yearbooks

1285. **The Best Writing on Mathematics 2013.** Mircea Pitici, ed. Princeton, N.J., Princeton University Press, 2014. 244p. index. $21.95pa. ISBN 13: 978-0-691-16041-2.

One does not often think of math and writing as going together. However, behind the formulas and equations there is much to be gained from studying the nature, meaning, and practice of mathematics and how it applies to today's world. This work brings together 20 of the most noteworthy articles on mathematics that came out in 2013. The contributors include both those established in the field and some new voices. The essays have been culled from math journals (e.g., *The Journal of Mathematics and the Arts*, *Math Horizons*), general science publications (e.g., *American Scientist*, *Scientific American*), and popular publications (e.g., *The Boston Globe*). They look into things like the history of mathematics, the philosophy behind it, and everyday occurrences of math. Some of the highlights of the 2013 edition include an article on math and fashion, an article on universal mathematical laws in complex systems, and the future of math in multimedia civilizations. It will be of interest to anyone looking for historical and philosophical insights into the world of mathematics, both on the general and scholarly level.—**Barbara Delzell**

1286.   **Building Blocks of Mathematics.** Chicago, World Book, 2013. 6v. illus. $169.00/set. ISBN 13: 978-0-7166-1431-9.

Using a graphic novel format, several comical math friends take readers through the basics of math. Addition, Subtraction, Fractions, Division, Multiplication, and Zero narrate their stories while they entertain and reinforce math concepts. All volumes cover multiple ways to perform each operation, and cross-reference operations to solve problems when possible. They rely heavily on word problems, number lines, and base ten computations. The set is better designed to reinforce previously taught concepts or to be utilized in small group settings than as an introduction for a new topic. The graphics are appealing, although they often miss a change to label a diagram that would help to reinforce a concept. The set is supplemented with a bibliography, glossary, list of Websites, and an index.—**Karen Gedeon**

1287.   Nahin, Paul J. **Will You Be Alive 10 Years from Now? And Numerous Other Curious Questions in Probability.** Princeton, N.J., Princeton University Press, 2013. 220p. index. $27.95. ISBN 13: 978-0-691-15680-4; 978-1-400-84837-9 (e-book).

In this book the author introduces the concept of probability in a fun and interesting way for students and general readers. Nahin presents 25 probability questions and then provides a lively discussion on each problem's background and solution. He shows in detail how various theories and computer experiments can work to solve the problem. All codes needed to solve the problem are located in the book with a detailed description of how it can be used to solve the puzzle. With wit and insight he explains the techniques used by mathematicians and scientists use to solve questions of probability.—**Linda W. Hacker**

36 Resource Sciences

Energy

Dictionaries and Encyclopedias

1288. **Encyclopedia of Energy.** Morris A. Pierce, ed. Hackensack, N.J., Salem Press, 2013. 4v. illus. index. $495.00/set. ISBN 13: 978-1-58765-849-5.

Targeted toward high school students, the outstanding feature of this set is its focus on the geography of energy. There is an article on the energy resources and consumption of every country in the world as well as each of the 50 states of the United States. This allows the reader to easily compare and contrast the use of alternative energy from one state to the next for instance, or note how Iceland transitioned to geothermal and hydropower for most of its energy needs. While there is a certain amount of variation between articles, mainly because of the nearly 200 international authors, this has minimal impact on its usefulness. In addition to the articles on the geography of energy, there are eight other categories of entries including biographies, the business of energy, and environmentalism. The geography of energy accounts for nearly half of the more than 560 articles. If you add the environmentalism articles, these two categories account for nearly two-thirds of all articles. The signed articles are 500 to 3500 words in length and contain brief bibliographies for further reading. The articles are non-technical and general in nature making this source accessible to high school students and the average reader. Purchase of the print edition entitles a school or library online access to the encyclopedia through the Salem Science platform (not reviewed). More information about Salem Science as well as sample articles can be found on the publisher Website.—**Mike Burgmeier**

Directories

1289. **Plunkett's Energy Industry Almanac.** 2014 ed. Jack W. Plunkett, ed. Houston, Tex., Plunkett Research, 2013. 600p. index. $349.99pa. ISBN 13: 978-1-60879-728-8.

Data aggregator Plunkett Research presents here 500 companies in the energy industries are detailed with data (one company per page). Each entry includes name, business specialty (e.g., alternative energy, exploration & production), types of business, address, telephone/fax/e-mail, five-year financials, and a textual overview of growth plans and special features that can run from 250 to 600 words. There is a lot of white space left on most pages. Companies are listed alphabetically with a single, interfiled index of subsidiaries, brand names, and affiliates. Entries are overwhelmingly headquartered in the United States, but there are some foreign-based operations. There is also a single-page list entitled "Hot Spots for Advancement for Women and Minorities." The initial 100 pages are divided into 3 chapters. The first covers major trends; the second offers industry statistics (overwhelmingly repackaged from the federal government); and the third acts as a directory of associations, organizations, government agencies, and contacts. If Plunkett almanacs have any value it is as an introductory compilation. They are designed as a general resource and meet that goal even though most of the material is readily available using existing reference sources, government documents, and the World Wide Web.—**Patrick J. Brunet**

Handbooks and Yearbooks

1290.   **Energy Statistics Yearbook 2009.** 53d ed. New York, United Nations, 2013. 632p. $130.00. ISBN 13: 978-9-21-061319-4.

The 2009 edition of this publication from the United Nations continues to provide an excellent understanding of the long-term trends of the energy situation in the world. A researcher would want to use the monthly and quarterly data found in the *Monthly Bulletin of Statistics,* which is also published by the United Nations, and previous editions to get a comprehensive view of the global energy situation. This yearbook provides data and statistics in table format from 2006 to 2009. The tables on solid, liquid, gaseous, and nuclear fuels, electricity and heat, and energy resources and reserves can help in government planning, commercial endeavors, environmental issues, and much more. Bringing together this amount of information is an enormous task and for some countries statistics are not available, but the extensive information provided is invaluable. The tables on new and renewable sources such as biodiesel, solar, wind, peat, and geothermal sources of energy could provide ideas on how to solve energy shortages. Country nomenclature, definitions, abbreviations and symbols, conversion tables, and useful graphs enhance this source that provides a good look at energy resources on a global scale. This outstanding publication will be useful in large public libraries, special libraries, and academic libraries.—**ARBA Staff Reviewer**

1291.   **International Handbook of Energy Security.** Hugh Dyer and Maria Julia Trombetta, eds. Northhampton, Mass., Edward Elgar, 2013. 560. index. 255.00. ISBN 13: 9781781007891.

This enlightening volume brings together a variety of international energy security experts to investigate the wide assortment of tangled security issues related to global energy and such topics as economics, politics, ethics, and concrete security. Key present-day problems, including human security, energy supply and demand, and the environment, are covered. Since wars, terrorism, geopolitical disputes, and piracy can disrupt the economies of any nation, it is imperative that all nations come together to mutually benefit the environment, their economies, and their safety in order to safeguard the limited resources of this planet. Broken down into seven parts—introduction; energy security issues; security of energy supply; security of energy demand; energy, the environment, and security; energy and human security; and conclusions—this handbook updates past insights and theories and introduces new issues in the complex world of energy security. The *Handbook* includes tables, figures, and an alphabetic index, and is available electronically. It is recommended for large public libraries and academic libraries.— **Diane J. Turner**

1292.   Scheckel, Paul. **The Homeowner's Energy Handbook.** North Adams, Mass., Storey, 2013. 288p. illus. index. $24.95pa. ISBN 13: 978-1-61212-016-4.

Every good book on the topic of home energy should include a section on energy conservation and this book addresses the topic well. The first five chapters, 30 percent of the book, covers energy audits, insulating, and tying together all aspects of home energy consumption. The remainder of the book provides details on 11 renewable energy technologies ranging from solar to biodiesel to biogas. The design and layout is pleasing and easy to read with numerous drawings to illustrate key points. The math and other engineering aspects are kept to a minimum. While this makes it more accessible for the beginner, those looking for more detailed calculation information will need to consult other sources. There are short two-page highlights for most chapters providing a closer look at some aspect of the topic, often providing the author's experience or giving the perspective of an expert in the field. Basic safety precautions are appropriately placed along with the occasional cautionary tale. This book should appeal to anyone who is new to the topic and wants to try their hand at a variety of small scale renewable energy projects. With a small price tag and the potential demand for checking this book out, libraries should consider purchasing for a circulating collection rather than adding it to a non-circulating reference collection.—**Mike Burgmeier**

1293.   **Understanding Electricity Series.** New York, Crabtree, 2013. multivolume. illus. index. $19.95/vol.; $8.95pa./set.

This four-volume series from Crabtree Publishing, a company known for their multivolume, nonfiction series designed specifically for children and young adults, provides information on how electricity is generated and its uses. So far the series covers the following concepts: What are Electrical Circuits?; What are Insulators and Conductors?; What is Electricity?; and What is Electromagnetism? With more in-depth descriptions of electricity, the text is written for upper elementary and middle school students. Each volume includes color photographs and easy-to-understand text, along with a quiz, a glossary, a further reading list, and a very short index, all of which can be used to teach young students basic researching skills. This series is recommended for elementary and middle school collections in public and school libraries where there is an interest in this type of information.—**Shannon Graff Hysell**

1294.   **World Energy Outlook 2012.** By the Organisation for Economic Co-operation and Development. Lanham, Md., Bernan Press, 2012. 700p. $210.00pa. ISBN 13: 978-92-64180-84-0.

This work provides authoritative projections on energy trends up through the year 2035. Created by the Organisation for Economic Co-operation and Development, it gives users insight into what these projections mean for energy security, economic development, and environmental sustainability. There is some discussion of climate change and its effect on energy, but the main focus is on oil, coal, natural gas, renewables, and nuclear power. Other key statistics include prospects for global energy demand, rate of production, trade, investment, and carbon dioxide emissions. These are broken down by region or country as well as by fuel and energy sector.—**Barbara MacAlpine**

Environmental Science

Catalogs and Collections

1295.   **Environmental Sciences and Pollution Management. http://www.csa.com/factsheets/ envclust-set-c.php.** [Website]. Ann Arbor, Mich., ProQuest. Price negotiated by site. Date reviewed: 2013.

This multidisciplinary database provides unparalleled and comprehensive coverage of the environmental sciences. Abstracts and citations are drawn from over 10,000 serials including scientific journals, conference proceedings, reports, monographs, books, and government publications. A wide variety of topics are covered in this database, including ecology, air quality, energy resources, and water resources. Coverage is from 1967 to the present with nearly 6,000 new records being added each month.—**James E. Bobick**

1296. **GreenFILE. http://www.greeninfoonline.com.** [Website]. Ipswich, Mass., EBSCO. Free. Date reviewed: 2013.

GreenFILE is a free multidisciplinary database that covers all aspects of human impact to the environment. It is designed to be used by professionals, students, and the general public and includes government documents and reports. The connections between the environment and a variety of disciplines such as agriculture, education, law, health, and technology can be seen in search results from over 470,000 records and full text for more than 5,500 records. Topics covered include global climate change, green building, pollution, sustainable agriculture, renewable energy, recycling, and more.—**ARBA Staff Reviewer**

1297. **National Library for the Environment. http://www.sustainable.org/environment/ biodiversity/378-national-library-for-the-environment.** [Website]. Free. Date reviewed: 2013.

This is a free, non-advocacy online environmental information service managed by the Committee for the National Institute for the Environment (CNIE), a nonprofit organization (http://www.ncseonline. org/NLE/). CNIE's mission is to improve the scientific basis for making decisions on environmental issues through the successful operation of a National Institute for the Environment (NIE). This Website provides seven free information resources: hundreds of up-to-date issue reports, environmental education programs and resources; environmental laws including local, state, federal and international; an in-depth resource on Population-Environment linkages; a virtual library of Ecology and Biodiversity; information on environmental conferences and meetings; and Environmental Careers and Jobs.—**James E. Bobick**

Dictionaries and Encyclopedias

1298. **America Goes Green: An Encyclopedia of Eco-Friendly Culture in the United States.** Kim Kennedy White, ed. Santa Barbara, Calif., ABC-CLIO, 2013. 3v. illus. index. $294.00/set. ISBN 13: 978-1-59884-657-7; 978-1-59884-658-4 (e-book).

Arranged thematically, volumes 1 and the first half of volume 2 of *America Goes Green* discuss 11 major topics: Activism and Community Green Efforts; Arts, Entertainment, and Media; Economics, Business, and Industry; Education and employment; Environment; Food and Drink; Health, Home, and Garden; Philosophy and Religion; Politics and Law; Science and Technology; Sports and Leisure. Interspersed are side bars on "greenovators" from Frederick Law Olmstead and Rachel Carson to Joseph R. Biden, Robert Kennedy Jr., and major Supreme Court decisions, such as *Sierra Club v. Morton* (1972).

The second half of volume 2 presents primary documents, arranged alphabetically by title. This interfiles federal, state, and local laws. Volume 3 is devoted to each state's green energy programs. The states are divided into five geographic regions. Concluding the volume are a glossary, a select bibliography (pp. 1191-1214), resources (mostly Websites of organizations), and a list of primary documents by theme. The index is quite hierarchical, and utilizes several cross-references.

For the purposes of this publication, "green" "refers to the development of practices and behaviors that are eco-friendly or ecologically positive for both the environment and human communities" (p. xix). Entries, written by 160 contributors, present debates, trends, viewpoints, and challenges for the green culture. In what amounts to the actual introduction, entitled "Social Pressures and Processes of 'Going Green' in America" (pp. xxi-xxxiii), Kathleen O'Halleran presents an overview and history of conservationism through laws, environmental movements, and the current trend in sustainability.

This encyclopedia addresses the positive changes and actions of the green movement. For instance, this work covers proactive movements and works like "Environmental Justice," "Green Publishing Efforts," "Green Jobs," "Carbon Footprint," the "Creation Care Movement," and "Biofuels." A wide range of religion is discussed—non-aligned, Christian, Jewish, Muslim and Buddhist. Articles that pertain to states (volume 3) present an overview, then illustrate issues (e.g., pollution), challenges (e.g., population growth), and solutions to environmental problems (e.g., sustainability). This set is excellent for exhibiting the positive perspectives of green initiatives in America. For more of the governmental activities and laws concerning detrimental treatment of the environment, readers should use the *Encyclopedia of the U.S. Government and the Environment: History, Policy, and Politics*, edited by Matthew Lindstrom (see ARBA 2012, entry 772). Although there is some overlap, each takes a distinct direction in its presentation of environmental issues.—**Ralph Hartsock**

Directories

1299. **Plunkett's Green Technology Industry Almanac.** 2014 ed. Jack W. Plunkett, ed. Houston, Tex., Plunkett Research, 2014. 400p. $349.99pa. ISBN 13: 978-1-60879-729-5.

Plunkett's Green Technology Industry Almanac is a newer addition to Plunkett Research's vast offering of industry almanacs and seems like a worthwhile industry survey to pursue since green technology is the wave of the future. Not written for in-depth analysis of the industry, the monograph instead provides students and researchers with self-contained segments readers can access without going through the entire book. While energy conservation is the key focus, the book also focuses on related topics in the area of recycling, water technology, building materials, heating and air conditioning, transportation, and manufacturing processes. Features of this volume include an industry trend analysis, statistical tables, profiles and directory information of leading companies, contact information for executives, a glossary, and a listing of industry associations and professional societies. Within this volume users will find statistics and information on such topics as corporate giants (e.g., Wal-Mart, General Electric) investments in green technology, new transportation technologies that cut emissions, and China's role as an emerging player in green technology. The typical entry includes company name, Web address, NAIC code, company ranking, types of business, brands, basic financial data, and contact information. Other useful aspects of the book include an index of subsidiaries, brand names, and affiliations, and an index of companies noted for promoting women and minorities.

The language is relatively jargon-free. The paper binding will not stand up to heavy use but the pages are thick with large clear type. Overall, this directory will complement the collections of large public and academic libraries.—**William C. Struning**

Handbooks and Yearbooks

1300. **The Environmental Resource Handbook, 2014.** 7th ed. Millerton, N.Y., Grey House Publishing, 2013. 1035p. index. $155.00pa.; $350.00 (online database; single user); $450.00 (print and online editions). ISBN 13: 978-1-61925-115-1.

Now in its 7th edition, this substantial resource updates and adds to information from earlier editions on environmental statistics and resources useful to all those interested in environmental issues. Covering associations, environmental health, law, statistics, research centers, trade shows, grants, Websites, consultants, green city rankings and green product catalogs, and much more, this handbook is a good place to start any research on the environment. It is broken down into two sections, with section 1 covering resources, where researchers can find everything from federal agencies to videos, and section 2 covering statistics and rankings, from lists of threatened and endangered animal species, to recycling profiles of 100 major cities. In all, there are more than 6,000 environmental listings and 171 tables and charts. A companion handbook of resources and statistical tables on countries outside the United States would be nice to have. The work concludes with a glossary and a list of abbreviations and acronyms, which is good to have to reference. The three indexes—subject, geographic, and alphabetical—makes this mass of information somewhat accessible, but it is easy for a user not accustomed to entry indexing to get confused between entry and page numbers. This resource is also available through the publisher's

GOLD database (Grey House On Line Databases). Here users can search the information in a variety of ways, including by keyword, organization name, and subject, just to name a few. This resource, updated every two years, continues to provide a great deal of valuable information for academic libraries with environmental programs and for large public libraries.—**Diane J. Turner**

1301.   **The Green Scene Series.** New York, Crabtree, 2013. multivolume. illus. index. $23.60/vol.; $7.95pa./vol.

This new series from Crabtree Publishing, a company known for their multivolume, nonfiction series designed specifically for children, provides a basic introduction to ways in which young students can join the green movement and become more aware of their environment. The volumes in the series discuss: going green at school, green gardening, what it means to be "green," living green at home, and green energy. These books are written with children in mind so they begin at the most basic level and answer questions that children will be interested in. Within each volume are plenty of color photographs and illustrations as well as sidebars full of additional information. Each volume ends with a glossary, resources to consult for further information, and a very short index, all of which can be used to teach young students basic researching skills. This series is recommended for elementary school libraries and juvenile collections in public libraries. They provide a good introduction to the basic concepts of environmentalism and ways in which children can participate in the green movement.—**Shannon Graff Hysell**

1302.   Spellman, Frank R., and Melissa L. Stoudt. **Environmental Science: Principles and Practices.** Lanham, Md., Scarecrow, 2013. 709p. index. $125.00. ISBN 13: 978-0-8108-8610-0; 978-0-8010-8611-7 (e-book).

Frank R. Spellman and Melissa Stoudt's *Environmental Science: Principles and Practices* demonstrates the interdisciplinary aspects of environmental science and how our air, water, and soil are affected by a complex array of factors. Providing the information about scientific principles, applications, concepts, and methodologies, this resource gives the student a more comprehensive idea of the interrelationship of human beings, technology, weather and a wide range of other variables and how all of these combined forces affect the differing environments in which human beings live on our planet. Because this source provides a detailed look at endangered species, hazardous wastes, acid rain, ozone depletion, and pollution of our air, water, and soil by manufacturing, pesticides, auto emissions, and more, it would be an excellent textbook or essential reference resource for faculty and students. The organization and special features enhance its value. Each chapter provides objectives, key terms, discussion questions, a bibliography, real-life examples, and suggested research topics for students. This volume, also available as an e-book, will help build a foundation for anyone interested in the current and emerging environmental issues that are changing and will continue to change the way we live.—**Diane J. Turner**

1303.   Spellman, Frank R., and Melissa L. Stoudt. **The Handbook of Environmental Health.** Lanham, Md., Scarecrow, 2013. 411p. index. $100.00; $99.99 (c-book). ISBN 13: 978-0-8108-8685-8; 978-0-8108-7915-7 (e-book).

Modern chemicals and technology support living in the contemporary society. These same substances also make people ill, damage plants and animals, and affect our environment. Written in plain English, this handbook is a comprehensive source on everyday environmental health issues.

It uses language for general readers, college students, environmental health practitioners, lawyers, public administrators, and regulators. When medical terms are introduced, the layperson's equivalent is enclosed in parentheses, such as *afebrile* (not having a fever). Environmental factors rarely enter into the clinician's differential diagnosis (p. x). International in scope, authors describe ailments that originated in diverse locations, such as Queensland fever. They also focus upon the symptoms rather than the industrial cause: black lung is covered, but not the industry from which it is derived—coal mining.

Environmental health is that segment of public health concerned with understanding and controlling the impacts of people on the environment, and of impacts of the environment upon people (p. 2). The introduction outlines environmental diseases from A to Z, highlighting allergies and asthma, lead and mercury poisoning, and the two sides of Zinc, which can be a deficiency or a dangerous surplus. Several toxins are succinctly defined, along with their effects.

A large portion of the text is devoted to occupational health (pp. 347-393), highlighting work-related diseases and workplace stresses, and the role of the environmental health practitioner. Much of the governmental data reflects conditions as recently as 2007. Authors frequently supply Websites for more up-to-date information. There is an entire chapter on radiation, from X-rays and other sources. Chapters conclude with "Discussion Questions" and "References and Recommended Reading," both print and online. Other chapters cover toxicology, epidemiology, food-borne disease, and air and water quality.

The index lists very few industries that have effects upon the environment, but lists several of the specific chemicals that do, along with their symptoms and causes of these symptoms. This volume will prove useful to college students, environmental health practitioners, lawyers, public administrators, and regulators.—**Ralph Hartsock**

37 Transportation

General Works

1304. **Plunkett's Automobile Industry Almanac.** 2014 ed. Jack W. Plunkett, ed. Houston, Tex., Plunkett Research, 2014. 580p. index. $349.99pa. ISBN 13: 978-1-60879-716-5.

Plunkett's Automobile Industry Almanac provides an overview of the automobile industry and the key players. It is intended to be a general guide and offers many easy-to-use charts and tables.

The opening chapters describe the state of the industry and the major trends and technologies affecting the industry; provide statistics from trade associations and government sources; and offer the industry contacts such as government agencies, associations, publications, job-hunting resources, and various information sources related to the industry. It includes information on recent car ad truck industry mergers and globalization efforts, information regarding automobile loans and insurance, and the affects of e-commerce in the automobile industry and the fact that most people now shop online before even stepping foot in a dealership. Chapter 4 is the core of this publication, and includes ranking charts and leading companies' profiles. The companies were selected from all U.S. and many foreign automobile and related industry segments: manufacturers; dealerships; financial services; and many others, including makers of trucks and specialty vehicles. Alphabetic and geographic indexes are provided for chapter 4. Each company profile includes the following: company name; ranks; business activities; types of business; brands/divisions/affiliations; names and positions of top officers; address; telephone and fax numbers; Website address; key financials; salaries/benefits; number of apparent women officers; growth plans; and office locations. There are two additional indexes at the end of the publications: index of firms noted as hot spots for advancement for women/minorities, and index by subsidiaries, brand names, and selected affiliations. The glossary at the beginning the publication covers basic industry terminology.

This almanac seems especially useful for market research and job hunting. The inclusion criteria of chapter 4 are not clear and the information provided is not in depth, but the volume provides a good overview of the automobile industry. This work is recommended for business reference collections.—**Mihoko Hosoi**

1305. **TRIS Online. http://trid.trb.org/.** [Website]. Free. Date reviewed: 2013.

TRIS Online is a public-domain, Web-based version of the Transportation Research Information Services (TRIS) bibliographic database, as a component of the National Transportation Library. Its purpose is to enhance transportation research, safety, and operations by sharing knowledge and information. The site currently provides access to more than 1 million records from sources worldwide. The site does not contain information on vehicle standards and specifications, patent information, market research, or military transport.—**James E. Bobick**

Ground

1306. Carpenter, Richard C. **Railroad Atlas of the United States in 1946. Volume 5: Iowa and Minnesota.** Baltimore, Md., Johns Hopkins University Press, 2013. 211p. maps. index. $70.00. ISBN 13: 978-1-4214-1035-7.

Railroad enthusiasts will find this atlas provides them with an incredible wealth of information concerning rail lines and routes in Iowa and Minnesota during the height of rail traffic in the late 1940s. A significant amount of detail is displayed on each map: station with names, mile markers, bridges, coaling stations, and interlocking towers are a few of the items in each map. Detailed maps of metropolitan areas help in managing complex track detail in urban development. Numbers for the adjoining maps are included on the top, bottom, and sides of the referenced page. Another unique feature that gives the work an intimate feel is the lettering on the maps. Generated by hand lettering, the work is highly detailed with information that sometimes becomes a bit crowded and difficult to read due to the lettering style. The work is completed with several indexes including coaling stations, interlocking stations, passenger and nonpassenger stations track plans, tunnels, and viaducts. All the indexes reference a map number along with the quadrant in which the feature is located.

The work will provide a fine addition to library collections that support interests in railroading, transportation issues, post-World War II history, or the Midwest region. With the interest shown in railroads by many in the country, this volume has the potential of becoming a popular resource for those interested in tracking down old railroad beds and routes in the Midwest.—**Gregory Curtis**

1307. Flory Jr., J. "Kelly". **American Cars, 1973 to 1980: Every Model, Year by Year.** Jefferson, N.C., McFarland, 2013. 949p. illus. index. $75.00. ISBN 13: 978-0-7864-4352-9.

The author of this tome has written several other volumes on the American automobile, including one on cars from 1946-1959 (2008) and one on the muscle cars of 1960-1962 (2004). This volume focuses on the fuel efficient automobiles made from 1973 to 1980, which were a result of soaring gas prices, tougher product regulations, and stiff foreign competition. Most can agree that by the early 1980s Americans were driving smaller, more fuel efficient cars with many more features than previous decades had seen.

Arrangement is chronological by year, and sub-arranged alphabetically by name of make. Entries include a short historical summary, production and financial data, detailed engineering specifications, a list of paint colors, and several small but clear black-and-white illustrations, mostly taken from manufacturers' advertisements. Heavily illustrated, the book has more than 1,300 photographs. All of the cars are American made; however, some were owned by foreign companies, such as the Dodge Colt, built by Mitsubishi. There is a thorough index. Since there are no doubt many Americans who share Flory's fondness for cars, there will be interest in this book in most public libraries.—**Paul B. Cors**

1308. **Superstar Car Series.** New York, Crabtree, 2013. multivolume. illus. index. $23.95/ vol;$10.95pa./vol.

This multivolume series from Crabtree Publishing, a company known for their multivolume, nonfiction series designed specifically for children and young adults provides information on six of the most well-known sports cars and muscle cars that will be of interest to young adults. New cars covered in the series include: Maserati, Bugatti, Aston Martin, and Caramo. Unless children are big car enthusiasts, it is unlikely they will be familiar with all of the new cars added to the series. With more in-depth descriptions of each car and motor type, the text is written for upper middle school and high school students. With the use of color photographs and easy-to-understand text, each volume covers the car and car maker's history, the evolution of the auto design, specialty cars, and the future of the line. Each volume concludes a timeline, a glossary, a further reading list, and a very short index, all of which can be used to teach young students basic researching skills. Earlier volumes in the series, such as those on the Ferrari, Corvette, and Mustang, are likely to garner more attention from children than these recently added volumes.—**Shannon Graff Hysell**

Author/Title Index

Reference is to entry number.

Subject Index

Reference is to entry number.

FOOD HABITS
Cocktails, 11th ed, 1086
Food & drink in American hist, 1087
Food lit, 1084
History of American cooking, 1094
New food lover's companion, 5th ed, 1092
Street food around the world, 1088

FOOD INDUSTRY
FAO statl yrbk 2013, 1090
Food & beverage market place 2014, 13th ed, 194
Plunkett's food industry almanac, 2014 ed, 1089

FOOD SCIENCE
Eating well, living better, 1091
Nutrition & food scis database [Website], 1085
Nutrition & health series, 1093
State of food & agriculture 2012, 1095
State of food insecurity in the world 2012, 1096

FOOTBALL
Historical dict of football, 712
Inside the NFL [Website], 689

FORD, HENRY
Quotable Henry Ford, 48

FOSSILS
If these fossils could talk series, 1273

FRANCE
Cultures of the world: France, 330
France, 103

FRANCE, LITERATURE
Historical dict of French lit, 920

FROGS
Frogs of the US & Canada, 1157

FRUIT
Vegetables, herbs, & fruit, paperback ed, 1097
What's wrong with my fruit garden? 1107

FUNDRAISING
Beyond bk sales, 543

GAMES
Cases on digital game-based learning, 1237
Chess results 1961-63, 705
Chess results 1964-67, 706
Chess results 1968-70, 707
Crash course in gaming, 519
Plunkett's games, apps & social media industry almanac, 2014 ed, 1239
Serious games & virtual worlds in educ, professional dvlpmt, & healthcare, 1240
Teen games rule! 532

GARDENING. *See also* **BOTANY; PLANTS**
American home landscapes, 1100
California native landscape, 1113
Dryland gardening, repr ed, 1102
Encyclopedia of planting combinations, repr ed, 1098
Garden, landscape & horticulture index [Website], 1121
Gardening for the birds, 1101
How to buy the right plants, tools & garden supplies, 1109
How to eradicate invasive plants, 1103
Organic methods for vegetable gardening in Fla., 1114
Plant breeding for the home gardener, 1119
Planting, 1112
Powerhouse plants, 1099
Practical botany for gardeners, 1131
Professional design gd to green roofs, 1106
Professional designer's gd to garden furnishings, 1111
Small garden handbook, 1120
Speedy vegetable garden, 1108
Teaming with nutrients, 1110
Timber Press gd to vegetable gardening in the mountain states, 1115
Timber Press gd to vegetable gardening in the NE, 1116
Timber Press gd to vegetable gardening in the Pacific NW, 1117
Timber Press gd to vegetable gardening in the SE, 1118
Tree gardens, 1105
Vegetables, herbs, & fruit, paperback ed, 1097
What's wrong with my fruit garden? 1107

GAYS
Feminist & queer info studies reader, 740
Gay male sleuth in print & film, new ed, 892
Historical dict of the lesbian & gay liberation movements, 741
LGBTQ families, 736
Make your own hist, 513

GENDER STUDIES
Gender studies database [Website], 721
GenderWatch [Website], 779
Handbook of research on gender & economic life, 159
Studies on women & gender abstracts [Website], 780

Plunkett's health care industry almanac, 2014 ed, 1188

HEALTH CARE - HANDBOOKS & YEARBOOKS. *See also* **MEDICINE – HANDBOOKS & YEARBOOKS**
Health & wellness in the 19th century, 1189
Health & wellness in the Renaissance & Enlightenment, 1190
Healthy living, 2d ed, 1192

HEALTH INSURANCE
HMO/PPO dir 2014, 26th ed, 1185
Weiss Ratings' gd to health insurers, Summer 2013, 206

HEALTH STATISTICS
Vital stats of the US 2012, 5th ed, 1193

HEART DISEASE
Heart disease, 1222

HEMINGWAY, ERNEST (1899-1961)
Fifty yrs of Hemingway criticism, 911

HERBS
Vegetables, herbs, & fruit, paperback ed, 1097

HEROES
Critical survey of mythology & folklore, 960

HISPANICS
Chicano database [Website], 357

HISTORY - AMERICAN
American decades: primary sources, 2000-09, 390
American eras: Civil War & Reconstruction 1860-77, primary sources, 391
American eras: industrial dvlpmt of the US, 1878-99, 392
American immigration, 383
American presidents, Washington to Tyler, 623
Articles of the Confederation, 393
Clothing through American hist, 416
Cornerstones of freedom series, 408
Daily life in the colonial city, 417
Daily life in the colonial south, 394
Declaration of Independence, 397
Encyclopedia of American studies [Website], 385
FreedomFlix [Website], 379
Great Depression, 409
Historical dict from the Great War to the Great Depression, 2d ed, 389
Magna Carta, 395
March of time [Website], 380

Mayflower Compact, 396
Mission-US [Website], 381
1960s, 410
100 people who changed 20th-century America, 378
Prohibition, 411
ProQuest hist vault [Website], 382
This is who we were: in the 1960s, 417
Thomas Paine's Common Sense, 397
2000s in America, 388
United States Constitution, 419
WPA—putting America to work, 413

HISTORY - ANCIENT
Civilization of ancient China, 442
Civilization of ancient Egypt, 443
Civilization of the Incas, 444

HISTORY - BIBLIOGRAPHY
Read on … hist, 855

HISTORY - MEDIEVAL
Daily life in a Medieval monastery, 429
Early Medieval world, 439
Medieval military technology, 2d ed, 608

HISTORY - WORLD
Atrocities, massacres, & war crimes, 438
History of the crusades [Website], 437
Kingfisher hist ency, 3d ed, 440
Perspectives on modern world hist series, 445
World hist series, 446

HOCKEY
European ice hockey championship results since 1910, 715
Historical dict of ice hockey, 716
Hockey hall of fame book of players, 714

HOLIDAYS
Celebrations in my world series, 976
Christmas ency, 3d ed, 973

HOLOCAUST
Jewish responses to persecution, v.3: 1941-42, 355

HORROR FILMS
Dracula's daughters, 1008
Horror show gd, 991

HORTICULTURE. *See also* **GARDENING; LANDSCAPING**
Garden, landscape & horticulture index [Website], 1121